P9-BYG-786

LET'S GO

■ PAGES PACKED WITH ESSENTIAL INFORMATION

"Value-packed, unbeatable, accurate, and comprehensive."

—The Los Angeles Times

"The guides are aimed not only at young budget travelers but at the independent traveler; a sort of streetwise cookbook for traveling alone."

—The New York Times

"Unbeatable; good sight-seeing advice; up-to-date info on restaurants, hotels, and inns; a commitment to money-saving travel; and a wry style that brightens nearly every page."

—The Washington Post

■ THE BEST TRAVEL BARGAINS IN YOUR BUDGET

"All the dirt, dirt cheap."

—People

"Let's Go follows the creed that you don't have to toss your life's savings to the wind to travel—unless you want to."

—The Salt Lake Tribune

■ REAL ADVICE FOR REAL EXPERIENCES

"The writers seem to have experienced every rooster-packed bus and lunar-surfaced mattress about which they write."

—The New York Times

"[Let's Go's] devoted updaters really walk the walk (and thumb the ride, and trek the trail). Learn how to fish, haggle, find work—anywhere."

—Food & Wine

"A world-wise traveling companion—always ready with friendly advice and helpful hints, all sprinkled with a bit of wit."

—The Philadelphia Inquirer

■ A GUIDE WITH A SPIRIT AND A SOCIAL CONSCIENCE

"Lighthearted and sophisticated, informative and fun to read. [Let's Go] helps the novice traveler navigate like a knowledgeable old hand."

—Atlanta Journal-Constitution

"The serious mission at the book's core reveals itself in exhortations to respect the culture and the environment—and, if possible, to visit as a volunteer, a student, or a teacher rather than a tourist."

—San Francisco Chronicle

LET'S GO PUBLICATIONS

TRAVEL GUIDES

Australia 9th edition
Austria & Switzerland 12th edition
Brazil 1st edition
Britain 2008
California 10th edition
Central America 9th edition
Chile 2nd edition
China 5th edition
Costa Rica 3rd edition
Eastern Europe 13th edition
Ecuador 1st edition
Egypt 2nd edition
Europe 2008
France 2008
Germany 13th edition
Greece 9th edition
Hawaii 4th edition
India & Nepal 8th edition
Ireland 13th edition
Israel 4th edition
Italy 2008
Japan 1st edition
Mexico 22nd edition
New Zealand 8th edition
Peru 1st edition
Puerto Rico 3rd edition
Southeast Asia 9th edition
Spain & Portugal 2008
Thailand 3rd edition
USA 24th edition
Vietnam 2nd edition
Western Europe 2008

ROADTRIP GUIDE

Roadtripping USA 2nd edition

ADVENTURE GUIDES

Alaska 1st edition
Pacific Northwest 1st edition
Southwest USA 3rd edition

CITY GUIDES

Amsterdam 5th edition
Barcelona 3rd edition
Boston 4th edition
London 16th edition
New York City 16th edition
Paris 14th edition
Rome 12th edition
San Francisco 4th edition
Washington, D.C. 13th edition

POCKET CITY GUIDES

Amsterdam
Berlin
Boston
Chicago
London
New York City
Paris
San Francisco
Venice
Washington, D.C.

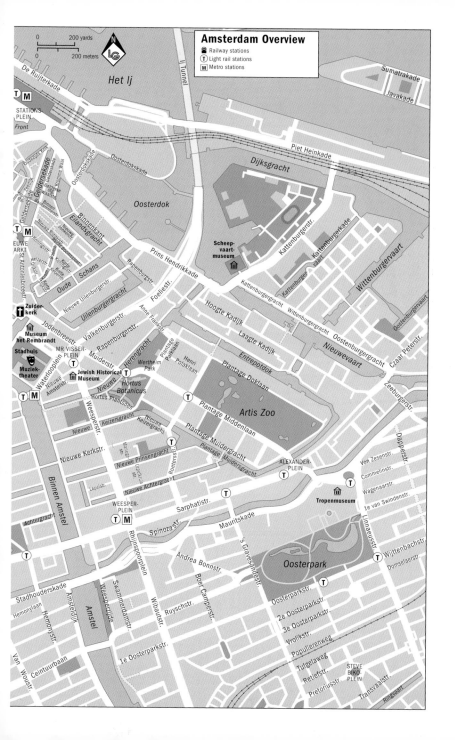

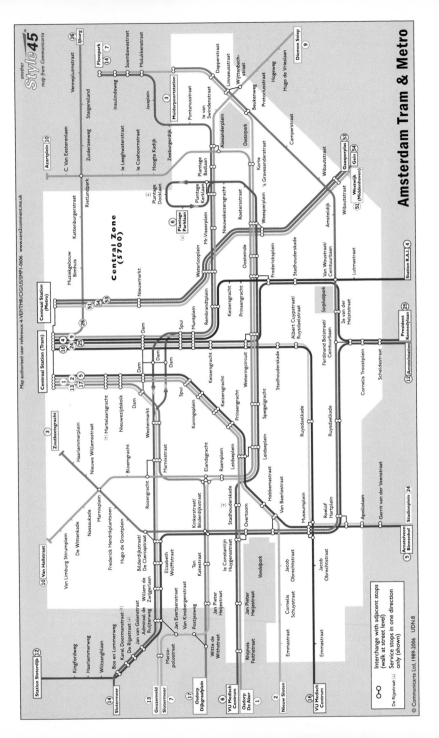

Amsterdam Tram & Metro

LET'S GO

AMSTERDAM

WITH COVERAGE OF
THE NETHERLANDS

NATHANIEL RAKICH EDITOR

RESEARCHER-WRITERS
JOHN A. DUNN
LUCY LINDSEY
RAVI RAMCHANDANI
KENNETH G. SAATHOFF

ANDREA TSURUMI MAP EDITOR
JULIE VODHANEL MANAGING EDITOR

ST. MARTIN'S PRESS ✖ NEW YORK

HELPING LET'S GO. If you want to share your discoveries, suggestions, or corrections, please drop us a line. We read every piece of correspondence, whether a postcard, a 10-page email, or a coconut. **Address mail to:**

> Let's Go: Amsterdam
> 67 Mount Auburn St.
> Cambridge, MA 02138
> USA

Visit Let's Go at **http://www.letsgo.com,** or send email to:

> feedback@letsgo.com
> Subject: "Let's Go: Amsterdam"

In addition to the invaluable travel advice our readers share with us, many are kind enough to offer their services as researchers or editors. Unfortunately, our charter enables us to employ only currently enrolled Harvard students.

CONTENTS

DISCOVER AMSTERDAM 1
When to Go 1
Neighborhood Overviews 2
  Oude Zijd 2
  Red Light District 2
  Nieuwe Zijd 3
  Scheepvaartbuurt 4
  Canal Ring West 4
  Central Canal Ring 4
  Leidseplein 5
  Rembrandtplein 5
  Jordaan 5
  Westerpark and Oud-West 6
  Museumplein and Vondelpark 6
  De Pijp 7
  Jodenbuurt and Plantage 7
Biking and Walking Tours 8
Suggested Itineraries 9

ESSENTIALS 15
Planning Your Trip 15
Safety and Health 24
Getting to the Netherlands 31
Getting Around the Netherlands 37
Keeping in Touch 44
Specific Concerns 47
Other Resources 52

LIFE AND TIMES 55
History of the Netherlands 55
The Netherlands Today 62

BEYOND TOURISM 77
A Philosophy for Travelers 77
Volunteering 78
Studying 83
Working 87

PRACTICAL INFORMATION .. 93
  Tourist and Financial Services 93
  Local Services 95
  Emergency and Communications 96

ACCOMMODATIONS 99
By Price 102
By Neighborhood 103
  Oude Zijd 103
  Red Light District 103

Nieuwe Zijd 105
Scheepvaartbuurt 108
Canal Ring West 109
Central Canal Ring 110
Leidseplein 111
Rembrandtplein 113
Jordaan 113
Westerpark and Oud-West 114
Museumplein and Vondelpark 116
De Pijp 118
Jodenbuurt and Plantage 118

FOOD 121
By Type 121
By Neighborhood 123
  Oude Zijd 123
  Red Light District 123
  Nieuwe Zijd 124
  Scheepvaartbuurt 125
  Canal Ring West 127
  Central Canal Ring 129
  Leidseplein 130
  Rembrandtplein 131
  Jordaan 132
  Westerpark and Oud-West 134
  Museumplein and Vondelpark 136
  De Pijp 137
  Jodenbuurt and Plantage 140

SIGHTS 143
  Oude Zijd 143
  Red Light District 144
  Nieuwe Zijd 146
  Scheepvaartbuurt 148
  Canal Ring West 149
  Central Canal Ring 152
  Leidseplein 152
  Rembrandtplein 153
  Jordaan 153
  Westerpark and Oud-West 154
  Museumplein and Vondelpark 154
  De Pijp 155
  Jodenbuurt and Plantage 158
  Greater Amsterdam 161

MUSEUMS 165
  Oude Zijd 165
  Red Light District 165
  Nieuwe Zijd 166
  Canal Ring West 168

Central Canal Ring 171
Jordaan 172
Museumplein and Vondelpark 174
Jodenbuurt and Plantage 176
Greater Amsterdam 181
Galleries 182
Canal Ring West 182
Central Canal Ring 182
Jordaan 183
Alternative Art Spaces 183

ENTERTAINMENT 185
Arts 185
Classical Music, Opera, and Dance 185
Live Music 187
Theater and Comedy 189
Film 190
Prostitution 192
Recreation and Gambling 194
Saunas and Spas 195
Coffee and Smart Shops 196
Oude Zijd 201
Red Light District 201
Nieuwe Zijd 202
Scheepvaartbuurt 205
Canal Ring West 205
Central Canal Ring 206
Leidseplein 207
Rembrandtplein 208
Jordaan 209
Westerpark and Oud-West 210
Museumplein and Vondelpark 210
De Pijp 210
Jodenbuurt and Plantage 211

SHOPPING 213
By Type 213
By Neighborhood 214
Oude Zijd 214
Red Light District 215
Nieuwe Zijd 215
Scheepvaartbuurt 216
Canal Ring West 216
Central Canal Ring 218
Jordaan 218
Westerpark and Oud-West 219
De Pijp 219
Jodenbuurt and Plantage 220
Sizes and Conversions 221

NIGHTLIFE 223
By Type 223
By Neighborhood 224
Oude Zijd 224
Red Light District 225
Nieuwe Zijd 227
Scheepvaartbuurt 229
Canal Ring West 229
Central Canal Ring 230
Leidseplein 230
Rembrandtplein 233
Jordaan 237
Westerpark and Oud-West 239
Museumplein and Vondelpark 240
De Pijp 240
Jodenbuurt and Plantage 241

DAYTRIPS 243
Aalsmeer 243
Zaanse Schans 245
Haarlem 249
Zandvoort Aan Zee 257
Lisse 259
Leiden 260
Noordwijk Aan Zee 268
The Hague (Den Haag) 269
Scheveningen 277
Delft 279
Rotterdam 285
Gouda 294
Utrecht 296
Arnhem 302
De Hoge Veluwe National Park 305
Groningen 306
Maastricht 313

WADDEN ISLANDS (WADDE-NEILANDEN) 320
Texel 320
Vlieland 324
Terschelling 325

APPENDIX 329
Climate 329
Measurements 329
Language 329

MAP APPENDIX 332

INDEX 345

HOW TO USE THIS BOOK

COVERAGE LAYOUT. *Let's Go: Amsterdam* divides up this dazzling city into neighborhoods. The **Discover** chapter is organized roughly as Amsterdam is laid out, from the inner Centrum to outlying neighborhoods. The **Accommodations, Food, Sights, Museums, Shopping,** and **Nightlife** chapters are broken down by neighborhoods in the same order (i.e., neighborhoods farther from the city center fall later in the chapter than neighborhoods closer to the city center). The **Entertainment** chapter is organized alphabetically according to genre, except for **Coffee and Smart Shops,** which are organized by neighborhood. Maps throughout the book provide helpful location reminders, both in Amsterdam chapters and in **Daytrips.**

TRANSPORTATION INFO. *Let's Go* mentions the nearest public transportation station, link, or line to as many establishments as possible. Amsterdam, however, is an extremely walkable (and bikeable!) city. For making connections between cities in the **Daytrips** chapter, information is generally listed under both the arrival and departure cities. Parentheticals provide the trip duration, frequency, and price. Consult the **Essentials** (p. 15) section for more general transportation info and the **Map Appendix** (p. 332) for maps, including a transportation map.

COVERING THE BASICS. The first chapter, **Discover Amsterdam** (p. 1), contains highlights of the city on the Amstel, complete with **Suggested Itineraries.** The **Essentials** (p. 15) section contains practical information on planning a budget, making reservations, and other useful tips for traveling in the Netherlands. Take some time to peruse the **Life and Times** (p. 55) chapter, which briefly sums up the history, culture, and customs of the Dutch. For study abroad, volunteer, and work options in the Netherlands, **Beyond Tourism** (p. 77) is all you need. **Practical Information** (p. 93) lists local services, while the **Appendix** (p. 329) has climate information, measurement conversions, and a glossary.

SCHOLARLY ARTICLES. Two contributors with unique regional insight wrote articles for *Let's Go: Amsterdam.* **Dr. Ivan Gaskell,** the Margaret S. Winthrop Curator in the Department of Paintings, Sculpture, and Decorative Arts at the Fogg Art Museum at Harvard University waxes poetic on Dutch artist Johannes Vermeer (p. 69). Former Let's Go Researcher-Writer and Dutch citizen **Hunter Maats** gives a suggestion for how to move beyond tourism (p. 82).

PRICE DIVERSITY. Our researchers list establishments in order of value from best to worst, with absolute favorites denoted by the *Let's Go* thumbs-up (🔊). Since the cheapest price does not always mean the best value, we have incorporated a system of price ranges for food and accommodations (p. viii).

PHONE CODES AND TELEPHONE NUMBERS. Amsterdam's area code is ☎020. In **Daytrips,** area codes for each region appear opposite the name of the region and are denoted by the ☎ icon. Phone numbers in text are also preceded by the ☎ icon.

A NOTE TO OUR READERS. The information for this book was gathered by *Let's Go* researchers from May through August of 2007. Each listing is based on one researcher's opinion, formed during his or her visit at a particular time. Those traveling at other times may have different experiences since prices, dates, hours, and conditions are always subject to change. You are urged to check the facts presented in this book beforehand to avoid inconvenience and surprises.

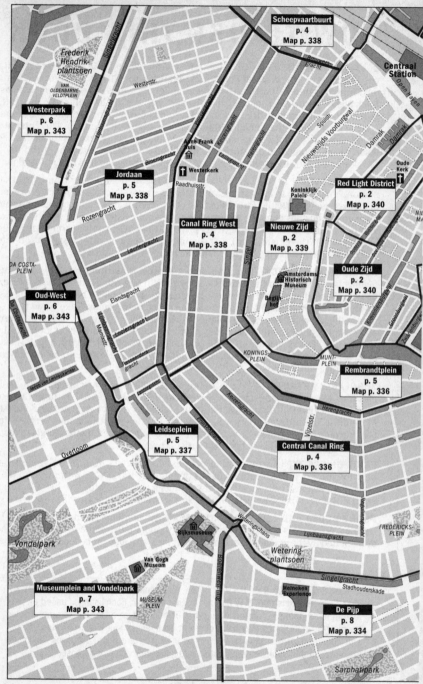

Scheepvaartbuurt
p. 4
Map p. 338

Centraal Station

Westerpark
p. 6
Map p. 343

Frederik Hendrik-plantsoen

VAN OLDENBARNE-VELDTPLEIN

Westerstr.

Jordaan
p. 5
Map p. 338

Anne Frank Huis

Westerkerk

Raadhuisstr.

Bloemgracht

Rozengracht

Canal Ring West
p. 4
Map p. 338

Koninklijk Paleis

Red Light District
p. 2
Map p. 340

Oude Kerk

Nieuwe Zijd
p. 2
Map p. 339

DA COSTA-PLEIN

Oud-West
p. 6
Map p. 343

Leidsegracht

Elandsgracht

Amsterdams Historisch Museum

Begijn-hof

Oude Zijd
p. 2
Map p. 340

KONINGS-PLEIN

MUNT-PLEIN

Rembrandtplein
p. 5
Map p. 336

Leidseplein
p. 5
Map p. 337

Overtoom

Central Canal Ring
p. 4
Map p. 336

Herengracht

FREDERICKS-PLEIN

Weteringschans

Vondelpark

Rijksmuseum

Weteringplantsoen

Van Gogh Museum

Singelgracht

Stadhouderskade

Museumplein and Vondelpark
p. 7
Map p. 343

MUSEUM-PLEIN

Heineken Experience

Lijnbaansgracht

De Pijp
p. 8
Map p. 334

Sarphatipark

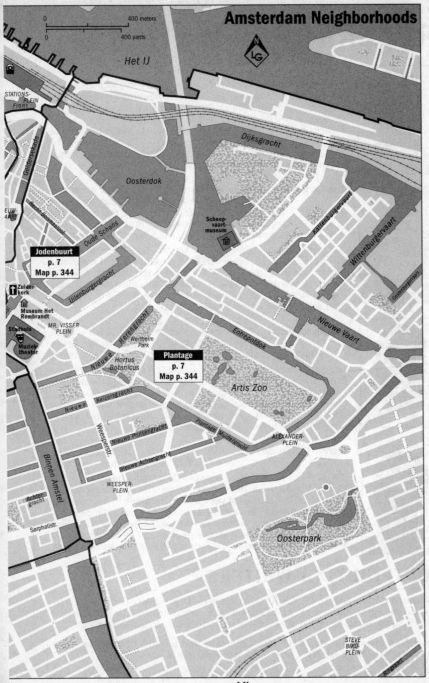

Amsterdam Neighborhoods

Het IJ

STATIONS-PLEIN Front

Dijksgracht

Oosterdok

Scheep-vaart-museum

Kattenburgervaart

Wittenburgervaart

Oude Schans

Jodenbuurt
p. 7
Map p. 344

Wittenburgergracht

Zuider-kerk

Museum Het Rembrandt

Nieuwe Vaart

MR. VISSER PLEIN

Stadhuis

Muziek-theater

Hexenfracht

Wertheim Park

Entrepotdok

Plantage
p. 7
Map p. 344

Nieuwe

Hortus Botanicus

Artis Zoo

Keizersgracht

Nieuwe

Weesperstr.

Nieuwe Prinsengracht

Plantage Muidergracht

ALEXANDER-PLEIN

Binnen Amstel

Nieuwe Achtergracht

WEESPER-PLEIN

Achter gracht

Sarphatistr.

Oosterpark

STEVE BIKO-PLEIN

RESEARCHER-WRITERS

John A. Dunn   *Canal Ring West, Central Canal Ring*

John went from one world-class city (New York) to another with sheer enthusiasm and a sharp sense of humor. This sci-fi aficionado did justice to Amsterdam's cultural crossroads with clean copy and his furious pedaling skills. Despite constantly being drenched by endless rains, he spun some hilarious stories that brightened up days both in Amsterdam and in the Let's Go office. He weaved his way among the cobblestones in the Nine Streets and the stoned in Canal Ring coffee shops with integrity unbefitting a Yankees fan.

Lucy Lindsey   *Bloemendaal aan Zee, De Pijp, Greater Amsterdam, Haarlem, Jodenbuurt and Plantage, Jordaan, Leidseplein, Museumplein and Vondelpark, Oude Zijd, Red Light District, Scheepvaartbuurt, Scheveningen, The Hague, Wadden Islands, Westerpark and Oud-West, Zaanse Schans, Zandvoort aan Zee*

A tried and true two-time Let's Go veteran, Lucy biked, biked, and biked until she could bike no more (read: crashed), but she always picked herself up to shoot off some delicious copy. From Klee to *klompen*, this art connoisseur could not stop uncovering Amsterdam's hidden jewels (and teaching her editors a thing or 500) even after finishing her assigned route.

Ravi Ramchandani   *Aalsmeer, Apeldoorn, Arnhem, De Hoge Veluwe, Greater Amsterdam, Groningen, Hooghalen, Leiden, Maastricht, Noordwijk aan Zee, Nieuwe Zijd, Rembrandtplein, Utrecht*

London, Amsterdam, Germany—Ravi traveled across Western Europe, working for four different Let's Go books in the process. He stayed "low" in the Netherlands while covering coffee shops, college towns, and—fearlessly—the world's largest flower trading floor. Ravi researched with skill and dedication, applying his enormous attention to solid and accurate copy.

Kenneth G. Saathoff   *Delft, Gouda, Lisse, Oude Zijd, Red Light District, Rotterdam*

Another Let's Go alum, Ken added the Netherlands to Saudi Arabia, Thailand, and Sweden on his travel resume. This avid outdoorsman didn't mind the change of pace though, drinking in the beautiful Dutch countryside and savoring some delicious Dutch desserts. This wizard with words couldn't even tear himself away, skipping his flight home for some extra exploration. Ken's editors could always count on him to send something titillating back to the office.

CONTRIBUTING WRITERS

Dr. Ivan Gaskell is the Margaret S. Winthrop Curator in the Department of Paintings, Sculpture, and Decorative Arts at the Fogg Art Museum at Harvard University. He is a respected scholar and commentator on the works of Dutch master painter Johannes Vermeer.

Hunter Maats is a graduate of Harvard University and a Dutch citizen. He was a Researcher-Writer for *Let's Go: Eastern Europe*, *Italy*, and *Mexico*.

ACKNOWLEDGMENTS

NATHANIEL THANKS. Thank you, ▇Julie, for the desserts, advice, and pure friendship. I owe you my sanity, my book, and, most importantly, my job. Thanks to my RWs, who always put themselves out there to make a great book. Thanks to Andrea for her patience and attention to detail. Thanks to Derek, my copyflow comrade, and to Noga, our copyflow guru. Thanks to Jake for coming to the rescue. Thanks to my family, just in general. Thanks to Molly for some musical quality time/rush hour traffic. Thanks to the pods: Money for always being welcoming; FRITA for parties late into the night; SPAM for its cozy chair and warm people; Europod for always having someone to talk to; Oosa for the entertainment; IRICO for my visits; Mapland for being neighborly; and Furniture, for obvious reasons. Thanks to Jenny for her aplomb; to Anne for babysitting; to Rachel for making me feel mature; to Sara for the chair (and that whole financial thing); to Calina for kindness; to Victoria for whale watching; to Tom for his values; to Vicki and Jansen for their god-like powers; to Patrick for knowledge; to Matt for wisdom; to Inés for breakfast; to Sergio for his laugh; to Vanessa, but I'm not sure why; to Pat for working late; to Vinnie for working later; to everyone else for this amazing community.

Then there's always someone who rolls it all into one, the consummate role model, the smartest teacher, and the most mindful friend, so thanks to Silvia, for everything.

ANDREA THANKS. Thank you to Mapland: Tom, Maisie, Joy, and Drew. Thanks to Nathaniel for his meticulous care of the maps—it made a big difference. Thank you Alexander, Sam, Phil, and Margaret for an awesome summer.

Editor
Nathaniel Rakich
Managing Editor
Julie Vodhanel
Map Editor
Andrea Tsurumi
Photographers
Vanessa Bertozzi, Kevin Connors, Frank Lee
Typesetter
Victoria Esquivel-Korsiak

LET'S GO

Publishing Director
Jennifer Q. Wong
Editor-in-Chief
Silvia Gonzalez Killingsworth
Production Manager
Victoria Esquivel-Korsiak
Cartography Manager
Thomas MacDonald Barron
Editorial Managers
Anne Bensson, Calina Ciobanu, Rachel Nolan
Financial Manager
Sara Culver
Business and Marketing Manager
Julie Vodhanel
Personnel Manager
Victoria Norelid
Production Associate
Jansen A. S. Thurmer
Director of E-Commerce & IT
Patrick Carroll
Website Manager
Kathryne A. Bevilacqua
Office Coordinators
Juan L. Peña, Bradley J. Jones

Director of Advertising Sales
Hunter McDonald
Senior Advertising Associate
Daniel Lee

President
William Hauser
General Managers
Bob Rombauer, Jim McKellar

ABOUT LET'S GO

NOT YOUR PARENTS' TRAVEL GUIDE

At Let's Go, we see every trip as the chance of a lifetime. If your dream is to grab a machete and forge through the jungles of Costa Rica, we can take you there. If you'd rather bask in the Riviera sun at a beachside cafe, we'll set you a table. We write for readers who know that there's more to travel than sharing double deckers with tourists and who believe that travel can change both themselves and the world—whether they plan to spend six days in Mexico City or six months in Europe. We'll show you just how far your money can go, and prove that the greatest limitation on your adventures is not your wallet, but your imagination.

BEYOND THE TOURIST EXPERIENCE

To help you gain a deeper connection with the places you travel, our fearless researchers scour the globe to give you the heads-up on both world-renowned and off-the-beaten-track attractions, sights, and destinations. They engage with the local culture only to emerge with the freshest insights on everything from local festivals to regional cuisine. We've also opened our pages to respected writers and scholars to hear their takes on the countries and regions we cover, and asked travelers who have worked, studied, or volunteered abroad to contribute first-person accounts of their experiences. In addition, we increased our coverage of responsible travel and expanded each guide's Beyond Tourism chapter to share more ideas about how to give back while on the road.

FORTY-EIGHT YEARS OF WISDOM

Let's Go got its start in 1960, when a group of creative and well-traveled students compiled their experience and advice into a 20-page mimeographed pamphlet, which they gave to travelers on charter flights to Europe. Four and a half decades later, we've expanded to cover six continents and all kinds of travel—while retaining our founders' adventurous attitude toward the world. Laced with witty prose and total candor, our guides are still researched and written entirely by students on shoestring budgets, experienced travelers who know that train strikes, stolen luggage, food poisoning, and marriage proposals are all part of a day's work.

THE LET'S GO COMMUNITY

More than just a travel guide company, Let's Go is a community. Our small staff comes together because of our shared passion for travel and our desire to help other travelers see the world the way it was meant to be seen. We love it when our readers become part of the Let's Go community as well—when you travel, drop us a postcard (67 Mt. Auburn St., Cambridge, MA 02138, USA), send us an e-mail (feedback@letsgo.com), or post on our forum (http://www.letsgo.com/connect/forum) to tell us about your adventures and discoveries.

For more information, visit us online: www.letsgo.com.

② PRICE RANGES ③ ④
① AMSTERDAM ⑤

Our researchers list establishments in order of value from best to worst; our favorites are denoted by the Let's Go thumbs-up (🖒). However, because the best value is not always the cheapest price, we have also incorporated a system of price ranges, based on a rough expectation of what you'll spend. For **accommodations,** we base our range on the cheapest price for which a single traveler can stay for one night. For **restaurants** and other dining establishments, we estimate the average amount a traveler will spend. The table tells you what you'll *typically* find in the Netherlands at the corresponding price range; keep in mind that no system can allow for every individual establishment's quirks, and you'll typically get more for your money in larger cities. In other words: expect anything.

ACCOMMODATIONS	RANGE	WHAT YOU'RE *LIKELY* TO FIND
①	under €36	Mostly hostels and really cheap hotels; expect a basic dorm-style room and a communal bath. You may have to provide or rent towels and sheets. There may be a lockout and curfew. Breakfast is sometimes included.
②	€36-55	Smaller hotels. You may have a private bathroom, or there may be a sink in your basic, comfortable room and a communal shower in the hall. Breakfast is usually included.
③	€56-77	Small hotels in more central areas, often on frequently traveled streets. Should have decent amenities, such as phone, TV, private bath, and respectable decor.
④	€78-100	Nicer hotels in convenient areas away from noisy, touristed streets. Well-decorated rooms and more attentive service.
⑤	above €100	Large hotels or upscale chains. If it doesn't have the perks you want, you've paid too much. Decor and service should be especially charming and comfortable.
FOOD	RANGE	WHAT YOU'RE *LIKELY* TO FIND
①	under €8	Mostly takeout food, like sandwiches, falafel, or Shawarma. Bakeries, dessert, and soup shops; some *eetcafes*.
②	€8-12	Small restaurants, standard *eetcafes*, and cheaper ethnic food with appetizers at a bar, low-priced entrees, and tapas. May be takeout or sit-down.
③	€13-17	Cheaper seafood and more upscale ethnic food, but you're likely paying for ambience. You'll probably have a waiter or waitress, so the tip will bump you up a few euro.
④	€18-22	Upscale restaurants with a decent wine list, tasteful decor, and good service. Pricier seafood and high-end ethnic cuisine. Probably no dress code, but avoid T-shirts and jeans.
⑤	above €22	Your meal might not exactly be budget, but there's a reason—beautiful surroundings, extensive wine list, and epicurean food that matches the decor. Dress nicely.

DISCOVER AMSTERDAM

Amsterdam's reputation precedes it—and what a reputation it is. Born out of a murky bog and cobbled together over eight centuries, the "Dam on the River Amstel" coaxes visitors with an alluring blend of grandeur and decadence. Thick clouds of marijuana smoke waft from subdued coffee shops, and countless bicycles zip past blooming tulip markets. Yet there is much more to Amsterdam than postcard stereotypes. A Golden Age of art flourished here, and here art remains. Against the backdrop of Vincent van Gogh's thick swirls and Johannes Vermeer's luminous figures, gritty street artists spray graffiti in protest. Squatters sharpen the city's defiant edge, while professional politicians push the boundaries of progressive reform. GLBT citizens blend seamlessly into a social landscape that defines tolerance but also faces difficult questions as the 21st century unfolds. With Muslim integration into Dutch secularism, the limits of liberalism in an interdependent world, and the endless fight to fend off the encroaching seas, this city has its work cut out for itself.

FACTS AND FIGURES

AGE: 733 years old in 2008

POPULATION: 743,027

TOTAL AREA: 207 sq. km

ETHNIC GROUPS: 173

PARKS: 28

FLOWER BULBS IN THEM: 600,000

TREES: 220,000

CANALS: 165

BRIDGES: 1281

POT SMOKERS: 5.2% of Netherlanders in any given year (compared with 12.3% of Americans)

HOUSEBOATS: 2500

WINDMILLS: 6

VAN GOGH PAINTINGS: 206

GALLERIES: 141

MUSEUMS: 51

GIANT CHESS PIECES: 32

COFFEE SHOPS IN 1960: 5

COFFEE SHOPS TODAY: Many, many more (some people estimate 500).

VISITORS PER YEAR: 16,000,000

DUTCH POPULATION: 16,000,000

DUTCH BIKES: 16,000,000

DUTCH PIGS: 14,000,000

DUTCH LAND BELOW SEA LEVEL: 27%

LEGAL PROSCRIPTIONS ON HOMOSEXUALITY: 0

WHEN TO GO

Though relatively moderate, the weather in the Netherlands nevertheless fluctuates from season to season; its only year-round characteristic is rain—and lots of it (for average temperatures and rainfall, see p. 329). Throngs of human and mosquito visitors pack the city's parks and streets in the summer high season (June-Aug.), when temperatures rarely exceed typical comfort levels. The crowds are thinner in the spring and fall, but dress gets bulkier. During these months, the

DISCOVER

Dutch are greeted almost daily with a playful, cool fog that usually dissolves into an ineffectual stream of sunshine by midday. In the depths of winter—and low season—mostly empty canals and streets frost over.

NEIGHBORHOOD OVERVIEWS

Amsterdam's cozy but confusing neighborhoods can be easily explored with help from its guiding canals. In the city center, water runs in concentric half-circles, beginning at Centraal Station. The **Singel** runs around the **Centrum,** which includes the **Oude Zijd** (Old Side), the infamous **Red Light District,** and the **Nieuwe Zijd** (New Side), which, oddly enough, is older than the Oude Zijd. Barely a kilometer in diameter, the Centrum overflows with brothels, bars, clubs, and tourists wading through wafts of marijuana smoke. The next three canals—the **Herengracht,** the **Keizersgracht,** and the **Prinsengracht**—constitute the **Canal Ring.** Its neighborhoods, which this book calls the **Central Canal Ring** and **Canal Ring West,** are home to beautiful canal houses, and nearby **Rembrandtplein** and **Leidseplein** sport classy nightlife that spans flashy bars and traditional *bruin cafes.* Just over the **Singelgracht, Museumplein** is home to the city's most renowned art museums as well as the verdant, sprawling **Vondelpark.** Farther out lie the more residential Amsterdam neighborhoods: to the west, the **Jordaan, Westerpark,** and **Oud-West;** to the east, **Jodenbuurt** and **Plantage;** to the south, **De Pijp** and far-flung **Greater Amsterdam.** Though these districts are populated by dense housing, they still boast excellent eateries and brilliant museums.

OUDE ZIJD

see map p. 340

Don't let the name Oude Zijd (Old Side) deceive you—the neighborhood is actually newer than the **Nieuwe Zijd** (New Side). With narrow, winding streets, picturesque canals, markets touting fresh cheese and produce, and snug footbridges beside raucous bars, coffee shops, and S&M sex shops, the Oude Zijd is simultaneously Amsterdam at its most genteel and its most decadent. The southern end of the **Kloveniersburgwal** and **Oudezijds Achterburgwal** canals are as serene as any in Amsterdam, merging into the historic buildings of the **University of Amsterdam.** To the north, the long and spindly **Zeedijk** is the heart of Amsterdam's **Chinatown,** boasting Asian acupuncture and massage parlors next to restaurants dishing out Chinese, Indonesian, Malaysian, and Thai food.

A little to the west, locals tend to congregate along **Nieuwmarkt,** one of Amsterdam's most popular squares, lined with casual yet sophisticated restaurants and cafes. On a nice day, the square is taken over by the cafes' terraces, as visitors lounge late into the warm summer nights. On the weekend, the square plays host to a popular open-air market peddling antiques, produce, and cheese. At the center of Nieuwmarkt, be sure to admire the **Waag,** a massive medieval weigh-house and modern-day restaurant.

RED LIGHT DISTRICT

see map p. 340

Welcome to Amsterdam's Red Light District, where the world's oldest profession meets modern global tourism. The neighborhood has existed in at least some form of sexual glorification, exploitation, and transaction since the 13th century. Amsterdam was then the seat of European maritime trade, and, with the frequent travels of so many lonely sailors and increasingly wealthy men, the sexual service industry began to take root.

Today in Amsterdam, prostitution is remarkably commercialized, regulated, and sanitized.

The fun really begins on **Warmoesstraat.** The street runs from St. Nicolaaskerk to Dam Sq. and serves as the debaucherous heart of Amsterdam, lined with bars (many of which offer Happy-hour discounts), coffee shops, backpacker hostels, and sex shops. The street is a type of staging ground for packs of young men getting ready to explore the brothels and sex theaters to the east, on **Oudezijds Voorburgwal** and **Oudezijds Achterburgwal.**

By day, the area is relatively tame, as families and older tourists ogle at the rows of crimson-curtained windows and blush as they pass the countless erotic shops and cinemas. But no visit to Amsterdam is complete without a visit to the Red Light District at night. As darkness descends upon the city, a faintly glowing pink haze enshrouds the neighborhood. Bars brim with hormone-charged young men guzzling Heineken by the pint, while crowds spill in from the nearby Zijds. The scene can be overwhelming or even jarring, with a frankness unseen or even unimagined by many visitors. But the entire spectacle takes places under the careful and manifold regulations of Dutch law: large groups of police stand guard, and surveillance cameras on the corners make sure nothing gets too out of control.

NIEUWE ZIJD

see map p. 340

The Nieuwe Zijd (New Side) gets its name from the **Nieuwe Kerk,** smack in the middle of the neighborhood. This side of the Centrum is technically older than the Oude Zijd, but its church, built in the early 15th century, is younger than the Oude Zijd's Oude Kerk—one of the earliest structures in the city. The Nieuwe Zijd is bordered on the east by Damrak, which turns into Rokin as it crosses **Dam Square,** Amsterdam's enormous plaza lined by the Nieuwe Kerk, the **Koninklijk Paleis,** and the **Nationaal Monument.** The messy tourist schmaltz closer to Dam fades with each successive street to the west: **Nieuwezijds Voorburgwal,** originally constructed as a bulwark against attack just outside the city center, is now a hub for nightlife; **Spuistraat** has its share of trendy cafes; **Kalverstraat** reigns as the Nieuwe Zijd's premier shopping district; and **Singel** is a mixed bag where hoity-toity restaurants lie not far from prostitutes beckoning from behind red-lit windows. Despite the neighborhood's proximity to tourist central, locals don't hesitate to miss out on the fun too. Book and art markets in the **Spui** offer a dose of serious culture just

BIZARRE AMSTERDAM

The Van Gogh Museum and Rijksmuseum are must-sees, but Amsterdam is also host to some rather eclectic museums. Convince your friends and family that your trip to Amsterdam has been truly edifying by sending them a postcard from the following (slightly different) collections:

1. Amsterdam Sex Museum, in the Nieuwe Zijd (p. 168). The birds and the bees—life-size.

2. Cannabis College, in the Red Light District (p. 166). Pot for dummies—and smarties.

3. CoBrA Museum, south of Amsterdam (p. 181). Cutting-edge art that's almost intelligible.

4. Electric Ladyland: The First Museum of Fluorescent Art, in the Jordaan (p. 172). A fluorescent collection to jolt the senses.

5. Foam Photography Museum, in the Central Canal Ring (p. 171). Dauntless photo exhibits.

6. Cat's Cabinet, in the Central Canal Ring (p. 152). Not for those with allergies.

7. Nationaal Brilmuseum, in the Canal Ring West (p. 170). The array of spectacles is a spectacle.

8. Pianola Museum, in the Jordaan (p. 173). Perhaps the world's only museum of player pianos.

9. Woonboot Museum, in the Jordaan (p. 173). See how the houseboat crowd lives it up.

10. Torture Museum, in the Nieuwe Zijd (p. 172). Painfully cheesy collection of torture devices.

blocks away from retail megastores. This combination of high and low, native and tourist is what makes the Nieuwe Zijd a not-to-be-missed destination.

SCHEEPVAARTBUURT

Amsterdam's Shipping Quarter—Scheepvaartbuurt, for those brave enough to attempt multiple, seemingly endless vowels—occupies a spot north of the Jordaan and Canal Ring. Most of the action centers on Haarlemmerstraat, rendering the neighborhood an easy place to explore for a day. This increasingly gentrified area has hip restaurants and smokeries just outside the tourist crush of Nieuwendijk. Venture south to the photogenic **Brouwersgracht,** at the top of the Canal Ring. At the **Korte Prinsengracht,** Haarlemmerstraat becomes **Haarlemmerdijk,** and the district becomes considerably more residential.

see map p. 338

CANAL RING WEST

If the Centrum is at the head of spectacular Amsterdam, the Canal Ring is the city's genteel heart. This is one of the most beautiful spots in Amsterdam, with rents—one of the highest per square foot in the world—to match. The Canal Ring West, also known by locals as the "Nine Streets" area, is a breath of fresh air (figuratively speaking) from the commotion of nearby **Dam Square.** Artists, young professionals, lovers, and tourists mingle in canal-side cafes or browse the neighborhood's countless shops. As the sun sets, however, a hush descends upon the Nine Streets, as the gentle canals reflect a faint glow from the lampposts and the night owls drift into nearby Leidseplein. **Prinsengracht,** the busiest of the four canals, tends to pull in the most visitors with its numerous cafes serving traditional Dutch cuisine; proximity to the popular **Anne Frank Huis** attracts visitors wandering in. Small boutiques line the neighborhood's streets; these shops typically specialize in homemade jewelry, candles, or soaps. Keep an eye out (or up) for the **Westerkerkstoren,** Amsterdam's tallest tower, which sits atop the famed **Westerkerk,** at the corner of Raadhuisstraat and Prinsengracht.

see map p. 338

TIP

NO RHYME, BUT ABECEDARIAN REASON. The three canals that make up the *grachtengordel* (canal girdle) go in alphabetical order as they fan out from the city center: Herengracht (Gentleman's Canal), Keizersgracht (Emperor's Canal), and Prinsengracht (Prince's Canal).

CENTRAL CANAL RING

The succession of canals that makes up the Central Canal Ring is a haven of tranquil historic homes, quiet hotels, and quirky neighborhood hangouts. This area lays claim to a stretch on the **Herengracht** known as the **Golden Bend,** so called because of the wealth of the 17th-century merchants who built especially wide and lavish canal houses there. **Keizersgracht** and **Prinsengracht,** south of Herengracht, as well as the trafficked **Singel** to the north, feature canal houses that are not as spectacular as their wealthy neighbors but that are no less historically or architecturally important. These buildings date back to as early as 1600 and are topped by many types of gables, among them the notable Dutch stylings of step gables and spout gables. The upscale interior tranquility of the Central Canal Ring gives way in two adjacent squares—**Leidseplein** and **Rembrandtplein**—touristed, action-filled centers of nightlife and cuisine.

see map p. 336

LEIDSEPLEIN

see map p. 337

Words cannot accurately describe Leidseplein, a raging plaza that very nicely encapsulates many of Amsterdam's best-known (or most stereotypical) traits. Chances are that you'll either love or hate Leidseplein, so named because it once marked the end of the road from Leiden to Amsterdam. On one hand, it offers Amsterdam's most densely concentrated assemblage of restaurants and nightlife, and the neighborhood is the prime gathering point for street performers and their tourist audiences. On the other, the hordes here can seem of the coarsest, loudest kind. Thankfully, Leidseplein is a clearly defined bubble on the southern curve of the much quieter Canal Ring. It is also just north of the cultured Museumplein.

REMBRANDTPLEIN

see map p. 336

Rembrandtplein proper is a grass rectangle surrounded by scattered flower beds, criss-crossed by pedestrian paths, and populated with half-dressed locals lazing about (when weather permits, of course). A bronze likeness of the famed master **Rembrandt van Rijn** and a 3D version of his famous painting *Night Watch* overlook the scene, but it's what surrounds the greenery that makes this neighborhood popular among locals and tourists alike. The area is littered with bars and cafes—establishments ranging from casual to upscale—and all are packed with lively night owls most nights of the week. Unfortunately, they are usually also unnecessarily expensive. By night, Rembrandtplein competes with Leidseplein for Amsterdam's hippest nightlife and partygoers, with a particularly rich concentration of ◪**GLBT** hot spots in the area. South and west of the square lies **Reguliersdwarsstraat,** dubbed by locals as "the gayest street in Amsterdam." It is quite a distinction, but one well earned, since gay men and women—with straight friends in tow—flock to the area. The city's younger gay community patronizes the clubs that sit just west of the intersection of Reguliersdwarsstraat and **Vijzelstraat,** as this area tends to house some of Amsterdam's hottest and least inhibited venues. **Amstel,** along the river of the same name, is home to a number of smaller GLBT bars. **Thorbeckeplein,** just off Rembrandtplein toward the **Herengracht,** has a small collection of clubs, party bars, and seedy strip clubs and cabarets. **Utrechtsestraat,** extending southward from Rembrandtplein into the Central Canal Ring, bears a concentration of great, less touristed restaurants.

STREET TRANSLATION. Many side streets in the Netherlands are prefixed by "Eerste" (1st) and "Tweede" (2nd) and followed by the name of the main street adjacent to them. On a map, these are denoted by 1e and 2e.

JORDAAN

see map p. 338

Head to the Jordaan when you need to relax in style. Amsterdam's most fashionable neighborhood is low-key and cozy; here, some of the city's best-preserved historical homes lean over the canals adorned by overflowing flower boxes. The area began in the 1600s as a working-class neighborhood and remained so until major gentrification in the 1990s, when it became the comely perch of Amsterdam's yuppie population (forcing out many of the area's wage-earning residents). To reach this infinitely charming and not-to-be-missed side of Amsterdam, take tram #13, 14, or 17 to **Marnixstraat** or **Westermarkt** or tram #10 to **Rozengracht** or **Bloemgracht.** On foot, you can walk from **Prinsengracht** past a succession of languid cafe-bars with canal-boat seating. Go farther west to explore quiet, narrow streets and secluded canals such as beautiful Bloemgracht. The part of the Jordaan to the north of Rozengracht features swinging nightlife while the south is a bit more subdued. The Jordaan boils down to a host of upscale studios, galleries, and cafes.

WESTERPARK AND OUD-WEST

see map p. 343

Not as traveled as more central parts of the city, the area north of Vondelpark and west of the Singelgracht spans several neighborhoods.Westerpark is the opposite of its southern neighbor: where the Oud-West has crowded, tightly packed streets, Westerpark is filled to the brim with winding canals and picturesque greens; where the Oud-West bristles like a small city, Westerpark breathes easy with the relaxed attitude of sedate suburbia. Westerpark's highlight is its eponymous park, which is a popular retreat for families on sunny summer days. Even farther west of Westerpark lie **Bos en Lommer** and **De Baarsjes,** sleepy residential neighborhoods with little to attract even the most curious traveler. **Rembrandtpark,** on the far edge of De Baarsjes, is relatively popular for local joggers and dog walkers. Closer to the Centrum, the Oud-West (Old West, bounded by Kostverlorenvaart, Hugo de Grootkade, Vondelpark, and Nassaukade) is a far cry from the scenic and stately neighboring Jordaan, but there are signs of gentrification and development everywhere, especially toward Westerpark and closer to downtown. With fewer bars and clubs than the Jordaan, it isn't the safest place at night (simply for the distance between establishments), but during the day the Oud-West comes vibrantly to life. A walk down **Kinkerstraat, Jan Pieter Heijestraat,** and the neighborhood's other major streets reveals the area's dazzling regional diversity, particularly when it comes to cuisine: Turkish delis, Ethiopian restaurants, and Surinamese supermarkets all abound in the area in and around the Oud-West.

MUSEUMPLEIN AND VONDELPARK

see map p. 342

Protected by the Singelgracht, which encircles the wild, spirited city core, Museumplein and Vondelpark occupy a quieter, more gentrified area of the city. The 19th-century home to wealthy Amsterdammers, the streets around Museumplein host some of the most beautiful and stateliest mansions in the city. Still, the neighborhood's real draws are the museums that line Museumplein, a flat expanse of green park that occupies roughly six square blocks. Towering over the park is the ornate, late 19th-century **Rijksmuseum,** with its world-class collection of Dutch Golden Age paintings, applied arts, and Asian objects. Along Van Baerlestraat, you'll find both the **Stedelijk Museum,** the city's main center for modern art (closed for renovation until at least 2009), and the immensely popular **Van Gogh Museum.** This peaceful neighborhood rounds out its potpourri of attractions with some of Amsterdam's most expensive shopping, as well as the city's world-famous concert hall, the **Concertgebouw.**

With meandering walkways and paved paths for both bikers and skaters, the Vondelpark, just southwest of Leidseplein, draws large crowds on any sunny day of the year. Located inside the Vondelpark is the **Openluchttheater,** or open-air theater, where music and dance shows, as well as all manner of film screenings, are held throughout the summer months. The excellent **Filmmuseum,** adjacent to the park, is home to the world's premier archive of Dutch cinema and features daily screenings from its holdings.

see map p. 333

DE PIJP

Venture outside the canal rings to De Pijp, a gentrifying neighborhood just beginning to spread its wings. This area has all the charms of a traditional European Latin Quarter, and its location has provided cheap housing to students, artists, and immigrants for decades. Ethnic eateries and cheap stores still abound, sharing streets with hip new bistros and lounges. **Ferdinand Bolstraat,** the neighborhood's main drag, is one such trendy street, while **Albert Cuypstraat** maintains some of its former grittiness. The street is home to the **Albert Cuypmarkt,** the largest outdoor market in Europe, where shopkeepers hawk food, household wares, and other sundries to huge crowds every day. **Sarphatipark,** a grassy and fountain-filled plot of park, lies in the heart of De Pijp. The enclave is best experienced by a relaxed stroll through the market or by wandering through the streets and stopping to pop into shops and cafes that catch your eye.

see map p. 344

JODENBUURT AND PLANTAGE

Amsterdam has always been a place of mixed blessings for the Jews, who arrived in the Netherlands in the early 17th century. In time, the area roughly bounded by the streets **Jodenbreestraat, Sint Antoniesbreestraat,** and **Waterlooplein** gained definition as a **Jewish Quarter (Jodenbuurt),** full of synagogues, theaters, shops, businesses, schools, and some 55,000 Jews. The quarter grew ever outward to include wealthier areas such as **Plantage Middenlaan** and **Nieuwe Keizersgracht.** When the Germans invaded Amsterdam in 1940, everything changed. The Nazis forced the residents of the Jodenbuurt into isolation, deportation, and mass extermination. Only 5200 Dutch Jews survived the war, and the Jodenbuurt, though still existing in name, would never be the same. Today the Quarter is home to a number of excellent museums and monuments chronicling the Jews and the Dutch resistance as well as to other sights like the **Stadhuis-Het Muziektheater** and the **Museum Het Rembrandt.**

To the southeast of the Jodenbuurt lies the verdant **Plantage.** This district is a leafy, shaded escape full of historical and ethnographic museums (namely the **Nationaal Vakbondsmuseum** and **Tropenmuseum**) as well as various centers for exploring the outdoors and nature. If you're yearning for a "rural"

THE HIDDEN DEAL

MORE MUSEUMS FOR LESS

Amsterdam, though often caricatured as a city of pot pilgrims, has more museums per square kilometer than any other city in the world. Visitors planning to hit up even just a handful of these museums may want to invest in a ■ **Museumjaarkaart (MJK).** An especially good deal for younger travelers, the pass (€35, under 25 €20, including the one-time "handling fee") entitles the holder to admission at most of the major museums in Amsterdam, including the Van Gogh Museum, Rijksmuseum, and the Museum Van Loon.

The pass is also valid at many first-rate museums all over the Netherlands—over 400 in total—like the Mauritshuis in The Hague, the Nederlands Architectuurinstituut in Rotterdam, the Frans Hals Museum in Haarlem, and the Bonnefanten Museum in Maastricht. The card is good for one year but can be worthwhile even for those staying one week (combined admission to just the Van Gogh Museum and Rijksmuseum is about the price of an under-25 card). To buy the MJK, bring a passport photo to most of the participating museums.

Realize, however, that although the MJK will save you money, it may not save you any time; card-holders still have to wait in line. For more information, check the Dutch-only www.museumjaarkaart.nl.

DISCOVER

side to Amsterdam, try the Plantage's outdoor spots, including the **Hortus Botanicus, Artis Zoo,** or sprawling **Wertheim Park.**

BIKING AND WALKING TOURS

The moment you step out of Centraal Station into the crush of tourists, locals, street performers, panhandlers, and miscellaneous characters, you'll immediately realize that this is not a city for drivers. One of the best ways to see the city, to understand Amsterdam's layout, and to appreciate all of its architectural beauty is to traverse the myriad canals and back alleys by foot. Amsterdam proper is laced with pedestrian walks, parks, and squares, all within close proximity to one another. Despite the city's daunting map layout, Amsterdam is smaller than you think. The walking tours in this guide offer suggested self-guided jaunts all over the city organized by various themes. The **Stoner's Tour of Amsterdam** (p. 198) gives you the city's best coffee shops and other sights to titillate and/or soothe your addled mind. If you'd rather get high-brow than high, try the **Sophisticated City Tour** (p. 150), a sampling of Amsterdam's most urbane museums, landmarks, and restaurants. **A History Lesson** (p. 178) puts you in touch with Amsterdam's past, from Jewish immigration in the 17th century and Golden Age affluence to the sometimes sordid, liberated present. Walkers beware: you'll have to jostle for space with bikers—and more than the occasional tram—for supremacy over labyrinthine pathways. The best way to cope with the sound of bike bells ringing in your ears is to succumb and become a cyclist yourself; **A Biking Tour of Amsterdam** (p. 156) starts off at the city's best bike rental shop and takes you on a whirlwind tour of the city.

▨ LET'S GO PICKS

MOST NAUSEATING DUTCH DELICACY: Raw herring.

GROOVIEST MUSEUM OWNER: Nick Padalino of Electric Ladyland (p. 172).

BEST WAY TO CHECK YOUR MATE: Playing oversized chess at Max Euwe-plein (p. 152).

MOST PAINFUL STOMACH CRAMP: All you can eat in an hour at Taste of Culture (p. 123).

BEST PLACE TO GET HIGH (LITERALLY): The 85m Westerkerkstoren (p. 149).

BEST PLACE TO SWEAR (IN DUTCH!) AFTER BURNING YOURSELF: Keizer Culinair, where you can learn how to cook a five-course meal (p. 86).

BEST PLACE TO SEE LOTS AND LOTS OF HAIR: Cockring (p. 226).

BEST ESCAPE: Texel (p. 320).

BEST PLACE TO GET DIRTY IN A BATH: Thermos Day sauna (p. 195).

MOST EMBARRASSING MUSEUM TO VISIT WITH YOUR FAMILY (EXCEPT YOUR QUIRKY AUNT ESTHER): The Amsterdam Sex Museum (p. 168).

BEST PLACE TO KICK PIGEONS: Dam Square, where you'll be swimming in them (p. 147).

HEADIEST DUTCH BREW: Wieckse Witte from Maastricht.

BEST CONVERTED CHURCH NOW DEVOTED TO SACRILEGE: Paradiso (p. 232).

BEST PLACE TO VIEW OLD DUTCH ARTISTIC GREATS: The Van Gogh Museum (p. 174).

BEST PLACE TO VIEW THE NEXT DUTCH ARTISTIC GREATS: The CoBrA Museum (p. 181).

BEST OF THE NETHERLANDS (7-9 DAYS)

Leiden (1 day)
One of Europe's most prestigious universities lends Leiden a bipolar personality– a serious intellectual center (with philosophy literally written on the walls) and a hopping party city (p. 260).

Wadden Islands (1-2 days)
As desolate as life gets in the gentrified Dutch countryside, the Wadden Islands present an enviable escape with glorious stretches of sandy white beaches (p. 320).

Haarlem (1 day)
This traditional Dutch town offers churches and other architectural delights to go with the most restaurants per capita in the Netherlands. Hit the beach at nearby Zandvoort or Bloemendaal if you choose, but don't miss the brilliant Frans Hals Museum.

Utrecht (1 day)
Only a 30min. train ride from Amsterdam, this study-by-day and party-by-night university town claims some of the Netherlands's best festivals as well as its own Museum Quarter (p. 298).

Amsterdam
☆

The Hague and Delft (1-2 days)
Brush up on international law at the Hague, the Netherlands's seat of government, home of the royal family, and location of the extraordinary Mauritshuis (p. 269). Delft, the birthplace of painter Johannes Vermeer, is a short tram ride away; it's one of the loveliest and best preserved Dutch towns (p. 279).

Maastricht (1 day)
Maastricht lies at the crossroads of the Netherlands, Belgium, and Germany and has a rich history to match. Its old cobblestoned feel, pub culture, and mysterious caves are worth the long train ride (p. 313).

Rotterdam (1 day)
The biggest port city in Europe, a center for modern architecture, a multicultural city: Rotterdam is as far from the Old World as it gets—at least in the Netherlands (p. 285).

BEST OF AMSTERDAM (3 DAYS)

Behind the Bookcase
Beat the crowds by getting up early for a pilgrimage to the **Anne Frank Huis** (p. 168), where the little diarist and her family went into hiding. The nondescript building escaped Nazi notice for two years yet is now anything but under the radar. Marvel at the wondrous **Westerkerk** (p. 149) on your way in or out.

Fetishizing Foray
Fade away into the **Red Light District** (p. 2) in the early evening to witness the bizarrely sanitized, adult-amusement-park feel of the area. Before hitting a club or coffee shop, be sure to admire the oddly placed **Oude Kerk** (p. 145)

END

START

Monument Central
Tourists and pigeons alike flock to **Dam Square** (p. 147) in the **Nieuwe Zijd** (New Side, which is actually older than the **Oude Zijd**, or Old Side). It's no wonder, since the plaza is surrounded by landmarks like the **Nationaal Monument** (p. 147), **Nieuwe Kerk** (p. 167), and **Royal Palace** (p. 147).

Livin' Large in Leidseplein
Mosey on over to the bright lights and loud sounds of **Leidseplein** (p. 5) for a delicious Dutch dinner (p. 130) and some decadent dancing (p. 230)

END

Picnic Partaking
Stroll over to the lush **Vondelpark** (p. 154) and munch on a late lunch from one of the area's restaurants or supermarkets (p. 136).

Night Watch
When the sun dips in the west, roll on over to the GLBT-friendly **Rembrandtplein** (p. 233) and its raging surroundings — the hottest streets for clubbing the night away.

END

START

Museum Hopping
What's worth sacrificing a lazy first day in Amsterdam? How about two of the world's most dazzling sites of artistic excellence, the **Rijksmuseum** (p. 175) and the **Van Gogh Museum** (p. 174)? You'll see more brush strokes than you ever thought possible — and more tourists, so go early!

Day 1: Masterpieces and Minglin'

Day 2: Frankly, My Dear, I Don't Give a Dam

Day 3: Ring Around the Canal

'Round the Square

Check out Amsterdam's other bustling forum, **Nieuwmarkt** (p. 143), for some excellent shopping and outdoor markets on weekends. Grab food inside the medieval fortress that dominates the square (p. 2) or walk down **Zeedijk** (p. 123) through Chinatown for all-you-can-eat chow.

(More) Art and Adoration

Extend your tour with an early-morning visit to the beautiful **Zuiderkerk** (p. 160) and Rembrandt van Rijn's former digs at the **Museum Het Rembrandt** (p. 177).

START

Judaic Jaunt

Head south toward the **Jewish Historical Museum** (p. 177) and the **Portugees-Israelietische Synagoge** (p. 159) to learn more about Dutch Jews' difficult history.

Vegetables, Animals, Minerals

Visit the sprawling and verdant **Hortus Botanicus** (p. 158) for a nutritious picnic from a nearby *eetcafe*. Visit the **Hollandsche Schouwburg** memorial (p. 159) on your way to the **Artis Zoo** (p. 159), an oasis of fun in an otherwise solemn neighborhood.

BEST OF THE REST (6 DAYS)

Day 4: Trail Blazer

Enjoy breakfast any time of day at **Barney's** (p. 205), everyone's favorite coffee shop, in the charming **Scheepvaartbuurt**. The so-inclined can take advantage of Amsterdam's densest concentrations of coffee shops in the nearby **Nieuwe Zijd** (p. 202) and **Jordaan** (p. 209). In central Jordaan, you'll find **Electric Ladyland** (p.172), a museum devoted to fluorescent art that will blow your befuddled mind. Cap off your galvanizing day with hearty Dutch grub at one of the Jordaan's cozy *bruin cafes* (p. 237).

Day 5: No Pipe Dream

Take an easygoing day to explore Amsterdam's most up-and-coming neighborhood, **De Pijp** (p. 7). At the **Heineken Experience** (p. 155), you'll have to dodge myriad tourists, but the novelty (along with the free beer) is well worth it. Browse through the largest outdoor market in Europe along the pedestrian **Albert Cuypstraat** (p. 219) before a taste of classy De Pijp food (p. 137) or pub life (p. 240).

Day 8: Off the Charts

Some of Amsterdam's best sights are actually on the periphery of this compact city. Hop on the tram (or take your bike!) down to **Amsterdamse Bos** (p. 161), the city's forest. Still on the edge of town, you can learn to appreciate the Netherland's fanatical passion for football (soccer) at **ArenA Amsterdam** (p. 162). On your way back home, check out one of Europe's great modern art movements at the **CoBrA Museum** (p. 181).

Day 9: Get Out of Town

Many excellent daytrips (p. 243) await your final days, from beaches and tulips to college towns and international justice. For suggested itineraries in the Netherlands's top daytrip destinations, see p. 9.

Day 6: Culture Overload

The Canal Ring boasts three not-to-be-missed museums within blocks of each other: **De Appel** (p. 172), the **Foam Photography Museum** (p. 171), and the **Museum Van Loon** (p. 171). Just steps away, you can see art that's still fresh in the Canal Ring's and the westerly Jordaan's **art galleries** (p. 182). Once evening comes, it's time to visit the **Stadhuis-Het Muziektheater** (p. 187) to watch an opera or the ballet; alternatively, head to the **Concertgebouw** (p. 186) for first-rate classical music.

Day 7: Gay Gallivanting and Sapphic Sauntering

It's impossible to explore all of GLBT Amsterdam in a day—or two, or even 200—but there's no harm in trying. Check in at one of Amsterdam's many GLBT hotels and check out sites like a gay bookstore (p. 50) or sauna (p. 195). Cruise over to the **COC** (p. 50) to learn about the latest in GLBT politics and culture and pay homage at **Pink Point** (p. 153) with its monument to gays and lesbians persecuted in WWII. Finally, lace up your party shoes to drink and dance at GLBT bars and clubs from the **Centrum** (p. 226) to **Rembrandtplein** (p. 234).

ESSENTIALS

PLANNING YOUR TRIP

ENTRANCE REQUIREMENTS
Passport (p. 16). Required for everyone who is not a citizen of Austria, Belgium, Denmark, Finland, France, Germany, Greece, Iceland, Italy, Luxembourg, Norway, Portugal, Spain, or Sweden. Nationals of these countries need only a government-issued ID.
Inoculations (p. 27). Not required, but a good idea.
Work Permit (p. 17). Required for all non-EU/EEA citizens, Bulgarians, and Romanians planning to work in the Netherlands.

EMBASSIES AND CONSULATES

DUTCH CONSULAR SERVICES ABROAD

Australia: 120 Empire Circuit, Yarralumla, ACT 2600 (☎+61 02 6220 9400; www.netherlands.org.au). Open M-Th 9am-12:30pm and 2-4pm, F 9am-12:30pm. **Consulates:** Level 23, Tower 2, 101 Grafton St., Bondi Junction, NSW 1355 (☎+61 02 9387 6644). Open M-F 10am-1pm. Other offices in Adelaide, Brisbane, Hobart, Melbourne, and Perth.

Canada: 350 Albert St., Ste. 2020, Ottawa, ON K1R 1A4 (☎613-237-5030; www.netherlandsembassy.ca). Open M-Tu and Th-F 9am-1pm. **Consulates:** 1 Dundas St. W., Ste. 2106, Toronto, ON M5G 1Z3 (☎416-598-2520; www.dutchconsulate.toronto.on.ca). Open M-F 9am-noon. Other offices in Winnipeg, London, and Kingston.

Ireland: 160 Merrion Rd., Dublin 4 (☎+353 01 269 3444; www.netherlandsembassy.ie). Open M-F 9am-12:30pm. **Consulates:** Mainport, Monahon Rd., Cork (☎+353 021 431 7900). 2nd office at Shipping Office, Dock Rd., Limerick (☎+353 061 315 315).

New Zealand: P.O. Box 840, at Ballance and Featherston St., Wellington (☎+64 04 471 6390; www.netherlandsembassy.co.nz). Open M-F 10am-12:30pm. **Consulates:** P.O. Box 3816, Equitable House, 1st fl., 57 Symonds St., Auckland (☎+64 09 379 5399). Open M-F 9:30am-1pm. 2nd office at P.O. Box 13734, Kenton Chambers, Ste. 105, 1st fl., 190-192 Hereford St., Christchurch (☎+64 03 963 1485). Open M-F 10am-1pm.

UK: 38 Hyde Park Gate, London SW7 5DP (☎+44 020 7590 3200; www.netherlandsembassy.org.uk). Open M-F 9am-5pm; passports M-F 9am-noon. **Consulates:** Thistle Court, 1-2 Thistle St., Edinburgh EH2 1DD (☎+44 0131 220 3226). 2nd location at All-Route Shipping Ltd., 14-16 West Bank Rd., Belfast BT3 9JL (☎+44 028 9037 0223). Other offices in Aberdeen, Birmingham, Cardiff, Guernsey, Hull, Liverpool, Manchester, and Southampton.

US: 4200 Linnean Ave. NW, Washington, D.C. 20008 (☎877-388-2443; www.netherlands-embassy.org). Open M-F 9am-5pm; passports M-F 9:30am-noon. **Consulates:** 1 Rockefeller Plaza, 11th fl., New York City, NY 10020 (☎212-246-1429; www.cgny.org). 2nd location at 11766 Wilshire Boulevard, Ste. 1150, Los Angeles, CA 90025 (☎310-268-1598; www.ncla.org). Other offices in Chicago and Miami.

15

CONSULAR SERVICES IN THE NETHERLANDS

Australia: Carnegielaan 4, The Hague (☎070 310 8200; www.australian-embassy.nl). Open M-F 8:30am-5pm.

Canada: Sophialaan 7, The Hague (☎070 311 1600; www.canada.nl). Open M-F 8:30am-1pm and 1:45-5:30pm.

Ireland: 9 Dr. Kuyperstraat, The Hague (☎070 363 0993; www.irishembassy.nl/html/00_frame_000.html). Open M-F 10am-12:30pm and 2:30-5pm; visas 10am-12:30pm.

New Zealand: Eisenhowerlaan 77N, The Hague (☎070 346 9324; www.new-zealandhc.org.uk/home.cfm?c=36). Open M-F 9am-12:30pm and 1:30-5pm.

UK: Lange Voorhout 10, The Hague (☎070 427 0427; www.britain.nl). Open M-F 9am-5:30pm. **Consulate:** Koningslaan 44, Amsterdam (☎020 676 4343). Open M-F 8:30am-1:30pm.

US: Lange Voorhout 102, The Hague (☎070 310 2209; http://thehague.usembassy.gov). Open by appointment only. **Consulate:** Museumplein 19, Amsterdam (☎020 575 5309; http://amsterdam.usconsulate.gov). Open M-F 8:30am-11:30am. Closed last W of every month.

TOURIST OFFICES

The **Netherlands Board of Tourism** is a helpful guide to the Netherlands's various attractions and the country's logistical hurdles.

US: 355 Lexington Ave., 19th fl., New York City, NY 10017 (☎212-370-7360; http://us.holland.com).

UK: P.O. Box 30783, London WC2B 6DH (☎020 7539 7950; www.holland.com/uk).

DOCUMENTS AND FORMALITIES

PASSPORTS

REQUIREMENTS
Citizens of Australia, Canada, Ireland, New Zealand, the UK, and the US need valid and current passports to enter the Netherlands and to re-enter their home countries. The Netherlands does not allow entrance to Americans, Australians, Canadians, and New Zealanders whose passports expire in under three months; returning home with an expired passport is illegal and may result in a fine.

NEW PASSPORTS
Citizens of Australia, Canada, Ireland, New Zealand, the UK, and the US can apply for a passport at any passport office or at selected post offices and courts of law. Citizens of these countries may also download passport applications from the official websites of their countries' governments or passport offices. Any new passport or renewal applications must be filed well in advance of the departure date, though most passport offices offer rush services for a very steep fee. Note, however, that "rushed" passports still take up to two weeks to arrive.

PASSPORT MAINTENANCE
Photocopy the page of your passport with your photo, as well as your visas, traveler's check serial numbers, and any other important documents. Carry one set of copies in a safe place, apart from the originals, and leave another set at home. Consulates also recommend that you carry an expired passport or an official copy of your birth certificate in a part of your baggage separate from other documents.

ONE EUROPE. European unity has come a long way since 1958, when the European Economic Community (EEC) was created to promote European solidarity and cooperation. Since then, the EEC has become the European Union (EU), a mighty political, legal, and economic institution. On May 1, 2004, 10 South, Central, and Eastern European countries—Cyprus, the Czech Republic, Estonia, Hungary, Latvia, Lithuania, Malta, Poland, Slovakia, and Slovenia—were admitted to the EU, joining 15 other member states: Austria, Belgium, Denmark, Finland, France, Germany, Greece, Ireland, Italy, Luxembourg, the Netherlands, Portugal, Spain, Sweden, and the UK. On January 1, 2007, two others, Bulgaria and Romania, came into the world, bringing the tally of member states to 27.

What does this have to do with the average non-EU tourist? The EU's policy of **freedom of movement** means that border controls between the first 15 member states (minus Ireland and the UK but plus Norway and Iceland) have been abolished, and visa policies harmonized. Under this treaty, formally known as the **Schengen Agreement,** you're still required to carry a passport (or government-issued ID card for EU citizens) when crossing an internal border, but once you've been admitted into one country, you're free to travel to other participating states. On June 5, 2005, Switzerland ratified the treaty but has yet to implement it. All 10 of the 2004 member states are slated to be added to Schengen in October of 2007 (although 2008 is more realistic). Britain and Ireland have also formed a **common travel area,** abolishing passport controls between the UK and the Republic of Ireland.

For more important consequences of the EU for travelers, see **The Euro** (p. 20) and **European Customs** and **EU customs regulations** (p. 18).

If you lose your passport, immediately notify the local police and the nearest embassy or consulate of your home government. To expedite its replacement, you must show ID and proof of citizenship; it also helps to know all information previously recorded in the passport. In some cases, a replacement may take weeks to process, and it may be valid only for a limited time. Any visas stamped in your old passport will be irretrievably lost. In an emergency, ask for immediate temporary traveling papers that will permit you to re-enter your home country.

VISAS AND WORK PERMITS

VISAS

EU citizens do not need a visa. Citizens of Australia, Canada, New Zealand, and the US do not need a visa for stays of up to 90 days, though this three-month period begins upon entry into any of the countries that belong to the EU's **freedom of movement** zone (above). Those staying longer than 90 days may purchase a visa through their consular service (p. 15). Visas good for either a one-year or a five-year stay in the Netherlands cost €60.

Double-check entrance requirements at the nearest embassy or consulate of the Netherlands (see **Embassies and Consulates Abroad,** p. 15) for up-to-date info before departure. US citizens can also consult http://travel.state.gov.

Entering the Netherlands to study requires a special student visa for some scholars. For more information, see **Beyond Tourism** (p. 77).

WORK PERMITS

Admission as a visitor does not include the right to work, which is authorized only by a work permit. For more info, flip on over to **Beyond Tourism** (p. 77).

ESSENTIALS

IDENTIFICATION

When you travel, always carry at least two forms of identification on your person, including a photo ID; a passport and a driver's license or birth certificate is usually an adequate combination. Never carry all of your IDs together; split them up in case of theft or loss and keep photocopies in your luggage and at home.

STUDENT, TEACHER, AND YOUTH IDENTIFICATION

The **International Student Identity Card (ISIC),** the most widely accepted form of student ID, provides discounts on some sights, accommodations, food, and transportation; access to a 24hr. emergency helpline; and insurance benefits for US cardholders. In the Netherlands, it can mean cheaper bike rentals, free drinks at a hostel bar, or even a free dessert at Burger King. ISIC applicants must be full-time secondary or post-secondary school students at least 12 years of age. Because of the proliferation of fake ISICs, some services (particularly airlines) require additional proof of student identity.

The **International Teacher Identity Card (ITIC)** offers teachers the same insurance coverage as the ISIC and similar but limited discounts. To qualify for the card, teachers must be currently employed and have worked a minimum of 18hr. per week for at least one school year. For travelers who are under 26 years old but are not students, the **International Youth Travel Card (IYTC)** also offers many of the same benefits as the ISIC.

Each of these identity cards costs US$22. ISICs, ITICs, and IYTCs are valid for one year from the date of issue. To learn more about ISICs, ITICs, and IYTCs, try www.myisic.com. Many student travel agencies (p. 32) issue the cards; for a list of issuing agencies or more information, see the **International Student Travel Confederation (ISTC)** website (www.istc.org).

The **International Student Exchange Card (ISE Card)** is a similar identification card available to students, faculty, and youths aged 12 to 26. The card provides discounts, medical insurance, access to a 24hr. emergency helpline, and the ability to purchase student airfares. An ISE Card costs US$25; call ☎ 800-255-8000 (in North America) or 480-951-1177 (from all other continents) for more info or visit www.isecard.com.

CUSTOMS

CUSTOMS IN THE EU. As well as freedom of movement of people within the EU (see p. 17), travelers in the first 15 EU member countries (Austria, Belgium, Denmark, Finland, France, Germany, Greece, Ireland, Italy, Luxembourg, the Netherlands, Portugal, Spain, Sweden, and the UK) can also take advantage of the freedom of movement of goods. This means that there are no customs controls at internal EU borders (i.e., you can take the blue customs channel at the airport), and travelers are free to transport whatever legal substances they like, as long as it is for their own personal (non-commercial) use—up to 800 cigarettes, 10L of spirits, 90L of wine (including up to 60L of sparkling wine), and 110L of beer. Duty-free allowances were abolished on June 30, 1999, for travel between the original 15 EU member states; this now also applies to Cyprus and Malta. However, travelers between the EU and the rest of the world still get a duty-free allowance when passing through customs.

Upon entering the Netherlands, you must declare certain items from abroad and pay a duty on the value of those articles if they exceed the allowance established by Dutch customs service. Note that goods and gifts purchased at **duty-free** shops abroad are not exempt from duty or sales tax; "duty-free" merely means that you need not pay a tax in the country of purchase. Duty-free allowances were abolished for travel between EU member states on June 30, 1999, but still exist for those arriving from outside the EU. Upon returning home, you must likewise declare all articles acquired abroad and pay a duty on the value of articles in excess of your home country's allowance. In order to expedite your return, make a list of any valuables brought from home and register them with customs before traveling abroad, and be sure to keep receipts for all goods acquired abroad.

Upon departure from the Netherlands, you can reclaim the money you shelled out due to value added taxes (p. 22) from large purchases taken back to your home country. The refund can extend to accommodations, food, and automotive expenses and can be applied for up to five years after your trip. Keep your receipts and check at VVV branches for details.

MONEY

CURRENCY AND EXCHANGE

The currency chart below is based on August 2007 exchange rates between local currency and Australian dollars (AUS$), Canadian dollars (CDN$), New Zealand dollars (NZ$), British pounds (UK£), and US dollars (US$). Check the currency converter on websites like www.xe.com or www.bloomberg.com or a large newspaper for the latest exchange rates.

EURO (€)		
AUS$ = €0.62		€1 = AUS$1.62
CDN$ = €0.69		€1 = CDN$1.46
NZ$ = €0.55		€1 = NZ$1.82
UK£ = €1.48		€1 = UK£0.68
US$ = €0.72		€1 = US$1.38

As a general rule, it's cheaper to convert money in the Netherlands than at home. While currency exchange should be available at Schiphol or your point of entry, it's wise to bring enough euro to last for the first 24 to 72 hours of your trip.

When changing money abroad, try to go only to banks or *bureaux de change* that have at most a 5% margin between their buy and sell prices. Since you lose money with every transaction, **convert large sums** (unless the currency is depreciating rapidly), but **no more than you'll need.**

If you use traveler's checks or bills, carry some in small denominations (the equivalent of US$50 or less) for times when you are forced to exchange money at disadvantageous rates but bring a range of denominations since charges may be levied per check cashed. Store your money in a variety of forms; ideally, at any given time you will be carrying some cash, some traveler's checks, and an ATM and/or credit card. All travelers should also consider carrying some US dollars (about US$50 worth), which are often preferred by local tellers.

TRAVELER'S CHECKS

Traveler's checks are one of the safest and least troublesome means of carrying funds. American Express and Visa are the most recognized brands. Many banks and agencies sell them for a small commission. Check issuers provide refunds if the checks are lost or stolen, and many provide additional services, such as toll-free refund hotlines abroad, emergency message services, and assistance with lost and stolen credit cards or passports. Traveler's checks are readily accepted in Amsterdam and in other large towns and cities in the Netherlands. Ask about toll-

THE EURO. The official currency of 13 members of the European Union—Austria, Belgium, Finland, France, Germany, Greece, Ireland, Italy, Luxembourg, the Netherlands, Portugal, Slovenia, and Spain—is now the euro.

The currency has some important—and positive—consequences for travelers hitting more than one euro-zone country. For one thing, money-changers across the euro-zone are obliged to exchange money at the official, fixed rate (see below) and at no commission (though they may still charge a small service fee). Second, euro-denominated traveler's checks allow you to pay for goods and services across the euro-zone, again at the official rate and commission-free.

At the time of printing, €1 = AUS$1.62 = CDN$1.46 = NZ$1.82 = UK£0.68 = US$1.38. For more info, check a currency converter (such as www.xe.com) or www.europa.eu.int.

free refund hotlines and the location of refund centers when purchasing checks, and always carry emergency cash.

American Express: Checks available with commission at select banks, at all AmEx offices, and online (www.americanexpress.com; US residents only). AmEx cardholders can also purchase checks by phone (☎800-528-4800). Checks available in Australian, British, Canadian, European, Japanese, and US currencies, among others. AmEx also offers the Travelers Cheque Card, a prepaid reloadable card. Cheques for Two can be signed by either of two people traveling together. For purchase locations or more information, contact AmEx's service centers: in Australia ☎29 271 8666, in New Zealand 09 367 4567, in the UK 1273 696 933, in the US and Canada 800-221-7282; from the Netherlands, dial 020 504 8000 or call the US collect at 336-393-1111.

Travelex: Visa TravelMoney prepaid cash card and Visa traveler's checks available. For information about Thomas Cook MasterCard in Canada and the US, call ☎800-223-7373, in the UK 0800 622 101; elsewhere, call the UK collect at +44 1733 318 950. For information about Interpayment Visa in the US and Canada call ☎800-732-1322, in the UK 0800 515 884; elsewhere, call the UK collect at +44 1733 318 949. For more information, visit www.travelex.com.

Visa: Checks available (generally with commission) at banks worldwide. For the location of the nearest office, call the Visa Travelers Cheque Global Refund and Assistance Center: in the UK ☎0800 895 078, in the US 800-227-6811; elsewhere, call the UK collect at +44 2079 378 091. Checks available in British, Canadian, European, Japanese, and US currencies, among others. Visa also offers TravelMoney, a prepaid debit card that can be reloaded online or by phone. For more information on Visa travel services, see http://usa.visa.com/personal/using_visa/travel_with_visa.html.

CREDIT, DEBIT, AND ATM CARDS

Where they are accepted, credit cards often offer superior exchange rates—up to 5% better than the retail rate used by banks and other currency exchange establishments. Credit cards may also offer services such as insurance or emergency help and are sometimes required to reserve hotel rooms or rental cars. Although the Dutch widely accept credit cards, many budget hotels require a stay of several nights or charge a surcharge if you want to use your credit card to pay your bill. We recommend making your reservation with a credit card but then paying in cash. **MasterCard** (a.k.a. EuroCard in Europe) and **Visa** are the most frequently accepted; **American Express** cards work at some ATMs and at AmEx offices and major airports.

The use of ATM cards is widespread in the Netherlands. Depending on the system that your home bank uses, you can most likely access your personal bank account from abroad. ATMs get the same wholesale exchange rate as credit cards, but there is often a limit on the amount of money you can withdraw per day (usually around US$500). There is typically also a surcharge of US$1-5 per withdrawal.

Debit cards are as convenient as credit cards but withdraw money directly from the holder's checking account. A debit card can be used wherever its associated credit card company (usually MasterCard or Visa) is accepted. Debit cards often also function as ATM cards and can be used to withdraw cash from associated banks and ATMs throughout the Netherlands.

The two major international money networks are **MasterCard/Maestro/Cirrus** (for ATM locations ☎800-424-7787 or www.mastercard.com) and **Visa/PLUS** (for ATM locations ☎800-847-2911 or www.visa.com). Watch out for transaction fees that are paid to the bank that owns the ATM.

PINS AND ATMS. To use a cash or credit card to withdraw money from a cash machine (ATM) in Europe, you must have a four-digit **Personal Identification Number (PIN).** If your PIN is longer than four digits, ask your bank whether you can just use the first four or whether you'll need a new one. **Credit cards** don't usually come with PINs, so if you intend to hit up ATMs in Europe with a credit card to get cash advances, call your credit card company before leaving to request one.

Travelers with alphabetic, rather than numerical, PINs may also be thrown off by the lack of letters on European cash machines. The following are the corresponding numbers to use: 1=QZ; 2=ABC; 3=DEF; 4=GHI; 5=JKL; 6=MNO; 7=PRS; 8=TUV; and 9=WXY. Note that if you mistakenly punch the wrong code into the machine three times, it will swallow your card for good.

GETTING MONEY FROM HOME

If you run out of money while traveling, the easiest and cheapest solution is to have someone back home make a deposit to your bank account. Failing that, consider one of the following options.

WIRING MONEY

It is possible to arrange a **bank money transfer,** which means asking a bank back home to wire money to a bank in the Netherlands. This is the cheapest way to transfer cash, but it's also the slowest, usually taking several days or more. Note that some banks may only release your funds in local currency, potentially sticking you with a poor exchange rate; inquire about this in advance. Wiring money in the Netherlands is about as straightforward and fast as it gets, especially at larger banks. Money transfer services like **Western Union** are faster and more convenient than bank transfers—but also much pricier. Western Union has many locations worldwide. To find one, visit www.westernunion.com or call in Australia ☎1800 173 833, in Canada and the US 800-325-6000, in the UK 0800 833 833, or in the Netherlands 0800 736 3666. To wire money using a credit card (Discover, MasterCard, Visa), call in Canada and the US ☎800-CALL-CASH, in the UK 0800 833 833. Money transfer services are also available to **American Express** cardholders and at selected **Thomas Cook** offices.

US STATE DEPARTMENT (US CITIZENS ONLY)

In serious emergencies only, the US State Department will forward money within hours to the nearest consular office, which will then disburse it according to instructions for a US$30 fee. If you wish to use this service, you must contact the Overseas Citizens Service division of the US State Department (☎202-647-5225, toll-free 888-407-4747).

ESSENTIALS

COSTS

The cost of your trip will vary considerably, depending on where you go, how you travel, and where you stay. The most significant expenses will probably be your round-trip (return) **airfare** to the Netherlands (see **Getting to the Netherlands: By Plane,** p. 31). Before you go, spend some time calculating a reasonable daily **budget.**

STAYING ON A BUDGET

To give you a general idea, a bare-bones day in the Netherlands (sleeping in hostels/guesthouses, buying food at supermarkets) would cost about US$50 (€35); a slightly more comfortable day (sleeping in hostels/guesthouses and the occasional budget hotel, eating one meal per day at a restaurant, going out at night) would cost US$90 (€65); and for a luxurious day, the sky's the limit. Don't forget to factor in emergency reserve funds (at least US$200) when planning how much money you'll need.

TIPS FOR SAVING MONEY

Some simpler ways include searching out opportunities for free entertainment, splitting accommodation and food costs with trustworthy fellow travelers, and buying food in supermarkets rather than eating out. Bring a **sleepsack** (p. 23) to save on sheet charges in European hostels and do your **laundry** in the sink (unless you're explicitly prohibited from doing so). Museums often have certain days once a month or once a week when admission is free; plan accordingly. In the summertime and on Queen's Day (April 30), there are tons of free concerts and events.

 BUDGET VOCABULARY. In Dutch, *korting* means "discount," while *gratis* means "free."

If you are eligible, consider getting an ISIC or an IYTC (p. 18); many sights and museums offer reduced admission to students and youths. For getting around quickly, bikes are the most economical option: renting a bike is cheaper than renting a moped or scooter. Don't forget about walking, though; you can learn a lot about a city by seeing it on foot. Drinking at bars and clubs quickly becomes expensive; it's cheaper to buy alcohol at a supermarket and imbibe before going out. That said, don't go overboard. Though staying within your budget is important, don't do so at the expense of your health or a great travel experience.

TIPPING AND BARGAINING

Service charges are included in all hotel, restaurant, and shopping bills as well as taxi fares, so tips are not necessary—but certainly accepted and appreciated. Taxi drivers are customarily tipped 10%, and bathroom attendants usually receive €0.10-0.20 per visitor. At restaurants, it's polite to leave a 10-15% tip. For small purchases, such as a drink in a bar or cafe, it's usually enough to round up the tab to the nearest euro.

TAXES

The quoted price of all goods and services in the Netherlands includes the **value added tax** (**BTW** in the Netherlands), which is set at 6% or 19% depending on the type of good or service purchased. The general tax rate—most often for larger goods (clothing, electronics, and jewelry)—is set at 19%. The going rate for some services (hotels) and smaller purchases like food, books, and tickets is 6%.

PACKING

Pack lightly: Lay out only what you absolutely need, then take half the clothes and twice the money. The Travelite FAQ (www.travelite.org) is a good resource for tips on traveling light. The online **Universal Packing List** (http://upl.codeq.info) will generate a customized list of suggested items based on your trip length, the expected climate, your planned activities, and other factors. Some frequent travelers keep a bag packed with all the essentials: passport, money belt, hat, socks, etc. Then, when they decide to leave, they know they haven't forgotten anything.

Luggage: Toting a **suitcase** or **trunk** is fine if you plan to live only in Amsterdam and explore from there, but it's not a great idea if you plan to move around frequently. In that case, a sturdy **frame backpack** is unbeatable. In addition to your main piece of luggage, a **daypack** (a small backpack or courier bag) is useful.

Clothing: No matter when you're traveling, it's a good idea to bring a warm jacket or wool sweater, a rain jacket (Gore-Tex® is both waterproof and breathable), sturdy shoes, and thick socks. Flip-flops or waterproof sandals are must-haves for grubby hostel showers, and extra socks are always a good idea. You may also want 1 outfit for going out and maybe a nicer pair of shoes. If you plan to visit religious or cultural sites, remember that you will need modest and respectful dress. Most nightlife establishments don't have stringent dress codes, though some have them for specific theme nights (e.g., leather).

Sleepsack: Some hostels require that you either provide your own linen or rent sheets from them. Save cash by making your own sleepsack: fold a full-size sheet in half the long way, then sew it closed along the long side and one of the short sides.

Converters and Adapters: In the Netherlands, electricity is 230 volts AC, enough to fry any 120V North American appliance. 220/240V electrical appliances won't work with a 120V current, either. Americans and Canadians should buy an adapter (which changes the shape of the plug; US$8) and a converter (which changes the voltage; US$10-30). Don't make the mistake of using only an adapter (unless appliance instructions explicitly state otherwise). Australians and New Zealanders (who use 230V at home) won't need a converter but will need a set of adapters to use anything electrical. For more on all things adaptable, check out http://kropla.com/electric.htm.

Toiletries: Condoms, deodorant, razors, tampons, and toothbrushes are often available, but it may be difficult to find your preferred brand; bring extras. Contact lenses are likely to be expensive and difficult to find, so bring enough extra pairs and solution for your entire trip. Also bring your glasses and a copy of your prescription in case you need emergency replacements. If you use heat-disinfection, either switch temporarily to a chemical disinfection system (check first to make sure it's safe with your brand of lenses), or buy a converter to 220/240V.

TOP 10 LIST

TOP 10 WAYS TO SAVE IN AMSTERDAM

Glimpsing Van Goghs and carousing in coffee shops can certainly be expensive, but fear not: *Let's Go* has culled some saving strategies to keep you on budget.

1. Buy food at **open-air markets,** but keep in mind they're more expensive on the weekends. Albert Heijn is not the cheapest supermarket, but its branches are easy to find; Euro Shopper is a consistently cheap food brand.

2. Patronize **coffee shops** farther outside the city center for cheaper prices; you can always bring your skunk back to a shop closer to the center to smoke.

3. Hang out **outside** in one of Amsterdam's 28 parks.

4. Find **free Internet** access in libraries or at cafes and coffee shops around the city.

5. Make your base **outside of the Centrum** in an area where restaurants and accommodations tend to be cheaper and less touristed.

6. At bars, order **draft beers** (Heineken, Dommelsch, etc.) or stock up on €3 wine at the supermarket.

7. Don't even think about **taking a cab** in this compact city.

8. Take advantage of **flyers and coupons** (in weekly papers, from promoters, or in some hip shops) that will allow you to bypass cover charges at clubs.

9. Ask hotels for **last-minute specials.** Say please.

10. Rent a bike to see the canals instead of overpaying for a boat cruise. After all, it's Amsterdam.

LIQUIDS IN THE AIR. Travelers should note new EU travel restrictions on liquids—including drinks, toiletries, and gels. At the time of printing, liquids could be transported only in containers of 100mL (3 fl. oz. in the US) or less. Each passenger could carry only as many containers as fit in a 1L (1 quart in the US) clear plastic bag. To avoid hassles, put as many of your liquids as possible in your checked luggage. Contact Schiphol Airport (p. 31) for the latest policy.

First-Aid Kit: For a basic first-aid kit, pack bandages, a pain reliever, antibiotic cream, a thermometer, a multifunction pocketknife, tweezers, moleskin, decongestant, motion-sickness remedy, diarrhea or upset-stomach medication (Pepto Bismol® or Imodium®), an antihistamine, sunscreen, insect repellent, and burn ointment.

Film: For those who have not yet surrendered to technology, film and developing in the Netherlands are relatively inexpensive, though you may consider bringing along enough film for your entire trip and developing it at home. Beware, however, that film and its developers are increasingly rare in this digital age. Although a digital camera requires a steep initial investment, it means you never have to buy film again. Just be sure to bring along a sufficiently large memory card and extra (or rechargeable) batteries. For more info on digital cameras, visit www.shortcourses.com/choosing/contents.htm. Less serious photographers may want to bring a disposable camera or two. Despite disclaimers, airport security X-rays can fog film, so buy a lead-lined pouch at a camera store or ask security to hand-inspect it. Always pack film in your carry-on luggage, since higher-intensity X-rays are used on checked luggage.

Other Useful Items: For safety purposes, you should bring a **money belt** and a small **padlock.** Basic **outdoors equipment** (plastic water bottle, compass, waterproof matches, pocketknife, sunglasses, sunscreen, hat) may also prove useful. **Quick repairs** of torn garments can be done on the road with a needle and thread; also consider bringing electrical tape for patching tears. If you want to do laundry by hand, bring detergent, a small rubber ball to stop up the sink, and string for a makeshift clothes line. Other things you're liable to forget include: an umbrella, sealable **plastic bags** (for damp clothes, soap, food, shampoo, and other spillables), an **alarm clock,** safety pins, rubber bands, a flashlight, earplugs, garbage bags, and a small calculator. A **cell phone** can be a lifesaver (literally) on the road; see p. 46 for information on acquiring one that will work in the Netherlands.

Important Documents: Don't forget your passport, traveler's checks, ATM and/or credit cards, adequate ID, and photocopies of all of the aforementioned in case these documents are lost or stolen (p. 16). If applicable, also check that you have a hosteling membership card (p. 100), driver's license (p. 18), travel insurance forms, and/or ISIC (p. 18).

SAFETY AND HEALTH

GENERAL ADVICE

In any type of crisis situation, the most important thing to do is **stay calm.** Your country's embassy (p. 15) is usually your best resource when things go wrong; registering with that embassy upon arrival in the country is often a good idea. The government offices listed in the **Travel Advisories** box (p. 26) can provide information on the services they offer their citizens in case of emergencies abroad.

LOCAL LAWS AND POLICE

The Netherlands has some of the most progressive laws in the world (see **Euthanasia Expanded,** p. 63), and visitors are often struck by the lack of moral legislation in the country and the efficiency of the legal system. That said, the Netherlands is a highly regulated country, both by criminal statutes and by cultural codes. If ever in doubt whether an activity is legally proscribed, ask one of the many helpful police officers continuously patrolling Amsterdam's streets, especially in the Red Light District. For emergency information, see p. 96.

DRUGS AND ALCOHOL

Trying to explain substance use in the Netherlands isn't rocket science—it's harder. The drinking age in the Netherlands is 16, but this has not led to rampant public drunkenness—at least among locals. It is poor form to stumble around in public under the influence, and doing so will immediately brand you a tourist.

The Dutch have always been at the forefront of progressive politics, and that position is rather evident today in its drug policy. In an attempt to create the safest environment possible for those who partake, the Dutch government tolerates soft drugs— they are highly regulated but not legalized. As a result, Amsterdam has now become a mecca for drug use and experimentation, though such a reputation has led to something of a local backlash against so-called "drug tourism." Amsterdam may be famous for its tolerance, but it is important to respect the city's customs in these sensitive areas.

Though Amsterdam is known as the hash capital of the world, marijuana is increasingly popular. Technically, pot is illegal in the Netherlands, but the country's current tolerance policy means that you are unlikely to face legal action if you carry no more than 30g (about 1 oz.) on your person and buy no more than five grams at a time at the country's coffee shops. Herbal drugs, such as mushrooms, are also tolerated in the Netherlands and are sold in smart shops. Both coffee shops and smart shops, however, are closely regulated (see **Know the Law**, p. 25). It is essential to note that **hard drugs—including heroin, ecstasy, or cocaine—are very much illegal and not tolerated,** and possession is treated as a serious crime. For full information on smoking and drug use, including drug culture and etiquette in the Netherlands, see p. 196. For information on the impending smoking ban, see **Up in Smoke?,** p. 238.

SPECIFIC CONCERNS

TERRORISM

Amsterdam is a major European city, and as such it takes the threat of terrorism very seriously. Although the Netherlands has seen nothing on the scale of the bombings in Madrid or London, its

THE LOCAL STORY

KNOW THE LAW

Amsterdam has a well-earned reputation for being an easy-going city but there are still limits to its liberality. The Dutch carefully regulate cannabis consumption, although deciphering the policy—a combination of prohibition and toleration— perplexes even some experts. Yet even if the specifics may be confusing, it's important to know some of the basics to avoid being caught in an undesirable position.

Coffee shops must follow these regulations: no advertising that a shop sells marijuana; no one under age 18 permitted; no hard drugs; no alcohol; and no aggression or disruptive behavior. Shops cannot store more than 500g of cannabis and cannot sell more than 5g to a person per day. Tokers should also know that they are personally allowed to possess up to 30g.

Laws and statutes regarding consumption of cannabis may differ among various municipalities and are constantly altered by local and national officials. Many Dutch cities regulate the proximity of coffee shops to schools, as well as their opening and closing times. Whether you're allowed to light up in specific places, such as in- and out-of-doors, is usually a matter of etiquette or an establishment's specific rules. As such it is important to ask reputable sources if you're unsure whether what you want to do is tolerated or legal. For a more complete rundown of drug use, see p. 196.

government has been on heightened alert since 2004. That year, a Muslim extremist assassinated director Theo van Gogh for his controversial film about Islam. Rumblings about Islamic fundamentalism have only grown with the increasing Dutch Muslim population (see **Low Country, High Tensions,** p. 64). Steps to curtail terrorism include the implementation of radiological portal monitors in Rotterdam and an agreement with the US to develop a program to facilitate travel between Schiphol and JFK airports. Travelers should be aware that the recent rise in tensions between Dutch natives and immigrants has resulted in numerous, often heated protests. Although you should do your best to avoid this sticky situation, remember that it is never possible to guarantee immunity from it. The box on **travel advisories** below lists offices to contact and websites to visit to get the most updated list of your home country's government's advisories about travel.

TRAVEL ADVISORIES. The following government offices provide travel information and advisories by telephone, by fax, or via the web:

Australian Department of Foreign Affairs and Trade: ☎612 6261 1111; www.dfat.gov.au.

Canadian Department of Foreign Affairs and International Trade (DFAIT): ☎800-267-8376; www.dfait-maeci.gc.ca. Call for their free booklet, *Bon Voyage...But.*

New Zealand Ministry of Foreign Affairs: ☎044 398 000; www.mfat.govt.nz.

United Kingdom Foreign and Commonwealth Office: ☎020 7008 1500; www.fco.gov.uk.

US Department of State: ☎888-407-4747; http://travel.state.gov. Visit the website for the booklet *A Safe Trip Abroad.*

PERSONAL SAFETY

EXPLORING AND TRAVELING

To avoid unwanted attention, try to blend in as much as possible. Respecting local customs (in many cases, dressing more conservatively than you would at home) may placate would-be hecklers. Familiarize yourself with your surroundings before setting out and carry yourself with confidence. Check maps in shops and restaurants rather than on the street. If you are traveling alone, be sure someone at home knows your itinerary and never tell anyone you meet that you're by yourself. When walking at night, stick to busy, well-lit streets and avoid dark alleyways. If you ever feel uncomfortable, leave the area as quickly and directly as you can.

There is no sure-fire way to avoid all the threatening situations you might encounter while traveling, but a good **self-defense course** will give you concrete ways to react to unwanted advances. **Impact, Prepare,** and **Model Mugging** can refer you to local self-defense courses in Australia, Canada, Switzerland and the US. Visit www.modelmugging.org for a list of nearby chapters.

If you are using a **car,** learn local driving signals and wear a seatbelt. Children under 40 lbs. should ride only in specially designed carseats, available for a small fee from most car rental agencies. Study maps before you hit the road and, if you plan on spending a lot of time driving, consider bringing spare parts and investing in a cellular phone and a roadside assistance program (p. 41). Park your vehicle in a garage or well-traveled area and use a steering wheel locking device in larger cities. **Sleeping in your car** is the most dangerous (and often illegal) way to get your rest. For info on the perils of **hitchhiking,** see p. 43.

POSSESSIONS AND VALUABLES

Never leave your belongings unattended; crime occurs in even the most safe-looking hostel or hotel. Bring your own padlock for hostel lockers and don't ever store valuables in a locker. Be particularly careful on **buses** and **trains;** horror stories abound about determined thieves who wait for travelers to fall asleep. Carry your bag or purse in front of you where you can see it. When traveling with others, sleep in alternate shifts. When alone, use good judgment in selecting a train compartment: never stay in an empty one and use a lock to secure your pack to the luggage rack. Use extra caution if traveling at night or on overnight trains. Try to sleep on top bunks with your luggage stored above you (if not in bed with you) and keep important documents and other valuables on you at all times.

There are a few steps you can take to minimize the financial risk associated with traveling. First, **bring as little with you as possible.** Second, buy a few combination **padlocks** to secure your belongings either in your pack or in a hostel or train station locker. Third, **carry as little cash as possible.** Keep your traveler's checks and ATM/credit cards in a **money belt**—not a "fanny pack"—along with your passport and ID cards. Fourth, **keep a small cash reserve separate from your primary stash.** This should be worth about US$50 (US$ or euro are best) sewn into or stored in the depths of your pack, along with your traveler's check numbers and photocopies of your passport, your birth certificate, and other important documents.

In large cities like Amsterdam, **con artists** often work in groups and may involve children. Beware of certain classics: sob stories that require money, rolls of bills "found" on the street, mustard spilled (or saliva spit) onto your shoulder to distract you while they snatch your bag. **Never let your passport and your bags out of your sight.** Hostel workers will sometimes stand at bus and train station arrival points to try to recruit tired and disoriented travelers to their hostel; never believe strangers who tell you that theirs is the only hostel open. Beware of **pickpockets** in city crowds, especially on public transportation and around the Red Light District, Leidseplein, and Centraal Station. Also, be alert in public telephone booths: If you must say your calling card number, do so very quietly; if you punch it in, make sure no one can look over your shoulder.

If you will be traveling with electronic devices such as a laptop computer or a PDA, check whether your homeowner's insurance covers loss, theft, or damage when you travel. If not, you might consider purchasing a low-cost separate insurance policy. **Safeware** (☎800-800-1492; www.safeware.com) specializes in covering computers and charges $90 for 90-day comprehensive international travel coverage up to $4000.

PRE-DEPARTURE HEALTH

In your **passport,** write the names of any people you wish to be contacted in case of a medical emergency and list any allergies or medical conditions. Matching a prescription to a foreign equivalent is not always easy, safe, or possible, so if you take prescription drugs, consider carrying up-to-date prescriptions or a statement from your doctor stating the medication's trade name, manufacturer, chemical name, and dosage. While traveling, be sure to keep all medication with you in your carry-on luggage. For tips on packing a **first-aid kit** and other health essentials, see p. 24.

IMMUNIZATIONS AND PRECAUTIONS

Travelers over two years old should make sure that the following vaccines are up to date: MMR (for measles, mumps, and rubella); DTaP or Td (for diphtheria, tetanus, and pertussis); IPV (for polio); Hib (for *Haemophilus influenzae* B); and HepB (for Hepatitis B). For recommendations on immunizations and prophylaxis, consult the Centers for Disease Control and Prevention (CDC; see below) in the US or the equivalent in your home country and check with a doctor for guidance.

USEFUL ORGANIZATIONS AND PUBLICATIONS

The American **Centers for Disease Control and Prevention** (**CDC;** ☎877-FYI-TRIP; www.cdc.gov/travel) maintains an international travelers' hotline and an informative website. Consult the appropriate government agency of your home country for consular information sheets on health, entry requirements, and other issues for various countries (see the listings in the box on **Travel Advisories,** p. 26). For quick information on health and other travel warnings, Americans can call the **Overseas Citizens Services** (M-F 8am-8pm; from US ☎888-407-4747, from overseas 202-501-4444) or contact a passport agency, embassy, or consulate abroad. For information on medical evacuation services and travel insurance firms, see the US government's website at http://travel.state.gov/travel/abroad_health.html or the **British Foreign and Commonwealth Office** (www.fco.gov.uk). For general health information, contact the **American Red Cross** (☎202-303-4498; www.redcross.org).

STAYING HEALTHY

Common sense is the simplest prescription for good health while you travel. Drink lots of fluids to prevent dehydration and constipation and wear sturdy, broken-in shoes and clean socks. There is little medical risk to traveling through the Netherlands, but you may want to take out travel insurance just in case. Citizens of the EU and Australia benefit from reciprocal health arrangements with the Netherlands; check at home to find out which medical and dental services are covered and how.

ONCE IN THE NETHERLANDS

ENVIRONMENTAL HAZARDS

Heat exhaustion and dehydration: Heat exhaustion leads to nausea, excessive thirst, headaches, and dizziness. Avoid it by drinking plenty of fluids, eating salty foods (e.g., crackers), abstaining from dehydrating beverages (e.g., alcohol and caffeinated beverages), and wearing sunscreen. Continuous heat stress can eventually lead to heat stroke, characterized by a rising temperature, severe headache, delirium and cessation of sweating. Victims should be cooled off with wet towels and taken to a doctor.

Sunburn: Always wear sunscreen (SPF 30 or higher) when spending excessive amounts of time outdoors. If you get sunburned, drink more fluids than usual and apply an aloe-based lotion. Severe sunburns can lead to sun poisoning, a condition that can cause fever, chills, nausea, and vomiting. Sun poisoning should always be treated by a doctor.

Hypothermia and frostbite: A rapid drop in body temperature is the clearest sign of overexposure to cold. Victims may also shiver, feel exhausted, have poor coordination or slurred speech, hallucinate, or suffer amnesia. *Do not let hypothermia victims fall asleep.* To avoid hypothermia, keep dry, wear layers, and stay out of the wind. When the temperature is below freezing, watch out for frostbite. If skin turns white or blue, waxy, and cold, do not rub the area. Drink warm beverages, stay dry, and slowly warm the area with dry fabric or steady body contact until a doctor can be found.

INSECT-BORNE DISEASES

Many diseases are transmitted by insects—mainly mosquitoes, fleas, ticks, and lice. Use insect repellents such as DEET and soak or spray your gear with permethrin (licensed in the US only for use on clothing). **Mosquitoes**—responsible for malaria, dengue fever, and yellow fever—can be particularly abundant in wet, swampy, or wooded areas, a bill that the Netherlands fits perfectly. **Ticks**—which can carry Lyme and other diseases—can be particularly dangerous in rural and forested regions away from the big Dutch cities. Like tourists, these critters tend to be most prevalent during the summer.

Tick-borne encephalitis: A viral infection of the central nervous system transmitted during the summer by tick bites (primarily in wooded areas) or by consumption of unpasteurized dairy products. The risk of contracting the disease is relatively low, especially if precautions are taken against tick bites.

Lyme disease: A bacterial infection carried by ticks and marked by a circular bull's-eye rash of 2 in. or more. Later symptoms include fever, headache, fatigue, and aches and pains. Antibiotics are effective if administered early. Left untreated, Lyme can cause problems in joints, the heart, and the nervous system. If you find a tick attached to your skin, grasp the head with tweezers as close to your skin as possible and apply slow, steady traction. Removing a tick within 24hr. greatly reduces the risk of infection. Do not try to remove ticks with petroleum jelly, nail polish remover, or a hot match. Ticks usually inhabit moist, shaded environments and heavily wooded areas. If you are going to be traipsing through these areas, wear long clothes and DEET.

Other insect-borne diseases: Lymphatic filariasis is a roundworm infestation transmitted by mosquitoes. Infection causes enlargement of extremities and has no vaccine. **Leishmaniasis,** a parasite transmitted by sand flies, can occur in Europe, but mostly in rural rather than urban areas. Common symptoms are fever, weakness, and swelling of the spleen, as well as skin sores. There is a treatment, but no vaccine.

FOOD- AND WATER-BORNE DISEASES
Prevention is the best cure: be sure that your food is properly cooked and the water you drink is clean. Although it is unlikely that there will be anything in the Dutch water (canal swimmers notwithstanding), you can peel fruits and vegetables before eating them and avoid tap water (including ice cubes and anything washed in tap water, like salad) if you're worried. Watch out for food from markets or street vendors that may have been cooked in unhygienic conditions. Other culprits are raw shellfish, unpasteurized milk, and sauces containing raw eggs. Buy bottled water or purify your own water by bringing it to a rolling boil or treating it with **iodine tablets;** note, however, that some parasites such as *giardia* have exteriors that resist iodine treatment, so boiling is more reliable. Always wash your hands before eating or bring a quick-drying purifying liquid hand cleaner.

Traveler's diarrhea: Results from drinking contaminated water or eating uncooked and contaminated foods. Symptoms include nausea, bloating, and urgency. Try quick-energy, non-sugary foods with protein and carbohydrates to keep your strength up. Over-the-counter anti-diarrheals (e.g., Imodium®) may counteract the problem. The most dangerous side effect is dehydration; drink 8 oz. of water with ½ tsp. of sugar or honey and a pinch of salt, try uncaffeinated soft drinks, or eat salted crackers. If you develop a fever or your symptoms don't go away after 4-5 days, consult a doctor. Consult a doctor immediately for treatment of diarrhea in children.

Giardiasis: Transmitted through parasites and acquired by drinking untreated water from streams or lakes. Symptoms include diarrhea, cramps, bloating, fatigue, weight loss, and nausea. If untreated, it can lead to severe dehydration.

Leptospirosis: A bacterial disease caused by exposure to fresh water or soil contaminated by the urine of infected animals. Able to enter the human body through cut skin, mucus membranes, and ingestion, it is most common in tropical climates. Symptoms include a high fever, chills, nausea, and vomiting. If not treated, it can lead to liver failure and meningitis. There is no vaccine; consult a doctor for treatment.

OTHER INFECTIOUS DISEASES
The following diseases exist in every part of the world. Travelers should know how to recognize them and what to do if they suspect they have been infected.

Rabies: Transmitted through the saliva of infected animals; fatal if untreated. By the time symptoms (thirst and muscle spasms) appear, the disease is in its terminal stage. If you are bitten, wash the wound, seek immediate medical care, and try to have the animal located. A rabies vaccine, which consists of 3 shots given over a 21-day period, is available and recommended for developing world travel, but it is only semi-effective.

AIDS and HIV: Acquired Immune Deficiency Syndrome (AIDS), the most infamous sexually transmitted infection, is usually preceded by a positive test for Human Immunodeficiency Virus (HIV). Thanks to the excellent Dutch health system and regulation of prostitution, HIV/AIDS is rare in the Netherlands, but the threat should never be dismissed; always practice safe sex. For detailed information on AIDS in the Netherlands, call the 24hr. (American) National AIDS Hotline at ☎800-342-2437.

Sexually transmitted infections (STIs): Gonorrhea, chlamydia, genital warts, syphilis, herpes, HPV, and other STIs are easier to catch than HIV and can be just as serious. Though condoms may protect you from some STIs, oral or even tactile contact can lead to transmission. If you think you may have contracted an STI, see a doctor immediately.

OTHER HEALTH CONCERNS

MEDICAL CARE ON THE ROAD

A **pharmacy,** *apotheek* in Dutch, can be found in all of Amsterdam's neighborhoods (see **Practical Information,** p. 93). If you need a **doctor** *(dokter)* for more serious health matters, call the local hospital for a list of local practitioners. If you are receiving reciprocal health care (p. 28), make sure you call a doctor who will be linked to the state health care system. Contact your health provider for information regarding charges that may be incurred. Note that the same medicines may have different names in the Netherlands than at home; check with your doctor before you leave. If you do not have insurance, go to the **Kruispost Medisch Helpcentrum,** a first-aid walk-in clinic for the uninsured (p. 97).

If you are concerned about obtaining medical assistance while traveling, you may wish to employ special support services. The *MedPass* from **GlobalCare, Inc.,** 6875 Shiloh Rd. E., Alpharetta, GA 30005, USA (☎800-860-1111; www.globalcare.net), provides 24hr. international medical assistance, support, and medical evacuation resources. The **International Association for Medical Assistance to Travelers** (**IAMAT;** US ☎716-754-4883, Canada 519-836-0102; www.iamat.org) has free membership, lists English-speaking doctors worldwide, and offers detailed info on immunization requirements and sanitation. If your regular **insurance** policy does not cover travel abroad, you may wish to purchase additional coverage.

Those with medical conditions (such as diabetes, allergies to antibiotics, epilepsy, or heart conditions) may want to obtain a **MedicAlert** membership (US$40 per year), which includes, among other things, a stainless steel ID tag and a 24hr. collect-call number. Contact the MedicAlert Foundation International, 2323 Colorado Ave., Turlock, CA 95382, USA (☎888-633-4298, outside US ☎209-668-3333; www.medicalert.org).

WOMEN'S HEALTH

Women traveling in unsanitary conditions are vulnerable to **urinary tract (including bladder and kidney) infections.** Over-the-counter medicines can sometimes alleviate symptoms, but if they persist, see a doctor. **Vaginal yeast infections** may flare up where it is hot and humid. Wearing loosely fitting trousers or a skirt and cotton underwear will help, as will over-the-counter remedies like Monistat® or Gynelotrimin®. Bring supplies from home if you are prone to infection, since they may be difficult to find on the road. **Tampons** (but not with applicators), **pads,** and **contraceptive devices** are widely available, but your favorite brand may not be stocked—bring extras of anything you can't live without. **Abortion** is legal in the Netherlands.

GETTING TO THE NETHERLANDS

BY PLANE

When it comes to airfare, a little effort can save you a bundle. Courier fares are the cheapest for those whose plans are flexible enough to deal with the restrictions. Tickets sold by consolidators and standby seating are also good deals, but last-minute specials, airfare wars, and charter flights often beat these fares. The key is to hunt around, be flexible, and ask about discounts. Students, seniors, and those under 26 should never pay full price for a ticket.

AIRPORT

The Dutch know how to make a good first impression; named best airport in the world in 2003, Amsterdam's sleek, glassy **Luchthaven Schiphol** (☎ 0900 0141, €0.40 per min., 020 794 0800 from outside the Netherlands; www.schiphol.nl) is the Netherlands's major hub for transatlantic flights and the fourth busiest airport in Europe. Signs (in English and Dutch) direct incoming travelers through the arrivals halls and into the vaulted, airy expanse of Schiphol Plaza, where tourist services abound. There's a branch of the **VVV** (p. 93) near the entrance to Arrivals Terminal 2, though lines can be long. You can **exchange cash** at ABN AMRO branches in the arrivals halls or in the lounge areas (☎ 020 446 6720; hours vary depending on location, but all are at least open daily 8am-7pm) or at the two GWK branches at Schiphol (☎ 0900 0566; at least open daily 7am-10pm). For **luggage storage,** head to the lockers throughout the plaza. (Storage €4-9 per 24hr., depending on size. 7-day max storage.) If you've misplaced your belongings, there are **lost and found** counters located in the lounges in the arrivals and departures levels. (Open daily by appointment 7am-6pm.) Schiphol Plaza also contains six **rental car** companies: Avis ☎ 020 655 6050; Budget ☎ 020 604 1349; Europcar ☎ 020 316 4190; Hertz ☎ 020 502 0240; National ☎ 020 316 4081; Sixt ☎ 020 405 9090. (All open daily at least 7am-11pm.) Price gouging abounds in the plaza's array of shops and restaurants, while the in-house casino serves to separate you from the rest of your funds.

The most efficient way to traverse the 18km between Schiphol and Amsterdam Centraal, in the middle of the city, is via the frequent **sneltreins,** a fast and smooth light rail connection (15-20min., €3.60). Purchase tickets at any of the kiosks that dot Schiphol Plaza and the arrivals halls. Board the trains by descending to underground platforms directly below the airport via elevator or escalators located smack in the middle of Schiphol Plaza. **Taxis** (☎ 653 1000; www.schipholtaxi.nl) also make the trek to Amsterdam. They congregate in front of the plaza. Prices tick upward unpredictably—fares to Centraal Station can reach €40. Taxis can be prohibitively expensive and should be avoided if possible.

AIRFARES

Airfares to Amsterdam peak between May and September; holidays are also expensive. The cheapest times to travel are November through March. Midweek (M-Th morning) round-trip flights run US$40-50 cheaper than weekend flights, but they are generally more crowded and less likely to permit frequent-flier upgrades. Not fixing a return date ("open return") or arriving in and departing from different cities ("open-jaw") can be pricier than round-trip flights. Patching one-way flights together is the most expensive way to travel.

If Amsterdam is only one stop on a more extensive globe-hop, consider a round-the-world (RTW) ticket. Tickets usually include at least five stops and are valid for about a year; prices range US$1200-5000. Try **Northwest Airlines/KLM** (☎800-225-2525; www.nwa.com) or **Star Alliance,** a consortium of 16 airlines including United Airlines (www.staralliance.com).

Fares for roundtrip flights to Amsterdam from the US or Canadian east coast in the high season cost US$1500-2500 and can drop to US$600-1000 in the low season; from the US or Canadian west coast, US$2000-3000/900-1100; from the UK, UK£70-100/60-80; from Ireland, €160-250/120-160; from Australia AUS$2000-3000/2500-3500; from New Zealand NZ$3000-4000/2700-3500.

BUDGET AND STUDENT TRAVEL AGENCIES

While knowledgeable agents specializing in flights to Amsterdam can make your life easy and help you save, they may not spend the time to find you the lowest possible fare—they get paid on commission. Travelers holding **ISICs** and **IYTCs** (p. 18) qualify for big discounts from student travel agencies. Most flights from budget agencies are on major airlines, but in peak season some may sell seats on less reliable chartered aircraft.

STA Travel, 5900 Wilshire Blvd., Ste. 900, Los Angeles, CA 90036, USA (24hr. reservations and info ☎800-781-4040; www.statravel.com). A student and youth travel organization with over 150 offices worldwide (check their website for a complete list), including US offices in Boston, Chicago, Los Angeles, New York City, Seattle, San Francisco, and Washington, D.C. Ticket booking, travel insurance, railpasses, and more. Walk-in offices are located throughout Australia (☎03 9207 5900), New Zealand (☎09 309 9723), and the UK (☎08701 630 026).

Travel CUTS (Canadian Universities Travel Services Limited), 187 College St., Toronto, ON M5T 1P7, Canada (☎888-592-2887; www.travelcuts.com). Offices across Canada and the US including in Los Angeles, Montreal, New York City, and Toronto.

USIT, 19-21 Aston Quay, Dublin 2, Ireland (☎01 602 1904; www.usit.ie). Ireland's leading student/budget travel agency, with 20 offices throughout Northern Ireland and the Republic of Ireland. Offers programs to work, study, and volunteer worldwide.

 FLIGHT PLANNING ON THE INTERNET. The Internet may be the budget traveler's dream when it comes to finding and booking bargain fares, but the array of options can be overwhelming. Many airline sites offer special last-minute deals on the Web. **KLM** (www.nwa.com), or Royal Dutch Airlines, is one airline that offers many options for travel to the Netherlands.

STA (www.statravel.com) and **StudentUniverse** (www.studentuniverse.com) provide quotes on student tickets, while **Orbitz** (www.orbitz.com), **Expedia** (www.expedia.com), and **Travelocity** (www.travelocity.com) offer full travel services. **Priceline** (www.priceline.com) lets you specify a price and obligates you to buy any ticket that meets or beats it; **Hotwire** (www.hotwire.com) offers bargain fares but won't reveal the airline or flight times until you buy. Other sites that compile deals include www.bestfares.com, www.flights.com, www.lowestfare.com, www.onetravel.com, and www.travelzoo.com.

SideStep (www.sidestep.com) and **Booking Buddy** (www.bookingbuddy.com) are online tools that can help sift through multiple offers; these two let you enter your trip information once and search multiple sites.

Air Traveler's Handbook (www.faqs.org/faqs/travel/air/handbook) is an indispensable resource on the Internet; it has a comprehensive listing of links to everything you need to know before you board a plane.

COMMERCIAL AIRLINES

The commercial airlines' lowest regular offer is the **APEX** (Advance Purchase Excursion) fare, which provides confirmed reservations and allows "open-jaw" tickets. Generally, reservations must be made seven to 21 days ahead of departure, with seven- to 14-day minimum-stay and up to 90-day maximum-stay restrictions. These fares carry hefty cancellation and change penalties (fees rise in summer). Book peak-season APEX fares early. Use **Expedia** (www.expedia.com) or **Travelocity** (www.travelocity.com) to get an idea of the lowest published fares, then use the resources outlined here to try to beat those fares. Low-season fares should be appreciably cheaper than the **high-season** (May-Sept.) ones listed here.

TRAVELING FROM NORTH AMERICA

Standard commercial carriers like **American** (☎800-433-7300; www.aa.com), **United** (☎800-538-2929; www.ual.com), and **Northwest** (☎800-447-4747; www.nwa.com) will probably offer the most convenient flights, but they may not be the cheapest (unless you snag a special promotion or airfare war ticket). Check **Lufthansa** (☎800-399-5838; www.lufthansa.com), **British Airways** (☎800-247-9297; www.britishairways.com), **Air France** (☎800-237-2747; www.airfrance.us), and **Alitalia** (☎800-223-5730; www.alitaliausa.com) for cheap tickets from destinations throughout the US to all over Europe. You might find an even better deal on one of the following airlines, if any of their limited departure points is convenient for you.

Icelandair: ☎800-223-5500; www.icelandair.com. Stopovers in Iceland for no extra cost on most transatlantic flights. For last-minute offers, subscribe to their email list.

Finnair: ☎800-950-5000; www.finnair.com. Cheap round-trips from North American cities to Amsterdam; connections throughout Europe, but especially fond of Helsinki.

Martinair: ☎800-627-8462; www.martinair.com. Fly from Miami or Orlando to Amsterdam from US$800.

TRAVELING FROM IRELAND AND THE UK

Because of the many carriers flying from the British Isles to the continent, we only include discount airlines or those with cheap specials here. The **Air Travel Advisory Bureau** in London (☎870 737 0021; www.atab.co.uk) provides referrals to travel agencies and consolidators that offer discounted airfares out of the UK. **Cheapflights** (www.cheapflights.co.uk) publishes airfare bargains.

Aer Lingus: Ireland ☎0818 365 000; www.aerlingus.ie. Return tickets from Dublin, Cork, Galway, Kerry, and Shannon to Amsterdam (€100-300).

bmibaby: UK ☎08702 642 229; www.bmibaby.com. Departures from throughout the UK. London to Amsterdam UK£80 round-trip.

easyJet: UK ☎08712 442 366; www.easyjet.com. Takes off from Belfast, Bristol, Edinburgh, Liverpool, and London for Amsterdam.

KLM: UK ☎08705 074 074; www.klmuk.com. Cheap return tickets from London and elsewhere to Amsterdam.

Transavia: UK ☎020 7365 4997; www.transavia.com. Short hops from Glasgow to Amsterdam (from UK£43 one-way) and London to Rotterdam (from UK£36 one-way).

TRAVELING FROM AUSTRALIA AND NEW ZEALAND

Singapore Air: Australia ☎13 10 11, New Zealand ☎0800 808 909; www.singaporeair.com. Flies halfway around the world to Amsterdam from Auckland, Christchurch, Melbourne, Perth, and Sydney via its namesake.

Thai Airways: Australia ☎1300 65 19 60, New Zealand ☎09 377 38 86; www.thaiair.com. Jet from Auckland, Melbourne, Perth, and Sydney to Amsterdam.

AIR COURIER FLIGHTS

Those who travel light should consider courier flights. Couriers help transport cargo on international flights by using their checked luggage space for freight. Generally, couriers are limited to carry-ons and must deal with complex flight restrictions. Most flights are round-trip only, with short fixed-length stays (usually one week) and a limit of a one ticket per issue. Most of these flights also operate only out of major gateway cities, mostly in North America. Generally, you must be over 18 (in some cases 21). In summer, the most popular destinations usually require a reservation about two weeks in advance (you can usually book up to two months ahead). Super-discounted fares are common for "last-minute" flights (three to 14 days ahead).

FROM NORTH AMERICA

Round-trip courier fares from the US to Amsterdam run about US$500. Most flights leave from New York City, Los Angeles, San Francisco, or Miami in the US; and from Montreal, Toronto, or Vancouver in Canada. The organizations below provide members with lists of opportunities and courier brokers for an annual fee.

Air Courier Association, 1767A Denver West Blvd., Golden, CO 80401, USA (☎800-211-5119; www.aircourier.org). 10 departure cities throughout the US and Canada to Amsterdam (US$329 for one-way). 1-year membership US$49.

International Association of Air Travel Couriers (**IAATC;** www.courier.org). From 7 North American cities to Western European cities, including Amsterdam. 1-year membership US$45.

Courier Travel (www.couriertravel.org). Searchable online database. Multiple departure points in the US to Amsterdam.

FROM THE UK, AUSTRALIA, AND NEW ZEALAND

The minimum age for couriers from the **UK** is usually 18. The **International Association of Air Travel Couriers** (www.courier.org; see above) often offers courier flights from London to Tokyo, Sydney, and Bangkok and from Auckland to Frankfurt and London. **Courier Travel** (see above) also offers flights from London and Sydney.

STANDBY FLIGHTS

Traveling standby requires considerable flexibility in arrival and departure dates. Companies dealing in standby flights sell vouchers rather than tickets, along with the promise to get you to your destination (or near your destination) within a certain window of time (typically 1-5 days). You call in before your specific window of time to hear your flight options and the probability that you will be able to board each flight. You can then decide which flights you want to try to catch, show up at the appropriate airport at the appropriate time, present your voucher, and board if space is available. Vouchers can usually be bought for both one-way and round-trip travel. You may receive a monetary refund only if every available flight within your date range is full; if you opt not to take an available (but perhaps less convenient) flight, you can only get credit toward future travel. Read agreements with any company offering standby flights with care, as tricky fine print can leave you in the lurch. To check on a company's service record in the US, contact the Better Business Bureau (☎703-276-0100; www.bbb.org). It's hard to receive refunds, and clients' vouchers will not be honored when an airline fails to receive payment in time.

TICKET CONSOLIDATORS

Ticket consolidators, or **"bucket shops,"** buy unsold tickets in bulk from commercial airlines and sell them at discounted rates. The best place to look is in the Sunday travel section of any major newspaper (such as *The New York Times*), where many bucket shops place tiny ads. Call quickly, as availability is extremely limited. Not all bucket shops are reliable, so insist on a receipt that gives full details of restrictions, refunds, and tickets and pay by credit card (in spite of the 2-5% fee) so you can stop payment if you never receive your tickets. For more info, see www.travel-library.com/air-travel/consolidators.html.

TRAVELING FROM CANADA AND THE US

Some consolidators worth trying are **Rebel** (☎800-732-3588; www.rebeltours.com), **Cheap Tickets** (www.cheaptickets.com), **Flights.com** (www.flights.com), and **TravelHUB** (www.travelhub.com). *Let's Go* does not endorse any of these agencies. As always, be cautious and research companies before you hand over your credit card number.

CHARTER FLIGHTS

Tour operators contract charter flights with airlines in order to fly extra loads of passengers during peak season. These flights are far from hassle-free. They occur less frequently than major airlines, make refunds particularly difficult, and are almost always fully booked. Their scheduled times may change, and they may be cancelled at the last moment (as late as 48hr. before the trip, and without a full refund). And check-in, boarding, and baggage claim for them are often much slower. They can, however, be much cheaper.

Discount clubs and fare brokers offer members savings on last-minute charter and tour deals. Study contracts closely; you don't want to end up with an unwanted overnight layover. **Travelers Advantage** (☎800-835-8747; www.travelersadvantage.com; US$90 annual fee includes discounts and cheap flight directories) specializes in European travel and tour packages.

BY BOAT

For the seafaring, ferries traverse the North Sea between the UK and the Netherlands. The fares below are **one-way** for **adult foot passengers.** Though standard return fares are usually just twice the one-way fare, **fixed-period returns** (usually within five days) are almost invariably cheaper. Ferries run **year-round. Bringing your bike** is usually free, but you may have to pay up to UK£10 in high season. For a **camper/trailer** supplement, you will have to add UK£20-140 to the "with car" fare.

DFDS Seaways: UK ☎08702 520 524; www.dfdsseaways.co.uk. Departs Newcastle at 5:30pm for Amsterdam (16hr., UK£19-39), but be there before 5pm.

P&O Ferries: UK ☎08705 980 333; www.posl.com. Daily ferries from Hull to Rotterdam (10hr.) from UK£100.

BY TRAIN

International trains arrive in Amsterdam's Centraal Station (p. 39) throughout the day, carrying everyone from business executives to pot pilgrims to toddler-toting parents. **Thalys** (www.thalys.com) runs trains from Paris Nord, Brussels Midi, and Antwerp Berchem to Centraal Station in Amsterdam (4¼hr., 5-8 per day, €41-101).

RESERVATIONS. While seat reservations are required only for selected trains (usually on major lines), you are not guaranteed a seat without one (usually US$5-30). You should strongly consider reserving in advance during peak holiday and tourist seasons (at the very latest, a few hours ahead). You will also have to purchase a **supplement** (US$10-50) or special fare for high-speed or high-quality trains. InterRail holders must also purchase supplements (US$3-20) for trains like EuroCity, InterCity, and many French TGVs; supplements are often unnecessary for Eurail Pass and Europass holders.

OVERNIGHT TRAINS. On night trains, you won't waste valuable daylight hours traveling, and you can avoid the hassle and expense of staying at a hotel. However, the main drawbacks include discomfort, sleepless nights, and the lack of scenery. **Sleeping accommodations** on trains differ, but typically you can either sleep upright in your seat (supplement about $2-10) or pay for a separate space. **Couchettes** (berths) typically have four to six seats per compartment (supplement about US$10-50 per person); **sleepers** (beds) in private sleeping cars offer more privacy and comfort but are considerably more expensive (supplement US$40-150). If you are using a railpass valid only for a restricted number of days, inspect train schedules to maximize the use of your pass: an overnight train or boat journey often uses up only one of your travel days if it departs after 7pm.

EURAIL PASSES. Eurail is **valid** in most of Western Europe, including the Netherlands (but not the UK). **Eurail Global Passes,** valid for a consecutive given number of days, are best for those planning on spending extensive time on trains every few days. Global passes valid for any 10 or 15 (not necessarily consecutive) days within a two-month period are more cost-effective for those traveling longer distances less frequently. **Eurail Pass Saver** provides first-class travel for travelers in groups of two to five (prices are per person). **Eurail Pass Youth** provides parallel second-class perks for those under 26.

EURAIL GLOBAL PASSES	15 DAYS	21 DAYS	1 MONTH	2 MONTHS	3 MONTHS
Eurail Pass Adult	US$675	US$879	US1089	US$1539	US$1899
Eurail Pass Saver	US$569	US$745	US$925	US$1309	US$1615
Eurail Pass Youth	US$439	US$569	US$709	US$999	US$1235

OTHER GLOBAL PASSES	10 DAYS IN 2 MONTHS	15 DAYS IN 2 MONTHS
Eurail Pass Adult	US$799	US$1049
Eurail Pass Saver	US$679	US$895
Eurail Pass Youth	US$519	US$679

Passholders receive a timetable for major routes and a map with details on bike rental, car rental, hotel, and museum discounts. Passholders often also receive reduced fares or free passage on many boat, bus, and private railroad lines.

The **Eurail Select Pass** is a slimmed-down version of the Eurail Pass: it allows five to 15 days of unlimited travel in any two-month period within three, four, or five bordering countries of 23 European countries. **Eurail Select Passes** (for individuals) and **Eurail Select Pass Savers** (for people traveling in groups of two to five) range from US$429/365 per person (5 days) to US$949/805 (15 days). The **Eurail Select Pass Youth** (second-class), for those ages 12-25, costs US$279-619. You are entitled to the same **freebies** afforded by the Eurail Pass, but only when they are within or between countries that you have purchased.

SHOPPING AROUND FOR A EURAIL. Eurail Passes are designed by the EU itself and can be bought only by non-Europeans almost exclusively from non-European distributors. These passes must be sold at uniform prices determined by the EU. However, some travel agents tack on a US$10 handling fee, and others offer certain bonuses with purchase, so shop around. Also, keep in mind that pass prices usually go up each year, so if you're planning to travel early in the year, you can save cash by purchasing before January 1 (you have three months from the purchase date to validate your pass in Europe).

It is best to buy your pass before leaving; only a few places in major European cities sell them, and at a marked-up price. You can get a replacement for a lost pass only if you have purchased insurance on it under the Pass Security Plan (US$14). Eurail Passes are available through travel agents, student travel agencies like STA (p. 32), and **Rail Europe** (Canada ☎800-361-7245, US 877-257-2887; www.raileurope.com) or **Flight Centre** (☎866-967-5351; www.flightcentre.com). It is also possible to buy directly from Eurail's website, www.eurail.com. Shipping is free to North America, Australia, New Zealand, and Canada.

OTHER MULTINATIONAL PASSES. If your travels are limited to the immediate vicinity of the Netherlands, regional passes are often good values. Check www.raileurope.com and www.eurail.com for the regional passes most applicable to the Netherlands, including the Benelux Tourrail Pass (p. 40).

If you have lived for at least six months in one of the European countries where **InterRail Passes** are valid, they prove an economical option. The Inter-Rail Pass allows travel within 30 European countries (excluding the pass-holder's country of residence). The **Global Pass** is valid for a given number of days (not necessarily consecutive) within a 10-day to one-month period. (5 days within 10 days, adult 1st class €329, adult 2nd class €249, youth €159; 10 days within 22 days €489/359/239; 1 month continuous €809/599/399). The **One Country Pass** limits travel within one European country (€33 for 3 days). Pass-holders receive free admission to many museums as well as **discounts** on accommodations, food, and many ferries to Ireland, Scandinavia, and the rest of Europe. Passes are available at www.interrailnet.com, as well as from travel agents, at major train stations throughout Europe, and through online vendors (www.railpassdirect.co.uk).

FURTHER READING & RESOURCES ON TRAIN TRAVEL.
Info on rail travel and railpasses: www.raileurope.com.
Point-to-point fares and schedules: www.raileurope.com/us/rail/fares_schedules/index.htm. Allows you to calculate whether buying a railpass would save you money.
Railsaver: www.railpass.com/new. Uses your itinerary to calculate the best rail-pass for your trip.
European Railway Server: www.railfaneurope.net. Links to rail servers through-out Europe.
The Netherlands Rail Planner: www.ns.nl/domestic/index.cgi. Input your desti-nation, date, and time of your desired travel and get a detailed train schedule. Prices only available for trips within the Netherlands.
Thomas Cook European Timetable: www.thomascooktimetables.com. Updated monthly, this publication covers all major and most minor train routes in Europe. Buy directly from Thomas Cook.

GETTING AROUND THE NETHERLANDS

Fares are either **one-way** or **round-trip.** "Period returns" require you to return within a specific number of days; "day return" means you must return on the same day. Unless stated otherwise, *Let's Go* always lists single fares. Round-trip fares on trains and buses in the Netherlands are simply double the one-way fare.

BY FOOT

Due to its snug size and its numerous sidewalks, Amsterdam is an immensely walkable city. Visitors are often amazed to find that they can traverse most of the city in only a few hours—even after taking a few breaks to eat and to gaze at the boats passing through the canals. Walkers should be careful, however, to yield to trams and bikes, which share Amsterdam's pristine paths with pedestrians. For themed walking tours of the city, see p. 150, p. 178, and p. 198.

BY BICYCLE

Bikes rule Dutch roads. The long, flat spaces that connect the Netherlands's cities and towns, as well as the bicycle-friendly streets that snake through the cities themselves, make cycling a cheap, convenient, and ecologically friendly mode of transport. Amsterdam's streets teem with bikes and bike paths, which can be easily navigated if you follow the basic rules.

First, observe and follow all street signs and stop lights. Amsterdammers violate these with impunity, thanks to instincts born from years of experience. Because you do not have this experience under your belt, a failure to observe traffic rules on Amsterdam's complicated road system may find you in an unexpected tête-à-tête with a tram or car. Second, remember that you must **yield to all traffic coming from the right,** whether car or bicycle. Third, always stay on the right side of the road. Fourth, beware of tram tracks—they're just wide enough for bike wheels to become wedged in between. If you do find your bike stuck, don't linger while a tram bears down on you—just get away. Be sure to signal all turns and stops lest you be rear-ended by an unassuming truck driver.

Finally, **always lock your bike**—bike theft is rampant in Amsterdam. All rental bikes come with locks and keys; use them even when you stop for a few moments. The majority of thefts take place when riders leave their bicycles unlocked briefly. Also keep in mind that most bike insurance does not cover bikes that are stolen with the key left on the bike; you have to produce the key to get back your deposit. Especially if you're locking your bike for an extended period, ensure that it is left in a quiet and safe spot, since locks don't always deter bike theft. If you have any questions regarding liability, ask a bike-rental salesperson for advice.

 I SEE THE (TWO-WHEEL) LIGHT. If you plan to ride your bike lawfully at night, you must obtain lights for both the front and the rear of your bike. If you are renting a bike, make sure it comes with these lights.

Unless Amsterdam is only one stop on a larger tour, it makes the most sense to rent or even purchase a bike (see **Practical Information,** p. 95). If you choose to bring your own, many airlines will count your bike as your second free piece of luggage; a few charge extra (around US$80 one-way). Bikes must be packed in a cardboard box with the pedals and front wheel detached; many airlines sell bike boxes at the airport (US$15). Most ferries let you take your bike for free or for a nominal fee, and you can always bring your bike on trains for €6. In addition to **panniers** (US$10-40), or baskets, to hold your luggage, you'll need a good **helmet** (US$15-50) and a **sturdy lock** (from US$25).

If you are nervous about striking out on your own, **CBT Tours,** 2506 N. Clark St. #150, Chicago, IL 60614, USA (☎800-736-2453; www.cbttours.com), offers full-package biking, culinary, hiking, and sightseeing tours (US$2000-2500) in the Netherlands. It is also possible to create a custom tour.

BY PUBLIC TRANSPORTATION

The hub for trams, buses, and the subway—as well as rail travel—is **Centraal Station,** a magnificent structure adorned with Baroque carvings and ornate gables at the end of Damrak. The area immediately around Centraal Station buzzes with activity; congested with locals, backpack-toting tourists, assorted beggars, hustlers, buskers, and preachers, it's a marvelous spot for people-watching. There's a branch of the **VVV** (p. 93) as well as **storage lockers** (€4-5, depending on size; 24hr. max.), and a GWK bank with **currency exchange.** For information on rail travel around the Netherlands, see p. 40.

Amsterdam's clean, efficient, and affordable public transportation—trams, buses, and the subway—runs daily approximately 6am-12:15am. The most convenient way to navigate Amsterdam's maze of canals and crooked streets is to use its highly efficient and comprehensive **tram system.** With over 20 lines, these streetcars traverse most of the main streets of the city, with tram stops located every few blocks. The currency of trams is the **strippenkaart,** a card with anywhere from two (€1.60) to 45 (€20.10) strips. The city is divided into several zones: Centrum, West, Oost (East), Noord (North), and Zuid (South); most of touristed Amsterdam falls within the Centrum zone. The number of strips you use up on your *strippenkaart* depends on the number of zones you traverse. Calculate your fare by looking at a map of the zones; you will need one strip for each zone you transverse, plus one (e.g., 1 zone costs 2 strips, 2 zones cost 3 strips, etc.). Have the appropriate number of strips stamped—either by the driver or at one of the many yellow machines. You will then have unlimited public transportation access for a period of time roughly proportional to the distance you're covering (1hr. for 1-3 zones, 1½hr. for 4-6 zones, 2hr. for 7-9 zones, 3hr. for 10-15 zones, and 3½hr. for 16+ zones). While the tram and bus operators may be lax about checking your tickets, the uniformed inspectors are not. If you're caught without a valid pass, you'll be slapped with a **€37.40 fine,** which you must produce on the spot.

You can buy a one-time *strippenkaart* when boarding any tram, but, if you're planning on navigating the city, it's advisable (and much cheaper) to buy in bulk (8 strips €6.40; 15 strips €6.80, under 12 and over 65 €4.50; 45 strips €20.10). Unlimited-use passes *(sterabonnement)* can be purchased for longer stays. You can purchase a *strippenkaart* or *sterabonnement* at **GVB (public transportation) offices,** train stations, and many city convenience stores, including Albert Heijn supermarkets. The same *strippenkaart* system is used to pay for public transportation throughout the Netherlands.

Confused and overwhelmed? For information and tram passes, head to the **GVB** on Stationsplein across from Centraal Station in the same building as the VVV. Be sure to ask for the special multi-colored tram map. (Information ☎0900 9292, €0.50 per min. Local info line ☎460 5959 operated M-F 9am-6pm. Open M-F 7am-9pm, Sa-Su 10am-6pm.)

The same basic system governs **buses,** which cover many of the same routes as trams but also travel to more distant locations in greater Amsterdam. While other public transport options shut down by 12:15am, **night buses** (single trip €3) rumble through the sleeping city until 7am. The zone transit system that governs Amsterdam applies to **long-distance buses** as well. Your *strippenkaart* can be used to travel throughout the country via bus; the number of strips required depends on the number of zones traversed.

The subway, known as the **Metro,** is only useful for a few locations in the downtown core. After departing south from Centraal Station, trains stop at Nieuwmarkt, Waterlooplein, and Weesperplein and then continue to Amsterdam's surrounding suburbs. If you find yourself in need of this service, simply look for the blue "M" sign and have your *strippenkaart* at the ready.

ESSENTIALS

In 2009, the Netherlands will move to an electronic fare system, sending the *strippenkaart* to a well-deserved retirement. Riders will prepay for a digital card, which they will tap at the turnstile at their point of entry and departure to automatically subtract their fare. The cost of the trip will depend on the distance between the two stations, not on the current zone system.

BY TRAIN

The Netherlands's national rail company is the efficient **Nederlandse Spoorwegen** (**NS;** ☎ 0900 9296, €0.35 per min.; www.ns.nl). Train service tends to be faster than bus service. *Sneltreins* are the fastest; *stoptreins*—surprise, surprise—make the most stops. One-way tickets are called *enkele reis*, normal round-trip tickets *retour*, and one-day return tickets (valid only on day of purchase but cheaper than normal round-trip tickets) are called *dagretour*. Tickets to all Dutch trains can generally be bought with a credit card from vending machines or at box offices, though the latter usually means longer lines. NS sells train passes solely for travel within the Netherlands. The **Zomertoer** (Summer Trip) allows unlimited one-week train travel July 1-August 31 (€59 for 2 people, €79 for 3 people). The Netherlands also gives students and youths (anyone under 26) discounted train tickets.

Trains in the Netherlands are generally comfortable, convenient, and reasonably swift. Shared second-class compartments are great places to meet fellow travelers. Trains, however, are not always safe; for safety tips, see p. 27. For long trips, make sure you are on the correct car, since trains sometimes split at crossroads. Towns listed in parentheses on European train schedules require a train switch at the town listed immediately before the parenthetical.

 TRAIN HOPS, TRAIN STOPS. Nederlandse Spoorwegen is the Dutch national rail company, operating the country's intercity train service. Their website has an English-language section where you can check train times and costs and get detailed door-to-door directions for all the stops in the Netherlands.

For Netherlands-only travel, the **Holland Railpass,** offered by many travel agencies, is good for three or five travel days in any one-month period (2nd-class travel for 3 days US$92, for 5 days US$146; ages 4-11 half-price). If your travels include a wider swath of turf, consider the **Benelux Tourrail Pass** for Belgium, the Netherlands, and Luxembourg (2nd-class travel 5 days in 1 month US$176, under 26 US$132; 25% discount for companion traveler). If you "lose" (i.e., do not buy) your train ticket and are caught by the authorities, it is possible to buy tickets on board; however, you will also have to fork over a €35 fine.

SHOULD YOU BUY A RAILPASS? Railpasses were conceived to allow you to jump on any train in Europe, go wherever you want whenever you want, and change your plans at will. In practice, it's not so simple. You still must stand in line to validate your pass, pay for supplements, and fork over cash for seat and couchette reservations. More importantly, railpasses don't always pay off. If you are planning to spend extensive time on trains hopping between big cities, a railpass will probably be worth it. But in many cases, especially if you are under 26, point-to-point tickets may prove a cheaper option. You may find it tough to make your railpass pay for itself in the Netherlands, where train fares are reasonable and distances short. If, however, the total cost of your trips nears the price of the pass, the convenience of avoiding ticket lines may be worth the difference.

RAIL-AND-DRIVE PASSES. In addition to simple railpasses, the Netherlands (as well as Eurail) offers rail-and-drive passes, which combine car rental with rail travel—a good option for travelers who wish both to visit cities accessible by rail and to make side trips into the surrounding areas. Prices range US$605-2056, depending on the type of pass, type of car, and number of people included. The price for children under 11 is US$182.50, and additional days cost US$72-105 each.

BY CAR

Visitors to Amsterdam without a death wish need not obtain a car. With Amsterdam's compact size and the prevalence of bicycles, it makes no sense to drive among its manic taxis, tiny canal-side alleys, absolute dearth of parking, and highest gasoline prices in the world. Travelers looking to explore the Netherlands as a country more thoroughly, however, may wish to rent a car if they need more space and mobility. Cars offer speed, freedom, access to the countryside, and an escape from the town-to-town mentality of trains. Although a single traveler won't save by renting a car, four usually will. If you can't decide between train and car travel, you may benefit from a combination of the two; RailEurope and other railpass vendors offer rail-and-drive packages. Fly-and-drive packages are also often available from travel agents or airline/rental agency partnerships.

DRIVING PERMITS AND CAR INSURANCE

INTERNATIONAL DRIVING PERMIT (IDP)
Foreign driver's licenses are typically acceptable to drive with in the Netherlands. However, it is useful (and in some cases mandatory) to have an International Driving Permit (IDP). Your IDP, valid for one year, must be issued in your own country before you depart. An application for an IDP usually requires one or two photos, a current local license, an additional form of identification, and a fee. To apply, contact your home country's automobile association. Be vigilant when purchasing an IDP online or anywhere other than your home automobile association. Many vendors sell permits of questionable legitimacy for higher prices.

CAR INSURANCE
Most credit cards cover standard insurance. If you rent, lease, or borrow a car, you will need a **Green Card,** or **International Insurance Certificate,** to certify that you have liability insurance and that it applies abroad. Green cards can be obtained at car-rental agencies, car dealers (for those leasing cars), some travel agents, and some border crossings.

RENTING A CAR

RENTAL AGENCIES
You can rent a car from a US-based firm (Alamo, Avis, Budget, or Hertz) with Dutch offices, from a European-based company with local representatives (Europcar), or from a tour operator (Auto Europe, Europe By Car, and Kemwel Holiday Autos) that will arrange a rental for you from a European company at its own rates. Multinationals offer greater flexibility, but tour operators often strike better deals. You can generally make reservations before you leave by calling major international offices in your home country. However, sometimes the price and availability information they give doesn't jive with what the local offices in the Netherlands will tell you. Try checking with both numbers to make sure you get the best price and the most accurate information possible. Local desk numbers are included in town listings; for home-country numbers, call your toll-free directory.

To rent a car from most establishments in the Netherlands, you need to be at least 21 years old. Some agencies require renters to be 25, and most charge those ages 21-24 an additional insurance fee (around US$25 per day). Policies and prices vary from agency to agency. Small local operations occasionally rent to people under 21, but be sure to ask about the insurance coverage and deductible and always check the fine print. At most agencies, all else that's needed to rent a car is a license from home and proof that you've had it for a year. Car rental in Europe is available through the following agencies:

Auto Europe: ☎ 888-223-5555 or 207-842-2000; www.autoeurope.com.

Avis: Australia ☎ 136 333; Canada 800-331-1212; New Zealand 0800 65 51 11; UK 0870 606 0100; US 800-331-1212; www.avis.com.

Budget: Canada ☎ 800-268-8900; UK 8701 565 656; US 800-527-0700; www.budgetrentacar.com.

Europe by Car: US ☎ 800-223-1516 or 212-581-3040; www.europebycar.com.

Europcar International, 3 Avenue du Centre, 78 881 Saint Quentin en Yvelines Cedex, France (UK ☎ 870 607 5000; US 877-940-6900; www.europcar.com).

Hertz: ☎ 800-654-3001 or 800-654-3131; www.hertz.com.

Kemwel: US ☎ 877-820-0668; www.kemwel.com.

COSTS AND INSURANCE

Picking up your car in the Netherlands is usually cheaper than renting in surrounding foreign hubs. It is always significantly less expensive to reserve a car from the US than from Europe. Ask airlines about special fly-and-drive packages; you may get up to a week of free or discounted rental. Luckily, the Netherlands has some of Europe's lowest car-rental rates; rental car prices start at around €30 per day from national companies and €20 from local agencies. Expect to pay more for larger cars and for 4WD. Cars with **automatic transmission** can cost up to €30 per day more than cars with manual transmission. Reserve ahead and pay in advance if at all possible. Always check if prices quoted include tax and collision insurance; some credit card companies provide insurance, allowing their customers to decline the collision damage waiver. Ask about discounts and check the terms of insurance, particularly the size of the deductible.

Many rental packages offer unlimited mileage, while others offer a limited number of kilometers per day with a surcharge per kilometer after that. Return the car with a full tank of gasoline (petrol) to avoid high fuel charges at the end. Be sure to ask whether the price includes **insurance** against theft and collision. Remember that if you are driving a conventional rental vehicle on an **unpaved road,** you are almost never covered by insurance; ask about this before leaving the rental agency. Be aware that cars rented on an **American Express** or **Visa/MasterCard Gold** or **Platinum** credit card in the Netherlands might *not* carry the automatic insurance that they would in some other countries; check with your credit card company. Insurance plans from rental companies almost always come with an **excess** for conventional vehicles, for younger drivers, and for 4WD. This means that the insurance bought from the rental company only applies to damages over the excess; damages up to that amount must be covered by your existing insurance plan. Many rental companies in the Netherlands require you to buy a **Collision Damage Waiver (CDW),** which will waive the excess in the case of a collision. **Loss Damage Waivers (LDWs)** do the same in the case of theft or vandalism.

National chains often allow one-way rentals (picking up in one city and dropping off in another). There is usually a minimum rental period and sometimes an extra drop-off charge of several hundred euro.

LEASING A CAR

For longer than 17 days, leasing can be cheaper than renting; it is often the only option for those ages 18 to 21. The cheapest leases are agreements to buy the car and then sell it back to the manufacturer at a prearranged price. As far as you're concerned, though, it's a lease and doesn't entail enormous financial transactions. Leases generally include insurance coverage and are not taxed. Expect to pay around US$1100-1800 (depending on size of car) for 60 days. Contact **Auto Europe, Europe by Car,** or **Kemwel** (p. 42) before you go.

BUYING A CAR

If you're brave and know what you're doing, **buying** a used car or van in the Netherlands and selling it just before you leave can provide the cheapest wheels for longer trips. Check with consulates for import-export laws concerning used vehicles, registration, and safety and emission standards.

ON THE ROAD

The Netherlands has well-maintained roadways, and the Dutch drive on the right side of the road. On maps, a green "E" indicates an international highway; a red "A," a national highway; and "N," another main road. Speed limits are 50km per hour in towns, 80km outside, and 100 or 120km on highways. Fuel comes in three types; some cars use benzene while others use gasoline or diesel fuel. Gasoline (petrol) prices vary from expensive to ridiculous, but they averaged about €1.50 per liter in cities at the time of printing. The **Royal Dutch Touring Association** (ANWB; ☎ 088 269 2888; www.anwb.nl) offers roadside assistance to members. For more info, contact the branches at Museumplein 5, Amsterdam (☎ 020 673 0844) or at Wassenaarseweg 220, The Hague (☎ 070 314 7147). For an informal primer on European road signs and conventions, check out www.travlang.com/signs. The **Association for Safe International Road Travel (ASIRT),** 11769 Gainsborough Rd., Potomac, MD 20854, USA (☎ 301-983-5252; www.asirt.org) can provide more specific information about road conditions. ASIRT considers road travel (by car or bus) to be relatively **safe** in the Netherlands. If you plan to drive a car while in the Netherlands, you must be 18 or older, and it is your responsibility that you and your passengers **buckle up;** it's the law.

DRIVING PRECAUTIONS. When traveling in the summer, bring substantial amounts of water (a suggested 5L of **water** per person per day) for drinking and for the radiator. For long drives to unpopulated areas, register with police before beginning the trek and again upon arrival at the destination. Check with the local automobile club for details. When traveling for long distances, make sure tires are in good repair and have enough air and get good maps. A **compass** and a **car manual** can also be very useful. You should always carry a **spare tire** and **jack, jumper cables, extra oil, flares,** a **flashlight,** and **heavy blankets** (in case your car breaks down at night or in the winter). If you don't know how to **change a tire,** learn before heading out, especially if you are planning on traveling in deserted areas. Blowouts on dirt roads are very common. If your car breaks down, **stay in your vehicle;** if you wander off, it's less likely trackers will find you.

BY THUMB

Let's Go strongly urges you to consider the risks before you choose to hitch. We never recommend hitching as a safe means of transportation, and none of the information presented here is intended to do so.

No one should hitch without careful consideration of the risks involved. Hitching means entrusting your life to a random person who happens to stop beside you on the road and risking theft, assault, sexual harassment, and unsafe driving. Some travelers report that hitchhiking allows them to meet local people and travel in areas where public transportation is sketchy. The choice, however, remains yours.

Hitchhiking at night can be particularly dangerous; experienced hitchers stand in well-lit places. For women traveling alone, hitching is just too dangerous. A man and a woman are a safer combination, two men will have a harder time, and three will go nowhere. Experienced hitchers pick a spot outside of built-up areas, where drivers can stop, return to the road without causing an accident, and have time to look over potential passengers as they approach. Hitching (or even standing) on super-highways is usually illegal: one may only thumb at rest stops or at the entrance ramps to highways. Finally, success will depend on appearance. Drivers prefer hitchers who are neat and wholesome-looking.

Most Western European countries offer a ride service, which pairs drivers with riders; the fee varies according to destination. **Eurostop** (www.taxistop.be/index_ils.htm), Taxistop's ride service, is one of the largest in Europe. Not all organizations screen drivers and riders; ask in advance.

KEEPING IN TOUCH

BY EMAIL AND INTERNET

An Internet connection is fairly easy to find in Amsterdam and other large Dutch cities. The best place for the Internet is in Amsterdam's wonderful libraries and Internet cafes (see **Practical Information,** p. 93, for listings). Although in some places it's possible to forge a remote link with your home server, most of the time this is a much slower (and thus more expensive) option than taking advantage of free **web-based email accounts** (e.g., www.gmail.com and www.hotmail.com). For lists of additional cybercafes in the Netherlands, check out www.cybercaptive.com or www.netcafeguide.com.

Increasingly, travelers find that taking their **laptop computers** on the road with them can be a convenient option for staying connected. Laptop users can call an Internet service provider via a modem using long-distance phone cards specifically intended for such calls. They may also find Internet cafes that allow them to connect their laptops to the Internet. Most excitingly, travelers with wireless-enabled computers may be able to take advantage of an increasing number of Internet "hot spots," where they can get online for free or for a small fee. Newer computers can detect these hot spots automatically; otherwise, websites like www.jiwire.com, www.wififreespot.com, and www.wi-fihotspotlist.com can help you find them. For information on insuring your laptop while traveling, see p. 27.

WARY WI-FI. Wireless hot spots make Internet access possible in public and remote places. Unfortunately, they also pose **security risks.** Hot spots are public, open networks that use unencrypted, unsecured connections. They are susceptible to hacks and "packet sniffing"—ways of stealing passwords and other private information. To prevent problems, disable ad hoc mode, turn off file sharing, turn off network discovery, encrypt your email, turn on your firewall, beware of phony networks, and watch for over-the-shoulder creeps. Ask the establishment whose wireless you're using for the name of the network so you know you're on the right one. If you are in the vicinity and do not plan to access the Internet, turn off your wireless adapter completely.

BY TELEPHONE

CALLING HOME FROM THE NETHERLANDS

You can usually make **direct international calls** from pay phones, but if you aren't using a phone card, you may need to feed the machine regularly. **Prepaid phone cards** are a common and relatively inexpensive means of calling abroad. Each one comes with a PIN and a toll-free access number. You call the access number and then follow the directions for dialing your PIN. To purchase prepaid phone cards, check online for the best rates; www.callingcards.com is a good place to start. Online providers generally send your access number and PIN via email with no actual "card" involved. You can also call home with prepaid phone cards purchased in the Netherlands (see **Calling Within the Netherlands,** p. 45).

 PLACING INTERNATIONAL CALLS. To call the Netherlands from home or to call home from the Netherlands, dial:

1. The **international dialing prefix.** To call from **Australia,** dial 0011; **Canada** or the **US,** 011; **Ireland, New Zealand,** the **UK,** or the **Netherlands,** 00.
2. The **country code** of the country you want to call. To call **Australia,** dial 61; **Canada** or the **US,** 1; **Ireland,** 353; **New Zealand,** 64; the **UK,** 44; the **Netherlands,** 31.
3. The **city/area code.** *Let's Go* lists the city/area codes for cities and towns in the Netherlands opposite the city or town name (in **Daytrips,** p. 243) and next to a ☎. If the first digit is a zero (e.g., 020 for Amsterdam), omit the zero when calling from abroad (e.g., dial 20 from Canada to reach Amsterdam).
4. The **local number.**

Another option is to purchase a **calling card,** linked to a major national telecommunications service in your home country. Calls are billed collect or to your account. To obtain a calling card, contact the appropriate company listed below. Where available, there are often advantages to purchasing calling cards online, including better rates and immediate access to your account. To call home with a calling card, contact the operator for your service provider in the Netherlands by dialing the appropriate toll-free access number (listed below in the third column).

COMPANY	TO OBTAIN A CARD:	TO CALL ABROAD:
AT&T (US)	800-364-9292 or www.att.com	0800 022 9111
Canada Direct	800-561-8868 or www.infocanadadirect.com	0800 022 9116
MCI (US)	800-777-5000 or www.minutepass.com	0800 022 9122
Telecom New Zealand Direct	www.telecom.co.nz	0800 022 4464
Telstra Australia	1800 676 638 or www.telstra.com	0800 022 2061

Placing a **collect call** through an international operator can be expensive, but it may be necessary in case of an emergency. You can frequently call collect without even possessing a company's calling card just by calling its access number and following the instructions.

CALLING WITHIN THE NETHERLANDS

The simplest way to call within the country is to use a coin-operated phone. **Prepaid phone cards** (available at newspaper kiosks and tobacco stores), which carry a certain amount of phone time depending on the card's denomination, usually save time and money in the long run. The computerized phone will tell you how much time, in units, you have left on your card. Another kind of prepaid telephone card comes with a PIN and a toll-free access number. Instead of inserting the card into the phone, you call the access number and follow the directions on the card. These cards can be used to make international as well as domestic calls. Phone rates typically tend to be highest in the morning, lower in the evening, and lowest on Sunday and late at night.

Pay phones in the Netherlands hurt (€0.30 per min.). You can buy a *telekaart* (phone card; €5, €10, and €25 installments available) virtually anywhere in the Netherlands, including at convenience stores, train stations, and the VVV. Some pay phones take credit cards or even—could it be?—coins. Calls from private phones are obviously subject to different rates, but if that private phone belongs to your hotel, you can bet on a charge that will make you pine for pay phones.

The cheapest option for phone calls are Internet-based providers such as **Vonage** (www.vonage.com) or **Skype** (www.skype.com), but they are subject to the whims of the World Wide Web.

CELLULAR PHONES

Using a cell phone is largely a matter of personal preference. Often, however, the convenience and peace of mind afforded by a cell phone is worth any extra cost or hassles. Prepaid mobiles can be expensive (€0.20 per min.), but it's usually free to receive calls, and text-messaging, even internationally, won't break the bank.

The international standard for cell phones is **Global System for Mobile Communication (GSM)**. To make and receive calls in the Netherlands, you will need a **GSM-compatible phone** and a **SIM (Subscriber Identity Module) card,** a country-specific, thumbnail-sized chip that gives you a local phone number and plugs you into the local network. Many SIM cards are **prepaid,** meaning that they come with calling time included and you don't need to sign up for a monthly service plan. Incoming calls are frequently free. When you use up the prepaid time, you can buy additional cards or vouchers (usually available at convenience stores) to "top up" your phone. For more information on GSM phones, check out www.telestial.com, www.orange.co.uk, www.roadpost.com, or www.planetomni.com. Companies like **Cellular Abroad** (www.cellularabroad.com) rent cell phones that work in a variety of destinations around the world, providing a simpler option than picking up a phone in-country. Alternatively, you can ask your cellular provider about adapting your personal phone to be able to make and receive calls in the Netherlands.

 GSM PHONES. Just having a GSM phone doesn't mean you're necessarily good to go when you travel abroad. The majority of GSM phones sold in the United States operate on a different **frequency** (1900) than international phones (900/1800) and will not work abroad. Tri-band phones work on all three frequencies (900/1800/1900) and will operate through most of the world. Additionally, some GSM phones are **SIM-locked** and will only accept SIM cards from a single carrier. You'll need a **SIM-unlocked** phone to use a SIM card from a local carrier when you travel.

TIME DIFFERENCES

The Netherlands is one hour ahead of Greenwich Mean Time (GMT). The Netherlands observes Daylight Saving Time, though it does so for a shorter period than does the US (meaning that just before and just after Dutch summer time, Amsterdam is five hours ahead of New York City).

4AM	5AM	6AM	7AM	8AM	NOON	1PM	10PM
Vancouver Seattle San Francisco Los Angeles	Denver Boise	Chicago Grace-land	New York City Toronto Boston	New Brunswick Halifax	London Dublin Tim-buktu	**Amsterdam** Monte Carlo Johannes-burg	Sydney Canberra Melbourne

BY MAIL

Post offices are generally open Monday through Friday 9am-5pm, and some are also open Saturday 10am-1:30pm. The main post office in Amsterdam is at Singel 250. (Open M-W and F 9am-6pm, Th 9am-8pm, Sa 10am-1:30pm.) To find out exact times for specific branches, call ☎ 0800 0417.

SENDING MAIL FROM THE NETHERLANDS

Airmail is the best way to send mail home from the Netherlands. Write "airmail" or "par avion" on the front. **Surface mail** is by far the cheapest and slowest way to send mail. It takes one to two months to cross the Atlantic and one to three to cross the Pacific—good for heavy items you won't need for a while, such as souvenirs that you've acquired along the way. International stamps cost €0.89, and your letters and postcards should reach European destinations within the week, North America within two weeks, and the rest of the world before the month is up.

SENDING MAIL TO THE NETHERLANDS

To ensure timely delivery, mark envelopes "airmail" or "par avion." In addition to the standard postage system whose rates are listed below, **Federal Express** (Australia ☎ 13 26 10, Canada and the US 800-463-3339, Ireland 1800 535 800, New Zealand 0800 733 339, the UK 08456 070 809; www.fedex.com) handles express mail services from most countries to the Netherlands. Sending a postcard or letter within the Netherlands costs €0.44.

There are several ways to arrange pickup of letters sent to you while you are abroad. Mail can be sent via **Poste Restante** (General Delivery) to almost any city or town in the Netherlands with a post office, and it is very reliable. Address Poste Restante letters like so:

> Vincent VAN GOGH
> Poste Restante
> Amsterdam, the Netherlands

The mail will go to a special desk in the central post office unless you specify a post office by street address or postal code. It's best to use the largest post office, since mail may be sent there regardless. It is usually safer and quicker, though more expensive, to send mail express or registered. Bring your passport (or other photo ID) for pickup; there may be a small fee. If the clerks insist that there is nothing for you, ask them to check under your first name as well. *Let's Go* lists post offices in the **Practical Information** chapter (p. 97).

American Express's travel offices throughout the world offer a free **Client Letter Service** (mail held up to 30 days and forwarded upon request) for cardholders who contact them in advance. Some offices provide these services to non-cardholders (especially AmEx Travelers Cheque holders), but call ahead to make sure. *Let's Go* lists AmEx locations in the **Practical Information** chapter; for a complete list, call ☎ 800-528-4800 or visit www.americanexpress.com.

SPECIFIC CONCERNS

SUSTAINABLE TRAVEL

As the number of travelers on the road continues to rise, the detrimental effect they can have on natural environments becomes an increasing concern. With this in mind, *Let's Go* promotes the philosophy of **sustainable travel.** Through a sensitivity to issues of ecology and sustainability, today's travelers can be a powerful force in preserving as well as restoring the places they visit.

Ecotourism, a rising trend in sustainable travel, focuses on the conservation of natural habitats and how to use them to build up the economy without exploitation or overdevelopment. Travelers can make a difference by doing research in advance and by supporting organizations and establishments that pay attention to their impact on their natural surroundings and that strive to be eco-friendly.

The organizations listed in the **Beyond Tourism** chapter (p. 77) focus on projects as diverse as wildlife preservation on the Wadden Islands to increasing ecological awareness among Amsterdam residents. Notably, Amsterdam is also home to the international office of the environmental advocacy organization Greenpeace.

ECOTOURISM RESOURCES. For more information on environmentally responsible tourism, contact one of the organizations below:

Conservation International, 2011 Crystal Dr., Ste. 500, Arlington, VA 22202, USA (☎ 800-406-2306 or 703-341-2400; www.conservation.org).

Green Globe 21, Green Globe vof, Verbenalaan 1, 2111 ZL Aerdenhout, the Netherlands (☎ 31 23 544 0306; www.greenglobe.com).

International Ecotourism Society, 1333 H St. NW, Ste. 300E, Washington, D.C. 20005, USA (☎ 202-347-9203; www.ecotourism.org).

United Nations Environment Program (UNEP), 39-43 Quai André Citroën, 75739 Paris Cedex 15, France (☎ 33 1 44 37 14 50; www.uneptie.org/pc/tourism).

RESPONSIBLE TRAVEL

The impact of tourist euro on the destinations you visit should not be underestimated. The choices you make during your trip can have powerful effects on local communities—for better or for worse. Travelers who care about the destinations and environments they explore should make themselves aware of the social, cultural, and political implications of the choices they make when they travel. Simple decisions such as buying local products instead of globally available ones, paying fair prices for products or services, and attempting to say a few words in Dutch can have a strong, positive effect on the community.

Community-based tourism aims to channel tourist euro into the local economy by emphasizing tours and cultural programs that are run by members of the host community and that often benefit disadvantaged groups. This type of tourism also benefits the tourists themselves, since it often takes them beyond the traditional tours of the region. The *Ethical Travel Guide* (UK£13), a project of **Tourism Concern** (☎ +44 020 7133 3330; www.tourismconcern.org.uk), is an excellent resource for information on community-based travel with a directory of 300 establishments in 60 countries.

Travelers to Amsterdam have the opportunity to promote and foster stronger ties between native Dutch inhabitants and the recent wave of Muslim immigrants from the Middle East. For more detailed information on programs and projects relating to responsible travel, check out our **Beyond Tourism** chapter (p. 77).

TRAVELING ALONE

There are many benefits to traveling alone, including independence and a greater opportunity to connect with locals. On the other hand, solo travelers are more vulnerable targets of harassment and street theft. If you are traveling alone, look confident, try not to stand out as a tourist, and be especially careful in deserted or very crowded areas. Stay away from areas that are not well lit. If questioned, never admit that you are traveling alone. Maintain regular contact with someone at home who knows your itinerary and always research your destination before traveling. For more tips, pick up *Traveling Solo*, by Eleanor Berman (Globe Pequot Press, US$18), visit www.travelaloneandloveit.com, or subscribe to **Connecting: Solo Travel Network,** 689 Park Rd., Unit 6, Gibsons, BC V0N 1V7, Canada. (☎604-886-9099; www.cstn.org. Membership US$30-48.)

WOMEN TRAVELERS

Women exploring on their own inevitably face some additional safety concerns, but it's easy to be adventurous without taking undue risks. If you are concerned, consider staying in hostels which offer single rooms that lock from the inside or in religious organizations with single-sex rooms. Stick to centrally located accommodations and avoid solitary late-night treks or metro rides.

Always carry extra cash for a phone call, bus, or taxi. **Hitchhiking** is never safe for lone women, or even for two women traveling together. Look as if you know where you're going and approach older women or couples for directions if you're lost or uncomfortable. If you're concerned, avoid coffee shops and anywhere having to do with the sex industry, as they can be particularly women-unfriendly.

Generally, the less you look like a tourist, the better off you'll be. Dress conservatively, especially in rural areas. Wearing a conspicuous **wedding band**—even if you are not hitched—sometimes helps to prevent unwanted advances.

Your best answer to verbal harassment is no answer at all; feigning deafness, sitting motionless, and staring straight ahead at nothing in particular will usually do the trick. The extremely persistent can sometimes be dissuaded by a firm, loud, and very public *"ga weg"* (hah vekh; "Go away!"). Don't hesitate to seek out a police officer or a passerby if you are being harassed. Memorize the emergency numbers in places you visit and consider carrying a whistle on your keychain. A self-defense course will both prepare you for a potential attack and raise your level of awareness of your surroundings (see **Personal Safety**, p. 26). Also be sure you are aware of the health concerns that women face when traveling (p. 30).

GLBT TRAVELERS

In terms of sexual diversity in Amsterdam, anything goes—and often. Darkrooms and dungeons rub elbows with saunas and sex clubs, though much more subdued options are the standard; in fact, many of the patrons at the more explicitly sexual venues are visitors to Amsterdam, not locals. Still, the Netherlands has the most tolerant laws for homosexuals in the world—for example, it became the first country to legalize gay marriage in 2001, converting all "registered same-sex partnerships" into full marriages. Countless services and establishments cater to GLBT visitors and native Amsterdammers alike.

Nonetheless, certain travelers—including drag queens and kings, other crossdressers, and transgendered visitors more generally—should take extra caution walking the streets at night, especially around and in the Red Light District. All GLBT visitors to Amsterdam should also be aware that, though the city is a haven of homosexual tolerance, the recent infusion of fundamentalist religiosity into the Dutch political dialogue has created an environment detrimental to complete acceptance of GLBT behaviors and visibility.

Listed below are contact organizations, mail-order catalogs, and publishers that offer materials addressing some specific concerns. **Out and About** (www.planetout.com) offers a weekly newsletter addressing travel concerns and a comprehensive site addressing gay travel concerns. The online newspaper **365gay.com** also has a travel section (www.365gay.com/travel/travelchannel.htm).

COC, Rozenstraat 14, Amsterdam (☎020 626 3087; www.cocamsterdam.nl), Founded in 1946, this oldest GLBT rights organization in the world exists as a social network and information center. See other listing in **Beyond Tourism,** p. 80. Open M-F 9am-5pm.

Gay and Lesbian Switchboard (☎020 623 6565) is available to answer questions, suggest events, or listen to personal problems. Staffed M-F noon-10pm, Sa-Su 4pm-8pm.

Gay Krant (☎421 0000; www.gk.nl). A travel service devoted exclusively to gay and lesbian travelers. Also sells an impressive array of magazines. Open M-Th 8:30am-5pm, F 8:30am-12:30pm.

Gay's the Word, 66 Marchmont St., London WC1N 1AB, UK (☎+44 020 7278 7654; http://freespace.virgin.net/gays.theword). The largest gay and lesbian bookshop in the UK, with both fiction and non-fiction titles. Mail-order service available.

Giovanni's Room, 345 South 12th St., Philadelphia, PA 19107, USA (☎215-923-2960; www.queerbooks.com). An international lesbian and gay bookstore with mail-order service (carries many of the publications listed below).

International Lesbian and Gay Association (ILGA), Avenue des Villas 34, 1060 Brussels, Belgium (☎+32 2 502 2471; www.ilga.org). Provides political information such as homosexuality laws of individual countries.

Vrolijk, Paleisstraat 135, Amsterdam (☎020 623 5142; www.vrolijk.nu). One of the biggest and best-known gay and lesbian bookstores in Europe. With an excellent selection of literature and periodicals spread over 2 floors, it's an ideal place to stop in for tips on what's hot and what's not in gay Amsterdam. Various knick-knacks abound; also houses a growing DVD selection. Shop online for books. Open M 11am-6pm, Tu-F 10am-6pm, Sa 10am-5pm, Su 1-5pm.

Xantippe Unlimited, Prinsengracht 290, Amsterdam (☎020 623 5854; www.xantippe.nl). General bookstore, but with a specialization in women and lesbians' issues. Open M 1-7pm, Tu-F 10am-7pm, Sa 10am-6pm, Su noon-5pm.

> ▼ **ADDITIONAL GLBT RESOURCES.**
> *Spartacus 2005-2006: International Gay Guide.* Bruno Gmunder Verlag (US$33).
> *Damron Men's Travel Guide, Damron Accommodations Guide, Damron City Guide,* and *Damron Women's Traveller.* Damron Travel Guides (US$18-24). For info, call ☎800-462-6654 or visit www.damron.com.
> *The Gay Vacation Guide: The Best Trips and How to Plan Them,* Mark Chesnut. Kensington Books (US$15).

TRAVELERS WITH DISABILITIES

Amsterdam is a particularly difficult city to navigate from a wheelchair. This otherwise tolerant and accommodating city has not yet made significant efforts for disabled travelers. The streets are narrow, the trams have steps and narrow doors, and only the better hotels have street-level entrances or elevators. Places that are wheelchair-accessible have been awarded the **International Symbol of Access (ISA).** Contact the Netherlands Institute for Care and Welfare (☎030 230 6311; www.nizw.nl) or the **Afdeling Gehandicaptenvoorlichting** (☎070 314 1420) for more information. Those with disabilities should inform airlines and hotels of their disabilities when making reservations; some time may be needed to prepare special accommodations. Call ahead to restaurants, museums, and other facilities to find out if they are wheelchair accessible. **Guide dog owners** should inquire as to the quarantine policies of each destination country.

Rail is probably the most convenient form of travel for disabled travelers in Europe: many stations have ramps, and some trains have wheelchair lifts, special seating areas, and specially equipped toilets. All Eurostar, some InterCity (IC) and some EuroCity (EC) trains are **wheelchair-accessible**, as are most trains in the Netherlands's national rail network. For those who wish to rent cars, some major **car-rental** agencies (e.g., Hertz) offer hand-controlled vehicles.

USEFUL ORGANIZATIONS

Accessible Journeys, 35 W. Sellers Ave., Ridley Park, PA 19078, USA (☎800-846-4537; www.disabilitytravel.com). Designs tours for wheelchair users and slow walkers. The site has tips and forums for all travelers.

AccessWise, Veesteeg 3B, Boven-Leeuwen (☎0900 040 1410; www.accesswise.org). Information for travelers with disabilities on traveling in the Netherlands and from the Netherlands through Europe. Currently, the website is only in Dutch, but call (€0.30 per min.)—they speak English.

Flying Wheels Travel, 143 W. Bridge St., Owatonna, MN 55060, USA (☎507-451-5005; www.flyingwheelstravel.com). Specializes in escorted trips to Europe for people with physical disabilities; plans custom trips worldwide.

Mobility International USA (MIUSA), P.O. Box 10767, Eugene, OR 97440, USA (☎541-343-1284; www.miusa.org). Provides a variety of books and other publications containing information for travelers with disabilities.

Nederlands Astma Fonds, Speelkamp 28, Leusden (☎033 434 1295; www.astmafonds.nl), has information on hotels and other accommodations that are suitable for those with asthma, bronchitis, or emphysema.

Society for Accessible Travel and Hospitality (SATH), 347 5th Ave., Ste. 610, New York City, NY 10016, USA (☎212-447-7284; www.sath.org). An advocacy group that publishes free online travel information. Annual membership US$49, students and seniors US$29.

MINORITY TRAVELERS

Amsterdam is an integrated, multicultural city. Surinamese, Indonesian, Moroccan, Turkish, African, and Antillean immigrants (and they are only the tip of the iceberg) have made their homes in Amsterdam, serving as a lasting reminder of Amsterdam's colonial history. But while Amsterdam has a reputation for tolerance, it also has a surprising streak of racism. The Netherlands, like many European countries today, is in the process of making tougher penalties for illegal immigrants—most of whom are minorities. This should not discourage non-Caucasian travelers from visiting the city—most Amsterdammers are very tolerant and welcoming—but minority travelers should be aware that their presence might elicit a less friendly reaction from some people.

DIETARY CONCERNS

While traditional Dutch food is hearty, heavy, and fish- and meat-based, the proliferation of international cuisine means vegetarians in the Netherlands should have no problem finding suitable selections in most restaurants. Indonesian food, in which Amsterdam is swimming, includes numerous vegetarian possibilities; Indian cuisine is also reliable. And despite their reputation for eating beef and raw fish, the Dutch have also adopted the Swiss tradition of fondue—a less healthful vegetarian option.

The travel section of the The Vegetarian Resource Group's website, at www.vrg.org/travel, has a comprehensive list of organizations and websites that are geared toward helping vegetarians and vegans traveling abroad. For more information, visit your local bookstore or health food store and consult *The Vegetarian Traveler: Where to Stay if You're Vegetarian, Vegan, Environmentally Sensitive*, by Jed and Susan Civic (Larson Publications; US$16). Vegetarians will also find numerous resources on the web; try www.vegdining.com and www.happycow.net for starters. Dutch websites include www.vegatopia.com and www.vegetariers.nl. The Dutch word for "vegetarian" is *vegetarisch*.

Eating kosher in Amsterdam is easily done—kosher delis, bakeries, and butchers are dispersed throughout the city. Many restaurants throughout the Netherlands, including larger cities like The Hague, are under the supervision of the Amsterdam Ashkenazi and Sephardic Rabbinates; all meat in the restaurants under Amsterdam rabbinical supervision is *glatt*. Travelers who keep kosher should contact synagogues in larger cities for information on kosher restaurants. Your own synagogue or college Hillel should have access to lists of Jewish institutions across the nation, or you can look one up at http://shamash.org/kosher. If you are strict in your observance, you may have to prepare your own food on the road. A good resource is the *Jewish Travel Guide*, edited by Michael Zaidner (Vallentine Mitchell; US$18). Travelers looking for halal restaurants may find www.zabihah.com a useful resource.

OTHER RESOURCES

Let's Go tries to cover all aspects of budget travel, but we can't put *everything* in our guides. Listed below are books and websites that can serve as jumping-off points for your own research.

WORLD WIDE WEB

Almost every aspect of budget travel is accessible via the web. In 10min. at the keyboard, you can make a hostel reservation, get advice on travel hot spots from other travelers, or find out how much a train from Amsterdam to Gouda costs.

Listed here are some regional and travel-related sites to start off your surfing; other relevant websites are listed throughout the book. Because website turnover is high, use search engines (e.g., www.google.com) to strike out on your own.

 WWW.LETSGO.COM Our website features extensive content from our guides; a community forum where travelers can connect with each other, ask questions or advice, and share stories and tips; and expanded resources to help you plan your trip. Visit us to browse by destination, find information about ordering our titles, and read blogs from our summer researchers!

THE ART OF TRAVEL

Amsterdam—The Channels: www.channels.nl. Virtual tour of Amsterdam, tourist and transportation information, and some hotel listings and reviews.

Backpacker's Ultimate Guide: www.bugeurope.com. Tips on packing, transportation, and where to go. Also tons of Netherlands-specific travel information.

BootsnAll.com: www.bootsnall.com. Numerous resources for independent travelers, from planning your trip to reporting on it when you get back.

City of Amsterdam Online: www.iamsterdam.nl. Maintained by the city, the site contains news from local government, links to sports and entertainment, and personalized suggestions by native Amsterdammers.

Expatica: www.expatica.nl. Devoted to the expatriate community in the Netherlands, this website is geared toward wealthier and older expats, but that doesn't change its omniscience. A good resource for English-language Dutch news.

How to See the World: www.artoftravel.com. A compendium of great travel tips from cheap flights to self defense to interacting with local culture.

How to Survive: www.howtosurviveholland.nl. Run by the folks over at Undutchables (p. 89) but less practical in nature. Contains humorous essays and introductions to various elements of Dutch culture written by foreigners.

Panoramsterdam: www.panoramsterdam.com. Hundreds of 360° views of Amsterdam.

TransArtists: www.transartists.nl. An information clearinghouse for artists seeking jobs, lodgings, and studios in the Netherlands. Classifieds postings and festival and workshop info.

Travel Intelligence: www.travelintelligence.net. A large collection of travel writing by distinguished travel writers.

Travel Library: www.travel-library.com. A fantastic set of links for general information and personal travelogues.

Visit Amsterdam: www.holland.com. Maintained by the Netherlands Board of Tourism, this comprehensive site has information on planning your trip and attractions in the city.

World Hum: www.worldhum.com. An independently produced collection of "travel dispatches from a shrinking planet."

INFORMATION ON THE NETHERLANDS

CIA World Factbook: www.odci.gov/cia/publications/factbook/index.html. Tons of vital statistics on the Netherlands's geography, government, economy, and people.

Geographia: www.geographia.com. Highlights, culture, and people of the Netherlands.

PlanetRider: www.planetrider.com. A subjective list of links to the "best" websites covering the culture and tourist attractions of the Netherlands.

TravelPage: www.travelpage.com. Links to official tourist office sites in the Netherlands.

World Travel Guide: www.travel-guides.com. Helpful practical info.

LIFE AND TIMES

Too many people demonize—or worship—Amsterdam as a world of sex, drugs, and rock 'n' roll. For sure, it has all of those things. But the Dutch legacy is rooted in two more profound pillars: internationalism and innovation. From its perch at the confluence of Europe, the Netherlands has experienced diffusion fueled by war, migration, occupation, and trade. There is no doubt that inherited peoples and ideas gave the Netherlands significant growing pains, but it is equally certain that, without them, the Golden Age could never have shone so brightly. From superiority on the seas to expertise on the easel, the Dutch have blazed their own unique path. At the same time, they have applied their ingenuity literally to cover new ground, claiming 2745 square miles of land from the North Sea through an intricate network of ocean-conquering dikes, canals, and pumps—land that was, in turn, quickly settled by international newcomers. The local adage, "God created the world, but the Dutch created the Netherlands," also applies to the fiercely independent attitude this geopolitical black sheep has forged for itself. The international flavors apparent to all visitors of Amsterdam are today joined by the innovative liberality of its daily life. Though this may circle back to indulgence, internationalism and innovation have lent Amsterdam and the Netherlands an unmistakable tint of sophistication.

HISTORY OF THE NETHERLANDS

IN THE BEGINNING

TRIBES AND TERPEN

The early history of the so-called **Low Countries**—modern-day Belgium, Luxembourg, and the Netherlands—is as murky and difficult to navigate as its boggy marshlands. Nomads first roamed the area 150,000 years ago, using primitive tools to hunt such native Dutch fauna as wood elephants and hippopotamuses. Their livelihood was rudely interrupted by the cold snap known as the Ice Age, delaying further Dutch development until 14,000 BC. Despite the moody nature of the sea, hunters and gatherers gave way relatively quickly—a few millennia or so—to settlements and agriculture. Native tribes like the **Frisians, Batavi,** and **Celts** had just made themselves comfortable when Julius Caesar stepped in to conquer them in 57 BC. The Low Countries were a constant source of frustration for the Romans; local tribes were uncooperative, the terrain was constantly flooded, and the weather was dreadful compared to sunny Italy's. Although local tribes had adapted to their surroundings by living on **terpen** (stone mounds used to keep lodgings above flood levels), Roman attempts to dam the land and build canals proved futile. Roman historian Pliny the Elder, perhaps suffering from sour grapes, wondered in writing "whether one should consider that country as part of the land or the sea."

100,000 BC
Though Amsterdam won't exist for another 101,275 years, inhabitants of the Low Countries are rumored region-wide to be chaotically impulsive, self-indulgent creatures of the night.

THE TIDE TURNS

NEW NEIGHBORS MOVE IN

Roman influence began to decline around AD 400 and vanished with an invasion by Germanic tribes, who by that time had unified to become collectively known as the **Franks** and the **Saxons.** Shortly after **Clovis I,** king of the Frankish Merovingians, ascended to the throne in AD 481, the Franks embarked on a crusade to eradicate all things pagan. The *Pactus Legis Salicae* (Law of the Salian Franks), a unique system of Roman and Christian law, paved the way for Christianity to make inroads into northern Europe. Missionaries were sent to local villages to seal the deal, some with more success than others. **Saint Willibrord,** one such proselytizer, became the first **Bishop of Utrecht** at the start of the 8th century. Upon Willibrord's death, **Saint Boniface** inherited his quest but, during an encounter with the Frisians, found himself meeting his maker sooner than he had hoped. Despite this initial hesitance to accept Christianity, the Frisians (and others) soon saw the light, firmly establishing Christianity's place in the Low Countries.

In AD 800, following nicely on Merovingian heels, **Charlemagne** took control of the Low Countries, vowing to execute anyone who still resisted Christian customs. A veritable megalomaniac, he envisioned himself assuming the legacy of the Roman emperors who had ruled hundreds of years earlier. Though Charlemagne ruled in name, his Dutch legacy is contested, for historians maintain that local officials in the Low Countries retained significant influence. Nevertheless, Charlemagne, gladly crowned as Holy Roman Emperor **Charles I** in AD 800, presided over an unprecedented cultural revitalization. Romanesque churches still stand in Nijmegen and Maastricht, physical remnants of this sliver of light in the Dark Ages.

The years after Charlemagne's death in 814 witnessed the decline of his Carolingian empire. The area's new rudderlessness presented a perfect opportunity for Scandinavian **Vikings** to plunder its decaying riches and take advantage of the disorganized central government. When Viking threats abated in the 10th century, the peace allowed towns to blaze their own individual paths ahead to economic prosperity without accountability to a federal power. Modern Dutch principalities became recognizable in the 11th century: the **County of Holland**—in which Amsterdam is located—was one of the first to form, along with **Flanders, Hainaut, Brabant, Liège, Utrecht,** and **Groningen.** From 1100 to 1400, the nobility flourished (the serfs less so) under the prevailing philosophies of feudalism and religious piety for local gain.

A TOWN IS BORN

In spite of Holland's emergence as a political body, the area that is now Amsterdam arrived a bit late to the party. Inspired by one of the worthier tribal practices, inhabitants who first settled at the mouth of the **Amstel River** in the 13th century

LIFE AND TIMES

AD 800
As the new ruler of the Low Countries, Charlemagne finds one way to achieve religious unity: by putting all remaining non-Christians to death.

AD 800s
Vikings do what Vikings do: attack and plunder.

built the first dam between the dikes on either side of the river in 1270. (Land reclamation projects such as this would continue for centuries, eventually accounting for 27% of the Netherlands's land area. The mechanical instruments used to pump the ocean out became another Dutch stereotype—the windmill.) The town grew as maritime trade flourished between northern Europe and Flanders, but it remained unnamed until 1275. At that date, now celebrated as Amsterdam's founding year, **Count Floris V** wrote in a tariff document of a town inhabited by people living near the *Aemstelledamme*—the "Dam on the River Amstel." The name eventually evolved into its current, easier-to-pronounce form. The city gained its charter around 1300 and continued to expand. Thanks to a booming economy fueled in part by proceeds from beer tolls, buildings like the Oude Kerk (p. 145) sprang up, and Amsterdam's population exploded to 12,000 by 1514. By the end of the 15th century, Amsterdam had become the largest and most important commercial center in Holland. **Emperor Maximilian I** was so indebted to Amsterdam's resources that he allowed the city to adorn itself with the imperial crown now featured prominently on its coat of arms.

WAR AND PEACE AND WAR

BURGUNDY TURNS TO RED

The French **Burgundian Dynasty** controlled the region following the decline of feudalism and the Holy Roman Empire in the Low Countries. Under French rule in the 1400s, Dutch provinces took small steps toward actual cooperation. Their representatives assembled in 1464 at the first meeting of what would become the Dutch parliament, the **States-General.** However, they still faced a long road to unity when, in 1477, the Burgundian territories were redigested into the Hapsburg Holy Roman Empire, which by then was ruled from the throne of very Catholic Spain. This might not have been a problem if not for the continental waves of discontent with the extravagances of the Catholic Church. It did not help matters that the genesis of the grumblings was partly attributed to a Dutch intellectual, **Erasmus of Rotterdam.** Martin Luther, who openly questioned the Catholic Church's indulgence system, was heavily influenced by this humanist scholar. When Luther posted his *95 Theses* to the door of a church in Wittenberg, Germany, poor Erasmus was attacked on both sides—by the Catholics for having incited Luther's radicalism and by the Lutherans for not aligning himself with their new faith. Erasmus's particular dilemma foreshadowed the years of religious turmoil that would follow during the radical Protestant Reformation.

In 1543, Spanish king **Charles V** created the **Political Union of the Netherlands** (present-day Belgium, Luxembourg, and the Netherlands) as part of his plot to conquer the world. This move made it clear that a Dutch identity was emerging from the North Sea fog, even though this particular federation soon fell victim to religious infighting. Years of salutary neglect had also

c. 1200
The site of the future Amsterdam is chosen when a boat carrying two men and a seasick dog comes ashore to escape a storm. The dog becomes the first of many to throw up in Amsterdam.

1452
A devastating fire consumes nearly three-quarters of Amsterdam. Residents decide to stop constructing buildings from timber.

LIFE AND TIMES

1568
William I, dubbed
"the Silent," lets
his loud actions
speak for him in
the revolt against
the Spanish.

left the Low Countries averse to foreign domination, something Charles's successor **Philip II** failed to realize. He was outraged at the Dutch rejection of Catholicism and set out to squelch the Protestant Reformation. Not surprisingly, dissidents were outraged right back, desecrating churches and destroying religious icons. Stern military reprisals from Philip's forces ignited a Dutch resistance against the Spanish government in 1568 that marked the beginning of a period of intermittent armed rebellion: the **Eighty Years' War,** led by **William I,** Prince of Orange.

William I led and personally funded a number of revolts in the country, but the city of Amsterdam remained loyal to Philip and hesitated to join the Dutch. After an especially encouraging victory at Leiden, William convened another meeting of Dutch delegates in 1576, the result of which was the **Pacification of Ghent**—a deal that not only bound the Low Countries together for a common cause but also established religious freedom. Despite an impressive history of eradicating any and all annoying faiths of the day, religious tolerance became a firm Dutch constant from that point forward. Of course, the Dutch record since then is not exactly spotless; in the 1578 **Alteration,** Amsterdam was less-than-agreeably converted to Protestantism—specifically the strict, ascetic Calvinism. Spanish citizens and many members of the Roman Catholic Church were deported from the city. Any remaining Catholics in Amsterdam were forced to practice in hiding, as their public worship areas were commandeered by the Protestants. The northern provinces, including Amsterdam, finally claimed their independence in the 1579 **Union of Utrecht,** and William was named the first leader of the **United Provinces of the Netherlands.** Left to their own devices, towns in the southern Low Countries like Antwerp in modern-day Belgium fell to Spanish invasion. The resulting exodus of Protestants and Jews from Antwerp to Amsterdam resulted in a surge of intellectual and cultural energy along the Amstel.

1613
The Netherlands
has a drinking
problem: because
water is too dirty to
drink, the average
Dutchman con-
sumes 250L of
beer annually.

Philip reacted to the union the way any proper tyrant would be expected to—he had William assassinated in 1584. The understandably angry Dutch waged war with Spain until 1609, when the uneasy **Twelve Years' Truce** established today's Dutch boundaries; after 1621, skirmishing resumed. Spain, however, was so distracted by the bigger, closer emerging power of France that they recognized Dutch independence in 1648.

GOLDEN AGE

The seeds of the Netherlands's future international commercial dominance were first cultivated in the 1590s, when two ships set sail from Amsterdam on separate voyages bound for **Indonesia.** They were but a harbinger of the Netherlands's imperial might. During the first half of the 17th century, while **Rembrandt van Rijn** was building an artistic legacy, two newly established merchant trading companies were securing an economic legacy on the international stage. Because of its fortuitously situated northern ports, the Netherlands was a prime candidate to assume the reins of the up-and-coming global trading enterprise. Both the Verenigde Oostindische Compagnie (VOC) or

Dutch East India Company, and the West-Indische Compagnie (WIC) or **West India Company,** founded in 1602 and 1621, respectively, began creating a vast network of Dutch trading posts throughout Southeast Asia, West Africa, and South America.

The VOC was the larger of the two companies and established major trading posts in India, Indonesia, Thailand, China, Sri Lanka, and Bengal, importing spices, silks, and cotton. The WIC traded slaves, gold, and ivory off the western coast of Africa and established busy ports in Brazil and Suriname. Dutch influence extended from economic subjugation to the political as well; Indonesia and Suriname were among the Dutch holdings overseas. The WIC even had a brief stint beginning in 1623 as the colonizers of **New Amsterdam** in North America. Dutch governor Peter Stuyvesant tried to whip the city's residents into obedient Calvinists until the English took over and renamed the city New York in 1664, though its grid structure remains a vestige of Dutch engineering. At the height of the Dutch trading empire, the navy numbered over 15,000 vessels (five times more than the British navy), guaranteeing it a monopoly over trade routes.

As a result of this newfound glory, Amsterdam became both the commercial and social capital of Europe. Religious freedom and abundant employment opportunities attracted immigrants from all over Europe. Portuguese, German, and Eastern European Jews seeking refuge from religious persecution flocked to the city, as did others seeking work in commercial enterprise. In this age of economic prosperity, aristocrats, merchants, and financiers built palatial homes along Amsterdam's canals and revitalized the city. Its population swelled from 50,000 in 1600 to 200,000 in 1650, accelerating an already booming economy. Artists also found the Netherlands a haven. In addition to Rembrandt, notable artists **Johannes Vermeer, Jan Steen,** and **Pieter de Hoogh,** among others, painted, chiseled, and carved out the Netherlands's reputation as a creative canvas (p. 68). Writers like **Constantijn Huygens** and poet **Joost van den Vondel** also flourished during this era. This blossoming of all things Dutch would last until the beginning of the 18th century.

END OF EMPIRE

Having jostled for supremacy with England in fits and starts, the Netherlands found their empire difficult to maintain when staring war in the face. Perhaps even more detrimental to the Netherlands, however, was peace with its naval rival and neighbor to the north. When the 1688 Glorious Revolution in England dethroned James II, **William III of Orange** (*stadhouder* of the United Provinces) was given the ultimate career advancement opportunity—an invitation to take the British throne with his wife, Mary. In England the Dutch now had an ally against the French, with whom they had waged intermittent war since 1672. In this new alliance, England was to focus its naval strengths in the war against France while the Netherlands levied its marsh—er, land—powers. Because England was the stronger member of the Anglo-Dutch alliance, William focused

LIFE AND TIMES

1626
The Dutch buy Manhattan Island from Native Americans for the equivalent of US$24. Today it is worth hundreds of billions of dollars.

1637
The Netherlands goes tulip-crazy: one bulb sells for US$76,000, as much as an entire estate. The florid bubble quickly pops, resulting in the first market crash in history, on par with the Wall Street crash of 1929.

1690
Smoking is banned in Haarlem. The people raise arms in protest, demonstrating the proud Dutch attachment to their puffables.

most of his energy on the British Isles. This did not sit too well with Netherlanders; tired of costly and bureaucratic wars, Amsterdam was rife with popular uprisings. In addition, the shift toward a terrestrial military was hardly healthful for the Dutch navy—and as went the navy, so went the Golden Age.

After the Netherlands attempted to trade with newly independent American rebels, the **Fourth Anglo-Dutch War** broke out in 1780. The British Admiralty finished the job started by years of neglect and wiped out what was left of the Dutch navy. With the defeat, Dutch international trade dominance was over. Domestically, the war's economic fallout served only to widen the deepening divide between upper and lower classes. The influence of the French Enlightenment, which touted the potential and reason of the individual and trumpeted the ideal of democratic rule, galvanized the 1780s **Patriot Movement.** The movement denounced the conservatism of the ruling Orthodox Protestant monarchy and those aristocrats loyal to **William V.** The upper crust quickly and brutally dispatched of this faux French Revolution—only to be ambushed by the real thing.

IN THE MIDDLE OF THINGS

DEMOCRACY GOES DUTCH

By 1795, Napoleon's French forces had swept through the Netherlands and brought it under their control. Napoleon put his brother Louis in charge of the territory and renamed it the **Batavian Republic.** Much to Napoleon's dismay, Louis encouraged the process of structural and political modernization for the Dutch, moving toward the democratization for which the Patriots had fought. In 1813, after Napoleon's string of military victories finally came to an abrupt and spectacular end, the Netherlands returned to autonomous rule. Governed by **King William I,** the **Kingdom of the Netherlands** was declared in 1815. Though William sought to maintain control over all of the Low Countries, Belgium stubbornly declared its independence in 1830; its status was confirmed when William begrudgingly signed a treaty recognizing the nation in 1839. So great was William's disappointment that he abdicated the throne in 1840.

1828
Coenraad Johannes van Houten invents "Dutch process" cocoa powder, revolutionizing the accessibility of chocolate.

Internal improvements and constitutional reform followed William's abdication. With the Industrial Revolution, dikes went up and canals went down. The Netherlands adopted the liberal charter it upholds today, making the monarch a servant to—rather than a master of—the States-General. Other significant political reforms were obtained with the **Pacification of 1917,** when universal male suffrage (with the women's vote following in 1919) and equal funding to religious and secular schools were established.

THE WORLD WARS

Despite pressures from both Britain and Germany, the Netherlands maintained its neutrality for the duration of **World War I.** The country escaped the disastrous fate suffered by its Low-

Country neighbor Belgium—another uncommitted nation—which was invaded in August of 1914. Following what was known as the "Great War," the Netherlands joined the **League of Nations** but was able to continue its policy of non-alignment.

During **World War II,** the Netherlands had no such luck. On May 10, 1940, the army of Nazi Germany crossed the borders of the still-neutral Netherlands and began bombing Dutch military facilities. Military resistance allowed the government and **Queen Wilhelmina** to flee en masse to England, where they formed a parliament in exile, but the Germans forced a Dutch surrender after only five long days. Rotterdam was leveled in short order, leaving the city to rebuild from scratch into its modern incarnation. The Germans occupied the Netherlands for most of the war, figuratively and literally flooding its delicate lands to make it more difficult for the Allies to invade neighboring Germany. In response, the Dutch created a clandestine—and largely unsuccessful—resistance movement that spanned various ideological groups in the country.

The Nazi occupation devastated Dutch society. The Nazis suppressed political opposition and began to persecute Jews, who were deported to concentration and extermination camps. Residents, however, stayed true to their history of tolerance: in one instance, Amsterdam dockworkers went on strike upon hearing of the deportation of Dutch Jews. This active resistance, which was met with military violence, was one of the few overt and organized acts of resistance that took place in the Netherlands during the war.

Amsterdam's longstanding Jewish community, centered in the Jodenbuurt, was essentially rendered non-existent by the Nazis. Fewer Jews from Amsterdam survived than in any other Western European city; of the 80,000 Jews in Amsterdam before Nazi occupation, only 5000 remained in the city after the war. Over 75% of the country's Jewish population did not survive the war, including diarist **Anne Frank,** who spent two years in hiding in an Amsterdam building (p. 168). Many structures in the Jodenbuurt have survived, but the area continues to lack its original identity more than 50 years after its residents were isolated and shipped off to Westerbork, a holding camp near Groningen, and then to death camps farther east.

ENDING ON A HIGH NOTE

Recovery from the war was slow but steady, and the Netherlands won the race to become the first country to pay off its Marshall Plan loans. The country was forced to rebuild many of its cities—especially Rotterdam (p. 285)—as well as to acknowledge that its overseas colonies had a right to self-determination after all. Indonesia earned its independence in 1949, and Suriname followed in 1975. Realizing that its policy of neutrality had not had the desired effects, the Netherlands soon abandoned it and joined **NATO.** Wilhelmina abdicated in favor of daughter Juliana in 1948. By the 1950s, the country, if not all of its citizens, had recovered, but the Netherlands was again plunged into turmoil, this time with a natural invasion. In 1953,

1928
The Olympic torch is lit for the first time at the 1928 Amsterdam Summer Olympics.

1940
The Netherlands's machine gun-equipped bicycles fail to repel a Nazi invasion.

LIFE AND TIMES

high waves and gale-force winds assaulted the coastlines, breaching dikes that protected the southwestern Netherlands and inundating the countryside. In the torrents of water, over 1800 people died, and the economy was devastated. The Netherlands rebounded, however, with the Delta Works project, a modern engineering marvel of dams and dikes. Its success has drawn attention from across the Atlantic as a model for New Orleans's recovery from Hurricane Katrina.

Amsterdam was at the forefront of the radical movements that erupted across much of the world in the 1960s. The counterculture **Provo** movement, followed by the more conventional hippies and other crusaders, influenced anti-war demonstrations in the US. They always remained playful and peaceful, and the influence of the Provos and their kin is widely credited with prompting Amsterdam's move to more liberal drug laws.

1964
The Provos propose the White Bicycle Plan to leave 20,000 bikes unlocked for public use. These are swiftly stolen.

Housing problems from the Netherlands's staggeringly high population density began after WWII and continued through the 1970s. The **squatters' movement** in Amsterdam became a significant political force in the 1980s; during its strongest moments, over 20,000 people occupied buildings without authorization in order to protest the exercise of eminent domain. On April 30, 1980, the day of **Queen Beatrix's** coronation, squatters organized huge demonstrations against the excessive spending on royal residences. Violence broke out in the streets of Amsterdam more than once as authorities attempted to put down this and other similar uprisings. Eventually, the movement died down as squatters realized that change was better effected through politics.

Throughout the continent, European nations decided that violence was not the answer and laid the groundwork for a European union. The Netherlands was a founding member of the European Economic Community (EEC) in 1957, and in 1992 the **Maastricht Treaty** was signed in that Dutch crossroads of a city (p. 313) to formally establish the **European Union (EU).** The slightly less watershed **Treaty of Amsterdam** set down some additional integration guidelines in 1997. Despite many trials (at the international courts in The Hague) and tribulations (such as the Dutch rejection of the European constitution in 2005), the Netherlands has seen its stature grow with the EU's, and both are now major players on the world stage.

THE NETHERLANDS TODAY

INTERNATIONAL JUSTICE

Present day
You join about 16 million other travelers in Amsterdam this year.

For a country only twice the size of New Jersey (even on dry days), the Netherlands continues to play an almost unfairly large role in international politics. The United Nations' **International Court of Justice (ICJ),** housed in the Vredespaleis (Peace Palace) in **The Hague** (p. 269), has overseen disputes between sovereign nations since 1946. Its 15 judges are elected to nine-year terms by a special UN assembly. Its highest profile defendant was undoubtedly Slobodan Milošević, the former leader of Yugoslavia who was found dead in his cell in 2006, cutting short his trial for the "ethnic cleansing" of Albanians. The court has focused heavily on the Balkans in recent years, trying and acquitting Serbia of the charge of genocide in Bosnia and Herzegovina. However, its reach extends across all areas of human rights, including giving the US a slap on the wrist for its handling of Mexican death-row inmates. (The American government has not appreciated the attention.) The Hague is a center for international justice even outside the ICJ; the Permanent Court of Arbitration, the International Criminal Court, Europol (the EU's international police force), and various ad hoc courts also call The Hague home.

DOMESTIC POLITICS

One of the most unique aspects of the Netherlands—but one of the least remarked in the popular press—is its coalition government, in which no one party gains absolute control of the electorate. The parliament house is divided into two chambers: the second chamber is popularly elected every four years, and the first is chosen by local councils. The makeup of the coalition is determined by which parties fare best in the second chamber elections; from the most popular party emerges the prime minister. In the 1960s, the coalition was led by the Catholic People's Party. The **Christian Democratic Appeal (CDA)** took control in 1977 and remained in power until it was upset in 1994 by the left-leaning Labor Party. Recent times have seen a move back to the right, and the CDA returned to the top spot following the 2002 elections. This shift to the right was most strikingly embodied by the trenchant politician Pim Fortuyn, who was assassinated in May 2002. In March 2003, Volkert van der Graaf, a vegan animal rights crusader, claimed sole responsibility for the assassination and was quickly convicted and sentenced to 18 years in prison. The CDA coalition still runs the country, helmed by **Prime Minister Jan Peter Balkenende.** The Cabinet, a collection of advisors to the prime minister, is the main force behind government policy. (While Queen Beatrix still sets agendas and must sign off on legislation, the monarch's role is largely ceremonial.) The party is also responsible for enacting the country's controversial anti-smoking legislation, which banned smoking on public transportation and in transportation depots in 2004. Attempts to extend the ban to commercial establishments such as bars, restaurants, and hotels—and even coffee shops—are progressing quickly and look to be law by 2008 (see **Up in Smoke?,** p. 238).

IN RECENT NEWS

EUTHANASIA EXPANDE

The Netherlands's (in)famous liber alism is once again under the micro scope. On April 1, 2002, the Termination of Life on Request and Assisted Suicide (Review Proce dures) Act, approved by the Dutch legislature a year earlier, entered into force. The central element of the law was to protect doctors who com ply with euthanasia requests, mak ing the practice unambiguously legal. The legislation made carefu exceptions—it is still illegal for for eigners and minors to seek euthana sia—but countless opponents worldwide remain up in arms.

One of the hottest topics cur rently on the table is the right o doctors and parents to make deci sions for those who can't yet utte their first words: newborns. For sev eral years, euthanasia proponents have advocated to make infan euthanasia legal in the cases o severely ill, impaired, or disabled babies. In 2005, a pair of doctors from Groningen published a set o guidelines (based on their own experience, no less) to be made law. The Groningen Protocol, as i came to be known, still presents a legal and ethical question closely considered by Dutch governing bodies. Legal or not, infant eutha nasia happens: the *New England Journal of Medicine* reported 22 cases between 1997 and 2004, a number many have called too low.

While this sensitive debate wil not end any time soon, it is clea that the Netherlands will continue to play the role of a Petri dish fo progressive reform.

LOW COUNTRY, HIGH TENSIONS

n a multicultural city like Amsterdam, the problems of race relations aren't always obvious on the surface, but ask any resident what he or she thinks about immigration, Islam, or the like, and you're likely to get a lengthy response.

In May 2002, conservative right-wing politician Pim Fortuyn was shot and killed by a radical animal rights activist, marking the first political assassination in the Netherlands since 1584. Fortuyn had publicly called Islam a "backward religion" and proposed an end to non-Western immigration to the Netherlands. National elections held nine days after his death saw the rise of reactionary anti-immigrant parties.

When nationalist filmmaker Theo van Gogh was fatally shot outside his apartment by an apparent Muslim radical in November 2004, the media frenzy, riots, and violence that followed threw the Netherlands into a tumult. Mosques, churches, and schools were attacked, and deep rifts between immigrants and natives widened. Van Gogh's killer left a note on his body threatening Ayaan Hirsi Ali, who subsequently went into hiding. Hirsi Ali, a Somali-born legislator, had collaborated with Van Gogh on the film *Submission*, a critique of Islam's treatment of women, and was well known for speaking out against genital mutilation and the oppression of women in Muslim commu-

RELIGION

In religious affairs, the current government of the Netherlands has stuck to tolerance more closely than some of its medieval counterparts did, and it has upheld the doctrine that freedom of religion is a fundamental right. Church and state are separate, and individuals have the right to practice as they wish, provided that their actions do not harm others. No single religion dominates: 31% of Dutchmen and Dutchwomen are Roman Catholic, 20% are Protestant, and 6% are Muslim—a number continuously on the rise with increased immigration from the Middle East. In keeping with its proud secularism, the Netherlands is also Europe's most godless country: 41% are non-practicers. Recently, religion—and its moral proscriptions and prescriptions—has violently emerged onto the Dutch political landscape. Theo van Gogh, a Dutch movie director, was killed in November 2004 after his film about Muslim women's position in society aired on national television (p. 66). The spark of the murder met the dry tinder of increasingly hostile relations between native and non-native Dutch society—or, more accurately, between secular and religious factions—and resulted in a conflagration of protests by religious groups throughout much of the country.

GLBT LIFE

Just over half a century after many of its GLBT citizens were deported and killed by the Nazis in WWII, today Amsterdam is undeniably one of the gay centers of the world—if not the capital. Legal protections—from age of consent to non-discrimination in the military to adoption policies—make no distinction between heterosexual and homosexual citizens. In 2001, Amsterdam also legalized the world's first gay marriage. Gay and lesbian clubs, hotels, restaurants, gyms, coffee shops, saunas, and other establishments grace almost every street and canal in the city proper. The annual ▼Pride Festival, which explodes into a flurry of unabashed canal-side revelry in early August, attracts hundreds of thousands of people of all sexual orientations, not to mention ages, ethnicities, and nationalities. Yet perhaps more indicative of the Dutch's tolerance, if not outright acceptance, of GLBT people and culture is the difficulty of distinguishing a specific "gay" scene in Amsterdam. While foreigners may be surprised to see two men walking hand-in-hand in public, Amsterdammers remain blithely unconcerned at this commonplace sight.

ARCHITECTURE

Amsterdam is an architectural and engineering wonder. The complexities of building a city on top of marshland have resulted in countless cricked necks whirling to see every architectural innovation. Canal-side houses were built with many large windows to help reduce the weight of the building on top of unstable topsoil. Tall, narrow houses were constructed at frightening angles to allow large pieces of furniture to be hoisted through windows without hitting the buildings. The hooks that served as pulleys still stick out from just about every canal house; some are still used. By the middle of the 16th century, a law was passed to limit the angle at which a house could be built to prevent buildings from falling into the streets.

The canal houses that remain today feature architectural elements dating from many different eras. Medieval houses were constructed with timber and clay, but as locals learned the hard way of the structures' flammability, brick construction became more prevalent. The only remaining elements of medieval construction are the timber facades of **Begijnhof 34** and **Zeedijk 1.** While space limitations and laws forced many houses to be impossibly narrow, the Herengracht features wider houses in the area called the **Golden Bend**—city officials bent the rules and let wealthy merchants build wider houses to fund the construction of the canal.

Under Charlemagne, the humble **Romanesque** style dominated churches and other buildings, but architects soon became bolder with the **Gothic** style, characterized by large windows, the pointed arch, and general immensity. Like other European artists of the period, Dutch architects stole some good ideas from the Italians during the **Renaissance. Hendrick de Keyser** left about as big a mark on Amsterdam as anyone can, designing the Zuiderkerk, the Westerkerk, the Noorderkerk, and the Bartolotti House (now the Theater Instituut Nederland). As a visitor to these sites can plainly see, his work was characterized by the elaborate ornamentation of building facades. In reaction to such extravagance came **Neoclassicism** in the Golden Age. Neoclassical Dutch houses resemble Greek and Roman temples, with columns and decorative scrolls. **Adriaan Dortsman** exemplified the style, constructing the (surprisingly sane) **Museum Van Loon** (p. 171) on Keizersgracht. During the 1700s, an interest in French design and architecture brought lighter decorations in the **Rococo** style to houses in the cities.

Nearly every visitor to Amsterdam has seen at least one work by 19th-century architect **Pierre**

nities. Van Gogh's death and threats against Hirsi Ali were cast as a major threat against free speech. Some Dutch writers and thinkers and many in Muslim communities have criticized Hirsi Ali for contributing to "Islamophobia" in the public discourse and for allying herself with anti-immigration politicians; others champion her support of women's rights.

Then there's Rita Verdonk, another conservative politician well-known for her tough policies. She has helped institute a tough new integration test for immigrants on Dutch culture and language, called for a ban on wearing a *burqa* in public, and said that only Dutch should be spoken in the streets. Many Dutch believe that her anti-immigrant record has directly resulted in the deaths of asylum seekers—hence graffiti reading, "Rita Verdonk, you have blood on your hands."

The Dutch approach the issues of race and immigration with varying degrees of level-headedness, compassion, and pragmatism, but the numbers don't lie: the Muslim population is growing (more than one million at last count), and about 100,000 people immigrate to the country per year. It remains to be seen to what extent reactionaries—and reactions to them—will threaten the famous Dutch constant of liberalism.

RACE AGAINST TIDE

While the debate over global warming remains murky, the Dutch are taking clear steps to prepare for its effects. As one of the Low Countries, the Netherlands has perhaps the most to lose from climate change; after centuries of land reclamation projects, 27% of the nation lies under sea level. Even a slight rise in ocean levels, such as scientists are beginning to detect, would transform the Netherlands into an underwater resort.

Even though international treaties and organizations are trying to prevent such an environmental catastrophe, progress has been slow. By the time international efforts reverse the perceived rise in planetary temperature, Amsterdam may have already become Atlantis. With that in mind, the Dutch have found at least one possible way to save their cities: make everything float.

The Netherlands has already begun testing a new type of floating home. The simple yet sturdy design allows the house to adapt to rising sea levels of up to five meters. Only a series of vertical poles bind the structure to the earth. When water comes along, the house, built of the lightest of materials, can slide up and down the poles with the tide. Although it remains to be seen if the plan can be implemented on a larger scale, it offers at least a glimmer of hope for the future; this way, if sea levels do rise, the Netherlands will remain afloat.

Cuypers. His Centraal Station and Rijksmuseum fuse Gothic and Renaissance styles. For **Hendrik Petrus Berlage** and his **Amsterdam School,** decoration functioned as a building's supports, not merely to hide them as Rococo ornaments did. Luckily for Amsterdammers, though, followers of Berlage's legacy were not such killjoys in their individual works. One of the most spectacular works created by Amsterdam School members **Piet Kramer, Johan van der Mey,** and **Michel de Klerk** is the **Scheepvaarthuis** (Shipping House). The building's design incorporates the street to resemble a ship's bow.

DANCE

The standard varieties of classical ballet and contemporary dance are spearheaded in the Netherlands by the **Dutch National Ballet** and the **Nederlands Dans Theater.** The Dutch National Ballet performs in the **Stadhuis-Het Muziektheater,** and the Nederlands Dans Theater uses venues throughout Amsterdam. Choreographers and dancers descend upon Amsterdam en masse every year; their avant-garde and eclectic styles are exhibited in fringe theaters and clubs that are often difficult to locate but worth the extra effort. Amsterdam is such a nimble city that even the street sometimes becomes a stage for dance performances. Though they have probably lost the spring in their step, famous Dutch choreographers include **Rudi van Dantzig** and **Hans van Manen.**

THEATER

Since the Dutch film industry has been, at times, threadbare (to say the least), Dutch actors have turned their efforts toward theater. Dutch theater has consequently seen rich talent throughout the years; a history of outdoor performances greatly benefited the genre's popularity. Since the 1960s, experimental theater has flourished in Amsterdam; live drama continues to boom. The scene is characterized by the prominence of many small companies. In Amsterdam, the **Theater Instituut Nederland** chronicles the history of Dutch actors and the stage. The **Hollandsche Schouwburg** was a popular venue for Dutch plays and operettas before WWII and is now a memorial to the transgressions it witnessed.

FILM

Long a relatively obscure aspect of Dutch culture, the film industry in the Netherlands recently became the focus of national and international debate over the limits of liberalism, the costs and benefits of immigration, and the region's increasing ethnic strife. The November 2004 murder of Theo van Gogh—the controversial director of *Submission: Part I* (2004), which portrays women's roles in Muslim society—shook the country to its ideological core. At the 2005 Rotterdam Film Festival, which opened only three months after the murder, audience members were screened with metal detectors before a viewing of *06/05* (2004), Van Gogh's fictional account of the 2002 assassination of right-wing politician Pim Fortuyn. Tensions continue to increase as publicity of the Dutch film industry expands.

Before 2002, Dutch films languished internationally, suffering from both underfunding and a lack of an international Dutch-speaking audience. Despite these constraints, a number of gifted directors have shot their way to cinema greatness, including filmmaker **Marleen Gorris,** whose *Antonia's Line* (1995) won an Academy Award for Best Foreign Language Film. On its heels was *Character* (1997), directed by **Mike van Diem,** which became the third Dutch Oscar winner in that category. **Johan van der Keuken,** known as JVDK to his fans, studied as a photographer and filmmaker in Paris before beginning a long career producing short films devoted to the perception of reality. **Joris Ivens** was both a masterful documentary director and an innovative cinematographer. One of Ivens's most notable works, *Rain* (1929), a 12-minute film composed solely of rainfall in Amsterdam, somehow took four months to produce. More modern movies starring the Dutch capital include *Diamonds Are Forever* (1971) and *Ocean's Twelve* (2004). With its greater accessibility and rivaling aesthetics, international directors also flock to film in Rotterdam; of most recent interest is *Who Am I* (1998), starring action-film star Jackie Chan.

The Netherlands is home to several prominent **film festivals,** including the International Film Festival Rotterdam (January), the Netherlands Film Festival (Utrecht, September), the Transgender Film Festival (Amsterdam, every other May, in odd years), the Holland Animation Film Festival (Utrecht, November), the International Documentary Film Festival Amsterdam (November), and CINEKID, an international film and television festival for children (Amsterdam, October).

LITERATURE

In terms of international recognition, Dutch literature faces the same *vraagstuk* (problem) as Dutch film or theater does: the language barrier. The most important Dutch moralist was **Erasmus,** whose humanist philosophy influenced Martin Luther. In theater, *Gijsbrecht van Aemstel* (1637) and *Lucifer* (1654), written by Amsterdam native **Joost van den Vondel,** figure among the most prominent of the Dutch Renaissance. Perhaps the most brilliant representative of Golden Age literature was **Pieter Corneliszoon Hooft,** whom the Dutch have honored by bestowing Amsterdam's swankiest shopping street with his name. Hooft, a poet and playwright, found a keeper in the Italian Renaissance style and triumphantly brought it back home to Amsterdam.

The **Multatuli Museum** in Amsterdam celebrates the life and works of **Eduard Douwes Dekker,** who took Multatuli (Latin for, roughly, "C'mon, I've been through a lot here") for a pen name. Multatuli used his experience in the Dutch East Indies as fodder for all of his novels, which attempted to expose the exploitation of natives in the Indonesian Dutch colonies. Unsurprisingly, then, *Max Havelaar* (1860), his most famous work, is the story of an official's attempts to expose the exploitation of natives in the Indonesian Dutch colonies. Needless to say, colonial authorities did not take kindly to Multatuli's biting criticism of imperialism and superior Dutch attitudes.

The atrocities of WWII prompted a surge of literary works, both reflective and accusatory. The most famous is the diary kept by **Anne Frank**—aptly named *The Diary of Anne Frank* (1947)—during her two years hiding from the Nazis in Amsterdam. Her diary is in select company as one of the few Dutch works to be widely translated into other languages.

In a jarringly juxtaposed vein, one of the bestselling works of Dutch 20th-century writing is the grabbingly titled *The Happy Hooker* (1971) by **Xaviera Hollander.** The autobiographical book chronicles her experiences as a call girl in the United States. Hollander has continued to popularize Dutch writing by penning articles for *Penthouse* magazine. Mainstream modern authors include **Willem Hermans; Gerard Reve,** author of *The Evenings* (1947); and **Harry Mulisch,** who wrote *The Assault* (1982), a story about a family shattered by a betrayal and a murder. The story's movie adaptation won an Academy Award for Best Foreign Language Film in 1987, the crowning achievement in Mulisch's already spectacular international reputation. One of Mulisch's more recent works is *Discovery of Heaven* (1992), a reflective, theological, and philosophical narrative with a decent dose of humor mixed in. For a more enlightened trip to the Netherlands, you can find many a Dutch opus at your local library.

MUSIC

The Netherlands has not produced composers to rival its neighbors' but instead has made great contributions in classical music performance. The world-class **Royal Concertgebouw Orchestra,** housed in the Concertgebouw performance hall in Amsterdam, is known for a daring program of classical and contemporary works. **The Netherlands Opera** performs at the Stadhuis-Het Muziektheater, often called the "Stopera," (which is luckily not named for audiences' reactions to performances).

Amsterdam's popular music scene is remarkably dynamic and cosmopolitan for a city with fewer than one million people. The Dutch colonial past lives on in a genre called **paramaribop,** which fuses Surinamese rhythms with jazz; paramaribop and Latin music appear at venues all over the city. Amsterdam also throbs all night and every night thanks to the myriad dance clubs and rave parties. Perhaps the biggest contribution to club music from the Dutch is the genre **gabber,** which resembles hardcore techno, but the number of beats per minute is mind-bogglingly high. **Neder Pop,** or Dutch pop, may sound like it belongs in the frozen treats aisle, but it has an international following—although it has always been less popular than British and American exports.

VISUAL ART

The Dutch have a long and varied history in art. Dutch painters are responsible for the departure from the International Gothic style, the development of the Northern Renaissance, and the perfection of **oil painting**—not to mention several entire museums worldwide. In general, Dutch artwork reflects the country's Calvinist tradition and is characterized by attention to the everyday rather than devoted to religious iconography.

VAN EYCK

One of the most famous Dutch painters was Johannes van Eyck. Though he didn't invent oil painting as once thought, he did use the medium to great effect, creating strikingly realistic details in his work. He was particularly adept at por-

on the trail of vermeer

Listening to "Visions of Johanna," I swore I heard Bob Dylan sing, "She's delicate and seems like a Vermeer." I wasn't surprised, because no other painter so pervades the contemporary Western imagination as the 17th-cen-

"Every time one of Vermeer's 31 works is exhibited, lines stretch around the block."

tury Dutchman Johannes Vermeer. His renderings of the intimate, domestic circumstances of women evoke interaction and introspection that suggest delicate and complex interior lives. "Like a Vermeer" has become shorthand for wistful and sensitive femininity with a hint of emotional vulnerability. Every time Vermeer's works, painted in Delft between 1653 and his death in 1675, are exhibited, lines stretch around the block. Scholars unanimously accept only 31 works as his, a small total by 17th-century Dutch standards. Painted at a rate of two per year, they were all considered statements, the results of intellectual contemplation as meticulous as their physical execution.

Visitors to Amsterdam and The Hague can see only seven Vermeers in just two museums. Any one of them is worth the trip—this is as good as art gets. The truly smitten can visit Vermeer's hometown Delft, but there are no Vermeers there. You won't find the exact house he painted in *The Little Street* (Rijksmuseum, Amsterdam), but you'll find plenty like it. Neither will you get precisely the same vantage point of the *View of Delft* (Mauritshuis, The Hague), but the harbor in front of

the city walls remains. Narrow streets open onto large squares dominated by huge medieval churches, and light from canals reflected into limpidly lit rooms vividly evokes Vermeer's physical world. The *View of Delft*, an imposing cityscape that set the standard for the genre, was the first Vermeer to enter a Dutch museum. King Willem I made funds available when it was auctioned in 1822 and decided that it should be placed in the royal gallery, the Mauritshuis, rather than in the Rijksmuseum. This was the work that first brought Vermeer to the attention of curators, dealers, and critics beyond the Netherlands. New railroads opened the country to tourism, and soon one French critic, Theophile Thoré, was urging visitors to see the *View of Delft* and two other paintings in the possession of the aristocratic Six

"Visitors to Amsterdam and The Hague can see seven Vermeers in two museums."

family in Amsterdam. The Sixes' policy of opening their collection to the public ensured that thousands of visitors could see *The Milkmaid* and *The Little Street* prior to their entry into the Rijksmuseum in 1908 and 1921, respectively.

We are also indebted to banker Adriaan van der Hoop. Among the paintings in his collection was the *Woman in Blue Reading a Letter*, bequeathed to the city of Amsterdam in 1854. Thoré knew only six paintings by Vermeer at this time, so he accepted Hoop's unsigned canvas after careful comparison with the others. The *Woman in Blue* is still owned by the city of Amsterdam, but it has been on loan to the Rijksmuseum since 1885. This brings to the fore a fact that easily eludes us: we take the identity of Vermeer's paintings for granted, but they are varied, so recognizing them as his work was no easy task. Nine years earlier, the Mauritshuis had acquired a painting that exemplifies the difficulty of identification: *Diana and her*

Vermeer acquired by the Mauritshuis in 1903, the gaze of its one figure meets our own as enigmatically and as devastatingly as any in art. *The Girl with a Pearl Earring* had been lost to sight since the late 17th century until it was offered, unattributed, at an auction in The Hague in 1881. A local collector bought it for all of two guilders. He bequeathed it to the Mauritshuis where it has since become the "Dutch Mona Lisa," emblematic, above all other works, of Vermeer's sympathetic account of the physical manifestation of young women's psyches. Although crushingly familiar from countless reproductions, this little painting—just 17½ by 15½ in.—flusters the heart. No more beautiful human achievement exists.

"Vermeer's paintings are varied, so recognizing them as his work is no easy task."

Companions, bought in 1876 as a Nicolaes Maes. The discovery of Vermeer's badly worn signature led to the correct attribution, but the dissimilarity between this scene and the *View of Delft*, hanging in the same room, led many to wonder if they were by the same artist. Not until the discovery of earlier similar works were scholarly doubts allayed.

In 1892, the Rijksmuseum acquired another Vermeer: *The Love Letter*. Uniquely in his body of work, Vermeer used the device of a view through a doorway to establish a private interior domain. A seated woman has just received a sealed letter from a maid standing behind her. Though the painting on the wall behind them, a sailing vessel on a calm sea, suggests that the course of love may well be running smooth, the recipient's expression is anxious and revelatory of an unguarded emotional moment. In *The Love Letter*, the exchange of glances is internal to the picture; in a

"She's delicate and seems like a Vermeer" brings visions of *Pearl Earring* to mind. But Dylan's diction is notoriously indistinct at times. I misheard—"...and seems like the mirror" is the true lyric— but it might as well mention the master of Delft. In so far as Vermeer's paintings mirror our desires, my version is true to their

"No more beautiful human achievement exists than the 'Dutch Mona Lisa.'"

contemporary reflections. Go to see the seven Vermeers. They will shimmer prismatically—unforgettably—in the mind of anyone who stands before them.

Dr. Ivan Gaskell is the Margaret S. Winthrop Curator at Harvard University's Fogg Art Museum.

traying the minutiae of architecture and nature, but, in doing so, he often neglected perspective. Because he is thought to have used living, breathing models, his figures aren't exactly the picture of grace, but they are still more realistic than those in the accuracy-minded Gothic tradition. To see Van Eyck paintings, visit Amsterdam's **Rijksmuseum** (p. 175).

The Betrothal of the Arnolfini, Van Eyck's most famous painting, from 1434, depicts an everyday scene of two people being promised to each other. He was likely present at the actual event and may have served as a sort of notary—the words *Johannes de Eyck fuit hic* ("Johannes van Eyck was here") appear on the back wall of the painting. This painting is also a precursor to Velazquez's *Las Meninas*, as the mirror in the back of the room shows a reflection of the scene along with the painter, beginning the tradition of the "painting of a painting."

BOSCH

Though only seven of the 40 paintings attributed to Hiëronymus Bosch bear his name (and zero are dated), he was legendary for his departure from the prevailing Flemish style embodied by Van Eyck. His symbolic triptychs presented terrifying scenes that mused pessimistically on human morality. Bosch's worlds were vividly gruesome and wildly fantastical, but he imbued his visions of demonic creatures with striking realism. As such, Bosch's work often evokes Surrealism, a movement that came some 400 years later.

The vivid, demon-filled *Temptation of St. Anthony*, foreshadowing 21st-century Amsterdam, presents man as tormented and tempted by sinful pleasures while St. Anthony himself resists and perseveres. Bosch's most famous work, *The Garden of Earthly Delights*, a three-part altarpiece, tells the history of the world, from creation to mounting human sins and the progression into hell. The work laments man's predisposition to pleasure in a dream-like haze; nudes and otherworldly beasts cavort across the paradisiacal middle panel and are confronted with a nightmarish hell on the right.

GOLDEN AGE

The Golden Age of the 17th century was one of the most glorious periods in Dutch painting. During the Reformation, religious authorities in northern Holland began to question whether painting should continue at all, as Protestants objected to pictures of religious figures or artwork in religious places. Parishes ceased to fund northern painters, though southern artists (still commissioned by the Catholic Church) continued using religious themes. Thus, Dutch artists turned to painting daily life and portraits. As the demand for religious paintings diminished and artists found that normally lucrative income source running dry, painters started creating pieces for wealthy private patrons rather than for God. Dutch paintings of this era are surprisingly small—save for Rembrandt's mammoth *Night Watch*—because they were made for private homes instead of public altars.

REMBRANDT

Rembrandt van Rijn, one of the most famous and talented artists in history, is looked upon by the Dutch with a pride that Italians reserve for Leonardo da Vinci. After an aborted attempt at being an ordinary student at the University of Leiden, the young Rembrandt took up the brush and soon became the most sought-after portrait painter in Amsterdam. In 1642, the same year he completed *Night Watch*, a representation of a military company standing guard, his upper-class wife Saskia van Uylenburgh died, and much of his elevated social status evaporated with her. Rembrandt's popularity soon declined as his work became more experimental, alienating his clientele. Though he declared bankruptcy in 1656 and lived in poverty, he was never completely rejected by the Amsterdam aristocracy, and he maintained a relatively high social status until his death in 1669.

In strictly technical terms, few artists have ever rivaled Rembrandt's talent in painting, etching, or drafting. He was part of a new generation of artists that established the **Realist Movement,** whose followers tried to portray the world as they actually saw it. Rembrandt's technique evolved greatly over his lifetime, but he is most famous for his constant skill with **chiaroscuro,** or elements of light and dark—mastered early in his career with *The Anatomy Lesson of Dr. Tulp* (1632), now at the **Mauritshuis** in The Hague. These contrasting lighting techniques allowed Rembrandt to reveal extraordinary emotional details in his subjects' faces—including his own. While other artists kept extensive records of their work and research, Rembrandt instead painted a series of self-portraits ranging from the time of his youth until right before he died—a visual autobiography of his personal and artistic development. Rembrandt tended to use coarse strokes and a darker palette, lending his paintings an air of brooding mystery. Many of his most famous works, including *Night Watch,* currently reside in the Rijksmuseum. For more on Rembrandt, visit the **Museum Het Rembrandt** (p. 177).

VERMEER

A contemporary of Rembrandt, Johannes Vermeer is known for painting everyday scenes with an extraordinary attention to detail. A slow worker, he studied every angle and curve of his subjects so as to better mirror nature on the canvas. Vermeer produced very few paintings, however, and only 35 have survived. One of his most famous paintings, *The Milkmaid* (1658), shows a woman in a Dutch household performing the simple and ordinary task of pouring milk. What the painting lacks in dynamicism of subject is more than made up for in its honesty. Vermeer was also behind the eminently recognizable *Girl with a Pearl Earring* (1665), which has been praised as the "*Mona Lisa* of the north." Its legacy has spawned a novel of the same name by Tracy Chevalier and an accompanying film—a veritable windfall for rabid fans of 17th-century Dutch art or Scarlett Johansson. These masterpieces are housed in the Rijksmuseum and Mauritshuis, respectively, along with a handful of his other works.

HALS

Frans Hals was one of the artists most greatly influenced by the religious turmoil in the Netherlands. To escape religious persecution, he fled the southern Netherlands to Haarlem; it was there that Hals carved out a niche as perhaps Holland's second-best portraitist.

Hals favored group portraits and used a painting technique characterized by coarser, "unrefined" brush strokes. In his *Pieter van den Broecke* (1633), he captured his subject in what appears to be an instantaneous moment, lending a sense of familiarity and spontaneity to the subject that uniquely brings him to life. Hals's *The Merry Drinker* (1630) appears in the Rijksmuseum and serves as a prime example of his expressive painting. His liveliness was an inspiration to both his contemporaries and a group centuries later known as the **Impressionists.** Hals's work was also co-opted by politicians: the robust subjects in *The Banquet of the Officers of the St. George Militia Company* (1616), now at the **Hals Museum** in Haarlem (p. 253), were hailed as model citizens for the new Dutch Republic.

POST-IMPRESSIONISM

Dutch art took a few hundred years off until **Vincent van Gogh,** born in Zundert, became the finest Dutch painter after Rembrandt. His early work, as exemplified by *The Potato Eaters* (1885), was more concerned with social commentary and more appropriate to his gloomy personality than his later paintings were. Upon moving to Paris in 1886, Van Gogh's style changed markedly. In the French capital, his **Post-Impressionist** work was characterized by his expressive use of bright, often harshly contrasting colors painted with rapid, thick brush strokes, as witnessed in his *Self-Portrait* and *Starry Night*, both of which date from 1889.

Van Gogh settled in Arles, France in the last years of his life; there he captured the dry, sunny landscape and the bright colored interiors of Provençal homes in *The Harvest* (1888) and *The Bedroom at Arles* (1888). Soon, however, the merriness turned to madness, and in the process of attacking his good friend with a razor blade, Van Gogh famously managed to chop off his own ear. Having sold only one painting in his lifetime, Van Gogh was no less of a spectacular failure when it came to suicide, surviving two full days after turning a gun on himself in 1890. Soon after his death, however, his works' worth was fully realized: *Portrait of Dr. Gachet* (1890) sold for US$82.5 million in 1990. For the most extensive collection of his works, visit Amsterdam's **Van Gogh Museum** (p. 174).

MODERN ART

Twentieth-century Dutch painting was dominated by the primary colors and rigid geometry of **Piet Mondrian.** Though his early paintings were largely composed of abstract nature scenes, by the end of his career, Mondrian's style had evolved into one in which forms were reduced to horizontal and vertical elements, exemplified in *Composition with Black, Red, Gray, Yellow, and Blue* (1920). Though his work may look like a second-grade project to the untrained eye, X-rays have recently revealed that Mondrian labored over the texture of his whites and the shades of his colors. Mondrian's search for purity of artistic essence was representative of the *De Stijl* (creatively, "the style") movement, which invaded the worlds of not only painting but also sculpture, architecture, and design.

The simplicity Mondrian contributed was countered by the zany and illusory drawings of **M.C. Escher.** Escher created impossible staircases, waterfalls without end, and tessellations that gradually morphed from polygons into living creatures. Art after WWII was marked by the group of writers and artists who called themselves **CoBrA,** after their native towns of Copenhagen, Brussels, and Amsterdam. CoBrA member **Karel Appel** painted in a bright, simplistic style similar to that of Joan Miró or Paul Klee.

SPORTS

FOOTBALL

Football (soccer) is the Dutch national sport, and, on the world stage, the Netherlands has enjoyed a long and almost glorious history. Amsterdam's team—and one of the nation's best—is **Ajax** (the Amsterdamse Football Club Ajax), which plays at the **Amsterdam ArenA.** In recent seasons, the team has vied with PSV Eindhoven for league supremacy, but its historical rival is Feyenoord of Rotterdam. The competition is taken so seriously that Rotterdammers have been known to use anti-Semitism to jeer the Jewish-associated Ajax; Amsterdammers have rebutted by extolling the Nazi demolition of Rotterdam. It is advised to stay above the fray; with football in the Netherlands, there is no such thing as stooping too low.

The Dutch national team, known as the **Oranje,** is arguably one of the better squads never to have won a World Cup. In the 1970s, the Dutch invention of "total football"—a relentless version of football where all players are involved in the offense and endlessly change positions—enabled the team to cruise to two World Cup championship games but fall flat both times. The recent past has witnessed mixed fortune for the team: the Netherlands, ousted in the quarterfinals in 1994, was knocked out in the semifinals in 1998. To the dismay of Dutch football fans, the Oranje failed to qualify for the 2002 World Cup in Korea and Japan, garnering the ignominious moniker "the 33rd team" (the best nation not to qualify). The national team recovered just enough to break the country's heart again in 2006, losing in the first single-elimination round. The Netherlands also co-hosted the Euro 2000 tournament and made it to the semifinals both then and in 2004. On big football days, the entire country shuts down, so beware of the Euro 2008 in June. Not all the country's residents pull for the Netherlands, however—its large immigrant populations fervently follow their own squads; expect television sets in all Dutch bars to blare non-stop football news during any big tournament.

OTHER SPORTS

When the canals freeze, Amsterdam becomes one big **ice skating** rink; since most residents own their own skates, rentals may be hard to find. Canal boats chug through the ice, though, and often only the Keizersgracht is left untouched for skaters. Those in good shape can skate to nearby towns. In Januaries when the weather is cold enough, the *Elfstedentocht* race covers 11 towns and 200km of frozen canals and rivers in Friesland for the brave of heart and frostbite-prone extremities.

A Dutch creation, **korfball**, is a bizarre amalgam of basketball (without backboards) and netball. Invented in 1901 by Amsterdam schoolteacher **Nico Broekhuysen**, korfball has been played on an international level since the 1970s. The **International Korfball Federation** has members from over 50 locales, from Armenia to the US.

Very naturally, the Dutch have a proud **cycling** tradition as well and have won the Tour de France twice. For homesick Americans, the Netherlands offers the best **baseball** league in Europe (though the rest of the continent seems not to care). Unfortunately, the Amsterdam Pirates take a back seat in the league to Rotterdam's Neptunus. The Netherlands also has a semi-professional **cricket** team that grabbed the last seed in the 2007 World Cup in the West Indies. It has won but two games in its World Cup history. **Rugby, tennis, golf, windsurfing,** and **field hockey** round out the Dutch athletic repertoire.

FOOD

Netherlandish nourishment is much more than just cheese—though Gouda and Edam are both native flavors—for it includes raw herring as well (with the occasional raw onion on the side).

Expect a lot of bread and cheese at breakfast and lunch and generous portions of meat and fish for dinner. Popular seafood choices include all sorts of grilled fish and shellfish, wholesome seafood stews, and, of course, raw herring. Other meals include the traditional *hutspot* (a concoction of mashed potatoes, carrots, and meat), *snert* (pea soup), and *frikandel* (the Netherlands's excuse for a sausage). In addition to classic Dutch fare, Amsterdam is full of ethnic food cultivated from a long imperialist past. Indonesian cuisine in particular has become a staple of life along the Amstel.

Between daily sittings, the Dutch conception of a light snack, often served in *eetcafes* (cafe-restaurants), includes *tostis* (piping hot grilled cheese or ham and cheese sandwiches), *broodjes* (familiar sandwiches), *bitterballen* (spiced meatballs with mustard dipping sauce), the scrumptious *oliebollen* (doughnuts), or *poffertjes* (small pancakes). To wet that palate, visit a *theehuis* (coffee shop that actually sells coffee and tea) or down a Heineken, the Netherlands's most famous beer. For dessert, don't tell your dentists about the syrupy *stroopwafel* cookies or *pannenkoeken*, the pancakes that can also make an excellent entree.

HOLIDAYS AND FESTIVALS

HOLIDAY OR FESTIVAL	DESCRIPTION	DATE
Queen's Birthday	A day of national pride. Orange clothing and street parties everywhere. Not the queen's real birthday.	April 30
WWII Remembrance Day	A solemn day for the Netherlands's WWII dead. A moment of silence is observed.	May 4
Liberation Day	A less depressing day celebrating of the country's liberation from Nazi occupation with public fêtes. Controversy often erupts over Dutch appeasement of their conquerors.	May 5
National Windmill Day	Windmills throw open their doors, and many have special (often educational) events.	2nd Tuesday in May
Amsterdam Gay Pride	3 days of tolerance and partying with a parade and street festivals for all sexual orientations.	Early August
Aalsmeer Flower Parade	Flower floats, flower art, and flowery music in the world's flower capital.	Early September
High Times Cannabis Cup	One long tokefest. At the end of the festival, awards are given to the best hash and marijuana.	November
Amsterdam Leather Pride	The premier gathering for "leather men." Features fetish parties and a lot of leather outfits.	November
Sinterklaas Eve	Dutch Santa Claus delivers candy and gifts to nice Dutch children. The naughty ones are kidnapped.	December 5

LIFE AND TIMES

BEYOND TOURISM

A PHILOSOPHY FOR TRAVELERS

HIGHLIGHTS OF BEYOND TOURISM IN THE NETHERLANDS

LEARN at the Netherlands's most prestigious universities (p. 84).

BATTLE racism, fascism, and nationalism in Dutch politics (p. 78).

EXHALE knowledge of marijuana into wide-eyed tourists (p. 80).

COOK a delicious meal of your choosing in a beautiful canal house (p. 86).

As a tourist, you are always a foreigner. While hostel-hopping and sightseeing can be great fun, you may want to consider going *beyond* tourism. Experiencing a foreign place through studying, volunteering, or working can help reduce that stranger-in-a-strange-land feeling. Furthermore, travelers can make a positive impact on the natural and cultural environments they visit. With this Beyond Tourism chapter, *Let's Go* hopes to promote a better understanding of the Netherlands and to provide suggestions for those who want to get more than a photo album out of their travels.

There are several options for those who seek to participate in Beyond Tourism activities. Opportunities for **volunteerism** abound with both local and international organizations. **Studying** in a new environment can be enlightening, whether it is through direct enrollment in a local university or an independent research project. **Working** is a way to immerse yourself in local culture while financing your travels.

As a **volunteer** in the Netherlands, you can participate in projects from unleashing your inner superhero and combating fascism to tilling Dutch farmland, either on a short-term basis or as the main component of your trip. Later in this chapter, we recommend organizations that can help you find the opportunities that best suit your interests, whether you are looking to get involved for a day or for a year.

Studying at a college or in a language program is another option. Though not as well known abroad as some other European university networks, the Dutch higher education system offers students extraordinary opportunities to study the application of cutting-edge social and scientific theories. As such, the Netherlands is a popular study-abroad destination because of the high quality of its certification, summer, graduate, and professional courses offered in English. Fittingly, international development, cultural cooperation, global economics, and sexuality studies all feature prominently at Dutch schools.

Many travelers structure their trips by the **work** available to them along the way, ranging from odd jobs on the go to full-time, long-term stints in cities. Those seeking work in Amsterdam should note that competition increases in the summer, and most employers strictly follow bureaucratic procedures for visa and work permits, perhaps due to recent attempts to curb squatting and drug abuse. All new employees should carry their passport or other form of identification to avoid trouble during inspections by tax and social security inspectors and immigration officers. To work in the Netherlands, foreigners must receive a civil service number (*burgerservicenummer;* BSN) from the local tax office (*belastingdienst*), both for themselves and for any family members. The process of getting work visas (p. 87), which may also be required, involves more red tape.

VOLUNTEERING

WHY PAY MONEY TO VOLUNTEER? Many volunteers are surprised to learn that some organizations require large fees or "donations." While this may seem ridiculous at first glance, such fees often keep the organization afloat, in addition to covering airfare, room, board, and administrative expenses for the volunteers. (Other organizations must rely on private donations and government subsidies.) If you're concerned about how a program spends its fees, request an annual report or finance account. A reputable organization won't refuse to inform you of how volunteer money is spent.

Pay-to-volunteer programs might be a good idea for young travelers who are looking for more support and structure (such as pre-arranged transportation and housing) or anyone who would rather not deal with the uncertainty implicit in creating a volunteer experience from scratch.

Volunteering can be a powerful and fulfilling experience, especially when combined with the thrill of traveling in a new place. Though the Netherlands is considered wealthy by international standards, there is no shortage of organizations confronting the country's very real issues such as immigration (see **Low Country, High Tensions**, p. 64) and global warming (see **A Race Against Tide,** p. 66). While many of the volunteer opportunities in the Netherlands require a strong command of the Dutch language, there are still several opportunities for English speakers.

Most people who volunteer in the Netherlands do so on a short-term basis at organizations that make use of drop-in or once-a-week volunteers. The best way to find opportunities that match your interests and schedule may be to check with **Vrijwilligers Centrale** (p. 83), an impressive national volunteer agency. Their free listing service will help you find a short- or long-term volunteer position in a range of local organizations such as day-care centers, human rights programs, and nursing homes. The national Dutch volunteer office also has a **hotline** (☎ 0900 899 8600, €0.20 per min.) that may be able to give you more general information. Another good way to search for volunteer organizations once in Amsterdam is to check the daily paper: every Saturday, newspapers like *Het Parool* and *De Telegraaf* post ads for service positions.

Those looking for longer, more intensive volunteer opportunities usually choose to go through a parent organization that takes care of logistical details and often provides a group environment and support system—for a fee. There are two main types of organizations—religious and non-sectarian—although there are rarely restrictions on participation for either. You can sometimes avoid high application fees by contacting the individual work sites directly. The websites **www.volunteerabroad.com** and **Action Without Borders** (www.idealist.org) allow you to search for volunteer openings both in the Netherlands and worldwide.

POLITICAL ACTIVISM

Perhaps unlike its lighthearted capital, the Netherlands's political scene is not all one big party. Travelers looking to flex some political muscle in the Netherlands have many options; the nation has a vibrant political culture with more than 10 active political parties. Supporting these parties is usually done on a volunteer basis, but there may be paid positions available for individuals with relevant experience. Parties are always in need of volunteers and will be especially happy if you show up during election season. Most of the parties also have active offices working with the European Parliament. Although we like to think that our blessing is the holy grail of Dutch politics, it is important to remember that *Let's Go* does not endorse any of the organizations listed here. This category has a lot of overlap; for instance, political parties often do work relating to (and hopefully helping) the environment or providing aid to health organizations.

Christian Democratic Appeal (CDA), Postbus 30453, 2500 GL The Hague (☎070 342 4888; www.cda.nl). This center-right party has become the biggest political party in the Netherlands. If you make it into the inner circle, try to shake the hand of its most famous member, Dutch Prime Minister Jan Peter Balkenende.

Christian Union, Postbus 439, 3800 AK Amersfoort (☎033 422 6969; www.christenunie.nl). A rightist religious party, the Christian Union believes that "a government that puts God's commands into practice serves society in the best way." Might be the closest thing to conservatism in the Netherlands.

Democrats 66, Postbus 660, 2501 CR The Hague (☎070 356 6066; www.democrats.nl). A liberal democratic party: internationalist, free-market, and supportive of government-reform programs. Would love volunteers who could restore it to its former glory.

Green Left, Postbus 20018, 2500 EA The Hague (☎070 318 3030; www.groenlinks.nl). Wins the prize for least obfuscated name; is both green and left. Part of a larger coalition of European Green Parties. Focuses on the environment and anti-violence.

Labor Party, Postbus 1310, 1000 BH Amsterdam (☎020 551 2155; www.pvda.nl). Left-of-center major opposition party. Social-democratic party of organized labor, workers' rights, social welfare programs, and more protectionist trade policy. Affiliated with the Socialist Party on the European level.

People's Party for Freedom and Democracy (VVD), Postbus 30836, 2500 GV The Hague (☎070 361 3006; www.vvd.nl). Sometimes confusingly labeled "conservative liberal," the VVD is best categorized on the right. Emphasizes individual freedom and supports free markets and economic liberalization, including supranationally.

Socialist Party, Vijverhofstraat 65, 3032 SC Rotterdam (☎010 243 5555; www.sp.nl). Leftist socialist party more radical than the Labor Party. Has grown in popularity to join Labour, VVD, and CDA at the top of the parliamentary ladder. Somewhere, Karl Marx would be smiling—had he not been an atheist.

SOCIAL ACTIVISM

Amsterdam may be famed for its tolerance, but its large immigrant populations from Indonesia, Suriname, the Ivory Coast, the Caribbean, the Far East—and so on—have not always been welcomed with bouquets of tulips. Countless organizations have emerged to battle discrimination and pull the underprivileged up by their bootstraps. Websites that list information on activist organizations (if not necessarily specific volunteer opportunities) also abound. **KIEM** (www.integratie.net) is a portal dedicated to integrating ethnic minorities in Amsterdam and promoting local tolerance for these groups (though, ironically, it is only in Dutch).

Dutch natives are by no means immune from disadvantage. GLBT citizens, women, and the homeless have all faced uphill climbs in the Netherlands, and many are still trudging. In order to level the Dutch terrain (flatter than it already is), we have also listed homeless shelter locations and organizations that are dedicated to helping locals.

Our listings here take advantage of Amsterdam's unique reputation for tolerance among persons of different ethnicities, religions, and sexual orientations. However, the fact that organizations dedicated to supporting tolerance have long existed in Amsterdam does not imply that discrimination or cultural intolerance in Amsterdam are problems of the past. Otherwise, they would have no need for you.

Amnesty International, Postbus 1968, 1000 BZ Amsterdam (☎020 626 4436; www.amnesty.nl). Despite its large reach, Amnesty has not lost sight of the little guy.

Dedicated to peace and asylum for refugees worldwide, Amnesty runs an office in Amsterdam that employs volunteers in research, fundraising, and publications.

COC Amsterdam, Rozenstraat 14, Amsterdam (☎020 626 3087; www.cocamsterdam.nl). The world's oldest organization dedicated to the support and solidarity of homosexuals and their families. Contact for involvement in support groups, gay pride activities, and publications.

Dutch Council for Refugees, Jacques Veltmanstraat 463, Amsterdam (☎020 346 7200; www.vluchtelingenwerk.nl). The local branch of the Dutch Council for Refugees often uses volunteers for office and administrative work.

Elandsstraat, Nieuwe Herengracht 20, Amsterdam (☎020 623 4757; opvangcentrum@planet.nl). Runs a day- and night-shelter for battered women, refugees, and other asylum seekers. Employs Dutch-speaking volunteers.

KAFKA, Postbus 14710, 1001 LE Amsterdam (☎065 168 2822; www.kafka.antifa.net). Seeks to metamorphose the Netherlands into an even more tolerant nation. Rallies against racism, nationalism, and 4 Dutch fascist parties. Organizes both research and documentation of neo-fascist incidents.

Art.1, Schaatsbaan 51, Rotterdam (☎010 201 0201; www.art1.nl). Named after Article 1 of the Dutch constitution, Art.1 is dedicated to keeping the government from ignoring the anti-discrimination clause within. A new organization combining the forces of the former National Bureau Against Racial Discrimination and similar regional bodies. Documents incidences of discrimination and encourages anti-discrimination groups.

Stichting Gered Gereedschap, Marius van Bouwdijk Bastiaansestraat 32, Amsterdam (☎020 683 9609; www.geredgereedschap.nl). Run entirely by volunteers and always eager for English speakers. Collects and refurbishes tools and work equipment to be sent to economically impoverished African communities.

UNITED for Intercultural Action, Postbus 413, 1000 AK Amsterdam (☎020 683 4778; www.unitedagainstracism.org). An international organization conveniently headquartered in Amsterdam. Enlists the volunteer efforts of over 560 European organizations in the struggle against nationalism, racism, and fascism. Organizes publications, campaigns, and conferences in support of migrants, minorities, and refugees, including the International Refugee Day and the Action Week Against Racism.

MEDICAL OUTREACH

Travelers interested in volunteering in health-related fields in Amsterdam often need to make longer commitments than volunteers in other fields, though health volunteers are often rewarded with long-lasting connections to local communities, the acquisition of useful professional skills, and the thanks of grateful patients.

AMOC/DHV, Stadhouderskade 159, Amsterdam (☎020 672 1192; www.amocdhv.org). AMOC's aim is to help addicts work and live with their addictions, and DHV was originally founded specifically to help Germans struggling with addiction in the Netherlands. Drop-In Centre and User Room staffed by volunteers, who also help with counseling, outreach, and networking.

Cannabis College, Oudezijds Achterburgwal 124, Amsterdam (☎020 423 4420; www.cannabiscollege.com). A marijuana information and resource center that employs volunteers. Keeps a comprehensive database on the legal and health issues surrounding marijuana consumption. Not an actual college, but staff educates curious tourists for free. See listing in **Museums,** p. 166.

HIV Vereniging Nederland, 1e Helmersstraat 17, Amsterdam (☎020 616 0160; www.hivnet.org). Safeguards the interests of individuals living with HIV/AIDS across the Netherlands.

Nederlandse Rode Kruis (Red Cross), Valkenburgerstraat 24, Amsterdam (☎020 622 6211; www.nrka.nl). Chapter of the international Red Cross. Volunteers provide free emergency medical treatment, organize blood donations, and participate in service projects such as swimming lessons for the disabled and assistance for asylum seekers.

Schorer, Sarphatistraat 35, Amsterdam (☎020 573 9444; www.schorer.nl). A resource for GLBT health concerns, especially HIV/AIDS. With the COC, maintains the **Gay and Lesbian Switchboard** (p. 50).

ENVIRONMENTAL CONSERVATION

In 1997, the Amsterdam Treaty established sustainable development as a priority for the European Union, and environmentalism is on the rise throughout the Netherlands. During the 1990s, the number of Dutch citizens belonging to an environmental organization rose to almost four million, a number still increasing today—not too shabby for a nation with a population under 17 million.

Action for Solidarity, Equality, Environment, and Diversity (A SEED) Europe, Postbus 92066, 1090 AB Amsterdam (☎020 668 2236; www.aseed.net). A SEED fights against the exploitation of people and the environment. Volunteers of all ages are accepted in this young, idealistic organization to participate in campaigns ranging from organic food advocacy to the World Bank boycott. Duration of participation flexible.

Both Ends, Nieuwe Keizersgracht 45, Amsterdam (☎020 623 0823; www.both-ends.org). Environmental action group encourages environment-friendly projects, especially in the developing world. Recruits small number of volunteers for fundraising, information exchange, campaigns promotion, research, and lobbying.

Friends of the Earth Netherlands, Nieuwe Looiersstraat 31, Amsterdam (☎020 550 7300; www.milieudefensie.nl). Organizes several events for volunteers to campaign for a cleaner Netherlands.

Greenpeace Nederland, Ottho Heldringstraat 5, Amsterdam (☎020 718 2000 or 0800 422 3344; www.greenpeace.nl). You've likely heard of Greenpeace, but you probably didn't know that its international headquarters are here. Active in a wide range of regional campaigns, from protesting genetically modified food to saving the whales.

International Union for the Conservation of Nature (IUCN), Plantage Middenlaan 2K, Amsterdam (☎020 626 1732; www.nciucn.nl). Umbrella funding organization that provides as many small grants as it can muster toward natural preservation. Its members include many large environmental activist groups.

IVN Nederland, Plantage Middenlaan 2C, Amsterdam (☎020 622 8115). This society of 125 professionals and 17,000 volunteers promotes environmental awareness through grassroots educational activities and 3 Dutch publications.

Wereld Natuur Fonds, Driebergseweg 10, Zeist (☎030 693 7333; www.wwf.nl). The Dutch branch of the World Wildlife Fund has regional offices throughout the country. Check out their up-to-date but exclusively Dutch website or call for the latest campaigns and volunteer opportunities in your area.

CULTURE

The Netherlands offers a few organizations that take volunteers under their cultural wing. These can be some of the most intimate experiences a traveler can have with a host country—we guarantee you'll feel even more Dutch than when you bought those wooden shoes.

IJAR, Postbus 75517, 1070 AM Amsterdam (☎061 221 4527; www.ijar.nl). Jewish Students and Youth Society seeks to bring Jewish youths together with various activities, events, and trips throughout the year.

in somebody else's clogs

It is fitting that what foreigners see as the hallmarks of Dutch culture—windmills, clogs, tulips, prostitutes, cheese, and marijuana—should come together in Amsterdam. This strange amalgam pretty much constitutes all that most people know about Holland.

Strictly speaking, however, Holland includes only two provinces of the 12 that make up the Netherlands. The number of people who confuse

"Take time out of your busy schedule to duck into a bar and talk with a native."

this distinction—conflating the country with the province—goes a long way toward proving my point: much more often than in the rest of Europe, foreigners shy away from getting to know the Dutch beyond a basic, cliché-ridden conception.

In fact, the romance and legend of many of our European neighbors has kept the Dutch off most people's radar completely. Not to sound bitter, but even Hollywood, an industry that has left almost no aspect of the world untouched, has decided that the Dutch simply don't sell. How many Frenchmen, Italians, Germans, and Brits do you see in the movies? Now, how many Dutchmen do you see in the movies? In my memory, there has been only one sizable Dutch character—Goldmember, the lead villain in the third *Austin Powers* movie. Throughout the movie, Goldmember repeats the same mantra over and over, asking whether it's "weird" that he's Dutch, as if to be Dutch is only and always to be "weird."

Not that Mike Myers is to blame. Frankly, I was glad we Dutch got a mention, let alone a leading character. But even if the movie managed to fixate on some uniquely Dutch foible, no one would have known. All the character can do is repeat that the Dutch are weird, and when the word "Dutch" conjures up images of weed and windmills, you can probably understand why. The Dutch, unlike so many other

nationalities, can't complain of being unfairly stereotyped. No cultural stereotypes exist against which to fight. The Dutch aren't misunderstood. They simply aren't understood at all.

Fortunately for visitors to Amsterdam, such a lack of understanding makes it very easy to move beyond tourism. Because many people know next to nothing about the Dutch, you can go beyond the average tourist's experience merely by making an effort to get to know them.

That's why it's so important for you to get beneath the surface of Dutch culture. This chapter directs you to many excellent and worthy ways to do this. Volunteering, working, studying abroad—all of these programs are great venues through which to learn more about the Dutch and about what makes Dutch culture, well, Dutch.

Or you can take a less structured approach. Why not actually get to *know* some Dutch folks? Take time out of your busy saving-the-world-one-seedling-at-a-time schedule to saddle up to a *bruin cafe* barstool and talk with a native Amsterdammer about something—anything. Chances are they'll engage you in conversation and probably surprise you with their effective use of the English language.

Don't be alarmed if your new friend is a little blunt, by the way. Many visitors often find the Dutch to be refreshingly brusque. Take it as a compliment that you're being taken seriously if you receive a stern, if inelegant, "No, that is wrong," when you inquire into the merits of topics from global affairs to celebrity gossip to pot politics.

In some ways I'm being flippant. But, honestly, the only way to go beyond tourism is to get to know the people. It may sound trite, but the more you put yourself out there trying to get to know Amsterdammers, the more rewarding your experience will be.

Hunter Maats, a Dutch citizen, has been a Let's Go Researcher-Writer in Northern Italy, Mexico, and Russia.

Nederlands Auschwitz Comité, Postbus 74131, 1070 BC Amsterdam (☎020 672 3388; www.auschwitz.nl). Dedicated to remembrance of the Holocaust through monuments, bulletins, and public awareness.

FOR THE UNDECIDED ALTRUIST

If reforming government, saving lives, and greening the world just don't do it for you, take a gander at the following catch-all volunteer agencies.

Concordia International, 19 North St., Portslade, Brighton, UK, BN41 1DH (☎+44 01273 422 218; www.concordia-iye.org.uk). A small non-profit charity, Concordia sponsors volunteer projects worldwide for residents of the UK. Dutch programs include public service and environmental protection.

SIW International Volunteer Projects, Willemstraat 7, Utrecht (☎030 231 7721; www.siw.nl). Offers 2- to 3-week programs for international visitors across the Netherlands. Help the disadvantaged, lend a hand to construction and restoration, or oversee cultural activities.

Vrijwillige Internationale Aktie (VIA), Marius van Bouwdijk Bastiaansestraat 56, Amsterdam (☎020 689 2760; www.via-nl.nl). The Dutch affiliate of **Service Civil International** (www.sciint.org), VIA uses teams of young volunteers to run progressively minded work sites in support of victims of social, economic, and political injustice. Most work sites are short-term 2- to 3-week projects; all encourage teamwork and cooperation among volunteers. Volunteers must apply through the office in their home country. Check the international website or contact one of the following offices: **Australia** ☎+61 296 991 129, www.ivp.org.au; **Canada** ☎613-737-6777, www.nocona.ca; **UK** ☎+44 113 246 9900, www.ivs-gb.org.uk; **US** ☎434-823-9003, www.sci-ivs.org.

Volunteers for Peace, 1034 Tiffany Rd., Belmont, VT 05730, USA (☎802-259-2759; www.vfp.org). Offers an average of 22 2- to 3-week programs in the Netherlands in work and refugee camps. Registration fee US$250 plus membership fee of US$30.

Vrijwilligers Centrale, Lissabonplantsoen 113, Haarlem (☎023 533 5826; www.vrijwilligerscentrale.nl). A huge volunteer agency with offices nationwide. Provides references and contacts according to your interests. More welcoming to foreigners than most.

STUDYING

VISA INFORMATION. Not a citizen of Australia, Canada, the EU, Iceland, Japan, Liechtenstein, Monaco, New Zealand, Norway, Switzerland, or the US? For a study of more than 3 months, you require a **student visa.** Apply several (at least 3) months in advance; your study program should provide all the necessary—and abundant—paperwork. A visa costs €250 plus whatever fees the program levies if applying through it; if you do it yourself, the visa will run €433. A residence permit for study (not for paid employment), required for non-EU/EEA citizens, costs €188 extra or €433 without a visa. Study of less than 3 months may require a Schengen Visa; inquire at your country's Dutch embassy.

Study-abroad programs range from basic language and culture courses to college-level classes, often for credit. In order to choose a program that best fits your needs, research as much as you can before making your decision—determine costs and duration as well as what kind of students participate in the program and what sort of accommodations are provided.

The best resource for English-language programs in the humanities, sciences, and social sciences is **NUFFIC,** Kortenaerkade 11, The Hague (☎070 426 0260; www.nuffic.nl), which caters to foreign students interested in studying in the Netherlands. Their comprehensive online search engine can help you find a course or degree program that matches your interests, time restrictions, location preferences, and budget. **Institutes of International Education,** which often offer instruction in English, are generally considered to be on par with renowned Dutch-language universities.

In programs that have large groups of students who speak the same language, there is a trade-off. You may feel more comfortable in the community, but you will not have the same opportunity to practice a foreign language or to befriend other international students. For accommodations, dorm life provides a better opportunity to mingle with fellow students, but there is less of a chance to experience the local scene. If you live with a family, there is a potential to build lifelong friendships with natives and to experience day-to-day life in more depth, but conditions can vary greatly from family to family.

UNIVERSITIES

Most university-level study-abroad programs are conducted in Dutch, although many programs offer classes in English and beginner- and lower-level language courses. Those who are relatively fluent in Dutch may find it cheaper to enroll directly in a university abroad, although getting college credit may be more difficult. University applicants are also frequently required to obtain the Dutch secondary-school diploma, or VWO, or an equivalent such as IB or British A-levels. You can search **www.studyabroad.com** for various semester-abroad programs that meet your criteria, including your desired location and focus of study. The following is a list of organizations that can help place students in university programs abroad or have their own branch in the Netherlands.

AMERICAN PROGRAMS

The Netherlands isn't the most wildly popular study-abroad destination, but it is on enough radar screens to remain desirable—and expensive. Bear in mind that some American schools still require students to pay them for credits obtained elsewhere. If you are an American student looking to study in the Netherlands, your college is often the best place to start your search.

American Institute for Foreign Study, College Division, River Plaza, 9 W. Broad St., Stamford, CT 06902, USA (☎800-727-2437; www.aifsabroad.com). Organizes programs for high-school and college study in universities in the Netherlands.

Center for Cultural Interchange, 746 N. LaSalle Dr., Chicago, IL 60610, USA (☎866-684-9675; www.cci-exchange.com). High-school abroad program for 1 semester or a full year. Promises lessons in Dutch and your own bicycle.

Central College Abroad, Office of International Education, 812 University, Pella, IA 50219, USA (☎800-831-3629; www.central.edu/abroad). Offers internships, summer, semester, and full-year programs in Leiden.

Council on International Educational Exchange (CIEE), 7 Custom House St., 3rd fl., Portland, ME 01401, USA (☎800-407-8839; www.ciee.org/study). Sponsors work, volunteer, academic, and internship programs in the Netherlands.

Institute for the International Education of Students (IES), 33 N. LaSalle St., 15th fl., Chicago, IL 60602, USA (☎800-995-2300; www.iesabroad.org). Offers full-year and semester programs in Amsterdam for college students. US$50 application fee. Scholarships available.

School for International Training, College Semester Abroad, Kipling Rd., P.O. Box 676, Brattleboro, VT 05302, USA (☎888-272-7881 or 802-258-7751; www.sit.edu/studyabroad). Semester-long programs in the Netherlands run US$12,900-16,000.

DUTCH PROGRAMS

The Dutch take education seriously, and, as a result, almost every large town and city in the country has excellent study-abroad programs. In particular, Utrecht, Groningen, Leiden, and Rotterdam rival Amsterdam's excellent options; the universities in these towns offer thousands of courses, in English and in Dutch, on every subject from international human rights to the postmodern critique of the "other." Not as famous but just as excellent as those other schools in neighboring France, Germany, and Britain, colleges in the Netherlands are comparatively easy to gain admission to and often cost less than their name-brand counterparts do.

Amsterdam-Maastricht Summer University, Keizersgracht 324, Amsterdam (☎020 620 0225; www.amsu.edu). Offers courses in numerous subjects, including art history, politics, journalism, language, and medicine during, yes, the summer.

Leiden University, Rapenburg 70, Leiden (☎071 527 2727; www.leiden.edu). The oldest university in the Netherlands has English-language instruction in several departments. Semester- and year-long programs for students with 2 or more years of university education. €4600 per semester, €8600 per year.

Universiteit Maastricht, Center for European Studies, Bonnefantenstraat 2, Maastricht (☎043 388 5282; www.ces.unimaas.nl). Runs summer and semester programs in English for college juniors and seniors.

University College Utrecht, Campusplein 1, Utrecht (☎030 253 9900; www.ucu.uu.nl). Subset of Utrecht University offers 3-year English-language BA and BS programs in the liberal arts and sciences. Exclusive, enrolling only 650 students at a time. Tuition varies but is always higher than you'd like, topping out at €17,734. VWO or equivalent required.

University of Amsterdam, Spui 21, Amsterdam (☎525 8080 or 525 3333; www.uva.nl/english). Amsterdam's largest university offers a full range of degree programs in Dutch and an only slightly more limited English selection for all degree-seekers. Open to college and graduate students. Students live either in university dormitories or in apartments. Tuition €9000 for most undergraduate programs and constantly on the rise. Discount for EU/EEA citizens. The university includes the **International School for Humanities and Social Sciences,** Prins Hendrikkade 189B, Amsterdam (☎020 525 3777; www.ishss.uva.nl), which boasts master's degree and summer programs like the Summer Institute on Sexuality, Culture, and Society.

Utrecht University, Postbus 80125, 3508 TC Utrecht (☎030 253 3550; www.uu.nl). Offers international bachelor's programs, master's, and Ph.D. programs in English and Dutch. Range of research programs, including biomedical sciences, social sciences, and the humanities. The bill runs €1538 for EU/EEA citizens for 2007-08; rest assured that this will go up. Others must shell out €5500-10,000. Also home to **Utrecht University Summer School,** Postbus 80148, 3508 TC Utrecht (☎030 253 4400; www.uu.nl/summerschool) and its courses in science, social science, and culture. Popular options include Dutch Culture and Society. Courses rarely longer than 2-3 weeks.

Vrije Universiteit Amsterdam, De Boelelaan 1105, Amsterdam (☎020 598 9898; www.vu.nl). Long menu of 100 master's degree programs, including 60 in English, that run 1-2 years. Tuition (€1230-1800 for EU/EEA citizens, €9000-12,000 otherwise) varies by program, in disciplines like science, law, and culture.

LANGUAGE SCHOOLS

Language schools can be independently run international or local organizations or divisions of foreign universities. They rarely offer college credit but remain a good alternative to university study for those who desire a deeper focus on the language or a slightly less rigorous courseload. These programs are also good for younger high-school students who might not feel comfortable with older students in a university program. Some worthwhile programs include:

Goethe Institut, Herengracht 470, Amsterdam (☎020 531 2900; www.goethe.de). This cultural center offers German-language courses, lectures, drama, and film.

Italian Cultural Institute, Keizersgracht 564, Amsterdam (☎020 626 5314; www.iicamsterdam.esteri.it). Add a little Romance to your life with ICI's Italian courses.

Maison Descartes, Vijzelgracht 2A, Amsterdam (☎020 531 9501; www.maisondescartes.nl). Music, expositions, symposia, and *cinema à la française.* Language courses and a multimedia library also available.

ALTERNATIVE STUDY ABROAD

For an alternative to a more traditional study-abroad program, check out these opportunities in agriculture, archaeology, art, and culinary technique. Also check out **www.nuffic.nl** for information on the Netherlands's "professional universities," known as **hogescholen,** which specialize in everything from finance to the arts.

The Academy of Fine Arts, Hortusplantsoen 2, Amsterdam (☎020 527 7220; www.bvo.ahk.nl). Instruction in drawing and painting. 4-year program qualifies students to be art teachers throughout Europe. Secondary-school diploma required. Art may be a universal language, but you'll need to know Dutch to enroll.

AgriVenture, 7710 5 St. SE #105, Calgary, Alberta, Canada (☎403-255-7799; www.agriventure.com). Runs an agricultural and horticultural exchange program. Applicants lucky enough to be picked are placed with a host family, receive room, board, and stipend, and learn Dutch farming techniques. Exchanges last 4-15 months.

Amsterdam Hogeschool voor de Kunsten, Jodenbreestraat 3, Amsterdam (☎020 527 7710; www.ahk.nl). The School of the Arts is an umbrella organization including some schools listed here. Note, however, that several academy classes—and websites—are presented in Dutch only. Tuition varies by program.

Binger Filmlab, Nieuwezijds Voorburgwal 4-10, Amsterdam (☎020 530 9630; www.binger.nl). A sort of dream camp for directors, writers, and producers from around the world. Offers 5-month programs taught in English on film theory and production for students with experience in the film industry. Surprisingly affordable, and scholarships are available. EU/EEA citizens €769, others €975.

Conservatorium van Amsterdam, Van Baerlestraat 27, Amsterdam (☎020 527 7550; www.cva.ahk.nl). School of Music accepts speakers of either Dutch or English into a melodic program of all genres of music. Admission by audition, examination, language certificate, and VWO or the equivalent.

Hague Academy of International Law, Carnegieplein 2, The Hague (☎070 302 4152; www.hagueacademy.nl). Study international law at the **Peace Palace** (p. 273)—not a bad campus, considering it's the home of the International Court of Justice and Permanent Court of Arbitration. 4 years of legal studies required. €750 for 1 of 2 3-week periods, €1400 for both. Room and board not included.

Keizer Culinair, Elandsstraat 169-173, Amsterdam (☎020 427 9276; www.keizerculinair.nl). 3 locations in Amsterdam and more throughout the Netherlands. Choose a sumptuous international feast, then learn to cook it under the guidance of a professional. Lunch €48. Dinner €60. Prices are per person, and there is a minimum depending on location. Wine tastings also available.

Nederlandse Jeugdbond voor Geschiedenis (NJBG), Prins Willem Alexanderhof 5, The Hague (☎070 347 6598; www.njbg.nl). Dutch Youth Association for History sponsors archaeological excursions and building restoration projects for members ages 9-26.

The Theater School, Jodenbreestraat 3, Amsterdam (☎020 527 7777; www.the.ahk.nl). Another branch of the Amsterdam School of the Arts. Offers degree programs in dance, theater, and technical media, almost exclusively run by active professionals. They will insist that you have a VWO equivalent and a solid grasp of Dutch.

WORKING

As with volunteering, work opportunities tend to fall into two categories. Some travelers want long-term jobs that allow them to integrate into a community, while others seek out short-term jobs to finance the next leg of their travels. In Amsterdam, those interested in long-term work are best off seeking employment in larger organizations or through internship programs that are willing to handle the red tape of work permits. Short-term work in Amsterdam largely feeds off the tourism industry. As always, it is important to keep your eyes and ears open for posts available via word of mouth. Bulletin boards and newspapers are also invaluable resources. Be sure to check out postings at the **Openbare Bibliotheek Amsterdam (Amsterdam Public Library),** Prinsengracht 587, just north of Leidsegracht, the **City Hall Information Center,** Amstel 1, in Waterlooplein, and the **University of Amsterdam.** Note that working abroad often requires a special work visa; see the box below for information about obtaining one.

VISA INFORMATION. First, the good news: if you're an EU/EEA citizen (save Bulgarians and Romanians), you need neither a visa nor a residence permit to work in the Netherlands (although they do make things run more smoothly). Other foreign nationals are required to have a work visa. Australian, Canadian, and New Zealand citizens ages 18-30 can apply to take part in the **Working Holiday Scheme,** which allows them to work in the Netherlands for 1 year. For US college students, recent graduates, and young adults, the simplest way to get legal permission to work in the Netherlands is through **Council Exchanges Work Abroad Programs** (www.ciee.org). Council Exchanges can help obtain a 3- to 6-month work permit/visa and also provide assistance finding jobs and housing. For stays over 3 months, a residence permit is also required for foreigners—except citizens of the US, Canada, New Zealand, Australia, and Japan. Apply several months in advance at your local Dutch embassy or consulate or with the Aliens Police Office in the Netherlands. The Dutch Ministry of Justice's Immigration and Naturalization Service runs a helpful website at **www.immigratiedienst.nl,** which is a good place to turn if you're stuck or things change.

LONG-TERM WORK

If you're planning on spending a substantial amount of time (more than three months) working in the Netherlands, search for a job well in advance. International placement agencies are often the easiest way to find employment abroad, especially for those interested in teaching English. Although they are often only available to college students, **internships** are a good way to segue into working abroad; although they are often un- or underpaid, many say the experience is well worth it. Be wary of advertisements for companies claiming to be able get you a job abroad for a fee—often the same listings are available online or in newspapers.

Once in the Netherlands, job searches usually begin by inquiring at city employment agencies, called *arbeidsbureaus* (AB). Foreigners can use the ABs only after obtaining a BSN. The easiest way to find the address of the nearest AB is to check the Dutch *Gouden Gids* ("Yellow Pages"). Another option is to contact the local *bureau voor de arbeidsvoorziening* (employment office).

CUTTING RED TAPE. Before you can obtain any government services while in the Netherlands, your papers must be in order. Keep multiple copies of all documentation—e.g., visas and employment guarantees—to expedite services.

English Language Jobs (☎018 230 0745; www.englishlanguagejobs.com). Founded in Amsterdam in 2000, English Language Jobs has listings of English-language jobs in the Netherlands and throughout Europe.

Intern Abroad (www.internabroad.com). A search engine for internship postings.

Specialty Travel Index, P.O. Box 458, San Anselmo, CA 94960, USA (☎888-624-4030 or 415-455-1643; www.specialtytravel.com). Has an extensive listing of "off-the-beaten-track" and "specialty" travel opportunities; the job listings for "Holland"—as they call it—mostly fall within the tourist industry.

TEACHING ENGLISH

Teaching jobs are difficult to obtain in Amsterdam, where highly skilled English speakers abound, and often don't pay well, although some elite private American schools offer competitive salaries. Volunteering as a teacher in lieu of getting paid is a popular option; even then, teachers often receive some sort of a daily stipend to help with living expenses. In almost all cases, you must have at least a bachelor's degree to be a full-fledged teacher, although college undergraduates can often get summer positions teaching or tutoring.

Many schools require teachers to have a **Teaching English as a Foreign Language (TEFL)** certificate. You may still be able to find a teaching job without certification, but certified teachers often find higher-paying jobs. Native English speakers working in private schools are most often hired for English-immersion classrooms where no Dutch is spoken. Those volunteering or teaching in public schools are likelier to work in both English and Dutch. Placement agencies or university fellowship programs are the best resources for finding teaching jobs. The alternative is to contact schools directly or to try your luck once you arrive in the Netherlands. The best time to look for the latter is several weeks before the start of the school year. The following organizations are extremely helpful in placing teachers in the Netherlands.

European Council of International Schools, 21 Lavant St., Petersfield, Hampshire GU32 3EL, UK (☎+44 1730 268 244; www.ecis.org). Association of hundreds of member schools worldwide. Website has directory of Dutch English-speaking schools.

International Schools Services (ISS), 15 Roszel Rd., P.O. Box 5910, Princeton, NJ 08543, USA (☎609-452-0990; www.iss.edu). Hires teachers for more than 200 overseas schools, including in Amsterdam, The Hague, and Rotterdam; candidates should have experience teaching or with international affairs. 2-year commitment expected.

Office of Overseas Schools, US Department of State, Room H328, SA-1, Washington, D.C. 20522, USA (☎202-261-8200; www.state.gov/m/a/os), keeps a comprehensive list of schools outside of the US and approved agencies that arrange placement for Americans to teach abroad.

SCHOOLS IN AMSTERDAM AND BEYOND

The Netherlands is home to a large number of English-speaking schools, be they international, American, British, or Dutch. While some schools interview and hire directly, most hire through recruitment fairs (see above).

American School of The Hague, Rijksstraatweg 200, Wassenaar (☎070 512 1060; www.ash.nl).

The British School in the Netherlands, Foundation School, Tarwekamp 3, 2592 XG The Hague (☎070 315 4040; www.britishschool.nl).

The British School of Amsterdam, Anthonie van Dijckstraat 1, Amsterdam (☎020 679 7840; www.britams.nl).

The International School of Amsterdam, Sportlaan 45, Amstelveen (☎020 347 1111; www.isa.nl).

The International School of The Hague, Wijndaelerduin 1, The Hague (☎070 338 4567 or 070 328 1450; www.ishthehague.nl).

Rijnlands Lyceum Oegstgeest, Apollolaan 1, Oegstgeest (☎071 519 3555; www.rijnlandslyceum.nl/oegstgeest), between The Hague and Leiden.

AU PAIR WORK

In the Netherlands, au pairs must be between 18 and 25 years of age and are not allowed to work more than eight hours per day or 30 hours per week in the household. Au pairs can stay in the Netherlands for a maximum of one year. They must be unmarried, have no dependents, and have a Dutch residence permit. They must not have previously had a residence permit. Au pairs work as live-in nannies, caring for children and doing light housework in exchange for room, board, and a small spending allowance or stipend. One perk of the job is that it allows you to get to know the Netherlands without the high expenses of traveling. Drawbacks can include long hours and mediocre pay—roughly €70-90 per week in the Netherlands. Much of the au pair experience depends on the family with which you are placed. For the lingually able, **www.aupair.nl** is a good starting point; otherwise, the agencies below should be useful in your quest for employment.

Au Pair in Europe, C/Los Centelles 45, Pta. 11, 46006 Valencia, Spain (☎+34 96 320 6491; www.planetaupair.com/aupaireng.htm). Offers au pair positions in the Netherlands to EU citizens only.

Childcare International, Ltd., Trafalgar House, Grenville Pl., London NW7 3SA (☎+44 020 8906 3116; www.childint.co.uk). Apply for Au Pair or Au Pair Plus programs.

InterExchange, 161 Sixth Ave., New York, NY, 10013, USA (☎800-287-2477; fax 924-0575; www.interexchange.org). Offers some summer programs, but most require commitments of at least 9 months. Has an agency in Amsterdam.

ADDITIONAL RESOURCES. Most of the search engines below are only in Dutch and are best for visitors who have already obtained their papers.

Content, Van Baerlestraat 83, Amsterdam (☎020 676 4441; www.content.nl). Includes jobs for non-Dutch speakers. Helpful walk-in facility too.

Dactylo (☎035 646 7300; www.dactylo.nl). Dutch website with job listings.

Manpower, Postbus 12150, 1100 AD Amsterdam (☎020 660 2222; www.manpower.nl). Numerous branches in Amsterdam, classified by employment sector. See Dutch-language website for the most appropriate address.

Randstad (☎020 569 5911; www.randstad.nl). Search by "function" and postal code in, yes, Dutch.

Researcher's Mobility Portal (www.eracareers.nl). An online portal to post your resume, read others' resumes, and find research-based jobs and careers in the Netherlands.

Undutchables, Singel 8, Amsterdam (☎020 623 1300; www.undutchables.nl). The most useful job recruitment agency for foreigners, placing people in jobs that require command of a language other than Dutch. Temporary and permanent jobs available.

Vedior Personeelsdiensten (☎035 646 7100; www.vedior.nl). Slightly flashier Dutch website that searches by keyword and postal code.

SHORT-TERM WORK

Traveling for long periods of time can be hard on the finances; therefore, many travelers try their hand at odd jobs for a few weeks at a time to help pay for another month or two of touring around. For several decades now, the Netherlands has been a mecca for young, bright-eyed EU nationals seeking short-term work. Amsterdam is full of recruitment and temp agencies, called **uitzendbureaus**, though a working knowledge of Dutch is often required. The *uitzendbureaus* advertise short-term jobs (fewer than 6 months or 1000hr.), though it is possible to extend employment up to one year. Jobs offered are usually unskilled and cater to foreigners with little experience. Be aware, however, that these *uitzendbureaus* often charge a percentage of your wage as a commission.

The **tourism industry** provides a substantial number of jobs to foreigners, who can work in hotels and hostels year-round. For these jobs, it is often best to go through establishments directly rather than through the *uitzendbureaus*. Certain hotels will also hire English speakers to work at the hotel and convince tourists at train stations to stay there. Another popular option is to work several hours a day at a hostel in exchange for free or discounted room and/or board. Most often, these short-term jobs are found by word of mouth or by expressing interest to the owner of a hostel or restaurant. Due to high turnover in the tourism industry, many places are eager for help, even if it is only temporary. *Let's Go* lists temporary jobs of this nature whenever possible; visit the **VVV** (p. 93) or check out the list below for some available short-term jobs.

FURTHER READING ON BEYOND TOURISM

Alternatives to the Peace Corps: A Guide of Global Volunteer Opportunities, by Paul Backhurst. Food First Books, 2005 (US$12).

The Back Door Guide to Short-Term Job Adventures: Internships, Summer Jobs, Seasonal Work, Volunteer Vacations, and Transitions Abroad, by Michael Landes. Ten Speed Press, 2005 (US$22).

Green Volunteers: The World Guide to Voluntary Work in Nature Conservation, ed. Fabio Ausenda. Universe, 2007 (US$15).

How to Get a Job in Europe, by Cheryl Matherly and Robert Sanborn. Planning Communications, 2003 (US$23).

How to Live Your Dream of Volunteering Overseas, by Joseph Collins, Stefano DeZerega, and Zahara Heckscher. Penguin Books, 2002 (US$20).

International Job Finder: Where the Jobs Are Worldwide, by Daniel Lauber and Kraig Rice. Planning Communications, 2002 (US$20).

Live and Work Abroad: A Guide for Modern Nomads, by Huw Francis and Michelyne Callan. Vacation-Work Publications, 2001 (US$16).

Overseas Summer Jobs 2002. Peterson's Guides and Vacation Work, 2002 (US$18).

Volunteer Vacations: Short-Term Adventures That Will Benefit You and Others, by Doug Cutchins, Anne Geissinger, and Bill McMillon. Chicago Review Press, 2006 (US$18).

Work Abroad: The Complete Guide to Finding a Job Overseas, by Clayton Hubbs. Transitions Abroad Publishing, 2002 (US$16).

Work Your Way Around the World, by Susan Griffith. Vacation-Work Publications, 2007 (US$22).

PRACTICAL INFORMATION

TOURIST AND FINANCIAL SERVICES

TOURIST OFFICES

Every town in the Netherlands has a **Vereniging voor Vreemdelingenverkeer (VVV),** or Dutch tourist office. While the brochures, maps, and tickets at these offices can be helpful, the employees may be weary of the crowds—and show it. Most VVVs are listed under their respective cities in **Daytrips** (p. 243); Amsterdam's (☎0900 400 4040, €0.40 per min.; www.amsterdamtourist.nl) are below.

Centraal Station, Stationsplein 15, at platform #2 inside Centraal. 6 counters, some of which can make last-minute reservations for accommodations. Open M-Th and Sa 8am-8pm, F 8pm-9pm, Su 9am-5pm.

Leidseplein/Stadhouderskade, Stadhouderskade 1, in Leidseplein. 2 counters for buying maps or tickets or getting free information. Open daily 10am-6pm.

Schiphol, Aankomstpassage 40, in Schiphol Airport in Arrival Hall 2. Buy train tickets from the airport to Centraal or book accommodations for your stay. Open daily 7am-10pm.

Stationsplein, Stationsplein 10. Across the tram tracks to the right when exiting Centraal Station. Once there, you can get help with hostel or hotel reservations, buy a Museumjaarkaart (see **More Museums for Less,** p. 7), or grab a map (€2). The busiest VVV, so expect a long wait here. Open daily 9am-5pm.

BOAT TOURS

Take a sunny day to watch the ducks float lazily by from one of Amsterdam's boat tours, the logical way to start off any trip to the city. Sailing through Amsterdam's many waterways will help you get a feel for its canal-dominated layout.

🛥**Amsterdam Canal Cruises** (☎626 5636; www.amsterdamcanalcruises.nl), boards opposite the Heineken Experience. Tram #16, 24, or 25 from Centraal. Exit at Ferdinand Bolstraat and backtrack 80m to Singelgracht. 1¼hr. tour. Lunch and dinner cruises available. €8, children €3.50. Open daily 9:30am-5:30pm.

Canal Bike (☎626 5574; www.canal.nl), at 4 moorings: Rijksmuseum, Leidseplein, Keizersgracht at Leidsestraat, and Anne Frank Huis. Canal Bike had the ingenious notion to combine the Dutch surplus of water with their natural tendency to pedal. Travel by paddle boat through Amsterdam's canals to see some of the city's top attractions. For 1-2 people €8 per hr., more than 2 people €7 per hr. €50 deposit. Printed route guides €2. Also offers boat tours of the city (day pass €16, for 10+ people €11), allowing you to hop on or off at various stops. Chill out aboard the jazz cruise (1½ hr., €45). Open daily high season 10am-9pm; low season 10am-7 or 8pm.

Lovers Boat Company, Prins Hendrikkade 25-27 (☎530 1090; www.lovers.nl). Offers several different options in canal travel. For €9, you can hop on a 1hr. canal cruise (every hr. 10am-5pm) that leaves from the main depot across from Centraal Station. If you're in the mood for history, the **Museumboot** (€17) picks up every 30min. at Centraal, Anne Frank Huis, Rijksmuseum, Bloemenmarkt, Waterlooplein, and the old shipyard. Patrons can board and disembark at all stops. For a romantic evening, try a candlelight cruise, which includes a drink (2hr., 9pm, €27.50), or a dinner cruise (2½hr., 7:30pm, €70), which both leave from outside Centraal.

BIKE AND BUS TOURS

In Amsterdam, bikes easily outnumber all other forms of transport. Thousands of them line the canals and wind through the streets, carrying tourists and locals to destinations all over the city. Bike and bus tours can take you on a whirlwind tour of the city's major attractions or get you out of the downtown area to see parts of the Netherlands you might never discover by train. For listings of bike-rental shops, see p. 96.

▨ **Mike's Bike Tours,** Kerkstraat 134 (☎622 7970; www.mikesbiketours.com). Popular tours of the city and surrounding areas led by hilarious, well-informed, friendly, and energetic guides out to make sure you enjoy your 2-wheelin' experience. 3-4hr. tours take you to all the major sights in Amsterdam, including more rural spots like a windmill and a cheese factory. Tours meet daily at the Rijksmuseum's rear entrance, at the base of the reflecting pool on the Museumplein. Mar.-Apr. and Sept.-Nov. 12:30pm; May-Aug. 11am, 4pm. Rain gear provided. 3-4hr. tours €29, including bikes; students €25. Traveler's checks and cash only.

▨ **Yellow Bike,** Nieuwezijds Kolk 29 (☎620 6940; www.yellowbike.nl). Tour Amsterdam by bike with an English-speaking guide or ride off into the sunset and into wine and cheese country. 3hr. tours of Amsterdam's major attractions leave Apr.-Oct. M-F and Su 9:30am, 1pm, Sa 9:30am, 2pm. If you've had your fill of the city, try one of the countryside tours, a 6hr., 22 mi. trek through the Netherlands's dikes, old villages, and windmills. 3hr. tour €19.50; 6hr. tour €27.50. Reservations recommended. Bike rental available from €10 per day. Open daily 8:30am-5:30pm.

Canal Bus (☎626 5574; www.canal.nl), affiliated with Canal Bike. Travels 3 routes with 11 stops at Amsterdam's most popular tourist spots; buy tickets at kiosks or on board. Especially worthwhile if you plan on doing heavy sightseeing over a 12hr. period. €18, children €11. Pass valid until noon the next day. Gives discounts at some museums, casinos, and restaurants. Open daily 10am-6pm, in summer 10am-9:30pm.

Lowlands Travel, Korvelplein 176, Tilburg (☎062 334 2046; www.lowlandstravel.nl). Every week, Lowlands Travel takes small groups on personalized 3- to 4-day tours of the Netherlands in the hope of revealing places untouched by souvenir shops and camera-wielding tourists. Several tours are available in a variety of different themes. Expeditions take you through the northern or southern Netherlands and Belgium. All tours include transportation, meals, and accommodations and start at €200.

Wetlands Safari (☎686 3445; www.wetlandssafari.nl). Takes visitors on a 5hr. bus-and-canoe tour out of Amsterdam into the marshes and wetlands of the Dutch countryside. The tour (€33) includes light lunch and loads of lush, beautiful scenery that will amaze even non-nature lovers. May 1-Sept. 15 M-F 9:30am from the Stationsplein VVV.

CURRENCY EXCHANGE

American Express, Damrak 66 (☎504 8777). Offers the best rates, no commission on American Express Travelers Cheques, and a €4 flat fee for all non-euro cash and non-AmEx traveler's checks. Open M-F 9am-5pm, Sa 9am-noon.

GWK Travelex, in Centraal Station. Other locations at Damrak 86, Kalverstraat 103, Leidseplein 1-3, and Schiphol Airport. €2.25 plus 2.25% commission for exchanges. Students with ISIC get 25% discount and no commission. 3% commission on traveler's checks. Centraal open M-Sa 7am-11:45pm, Su 9am-11:45pm; Damrak daily 10am-10pm; Kalverstraat M-Sa 9am-6pm, Su 10:30am-5pm; Leidseplein daily 8:30am-10pm; Schiphol 24hr.

Pott-Change, Damrak 95 (☎626 3658). No commission on cash; €1.50 flat fee on traveler's checks. Open M-F 8:15am-8pm, Sa-Su 9:15am-8pm.

BANKS

Banking hours in Amsterdam are usually Monday, Wednesday, and Friday 9am-5pm and Thursday 9am-7pm.

ABN AMRO Bank, Dam 2, Leidsestraat 1, and Schiphol Airport (☎523 2900). Currency conversion, but no traveler's checks. Open M 11am-5pm, Tu-F 9am-5pm.

GWK, Centraal Station (☎627 2731) and Julianaplein 1 (☎693 4545). Currency conversion and traveler's checks exchanged. Centraal Station open M-W and Sa-Su 7am-10:45pm; Julianaplein M-Sa 7:30am-8pm, Su 10am-6pm.

Rabobank, Nieuwmarkt 20, Frederiksplein 54, and Dam 16 (☎777 8899). No currency exchange. ATM service only. Hours vary depending on branch; in general, open M-F 10am-6pm.

LOCAL SERVICES

BIKE RENTAL

Tired of being left out of the fun? If you can't beat 'em, join 'em. After some time as a pedestrian in Amsterdam, you'll get to *become* the wheeled menace yourself with help from the following:

 Frédéric Rent a Bike, Brouwersgracht 78 (☎624 5509; www.frederic.nl), in the Scheepvaartbuurt. From Centraal Station, head down Damrak and turn right at Nieuwendijk. Turn left after you cross the Haarlemmersluis bridge and follow Brouwersgracht for about 7 blocks; it's on the right. Part bike-rental establishment, part tourist office, Fred's is an excellent source of information and transportation. In addition to renting bikes, the friendly and helpful staff provides street maps, cycling know-how, and information suited to customers' particular interests. Bikes €10 per day, including lock and theft insurance, or €40 per week. Online reservations available. No deposit (though ID or credit card imprint is required). Open daily 9am-6pm. Accepts AmEx/MC/V for imprint, but payment must be in cash.

Bike City, 68-70 Bloemgracht (☎626 3721; www.bikecity.nl), in the Jordaan. Great rates on pedal, 3-speed, and 7-speed bikes, from €10 for 24hr. to €44.50 for 5 days. Bike rental comes with 2 good locks: use them! Bring a passport or other government-issued ID. Deposit €25. Open daily 9am-6pm. AmEx/MC/V with 5% surcharge.

> **✦TIP✦ BIKE-LOCKING BLUNDERS.** When you park your bike, remember where you left it. It's more common than you may think to forget at which of Amsterdam's countless canal-side locations you locked it up. Especially if you rented it, make sure to remember what your bike looks like—with over 600,000 bikes crowding Amsterdam's streets, they all begin to blur together.

Damstraat Rent-a-Bike, Damstraat 22 (☎625 5029; www.bikes.nl). Head south down Damrak from Centraal Station until you hit Dam Sq.; from there, go left across the square onto Damstraat. Good deals on a variety of bikes, from generic city cycles to luxury 21-speeders. Rentals from €3.50 for 1hr., €7 per day, €31 per week. Credit card imprint or €25 and an ID required as deposit. Open daily 9am-6pm.

Holland Rent-a-Bike, Damrak 247 (☎622 3207), in the basement of the Beurs van Berlage. Offers cheap rentals very close to Centraal Station. Bikes €6.25 per day, €32.50 per week; €100 or €30 plus an ID for deposit. Open M-F 7am-7pm, Sa 8am-6pm, Su 9am-6pm. AmEx/MC/V.

Mac Bike, Marnixstraat 220, Weteringschans 2, Mr. Visserplein 2 (☎626 6964; www.macbike.nl). This popular chain of bicycle-rental stores offers a variety of options, from 3hr. (€6) to 7-day rentals (€30). Beware of labeling yourself a tourist by riding one of the bikes that has a red "Mac Bike" logo on the front. For 50% of the rental price, you can insure your bike against theft and avoid paying the replacement fee of €300-600. Also sells and repairs bikes. Deposit €30. Open daily 9am-6pm. AmEx/MC/V.

LIBRARY

Openbare Bibliotheek Amsterdam, Prinsengracht 587 (☎523 0900). The main branch of the city's public library system is the only one in the city center proper. Free Internet access can be reserved for a 30min. slot at the information desk. Relax in the reading room and catch up on the latest news over a cup of coffee at the inexpensive cafe. Has an adequate selection of English-language magazines and fiction. Open M 1-9pm, Tu-Th 10am-9pm, F-Sa 10am-5pm; Oct.-Mar. also Su 1-5pm.

LAUNDROMATS

If you're running out of clean clothes, you should have no trouble finding a *wasserette* (laundromat) in your area. Below are just a few examples.

Rozengracht Wasserette, Rozengracht 59 (☎638 5975), in the Jordaan. Go left down Rozengracht from Westermarkt. You can do it yourself (wash €6, with dry €7 per 5kg load) or have it done for you (€8 for 5kg). Open daily 9am-9pm. Cash only.

Wasserette/Launderette, Oude Doelenstraat 12 (☎624 1700). From Dam, take Damstraat toward the Oude Zijd; the laundromat is on your right just before Oudezijds Achterburgwal. Convenient *wasserette* for those staying in the Red Light District, Oude Zijd, or the northern Nieuwe Zijd. Wash and dry €7. Self-service only. Open M-F 8:30am-7pm, Sa 10am-5pm. Cash only.

Wasserette-Stomerij De Eland, Elandsgracht 59 (☎625 0731), in the Jordaan. From the Westermarkt tram stop, turn left at Prinsengracht; after the second bridge, turn right at Elandsgracht. Self-service only. €5 for 4kg, €7 for 6kg. Open M-Tu and Th-F 8am-8pm, W 8am-6pm, Sa 9am-5pm.

EMERGENCY AND COMMUNICATIONS

EMERGENCY

Emergencies: ☎112. Free from all pay phones.

POLICE

Hoofdbureau van Politie, Elandsgracht 117 (☎559 9111), at the intersection with Marnixstraat. Police headquarters. Call the national non-emergency line, ☎0900 8844, to be connected to the station nearest you or to the rape crisis department.

CRISIS LINES

General counseling at Telephone Helpline (☎675 7575). Open 24hr. Rape crisis hotline (☎612 0245) staffed M-F 10:30am-11pm, Sa-Su 3:30-11pm. Drug counseling at the Jellinek Clinic (☎570 2378). Open M-F 9am-5pm.

AIDS Helpline (☎0800 022 2220). Advice and information about AIDS. Open M-F 2-10pm.

HIV-Plus Line (☎685 0055). Information about HIV and help for those worried about the virus. Open M, W, F 1-4pm, Tu and Th 8-10:30pm.

LATE-NIGHT PHARMACIES

Those looking for a pharmacy should keep their eyes out for an *apotheek* sign. Most are open Monday through Friday 8:30am-5:30pm and sell toiletries, first-aid supplies, and condoms in addition to filling prescriptions. The city's two major chains are **Nassau Apotheek** and **Da Apotheek.** While no single dedicated 24hr. pharmacy exists in the city, the 24hr. Afdeling Inlichtingen Apotheken hotline (☎694 8709) will direct you to the nearest pharmacy.

MEDICAL SERVICES

Academisch Medisch Centrum, Meibergdreef 9 (☎566 9111). A clinic easily accessible by bus #59, 60, 120, or 158 from Centraal (ask the driver to announce the medical center). Arranges for hospital care.

Centrale Doktorsdienst (☎592 3355). 24hr. medical help for non-urgent matters. English-speaking staff will advise on appropriate treatment.

Kruispost Medisch Helpcentrum, Oudezijds Voorburgwal 129 (☎624 9031). From Centraal Station, turn left at the Victoria Hotel and follow the street until Oudezijds Voorburgwal on your right. This walk-in clinic offers first aid to uninsured travelers only. Open daily 7am-9pm.

STD Line, Groenburgwal 44 (☎555 5822), offers phone counseling and, if you call ahead for an appointment, a free testing clinic. Open for calls M-F 9am-12:30pm and 1:30-5:30pm.

Tourist Medical Service (☎592 3355). Offers 24hr. referrals for visitors to Amsterdam.

INTERNET ACCESS

Internet access is fairly abundant in Amsterdam, but spacious Internet cafes are hard to come by. Most Internet access can be found in the city's numerous coffee shops. The following all have more than five computers and are sure to meet your needs, whether you're a gamer or a scholar.

easyInternetcafé, Damrak 33 (☎320 8082; www.easyeverything.com). Houses webcams and 144 PCs on several floors. €1 per 22min., €6 for 24hr., €10 for 1 week, €22 for 20 days. Open daily 9am-10pm.

The Mad Processor, Kinkerstraat 11-13 (☎421 1482; www.madprocessor.com), in Oud-West. Open later than most Internet spots in Amsterdam and boasts a beautiful canal-side location. Gamers and geeks will love the Mad Processor for having the newest computer games plus a hip-hop soundtrack. Play your favorites while meeting local players. It's also one of the few spots with outlets for plugging in your laptop and floppy disk drives. High-speed Internet on your laptop or their desktops €4 per hr. Printing €0.50 per page. Open daily noon-2am. Cash only.

Cyber Cafe Amsterdam, Nieuwendijk 19. From Centraal, turn right at the Victoria Hotel, left at Martelaarsgracht, and right on Nieuwendijk. This is a crowded yet personable cyber cafe with Internet (€1 per 30min.) at 12 computers. Open M-Th and Su 10am-1am, F-Sa 10am-3am. Cash only.

Internet Cafe, Martelaarsgracht 11 (☎627 1052; www.internetcafe.nl). From Centraal, turn right at the Victoria Hotel and then left on Martelaarsgracht. 30min. of speedy Internet €1. 20min. of Internet ½ off with drink purchase (€1.60-5). Open M-Th and Su 9am-1am, F-Sa 9am-3am.

POST OFFICES

Post offices are generally open Monday through Friday 9am-5pm and sometimes Saturday 10am-1:30pm. Larger branches may stay open later. Post offices can be recognized by their red-and-blue signs and often house a postbank where you can exchange currency. For further info, call the information hotline (☎0800 0417). For information on mail rates and delivery, see p. 47.

Hoofdpostkantoor, Singel 250, at Raadhuisstraat. Main post office. Open M-W and F 9am-6pm, Th 9am-8pm, Sa 10am-1:30pm.

ACCOMMODATIONS

Many of the accommodations in these listings are converted canal houses with unbelievably steep staircases. Although many of Amsterdam's canal-side hotels and hostels are criticized for their tight quarters, they offer affordable accommodations highlighted by beautiful views. What they sacrifice in space, canal-side locales compensate for with unparalleled access to the beautiful side of the city.

Unless otherwise indicated, these lodgings do not have elevators, which means that you will likely have to lug your baggage up at least two imposing flights of stairs. That mammoth suitcase on wheels won't seem so convenient while crawling up to the fourth floor—when packing, consider a backpack or two smaller pieces of luggage instead. Some of the shared bathrooms have antechambers so you can get dressed fresh from the shower. Shower shoes to prevent athlete's foot are also essential, and those squeamish about nudity should also pack a big towel.

Many of the smaller hotels in Amsterdam only accept credit cards with a hefty surcharge of 3-6.5%. These establishments are not trying to cheat their customers, nor are they afraid of last-minute cancellations. Card companies make it difficult for credit cards to be worthwhile for small establishments, so these hotels try to charge patrons the same amount that the company charges them. We attempt to list all surcharges at all hotels, but even ones without extra charges will provide incentives like free breakfast or cheap drinks at their in-house bars as encouragement for customers to pay in cash. Some hotels will require full payment for your entire stay up front. The summer months and the few days before Christmas until New Year's Day are usually considered to be the high season, when hostel and hotel prices are higher.

For each neighborhood, hostels, hotels, and B&Bs are listed together in descending order of quality. Since this is Amsterdam, we have indicated where hotels are specifically for ☑GLBT patrons, though it is against the law in Amsterdam for establishments to discriminate based on sexual orientation.

HOSTELS

Many hostels are laid out dorm-style, often with large single-sex rooms and bunk beds, although private rooms that sleep two to four are becoming more common. They sometimes have kitchens and utensils for your use, bike or moped rentals, storage areas, transportation to airports, breakfast and other meals, laundry facilities, and Internet access. There can be drawbacks: some hostels close during certain daytime "lockout" hours, have a curfew, don't accept reservations, impose a maximum stay, or, less frequently, require that you do chores. In the Netherlands, a dorm bed in a hostel will average around €20-30 and a private room around €40-70. To find a good deal, see our listings below or try **www.hostels-amsterdam.nl.**

 A HOSTELER'S BILL OF RIGHTS. There are certain standard features that we do not include in our hostel listings. Unless we state otherwise, you can expect that every hostel has no lockout, no curfew, a kitchen, free hot showers, some system of secure luggage storage, and no key deposit.

HOSTELLING INTERNATIONAL

Joining the youth hostel association in your own country (listed below) automatically grants you membership privileges in **Hostelling International (HI)**, a federation of national hosteling associations. HI hostels are scattered throughout the Netherlands and offer discounted prices to members. HI's umbrella organization's website (www.hihostels.com), which lists the web addresses and phone numbers of all national associations, can be a great place to begin researching hosteling in a specific region. Other comprehensive hosteling websites include www.hostels.com and www.hostelplanet.com.

Most HI hostels also honor **guest memberships**—you'll get a blank card with space for six validation stamps. Each night you'll pay a nonmember supplement (one-sixth the membership fee) and earn one guest stamp; get six stamps and you're a member. This system works well in most of Western Europe, but you may need to remind the hostel reception. A new membership benefit is the FreeNites program, which allows hostelers to gain points toward free rooms. Most student travel agencies (p. 32) sell HI cards, as do all of the national hosteling organizations listed below. All prices listed below are valid for **one-year memberships** unless otherwise noted.

Australian Youth Hostels Association (AYHA), 422 Kent St., Sydney, NSW 200 (☎02 9261 1111; www.yha.com.au). AUS$52, under 18 AUS$19.

Hostelling International-Canada (HI-C), 205 Catherine St., Ste. 400, Ottawa, ON K2P 1C3 (☎613-237-7884; www.hihostels.ca). CDN$35, under 18 free.

An Óige (Irish Youth Hostel Association), 61 Mountjoy St., Dublin 7 (☎830 4555; www.irelandyha.org). €20, under 18 €10.

Hostelling International Northern Ireland (HINI), 22-32 Donegall Rd., Belfast BT12 5JN (☎02890 32 47 33; www.hini.org.uk). UK£15, under 25 UK£10.

Youth Hostels Association of New Zealand Inc. (YHANZ), Level 1, 166 Moorhouse Ave., P.O. Box 436, Christchurch (☎0800 278 299 from NZ only or 03 379 9970; www.yha.org.nz). NZ$40, under 18 free.

Scottish Youth Hostels Association (SYHA), 7 Glebe Cres., Stirling FK8 2JA (☎01786 89 14 00; www.syha.org.uk). UK£8, under 18 UK£4.

Youth Hostels Association (England and Wales), Trevelyan House, Dimple Rd., Matlock, Derbyshire DE4 3YH (☎08707 708 868; www.yha.org.uk). UK£16, under 26 UK£10.

Hostelling International-USA, 8401 Colesville Rd., Ste. 600, Silver Spring, MD 20910., USA (☎301-495-1240; www.hiayh.org). US$28, under 18 free.

 BOOKING HOSTELS ONLINE. One of the easiest ways to ensure you've got a bed for the night is by reserving online. Click to the **Hostelworld** booking engine through **www.letsgo.com,** and you'll have access to bargain accommodations from Argentina to Zimbabwe with no added commission.

HOTELS, GUESTHOUSES, AND PENSIONS

Hotel singles in the Netherlands cost about €50-80 per night, doubles €70-100. You'll typically share a hall bathroom; a private bathroom will cost extra, as may hot showers. Some hotels offer "full pension" (all meals) and "half pension" (no lunch). Smaller **guesthouses** and **pensions** are often cheaper than hotels. If you make **reservations** in writing, indicate your night of arrival and the number of nights you plan to stay. The hotel will send you a confirmation and may request payment for the first night. Often it is easiest to make reservations over the phone with a credit card.

OTHER TYPES OF ACCOMMODATIONS

BED & BREAKFASTS (B&BS)

For a cozy alternative to impersonal hotel rooms, B&Bs (private homes with rooms available to travelers) range from acceptable to sublime. Rooms in B&Bs

generally cost €80-100 for a single and €120-160 for a double in the Netherlands. Any number of websites provide listings for B&Bs; check out **InnFinder** (www.inncrawler.com), **InnSite** (www.innsite.com), **Pamela Lanier's Bed & Breakfast Guide Online** (www.lanierbb.com), **www.bedandbreakfast.com**, or **www.find-an-amsterdam-bed-and-breakfast.nl.**

UNIVERSITY DORMS

Many **colleges** and **universities** open their residence halls to travelers when school is not in session; some do so even during term-time. Getting a room may take a couple of phone calls and require advanced planning, but rates tend to be low, and many offer free local calls and Internet access. Some Dutch institutes of higher learning worth contacting are the University of Amsterdam (☎ 020 525 8080), Utrecht University (☎ 030 253 3550), and Leiden University (☎ 071 527 2727).

HOME EXCHANGES AND HOSPITALITY CLUBS

Home exchange offers the traveler various types of homes (houses, apartments, condominiums, villas, even castles in some cases) plus the opportunity to live like a native and to cut down on accommodation fees. For more information, contact HomeExchange.com Inc., P.O. Box 787, Hermosa Beach, CA 90254, USA (☎ 310-798-3864 or toll-free 800-877-8723; www.homeexchange.com) or Intervac International Home Exchange (☎ 026 334 3272; www.intervac.com).

Hospitality clubs link their members with individuals or families abroad who are willing to host travelers for free or for a small fee to promote cultural exchange and general good karma. In exchange, members usually must be willing to host travelers in their own homes; a small membership fee may also be required. **The Hospitality Club** (www.hospitality-club.org) is a good place to start. **Servas** (www.servas.org) is an established, more formal, peace-based organization and requires a fee and an interview to join. An Internet search will find many similar organizations, some of which cater to special interests (e.g., women, GLBT travelers, or members of certain professions). As always, use common sense when planning to stay with or host someone you do not know.

LONG-TERM ACCOMMODATIONS

Travelers planning to stay in the Netherlands for extended periods of time may find it most cost-effective to rent an **apartment**. A basic one-bedroom (or

FROM THE ROAD

BEDUTCHED?

It looks like English, smells like English, and even sounds like English (a little), but once you arrive in Amsterdam, you'll soon realize that Dutch is definitely not English. However, after months glued to the strange vowel combinations and odd "j" placements in this book, I think I can spare you the frustration of having to learn it all from painful experience.

Brug: A bridge.
Bruin cafe: Brown cafe, a very chill Dutch nightspot.
Centrum: Downtown.
Eetcafe/Eethuis: An eatery! See **Food Translation,** p. 127.
Gezellig: Cozy. Aww.
Gracht: Canal. Don't fall in.
Hof: Courtyard. Ideal for quiet relaxation.
Hofje: An almshouse. Ideal for quiet relaxation (really).
Kerk: Church.
Plein: Nothin' fancy; a town square.
Rijwiel: Bicycle.
Shawarma: OK, not Dutch; a Middle Eastern shaved meat that's everywhere in Amsterdam.
Straat: A suffix that's everywhere on Dutch maps, and, no surprise, it means street.
Strip: Currency for public transportation; part of a *strippenkaart.*
Verdampers: Vaporizers to squeeze every drop of THC from your marijuana. Careful.
Wasserette: Laundromat.
Weg: A lane; not quite a *straat.*
    —*Nathaniel Rakich*

studio) apartment in Amsterdam will range €500-1500 per month. Besides the rent itself, prospective tenants usually are also required to front a security deposit (frequently one month's rent). The websites **www.craigslist.org, www.find-an-amsterdam-apartment.nl, www.simplyamsterdam-apartments.nl,** and **www.kamernet.nl** are popular places to find listings. Expat websites, newspaper ads, and online realtors also list long-term accommodations; be sure to ask for pictures and the exact location of the apartment before agreeing to rent. See p. 52 for more websites.

BY PRICE

UNDER €36 (❶)

▨ Aivergo Youth Hostel (106)	NZ
Bob's Youth Hostel (106)	NZ
Budget Hotel Tamara (107)	NZ
De Witte Tulp Hostel (105)	RLD
Durty Nelly's Hostel (104)	RLD
▨ Flying Pig Downtown (106)	NZ
Flying Pig Palace (116)	MV
▨ Frédéric Rent a Bike (108)	SVB
Frisco Inn (105)	RLD
Hostel Cosmos (107)	NZ
▨ Hotel Abba (114)	WO
Hotel Aspen (109)	CRW
▨ Hotel Bema (116)	MV
Hotel Brian (107)	NZ
Hotel Groenendael (107)	NZ
▨ Hotel Impala (111)	LP
Hotel My Home (108)	SVB
Hotel Old Quarter (104)	RLD
Hotel Pax (110)	CRW
Hotel Wijnnobel (117)	MV
International Budget Hostel (112)	LP
Marnix Hotel (113)	LP
Meeting Point Youth Hostel (105)	RLD
The Shelter Jordan (114)	JD
▨ Stayokay Amst. Stadsdoelen (103)	OZ
▨ Stayokay Amst. Vondelpark (116)	MV
Tourist Inn (107)	NZ
The Winston Hotel (105)	RLD

€36-55 (❷)

▼ANCO Hotel and Bar (104)	RLD
▨ City Hotel (113)	RP
De Oranje Tulp (108)	NZ
▨ Hemp Hotel (110)	CCR
Hotel Asterisk (110)	CCR
Hotel Belga (109)	CRW
▨ Hotel Brouwer (106)	NZ
Hotel Continental (108)	NZ
Hotel Crystal (115)	WO
Hotel Di Ann (110)	CRW
Hotel Hegra (109)	CRW
Hotel La Boheme (112)	LP
Hotel Museumzicht (116)	MV

Hotel Plantage (119)	JP
▨ Hotel Royal Taste (103)	OZ
Hotel The Crown (104)	RLD
Hotel Titus (113)	LP
Hotel Van Onna (114)	JD
Hotel Vivaldi (118)	LP
Jupiter Hotel (115)	WO
Leidseplein Hotel (113)	LP
Old Nickel (104)	RLD
▨ Quentin Hotel (111)	LP
Westertoren Hotel (110)	CRW

€56-77 (❸)

Apple Inn Hotel (118)	MV
▨ Bicycle Hotel (118)	DP
Euphemia Budget Hotel (110)	CCR
▨ Freeland (111)	LP
▨ ▼The Golden Bear (110)	CCR
The Greenhouse Effect Hotel (104)	RLD
Hotel Acacia (114)	JD
Hotel Adolesce (119)	JP
Hotel Barbacan (119)	JP
Hotel Bellington (117)	MV
▨ Hotel Clemens (109)	CRW
Hotel d'Amsterdam (115)	WO
Hotel de la Haye (112)	LP
Hotel Kap (111)	CCR
Hotel Kooyk (113)	LP
Hotel Monopole (113)	RP
Hotel Omega (117)	MV
Hotel Rembrandt (119)	JP
Hotel Vijaya (105)	RLD
▨ King Hotel (111)	LP
▨ Luckytravellers Fantasia Hotel (118)	JP
▨ Nadia Hotel (109)	CRW
Ramenas Hotel (108)	SVB
Thorbecke Hotel (113)	RP

€78-100 (❹)

Hotel de Paris (112)	LP
Hotel Europa 92 (117)	MV
Hotel Hoksbergen (107)	NZ
Hotel Internationaal (105)	RLD
Hotel Princess (115)	WO

Hotel Rokin (107)	NZ
Hotel Sarphati (118)	DP
🏠 Wiechmann Hotel (109)	CRW

ABOVE €100 (❺)	
The Bridge Hotel (119)	JP
🏠 Hotel de Filosoof (114)	WO
Hotel Nova (106)	NZ
Tulip Inn Amsterdam Centre (115)	WO

CRW Canal Ring West **CCR** Central Canal Ring **DP** De Pijp **JP** Jodenbuurt and Plantage **JD** Jordaan **LP** Leidseplein **MV** Museumplein and Vondelpark **NZ** Nieuwe Zijd **OZ** Oude Zijd **RLD** Red Light District **RP** Rembrandtplein **SVB** Scheepvaartbuurt **WO** Westerpark and Oud-West

BY NEIGHBORHOOD

OUDE ZIJD

Serenity is not easy to find in the Oude Zijd. Especially on weekends, crowds stay out well into the wee hours of the morning. If you want peace and quiet, try to get a hotel at the southern end of the **Kloveniersburgwal** or **Oudezijds Achterburgwal,** which are still within easy walking distance of the area's attractions but far enough away to offer some respite. Just be careful that you're getting quality for your money; many of the hotels in the Oude Zijd target young, naive tourists.

see map p. 340

🏠 **Stayokay Amsterdam Stadsdoelen,** Kloveniersburgwal 97 (☎624 6832; www.stay-okay.com/stadsdoelen). Tram #4, 9, 16, 24, or 25 to Muntplein. From Muntplein, proceed down Nieuwe Doelenstraat; Kloveniersburgwal will be on your right over the bridge. Just outside the chaos of the Red Light District but still a stone's throw away. A good hostel if you want to stay in (relatively) quiet environs. This branch of the chain sleeps 158 and provides clean, drug-free lodgings for reasonable prices. Don't expect the modern digs of most Stayokays; Stadsdoelen is housed in a genuine canal house, and rooms feel older and more worn (although still comfortable and clean). Pool table, TV room, and bar open 6pm-midnight (2nd drink free with a ticket from reception). Discounted museum passes and transportation tickets. Breakfast, lockers, and linens included. Locker deposit €20 or passport. Kitchen and laundry facilities. Internet access €5 per hr. Reception 24hr. Co-ed or single-sex 8- to 20-bed dorms €24.50-26.50. €2.50 HI discount. MC/V. ❶

🏠 **Hotel Royal Taste,** Oudezijds Achterburgwal 47 (☎623 2478; www.hotelroyal-taste.nl). Just across the canal from the Red Light District (neon sign and all). Provides clean, comfortable, and almost fancy accommodations at reasonable prices. Popular with British weekenders and American tourists. Bar downstairs features a big-screen TV sporting football or rugby games. Expansion into 2 nearby buildings planned for 2008. Breakfast €7.50. Singles with sink €50, with full bath €60; doubles with bath €100-110, with canal view €120; triples €150-165; quads €190. Cash only. ❷

RED LIGHT DISTRICT

In the middle of the action, many of the several digs along **Warmoesstraat** offer the potential for a lot of fun, especially the establishments that keep their downstairs bars open late for guests. However, the accommodations here are as expensive as any in the rest of the city. They're usually booked solid through the summer months, and while it may initially seem convenient to shack up across the street from a brothel, the proximity to the heart of the Red Light District can become a

see map p. 340

little distracting and disorienting. These hotels are usually popular places for big groups of men, so the atmosphere can be a bit unruly—although, for some visitors, this can mean an even better time.

 ROOM FOR ONE MORE. If stuck looking for a hotel room or hostel bed in Amsterdam, there are many places to turn. Several hostels line **Warmoesstraat,** and there are several budget hotels along **Raadhuisstraat** in the Canal Ring West. Another good resource is **Hotelrunners,** Warmoesstraat 88, a budget hotel reservation service. (☎330 0233; www.hotelrunners.com.)

Hotel The Crown, Oudezijds Voorburgwal 21 (☎626 9664; www.hotelthecrown.com). This Moroccan-owned hotel provides handsome digs in a fun, if at times rowdy, atmosphere. Loads of British tourists stay here for its convenience to the action. Bar open M-Th and Su until 1am, F-Sa until 3am, with pool table and dartboard. Beer €4 per pint. Mixed drinks from €2.50. Beds €40-55 per person in rooms that sleep 1-3 people; rooms with hall showers €10 less. AmEx/MC/V. ❷

The Greenhouse Effect Hotel, Warmoesstraat 55 (☎624 4974; www.the-greenhouse-effect.com). A funky hotel (with in-house coffee shop) popular with Amsterdam's drug tourists. Each room is individually decorated with a different artistic theme (Arabian, Chinatown, Tropical, Outer Space, etc.); the hotel's repeat customers all have favorite rooms they come back to. Hotel guests are treated to an all-day Happy hour at the downstairs bar, which doubles as reception (pints €2.30). See website for discounts. Rooms located above, across the street from, and a 5min. walk from the bar. Singles €65, with bath €75; doubles €95; triples with bath €130; 2- to 4-person apartments €135-190. AmEx/MC/V. ❸

Durty Nelly's Hostel, Warmoesstraat 115-117 (☎638 0125; www.xs4all.nl/~nellys). From Centraal Station, go south on Damrak, turn right on Brugsteeg, and veer right on Warmoesstraat; Nelly's is 2 blocks down on the left. Cozy hostel above its own Irish pub (p. 226) sleeps 42 in clean, co-ed accommodations. Popular with young travelers. Breakfast and linens included. Locker deposit €10. Reception 24hr. at bar, where guests can drink after hours. Internet reservations only. Dorms €25-45. AmEx/MC/V. ❶

ANCO Hotel and Bar, Oudezijds Voorburgwal 55 (☎624 1126; www.ancohotel.nl). A 5min. walk from the leather district. This extremely well-maintained, ▼**gay,** men-only hotel has crisp apartment-style accommodations, canal views, and free cable TV. The downstairs bar (open 9am-10pm), lined with erotic posters, is a good springboard for a wild evening of clubbing. Breakfast included. 3- to 4-person dorms €43; singles €65; doubles €90, with private bathroom, kitchenette, and minibar €135. AmEx/MC/V for stays over 2 nights. ❷

Hotel Old Quarter, Warmoesstraat 22 (☎626 6429; www.oldquarter.com). Smaller rooms are snug but homey; larger ones are clean, classy, and bright. All rooms include TV and phone, and some have a strikingly good view of the canal. Biggest attraction: a small elevator that makes it wheelchair-accessible, a rarity in this city of steep-stairwelled canal houses. All triples and quads have cable TV. Downstairs *bruin cafe* provides a great place to watch a football match (kitchen open 9am-11pm). M night jazz jam sessions. Breakfast included. Reception 24hr. Singles from €35; doubles from €70; triples from €125; quads €160. AmEx/MC/V. ❶

Old Nickel, Nieuwebrugsteeg 11 (☎624 1912). From Centraal, turn left onto Prins Hendrikkade and then bear right onto Nieuwebrugsteeg. Magnetic hotel in a quiet corner of the neighborhood. Downstairs bar, with deep oak paneling and heavy red curtains, gives the hotel's reception a regal feel at a budget price. Single rooms are tiny; larger rooms are sunny. Breakfast included. 4am curfew; no curfew in additional rooms down the street. All facilities are shared. Singles €40-50; doubles €80-100; triples €105-150; quads €140-200. AmEx/MC/V. ❷

Frisco Inn, Beursstraat 5 (☎ 620 1610). From Centraal Station, go south on Damrak, left at Brugsteeg, and right onto Beursstraat. Small, central hotel behind the Beurs van Berlage. On one of the quietest streets in the Red Light District. Rents 27 beds in solid but small newly renovated rooms. Downstairs bar sells beer (€2). Breakfast €4-10. All rooms have new bathrooms, safe, and TV. Reception 24hr. at bar. Singles and doubles €35-50 per person. AmEx/MC/V. ●

The Winston Hotel, Warmoesstraat 129 (☎ 623 1380; www.winston.nl). A budget hotel that goes out of its way to make sure your experience is unique. Each room in the Winston is individually decorated in a different artistic style. A perfect location between Dam Sq. and the Red Light District. Visit **Club Winston** (p. 226), an affiliated happening nightspot, just next door. Breakfast included. Dorms €20-30; singles €60-75; doubles €80-120; triples €90-140; quads €110-177. AmEx/MC/V. ●

Hotel Vijaya, Oudezijds Voorburgwal 44 (☎ 626 9406 or 638 0102; www.hotelvijaya.com). Clean and basic rooms on the fringe of the bustle, but still very much within the Red Light District. Enjoy the casual and reasonably priced Indian restaurant downstairs for a 10% discount. All rooms with TV and private bathroom. Breakfast included. Singles €75; doubles €110; triples €145; quads €165; quints €210. In low season, all about €10 less. AmEx/MC/V. ❸

Hotel Internationaal, Warmoesstraat 1-3 (☎ 624 5520; www.hotelinter.nl), located right at the start of Warmoesstraat, close to Centraal Station. Downstairs bar has old-time charm (open M-Th and Su 10:30am-1am, F-Sa 10:30am-3am). Rooms themselves are small but very clean, adding a touch of personality with attractively exposed rafters. Breakfast €7.50. Doubles and triples €85-150. AmEx/MC/V. ❹

Meeting Point Youth Hostel, Warmoesstraat 14 (☎ 627 7499; www.hostel-meetingpoint.nl). A no-frills hostel popular with young backpackers. 111 beds available in 8- to 18-bed increments. Newly renovated bathrooms on the top 2 floors. Downstairs bar exclusively for guests open 24hr., with pool table and dartboard. Breakfast €2.50, served until noon. Lockers (large lockable barrels) €3. Towel rental €0.50. Internet access €1 per 30min. 18+. Check-out 10am. Dorms €16-21. AmEx/MC/V. ●

De Witte Tulp Hostel, Warmoesstraat 87 (☎ 625 5974; www.wittetulp.nl). Very basic budget digs without even the hint of luxury; these rooms at these prices should be used only as a last resort. Mind-bogglingly small but private rooms. Downstairs pub serves drinks (beer €4.50 per pint; liquor €3.50-5.50 during the afternoon Happy hour) and snacks; hotel guests receive a 25% discount on all drinks and food. Shared facilities. Breakfast €3.50. Linens included. 6-bed dorms Apr.-Sept. €35; Oct.-Mar. €20. Doubles €45. Weekends €5 more. AmEx/MC/V. ●

 THE REAL DEAL. Throughout Amsterdam, but especially around the Oude Zijd and the Red Light District, many hostels and hotels have bars on the ground floor. It is common practice for these bars to close to the public around 2am but to keep the facility open later for hotel patrons. Most of these bars, however, aren't nearly as good as their stand-alone counterparts. –Ken Saathoff

NIEUWE ZIJD

A good traditional hotel is hard to find in the Nieuwe Zijd: largely disappointing options run from grimy to pricey. While some of the Nieuwe Zijd accommodations call themselves "inns" or "hotels," many listed below offer dorm-style rooms or small, budget rooms without ensuite bathrooms. For a solid room to yourself, try the apartments at Bob's or the private rooms in Hotel Brouwer.

see map p. 340

Flying Pig Downtown, Nieuwendijk 100 (☎ 420 6822; www.flyingpig.nl). From the main entrance of Centraal Station, walk toward Damrak. Pass the Victoria Hotel and take the 1st alley on your right. At the end of that alley, you'll find Nieuwendijk. Exceptionally friendly staff, knockout location, and a stylish and hip decor make the Flying Pig Downtown a perennial favorite among party-hardy backpackers. Almost always a full house: plan on booking ahead or at least try to check in by 10am. Caters to a younger set, mostly 18- to 28-year olds who flock here for the spacious dorms. Sprawling, gorgeous social space and bar filled with pillows is ideal for reading and watching the parade go by on the avenue outside the bar (open M-F until 4am, Sa-Su until 5am). Tu and F-Sa loud DJs spin tunes. Breakfast included; also a kitchen where you can make your own meals. Key deposit, including a locker, €10. Linens included. Free Internet access. One women-only dorm available. 16- to 22-bed dorms €21; 8- to 10-bed dorms €24; 4- to 6-bed dorms €27; singles and twins €76. ISIC holders receive a free beer at the bar in summer and a 5% discount in winter. AmEx/MC/V. ❶

Hotel Brouwer, Singel 83 (☎ 624 6358; www.hotelbrouwer.nl). From Centraal Station, cross the water, go right on Prins Hendrikkade, and turn left onto Singel. Small hotel right off the canal run by the same family for 3 generations; easily the best hotel in the neighborhood. 8 gorgeously restored rooms, each with private bathroom, canal view, and named for a Dutch painter. Choose from Vermeer, Van Gogh, Mondrian, and Escher, among others. Elevator. Breakfast included in a charming dark-wood dining room. Rooms for 1 person €55; for 2 people €90; for 3 people €115. Cash and traveler's checks only. ❷

Aivergo Youth Hostel, Spuistraat 6 (☎ 421 3670). An Arabian Nights theme permeates brightly tiled bathrooms and burnt sienna walls sprinkled with jewels for a uniformly cool vibe. Huge, perfectly clean dorm rooms decorated with gauzy purple curtains. Morning coffee and tea free. No breakfast, but a microwave and fridge are available for guest use. Sheets and towels included in female dorms; €1 in mixed dorms. Free lockers and Internet access. Dorms €25-40; sole double €60. Cash only. ❶

 TIP

UNDER THE RAINBOW. Many, though not all, GLBT establishments customarily hang a rainbow flag outside or over their door, while some prominently display pink triangles. Don't assume, however, that all rainbow flags signal that an establishment is gay-friendly; rainbow flags can also represent peace.

Bob's Youth Hostel, Nieuwezijds Voorburgwal 92 (☎ 623 0063). From Centraal Station, head down the rightmost artery and veer left at Martelaarsgracht; bear left when it splits and becomes Nieuwezijds Voorburgwal. Provides bare-bones necessities to its backpack-toting clientele. For a more private experience in a similarly great location, the hostel also rents spacious, furnished apartments with shared kitchens. The subterranean reception area, covered in drawings, notes, and graffiti, doubles as a guest living room. Free luggage storage. Breakfast (eggs, toast, and jam) included. Lockers included with a €10 deposit. Linens included, but bring a towel. Key deposit €10. 2-night min. weekend stay; 7-night max. stay. Reception 8am-3am. No reservations; arrive before 10am or call early to stand a chance of getting a room. 1 women-only dorm. Dorms €21; doubles with shared bath €70; triples with private bath and shared kitchen €90. ❶

Hotel Nova, Nieuwezijds Voorburgwal 276 (☎ 623 0066; www.novahotel.nl). Exceptionally large, clean accommodations a stone's throw from the city center and the pleasant Spui. The price is certainly not budget friendly, but these slick, modern rooms may provide much-needed respite from other dingier options. Make sure to get good directions to your room at reception: Nova is a 60-room labyrinth. All rooms come with bathroom, fridge, phone, and TV. Breakfast included. Singles €120; doubles €165; triples €205; quads €240. AmEx/D/MC/V. ❺

Tourist Inn, Spuistraat 52 (☎421 5841; www.tourist-inn.nl). From Centraal Station, turn right at Prins Hendrikkade and left at Martelaarsgracht. A couple of blocks ahead, keep right onto Spuistraat. A great, friendly value for backpackers and families. Its 11 dorms and 11 private rooms are comfortable places to roost. A recent major renovation means modern bathrooms, new TVs, carpets, lockers, and furniture; the hotel feels clean and newer than most nearby options. Small elevator. Breakfast included. Laundry facilities around the corner; linens and a towel included. Lockers €1.20 per day, plus €30 deposit. Reception 24hr. Walk-ins welcome, but reservations are strongly advised, particularly in summer. Dorms €20-35; singles €50-100; doubles €80-90; triples €105-150; quads €140; quints €125-175; 6-person rooms €150-210. Prices depend on season. AmEx/MC/V. ❶

Hotel Groenendael, Nieuwendijk 15 (☎624 4822; www.hotelgroenendael.com). Turn right on the main street out of the station, go left at Martelaarsgracht, and then head right on Nieuwendijk. Mellow hotel near Centraal Station on one of the area's most commercial streets. Uses shaggy throw rugs for tablecloths in the dining room. Rooms—some with balconies, all with sink—are in fairly good shape. Some overlook Nieuwendijk and can be a little noisy, especially on weekends. Plenty of small, clean bathrooms, mostly off shared hallways. Breakfast included and served 8:30-10am in a lounge decorated with international knick-knacks. Free towels and access to safe. Room key deposit €5. Singles €35; doubles €60; triples €90. Cash and traveler's checks only. ❶

Budget Hotel Tamara, Nieuwezijds Voorburgwal 144 (☎624 2484; www.hostelsclub.com). Friendly Irish staff welcomes backpackers to Amsterdam in true budget style. Guests get a free drink at the Blarney Stone Pub. Free tea and coffee in the morning. Small lounge on 1st fl. has Sky TV, beaming mostly sports games. All rooms with washbasin. Internet access €2 per 30min. Reception 24hr. Dorms €30; singles €45; doubles €50; triples €75; quads €100. Cash only. ❶

Hostel Cosmos, Nieuwe Nieuwstraat 17 (☎625 2438; www.hostelcosmos.com), between Nieuwendijk and Nieuwezijds Voorburgwal, a few blocks north of Dam Sq. 30 beds in 6 clean rooms. The staff is very friendly and has a large collection of DVDs, which they are happy to play for you in the reception area; their plan is to install DVD players in all rooms. Some rooms with TV. Free maps and free walking tour. Ages 18-35 only. Breakfast included. Lockers €1. Internet access €1 per 30min. 7-night max. stay. Reception 24hr. Reserve online. 8-person dorms €27.40-32.20; 6-person dorms €28.40-33.40; doubles €38.40-44.50. Prices depend on season. Cash only. ❶

Hotel Rokin, Rokin 73 (☎626 7456; www.rokinhotel.com). Centrally located just a few blocks south of Dam Sq. Clean, comfortable digs come with bathroom, safe, and TV. Continental breakfast included in a pleasant dining room. Free Internet access and Wi-Fi. Singles M-Th €85-110, F-Su €90-110; doubles M-Th €115-135, F-Su €140-165; triples M-Th €150-175, F-Su €175-190. Prices depend on season. AmEx/MC/V. ❹

Hotel Hoksbergen, Singel 301 (☎626 6043; www.hotelhoksbergen.nl). Tram #1, 2, or 5 to Spui. On the east side of the Singel, between Rosmarijnsteeg and Paleisstraat. This quaint, 300-year-old canal house offers its patrons a bathroom, phone, and flat-screen TV in every room—not too bad at all, even if the price is steep for such tight quarters. Also provides apartments for larger parties. Full Dutch breakfast (breads, cheese, ham, and tea) included. Singles €84; doubles €95-119; triples €143; 4- to 6-person apartments €165. Oct.-Apr. prices are 15-20% lower. AmEx/MC/V with 5% surcharge. ❹

Hotel Brian, Singel 69 (☎624 4661; www.hotelbrian.com). From Centraal Station, turn right at the Victoria Hotel and then left onto Singel. Extremely basic communal digs in a friendly, low-key hotel. Beware of extremely tiny staircases. Picturesque canal-side location and low price make these tiny crash pads a little more interesting. Breakfast, coffee, and tea included all day. Free Internet access. Key deposit €20. Reception 8am-11pm. Singles €35-40; doubles €50-54; triples €75-81; quads €100-108. Prices depend on season. Cash only. ❶

Hotel Continental, Damrak 40-41 (☎ 622 3363; www.hotelcontinental.nl). Damrak location puts you right near the action, 5min. from Centraal Station. More upscale than standard budget digs, with small but comfy rooms that are decorated with more than a bit of style. Each of 26 rooms with TV and phone. Some doubles and triples have private bath. Reception 24hr. Check-in 2pm-midnight; call ahead if arriving later. Check-out 10am. 48hr. cancellation policy. Singles €50-110; twins €65-150; doubles €65-160; triples €85-190; quads €110-240. AmEx/MC/V with 5% surcharge. ❷

De Oranje Tulp, Damrak 32 (☎ 428 1618; www.oranjetulp.nl). Located 3min. down the main street heading straight out of Centraal and hidden above a restaurant. With the noise of Damrak within earshot, De Oranje Tulp may not be a 1st choice, but it can be an effective, centrally located crash pad following nights of excessive debauchery. Though the rooms are a bit dated and lack character, most have bath, and all have TV. Guests receive discounts on dinner in the restaurant downstairs. Breakfast included. Prices vary significantly by season. Singles €50-80; doubles €60-110; triples €90-150; quads €100-180; quints €125-225. AmEx/MC/V. ❷

SCHEEPVAARTBUURT

Just northwest of the city center, the Shipping Quarter is steps from the action of the Centrum and Centraal Station but far enough away to let those nesting here feel some distance from the madness.

see map p. 338

▨ **Frédéric Rent a Bike,** Brouwersgracht 78 (☎ 624 5509; www.frederic.nl). "Rent a Bike" is a loose term 'round Frédéric's parts— apparently, it can also mean hotel. The best option is to stay in 1 of 3 lived-in, homey, and cheerful rooms in the back of the rental shop—each named after a different painter (Chagall, Picasso, and Mondrian); 1 has private bath with sauna jets (and a water bed) while the other 2 share a bath. Upon your arrival, the staff will provide a complimentary map and tips on good restaurants and museums in the area. At reception, you'll also find a bar with drinks, rolling papers, smokes, games, soap, towels, and anything else you need. If the rooms are occupied, Frédéric can also book you a room, apartment, or houseboat in various privately listed locations around the city for a 15% commission. All but 1 of these have a kitchen or cooking space, so even with the commission you may be able to save money. Another cheap option is to stay with Frédéric's parents in 1 of 2 rooms in their home. Visit Frédéric's website for virtual tours of the accommodations, reservations, and lots of information about Amsterdam. In the apartments, linens are changed once per week. Reception 9am-6pm. Bikes €10 per day. *Chez* Frédéric's parents €35; singles €40-50; doubles €60-100; houseboats for 2-4 people €100-160. Apartments available for short-term stays from €140 for 2 people to €225 for 6. Cash only; AmEx/MC/V required for reservation. ❶

Ramenas Hotel, Haarlemmerdijk 61 (☎ 624 6030; www.hotelramenas.nl). Walk from Centraal Station along Nieuwendijk as it turns into Haarlemmerstraat and then Haarlemmerdijk. Above an average cafe of the same name, Ramenas rents simple rooms that get the job done. Clean hall bathrooms and comfortable rooms, although they are up some very steep steps. Ask for reception behind the bar in the cafe. Breakfast included. Reservations via website. Prices fluctuate depending on the time of week and the season. Doubles €65-100, with bath €70-125; triples €75-135/85-150; quads €120-200; quints €125-225. MC/V. ❸

Hotel My Home, Haarlemmerstraat 82 (☎ 624 2320; www.amsterdambudgethotel.com). From Centraal Station, head south on Nieuwezijds Voorburgwal, turn right on Nieuwendijk, and continue across the Singel; your new home is 1 block on your left. Budget digs in a friendly, low-frills environment. The hall bathrooms are clean, and the big social space gives the hotel a community feel. Breakfast, complete with a bottomless cup of coffee, included and served 8:30-10am. Friendly staff can provide complimentary maps as well as the inside scoop on the city scene. Linens and towels included. Free Internet and pool table in reception. Reception 8:30am-1pm and 6-11pm. Online reservations available. 4- to 5-person dorms €25; 3-person dorms €28-30; doubles €57, with shower €60. Cash only. ❶

BIKE-FRIENDLY BEDS. Bring your own bike to the **Bicycle Hotel** (p. 118). You can even park it in the bike parking garage across the street.

CANAL RING WEST

Despite the Canal Ring West's limited area, several small hotels have managed to squeeze into the neighborhood. Try to book at least two weeks in advance, especially when the weather heats up. Though most accommodations are expensive, some bargains still exist. **Raadhuisstraat,** near Westerkerk in the heart of the district, could be considered "hotel row," with eight hotels on the strip.

see map p. 338

Nadia Hotel, Raadhuisstraat 51 (☎620 1550; www.nadia.nl), on the corner of Raadhuisstraat and the Keizersgracht. Tram #13 or 17 to Westermarkt. One of the classiest hotels in the area. Elegantly decorated with an attentive staff. Each well-kept, cozy room includes TV, fridge, and safe. Breakfast and Wi-Fi included. Book 2-3 weeks in advance. Weekday high-season singles €75; doubles €115; triples €150. Higher prices for balcony or rooms with canal views and on weekends. AmEx/MC/V. ❸

Hotel Clemens, Raadhuisstraat 39 (☎624 6089; www.clemenshotel.nl). Tram #13 or 17 to Westermarkt. Of all the small hotels along Raadhuisstraat, this is one of the best for your money. Each well-kept room boasts a long list of luxuries: phone, fridge, TV, safe, shower, and hair dryer. Breakfast €5. Free Internet access; laptop rental available at reception (€8). Key deposit €20. 3-night min. stay on weekends. Only holds 20 guests, so book up to a month in advance. Singles €60; budget doubles €75; deluxe doubles €120; budget triples €130; deluxe triples €150. AmEx/MC/V. ❸

Hotel Hegra, Herengracht 269 (☎623 7877; www.hegrahotel.com). Tram #1, 2, or 5 to Dam. Follow Raadhuisstraat to Herengracht and turn left. Small family hotel on a lovely canal. 11 basic rooms, most with shower but no toilet. May seem claustrophobic, but no smaller than other canal-side hotels. Breakfast included. Singles €50; doubles €65; triples with bath €130. AmEx/MC/V. ❷

Hotel Aspen, Raadhuisstraat 31 (☎626 6714; www.hotelaspen.nl). Tram #6, 13, or 17 to Westermarkt. Most of the snug rooms have bath (except singles and 1 small double). Reserve 2 weeks in advance via email. Singles €35; doubles €50-80; triples €85-95; quads €95-110. Cash only in summer. AmEx/MC/V in winter. ❶

Hotel Belga, Hartenstraat 8 (☎624 9080; www.hotelnet.nl). Tram #1, 2, or 5 to Dam. Walk away from the palace on Raadhuisstraat. Turn left at Herengracht and take the 1st right on Hartenstraat. Rooms are large and sunny with TV, phone, and safe. Shared bath. Ask for a canal view. Breakfast included. Reception 8am-midnight. Singles €41-57; doubles €62-84; triples with bath €115. AmEx/MC/V. ❷

Wiechmann Hotel, Prinsengracht 328-332 (☎626 3321; www.hotelwiechmann.nl). Tram #1, 2, or 5 to Prinsengracht; turn right and walk along the left side of the canal. "Quaint" really does best describe Wiechmann, decorated with impressive antiques, including a large grandfather clock and full knight's armor. Features a lovely living room for reading and relaxing. Enjoy breakfast (7am-10am) in the hotel's spacious eating area overlooking the canal. Rooms have bath. Free Internet. Key deposit €20. 2-night min. stay on weekends. Book 2-3 weeks in advance and ask for a canal view. Singles €80-100; doubles €130-150; family rooms €180-200. MC/V. ❹

Hotel Di Ann, Raadhuisstraat 27 (☎623 1137; www.diann.nl). Tram #13 or 17 to Westermarkt. A delightful breakfast area, which boasts an elegant balcony and a large flat-panel TV, gives this establishment a unique character. Although far from spacious, each room have bath. Free Internet access. Singles €50-75; doubles €85-120; triples €125-150; quads €150-175. Prices vary; call ahead to avoid surprises. AmEx/MC/V. ❷

Westertoren Hotel, Raadhuisstraat 35B (☎624 4639; www.hotelwestertoren.nl). Tram #13 or 17 to Westermarkt. Best for groups, Westertoren boasts a handful of "family" rooms that sleep up to 6. Tea and coffee in room. Various combinations of shared or private bath; check website for details. Dutch breakfast brought to each room daily. 3-night min. stay on weekends. Book very early, especially in summer. Singles €40; doubles €60; triples €90; family rooms (4-6 people) €25 per person. AmEx/MC/V. ❷

Hotel Pax, Raadhuisstraat 37 (☎624 9735). Tram #13 or 17 to Westermarkt. Budget hotel with cot beds for walk-in reservations. Rooms have sink and TV, but showers and toilets are communal. Check yourself out in the eerie, mirror-lined hallway. Reception closes around 8pm, but guests are given a key to enter the building. Prices vary with season. Singles €25-70; doubles €65-95; triples €69-99; quads €70-109. AmEx/MC/V with 3.5% surcharge. ❶

CENTRAL CANAL RING

Although few hostels exist in this neighborhood adjacent to Amsterdam's main tourist attractions, the ones that do are affordable, lovely accommodations close to the city's busiest tourist centers. These inexpensive pads are a good deal, especially if you're traveling in pairs.

see map p. 336

▧ **Hemp Hotel,** Frederiksplein 15 (☎625 4425; www.hemp-hotel.com), next to the National Bank. Tram #4, 6, 7, 10, or 20 to Frederiksplein. Be sure to book as far in advance as possible, because this small hotel offers visitors an affordable and unforgettable experience. Each room is designed and decorated according to a different cultural theme. While reveling amid all things hemp, you can imagine yourself in such exotic locales as the Caribbean, Morocco, and Afghanistan. Unwind as you sip—what else?—hemp beer and chat with local expats in the cozy hotel bar. Breakfast—featuring yummy hemp bread—is included and served from 11am-noon. Hotel bar open 11am-3am. Their only single costs €50; doubles €65-80. MC/V with 5% surcharge. ❷

▧ **Hotel Asterisk,** Den Texstraat 16 (☎626 2396 or 624 1768; www.asteriskhotel.nl). Tram #16, 24, or 25 to Weteringcircuit. Turn left at the roundabout and proceed to Den Texstraat. A beautiful, well-kept hotel whose spacious and pristine rooms are a steal. Each room includes TV, phone, and safe. The hotel's friendly, professional staff is a great resource for information about Amsterdam. Breakfast included with reservation. High-season singles €45-59, with shower or toilet €49-64; doubles €59-79, with bath €84-129; triples €99-144; quads €119-165. MC/V with 4% surcharge. ❷

▧ **The Golden Bear,** Kerkstraat 37 (☎624 4785; www.goldenbear.nl). Tram #1, 2, or 5 to Prinsengracht, backtrack 1 block to Kerkstraat and turn left. Located just outside the rollicking ruckus of the Leidseplein, the Golden Bear opened in 1948 as Amsterdam's oldest openly ▼**gay** hotel. With its welcoming and informed staff, the Bear guides its patrons through Amsterdam's swinging nightlife and copious cultural offerings. Rooms are renovated and refurnished on a regular basis, keeping the hotel fresh and beautiful. All rooms feature brightly painted walls along with phone, safe, TV, VCR, and DVD player. Continental breakfast included, served 8:30am-noon. Singles from €60, with bath €105; doubles €62-132; twins €71-94. ❸

Euphemia Budget Hotel, Fokke Simonszstraat 1-9 (☎622 9045; www.euphemiahotel.com). Tram #16, 24, or 25 to Weteringcircuit. Backtrack on Vijzelstraat and turn right on Fokke Simonszstraat. Seriously spartan digs in a former monastery. Rooms are modest, clean, and affordable. Continental breakfast €5. Free Internet with your own laptop or €1 for 15min. at the hotel computer station. Reception 8am-11pm. Doubles with bath €70-120; triples €75-138; quads €100-184. Prices depend on season, availability, and type of room. 10% discount on the 1st night with website reservation. AmEx/MC/V with 5% surcharge. ❸

Hotel Kap, Den Texstraat 5B (☎624 5908; www.kaphotel.nl). Tram #16, 24, or 25 to Weteringcircuit. Go left down Weteringschans, right at 2e Weteringplantsoen, and left at Den Texstraat. Offers clean, comfortable, and spacious rooms on a quiet, residential street removed from the noise of the surrounding area. Breakfast included and served in a lovely lounge 8-10:30am. TV in each room, but no phones. Reception 8am-10:30pm. Check-out 11am. Depending on space and facilities, singles €60; doubles €98; triples €132; quads €142. AmEx/MC/V with 5% surcharge. ❸

 DUTCH DOORS. Addresses on one side of the street don't necessarily correspond with those on the other, so if you see #346 while searching for 347, don't expect your destination to be directly across the way!

LEIDSEPLEIN

Leidseplein is a touristy theme park of a neighborhood, so staying here can either be a lot of fun or just really loud. If you want proximity to the restaurants and nightlife with less of the craziness, head to **Leidsekade**, which is home to many reasonably priced rooms facing the Singelgracht. Most hotels will lower their prices during the week, for bookings at the last minute, or if business is slow.

see map p. 337

Freeland, Marnixstraat 386 (☎622 7511; www.hotelfreeland.com). Something feels palpably different at Freeland, and it's not just the well-developed flower theme; this is a happy, fresh, and well-run establishment. All rooms come with DVD player and private bath. Most rooms have A/C, and some doubles have tubs. Breakfast included. Free Internet in lobby; Wi-Fi throughout the hotel. Singles €65-80; doubles €90-110; triples €115-130. Ask for the special double with a sunroom, which costs the same as a regular double. Book early. AmEx/MC/V. ❸

Quentin Hotel, Leidsekade 89 (☎626 2187; www.quentinhotels.com). Located in a renovated canal-side mansion, Quentin looks and feels more like a hotel than its neighbors. Many of the comfortable rooms have desks and cable TV, and the high ceilings and huge gilt-framed mirrors help dress the place up. Has an elevator, unlike many other hotels in the area. Continental breakfast €7. Reception 24hr. Singles €40, with bath €65; smaller doubles with bath €75, larger doubles without bath €85, larger doubles with bath €99; triples with bath €125. Great last-minute rates. AmEx/MC/V. ❷

King Hotel, Leidsekade 85-86 (☎624 9603; www.hotel-king.nl). Enjoy spacious rooms, many with a canal view, in a spotless, recently renovated hotel. The King is an excellent value; rooms are clean and well-equipped with private facilities, TV, phone, safe, and hair dryer. Breakfast included in a cozy eating area, although they stop serving at 9:30am. Reception 10am-10pm. Singles €70; standard doubles €85, larger doubles €95, with canal view €105. MC/V with 6% surcharge. ❸

Hotel Impala, Leidsekade 77 (☎623 4706; www.hotel-impala.nl). A cozy 12-room hotel in a refurbished canal house. Suites here are comfortable, but it's the friendly service you'll want to write home about. Large homemade breakfast €8 in the sunlight-bathed kitchen area, also used as a hangout spot for the Impala's herds of guests. Dorms €22.50; doubles €75; triples €110; quads with bath and breakfast included €140. AmEx/MC/V with 5% surcharge. ❶

Hotel La Boheme, Marnixstraat 415 (☎624 2828; www.la-boheme-amsterdam.com). Tram #1, 2, or 5 to Leidseplein. Take a right after the theater onto Marnixstraat. Clean, well-run hotel with a young and friendly vibe. Cafe and bar in lobby. All rooms have phone and TV. Breakfast included. Free Wi-Fi. €20 key deposit. Reception 8am-11pm. Singles with shared bath €55-60; twin doubles with bath €100-115; spacious triples with bath €135-145. Look for specials on their website and call to reserve, since last-minute specials crop up occasionally. MC/V. ❷

Hotel de la Haye, Leidsegracht 114 (☎624 4044; www.hoteldelahaye.com). Tram #1, 2, or 5 to Leidseplein. Walk up Marnixstraat 1 block and turn right. Combines the convenience of Leidseplein and the serenity of a canal view. Sink and TV in each room. Rooms with many beds can get a little cramped. Breakfast included in a pretty yellow room with a canal view and fresh flowers. 3-night min. stay. Payment required for whole stay on arrival. Reception 8am-10pm. Prices fluctuate depending on the season and time of week; booking over the phone is a good idea, in case of special or last-minute deals. Singles €60-95; doubles €79-125, with bath €110-145; triples €115-130/145. AmEx/MC/V with 5% surcharge. ❸

International Budget Hostel, Leidsegracht 76 (☎624 2784; www.internationalbudgethostel.com). Tram #1, 2, or 5 to Prinsengracht. From the tram, turn right and walk to Leidsegracht. Rooms here aren't spacious or lavishly decorated, but exposed ceiling beams and ample light give them a homey feel. Dorm rooms cram 4 beds into the same space, as do the more comfortable (but costlier) twins. Dorm-quality shared facilities. Breakfast (various options €3-8) served 9am-noon. Safe available. Lounge with TV, vending machines, telephone, and Internet (€1 per 15min.) open 9am-11pm. Locker key deposit €10. Padlock €5. In summer, 3-night min. stay starting F or 2-night min. stay starting Sa. Reception 9am-11pm. 4-person dorms July-Aug. €30, Sept.-June €28; twin rooms with shared bath €70. AmEx/MC/V with 5% surcharge. ❶

Hotel de Paris, Marnixstraat 372 (☎622 5587; www.hoteldeparis.nl). A touch of Parisian elegance only a few blocks from Leidseplein. The claret-and-gold wallpaper and red velvet in the lobby will tip you off to this hotel's rather grand ambitions; the rooms don't quite live up to the hype, but they're clean, comfortable, and certainly a step up from the Marnix next door. All rooms with bath. Breakfast included. Singles €95; doubles M-Th €125, F-Su €160; triples M-Th €145, F-Su €165; quads M-Th €175, F-Su €225. AmEx/MC/V with 3% surcharge. ❹

Leidseplein Hotel, Korte Leidsedwarsstraat 79 (☎627 2505; www.leidsepleinhotel.nl). What this somewhat plain hotel lacks in decoration or presentation it makes up for with location, location, location. Stay out late and return to clean digs smack in the heart of Leidseplein's restaurant and club district. All rooms come with TV and private bath. Breakfast €5. Pay on arrival. Singles €50; doubles €90; quads €120-140. MC/V with 3% surcharge. ❷

Marnix Hotel, Marnixstraat 382 (☎616 0661). Though it feels a little cramped, budget travelers appreciate the Marnix's rock-bottom prices. For double or triple rooms, you might do best to look elsewhere, but you're unlikely to find a cheaper dorm room in Leidseplein. Breakfast €5 in a small room. Free Internet on a single computer. For 6-person groups, the entire dorm room can be reserved. Dorms €23-30; twin rooms €90, with bath €100; triples €100-120; quads €120-140. AmEx/MC/V. ❶

Hotel Kooyk, Leidsekade 82 (☎623 0295). A small, peaceful hotel overlooking the canal. Perfectly adequate rooms come with TV and sink. Not every floor has a shower, so you may have to squeak up or down the stairs. Breakfast included. Doubles €70; triples €90; quints €135; 6-person rooms €150. MC/V. ❸

Hotel Titus, Leidsekade 74 (☎626 5758; www.hoteltitus.nl). Tram #1, 2, or 5 to Leidseplein. Walk past the theater on your right, take a right onto Marnixstraat, and then swing left onto Leidsekade. The Titus's somewhat bare and run-down rooms come equipped with TV and phones. Lounge and breakfast area boasts a big-screen TV and a canal view. Breakfast included. Reception 8am-midnight. Singles €45; doubles €75-90; triples €120; quads €140. AmEx/MC/V with 5% surcharge. ❷

REMBRANDTPLEIN

Budget accommodations are scarce in Rembrandtplein and its surroundings. The area doesn't have the heavy concentration of hotels and hostels found in surrounding neighborhoods such as Leidseplein and the Oude Zijd, but there are a few good choices in the vicinity of the Rembrandt statue.

see map p. 336

City Hotel, Utrechtsestraat 2 (☎627 2323; www.city-hotel.nl). Classy, spacious accommodations above a pub on Rembrandtplein. Many rooms have great views of the square, and the ones on higher floors overlook the city skyline. Popular with young travelers. Rooms, hall baths, and showers all immaculately kept. Breakfast included in a spacious dining room with views of the square. Rooms without bath share facilities with 1 other room. Reception 24hr. 2- to 8-person rooms €45 per person. AmEx/MC/V. ❷

Thorbecke Hotel, Thorbeckeplein 3 (☎623 2601; www.thorbeckehotel.nl). Located in the center of Rembrandtplein's nightlife crush, on a busy square lined with party bars (and its own downstairs). Ideal location for partygoers, smack-dab in the middle of the action. All rooms neat and clean with TV and kettle. Breakfast included. Singles €65, with bath €85; doubles €85/110; triples with bath €135. 6-person suite with small balcony €300. AmEx/MC/V with 5% surcharge. ❸

Hotel Monopole, Amstel 60 (☎624 6271; www.hotel-monopole.nl). Tram #4 or 9 to Rembrandtplein. From Rembrandtplein, go north on Halvemaansteeg and head right when you hit the river. The location right by the Amstel offsets simple rooms with flowered bedspreads and pastel walls. Not all rooms have canal views, so make sure to ask ahead. Comfortable living room on 1st fl. All rooms with TV, some with bath. Breakfast included and delivered to door. Singles €65-85; doubles €85-125; triples €125-155; quads €145-185. Prices vary by season. MC/V with 5% surcharge. ❸

JORDAAN

Lodgings in the Jordaan generally afford peace and quiet a comfortable distance from the frenzied city center.

Hotel Van Onna, Bloemgracht 104 (☎626 5801; www.vanonna.nl). Tram #13, 14, or 17 to Westermarkt; also close to the Bloemgracht stop on tram #10. No television and no smoking equal a peaceful night's rest in either of the 2 historic canal houses in which Hotel van Onna has rooms. The friendly owner grew up in the Jordaan and is happy to chat about the history of the area or share advice on local restaurants. Cozy rooms all have private bathrooms. Despite the trek upstairs, ask for a top-floor room. Ceilings there are sloped by the building's original wood beams, and the view stretches out over the entire Jordaan. Breakfast included. Reception 8am-11pm. Singles €45; doubles €90; triples €135; quads €180. Cash only. ❷

see map p. 338

The Shelter Jordan, Bloemstraat 179 (☎624 4717; www.shelter.nl). Tram #13, 14, or 17 to Marnixstraat; follow Lijnbaansgracht (off Rozengracht) for 50m, then turn right on Bloemstraat. This well-run Christian hostel's prices can't be beat, especially in the Jordaan. The staff is composed of Christian ministry volunteers, but there is no obligation to participate in any of the hostel's religious activities. Best suited for those under 35. No drugs or alcohol. Umbrella rental €0.50. Currency exchange with no commission. Breakfast included 8-10:30am. Lunch €3.75; dinner €4.75. Lockers with €5 key deposit and free storage for larger bags and packs. Sheets €2. Cafe with Internet access (€0.50 per 20min.) and a piano. 1-month max. stay. 14- to 20-bed single-sex dorms Sept.-May €18; June-Aug. €19.50. MC/V with 5% surcharge. ❶

Hotel Acacia, Lindengracht 251 (☎622 1460). Tram #3 to Nieuwe Willemsstraat. If watching the houseboats peacefully rocking along the canals of the Jordaan isn't enough for you, try living in one. Acacia has 2 lovely houseboats, 1 new and 1 old, with rooms for 2-4 people; ideal for families untroubled by motion sickness. On land, very simple but perfectly comfortable rooms in a quiet location all come with private bath. Studios and houseboats include small kitchenette. Breakfast included. 3-night min. stay unless booking at the last minute. Hotel singles €65; doubles €80; triples €99; quads €120; quints €130. Studio doubles €90; triples €105. Houseboat doubles €95-110; triples €115; quads €130. MC/V with 5% surcharge. ❸

> **⚑TIP▸** **PROCRASTINATORS, REJOICE.** Rooms in Amsterdam are almost always cheaper when booked at the last minute, although only same-day reservations qualify. If you don't mind flying by the seat of your pants, you may find a great deal.

WESTERPARK AND OUD-WEST

Staying in accommodations west of the Canal Ring means you'll have a pleasantly short walk to shopping and nightlife in Leidseplein and the attractions of Museumplein, often at lower prices. Nevertheless, the neighborhood is still fairly rough-edged and commercial.

see map p. 343

 Hotel Abba, Overtoom 122 (☎618 3058; www.abbabudgetho-tel.com). Tram #1 or 6 to 1e Constantijn Huygensstraat; Abba is across the street. A budget hotel with a clean, welcoming feel. An attractive option with its proximity to Leidseplein and the museums. Free safe at reception. Breakfast included 8-9:30am. Reception until 11pm. Credit card needed for reservation. Singles €35-50; twins €65-80; special family-style quints €35 per person. Cash only. ❶

 Hotel de Filosoof, Anna Vondelstraat 6 (☎683 3013; www.hotelfilosoof.nl). Each room in this lovely hotel is dedicated to a different philosopher; choose from Nietzsche, Wittgenstein, "Clouds"—a room dedicated to Aristophanes, Socrates, and Magritte—and many more. It may sound gimmicky, but this hotel Kant be beat—as long as you don't lie awake all night pondering your existence. There's a pretty garden out back and an even prettier garden (Vondelpark) just steps away. All rooms with cable TV, phone, and bath. Breakfast included. Singles €125; small doubles €108, larger doubles €175. ⑤

Hotel d'Amsterdam, 2e Helmersstraat 4 (☎616 0125; www.hoteldamsterdam.com). This 16-room hotel's budget digs are clean and comfortable and come in different sizes for different wallets. Unlike the Crystal next door, d'Amsterdam has an elevator (with an awesome cell-phone-inspired button display). Breakfast included. Ensuite bath in all rooms. Small doubles €60, larger doubles €90; triples €130. MC/V. ❸

Jupiter Hotel, 2e Helmersstraat 14 (☎618 7132; www.jupiterhotel.nl). A bit of a misnomer. This nice little hotel boasts a pretty breakfast area and a scenic residential location with a garden out back. Breakfast included. Credit card needed for reservation. High-season single €49, with bath €59; doubles €69/94; triples with bath €124; quads with bath €149. Cash only. ❷

Tulip Inn Amsterdam Centre, Nassaukade 387-390 (☎530 7888; www.tulipinnamsterdamcentre.com). Tram #1, 2, 5, 6, 7, or 10 to Leidseplein. A 3-star, 70-room hotel, the Tulip Inn caters to the business traveler, although there is a large lobby with busy bar open until 1am. No drugs of any kind allowed. All rooms with ensuite bath, phone, TV, and safe. Adapters available at reception. Luggage room available for storage. Breakfast buffet included 7-10am. Free Wi-Fi and Internet terminals in lobby. Reception 24hr. Rooms can be cheaper if booked far in advance. High-season singles from €129; doubles from €139. Low-season singles from €89; doubles from €99. AmEx/MC/V. ⑤

Hotel Princess, Overtoom 80 (☎612 2947; hotelprincess@planet.nl). Tram #1 or 6 to 1e Constantijn Huygensstraat. All rooms share a toilet and shower. Like all good princesses have, rooms overlooking busy Overtoom have tiny balconies. Breakfast included 8-10am in a nice breakfast room looking out over the intersection of Overtoom and 1e Constantijn Huygensstraat. Pay on arrival. Doubles €80-90; bunk-bed triples €110-120; bunk-bed quads €130-140. Cash only. ❹

Hotel Crystal, 2e Helmersstraat 6 (☎618 0521; hotelcrystal@planet.nl). Tram #1, 2, 5, 6, 7, or 10 to Leidseplein. With the American Hotel on your right, cross the bridge and make a right; it's the 3rd street on your left. 17-room hotel lies within short walking distance of Leidseplein, Museumplein, and Vondelpark. Operated by the same owner as the Hotel Princess. The rooms aren't palatial, but they're comfortable, especially those with private bathrooms. The hall bathrooms are well maintained; all rooms with sinks. Breakfast

FROM THE ROAD

LEARNING TO BIKE THE HARD WAY

It was raining, as usual. I was biking along Prinsengracht when the car next to me suddenly swerved. The next thing I knew, my left shoe was 20 ft. away, and I was peeling my face off a canal-house door. Don't let this happen to you.

You'll inevitably see people biking down the wrong side of a canal or one-way street, running red lights, and playing chicken with trucks. But, as I witnessed, this is actually pretty dangerous. To avoid smashing face-first into a canal house, add a couple minutes to your trip and bike sanely.

But first, I suggest getting a single-speed bike; in case you haven't noticed, the Netherlands is really flat. Also check for lights in the front and back—you can be ticketed for not using lights at night, but mostly they're just safe. And take my word for it: get two locks—one for each wheel—and secure your bike to something sturdy. Highly intoxicated revelers have been known to throw bikes in the canals. Thanks, guys.

My other advice is always to bike perpendicular to tram rails so your wheels don't get caught in them. Be careful of taxis and mopeds, which weren't exactly careful of me. Learn and use hand signals—all the cool kids do, and I had fun with them!

But don't let my horror stories intimidate you. Face it: you need to cycle in Amsterdam. Bike-ness is next to godliness here, and a bike condenses the city to a manageable size.

—Lucy Lindsey

included. Credit card needed for reservation. High-season singles €50; doubles €70; twins with bath €102; triples with bath €130; spacious quads with bath €150. Low-season singles €30; doubles €64; twins with bath €73; triples with bath €95; spacious quads with bath €113. Cash only. ❷

MUSEUMPLEIN AND VONDELPARK

This beautiful, peaceful neighborhood is a great location to launch your Amsterdam exploration. Next to the city's most famous museums and just across the river from *the* nightlife hot spot (Leidseplein), it may seem surprising that bargains are available even in this prime part of town.

see map p. 342

■ **Stayokay Amsterdam Vondelpark,** Zandpad 5 (☎589 8996; www.stayokay.com/vondel-park), bordering Vondelpark. Tram #1, 2, or 5 to Leidseplein, walk to the Marriott, and take a left. Walk a block and turn right onto Zandpad just before the park. A palatial, spotless hostel with exceptionally clean rooms and a professional staff. Dorm room capacities range 2-20 people; all can be made single-sex and have bath. The massive hostel has a lobby lounge, bar with terrace on the park, TV/rec room, and smoking room (the rest of the hostel is non-smoking). Elevator access. Bike rental €8 per day. Lockers in the lobby €3; bring a padlock for room lockers. Breakfast and linen included; towels €3. Internet access €0.50 per min. Reception 7:30am-midnight. Hostel fills up quickly—make a reservation in advance online or by phone. 12- to 14-person dorms in high season €24; 6- or 8-person dorms €26; quads €29; twins €79.50. Prices can fluctuate depending on day of the week and capacity. €2.50 HI discount. MC/V. ❶

■ **Hotel Bema,** Concertgebouw 19B (☎679 1396; www.bemahotel.com). From Centraal Station, tram #16 to Museumplein; the hotel is just to the left of the imposing Concert-gebouw, across from the main taxi stand. Bema is a charming 7-room hotel with airy accommodations (complete with high ceilings and skylights), a very friendly staff, and a funky neo-hippie style. Breakfast included. Reception 8am-midnight. Singles €35-45; doubles and twins €65, with shower €90; triples €85/100; quads with shower €100-115. Bema also has several apartments around the city equipped with kitchenettes for rent. Ask for prices. AmEx/MC/V with 5% surcharge. ❶

Flying Pig Palace, Vossiusstraat 46-47 (☎400 4187; www.flyingpig.nl). Tram #1, 2, or 5 from Centraal Station to Leidseplein, walk over the bridge to the Marriott, and turn left. Go past the entrance to the park and then take the first right onto Vossiusstraat. The Palace is down a long block on your left. This is your place if you believe that an enjoyable hostel experience will come only when pigs fly. Not as clean or as wild as the Flying Pig Downtown (p. 106) but has the same communal, friendly attitude in a tranquil setting, with bird songs floating over from the park. Flying Pig hostels are for travelers over the age of 18. The cozy bar with rugs, books, and pillows at 1 end is the Pig's unofficial meeting spot; head to Happy hour from 8-9pm to unwind after a day of touring. All rooms co-ed with shared kitchen. Ample breakfast included. Free Internet. Reception 8:30am-9:30pm; 24hr. check-in possible. Stop by between 8-10am or call at 8:30am to reserve for the same night; you can also reserve over the Internet, but in the high season the Pig recommends that you call or stop by in the morning instead. Queen-sized bunk beds in some dorms (sleeps 2 for the price of 1½). High-season 14-bed dorms €24; 10-bed dorms €27; 8-bed dorms €29; 4-bed dorms €32; double with bath €36. For long-term stays, ask about doing work in exchange for rent. AmEx/MC/V. ❶

Hotel Museumzicht, Jan Luijkenstraat 22 (☎671 5224; www.hotelmuseumzicht.nl). Bus #197 directly from Schiphol Airport to Hobbemastraat. From Centraal Station, take tram #2 or 5. Small, charming house with old-fashioned personality and helpful staff; a stone's throw (literally, from some rooms' windows) from the Rijksmuseum. The beautiful window-lined breakfast room might tempt you to stay beyond *ontbijt*.

Breakfast included. Reception 8am-11pm. Singles €48; doubles €78, with bath €98; triples €99/124. AmEx/MC/V with 5% surcharge. ❷

Hotel Bellington, PC Hooftstraat 78-80 (☎671 6478; www.hotel-bellington.com). From Schiphol Airport, bus #197 to Hobbemastraat; from Centraal, tram #2 or 5. The only thing higher than the prices on Hooftstraat, Bellington is a well-groomed hotel situated above the city's ritziest shops; best rooms have windows with views of the thoroughfare. A bargain with well-preserved rooms in perfect proximity to museums, Vondelpark, and the steepest shopping around. Phone and TV in each room. Breakfast included. Reception 8am-11pm. Doubles €65, with bath €85-110; triples €85-110; quads €120-135. AmEx/MC/V. ❸

Hotel Omega, Jacob Obrechtstraat 33 (☎664 5182). Tram #16 to Jacob Obrechtstraat. Hotel Omega is in a beautiful tree-lined neighborhood, near Vondelpark in one direction and the Museumplein in the other. Close to several small eateries and cafes. Rooms here are comfortable and clean and include TV, phone and fridge; some have A/C or balcony windows, both at no extra charge. The staff is friendly, and there's a pleasant garden terrace out back. Singles €60-100; doubles €110-130. AmEx/MC/V. ❸

 KNOCK, KNOCK. Almost all hotels and hostels keep their front doors locked at all times, but it's not because they don't like you as a person. If you find yourself locked out, you can always be buzzed in, though you may want to let the night staff know before departing that you're going to be out late.

Hotel Wijnnobel, Vossiusstraat 9 (☎662 2298 or 673 4115). Follow directions to the Flying Pig Palace, and you will come to this hotel first on Vossiusstraat. Hotel Wijnnobel possesses both the charms and the drawbacks of being old-fashioned. With fireplaces, antique wood, high ceilings, big, beautiful windows, and a garden in the back, this hotel has the warm feel of a home. But nothing here is mechanized—that means no phones, no TV, no website, and no credit cards. It feels a little cramped, and beds are well-worn. Huge, airy shared bathrooms have bathtubs. The smaller and higher up the room is, the cheaper. All 11 rooms share facilities on each floor. Breakfast included. Singles €35; doubles €60-75; triples €90; quads €120; quints €150. Ask about price reductions during the low season. Cash only. ❶

Hotel Europa 92, 1e Constantijn Huygensstraat 103-105 (☎618 8808; www.europa92.nl), between Vondelstraat and Overtoom. Tram #1 or 6 to 1e Constan-

LOCAL LEGEND

SAINT RACIST?

Many countries celebrate the arrival of a legendary gift-bearing character around Christmastime. The Netherlands is no exception—its version is called "Sinterklaas." But Sinterklaas can't deliver presents alone: he needs help. Help, however, comes in the form of political controversy.

Sinterklaas's helper is named Zwarte Piet, or "Black Pete." Zwarte Piet is black with dark, curly hair, and he sports gold hoop earrings. In holiday parades, Piet is often portrayed by whites (donning black face paint and afro wigs) as Sinterklaas's impish, disobedient servant. He is also an object of fear, threatening to take bad children away to Spain with him.

Outcries against Sinterklaas's black helper began in the 1970s, coinciding with increasing numbers of Surinamese immigrants. Piet's dark skin is the crux of the debate. Piet apologists claim that his dark skin is due to soot from chimney gift-deliveries; others point to the traditionally darker skin tones of Moors in Spain, Piet's land of origin.

Whatever the case, in a country increasingly fraught with tensions, Zwarte Piet's days may be numbered: in 2006, during Sinterklaas's nationally televised arrival in the Netherlands, the jolly old elf was assisted by a retinue of orange, blue, and green Petes. However, these awkwardly named "Colored Petes" have yet to prove their lasting power.

tijn Huygensstraat. Converted from 2 adjacent houses into 1 labyrinthine hotel. Clean rooms all come with phone, TV, hair dryer, and private bath. Tiny elevator means you carry your luggage for no more than ½ flight of stairs. Large garden terrace. Breakfast included with certain reservation packages; otherwise, it is a hefty €9. Singles €80-95; doubles €110-145; triples €135-185. AmEx/MC/V with 4% surcharge. ❹

Apple Inn Hotel, Koninginneweg 93 (☎662 7894; www.apple-inn.nl). Tram #2 to Emmastraat, then walk 200m further in the direction of the tram. Further afield than other hotels in the area, the Apple Inn will nevertheless put you in a peaceful, residential neighborhood and directly across from Vondelpark. The 32 rooms are basic but clean and include modern and spotless bathrooms (some with tubs!). Rooms include TV, phone, and hair dryer. Breakfast included. High-season singles €85-100; doubles €105-140; triples €135-175; quads €175-190. Low-season singles €65-85; doubles €85-100; triples €128-140; quads €156-175. AmEx/MC/V with 2% surcharge. ❸

DE PIJP

Staying in De Pijp may be a bit of a hike from Centraal Station and the playground that is the Centrum, but De Pijp's proximity to inexpensive eateries and to the Rijksmuseum—not to mention the best open-air market in Amsterdam—makes a bit of added distance more than worth the trek.

see map p. 333

▨ **Bicycle Hotel,** Van Ostadestraat 123 (☎679 3452; www.bicyclehotel.com). Tram #16 or 24 to Albert Cuyp. Bicycle's draws include clean digs and spotless bathrooms, plus a large, airy common room and leafy garden. A 2-wheeler-friendly hotel (as its name implies); includes free parking in its bike garage and maps of recommended bike trips. Bicycles available to rent (€7.50 per day). Sink and TV in all rooms. Breakfast included (served 8-10am). Free Internet and safe. 3-night min. on weekends. Singles €65, with bath €95; doubles €80-115; triples €95-130. 4-person canal house in the Plantage €130. AmEx/MC/V with 4% surcharge. ❸

Hotel Sarphati, Sarphatipark 58 (☎673 4083). Tram #25 stops right in front of the hotel. Comfortable rooms can be a bit small, but the real draw is its location. Beautiful and largely untouristed Sarphatipark is across the street, and the trendy bars and cafes of Van Der Helststraat are only steps away. Ask for a room over the back garden for extra seclusion. 16 rooms come with phone, TV, safe, hair dryer, and bathroom; some have A/C and tub. Breakfast included. Singles M-Th €80, F-Su €90; doubles M-Th €100, F-Su €135. Low-season prices considerably lower. MC/V with 5% surcharge. ❹

Hotel Vivaldi, Stadhouderskade 76 (☎577 6300). Tram #16, 24, or 25 from Centraal Station. Directly across from the Heineken Experience, Vivaldi features 24 simple rooms, all with TV, phone, and bath; some have patios or delicious canal views. Breakfast included (served 8:30-10am). Reception 24hr. Singles €55-95; doubles €65-105; triples €85-125; family rooms €105-145. AmEx/MC/V with 5% surcharge. ❷

JODENBUURT AND PLANTAGE

Since they are off the main tourist circuit, the Jodenbuurt and Plantage offer fewer places to stay; however, the available accommodations are often a good value. Some respectable hotels snuggle up to the Artis Zoo, while others hug Nieuwe Keizersgracht, close to the Amstel River.

see map p. 344

▨ **Luckytravellers Fantasia Hotel,** Nieuwe Keizersgracht 16 (☎623 8259; www.fantasia-hotel.com). Tram #9 or 14 to Waterlooplein. Has a younger, more laid-back feel than most hotels in the neighborhood. Rooms have an eclectic, homemade design and vary in size; smaller rooms and rooms on the 5th fl. are cheaper. Facilities include radios, phones, coffeemakers, and safe. You'll be an even luckier traveler if you can snag one of the rooms with a canal view. Breakfast included. Singles €65-75; doubles €85-95; triples €120-130; quads and family rooms €150. AmEx/MC/V with 3% surcharge. ❸

Hotel Adolesce, Nieuwe Keizersgracht 26 (☎ 626 3959; www.adolesce.nl). This pristine, quiet, completely angst-free 10-room hotel is located in an old canal house just steps away from the Amstel River and Amsterdam's famous Magere Brug. The lobby includes a small bar. No drugs of any kind allowed. All rooms with sink, TV, and phone; many are spacious enough for a sofa and desk. Limited breakfast (coffee, tea, fruit, and biscuits) included and served all day. Reception open 8:30am-1am; pay on arrival. Singles €65-75; doubles €85-95; triples €125. MC/V. ❸

The Bridge Hotel, Amstel 107-111 (☎ 623 7068; www.thebridgehotel.nl). This large, modern hotel is a stylish step up from the nearby competition. Although its name may denote what you want to jump off of when you get the bill, the Bridge is worth the splurge. Deluxe rooms are well outfitted with a desk, a breakfast table, and, usually, a canal view—be sure to ask! Friendly, professional staff. All rooms come with TV, telephone, and private bath. Breakfast and city tax included. Deluxe singles €110; standard twins €110, deluxe twins €120; deluxe triples €165. AmEx/MC/V. ❺

Hotel Plantage, Plantage Kerklaan 25A (☎ 620 5544; www.hotelplantage.nl). Tram #9 or 14 to Plantage Kerklaan. Budget hotel across from the Artis Zoo with few extra frills but competitive prices and a younger crowd. No breakfast, but **Café Koosje** downstairs (p. 141) opens at 9am. Private bath in all rooms. Reserve online only. High-season singles €55; twins €70; quads €140; quints €155. MC/V with 2% surcharge. ❷

Hotel Rembrandt, Plantage Middenlaan 17 (☎ 627 2714). Tram #9 or 14 to Plantage Kerklaan. A reception room filled to the brim with books welcomes travelers to this quiet hotel, situated just steps from the Artis Zoo and peaceful Wertheim Park—or, should you so desire, the tram to the Centrum. Rooms are well-kept with modern bathrooms, TV, and phone, but there is quite a size difference between the small and large doubles. Breakfast included in the beautiful antique dining room. Singles €75; small doubles €95, large doubles €115; triples €140; quads €165. MC/V. ❸

Hotel Barbacan, Plantage Muidergracht 89 (☎ 623 6241; www.barbacan.nl). Tram #9 or 14 to Plantage Kerklaan. This quiet hotel's rooms are unremarkable but do the trick with all the standard amenities, including bathroom. Internet access €2.50 per 30min. Doubles €70-90, with bath €100-120; triples €110-120/130-140; quads €130-140/155-165. AmEx/MC/V with 5% surcharge. ❸

FOOD

When it comes time to sit down for a meal, you'll thank your lucky stars that colonial history and a medley of immigrants have diversified your choices. In fact, in most areas the sheer number of options—from Shawarma snack bars to Argentine steakhouses to pan-Asian noodle joints—can be dizzying. An adventurous palate will serve you best as you navigate the jumble of Surinamese, Italian, Tibetan, and Ethiopian restaurants—among others. Though Dutch food is common in the city, it's not nearly as exciting, or often as well prepared, as some of the selections from the former Dutch empire. Indonesian cuisine, omnipresent throughout Amsterdam, is one of the surest and tastiest bets for vegetarians and vegans, as traditional Dutch cuisine is hearty, heavy, meaty, and wholesome.

Dutch restaurants overlap with nightlife in Amsterdam's classic *bruin cafes*, which, along with *eetcafes*, are the best source for traditional Netherlandish fare (p. 74). These laid-back places to sit down contrast with the Centrum's many takeout stands of varying quality. The listings below, listed by neighborhood in descending order of value, are some of the city's best bets—both for a quick bite and a place to take your parents.

The cheapest way to eat in Amsterdam, though, is at one of its ubiquitous grocery stores. **Albert Heijn** supermarkets line the streets and are immediately recognizable by their large, blue signs. Two of the most popular can be found in Dam Square and underneath Museumplein. Check for more branches at www.ah.nl. (Hours vary by location.) **Dirk van den Broek** is a large, basic supermarket that's cheaper than Albert Heijn. You can see its locations throughout Amsterdam at www.dirk.nl. (Most open M-Sa 8am-6pm; larger stores open later and on Su.)

TIP

RIP-OFF? NOT REALLY. Many supermarkets charge around €0.25 for a plastic grocery bag in an effort to reduce their use and help the environment. If you want a bag to carry your food home, ask for one as the cashier is ringing you up, and he'll charge you.

BY TYPE

AFRICAN	
Abyssinia Afrikaans Eetcafe (135)	WO ❸
Addis Adaba Restaurant (134)	WO ❷
Axum (129)	CCR ❷
Eetkunst Asmara (140)	JP ❷
🍽 Rainarai (133)	JD ❶
Restaurant Zina (136)	WO ❹

AMERICAN	
Café Americain (130)	LP ❹
🍽 Eat at Jo's (130)	LP ❸
🍽 Harlem: Drinks and Soulfood (126)	SVB ❸

BAKERIES	
Bagels & Beans (137)	MV ❶
Bakkerij Mediterrane (126)	SVB ❶
Bakkerij Paul Année (128)	CRW ❶

BAKERIES, CONTINUED	
De Taart van m'n Tante (139)	DP ❶
🍽 Lanskroon (129)	CCR ❶

CAFES AND SANDWICHES	
Aguada (141)	JP ❷
Belgica (131)	LP ❷
🍽 Cafe-Restaurant Amsterdam (134)	WO ❸
Cafe de Koe (133)	JD ❷
🍽 Cafe Vertigo (136)	MV ❶
De Balie (130)	LP ❸
De Groene Olifant (141)	JP ❶
🍽 Foodism (127)	CRW ❷
Het Blauwe Theehuis (136)	MV ❶
La Place (125)	NZ ❶
Plancius (140)	JP ❸
Roem (133)	JD ❷

FOOD

CAFES AND SANDWICHES, CONT'D
Small World Cafe (126) — SVB ❶
Soup En Zo (140) — JP ❶
Theehuis Himalaya (124) — RLD ❶
TisFris (141) — JP ❷

CHEESE
De Kaaskamer (128) — CRW ❶

CHINESE
Nam Kee (123) — OZ ❶
Nam Tin (140) — JP ❷
New Season (124) — RLD ❷
Sea Palace (140) — JP ❹
Taste of Culture (123) — OZ ❷

DELIS
De Avondmarkt (134) — WO ❶
J.J. Ooyevaar (130) — LP ❶
🦪 Peperwortel (134) — WO ❷
🦪 Van Dobben (131) — RP ❶

DESSERT
Jordino (126) — SVB ❶
Peppino Gelateria (139) — DP ❶

DUTCH
Bloem (141) — JP ❺
Café Koosje (141) — JP ❷
🦪 Cafe Latei (123) — OZ ❶
Carousel Pancake House (129) — CCR ❶
De Reiger (133) — JD ❹
De Soepwinkel (137) — DP ❶
🦪 Hein (127) — CRW ❸
Het Molenpad (128) — CRW ❸
Pancake Bakery (127) — CRW ❷
🦪 Pannenkoekenhuis Upstairs (125) — NZ ❷
The Pantry (131) — LP ❷
Westers (135) — WO ❸

FUSION/GLOBAL
🦪 In de Waag (123) — OZ ❹
Nieuw Albina (138) — DP ❶
Spanjer en Van Twist (128) — CRW ❸
Warung Spang Makandra (138) — DP ❷
Wolvenstraat 23 (127) — CRW ❶
Zouk (135) — WO ❸

INDIAN AND PAKISTANI
Balraj (126) — SVB ❸
🦪 Bombay Inn (130) — LP ❷
Dosa (135) — WO ❸
Koh-i-noor (128) — CRW ❸

INDONESIAN
Aneka Rasa (123) — RLD ❷
Bojo (130) — LP ❷
Esoterica (135) — WO ❷
Padi (126) — SVB ❷
Sie Joe (125) — NZ ❶

IRISH
Tig Barra (136) — WO ❷

ITALIAN
🦪 Abe Veneto (140) — JP ❷
Cinema Paradiso (133) — JD ❷
Il Panorama (128) — CRW ❸
🦪 Ristorante Caprese (125) — NZ ❸
🦪 Ristorante Pizzeria Firenze (131) — RP ❶
Yam Yam (134) — WO ❷

JAPANESE
Go Sushi (136) — MV ❷
Shinto (139) — DP ❷
Tomo Sushi (132) — RP ❹

JUICE
Frood (125) — NZ ❶
Jay's Juice (126) — SVB ❶
La Fruteria (125) — NZ ❶

MEDITERRANEAN
🦪 Cafe De Pijp (137) — DP ❸
Poco Loco (123) — OZ ❸
Prego (127) — CRW ❹
Trez (138) — DP ❹

MEXICAN AND CARIBBEAN
Chicanos (131) — LP ❸
La Margarita (132) — RP ❹
Rose's Cantina (131) — RP ❹

MIDDLE EASTERN AND KOSHER
🦪 Bazar (137) — DP ❷
Ben Cohen Shawarma (133) — JD ❶

SPANISH AND PORTUGUESE
Mas Tapas (140) — DP ❸
Tapa Feliz (137) — MV ❸

THAI AND SOUTHEAST ASIAN
Cambodja City (139) — DP ❷
🦪 NOA (129) — CCR ❸
Rakang (133) — JD ❹
Thai Restaurant Phuket (132) — RP ❷
Top Thai (128) — CRW ❸

TIBETAN
Tashi Deleg (129) — CCR ❹

TURKISH AND KURDISH
Kismet (134) — WO ❶
Saray (138) — DP ❸
Zagros (139) — DP ❷

VEGETARIAN AND VEGAN
🦪 De Vliegende Schotel (133) — JD ❷
De Waaghals (138) — DP ❸
Golden Temple (129) — CCR ❷
Green Planet (125) — NZ ❸
Restaurant de Bolhoed (133) — JD ❸

FOOD

CRW Canal Ring West CCR Central Canal Ring DP De Pijp JP Jodenbuurt and Plantage JD Jordaan LP Leidseplein MV Museumplein and Vondelpark NZ Nieuwe Zijd OZ Oude Zijd RLD Red Light District RP Rembrandtplein SVB Scheepvaartbuurt WO Westerpark and Oud-West

BY NEIGHBORHOOD

OUDE ZIJD

There's plenty of food in the Oude Zijd, but most options are less tempting. In nice weather, a popular option is one of the several restaurants with large outdoor terraces along **Nieuwmarkt**. Another good area for grub is Chinatown, mainly centered on **Zeedijk**, which has excellent Asian fare in all price ranges.

see map p. 340

■ **Cafe Latei,** Zeedijk 143 (☎625 7485; www.latei.net). At this unique cafe and curiosity shop, nearly everything is for sale—even your plate. The brainchild of 2 vintage knick-knack enthusiasts, Cafe Latei is ideal for a quick bite or leisurely conversation. Hanging lamps, old-fashioned crockery, and wall hangings may come and go, but the affable atmosphere remains. Sandwiches, made with goat cheese, chorizo, and other fine ingredients, around €3. All-day continental breakfast €6.40. Fresh juices €2-4. Th couscous nights; call for other special events. Open M-F 8am-6pm, Sa 9am-6pm, Su 11am-6pm. ❶

■ **In de Waag,** Nieuwmarkt 4 (☎452 7772; www.indewaag.nl). A high-class restaurant in a weigh-house from 1488. See **In de Waag,** p. 124. ❹

Taste of Culture, Zeedijk 109 (☎638 1466). 2nd location at Rokin 152 (☎638 1249). It's easy to imagine that many an eating contest has been inspired by Taste of Culture's tempting offer: all you can eat in 1hr. for only €8.50. Start with the dim sum (dumplings or egg rolls) and then move on to heartier dishes (chicken drumsticks or egg fried rice). Plenty of vegetarian options. If you're looking for table service, however, you've come to the wrong place; this restaurant is strictly about the buffet, on your right as you walk in. Drinks €1.50. Open daily noon-11pm. Cash only. ❷

Poco Loco, Nieuwmarkt 24 (☎624 2937). A popular restaurant and bar facing Nieuwmarkt, with a Mediterranean menu that changes seasonally. Selection of club sandwiches €6.75. Popular tapas €3-5. Dinner entrees €12.50-20. Check for the daily specials like €10 dinner entrees. Reservations recommended on weekends. After dinner, lounge on the terrace with a glass of beer (€2). Open M-Th and Su 10am-1am, F-Sa 10am-3am. ❸

Nam Kee, Zeedijk 111 (☎624 3470, www.namkee.nl). 2nd branch nearby on Geldersekade 117 (☎639 2848). A popular but affordable Chinatown favorite. Unencumbered by fancy decor but armed with a full battery of Chinese favorites, from fish ball soup (€3.50) to chicken in black bean sauce (€8.50). A great place to grab an inexpensive sit-down dinner. Open 11:30am-midnight. Cash only. ❶

F O O D

RED LIGHT DISTRICT

Although the Red Light District didn't become famous for its food, you can still fill up at the Shawarma, pizza, or falafel huts cluttering **Warmoesstraat** or at one of the following. If something about eating in the heart of Europe's sex capital makes you a little queasy, just don't look up from the table.

Aneka Rasa, Warmoesstraat 25-29 (☎626 1560). If the grime of Warmoesstraat is beginning to take its toll, you'll appreciate this

see map p. 340

IN DE WAAG

Dine in medieval elegance when you step into the formidable castle that magnificently stands at the center of Nieuwmarkt. ▓In de Waag is a pleasurable culinary experience in Amsterdam's oldest secular structure. In 1488, the building served as the eastern gate into the city; 16 years after the walls were torn down in 1601 to allow for expansion, the building became a weigh-house. Later, it served as a municipal archive, fire station, history museum, and medical amphitheater—Rembrandt's *The Anatomy Lesson of Dr. Tulp* was painted here during one such medical session.

Since 1996, though, visitors have experienced the stately elegance of the centuries-old building by way of a delicious meal or a relaxed drink in the enormous interior restaurant. The basic lunch menu has sandwiches and salads (€5-10; burger and fries €11.50), served under more than 300 candles hanging from the ceiling. The casual patrons pack between stone walls and long wood tables to delight in a satisfying dinner menu that changes with the seasons; expect dishes like sea bass for around €20. If you're so inclined, bring your laptop to surf the web while you dine, but doing so just seems so uncouth amid such perfect, antiquated elegance.

Nieuwmarkt 4 (☎452 7772; www.indewaag.nl). Open daily 10am-midnight. Lunch served 10am-5pm; dinner 6-10:30pm.

clean, relaxed Indonesian joint with its very friendly staff. You and a friend can chow down on the popular *rijsttafel* for a relatively inexpensive €16.80-17.80 per person. Other main dishes, like the popular beef in spicy coconut sauce, satisfy the palate (€11.60-12.50). Plenty of tasty vegetarian plates as well (€7.50-8.40). Open daily 5-10:30pm. AmEx/MC/V. ❷

Theehuis Himalaya, Warmoesstraat 56 (☎626 0899; www.himalaya.nl). Though it appears to be just a New Age book shop, this small storefront belies an exceptionally large interior. The backroom houses a Buddhist-themed theehuis, serving light vegetarian and vegan lunches. With 25 varieties of tea and soothing music playing, the shop feels 29,029 ft. above the lurid grit of Warmoesstraat. Tasty sandwiches and bagels (€3-5) as well as delicious pastries (€1.50-3). Open M noon-6pm, Tu-W and F-Sa 10am-6pm, Th 10am-8pm, Su noon-5:30pm. AmEx/MC/V. ❶

New Season, Warmoesstraat 39 (☎625 6125). The seating area may be small, but the menu is anything but limited. There is no shortage of hard-to-pronounce choices at this pan-Asian, family-style sit-down eatery. Menu includes Cantonese, Szechuan, Thai, and Malaysian dishes. Main courses around €9-13.50. Vegetarian plates €5.50-6.50. Try the sizzling Teppan meals for €16-18.60. Open daily 11am-11pm. AmEx/MC/V. ❷

NIEUWE ZIJD

Almost all of the Nieuwe Zijd's dining options, whether fast-food or otherwise, cater to tourists. For a more authentic dining experience, stay away from Damrak, running down from Central Station, Nieuwendijk,

see map p. 340

parallel to Damrak north of Dam Sq., and Kalverstraat, the area's major shopping street, which runs down from Dam. These three streets are the main tourist arteries of the Nieuwe Zijd and possess every type of pizza, hamburger, and falafel imaginable. For a quieter meal, try the restaurants lining **Nieuwezijds Voorburgwal** or **Spuistraat,** running parallel to Damrak to the east, or any of the smaller lanes jutting out from these streets.

▓**Pannenkoekenhuis Upstairs,** Grimburgwal 2 (☎626 5603). 2min. walk from the Rokin tram stop. This tiny nook caters to the creative traveler, with vintage photos of Dutch royalty, only 4 tables, and antique teapots hanging from the ceiling. The traditional pancakes are said to be among the best in Amsterdam, but running up to €9 apiece, they don't accommodate slimmer budgets. If you bring an old teapot as an offering, you'll get a free powdered-sugar pancake. Take the ultimate lunchtime plunge with the Miranda (pear, egg nog, chocolate sauce, and whipped cream; €8.50). Open M and F noon-7pm, Sa noon-6pm, Su noon-5pm. ❷

Ristorante Caprese, Spuistraat 259-261 (☎620 0059). From Dam Sq., follow Spuistraat south a few blocks. Authentic Italian food, relaxed jazz, and comforting candlelight in a setting favored by a large number of locals and tourists alike. The chef's homemade pastas and tomato sauce and the restaurant's inexpensive glasses of wine (€3) make Ristorante Caprese an excellent spot to unwind for dinner or a relaxing weekend lunch. You won't find pizzas at this family-run escape, but main pasta dishes run €10-11, and all meat is raised organically. Meat and fish dishes, served with salad and french fries, €18-22. Open daily 5pm-1am. Kitchen closes at 11:45pm. ❸

Green Planet, Spuistraat 122 (☎625 8280; www.greenplanet.nl). This diehard vegetarian restaurant aims to be as environmentally sound as possible. Advertises itself as "more than a restaurant, a lifestyle"—one you might consider converting to after tasting its Asian stir-fry (€15.50). Uses biodegradable packaging for takeout. Salads start at €5.50; add ingredients for €2.50-4.50 each. Lots of vegan options. Organic wines and beers from €2.50. Open M-Sa 5:30pm-midnight. ❸

Sie Joe, Gravenstraat 24 (☎624 1830), between Nieuwendijk and Nieuwezijds Voorburgwal, behind the Nieuwe Kerk. Pronounced like "see you": a phonetic Dutch transcription of the owners' hopes that you'll be back for more. At this warm, family-run joint, you probably will be. Serves up great Indonesian lunch and early dinner at good prices, especially compared with nearby, tourist-oriented Indonesian stops. In this cozy lunch cafe, vegetarians should sample the delectable *gado gado* (mixed vegetables in peanut sauce; €7). *Tjendol* (a delicate drink made of soft green noodles, palm sugar, coconut milk, and crushed ice) €3. Lamb and chicken *satay* just €7. Open M-W and F-Sa 11am-7pm, Th 11am-8pm. ❶

La Place, Kalverstraat 201 (☎622 0171; www.laplace.nl). From the Muntplein tram stop, take Kalverstraat northwest; the restaurant is on your right. In the Vroom & Dreesmann department store, with another entrance on Kalverstraat. Don't expect culinary advice from the security guards at the door; at this upscale cafeteria, they're there to protect the merchandise, not to serve you. Sumptuous market-style buffet boasts sandwiches (€2.60-4.50), pizza (€6.25), a wide range of salads (€3.35-6.35), and meat and fish entrees (€8-10). Curry and noodle bars satisfy international palates. You can even get a glass of wine with your meal (€2.40). Ample indoor seating on 3 floors in a variety of different settings and rooms, including a small terrace overlooking Kalverstraat. Menu and prices change with the season. Open M 11am-8pm, Tu-W and F-Sa 9:30am-8pm, Th 9:30am-9pm, Su 11am-8pm. AmEx/MC/V. ❶

La Fruteria, Nieuwezijds Voorburgwal 141 (☎623 2917), north of Dam against the Nieuwe Kerk. Selling shakes with names like Allegria, Sunshine, and Oasis, you'll be hard-pressed not to leave this small store with a smile on your face. This colorful store sells delicious fruit shakes and juices freshly made from organic produce. Small €3; medium €3.50; large €4; 1L bottle €7. Complement your shake with reasonably priced fruit salad (€3-4) or fruit, yogurt, and muesli (€3-4.30). Open M-Sa 9am-7pm, Su 10am-7pm. Cash only. ❶

Frood, Korte Lijnbaanssteeg 4-6 (☎320 1934), between Nieuwezijds Voorburgwal and Spuistraat, north of Dam and just around the corner from Bob's Youth Hostel. Snug spot off a small side street vends fresh fruit juices, smoothies, and vegetable shakes (€3-3.60) alongside fruit salad (€2.50). For those who are extremely health-conscious, wheatgrass is on tap (1 shot €2.50). Open M-F 8:30am-5:30pm, Sa 10am-5:30pm. ❶

SCHEEPVAARTBUURT

The Scheepvaartbuurt's main drag, Haarlemmerstraat, is home to a truly international spectrum of cuisine, featuring tastes from the American South to Northern Africa. To get to the Scheepvaartbuurt's plentiful restaurants and bars from

see map p. 338

FOOD

Centraal Station, take a right on Prins Hendrikkade, then a left, and then an immediate right onto Nieuwendijk, which turns into Haarlemmerstraat as it crosses the Singel. Haarlemmerstraat turns into Haarlemmerdijk at Korte Prinsengracht. Alternatively, head north from the Jordaan on Prinsengracht, which intersects the street two blocks past the Brouwersgracht.

▩ **Harlem: Drinks and Soulfood,** Haarlemmerstraat 77 (☎330 1498), at the Herenmarkt. Spelled the bizarre, American way (with a single "a"), Harlem serves American Southern soul food, like catfish and macaroni and cheese, infused with Cajun and Caribbean flavors. Practice your drawl with the bartenders next to the chalkboard menu or head outside to the patio for a prime view of Haarlemmerstraat. Rotating dinner menu boasts about 10 creatively prepared and generously portioned dishes, each with a large helping of delicious rice and vegetables (€11-17). Lighter lunch includes the rotating soup of the day (€4.75) and an array of club sandwiches (€4.40-7.50), as well as unique salad selections like the Marvin Gaye (€6.50). Especially packed Th night. Open M-Th 10am-1am, F-Sa 10am-3am, Su 11am-1am. Kitchen closes 10pm. MC/V. ❸

Small World Cafe, Binnen Oranjestraat 14 (☎420 2774; www.smallworldcatering.nl). 1 block off Haarlemmerdijk. A tiny shop with some big and hearty sandwiches, Small World can fill the street outside with happy lunchtime customers on a warm day. Other than a few stools, there's no seating inside the shop, but there are ample chairs and room to chat outside under the awning. Sandwiches from tuna salad (€5.25) to meatloaf (€6). Daily soup around €4. Cakes and desserts €3.25. Open Tu-Sa 10:30am-8pm, Su noon-8pm. Cash only. ❶

Bakkerij Mediterrane, Haarlemmerdijk 184 (☎620 3550), near the end of the street, opposite The Movies. This tiny Moroccan bakery sells cheap and delicious coffee, breads, Moroccan and Dutch pastries, and excellent croissants. Busy during breakfast; the walls are covered with pictures of the smiling faces of regular customers. Everything under €3. Open M-Sa 8am-7:30pm, Su 8am-6pm. Cash only. ❶

Balraj, Haarlemmerdijk 28 (☎625 1428). Top-rate North Indian and Punjabi cuisine in a narrow space that's usually jammed with locals. Though the prices are on the heftier side, they generally remain stable, and the quality of the rations, wide selection, and intimate table settings can make up for throwing down extra cash. Chicken tikka masala €14.25. Spicy lamb *madras* €12.75. Each main dish comes with basmati rice, chapati bread, and *daal*. *Biryani* dishes—both lamb and chicken—are aromatic, simmered with cardamom and coconut and served with sides of curd and lentils (€12.50-13.50). Vegetarian dishes are less expensive: *saag paneer* and *alu mattar* each €10.75. Open daily 4-10pm. Cash only. ❸

Padi, Haarlemmerdijk 50 (☎625 1280). Locals rave about this Indonesian *eethuis* lined with Indonesian fans and rustic wood decor. Padi's menu goes on and on with inexpensive appetizers (€2-5) and a wide range of classic Indonesian offerings. Try chicken, pork, or even goat *satay* (€3.75-4.50) or go for some of Padi's vegetarian offerings. The traditional Indonesian *rijsttafel* costs less here than at many other restaurants (€14.75 for 1, €27.50 for 2). Open daily 5-10pm. Cash only. ❷

Jay's Juice, Haarlemmerstraat 14 (☎623 1267). Jay, the self-proclaimed "king of juice," presides over this den of good vibes where everything, as Jay says, "comes from the heart." Jay's Booster features tomato, ginger, carrot, and celery; add ginseng, guarana, or even horny goat grass (10mg of herbal Viagra) if you're in the mood—or would like to be (each €0.50). Try a shot of pressed wheatgrass juice for €2; Jay grows the grass himself. Buy 10 juices and get 1 free. Juices available in 0.3L (€2.30-3.55), 0.5L (€3.10-4.60), or 1L (€5.50-8.20) bottles. Open daily 8am-7pm. Cash only. ❶

Jordino, Haarlemmerdijk 25 (☎420 3225). This chocolateria sells an enticing smorgasbord of decadent, delectable confections. Ice cream and *gelato* (1 scoop €1.25; each additional scoop €0.75) made with seasonal ingredients. The real draws are the beautifully garnished plates of handmade chocolate (100g bags €3.50-4.10). Open M and Su 1-7pm, Tu-Sa 10am-7pm. ❶

CANAL RING WEST

The Canal Ring West, escaping the touristy blight suffered by its neighbors to the east, has a down-to-earth blend of traditional Dutch and ethnic cuisines. You can still find some tourist traps without too much effort, but the restaurants below are some of the choicest in the district.

see map p. 338

🍴 **Foodism,** Oude Leliestraat 8 (☎427 5103). Bright green walls, red tables, and a cozy, alternative atmosphere surround a friendly staff that serves up a variety of vegetarian dishes and inspired pasta platters (€10-13). Breakfast served all day (coffee, orange juice, bagel, scrambled eggs, and mushrooms; €9.50). Ask for a bottle of pumpkin seed oil, a favorite ingredient of the owner. You can bring your food to Café Zool, the bar across the street. Open M-Sa 11:30am-10pm, Su 1-10pm. Cash only. ❷

🍴 **Hein,** Berenstraat 20 (☎623 1048). If you miss home-cooked meals, you've come to the right place. Watch fresh food prepared in the open kitchen from of the seating area. The menu changes daily, subject to the owner's tastes. Entrees average €10. Sample the fresh selection of pies and cakes (€3). Strudel with spinach and feta cheese (€7.50) is popular. Open M-Sa 8:30am-4pm, Su 9am-4pm. Reservations accepted. Cash only. ❷

Wolvenstraat 23, Wolvenstraat 23 (☎320 0843). This sophisticated establishment is one of the trendiest attractions in the Canal Ring West. White walls adorned with colorful abstract artwork, white velvet couches, and intimate tabletop candles give this restaurant a casual yet urbane feel. Lunch here means sandwiches (€2-5.20), salads (€6), and omelettes (€3-4). Dinner features a wide selection of Asian cuisine. Popular with locals, tourists, and starving artists. Turns into a bar after 10pm. Lunch menu 8am-3:30pm, dinner 6-10:30pm. Open M-Th 8am-1am, F 8am-2am, Sa 9am-2am, Su 10am-1am. Cash only. ❶

The Pancake Bakery, Prinsengracht 191 (☎625 1333). This haven for pancake lovers resides in a 17th-century canal-side warehouse of the Dutch East India Company. Choose from over 40 varieties of pancakes, ranging from peaches to brandy to ham and cheese (€6-9). Also has a selection of international pancakes like Greek lamb gyro or Hawaiian pineapple (€12.50). Enjoy your food in the upstairs seating area overlooking the grand Prinsengracht canal. Open daily noon-9:30pm. AmEx/MC/V. ❷

Prego, Herenstraat 25 (☎638 0148). Dine in style at this intimate, elegantly decorated restaurant, serving a banquet of Mediterranean seafood dishes. Entrees

FOOD TRANSLATION

Dutch menus often have translations, but you may still run into some unappetizing situations. Here are some key words to help you navigate the menu.

Applegebak: Apple pie, sometimes served with whipped cream.

Bruine bonen met stroop: Brown beans with syrup. Yum.

Broodje: A sandwich; usually refers to a small bun or roll, commonly filled with ham and cheese.

Bitterballen: Deep-fried, crispy outside gives way to a casserole-textured inside of mashed meat.

Erwtensoep: Pea soup. A wintertime favorite. Extraordinarily thick soup considered best when the spoon sticks straight up.

Hutspot and **Stamppot:** Two very traditional Dutch meals made with mashed potatoes, vegetables, and sometimes wurst.

Jenever: Traditional Dutch liquor; granddaddy of gin.

Kaas: Cheese.

Kip: Chicken.

Kroket: Crispy fry on the outside, chewy filling of cheese or meat.

Rundvlees: Beef.

Pannenkoeken: Thin, warm pancakes. Classically served with butter and powdered sugar.

Poffertjes: Mini pancakes served with butter, sugar, and syrup.

Rijsttafel: Indonesian "rice table": rice with between 10 and 25 smaller spicy side dishes.

Tostis: An inexpensive classic, usually involving ham, cheese, butter, and two slices of white bread smushed together in a grill.

€19-25. Slightly raised floor allows diners, including a sizable contingent of expats, to watch the chefs at work. Ask the waiters for a wine recommendation from their varied selection. Open daily 6-10pm. ❹

De Kaaskamer, Runstraat 7 (☎ 623 3483). A visit to the Netherlands is never complete without a taste of its famous cheeses, and with over 300 variations to choose from, the selection at this small but well-stocked shop is unlikely to disappoint. Prices range from €1.25-10 per g. Also sells 22 types of olives, a selection of nuts and dried fruits, and an array of wines. The perfect place to pick up a snack to eat by the canals. Open M noon-6pm, Tu-F 9am-6pm, Sa 9am-5pm, Su noon-5pm. Cash only. ❶

Bakkerij Paul Année, Runstraat 25 (☎ 623 5322). The smell of freshly baked bread fills this small neighborhood bakery. All products are baked on the premises, and most are prepared with organic products. Try the giant chocolate croissants (€1.25) or take home a bag of their specialty, honey-roasted granola (€3.50). Small sandwiches (€2.50) often sell out by 2pm. Open M-F 9am-6pm, Sa 9am-5pm. Cash only. ❶

Spanjer en Van Twist, Leliegracht 60 (☎ 639 0109). High ceilings, a lofted seating area, large windows, and a professional crowd give this restaurant a chic, hip feel. Generous portions and tasty food, but at a cost. Lunch offers a variety of sandwiches and salads (€3-8). Dinner includes a grilled rib-eye steak with tuna butter, french fries, and salad (€14.50). Also a full selection of tapas (€11.25). For dessert, try the selection of homemade cakes (€3.20). Lunch served M-F 11am-4pm, Sa-Su 11am-5pm. Dinner M-F 6-10pm, Sa-Su 5-10pm. MC/V. ❸

Koh-i-noor, Westermarkt 29 (☎ 623 3133). Offering a taste of traditional Indian culture with authentic music, vibrant paintings, and colorful tapestries, Koh-i-noor serves an endless variety of Indian delicacies from its long menu. Sit inside to absorb the laid-back atmosphere and delicious smells or outside to enjoy the view. Try the fish *dhansak* (€13.50) or the chicken *tikka tandoori* while digesting cultural and geographical facts from the informative "India At A Glance" placemat. Menu also available for take-out. Open daily 5-11:30pm. AmEx/MC/V. ❸

Het Molenpad, Prinsengracht 653 (☎ 625 9680). The Dutch word *gezelligheid* (coziness) was created to describe eateries like this. Escape from the bustle and take your meal to the wooden benches out back. In mid-summer, locals fill up the canal-side seats in front, and, in winter, they gather at this traditional *bruin cafe*'s inviting bar. Usual *eetcafe* offerings (soup €4.75; entrees €13-16; dessert €6) go well with a *vaasje* of beer (€1.90). Lunch served until 4pm. *Tostis* €2-3. Sandwiches €4-5. Salad €8-14. Dutch snacks like *bitterballen* (€3.40) available 3-10:30pm. Open M-Th and Su noon-1am, F-Sa noon-2am. Cash only. ❸

Top Thai, Herenstraat 22 (☎ 623 4633). Serves traditional Thai cuisine in a spacious and beautifully decorated setting. Sate your palate with pad thai variations (€6-10), entrees like the Flying Chicken (€15.50), Thai Hot Beef (€14.50), or the eclectic Top Thai Pearls, a sampler of the restaurant's appetizers (€7). Takeout available; call ahead. Open daily 4:30-10:30pm. MC/V. ❸

Il Panorama, Herengracht 194 (☎ 627 9577). A taste of Italy in the Netherlands, this corner restaurant has a large, varied selection of hearty sandwiches (€4-6), titanic pizzas (€7-11), and pastas (€9-13) to suit all tastes. Daily dessert menu includes home-made chocolate mousse (€3.75). For dinner, try one of the delicious meat dishes (€14-20). Open M-Sa noon-11pm, Su 1-11pm. Cash only. ❸

DIP OUT OF YOUR POCKET. If you want mayo with your fries (as the locals do), or even just ketchup (which may appear to you more like tomato sauce), you are likely to pay up to €0.35 for it. Just think of it as a healthy respect for condiments that's lacking in the rest of the world.

CENTRAL CANAL RING

Vegetarian and Indonesian options abound between the moats; if their prices are too steep for your wallet, a decent pizzeria is generally just a block or two away.

see map p. 336

■ **Lanskroon,** Singel 385 (☎623 7743), at the Spui. Locals have been getting their fix of traditional Dutch pastries at this famed *banketbakkerij* since 1958. Stop by after a long day or come for a mid-afternoon snack to enjoy *stroopwafels* (honey-filled cookies; €1.50), fresh fruit pies (€2.50), exotically flavored sorbets, and other delights made on-site. Open Tu-F 8am-5:30pm, Sa 9am-6pm, Su 10am-6pm. Cash only. ❶

■ **NOA,** Leidsegracht 84 (☎626 0802; www.withnoa.com), just outside the Leidseplein hype. NOA (Noodles of Amsterdam) is an artsy, elegant restaurant that serves up a diverse menu of pan-Asian dishes. Though pricey, the good food and hip atmosphere will soften the blow. Urbane gourmands sink into plush sofa seats around dainty tables to enjoy pad thai (€15.50) and salads (€13). Everything on the menu €6-16.75. Get your mixed-drink fix here—they make great caipirinhas, apple martinis, and mojitos (€7-9). Open Tu-Th and Su noon-midnight; F-Sa noon-1am. AmEx/MC/V. ❸

Golden Temple, Utrechtsestraat 126 (☎626 8560), between Frederiksplein and Prinsengracht. A lovely vegetarian shrine to light and healthful consumption. Separate breakfast, lunch, and dinner menus offer you the opportunity to visit at your convenience. Relax as you sip a yogi chai tea (€2.10), or try the more substantial Indian *thali,* which allows you to mix and match a meal from various vegetarian or vegan regional delicacies (€12.50). Complete your meal with a scoop from the daily selection of vegan ice creams (€2.25). Hearty pizzas €6.50-9.50. No alcohol served. Open daily 10am-9:30pm. AmEx/MC/V. ❷

Coffee and Jazz, Utrechtsestraat 113 (☎624 5851). With an elegant, candlelit interior, Coffee and Jazz welcomes a persistent stream of faithful local and tourist patrons. Relax amid the bamboo furniture and smooth jazz (the restaurant even produces its own CD) while choosing from a variety of menu options that fuse the Indonesian and the Dutch. Homeland ingredients like fresh mackerel are prepared Indonesian-style, sharing the menu with tender beef *satay* (€10.50). Delectable fruit shakes (€4.50) blend mango, banana, and orange—and are big enough for 2. Call ahead for dinner reservations; on a nice day, enjoy your meal outside on the bustling Utrechtsestraat. Open Tu-F 9:30am-8pm, Sa 10am-4pm. ❷

Axum, Utrechtsedwarsstraat 85-87 (☎622 8389; www.axumrestaurant.nl). Tram #4 to Frederiksplein. Go north on Utrechtsestraat for a block, then turn right on Utrechtsedwarsstraat. Wonderful family-run eatery serving great Ethiopian fare. Use your hands to scoop up your food with tart *injera* while marveling at the authentic Ethiopian decorations. Well-spiced entrees (€11-14) come in steaming pots and include small sides of lentils, salad, and veggies. *Wot*'s up here on a regular basis with highlights like *yebeg wot* (zesty lamb; €11) and *doro wot* (zesty chicken; €9.75). Vegetarians, rest assured; Axum offers a variety of veggie options, such as the *shiro wot* (fried, mashed chickpeas in Ethiopian herbs; €9.75). Split Ethiopian-style coffee with a friend (€5, serves 2-3 people) to top off your meal. Open M-F 5:30-11pm, Sa-Su 5:30-11:30pm. ❷

Tashi Deleg, Utrechtsestraat 65 (☎620 6624). Choose from 2 separate menus—Indonesian or Tibetan—at this pricey but relaxed eatery illuminated by silver bird's-nest chandeliers. For a simple meal, try the *cha sha tse* (boneless chicken curry; €12), a Tibetan 3-course menu (€19.50), or a filling Indonesian *rijsttafel* (rice accompanied by 5 or more small dishes; €15-23.50). Balance the food with tart *tib chang* (Tibetan rice beer; €1.75) or the house specialty, buttered tea. Open Tu-Su 3-11:30pm. V. ❹

Carousel Pancake House, Weteringcircuit 1 (☎625 8002). Tram #6, 7, 16, 24, or 25 to Weteringcircuit. Delectable pancakes are the main attraction at this warm, inviting, doughnut-shaped *eethuis* named for its model merry-go-round. The location in the

FOOD

greenery of Weteringcircuit makes this tourist attraction an ideal place to enjoy delicious food and the beauty of nature. The *pannenkoeken*—large, buttery, and warm—are served with a variety of toppings, from fruit to bacon to cheese (€3.50-8). For dessert, split a fluffy Carousel pancake (€8), which arrives smothered in fruit preserves and 3 ice-cream scoops. Open daily 10am-8:30pm. Cash only. ❶

LEIDSEPLEIN

If you're looking for an undiscovered culinary gem, look elsewhere. Expensive tourist menus are everywhere you turn in Leidseplein, and there are always plenty of tourists to eat them up. Here we list a few good deals among the madness and a few small refuges from the massive maelstrom. If you simply want a quick bite and some food in your belly, two international fast-food joints on Leidsestraat serve good-quality and surprisingly tasty meals for €4-7: at **Maoz Falafel** (see **The Wonderful Mensch of Maoz**, p. 132), you'll find falafel, hummus, and *frites*. (Open M-Th and Su 11am-1am, F-Sa 11am-3am. Cash only.) **Wok to Walk,** Leidsestraat 96, serves fried rice and noodle dishes with a variety of meat and vegetable options. (www.woktowalk.com. Open M-F 11:30am-1am, 11:30am-3am. Cash only.)

see map p. 337

☒ **Eat at Jo's,** Marnixstraat 409 (☎624 1777; www.melkweg.nl), inside Melkweg (p. 232). Tram #1, 2, 5, 6, 7, or 10 to Leidseplein. Turn down the smaller side street to the left of the grand Stadsschouwburg theater. An enclave of cool just outside Leidseplein. Milwaukee-born chef Mary Jo first came to Melkweg when her musician husband played there. Today the couple feeds musicians, hipsters, and little old ladies alike with a multiethnic, freshly prepared menu that changes daily. Bands often grab a bite to eat after a performance at Melkweg. Recent guests include Dido, Tom Jones, and Coldplay. Soups (€4.40) and numerous vegetarian options (entrees €13) earn rave reviews. Open W-Su noon-9pm. Cash only. ❸

☒ **Bombay Inn,** Lange Leidsedwarsstraat 46 (☎624 1784). Bombay Inn stands out for delicately spiced dishes at excellent value. The choice for budget travelers is clear: just ask for the generous "tourist menu" and gorge on 3 courses. Includes *papadum* and soup, chicken or lamb curry, mixed rice, salad, and coffee or dessert (chicken menu €8.50; lamb menu €9.50; 2-person menu available). Veggie sides such as *alu palaak* and *saag paneer* come cheap as well (€5.50). Rice (€2.25) and other extras not included. Open daily 5-11pm. AmEx/MC/V. ❷

Café Americain, Leidsekade 97 (☎556 3116; www.amsterdamamerican.com), inside, but spelled differently from, the American Hotel, overlooking Leidseplein on the corner of Marnixstraat. Still home to original 1902 Tiffany lamps, wall murals, and reading tables, Café Americain is a monument to Art Deco sophistication. Stop by for a drink or a snack in the dark and atmospheric space—where Humphrey Bogart himself would feel at home—or on the pleasant terrace in good weather (but make sure to take a peek inside before you leave). Dinner is a considerably more expensive and formal affair. Beer €3. Assorted warm snack platter €8. Dinner entrees from €17. Open M-F 6:30am-11:30pm, Sa-Su 7am-11:30pm. Kitchen closes at 10pm. AmEx/MC/V. ❹

J.J. Ooyevaar, Lange Leidsedwarsstraat 47 (☎623 5503). A simple deli counter at the back of a small convenience store. Surrounded by fancy restaurants, it's easy to miss, but J.J. Ooyevaar is the best (and only) place near Leidseplein for lunch under €3. Endless varieties of sandwiches on many different kinds of bread, from the ham and cheese *broodje* (€2) to the mozzarella, tomato and pesto ciabatta (€2.65). Open M-F 8:30am-6pm, Sa-Su 8:30am-5pm. Cash only. ❶

De Balie, Kleine-Gartmanplantsoen 10 (☎553 5131; www.debalie.nl). This art-house cinema and cultural center is also home to a hip and affordable cafe, restaurant, and bar that attracts many of the hip and affable patrons. Snacks or a lunch in the cafe (*tostis* with cheese, tomato, and turkey sausage €3.75) won't set you back more than €5. At dinner, get €2 off the set menu (a starter, main course, and coffee; €19.50) with a ticket stub from De Balie or Paradiso. Outdoor seating. Cafe menu available 11am-4pm. Dinner 4-10pm. Open daily 10am-1am. Cash only. ❸

Bojo, Lange Leidsedwarsstraat 51 (☎622 7434). Bojo is the most laid-back Indonesian restaurant in Leidseplein. The food, served in large portions, keeps the restaurant packed until late. You can't go wrong with the tender savory lamb or chicken *satay* smothered in peanut sauce (€6). House fave *ayam banjar* features chicken in a sweet and spicy sauce (€10.25). *Lychees* make for a great dessert (€2). Open M-Th 4pm-2am, F 4pm-4am, Sa noon-4am, Su noon-2am. AmEx/MC/V. ❷

Belgica, Kleine-Gartmanplantsoen 25 (☎535 3290; www.belgica.nu). The space beyond the revolving door of this quiet brasserie seems about as far as Belgium when it comes to escaping the madness of Leidseplein. Come here for a nice drink (8 beers on tap from €2.20) or bite to eat—try a "soup bowl bun" filled with *chile con carne* (€7.50). Open daily 7am-1am. Kitchen closes at 12:30am. Cash only. ❷

Chicanos, Korte Leidsedwarsstraat 105 (☎626 1104). Slightly tacky cowhide furnishings and an American cowboy hue give away its tourist emphasis, but some good deals on tasty Tex-Mex dishes are available. Try the pre-arranged "student menu": choose between spare ribs, chicken, or steak with chips, salad, and a small beer (M-Th €10.25) or all-you-can-eat spare ribs with potato wedges and a salad (€17). Good place to go with a group. Open M-F 5-11pm, Sa 12:30-11pm, Su 12:30-10:30pm. ❸

The Pantry, Leidsekruisstraat 21 (☎620 0922). If the seemingly endless selection of Indian, Indonesian, and Middle Eastern restaurants leaves you yearning for more traditional Dutch fare, head to The Pantry. Start your meal with smoked eel on toast (€7.50) and then choose from a selection of typical Dutch platters like *hutspot,* a boiled mix of mashed potatoes, stewed beef, carrots, and onions (€11). Small and often very crowded; reservations recommended. Open M-F 5-11pm, Sa-Su noon-11pm. ❷

REMBRANDTPLEIN

The Rembrandtplein area overflows with countless restaurants and pubs, but only a few of these offerings are worth a try, even with the promise of the area's prime people-watching. Utrechtsestraat, running south of Rembrandtplein in the southeast corner, is where you will find some of the best and least touristed restaurants.

see map p. 336

■ **Ristorante Pizzeria Firenze,** Halvemaansteeg 9-11 (☎627 3360; www.pizzeria-firenze.nl). Just off Rembrandtplein, next to Montmartre (p. 234). A delightful little Italian restaurant and pizzeria, complete with murals of the Italian countryside, friendly service, and simply unbeatable prices. 25 types of pizza (€4.60-8) and pasta (€5.25-8). Lasagna €8.50. Glass of house wine €2.25. One of the least expensive stops for a sit-down meal anywhere in Rembrandtplein. Open daily 1-11pm. MC/V. ❶

■ **Van Dobben,** Korte Reguliersdwarsstraat 5-9 (☎624 4200). For quick, no-frills food on the cheap, this old-fashioned deli and neighborhood cafeteria is the perfect stop. Van Dobben has been serving customers since 1945, and almost everything on the menu is under €5. Choose from the large selection of sandwiches under €3, including roast beef (€3) and ham (€2.80). The stone tabletops, tiled walls, and meat-cutting machines give the place a classic, clean feel. If you're in a hurry, they'll pack up your meal. Open M-Th 9:30am-1am, F-Sa 9:30am-2am, Su 11:30am-8pm. Cash only. ❶

Rose's Cantina, Reguliersdwarsstraat 40 (☎625 9797; www.rosescantina.com). Tram #1, 2, or 5 to Koningsplein or #4, 9, 14, 16, 24, or 25 to Muntplein. A large open restaurant that is something of a neighborhood institution, with high ceilings and a gigantic

FOOD

THE WONDERFUL MENSCH OF MAOZ

During Hanukkah, so the story goes, a day's worth of oil lasted eight full days. At **Maoz Falafel**, hungry travelers can make their sandwiches last nearly as long. Owned by two Israeli brothers, Maoz is an Amsterdam-based chain that has recently spread to locations in Australia, Europe, and the US. Maoz is known for its endlessly replenishing salad bar, fresh homemade falafel, healthful veggies, and incomparably low prices. Three falafel with salad cost €3.50, and a falafel sandwich runs €4. With the right technique, you can make these dishes your daily meal. Ordering any falafel gives you access to the all-you-can-stack salad bar. Pile up a Middle Eastern dagwood of couscous, carrots, tomatoes, spicy onions, beets, peppers, and tahini—and don't be shy about going back for seconds. Expert stackers say the secret is leaving the pita intact; that way, there's room for the second trip.

Maoz locations are spread throughout the center of Amsterdam. Around lunch and dinner times, arrive early unless you want to wait. Locations outside Centraal Station (☎623 0793), Muntplein 1 (☎420 7435), Leidsestraat 85 (☎427 9720), 1e Van Der Helststraat 43 (☎676 7612), Oudebrugsteeg 30 (☎625 0717), and Ferdinand Bolstraat 67. Open daily 11am-11pm, but hours vary by location.

bar. Quieter garden terrace in back for warmer nights. The mood is always lively, accentuated by sultry salsa music (and dip). Though the food is mostly classic Tex-Mex, it also includes hamburgers and salads. €17.50 gets you a choice of 2 out of 3: quesadillas, enchiladas, or tacos, served with sides of rice, black beans, and guacamole. Fajitas €19.50. Margaritas are small, but quality and presentation take precedence. All mixed drinks €6.50. To start the party early, order a 1L margarita pitcher (€41.50). Reservations recommended, especially on weekends. Open Tu-Su 5pm-midnight. Kitchen open 5-10pm. AmEx/MC/V. ❹

La Margarita, Reguliersdwarsstraat 49 (☎623 0707). La Margarita is a lighthearted, family-run Caribbean restaurant that serves creative meals native to the islands. Colorful walls, straw umbrellas, and vibrant greenery add an authentic touch accentuated by rollicking music and a friendly staff. Try tropical dishes such as marinated red snapper (€18.25). All entrees (€15-20) include rice, beans, sweet potatoes, plantains, and tropical vegetables. Abundant vegetarian dishes €15. Extensive drink menu; most mixed drinks €6.30. 3-course buffet €20. Reservations recommended. Open M-Th and Su 5pm-1am, F-Sa 5pm-3am. Kitchen closes at 11pm. AmEx/MC/V. ❹

Tomo Sushi, Reguliersdwarsstraat 131 (☎528 5208). Hip sushi joint with stylish, minimalist furnishings. The salsa music, though somewhat incongruous, fits the relaxed, clean vibe. Sushi and/or *sashimi* combos €15.50-27; most about €22. *Nigiri* (including scallop and yellowtail) €1.40-3.70. 6-piece *maki* sushi €3.70-9.20. Salmon roll €4.80. Tempura €18. Cleanse your palate with green tea ice cream (€5). Domestic beer €2.80. Imported Japanese beer €3.80. Warm sake €5. Open daily 5:30-11:30pm. Reservations recommended. AmEx/MC/V. ❹

Thai Restaurant Phuket, Reguliersdwarsstraat 11 (☎626 5010), at the northern end of Reguliersdwarsstraat. Nestled amid some of Amsterdam's most bustling nightlife, this simple Thai place is a good stop for affordable, high-quality food. Try the "tourist menu" (choice of spring rolls or vegetable soup with vegetables, white rice, and curry chicken or fried pork; €11.50). Pad thai €10.50-15. Open daily 3-11pm. AmEx/MC/V. ❷

JORDAAN

It's worth heading out west to the Jordaan for sophisticated eats on an outdoor terrace. Cuisine here tends to be more discriminating than in the Centrum, though not necessarily more expensive.

see map p. 338

■ **De Vliegende Schotel,** Nieuwe Leliestraat 162-168 (☎ 625 2041; www.vliegendescho-tel.com). The name may be alien (it means "The Flying Saucer," by the way), but De Vliegende Schotel's food is simple, organic, and delicious. With faves like tempura and goulash, this casual vegetarian restaurant's diverse menu is ideal for a quick bite. Ample brightly colored tables and chairs. Soups and starters from €2.50. Entrees, including cheese fondue, from €9.40. Beer €2. Wine €3 per glass. Open daily 5-11:30pm. Kitchen closes at 10:15pm. AmEx/MC/V. ❷

■ **Rainarai,** Prinsengracht 252 (☎ 624 9791; www.rainarai.nl), on the corner of Laurier-gracht. This small but special Algerian restaurant, market, and deli serves absolutely delicious food. On sunny days, Rainarai lays out oriental carpets on the sidewalk for uber-relaxed eating and people-watching. The 7 daily dishes (made with fresh ingredi-ents like quail, artichokes, tomatoes, or sole) can be taken to go (around €4 per kg), or you can choose a combination to be consumed at a luxurious spot out by the canal (3 dishes €8.50). Open daily 10am-10pm. Cash only. ❶

Rakang, Elandsgracht 29 (☎ 620 9551). Rakang is an elegant, authentic, and upscale Thai restaurant, but that's not the half of it: the next door down is the **takeout counter** ❶, where you'll find one of the best deals for food in the Jordaan. Main dishes €3.50; snacks like spring rolls €1. Set menu of rice, vegetables, and two main dishes €8.50. Yeah, it blew our minds too. Open daily 4:30-10:30pm. If you decide to go for the sit-down, family-style dinner, you'll find appetizers €6-12 and entrees €18-22. Many *prix-fixe* menu choices. Open daily 6-10:30pm. ❹

De Reiger, Nieuwe Leliestraat 34 (☎ 624 7426). Although it won't come cheap, you'll be hard-pressed to find a more delicious dinner in the Netherlands. A very local, very busy restaurant, bar, and *bruin cafe,* but the food here is no joke. Perfectly cooked rack of lamb €19.50. Mustard soup €6. Open daily 5pm-1am, lunch Sa from 11am with a cheaper menu of *broodjes* (€2.50) and main dishes like *carpaccio* (€6). Kitchen closes at 10:30pm. Cash only. ❹

Cinema Paradiso, Westerstraat 186 (☎ 623 7344; www.cinemaparadiso.info). Word of mouth has filled this cavernous, windowless former cinema with fans of its purist Italian food and candlelit charm. Antipasti €4-10. Bruschetta for 2 €10. Pasta €9-15. No res-ervations for parties of fewer than 8 people, so be prepared for a wait unless you arrive early. Open Tu-Su 6-11pm. AmEx/MC/V. ❷

Roem, 126 Prinsengracht (☎ 427 7955). This people-watching hot spot features a prime canal location and inexpensive eats. 3 price levels for sandwiches, from €4 *broodjes* to big €7 clubs. Chocolate truffle pie—a time-tested locals' favorite—€3.50. Dinner entrees around €12; salads €7-11. Enjoy a glass of wine (€2.50) or a beer (€2) later in the evening, when the restaurant becomes more of a destination for drinkers. M-Th and Su 10am-1am, F-Sa 10am-3am. Cash only. ❷

Ben Cohen Shawarma, Rozengracht 239 (☎ 627 9721). Tram #10 to Rozengracht or #3, 14, or 17 to Marnixstraat. Open late and won't break the bank. Yummy, simple Sha-warma (€4.50) and french fries. Open daily 5pm-3am. ❶

Restaurant de Bolhoed, Prinsengracht 60-62 (☎ 626 1803). Perennial contender for the best in vegetarian and vegan fare—fresh, flavorful, and lovingly prepared. The canal-side setting is lovely, but so is the cozy interior, shielded from the street by overgrown leafy vines. Besides a variety of pastas, casseroles, and Mexican dishes (€12.50-15), the key attractions are freshly squeezed juices and organic and vegan desserts made daily. Be sure to try the banana cream pie (€4.50). Generous portions in the vegan meal of the day (€17.50). Set menus from €21. Dinner reservations necessary; last reservation 9pm. Open M-F and Su 11am-10pm, Sa 10am-10pm. Cash only. ❸

Cafe de Koe, Marnixstraat 381 (☎ 625 4482; www.cafedekoe.nl). A relaxed crowd, rock music, and some *koeien* (*koe* means "cow") make this 2-level tavern a happening spot. The first of a string of hip bars lining Marnixstraat on the way to Leidseplein, Koe is usu-

FOOD

ally busy but not overwhelming. Live music most Su (call ahead for info); music trivia "pop quiz" last Su of the month. More attractive for a sit-down dinner than most bars. Try the daily special (€9.50) or choose from meat, fish, veggie, and pasta dishes (€8-12) like the ostrich steak (€14.50). Remember to tip—the waitstaff, not the cows. Cafe open M-F and Su 4pm-1am, Sa 4pm-3am. Kitchen open 6-10:30pm. AmEx/MC/V. ❷

WESTERPARK AND OUD-WEST

They're a bit of a hike from the center of Amsterdam, but the Westerpark and Oud-West neighborhoods dish up high-quality cuisine, especially for East African and Middle Eastern fare. The best places line the **Overtoom** and the three **Helmersstraats,** while **Jan Pieter Heijestraat** hosts many takeout joints. **Kinkerstraat** is also packed with ethnic eateries.

see map p. 343

🔳 **Cafe-Restaurant Amsterdam,** Watertorenplein 6 (☎682 2667; www.cradam.nl). Worth the trek out to Van Hallstraat in Westerpark, the terminus of tram #10, this converted water-pumping station has inherited wonderfully high ceilings and a minimalist charm from its industrial roots. Surprisingly casual and child-friendly, with a continental menu of meat, fish, and vegetable choices (€10-20) that changes seasonally. Part of the massive restaurant is without tablecloths and has more of a cafe feel (hence the name); people linger here for hours with a book and a latte. The terrace is particularly enjoyable, with a natural feel along a small grassy marsh. Reservations can be made on the website. Free Wi-Fi. Open M-Th 10:30am-midnight, F-Sa 10:30am-1am. Kitchen open M-Th until 10:30pm, F-Sa until 11:30pm. AmEx/MC/V. ❸

🔳 **Peperwortel,** Overtoom 140 (☎685 1053; www.peperwortel.nl). 1 block from 1e Constantijn Huygensstraat. Peperwortel is a deli-slash-restaurant and a foodie's paradise. Rotating menu of entrees (around €9.50) features dishes like Indonesian beef or couscous and ratatouille, and each comes with rice, pasta, or potatoes and a vegetable. Have them pack it up so you can take it to Vondelpark across the street, or you can eat on one of their tables outside. Open M-F 4-9pm, Sa-Su 3-9pm. Cash only. ❷

Kismet, Kinkerstraat 350 (☎683 9975). Tram #7 or 17 to Jan Pieter Heijestraat. Small, utterly unpretentious place serving Turkish food; you'd never guess to go in here, but the food is excellent and quite cheap. You can sit to eat at a simple table or take it to go. Try the Turkish pizza (€1.75) and the large selection of homemade Turkish treats like grape leaves (3 for €1) and amazing baklava (€2.50). Combo menus €5.50. Open daily 9am-9pm. ❶

Yam Yam, Frederik Hendrikstraat 88-90 (☎681 5097; www.yamyam.nl). Yam Yam is a small, relatively unadorned trattoria, and while you may be unimpressed by the decor, you are likely to be won over by the delicious food. Pizza is the specialty here (around €15 per pie), but all manner of Italian food is on the menu, from bruschetta to tiramisu. The Yam Yam pizza (€13.50), made with truffle sauce, is especially fantastic. Open Tu-Su 6-10:30pm. MC/V. ❷

De Avondmarkt, De Wittenkade 94-96 (☎686 4919). One of the largest night shops in Amsterdam, this late-night grocery and delicatessen boasts all the essentials of a small supermarket (jam, bread, snacks, and so on), with a full menu of hot food and an extensive wine collection. Munch on over 80 kinds of cheeses (€4.50-30 per kg) or buy hot, ready-to-eat spare ribs (€1.10 per 100g), lasagna (€9 per kg), or a wide variety of other home-cooked foods in portions that could feed Amsterdam. All bread is freshly baked on premises. There is also a collection of organic fruits, milks, and other products. Open M-F 4pm-midnight, Sa 4pm-3am, Su 4pm-2am. ❶

Addis Ababa Restaurant, Overtoom 337 (☎618 4472). This popular, unassuming restaurant is owned by an Ethiopian couple; it isn't anything fancy, but it won't break the bank either. Try the *gomen wot,* spinach with cottage cheese, lentils, vegetables, and salad, served with *injera,* traditional Ethiopian bread. Entrees €7.50-10.50. Combo meals €12. Open 5-11pm. ❷

Esoterica, Overtoom 409 (☎689 7226). Tram #1 or 6 to Rhijnvis Feithstraat. Walk 3 blocks on Overtoom away from the canal; Esoterica is worth every step. There's no obvious sign; look for it on the corner of Schoolstraat. All the food is freshly prepared at this eccentric, placid spot specializing in vegetarian and Indonesian cuisine. Browse the eclectic book collection or the variety of paintings on display by local artists. Chess tournaments every Su afternoon. Appetizers €2.40-5. Main dishes €7.50-8.50. Indonesian *rijsttafel* €13.50. Vegan options also available. Open W-Su 2-10pm. Cash only. ❷

Dosa, Overtoom 146 (☎616 4838; www.dosasouthindian.nl). Tram #1 or 6 to 1e Constantijn Huygensstraat. Serves straightforward South Indian cuisine in a pleasant setting. One of the few Indian restaurants around with a selection of southern specialties. Try one of the six varieties of *dosa,* a South Indian savory pancake (€12-16). Plenty of vegetarian choices and a surprisingly large variety of *naan* (€1.50-4). For dessert, try *kheer,* the traditional Indian rice pudding (€3), or homemade Indian ice cream (*kulfi;* €3-4.50). Sides hover around €6; entrees about €13. Delivery available to nearby Leidseplein hotels daily until 10:30pm. Open M-F 3:30-11:30pm, Sa-Su noon-11:30pm. Kitchen closes daily 11pm. AmEx/MC/V. ❸

Zouk, 1e Constantijn Huygensstraat 45 (☎689 1133). Tram #1 or 6 to 1e Constantijn Huygensstraat. Like its sister Cafe de Pijp (p. 137), Zouk doesn't take its trendiness too seriously. Dinner of rib-eye steak, Thai, or Mexican at this casual, stylish spot will run you €12-16. The menu changes seasonally, but there is always at least 1 vegetarian dinner option. Range of lunch sandwiches €3-5. Beer €2. Caipirinhas €5. Open M-Th and Su noon-1am, F-Sa noon-3am. Kitchen closes daily 10pm. Cash only. ❸

Abyssinia Afrikaans Eetcafe, Jan Pieter Heijestraat 190 (☎683 0792). Tram #1 or 6 to Jan Pieter Heijestraat. Bamboo walls, African lamps, and dark wood tables accompany authentic Ethiopian food in this dimly lit, intimate restaurant. Enjoy an extensive menu, including many vegetarian options (entrees €9.50-15). Eat off a platter of tasty *injera* (fermented pancakes) with your hands. African beers €3. Reservations suggested. Open daily 5pm-midnight. AmEx/MC/V. ❸

Westers, 1e Constantijn Huygensstraat 35-37 (☎612 1691). Tram #1 or 3 to Overtoom. Westers has the cozy feeling of a *bruin cafe* but in a sizable space with big windows, plus a typical Dutch menu and a pleasant outdoor terrace. Several vegetarian options available. Appetizers and salads run €6-8; entrees around €9-15. Try the €13 daily special for a good value. 10 types

ON THE MENU

ONE WAFEL, EXTRA STROOP

While many European countries are world-renowned for their signature baked goods, the Netherlands generally doesn't rank high on the list. However, while the sturdy and delectable *stroopwafel* is not exactly a household name abroad, this well-kept secret may be the tastiest part of your visit to the Low Countries.

According to legend, the *stroopwafel* was invented in 1784 in Gouda, when a baker collected his leftover scraps of dough to make a delicately pressed cookie, which he split in half and filled with a caramel syrup. Over the next few years, he honed the recipe, immortalizing it throughout the Netherlands. Fragrant with cinnamon and other spices, the dough is pressed into very thin waffle molds, filled with caramel, and sandwiched together. While you will usually see *stroopwafels* with a diameter of four inches in sealed packages of 10 or 12, some bakeries also make special 10 in. *stroopwafels.* These versions stand alone, fresh and untarnished by a paper or plastic container, and scream to be eaten.

However, *stroopwafels* are delicious even from the package, especially with afternoon tea or coffee. You can even get a freshly baked taste if you place the *stroopwafel* over your steaming mug until it becomes warm and gooey. Yum!

of lunch sandwiches for €2.50. Beers start at €1.80. Open M-Th 11am-1am, F-Su 11am-2am. Kitchen closes at 10:30pm. Cash only. ❸

Tig Barra, Overtoom 31 (☎ 412 2210; www.tigbarra.nl). Tram #1 or 6 to 1e Constantijn Huygensstraat. Walk toward the Singelgracht, and Tig Barra will be on the right side of the street. A monument to the Emerald Isle; look for Irish flags flying over the door at this full-on Irish pub and restaurant. Abide by the "homage to the gargle" painted above the bar and have a pint of Guinness (€4.30) alongside Irish pub grub (€8-11.50). Catch Irish football matches on the big-screen TV. Bollycotton fish pie €11.50. Beef-and-Guinness pie €12. Breakfast served any time of the day for late risers; enjoy the heaping "Irish Breakfast": eggs, sausages, bacon, beans, mushrooms, tomatoes, hash browns, and toast (€12). Weekly live music from local and traditional Irish musicians; call ahead for info. Open daily 10am-1am. ❷

Restaurant Zina, Bosboom Toussaintstraat 70 (☎ 489 3707; www.restaurantzina.com). For a much more elegant taste of Middle Eastern cuisine than Shawarma and falafel stands offer, try this sleek new restaurant owned by one of Amsterdam's better-known North African chefs. You won't get a heaping meal for a budget price here, but the Tunisian and Moroccan cuisine is prepared with loving care, and it shows. Entrees €16-21. Reservations strongly recommended. Open Tu-Su 6:30-10pm. AmEx/V. ❹

MUSEUMPLEIN AND VONDELPARK

If you're looking for a quick bite while gallery-hopping in the area, Museumplein's major museums all have cafes with unexceptional food. Lining the surrounding park and boulevards, food stands offer equally unexceptional but somewhat cheaper and greasier food (sandwiches and hot dogs; €2-3). You might want to stock up on snacks at the **Albert Heijn** supermarket on Van Baerlestraat, near the Concertgebouw; above it is a slanted, grassy plain perfect for picnicking. For more quality sit-down fare, try one of the following area eateries.

see map p. 342

🏵 **Cafe Vertigo,** Vondelpark 3 (☎ 612 3021; www.vertigo.nl). Adjacent to the Filmmuseum and overlooking a placid duck pond toward the north (by northwest) corner of the park, Vertigo's expansive, tree-lined terrace and balcony are perfect places to kick back and eye the birds through the rear window. If you're lucky, in the warmer months you can listen spellbound to a pianist playing Liszt or Mozart on the terrace—these musicians don't get stage fright. Forgo the cafe's pricier dinner menu in favor of the filling lunch sandwiches (BLTC—C is for chicken—€5.50) and tasty snacks (spring rolls €3.50). Basket lunches for a picnic are available from €17.50 (visit www.citypicknick.nl or dial M, and then the rest of the number, for reservations). Without a shadow of a doubt, you'd have to be psycho to skip Vertigo. Sept.-Mar. Sa disco nights. Lunch until 5pm, soups and salads available 5-6pm, and dinner 6-10pm. Open daily 10am-1am. MC/V. ❶

Het Blauwe Theehuis, Vondelpark 5 (☎ 662 0254; www.blauwetheehuis.nl). In the middle of the park, just south of the open-air theater. Through the trees in the park, you may glimpse a linoleum flying saucer full of people having a good time. This is in fact Het Blauwe Theehuis, a cafe-bar with circular terraces. Lunch sandwiches (€4) and evening tapas (€3-4) are pretty standard, but stop by Het Blauwe for a drink instead. Chill on the outdoor patio in the warmer months or, in winter, watch people pass in the park from upstairs. DJ Su night. Open M-Th and Su 9am-midnight, F-Sa 9am-2am. Lunch starts at 11am; kitchen closes at 10pm. Cash only. ❶

Go Sushi, Johannes Verhulststraat 35 (☎ 471 0035). Tram #16 to Jacob Obrechtstraat. No relation to the famous London conveyor-belt sushi chain Yo! Sushi, Go Sushi is a tiny "Japanese Eetwinkel" tucked into a quiet street. Yummy sushi is made to order right before your eyes. 3 pieces of *maki* €1.90-2.60. *Nigiri* €1.20-3. 10-piece sushi "lunchbox" €9 or full-meal Bento box €12.50. Takeout available, or eat in at the tiny bar. Open M-F noon-7pm. Cash only. ❷

Bagels & Beans, Van Baerlestraat 40 (☎675 7050), 1 block from the Concertgebouw toward the Vondelpark. The original store of a successful Amsterdam chain, Bagels & Beans's simple combination provides two perennial favorites: great coffee and better bagel sandwiches—and they're both cheap. Head here after a morning on the Museum-plein. Bagel with avocado, tomato, and cheese €4.40. Bagel with chocolate sprinkles and butter €2.30. Free Wi-Fi. Live jazz W at 3:30 and 6:30pm on the back patio. Open May-Sept. M-F 7:59am-6:02pm (we kid you not), Sa-Su 9:31am-6:02pm; Oct.-Apr. M-F 8:28am-6:01pm, Sa-Su 9:31am-5:59pm. ❶

Tapa Feliz, Valeriusstraat 85HS (☎364 1283). Tram #16 to Emmastraat. Advertising itself as a tapas bar and international restaurant, Feliz serves multicultural dishes in a polychromatic tiled 2-floor restaurant. Linger over sangria (0.5L for €8) and tapas (olives €2.50; chorizo €5.50) with the locals on Feliz's pleasant terrace. Warm sand-wiches at lunchtime (€4-6.25) are kinder to the wallet than the expensive dinner entrees, though the large paella (€18.50) is nicely spiced and big enough to share. Artisan brown bread with garlic mayonnaise €3. The wine list is long and reasonably priced at €18-30 per bottle; a chilled rose is always included in the summertime. Lunch daily 11:30am-3pm. Dinner M-F 5:30-10:30pm, Sa-Su 3:30-10:30pm. AmEx/MC/V. ❸

DE PIJP

The food scene in De Pijp is unbeatable. The sheer number of flourishing restaurants is astounding in what was once con-sidered a downtrodden area; the explosion of eateries reflects the neighborhood's upward mobility. Scores of no-frills eth-nic joints share streets with more expensive, elegantly appointed restaurants serving "international cuisine," a term implying culinary influences from Thailand to Greece. For a

see map p. 333

reasonably priced meal, choose from Kurdish, Surinamese, or Cambodian cuisine along the **Albert Cuypstraat** east of the market. If plush mixed drinks are more your speed, hit **Ferdinand Bolstraat** for more highly priced selections. Both inexpensive and more upscale options are included below.

Cafe De Pijp, Ferdinand Bolstraat 17-19 (☎670 4161). Tram #16, 24, or 25 to Stad-houderskade. A hip and sociable restaurant in the heart of De Pijp—unsurprisingly, this isn't the place to come for a quiet night out. Good Mediterranean-influenced food is complimented by even better company. Soup of the day €4. Popular tapas starter for two €15. Entrees €13-15. Mixed drinks €5. Open M-Th 3:30pm-1am, F 3:30pm-3am, Sa noon-2am, Su noon-1am. Cash only. ❸

Bazar, Albert Cuypstraat 182 (☎664 7173). Tram #16, 24, or 25 to Albert Cuypstraat. Bazar is a massive, high-ceilinged wonder housed in the open space of a former church just off the bustling Albert Cuypmarkt. The menu features excellent and inexpensive cuisine from North Africa, Lebanon, and Turkey, and the decor runs the gamut from a large Coca-Cola sign in Arabic to beautifully ornate, oversized Arabian lamps. The lunch special is a mere €10 per person (min. 2 people). Breakfast (think Algerian pancakes and Turkish yogurt) and lunch start at €3.50. Main dinner courses around €10. Be on the safer side and make reservations for dinner. Open M-Th 9am-1am, F-Sa 9am-2am, Su 9am-midnight. ❷

De Soepwinkel, 1e Sweelinckstraat 19F (☎673 2293; www.soepwinkel.nl), just off Albert Cuypmarkt. A hip kitchen that elevates soup-making to a fine art. The simple bench-and-table decor focuses your attention on the mouthwatering selection of all-nat-ural homemade soups, from Indonesian chicken soup to gazpacho. 6 specialties change every month but always include vegetarian options and a soup for kids. All

FOOD

THE BIG SPLURGE

DE KAS

An expensive meal isn't hard to come by in Amsterdam (in fact, depending on your budget, any meal in Amsterdam may be expensive), but if you're looking for a delicious meal in an unusual space, a trip out to De Kas is more than worth the time and money. De Kas isn't easy to find—it's probably farther from the city than the average tourist to Amsterdam would ever go—but that makes its solarium, looking out into the green park, seem a world away from the urban sprawl.

The restaurant itself is a working, functioning greenhouse, so the building is filled to the brim with light and greenery. Two greenhouses filled with tomato plants, basil, and lemon trees flank the main central space, where the glass-walled kitchen faces the large, high-ceilinged dining room. The greenhouse sits in Frankendael Park, a wide-open expanse surrounded by ponds and trees, so it feels secluded from the surrounding roads. Outside the buildings is a small, meticulously kept herb garden where patrons can eat when the weather is nice enough.

What makes this place even more special is its history. Once a marshy swampland, the area became the Golden Age site of wealthy Amsterdammers' summer homes in the 17th century. In 1926, the Amsterdam Municipal Nursery erected its greenhouse complex here. In 1997, develop-

served with fresh bread (prices range from €3.75 for a small vegetarian soup to €10.50 for a large meaty one). Non-soup menu includes quiche (€2.50) and a brie, apple, and walnut sandwich (€3.50). Open M-F 11am-8pm, Sa 11am-6pm. Cash only. ❶

Warung Spang Makandra, Gerard Doustraat 39 (☎670 5081; www.spangmakandra.nl). Tram #16, 24, or 25 to Albert Cuypstraat. The friendly owner of this tiny shop is happy to translate the Dutch-only menu of inexpensive Javanese-Surinamese rice and noodle dishes. Takeout is available, but the interior is comfortable and pleasant, dressed up like its neighbors but with dishes at ½ the price. Noodle soups €4.50. *Roti* (a South Asian bread) €4-6. Dinner specials €7.50-€10. Cash only. ❷

Trez, Saenredamstraat 39-41 (☎676 2495), just off Frans Halsstraat. If in the mood for a meal on the classier side, head off the main drag to Trez's Mediterranean cuisine. The restaurant's white facade overflows with gorgeous flowers spilling onto the sidewalk. Inside, the service is professional and the food prepared in an exposed kitchen in the center of the space. Split a "Trez Plateau" (3 tiers of fish, meat, and vegetables; €12.50) to start your meal. Main courses €16-20; charming chefs have been known to deliver your meal to your table themselves. Open daily 6-10pm or later. MC/V. ❹

De Waaghals, Frans Halsstraat 29 (☎679 9609). Since 1981 this specialty vegetarian restaurant has made every attempt to use organic ingredients and provide vegan options—whether this makes it a waaghals ("daredevil") is up to you. 3 chefs create a new menu featuring seasonal fruits and veggies at least every 2 months as well as a monthly dish that is a vegetarian interpretation of a particular country's cuisine. Meals range around €10-17.50. Try to call ahead for reservations on weekends. Open Tu-Su 5-9:30pm. Cash only. ❸

Nieuw Albina, Albert Cuypstraat 47-49 (☎379 0223). Tram #16, 24, or 25 to Albert Cuypstraat. Never mind the decor—or lack thereof. This is a budget traveler's paradise of cheap, good food, with a near-constant stream of customers. Surinamese and Chinese specialities are combined for a popular menu of soups, roti, rice, and noodles (€4-10). Open M and W-Su noon-10:30pm. Cash only. ❶

Saray, Gerard Doustraat 33 (☎671 9216). Tram #16, 24, or 25 to Albert Cuypstraat. This small establishment has been serving Turkish delicacies for more than 30 years. The menu mainly focuses on grilled options for main courses (€9-14.50), but you can start off enjoying Saray's delicious homemade bread or sampling any of the starters (such as the *sigara boregi*, cigar-shaped pastries filled with egg, feta, and parsley; €3.40). Wash it down with Efes, the Turkish national beer (€2) or with a Turkish liqueur (€2.70). Takeout available. Open daily 5-11pm. AmEx/V. ❸

Zagros, Albert Cuypstraat 50 (☎670 0461). Tram #16, 24 or 25 to Albert Cuypstraat. Here's your chance to experience little-recognized Kurdish cuisine. The food is influenced by the 5 countries in the Kurdish cultural sphere—Turkey, Iran, Iraq, Syria, and Armenia (check out the map if you need to brush up on your geography)—in a plain but appealing candlelit atmosphere. Plenty of veggie options available. Lamb dominates the menu: grilled lamb chops come with couscous and salad (€12.50); *beste berxe* includes cubed and marinated lamb, rice, and a salad (€11.50). Try the sticky, sugary baklava if you're not already full (€3.50). Takeout available. Open Tu-Su 5pm-midnight. Kitchen closes 10:30pm. Cash only. ❷

De Taart van m'n Tante, Ferdinand Bolstraat 10 (☎776 4600; www.detaart.com). Tram #16, 24, or 25 to Stadhouderskade. There's no better place to step in out of the rain. This successful made-to-order cake business sells cakes by the slice in their cafe (apple tart €4, made "tipsy" with amaretto €4.30; pecan pie €4.50). Colorful tablecloths, flowers, and fabulously decorated cakes in the window give the space a sugary sweet glow. Open daily 10am-6pm. Cash only. ❶

Peppino Gelateria, 1e Sweelinckstraat 16 (☎676 4910). Tram #16, 24, or 25 to Albert Cuypstraat. 2 silver *gelato* machines in Peppino's window constantly blend fresh cream and fruit to make the finest Italian-style *gelato* around. 24 flavors made each day, from lemon to chocolate chip (€0.90 for 1 scoop; €1.50 for 2). Cappuccinos and macchiatos are available as well. Open daily 11am-11pm. Cash only. ❶

Cambodja City, Albert Cuypstraat 58-60 (☎671 4930). Tram #16, 24, or 25 to Albert Cuypstraat. Cambodja City serves up halal specialties from Thailand, Vietnam, and—wait for it—Cambodia at a great value. Food is good, cheap, and generously portioned—perfect for takeout to Sarphatipark. Vietnamese noodle soup is loaded with chicken-beef balls and makes for a full meal (€9.50). Thai chicken or lamb curry €9.50. Entrees under €13.50. Special dinners for 2-4 people: 10 choices for €34-40. Open daily 5-11pm. Cash only. ❷

Shinto, Govert Flinckstraat 153 (☎670 4690). Sushi bars are surprisingly rare finds in a neighborhood packed with ethnic eateries. This straightforward, immaculate spot satisfies yens for miso and eel. The combo meals (€8-20.50) are made with fresh ingredients before your eyes. Sake €4.50. Takeout and delivery available. Free delivery with a purchase of more than €15. Open daily 4-10pm. Cash only. ❷

ers threatened to tear that down to make way for new housing before the restaurant-to-be claimed the plot. Four years and many extensive renovations later, De Kas opened, with a new set of greenhouses built using the old floor plans and the original chimney still standing.

The restaurant makes every effort to use local and organic ingredients in its cooking, including fruits and vegetables from their own farmland in North Holland. There is only one set meal served every day; for lunch, this includes three starters and a main course, supplemented by bread, olive oil, and olives. For dinner, the menu includes several small starters, an entree, and a dessert. Dishes may include heirloom tomatoes with halibut and an olive tapenade; buffalo mozzarella served with a selection of beets; or catfish wrapped in prosciutto with fresh beans and gnocchi.

Kamerlingh Onneslaan 3 (☎462 4562). Tram #9 to Hogeweg. Look for the greenhouses through the trees and enter the park by either footbridge over the water. Lunch menu €35, dinner menu €47.50. Wine from €4 per glass. Dessert €8. Open M-F noon-2pm and 6:30-10pm, Sa 6:30-10pm. Reservations recommended. AmEx/MC/V.

Mas Tapas, Saenredamstraat 37 (☎664 0066; www.diningcity.com/amsterdam/mas-tapas/en/index.html). Tram #16, 24, or 25 to Albert Cuypstraat. This spot aims for quaint, with lavender whitewashed walls and tiled folding tables and chairs. Apparently, the formula works; the place is usually jam-packed. Selection of 12 tapas (€4 each; €19.50 for 5) includes garlicky mushrooms, oysters in cava, and *estofado de pescado* (fish stew with gambas, fennel, and clams). Salads €8.50-9.50. Brandy de Jerez €3.25. Wine €2.75-3.75 per glass. Open daily 4pm-midnight. Cash only. ❸

 LAND OF THE MIDNIGHT MEAL. If you find yourself sitting alone in a restaurant at 7pm in the summer, don't worry that it's an uncool place to have dinner. Because it doesn't get dark until around 10:30pm, locals eat later—restaurants start to get full between 8 and 9pm.

JODENBUURT AND PLANTAGE

Although they may lack the selection or volume of some of Amsterdam's other neighborhoods, the Jodenbuurt and Plantage still host some reputable restaurants. Start sniffing around at Plantage Kerklaan, across from the Artis Zoo.

see map p. 344

🏆 **Abe Veneto,** Plantage Kerklaan 2 (☎639 2364). A welcome treat for any budget-wary traveler, this restaurant matches a friendly entourage of proprietors and a cosmopolitan atmosphere with absolutely terrific food. Choose from a dizzying selection of more than 45 freshly made pizzas (€5-9.50), pastas (€7-9.50), and salads (under €5). Wine by the bottle or the carafe (½-carafe €6.50). Takeout and delivery available to nearby hotels or for eating in a nearby park. Open daily noon-midnight. Cash only. ❷

Eetkunst Asmara, Jonas Daniel Meijerplein 8 (☎627 1002). Operated by a group of Eritrean immigrants, this small restaurant provides a delicious alternative option to the *broodjes* and *ciabattas* of nearby cafes. Enjoy personally prepared East African specialties (such as beef with assortment of mild herbs; €9) served on *injera*, a spongy traditional East African bread. Meat, fish, and vegetarian options available. Conclude your meal with a ceremonial pot of tea (€4). Open daily 6-11pm. Cash only. ❷

Soup En Zo, Jodenbreestraat 94A (☎422 2243). Let your nose guide you to the amazing broth at this tiny soupery. Homemade soup and fresh bread make a great lunch combo, especially for vegetarians. Several soups and sizes (€2.70-6) with free bread and delicious toppings (coriander, dill, cheese, nuts). If the soups don't tempt you, they have a small selection of salads (under €6). The restaurant is only a takeout counter, but you can munch your meal on their front patio in good weather. Check out their other location at Nieuwe Spiegelstraat 54. Open M-F 11am-8pm, Sa-Su noon-7pm. ❶

Plancius, Plantage Kerklaan 61A (☎330 9469). 19th-century hot spot Plancius carries the torch into today with chic design and stylish, international breakfasts (on weekends), lunches, and dinners. Menu changes every few months; past favorites include shrimp croquettes with caper mayonnaise (€8). Popular sandwiches €3-5; pasta €8. Dinner entrees €15-20. Open daily 10am-2am; breakfast and sandwiches 10am-4:30pm, lunch 10am-6pm, dinner 6-10pm. ❸

Nam Tin, Jodenbreestraat 11-13 (☎428 8508). Nam Tin isn't your everyday Chinese takeout: Confucian statues and dragon figurines bedeck a large, elegant Chinese banquet hall filled with Chinese-speaking patrons. Most important of all, though, is the genuine, delectable Cantonese cuisine. Dim sum like *ha kau* (shrimp dumplings; €4) and *ba pao* (roast pork in steamed buns; €3) served noon-5pm. Noodle soups €7-12. Open M-Sa noon-midnight, Su noon-11:30pm. Kitchen open daily noon-10pm. Cash only. ❷

Sea Palace, Oosterdokskade 8 (☎626 4777; www.seapalace.nl). A gargantuan palace floating on the water in gaudy pagoda style, topped only by its ornate, gilded, and carved interior. The incredible restaurant itself is the main attraction, but the edibles will certainly not disappoint. The *Odyssey*-length menu offers Chinese and Indonesian cuisine. Pick from *prix-fixe* meals (from €57 for 2 people to €525 for 10 people) or mix and match from the endless selection. Soups €3-4.20. Entrees €13.50-35.50. Dim sum served noon-4pm (€3-5). The upstairs terrace provides good views of Amsterdam's old harbor. Open daily noon-11pm. Kitchen closes at 10:30pm. AmEx/MC/V. ❹

Café Koosje, Plantage Middenlaan 37 (☎320 0817; www.cafekoosje.nl). A pleasant place to grab breakfast, lunch, dinner, or a drink in the classic wooden interior or outside at the sociable sidewalk tables. For lunch, you'll find *ciabattas* (€3-5) and the soup of the day (€4). For dinner, Koosje dishes up a more serious menu (entrees €10-15). At night, drinkers hit the full bar, with patrons as varied as students to nursing-home residents from down the street. Open M-Th and Su 9am-1am, F-Sa 9am-4am. MC/V with 3% surcharge. ❷

Bloem, Entrepotdok 36 (☎330 0929; bloem36@planet.nl). Keep the zoo on your right and follow Plantage Kerklaan until it crosses the canal. Bloem looks out over the Entrepotdok canal, a 19th-century center for trade and transit; the recent revitalization of the warehouses and docks in this area has brought in charming *eetcafes* like Bloem that are beautiful spots on a warm night. The €25 set menu pairs entrees like portobello mushrooms filled with pumpkin, blue cheese, and herb pilaf with a soup, a starter, and a dessert. At dinner, there's always a €10 menu of rotating specials. Open noon-last customer. Kitchen closes at 10pm. MC/V. ❺

De Groene Olifant, Sarphatistraat 510 (☎629 4904; www.degroeneolifant.nl). The Green Elephant is at the other end of the Artis Zoo near the Tropenmuseum, but it definitely doesn't lack for customers or atmosphere. Stop by for a sandwich (ham, red onion, tomato, and egg or mozzarella and pesto €5) or some nuts (wide selection €1-3) or join the crowds for a drink on the open patio as the sun begins to set. Open daily 11am-4pm and 6-10pm. Cash only. ❶

TisFris, Sint Antoniesbreestraat 142 (☎622 0472). Watch the world go by on foot, in cars, and by boat and bike on the large terrace or through the enormous windows facing Sint Antoniesbreestraat. Plenty of options for vegetarians and vegans. Signature oven-grilled sandwiches €4-5. Warm goat cheese salad with croutons, honey, and walnuts €9. Also a small selection of larger "3-layer" sandwiches (smoked salmon, rocket, and cream cheese €8). Don't worry, rocket is just a vegetable. Open M-Sa 9am-7pm, Su 10am-7pm. Cash only. ❷

Aguada, Roetersstraat 10 (☎620 3782). Cheese fondues (€9-11), salads (from €4), and tasty grills (from €11) are part of the rotating menu at this comfy cafe across the street from the University of Amsterdam. Starters, including vegetarian meatballs or *gambas al ajillo,* €2-6. Open daily 10am-4pm and 6-11pm. So untouristed that it closes for lunch in the summer months. Kitchen closes at 10pm. Cash only. ❷

SIGHTS

Amsterdam is not a city of traditional sights—if you want to join the sweating masses in endless lines to catch a glimpse of a postcard monument, you've come to the wrong place. But don't be fooled: this city—as a collection of nearly 100 interlocking islands—is a sight in itself. The dazzling engineering feat of merely keeping dry isn't the only draw, however. For sites merely to marvel at, turn to **Accommodations** (p. 99), **Food** (p. 121), **Museums** (p. 165), **Entertainment** (p. 185), **Shopping** (p. 213), or **Nightlife** (p. 223)—in short, everywhere in Amsterdam has a story. Today, many of Amsterdam's most impressive sights are those that chronicle the city's expanding liberalism as it confronted, and continues to confront, a difficult colonial heritage and an ever-evolving multicultural present.

OUDE ZIJD

If you can see past the neon lights and through the thick haze of smoke that hangs back over the Red Light District, you'll be able to dig up a bit of the past in the Oude Zijd. Although many have been claimed by the University of Amsterdam, most of the compelling and historically significant buildings in the south have remained intact. While closed to the public, the canal houses in particular boast pleasantly picturesque facades.

see map p. 340

⬛ NIEUWMARKT. On the border between the Oude Zijd and the Jodenbuurt, Nieuwmarkt is one of Amsterdam's most beloved squares, lined with cafes, restaurants, markets, and coffee shops. On warm summer days, crowds pack the forum's endless terraces. While in Nieuwmarkt, be sure to stop and to take a look at the **Waag** (the giant fortress in the center; it's hard to miss), Amsterdam's largest surviving medieval building. Dating from the 15th century, the Waag came into existence as one of Amsterdam's fortified city gates (at the time known as Sint Antoniespoort). As Amsterdam expanded, the gate became obsolete, and it was converted into a house for public weights and measures. At the end of the 17th century, the Surgeon's Guild built an amphitheater at the top of the central tower to house public dissections for the (overly) curious masses as well as private anatomy lessons—famously depicted by **Rembrandt van Rijn's** *The Anatomy Lesson of Dr. Tulp*, which the guild commissioned. The Waag has also housed a number of other sites, including the Jewish Historical Museum and the Amsterdam Historical Museum. Today, it is home to **⬛In de Waag** (p. 124), an outstanding restaurant and cafe. *(Metro to Nieuwmarkt.)*

SINT NICOLAASKERK. A burst of color emanates from the stained-glass windows over the impressive columned altar of this relatively new Roman Catholic church. Designed by A.C. Bleys and completed in 1887 to honor the patron saint of sailors, it replaced a number of Amsterdam's secret Catholic churches from the era of the Alteration (p. 58). Designed in the Neo-Renaissance style, the structure humbles visitors with stern black marble columns, a domed ceiling, and wooden vaults that create a heavy but grand interior. The magnificent cupola, made from Belgian glass in 1890, is the only glass cupola in the Netherlands. The walls of the church are art themselves, lined with magnificent murals depicting the life and story of St. Nicolaas. Take time to admire the church's massive 2300-pipe organ, designed by William Sauer. *(Prins Hendrikkade 73. 2min. walk from Centraal Station; turn left when you exit Stationsplein. ☎624 8749. Daily service 12:30pm; Su mass 10:30am Dutch, 1pm Spanish. Organ festival July-Sept. Sa 8:15pm. Contemporary and classical organ concerts occasionally Sa 3pm—call ahead. Open M 1-4pm, Tu-F 11am-4pm, Sa noon-3pm. Organ festival €6.)*

FO GUANG SHAN HE HUA TEMPLE. While Amsterdam's Chinatown might be small, the city is home to approximately 20,000 Chinese residents, most of whom hail from Hong Kong. Amsterdam's first house of Buddhist worship, affiliated with the Taiwan-based Fo Guang Shan Buddhist Order, was opened by Queen Beatrix on September 15, 2000. The temple is intended to "encourage both spiritual development and cultural exchange." Most visitors just stop to peek in at the one-room temple, but classes on Buddhism and Chinese are available, as are guided tours, given on Saturday between 2 and 4pm or by appointment for groups of 10 or more. Look for the striking gold-and-red facade from the street. *(Zeedijk 106-118, just north of Nieuwmarkt. ☎ 420 2357. Services Su 10:30am open to the public. Open Tu-Sa noon-5pm, Su 10am-5pm. Free.)*

OTHER SIGHTS. The **Oudemanhuispoort** (Old Man's Gateway) refers to a covered pedestrian walkway that runs between Kloveniersburgwal and Oudezijds Achterburgwal, as well as the gate that guards it. The building was once an almshouse for elderly men and women and later housed the Rijksmuseum's collection for a time; in the 18th century, it became Amsterdam's first shopping mall. It now houses a used-book, postcard, and art market, moved here in 1875 from Rembrandtplein. There are reams of paperbacks ranging from esoteric philosophy to trite love stories in a variety of languages (p. 214). Also check out the peaceful courtyard off the market, part of a University of Amsterdam school building. Walled in on three sides by the Voorburgwal, Achterburgwal, and Grimburgwal canals, **Huis aan de Drie Grachten,** the "House on the Three Canals," was erected in 1609. The Huis is a geometrical oddity; three of the four sides feature step-gables, arranged so that one gable looks out onto each canal. *(Oudezijds Voorburgwal 249.)* The elaborate ornamental gate of **Sint Agnietenkapel** promises seclusion from the whirlwind of the Oude Zijd. Erected in 1470, the building features a disproportionately angled facade. Now owned by the University of Amsterdam, the building is open to the public when school is in session. *(Oudezijds Voorburgwal 231.)* In 1660, the brothers Louis and Hendrick Trip used the money they made in the arms trade to commission the massive and imposing building now known as the **Trippenhuis.** The coal-black facade appears to belong to a single building but really covers two, one for each brother; look for both weapons and olive branches in carvings on the facade. From 1815 to 1885, the building doubled as the Rijksmuseum. *(Kloveniersburgwal 29.)* By comparison, glance over at the other side of the canal, where the **Kleine Trippenhuis,** 2.44m wide, still stands. This impossibly narrow building was once home to the brothers' coachman. *(Kloveniersburgwal 26.)* Farther north along the canal, the former headquarters of the Dutch East India Company reside at the **Oost-Indisch Huis** (East Indies House); the enormous building is now only used for University of Amsterdam classes. *(Kloveniersburgwal 48.)*

 AFTERNOON DELIGHT. If curious about how the Red Light District operates but wary of visiting at night, try going in the late afternoon. You'll still get a feel for the neighborhood, but the district won't be quite as intense.

RED LIGHT DISTRICT

If you have come to witness the spectacle, there's no better time to appreciate the Red Light District than at night. Though prostitutes work all through the day, it's only after dark that the area actually takes on a red radiance, sex theaters throw open their doors, and the main streets are so thick with people that you may have to slip out to Damrak for some air—and that's saying something. It's a heavily touristed area, though the promise of seediness remains largely unfulfilled because of the

see map p. 340

unabashed openness of the window prostitutes. If you're looking to dip your toes in the carnality of the Red Light District, there are always **sex shows,** in which actors perform strictly choreographed fantasies on stage. The most famous live sex show takes place at **Casa Rosso,** Oudezijds Achterburgwal 106-108. (☎627 8954; www.janot.com. Open M-Th 8pm-2am, F-Sa 8pm-3am. €35, with 4 drinks €45.) The Red Light District offers quite a bit at its fringes as well, where the crimson glow fades and some of the most historic buildings still stand. During the day, the district is comparatively flaccid, though you can get an eyeful at any time. Tourist families parade down **Oudezijds Achterburgwal** under the impression that, if it must be seen, it's better to take the kids in the daylight hours. Police patrol the area 24hr.; they are usually in control of any disturbance within a few minutes. If you can't wait until nighttime to start guzzling, check out **De Bekeerde Suster,** Kloveniersburgwal 6-8, a brewery whose name translates to The Reformed Sister. Call ahead to reserve space on a tour of the elegant distillery. (☎423 0112; www.debekeerdesuster.nl.)

OUDE KERK. Reopened to the public in 1999, the Oude Kerk may come as a welcome shock. Located smack in the middle of the otherwise lurid Red Light District, it may be the only church in the world completely bounded by prostitution sites. History breathes in this stunning structure with an enormous, yawning interior and magnificent stained-glass windows. Erected in 1306, the Oude Kerk was the earliest parish church built in Amsterdam, but it is now a center for cultural activities, hosting photography and modern art exhibits. At the head of the church is the massive **Vater-Müller organ,** which was built in 1724 and is still played for public concerts. Saskia van Uylenburgh, Rembrandt van Rijn's first wife, and Kiliaen van Rensselaer, a founder of New York City, were both buried in tombs here. The Gothic church has seen hard times, having been stripped of its artwork and religious artifacts from 1566 to 1578, during the Alteration. Between then and now, the Protestant church has served a number of functions: a home for vagrants, a theater, a market, and a space for fishermen to mend broken sails. Today, there is still an empty, spare feeling inside the building (ideal for the changing art exhibits that currently grace the hall), but the church is nevertheless one of the most impressive and prominent structures in the city. *(Oudekerksplein 23. From Centraal Station, walk down Damrak, take a left at the corner of Oudebrugsteeg just before the Beurs van Berlage, and turn right on Warmoesstraat; at the next left is the church. ☎625 8284; www.oudekerk.nl. Open M-Sa 11am-5pm, Su 1-5pm. €4.50, students and over 65 €3.50, under 12 free. Additional charge for exhibits.)*

FROM THE ROAD

TAKE IT AS RED

As the "Condomerie of the Golden Fleece" can attest, Amsterdam's Red Light District has achieved an almost epic reputation for debauchery. For me, it was a bit alarming to turn past a beautiful tree-clad canal only to be greeted by a beautiful bikini-clad woman. Luckily, people turned out to be friendly: Two strangers had already smiled and waved at me. Then they tried to sell me ecstasy.

The surprises kept on coming. I bumped into odd reminders of religion on this supposedly sin-drenched stretch. Walking past an adult video store, I heard the bells of the Oude Kerk practically in my ears. "God is my ruler," read a 1648 plaque—on the side of the Erotic Museum.

The most surprising thing about the district, though, may be its normality. You might be startled by the sudden appearance of flesh in those eerie red-lit windows, but more often you'll catch the prostitutes text-messaging or socializing rather than soliciting. The illegal drug pushers end up a little more polite than you might expect. And maybe, sandwiched between the leather bar and the porno theater, you'll find a tidy grandmotherly cafe proudly making its own scones and jam. The odd twist of Amsterdam is that, by permitting what is usually forbidden, it removes much of the "dirtiness" from the taboo. Suddenly, the Red Light District has stopped being offensive or shocking, and you realize: it's just another neighborhood.

—*Ken Saathoff*

> **TIP** **FLESH PHOTOGRAPHY.** As tempting as it may be, do not take pictures in the Red Light District, especially of prostitutes. Taking pictures is incredibly rude and can land the picture-taker in trouble.

NIEUWE ZIJD

see map p. 340

Despite being home to several of Amsterdam's important historical landmarks, the New Side is one of the city's most heinously overpopulated, commercial neighborhoods. Hordes of panting tourists fresh off the train from Centraal Station descend upon **Damrak** and **Nieuwendijk,** two major pedestrian corridors, in search of the neighborhood's innumerable coffee shops and budget hotels. If you manage to stick to the quieter side streets—as well as to the slightly less congested **Spuistraat** and **Nieuwezijds Voorburgwal**—an afternoon in the Nieuwe Zijd can be entertaining; just keep your hand to your purse and avert your gaze from the sea of H&M shopping bags. The neighborhood's heart and soul is the bustling **Dam Square,** flanked on either side by two of the city's more significant monuments, the **Koninklijk Paleis** (Royal Palace) and the **Nieuwe Kerk,** as well as the **Nationaal Monument.** On any given summer day, this expanse of white cobblestone is full of buskers, pickpockets, babies, shoppers, dogs, and street vendors. In the past, the square has seen executions, protests, markets, and celebrations, as well as the erection and destruction of both the first town hall (now the Royal Palace) and the public weights and measures house. (Louis Bonaparte, king of the Netherlands until his abdication in 1810, razed the latter on the logic that the hall spoiled his view from the palace.) Visiting the area can consume the better part of a day, especially if you nurse a mojito in the back room of one of the area's swank bars or take the time to try out perfumes at the **Magna Plaza Shopping Center,** originally constructed in 1899 as a post office. (Open M 11am-7pm, Tu-Sa 10am-7am, Su noon-7pm.)

■ **BEGIJNHOF.** You don't have to take vows to enter this secluded courtyard in the 14th-century home of the Beguines—a sect of free-thinking and religiously devoted laywomen. Though tour groups, bicycles, and cameras are all prohibited here, the casual visitor will be rewarded with access to one of the area's more attractive sights. The peaceful Begijnhof's rosy gardens, beautifully manicured lawns, gabled houses, and tree-lined walkways afford a much-needed respite from the bustling excesses of the Nieuwe Zijd. The women who currently live in the Begijnhof are not required to be Catholic, but when the site was founded in 1346, its residents were considerably more sequestered. While they didn't take vows, they devoted themselves to a life of religious contemplation, charity, and manual labor. *(From Dam, take Nieuwezijds Voorburgwal south 5min. to Spui, turn left, and then go left again on Gedempte Begijnensloot; the gardens are on the left. Alternatively, follow signs to Begijnhof from Spui. No guided tours, bikes, or pets. Open daily 9am-5pm. Free.)* One of the oldest houses in Amsterdam, **Het Houten Huys** (The Wooden House), built in 1475, is located on the premises, though most of the other homes were rebuilt (after a considerable delay) in the 17th and 18th centuries following major fires in the 1400s. *(☎ 623 5554. Open M-F 10am-4pm.)* While there, visit the court's two churches. The **Engelsekerk,** the English Presbyterian church, holds one of the city's few all-English services. The building is believed to date from 1419, when it served as the Begijnhof's Catholic chapel. In 1607, as a result of the Reformation, the Beguines were forced to turn it over to Amsterdam's English-speaking Presbyterians. It was enlarged in 1665 and restored 30 years ago. *(Begijnhof 48. ☎ 624 9665. Open for prayer Su 10:30am.)* Across from the Engelsekerk is the **Begijnhofkapel,** constructed in 1671 from two houses. It was once one of Amsterdam's *schuilkerken*, hidden churches performing Catholic services. *(Begijnhof 30. ☎622 1918. Open M 1-6:30pm, Tu-F 9am-6:30pm, Sa-Su 9am-6pm. Services Su 10am in Dutch, 11:30am in French. Free.)*

DAM SQUARE AND KONINKLIJK PALEIS. Next to the Nieuwe Kerk (p. 167) on Dam Sq. is the Koninklijk Paleis, one of Amsterdam's most impressive architectural feats. The palace is closed for renovations until 2009, but even the edifice's exterior bursts with architecture and history. The building was opened in 1655 and fully completed 10 years later. It originally served as the town hall, but it was no ordinary municipal building. In a city at the center of a burgeoning worldwide trade and governed by a group of magistrates, the town hall became the most important government building in the city. Its architect, Jacob van Campen, aimed to replace the entrenched Amsterdam Renaissance style with a more Classicist one and looked to Rome for his example. Compare this palace to the **Westerkerk,** up Raadhuisstraat from Dam, at Prinsengracht (p. 149). It did not become a palace until the arrival of finicky Louis Napoleon in 1808, who had it renovated and remodeled to better serve as a royal residence. Today, Queen Beatrix still uses the building for official receptions, though she makes her home in The Hague. Inside, the airy, white-marble Citizen's Hall was intended, by virtue of its celestial floor maps and allegorical sculptures, to be the universe contained in a single room (with the Netherlands, of course, at the center). Across Dam Sq. is the Dutch **Nationaal Monument,** unveiled on May 4, 1956, to honor Dutch victims of WWII. Inside the 22m white stone obelisk is soil from all 12 of the Netherlands's provinces and the Dutch East Indies. Along the back of the monument, you'll find the provinces' crests bordered by the years 1940 and 1945. In addition to this reminder of Dutch suffering during the war, the monument is one of Amsterdam's central meeting and people-watching spots. The square itself is worth gawking at, if only for the sheer volume of *Homo sapiens* and *Columba livia*, whose flocking patterns are eerily similar. On the northeast corner of Dam sits **Madame Tussaud's Wax Museum,** a branch of the massive Brit-owned collection of wax figures of historical personalities, celebrities, and world leaders. *(Tram #5, 13, 17, or 20 to Dam.)*

SPUI. Pronounced "spow," this tree-lined, cobblestone square—perfect for quiet lounging on summer afternoons—is home to an art market on Sundays, hosts a book market on Fridays, and is surrounded by bookstores—notably the slick, international **Athenaeum Boekhandel** as well as the **American Book Center**

THE LOCAL STORY

LASER 3.14

You may have noticed Laser 3.14's graffiti scrawled around Amsterdam on construction sites, crumbling buildings, and derelict spaces. Let's Go asked the artist to unravel his cryptic poetry. For more information, visit www.laser314.com.

LG: How do you write your stuff and choose the site for each piece?

A: I didn't want someone to have to be a graffiti writer to decipher my work. I started out as a painter, and I used to make captions for my paintings, and that's how this form evolved. And I really like the impermanence of what I do; because I write on temporary spaces, the pieces as a whole make up this kind of shifting, dynamic poem, and it's something even I can't control.

LG: How have people responded to your work?

A: The police don't bother me because I write on places that are falling apart. It's great when someone writes me an email to say that they like my work, but I like even more when people actually interact with it. I wrote, "Tradition can be a prison" on a builder board, and somebody blacked it out; I put it up again, and again it was blacked out. When I wrote, "Hatred is an underestimated devotion," somebody crossed out "hatred" and wrote "love." I've had some interesting responses.

(p. 215). The Begijnhof (p. 146) is sometimes accessible through a small door off the northern side of the square. Look out for **Het Lievertje** (The Little Urchin), a small bronze statue by Carel Kneulman that became a symbol for the Provos, a Dutch counter-culture movement (p. 62), and was the site of many meetings and riots in the 1960s. *(Tram #1, 2, 4, 5, 9, 14, 16, 24, or 25 to Spui.)*

BEURS VAN BERLAGE. Architecture buffs will salivate over this old stock and commodities exchange, designed by Hendrik Petrus Berlage and constructed between 1896 and 1903. The unadorned edifice went on to have an impact on later Modernist architecture. It was also influential for the techniques developed to sustain its massive weight in the porous Amsterdam soil. In 2000, a wide tunnel was built under the structure, continuing the everlasting Dutch battle with the elements. The Beurs van Berlage is now home to the Dutch Philharmonic Orchestra and moonlights as an exhibition space. The recently renovated halls also provide room for events such as craft fairs and conferences; check the website for details. Today, the Beurs can only be viewed during an event or performance (p. 186), although a cafe has opened on its south side. *(Damrak 277, near Dam Sq. ☎ 530 4141; www.beursvanberlage.nl. Cafe open daily 10am-6pm.)*

LOCK AND RIDE: A GUIDE. When securing your bike, make sure the lock goes through the main frame of the bike *and* through the front tire. If you only lock the frame, your front tire is left vulnerable; if you only lock the front tire, the rest of your bike is an easy target for thieves. Lock your bike to a heavy fence or one of the special bike racks; ask a local, a shop's proprietor, or a passing police officer if you're unsure where you can legally lock your bike.

SCHEEPVAARTBUURT

Just north of the Jordaan and west of the Centrum, Amsterdam's **Shipping Quarter** functioned as the conduit for the city's thriving maritime commerce during the 18th and 19th centuries. When Amsterdam's shipping industry shifted away from the banks of the IJ in the late 1800s, the area was abandoned. Though the flow of commerce subsided, the toughness often associated with ports of call remained

see map p. 338

throughout the end of the 20th century; the Scheepvaartbuurt underwent various gritty transformations, housing little more than an assortment of criminals and junkies. But thanks to urban renewal (and an outpouring of investment from the city's coffers), the Scheepvaartbuurt now boasts some of the city's best restaurants, coffeehouses, and shopping venues, all without the crowds, lines, and tourism that pervade neighborhoods closer to the center.

The Shipping Quarter begins where Nieuwendijk intersects with the Singel and where the district's main drag—**Haarlemmerstraat**—begins. The area has quite a different feel than the neighboring bustle of the city center to the east or the Jordaan to the south; its bustle is lively without being packed with tourists, and its pockets of tranquility are never self-conscious. The eastern part of Haarlemmerstraat is the most vibrant; it is here where architects and entrepreneurs have worked their magic. The district's western half, where Haarlemmerstraat becomes Haarlemmerdijk across the Korte Prinsengracht (a crucial and confusing fact for navigating local addresses), is significantly more residential. The area's maritime past has largely been forgotten; the only reminders are lone, bronze, ship-related monuments—propellers, anchors, and nautical steering wheels—that dot the street corners. Amid the bustle, it's easy to forget that the Scheepvaartbuurt is bordered on the south by one of Amsterdam's most beautiful canals, **Brouwersgracht.** It's an ideal place to relax, only two blocks and yet a world away from Haarlemmerstraat's frenetic urban pace.

Few sights appear along Haarlemmerstraat—though the street, with its unparalleled collection of eateries and coffee shops, is still worth beholding. Stop at the **West-Indisch Huis** (West Indies House), Haarlemmerstraat 75, at Herenmarkt. The white, ornately gabled structure dates to 1617 and originally functioned as the headquarters of the Dutch West Indies Company, back when the Dutch ranked among the world's most enterprising imperialists.

CANAL RING WEST

There are some 2200 buildings in the canal ring, 1550 of which have been named national monuments, making the Canal Ring West a sight in itself. Begin at Westermarkt (tram #13 or 17 from Centraal), the jumping-off point for all touristic sites.

■**WESTERKERK.** This stunning Protestant church was designed by Roman Catholic architect Hendrick de Keyser and completed in 1631. It stands as one of the last structures built in the Dutch Renaissance style, which can be distinguished by its use of both brick and

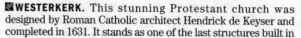

see map p. 338

stone. The blue and yellow imperial crown of Maximilian of Austria—the Hapsburg ruler of the Holy Roman Empire in the late 15th century—rests atop the 85m tower, which has become a patriotic symbol for the citizens of Amsterdam. Rembrandt is believed to be buried here, but no one knows exactly where, so watch your step. In contrast to the decorative exterior, the Protestant church remains properly sober and plain inside; it is still used by a Presbyterian congregation. Make sure to climb the **Westerkerkstoren** as part of a 30min. guided tour for a breathtaking view of the city. The tower is home to 47 bells, including Amsterdam's heaviest, which weighs in at 7509kg. During WWII, the bells were removed to prevent them from being melted down into munitions. Every Tuesday from noon until 1pm, the carillon (the musical instrument that controls the bells) is played for a lovely hour of resonant music. *(Prinsengracht 281, on the corner of Prinsengracht and Westermarkt. Trams #13, 17, or 20 to Westermarkt. ☎624 7766. Open Apr.-Sept. M-F 11am-3pm; July-Aug. M-Sa 11am-3pm. Tower closed Oct.-Mar. Tower tours Apr.-Sept. every 30min. 10am-5:30pm. €5.)*

FELIX MERITIS. This imposing, four-columned classical structure was built in 1789 to house the Felix Meritis Society of arts and sciences. A monument to Enlightenment ideals, the building once served as a cultural center for the city's intellectual elite. After somehow ending up the headquarters for the Dutch Communist Party during post-WWII reconstruction, Felix Meritis returned to its original function. The center now hosts cultural events, debates, classical and world music concerts, and art exhibits, mostly focusing on modern politics. Meritis even houses a summer university which offers two- to three-day courses in English (including intensive Dutch for non-native speakers; see www.amsu.edu). The institute's canal-side cafe serves as a forum for impromptu political and intellectual discussions. *(Keizersgracht 324. ☎626 2321; www.felix.meritis.nl. Open M-F 9am-7pm.)*

INSTITUTE FOR WAR DOCUMENTATION. This mansion, built by a wealthy Dutch tobacco planter in the 1890s, now houses an extensive collection of Dutch war archives and photographs. There is also a library containing English-, French-, and German-language books. The institute's assembly focuses primarily on WWII, though there is a growing collection of archives focusing on Dutch military activities in the former Yugoslavia and the East Indies. The study and library are both open to the public, but you will find that students and professors comprise most of the studious crowd. *(Herengracht 380. ☎523 3800; www.oorlogsdoc.knaw.nl. Open M 1-6pm, Tu-Th 9am–6pm, F 9am-5pm. Free.)*

TIME: One day.

SEASON: Year-round. The canals are particularly pleasant in spring and fall, with picturesque foliage and temperate weather.

SOPHISTICATED CITY TOUR

Amsterdam is not a pretentious city. Its sophistication is simple, unaffected, and relaxed—perfect for a leisurely walk. This walking tour takes you through Golden Age art, the history of the Central Canal Ring, and the hot spots of De Pijp, the city's most up-and-coming neighborhood.

1. REMBRANDTPLEIN. Somewhat incongruously, the tour begins here, surrounded by the Rembrandtplein's gaudy nightclubs, backpacked tourists, and locals of every stripe—not quite the sophistication this walking tour has in mind. Turn your eyes skyward to the statue of the square's namesake, master painter Rembrandt van Rijn, bid the throngs of photo-snapping, drink-sipping revelers goodbye, and take a cathartic dip into urbane Amsterdam (p. 5).

2. GOLDEN BEND. A stretch of houses on the Herengracht between Leidsestraat and Vijzelstraat is known as the Golden Bend because of the affluence of its 17th-century inhabitants and the opulence of the homes they built. Though very few of the structures here are open to the public, survey the elegant, doubly wide houses on this picturesque stretch of the "Gentleman's Canal," particularly #495 for its rare balcony, #507, which was former mayor Jacob Boreel's house and looted in 1696 when he introduced a burial tax to the city, and #527, where Tsar Peter the Great spent a night at the Russian ambassador's house (p. 152).

3. CAFÉ AMERICAIN. Café Americain, the cafe of choice for well-heeled Amsterdammers and artists for over 100 years, is all dark wood, marble, Art Deco light fixtures, and stained glass. While you may not want to stop here for dinner or a multi-course meal (unless you're looking to splurge), a classy libation and a warm Dutch snack platter for two (€8) outside on the square overlooking Leidseplein is a restful delight. The marble fountain, it should be noted, is just as easily enjoyed with a snack from a stand across the street (p. 130).

4. RIJKSMUSEUM AMSTERDAM. Marvel at Rembrandt's shadowy, dynamic *Night Watch* and Johannes Vermeer's luminous, shimmering *Milkmaid* in the National Museum. Both exemplify the Golden Age boom of subsidy and interest in the arts. Make sure to check out two of the three surviving dollhouses from the period, which cost astronomical sums to create. The building is also a sight in itself: this huge neo-Gothic structure designed by Pierre Cuypers is one of the most readily identifiable landmarks in Amsterdam (p. 175).

5. PRINSENGRACHT. Compare the skinnier residential houses on the "Prince's Canal" with their more opulent Herengracht counterparts. Along Prinsengracht, a number of houseboats—long used to alleviate crowding in the city center—still house occupants throughout the year.

6A. MUSEUM VAN LOON. Revel in the lavishly appointed splendor of a canal house and its garden just as it appeared in the Golden Age. This museum preserves the residence of the Van Loon family, whose ancestors founded the Dutch East India Company and had a particularly cultivated, expensive interior designer. If you look closely, you can find the names of the original owners of the canal house engraved into the ornate gilt banister along the central staircase (p. 171).

6B. FOAM PHOTOGRAPHY MUSEUM. Sophistication in art doesn't require oil paints, porcelain, or hundreds of years; across the canal from the Museum Van Loon, the FOAM Photography Museum proves that contemporary photography is just as classy (and certainly a lot hipper). Rotating exhibits range from street art to war photography to portraiture—a nice point of comparison to the Golden Age portraits across the canal (p. 171).

7. CONCERTO AND GET RECORDS. No matter how you might define sophistication in music, Concerto's got it. Filling almost half a block with CDs, DVDs, records, and a staff who knows their stuff, this 30-year-old institution is the place to buy good taste in music, if you don't have it already. Listening stations are available to play anything in the store, so you may find yourself

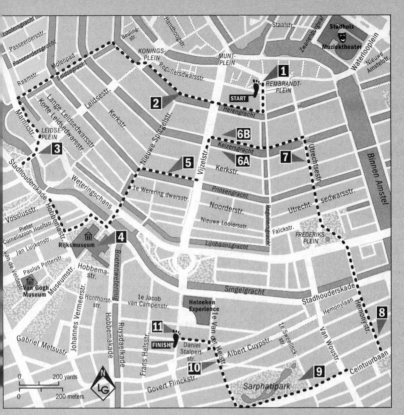

here longer than planned. Step across the street to Get Records, a store under the same management with a superlative selection of rock 'n' roll (p. 218).

8. YO YO. Lighting up a joint hardly seems like the soigné thing to do—at least at other coffee shops. This airy, homey establishment is so warm and friendly it's almost wholesome. (Normal) brownies, praiseworthy coffee, quiche, or (and?) deservedly famous apple pie complete a particularly refined smoke (p. 210).

9. SARPHATIPARK. Wait out the high by the sinuous pond in this small but beautifully manicured park named for the philanthropist Dr. Samuel Sarphati. Careening wildly through gentrified De Pijp while under the influence is simply uncouth, even if you do meet the riff-raff of tourists spilling out from the Heineken Experience. The Sarphatipark is largely neglected by tourists, so expect to have the willow trees and grassy lawns mostly to yourself; nothing says sophistication quite like exclusivity (p. 155).

10. CHOCOLATE BAR. This hyper-chic bar in the heart of De Pijp is packed with crowds of local hipsters lounging outdoors. Winning DJs spin nearly every night here. Try one of the 12-15 mixed drinks (€6.50) or fresh fruit shakes (€2.80). After enjoying a drink or two, you'll be ready for dinner (p. 240).

11. CAFE DE PIJP. This low-key eatery positively breathes cultured charm. Soups and innovative appetizers give way to sumptuous main courses; melting desserts are a perfect way to polish off a particularly refined day. If you have the need for more sophistication, De Pijp boasts some of the city's hippest bars and lounges, perfect for an evening among equally classy urbanites (p. 137).

> **TIP** **FOREIGNER'S DILEMMA.** Believe people when they say that almost everyone in Amsterdam speaks some English. "Do you speak English?" may be interpreted as a condescending question and met with a cold response.

CENTRAL CANAL RING

see map p. 336

Two of Amsterdam's most famous bridges span the Amstel near City Hall in the Central Canal Ring. At Amstelstraat, the **Blauwbrug** (Blue Bridge), adorned with detailed nautical carvings, stretches across the river. Capped with ornate blue-and-gold crowns, it offers one of the city's more spectacular river views. To the right of this bridge is the **Magere Brug** (Skinny Bridge), which sways precariously above the water. The Magere is the oldest of the city's many pedestrian drawbridges and the only one still operated by hand. Its original construction in 1670 replaced an even older, skinnier bridge that was built—according to city lore—for two sisters who lived on opposite sides of the canal and sought a convenient way to pay each other visits.

Along the Herengracht, it's hard to miss the **Golden Bend,** if only because its relatively spacious canal houses appear to be the only habitable ones in the neighborhood. In the 17th century, residents of Amsterdam were taxed according to the width of their homes, and houses could not be more than one plot (a few meters) wide. To encourage investment in the Herengracht's construction, the city government allowed its elite to build homes that were twice as wide along the new canal. During June, the popular **Amsterdam Canal Garden Foundation** (www.amsterdamsegrachtentuin.nl) opens up about 20 of the private back gardens to the public, and people throughout the Netherlands come to see these tiny hidden treasures of landscape (3-day pass €10). The rest of the year, you can get a taste of Golden Age canal life at **Museum Van Loon** (p. 171).

CAT'S CABINET. Housed in the only public building on the Central Canal Ring's scenic Golden Bend, the Cat's Cabinet is an eccentric shrine to all things feline. The Cabinet displays cat-themed *objets d'art*, including cat portraits, statues, knick-knacks, and even a mummified Egyptian cat (less an *objet d'art* than a corpse). The collection was started by a businessman with an unusually strong attachment to his cat, which he named J.P. Morgan; check out Morgan's mug gracing the doctored dollar bill in the museum. After 18 years of eating, sleeping, and showering with his cat, the businessman opened the bottom two floors of his beautiful canal-side mansion when Morgan died in 1990. Feline lovers will purr in appreciation at the collection (and at the six tabby cats who reside in the Cabinet), but it might cause others to take a catnap. *(Herengracht 497. ☎ 626 5378; www.kattenkabinet.nl. Open M-F 10am-2pm, Sa-Su 1-5pm. €5, under 12 €2.)*

LEIDSEPLEIN

see map p. 337

Leidseplein proper is a crush of cacophonous street musicians, blaring neon lights, and ringing, clanging trams. Daytime finds the square packed with countless shoppers, smokers, and drinkers lining the busy sidewalks. When night falls, tourists flock to the square while locals fade to the less populated surrounding streets. A slight respite from the hordes is available just east of Leidseplein along Weteringschans at **Max Euweplein.** Named after the famous Dutch chess master Max Euwe, the square sports an enormous chess board with oversized pieces. One of Amsterdam's more bizarre public spaces, it is notable both for the tiny park across the street (where bronze iguanas provide amusement) and for the motto inscribed above its pillars: *Homo sapiens non urinat in ventum* ("a wise man does not pee into the wind").

REMBRANDTPLEIN

see map p. 336

AMSTEL DIAMONDS. Diamond-factory tours are just about the only way visitors can get into a diamond workshop without becoming an apprentice. A small diamond manufacturer that has worked on the river since 1876, Amstel offers free guided tours of its manufacturing center. The short yet fascinating tour will teach you how diamonds are formed as well as what determines the value of each gem. *(Amstel 206-208. Take any Metro line to Waterlooplein and exit toward the Stadhuis-Het Muziektheater. ☎623 1479. Open M-Sa 9:30am-5pm, Su 10am-5pm. Tours daily, but times vary.)*

JORDAAN

see map p. 338

The Jordaan's restored gabled homes and flower-filled terraces, its mellow canals and tiny galleries—these are among the most memorable sights in this upscale neighborhood once reserved for the city's impoverished citizens. The whole area is suffused with gentrified calm, but **hofjes** in the Jordaan are particularly ideal for finding a moment of silence. Before the Alteration (p. 58), these almshouses were subsidized by the Catholic Church to serve as housing for the poor and the elderly. For maximum tranquility, step behind the nondescript green door that separates **Sint-Andrieshof**, Egelantiersgracht 107-145, from the street and take a slow stroll around the gentle garden beneath austere sloping roofs. Be quiet, though—the courtyard has the hushed solemnity of a church, which probably has less to do with its holy history than with the private residences that now enclose it. (Open daily 9am-6pm. Free.)

HOMOMONUMENT AND PINK POINT. Since 1987, the Homomonument has marked Amsterdam as a testament to the strength and resilience of the homosexual community. Conceived by Karin Daan, its pale pink granite triangles allude to the symbols homosexuals were required to wear in Nazi concentration camps. Her design was chosen out of numerous entries partly for its underlying theory that the structure would become a part of its surroundings. Time has proven Daan correct: the three triangles, 33 ft. on each side, integrate with the bend in the canal's quay wall, and, in the space between them, daily activity continues.

THE HIDDEN DEAL

RIDE WITH SAINT NICK

Canal boat rides abound as one of the premier tourist activities to explore Amsterdam. Unfortunately, they rarely live up to the hype; it's easy to get lost in a sea of photo-snapping tourists and multiple languages blaring over the intercom. Seeing Amsterdam from the water is a unique, worthwhile experience, and unless you make a wealthy boat-owning friend, the **Saint Nicolaas Boat Club** is one of your best bets for a trip out on the waterways.

The Saint Nicolaas Boat Club is a nonprofit organization dedicated to preserving and sharing the spirit of the canal lifestyle by providing an intimate floating experience. The boats, called *tuindersvletten*, are small iron barges and were originally used to ferry materials and market goods around the city. The boats carry up to 10 people, and their size translates into the ability to go where big cruise ships can't. No other opportunity exists to see the canals in such a cozy setting.

Guests are encouraged to bring food and drink aboard for the ride (1¼-1½hr.). Since the boat captains are volunteers, there is no set schedule for rides. The only way to book rides is to inquire at Boom Chicago (p. 189) in Leidseplein; they can provide information and put you in contact with the Boat Club.

The cost? Whatever you choose to give, but donations are this organization's only source of income. See www.amsterdamboatclub.com for more info.

The raised triangle points to the **COC** (Dutch Association for the Integration of Homosexuality; p. 50), one of the oldest gay rights organizations in the world. The ground-level triangle points to the **Anne Frank Huis** (p. 168) and reads, *Naar Vriendschap Zulk Een Mateloos Verlangen*, a line from a poem by Jacob Israël de Haan that translates, "such an endless desire for friendship." The triangle with steps into the canal points to the **Nationaal Monument** (p. 147) on the Dam, a reminder that homosexuals were among those sent to concentration camps. The Homomonument serves as a tripartite memorial to men and women persecuted for their homosexuality in the past, a confrontation with continuing discrimination in the present, and an inspiration for the future. On Queen's Day (Apr. 30) and Liberation Day (May 5), massive celebrations surround the monument.

If the Homomonument serves as a valuable testimony to the ongoing civil rights struggle of homosexuals worldwide, then its neighbor, Pink Point, stands as a reminder of everything vibrant and fun about GLBT life in Amsterdam. Since 1998, the Pink Point kiosk has served as a clearinghouse for information on homosexual happenings in the city and beyond. Pick up free listings of GLBT bars, clubs, restaurants, and cultural life or the 134-page *Bent Guide* (€14), an extensive collection of listings and advice on GLBT tourism in Amsterdam. The kiosk also sells a great selection of souvenirs, postcards, and knick-knacks. Start here if you're attending the gay pride festival in the first weekend of August; the party lasts all weekend, culminating in a Sunday celebration at the Stadhuis-Het Muziektheater. *(In front of Westerkerk. Tram #13, 14, or 17 to Westermarkt. Pink Point ☎ 428 1070; www.pinkpoint.org. Open daily noon-6pm.)*

WESTERPARK AND OUD-WEST

The Westerpark neighborhood is mostly residential, but its park is worth a visit. Take tram #3 to Haarlemmerplein and glide through the gates—tall, wavy, blue monstrosities—into a wide expanse of green. Banks of thick grass slope into the Haarlemmervaart, which looks more like a river than a canal, and any number of winding dirt paths invite visitors to wander down them. In the center of it all is a large pond filled with ducks and fish, along with numerous interesting statues. Benches line the pond, and a large playground attracts parents with their children. It's an excellent place to while away an afternoon. Just beyond the park is the sprawling **Westergasfabriek** along Haarlemmerweg; the complex is a former gas works made up of a series of buildings first constructed in 1883. Redeveloped and reopened for public use as a cultural center in 2003, they now contain several cafes and a movie theater and play host to big open-air concerts and festivals in the summer. For entertainment details, see p. 188.

see map p. 343

BIKE THE DIKES. Biking is the fastest mode of transportation in the city surrounded by water. If you are staying for more than a few days, renting a bike is a good way to see the city. Be sure to follow all traffic signs; if in doubt, ask a police officer where you can and cannot bike. For more two-wheelin' tips, see **Learning to Bike the Hard Way,** p. 115.

MUSEUMPLEIN AND VONDELPARK

■**VONDELPARK.** With meandering walkways, green meadows, several ponds, and a 1.5km paved path, this leafy park—the largest within the city center—is a lovely meeting place for children, skaters, seniors, stoners, soccer players, sidewalk acrobats, and, sometimes, the homeless. Named after one of the Netherlands's most celebrated authors and playwrights, Joost van den Vondel, Vondelpark has, in addition to a few good outdoor cafes (p. 154), an open-air theater where visitors can enjoy free music and dance concerts Thursday through Sunday during the summer (p. 190). "English-style" landscaping aims to convince visitors that they are actually surrounded by nature and not just city trees, and it succeeds in the style of London's Hyde Park or New York City's Central Park. Every Friday, you can meet up with about 350-600 in-line skaters at 8pm by the Filmmuseum (p. 176) for a group skate through Amsterdam. If you just can't wait until the weekend, spend an afternoon in the park on a nice day and you're sure to catch some radical zig-zagging footwork. For the less daring, try wandering around the hexagonally shaped, beautifully maintained rose gardens. There's also a special children's play area toward the center of the grounds. *(In the southwestern corner of the city, outside the Singelgracht. Take tram #1, 2, 3, 5, 6, 12, or 20; just a short walk across the canal and to the left from Leidseplein. www.vondelpark.org. Theater ☎673 1499; www.openluchttheater.nl.)*

COSTER DIAMONDS. Coster is one of Amsterdam's largest and most popular diamond centers. Take a free tour—in your choice of 25 languages—of the factory's large diamond-cutting and polishing studio before sipping a drink in its lovely cafe or browsing the showroom. Indeed, diamond factories are great places to purchase the gem, offering wholesale prices that eliminate significant taxes for out-of-country tourists. Be sure to ask for a VAT receipt for a later refund. *(Paulus Potterstraat 2-8. ☎305 5555; www.amsterdam-diamonds.com. Open daily 9am-5pm.)*

DE PIJP

To the south of the tourist-filled canal rings, De Pijp ("The Pipe") is a mash of ethnicities and cultures. Constructed in the 19th century to ease cramped working-class housing in the Jordaan, De Pijp is now home to more upper-crust overflow. Nevertheless, De Pijp is far from abandoning its labor-class roots. Though real-estate prices have soared in recent years, De Pijp continues to be a neighborhood of choice for artists,

see map p. 333

immigrants, and expats. Its narrow, pipe-like streets of row houses, widely thought to be the origin of its name (the actual origin is unknown), are peppered with inexpensive ethnic food joints and discount stores.

De Pijp is a find for bargain hunters and would-be bohemians. Boutiques selling vibrant silks and ethnic prints at low prices entice the most discerning fashionistas. Bargains on everything from furs to fruit can be found at the **Albert Cuypmarkt,** located along Albert Cuypstraat between Ferdinand Bolstraat and Van Woustraat; this massive market is worth a visit even if you don't have time to tour the entire neighborhood. To avoid the crowds, stroll along the waterways and paths of the small and peaceful **Sarphatipark,** located a few blocks to the south of the bustling market. As in all unlit expanses, avoid walking through the park after sunset.

HEINEKEN EXPERIENCE. Busloads of tourists pour in daily to discover that beer is not made in the Heineken Brewery. Plenty is served, however. The factory stopped producing here in 1988 and has turned the place into a corporate altar, an amusement park devoted to their green-bottled beer. In the Experience, visitors guide themselves past holograms, virtual reality machines, and other multimedia treats that inform you of more than you ever needed to know about the Heineken corporation and beer production. There's even a kiosk where you can email a video of yourself singing on a boat on the Amstel to ignorantly envious friends. Some of the attractions can get wonderfully absurd (e.g., the Bottle Ride, designed to replicate the experience of becoming a Heineken beer), but you'll eventually go along with it and have fun—after a few drinks. A visit includes three beers or soft drinks and a souvenir, all of which is in itself well worth the price of admission. To avoid the crowds, come before 11am and take your alcohol before noon like the real fans do. *(Tram #16, 24, or 25 to Stadhouderskade. ☎523 9666; www.heinekenexperi-*

A BIKING TOUR OF AMSTERDAM

Anyone who has ridden a bicycle in a less bike-friendly city will be blown away by Amsterdammers' respect for the mechanical miracle of the bicycle. This tour starts and ends at **Frédéric Rent a Bike** (p. 95). Begin your tour by biking down **Prinsengracht**. Turn left onto **Reestraat** and continue over the **Singel** to **Dam Square**.

1. DAM SQUARE. Amsterdam's central square is surrounded by the Nieuwe Kerk, Nationaal Monument, and Koninklijk Paleis, home to the Dutch royal family. The square was originally—you guessed it—a dam in the Amstel River, built in the 13th century. Since then it has become a gathering place for famous buildings, pigeons, hippies, tourists, and beautiful architecture (p. 147).

2. SPUI. Go back toward Singel, turn left on Nieuwezijds Voorburgwal, and go south for a few minutes. The Spui is home to a Friday book market and a Sunday art market. Ride back to the Canal Ring West via Heistraat. Turn left onto Herengracht and right onto Leidsegracht; pause at the beautiful intersection at Keizersgracht (p. 147).

3. DE APPEL. Continue down Leidsegracht, turn left at Keizersgracht, and veer left on Nieuwe Spiegelstraat. De Appel is the venue for everything interesting in the contemporary art world—if you bike quickly, the artists will probably still be at it when you get there (p. 172).

4. GOLDEN BEND. This stretch of Herengracht, between Leidsestraat and Vijzelstraat, is known as the "Golden Bend" because of its opulent houses. Officials bent strict house-width rules for wealthy citizens who were willing to invest in the construction of the Herengracht (p. 152).

5. MAGERE BRUG. Turn right at Utrechtsestraat and then left at Prinsengracht. Continue until you hit the Amstel. Turn left; the Magere Brug (Skinny Bridge) is on your right. Although the former, skinnier Skinny Bridge was replaced in 1871, this slightly fatter bridge is still the oldest of the city's pedestrian bridges and the loveliest place to contemplate passing boats (p. 152).

6. NIEUWMARKT. Cross the bridge, turn left, and head north along the Amstel. Go left around the far side of the Stadhuis and cross the bridge at Staalstraat. When you hit Groenburgwal, turn right, right again at Raamgracht, and then left at the first bridge. Turn left to double back along Raamgracht. Turn right at Kloveniersburgwal and follow it to Nieuwmarkt, an open-air market. At Nieuwmarkt, you'll pass De Waag, a beautiful old building that used to be one of the city gates and a weighing station. Finally, head back to Frédéric via Zeedijk (p. 143).

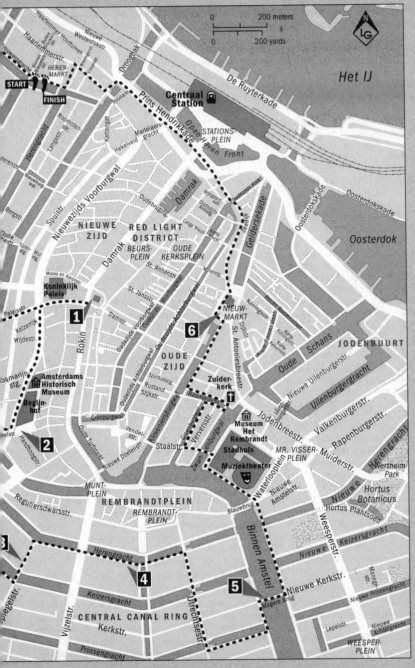

157

ence.com. Open in summer daily 10am-7pm, last entry at 5:45pm; otherwise Tu-Su 10am-6pm, last entry at 5pm. Under 18 must be accompanied by a parent. €11. MC/V.)

JODENBUURT AND PLANTAGE

The Jodenbuurt and Plantage neighborhoods, with their extensive green spaces and varied, excellent assortments of museums, differ greatly from the city center. The Jodenbuurt, or Jewish Quarter, was home to nearly all of the city's Jews until WWII, when Nazi forces deported 70,000 of them to concentration camps. Until that time, **Mr. Visserplein** and **Waterlooplein** were the de facto centers of the Judaic community's dynamic cultural life, though the quarter was not home to only Jewish inhabitants. **Rembrandt van Rijn** lived at **Jodenbreestraat 4,** and his Ashkenazi neighbors were frequent subjects of his paintings. The quarter's lively and subsequently solemn past is commemorated by a host of monuments and remembrances. Post-war developers unfortunately all but neglected the Jodenbuurt. In contrast to the narrow cobblestoned streets of the Centrum, the modern-day Jodenbuurt is less attractive, marked by its ill-designed, bleak streets.

see map p. 344

The Plantage, by contrast, is positively lush with verdant spaces. The land originally provided wealthy 17th-century Canal Ring residents with plots for gardens and parks so they could escape from the city—hence the name "Plantation." One of the most prominent horticultural spaces, **Hortus Botanicus,** was founded here in 1638 as a medicinal garden. As metropolitan limits pushed outward in the 1850s, the region became one of the city's first suburban developments. Members of the merchant class lived in elegant villas that lined wide, tree-lined streets. Today, the Plantage is home to **Artis Zoo** and to its own fine assemblage of museums.

■ **HORTUS BOTANICUS.** With over 4000 species of plants, this outstanding botanical garden is a terrific place to get lost. Visitors can wander past lush palms, flowering cacti, and working beehives or stroll through simulated ecosystems, a rock garden, a rosarium, an herb garden, a three-climate greenhouse, and a butterfly room. Originally established as "Hortus Medicus," a medicinal garden for the town's physicians, the plot has grown into a sprawling collection of meticulously labeled plants held in beautifully designed greenhouses. Many of its more exceptional specimens, including a smuggled Ethiopian coffee plant whose clippings spawned the Brazilian coffee empire, were gathered during the 17th and 18th centuries by members of the Dutch East India Company. Don't miss Hortus's **Welwitschia mirabilis,** a rare desert plant from Namibia that sprouts only two leaves over a life span of more than 2000 years. This one is only around 20 years old, but in a couple millennia it will still be growing. In late summer, check out the giant water lily, **Victoria amazonica,** planted anew every year. The pleasant cafe, housed in a former orangery (a greenhouse used for citrus), has outdoor seating when weather permits and €1-6 sandwiches and snacks. *(Plantage Middenlaan 2A. Tram #7, 9, or 14 to Waterlooplein/Plantage Parklaan and follow the "Hortus Botanicus" signs. ☎ 638 1670; www.dehortus.nl. Open Feb.-June and Sept.-Nov. M-F 9am-5pm, Sa-Su 10am-5pm; July-Aug. M-F 9am-9pm, Sa-Su 10am-9pm; Dec.-Jan. M-F 9am-4pm, Sa-Su 10am-4pm. Guided tours in English Su 2pm €1. €6, ages 5-14 and seniors €3. Cafe open M-F 10am-5pm, Sa-Su 11am-5pm; in summer also daily 6-9pm.)*

■ **GASSAN DIAMONDS.** In the late 19th and early 20th centuries, Amsterdam was a major world diamond center, with massive quantities of the precious gem brought in from colonial exploits in Africa. The rocks were mainly cut and sold in the Jodenbuurt, particularly around Waterlooplein. Gassan is the best of the remaining factories, with an impressive showroom and particularly friendly tour guides. Every few minutes, free one-hour tours depart and fill visitors with plenty of interesting information—and complimentary drinks. Rightly so, the tours fill up quickly, so reserve in advance. *(Nieuwe Uilenburgerstraat 173-175, behind the flea market at Waterlooplein. Take any Metro line to Waterlooplein, exit toward Jodenbreestraat, and take Nieuwe Uilenburgerstraat east. ☎ 622 5333; www.gassandiamonds.com. Open daily 9am-5pm.)*

HOLLANDSCHE SCHOUWBURG. Now a poignant memorial to Amsterdam's Holocaust victims, Hollandsche Schouwburg opened at the end of the 19th century as a Dutch theater on the edge of the old Jewish quarter. In 1941, the Schouwburg underwent a terrible metamorphosis when Nazi occupiers converted it into the Joodsche Schouwburg, the city's sole establishment to which Jewish performers and Jewish patrons were granted access. Not long after, the building was changed into an assembly point for Dutch Jews who were to be deported to **Westerbork,** the transit camp to the north (p. 312). The majority of those passing through met their ends in the concentration camps of Auschwitz, Bergen-Belsen, or Sobibór. At the end of the war, the theater was destroyed, and all that remains of the original structure is a skeleton of crumbled brick walls.

A stone monument now occupies the space where the theater's stage used to be, and poplar trees grow in the one-time courtyard. A memorial room, in which 6700 surnames of victims who were deported from this site are engraved and illuminated behind an eternally lit flame, reminds visitors of the extraordinary toll of WWII. Upstairs is a small exhibition that details the gradual isolation and ultimate death of the majority of Dutch Jews who first entered the theater as prisoners, and some video monitors reveal their firsthand accounts through short interviews. *(Plantage Middenlaan 24. Tram #9 or 14 to Plantage Kerklaan. ☎ 531 0430; www.hollandscheschouwburg.nl. Open daily 11am-4pm; closed on Yom Kippur. Free.)*

ARTIS ZOO. Artis is the oldest zoo and park in the Netherlands; it is also a zoological museum, a museum of geology, an aquarium, and a planetarium. A day of good weather is enough to make the Artis complex worth a visit, especially for children (and perhaps adults) sick of historical landmarks. The zoo's got all the big guns: a polar bear, several massive gorillas, elephants, giraffes, a whole building full of scary bugs, and hundreds of free-roaming schoolchildren—be careful not to trip over any as you stroll the grounds. During WWII, up to 300 Jews were hidden in the zoo's empty cages. *(Plantage Kerklaan 38-40. Tram #9 or 14 to Plantage Kerklaan. ☎ 523 3400; www.artis.nl. Open daily 9am-5pm, during daylight saving time 9am-6pm. €17.50, ages 3-9 €14, seniors €16.50, under 3 free. Guidebooks €2.50. AmEx/MC/V.)*

PORTUGEES-ISRAELIETISCHE SYNAGOGE. Amsterdam's early Sephardic Jewish community, mainly refugees fleeing religious persecution in Spain, founded this large synagogue, known as the Esnoga (the Portuguese word for synagogue), in 1675. The beautifully maintained structure still holds services on Saturdays and holidays, and it has remained largely unchanged since its founding. Despite the destructive force of the Nazi occupation during WWII, the synagogue was somehow left unharmed. One of the few tangible remnants of Amsterdam's once-thriving Jewish community, the synagogue features a plain but beautiful *chuppah* (a Jewish wedding canopy) crafted from Brazilian jacaranda wood and donated in 1956. The large worship hall is free to walk through and features massive brass candelabras and an architectural style similar to the arches of Amsterdam's canal houses. Descriptions of the various elements of the synagogue, along with a small but informative exhibit of artifacts and narratives from the synagogue's more than 300 years of history, help visitors place the synagogue in historical context. A video presentation gives some background on Amsterdam's Jewish community as an introduction to your visit.

Just after you leave, take a look at **The Dockworker.** Unveiled in 1952, this bronze statue just behind the synagogue memorializes the strike held by the

Amsterdam dockworkers in February 1941. The men were among the first groups in Amsterdam to respond to the German occupation—specifically to the arrest of over 400 Jewish men at the order of the German chief of police. *(Mr. Visserplein 1-3. Tram #9 or 14 to Waterlooplein. ☎ 624 5351; www.esnoga.com. Open Apr.-Oct. M-F and Su 10am-4pm; Nov.-Mar. M-Th and Su 10am-4pm, F 10am-3pm. €6.50, students, seniors, and Museumjaarkaart holders €5, under 17 €4.)*

ZUIDERKERK. Tucked away on a quiet square surrounded by trees and small apartments, the Zuiderkerk dominates the surrounding neighborhood with its elegant spire. Constructed between 1603 and 1614 and designed by architect Hendrick de Keyser, it was the first Protestant church to be built after the Reformation. During and after the Netherlands's harsh winter of 1944-45, in which temperatures and foodstuffs reached record lows, the building was a makeshift morgue. Its tower is open in summer and boasts some of the best views of the city. Zuiderkerk houses the Municipal Information Center for Physical Planning and Housing and features exhibits on the history and planning of Amsterdam's neighborhoods—as well as future plans for the city's growth. Call ahead to arrange a viewing of a video and short talk on Amsterdam's city planning, free on Saturdays after 2pm. *(Zuiderkerkhof. From Nieuwmarkt, head southwest on Kloveniersburgwal and turn left at Zandstraat; the church will be on your left. ☎ 552 7987, tower tours 689 2565; anna@buschermalocca.nl. Planning office open M 11am-4pm, Tu-W and F 9am-4pm, Th 9am-10pm. Free. Guided tower tours Apr.-Sept. M-Sa noon-3:30pm every 30min. €6, ages 6-12 €3. Under 9 need adult supervision.)*

BROUWERIJ 'T IJ. This former bathhouse and current daytime bar is a no-frills, die-hard brewery for the serious enthusiast. Situated on the body of water known as 't IJ, the building bears the sign of the Brouwerij 't IJ: an ostrich and its egg. Some say the logo derives from the similarity between the sound of " 't IJ" and the Dutch *de ei*, which means "the egg." There's plenty of lively conversation from the locals who pack the bar and large canal terrace. Bring your camera, because, after sampling the Brouwerij's nine home brews (six regulars and three seasonal beers for €1.70-3 each), you're sure to have a foggy memory of this unique brewery. The building is also adjacent to the massive De Gooyer Windmill, a corn mill built in 1725 and an interesting sight in its own right. *(Funenkade 7. Bus #22 out to the Zeeburgerstraat stop. Walk behind the windmill. ☎ 622 8325 or 320 1786. Open W-Su 3-7:45pm. Tours F 4pm. Free.)*

 LET'S GET AROUND. *Amsterdam Op de Fiets* is an excellent map of the city; it labels good biking routes, bike repair shops, and loads of non-biking-related things like movie theaters and public pools. Pick it up at Pied a Terre (p. 219), Bike City (p. 95), or any map shop.

WERTHEIM PARK. This small park on the Nieuwe Herengracht canal is a great place to stretch out on a sunny day. One of several wonderful green spaces in the Plantage, Wertheim Park provides a contemplative spot for visitors to sit. The park is home to the **Nooit Meer Auschwitz** (Auschwitz Never Again) monument, a small glass memorial that holds the ashes of Auschwitz victims. A mirror of broken glass reflecting a shattered image of the sky, symbolic of the heavens' inability to reckon the horror of the Holocaust, covers the ashes. *(Plantage Middenlaan, across from Hortus Botanicus. Open daily 8am-sundown.)*

STADHUIS-HET MUZIEKTHEATER. Nicknamed the "Stopera" (a combination of Stadhuis and opera) by protesters who objected to the demolition of historic buildings in the old Jewish quarter before the complex opened in 1986, the Amstel-bound Muziektheater is home to the Netherlands Opera and the National Ballet. Enthusiasts can tour the performance and backstage spaces of both companies,

SIGHTS

sampling wigs, props, and costumes from past performances every Saturday at noon. The rotund red-brick, marble, and glass complex also houses Amsterdam's city hall, or Stadhuis. For information on performances, see p. 186. *(Waterlooplein. Tram #9 or 14, or any Metro line, to Waterlooplein. Box office ☎ 625 5455; www.hetmuziektheater.nl. Box office open M-Sa 10am-6pm, Su and holidays 11:30am-2:30pm, or until curtain on the day of a show. Tours last 75min.; €4.50, ages 7-12 free. AmEx/MC/V.)*

ARCAM (ARCHITECTUURCENTRUM AMSTERDAM).
Staffed by professionals with training in design, ARCAM is a solid resource for anyone interested in learning more about Amsterdam's vibrant architecture. While the center is not a museum, it hosts a number of changing exhibitions, lectures, and discussions that provide guests and residents of the city with some insight into what's behind (and inside) Amsterdam's newest and oldest structures. ARCAM also sells a detailed architectural map of the city (€7.50) and several printed guides (€10-12) that can help you make the most of your exploration. Although they do not provide tours of the city themselves, they are happy to refer people to the tour companies they think do the best job. *(Prins Hendrikkade 600. Tram #9 or 14 to Waterlooplein. ☎ 620 4878; www.arcam.nl. Open Tu-Sa 1-5pm; closed on bank holidays. Wheelchair-accessible. Free.)*

MOZES EN AARONKERK (MOSES AND AARON CHURCH).
Once a prominent Catholic church in the heart of the Jewish Quarter, this daunting piece of Neoclassical architecture was built in 1841 and is the only Christian edifice in the Jodenbuurt proper. The church no longer hosts an active congregation and so is not regularly open to the public. The site now hosts exhibitions, symposia, social service groups, and an adult-education center. Moses and Aaron was once graced with concerts by Franz Liszt and Camille Saint-Saëns, and it carries on its lively musical past into the present with frequent performances. Call or check the website for information on upcoming events. *(Waterlooplein 207. Tram #9 or 14 to Waterlooplein. ☎ 622 1305; www.mozeshuis.nl. Concert prices vary but can be as low as €4.)*

GREATER AMSTERDAM

It doesn't hurt to leave the chaotic Canal Ring sometimes. Here are some major sights that just don't fit on our maps.

AMSTERDAMSE BOS (AMSTERDAM FOREST).
Sculpted in 1934, the forest impressively spans 10 sq. km southwest of the city center. With 19km of bike trails, excellent picnic spots, weaving waterways, a small petting zoo, and a picturesque pan-

THE HIDDEN DEA[L]

BIKE BUY-BACKS

If Los Angeles is the city of th[e] automobile, Amsterdam is the city of the bicycle. Everyone—from old ladies bringing home grocer ies to professionals on their wa[y] to work—rides a bike. It is th[e] quickest and easiest way to ge[t] around town, and almost all o[f] the city is accessible by bike[.] Moreover, the proliferation of two wheelers translates into fewe[r] toxin-emitting cars and trucks on Amsterdam's small streets.

If you plan on staying i[n] Amsterdam for more than a fe[w] days or want to see a big chunk o[f] the city quickly, rent a bicycle. I[f] your stay extends past a few days however, bike rentals can becom[e] prohibitively expensive, and you[r] best bet may be to purchase a[ ]used bike from an area shop.

A decent used bike can be pur chased within Amsterdam cente[r] for about €140. The importan[t] trick, however, is to check wit[h] the bike shop about buy-backs[.] Often, if you return your bike i[n] good condition within a certai[n] period, you can receive as muc[h] as half the price back. One popu lar shop is **Damstraat Rent-a Bike,** Damstraat 22 (☎ 62[5] 5029; www.bikes.nl), whos[e] bikes range €130-300 (p. 95).

Not all shops have a buy-bac[k] option, so be sure to ask before pu[r] chasing. Also remember to sav[e] your receipt, or else it is unlikely tha[t] you will get a fair return price.

LOCAL LEGEND

DUTCH GIANTS

When visiting the Netherlands for the first time, you might feel that you're constantly in the midst of a swarm of giants. The country may be small, but its people certainly are not. The Dutch have the highest average height of any nationality on earth: 6' 1" for men and 5' 8" for women. This means that they are considerably taller than Americans, whose men average 5' 9" and women 5' 5".

A 2004 article in the New Yorker put forth several theories to explain this phenomenon. One attributes the height to the Netherlands's flat geography; inhabitants of flat areas tend to be taller, whereas mountain dwellers are often shorter. Another theory connects it to the Dutch affinity for dairy products; a German study has found a correlation—if you can believe it—between height and cow population. The article, however, posited that the likeliest explanation lies in the Netherlands's universal health care and social welfare systems. The Dutch growth spurt began in the mid-1800s, just as the nation's first social welfare system began. As access to better health care broadened and the nutritional value of meals increased, so too did Dutchmen's average height. Studies also indicate that Americans lose most ground to the Dutch during infancy, when pediatric health care is most vital, and during the teenage years, probably due to Americans' fattier and less healthful diets.

cake house, these woods may well be the city's best-kept secret. The expansive green space feels more like a park than a forest at times, with several football pitches and roads covering the land; however, many quiet acres do provide a much-needed repose from the city of red lights. With six pedestrian routes and 13 bike paths, the forest provides a natural environment for daily exercise. Upon entering the forest at Van Nijenrodeweg, you'll see an odd, dark, wood building on your left; this is the **Visitors Center,** an excellent source of information about the park. The helpful map of the Bos is €5. (☎545 6100; www.amsterdamsebos.nl. Open Tu-Sa noon-5pm, Su 10am-5pm.) From the Visitors Center, you'll see the Bosbaan Canal, used as a practice area for local rowing teams. **Rental bikes** are available at the main entrance at Van Nijenrodeweg. (☎644 5473; e.waaijer@arjo.nl. €4 per hr., €6 per 2hr., €9 per day.) Better yet, dip your feet in the Grote Vijver, a 20min. walk from the main entrance along the left side of the Bosbaan canal, with 3hr. **canoe, water bike,** or **electric boat** rides. (☎645 7831; www.kanoverhuur-adam.nl. 2 people per canoe, €8; 2 people per water bike, €8; 5 people per electric boat, €22.) At the opposite end of the Bosbaan from the Visitors Center is **Boerderij Meerzicht,** a combined *pannenkoekenhuis* and petting zoo. Pancakes in the large but homey restaurant run €4.80-9, sandwiches go for €3-4.20, and *thee* and *koffie* cost €2. At the "petting" zoo next door, actual petting isn't always permitted, but you can always feed the deer and goats through the fence. (☎679 2744. 1st pancakes served 11am. Open daily 10am-7pm.) The nearby **openluchttheater** (open-air theater) puts on a different Shakespearean play (in Dutch) every summer; check the website for the current production and playing times. (☎643 3286; www.bostheater.nl.) In the same building as the Visitors Center is the **Bosmuseum,** a fun spot for kids with interactive nature exhibits, including an underground tunnel that allows visitors of all ages to explore life beneath the earth's surface. (☎676 2152. Open Mar.-Oct. daily 10am-7pm; Nov.-Feb. F-Su 10am-6pm.) The forest offers plenty of green for field hockey, cricket, and tennis and has numerous fishing ponds. Keep the scale of the park in mind; if you're walking, you will have to trek a fair distance before reaching the first sights. (Main entrance at Nieuwe Kalfjeslaan 4. Bus #170 or 172 from Centraal, Dam, Westermarkt, Leidseplein, Museumplein, or Stationsplein to Van Nijenrodeweg—or just ask for Amsterdamse Bos. ☎545 6100; www.amsterdamsebos.nl.)

ARENA STADIUM. The Dutchman's undying passion for football—soccer to some—is magnificently demonstrated by the state-of-the-art, 52,000-

seat stadium built in Amsterdam's outskirts in 1996. ArenA, a massively modern creation, even boasts Europe's first mobile domed roof that slides open or closed depending on weather conditions. For a small nation, the Netherlands enjoys a distinguished football history, having reached two back-to-back World Cup finals in 1974 and 1978 (p. 73). Amsterdam's love for "the beautiful game" is devoted to the Amsterdamsche Football Club (AFC) **Ajax,** the Netherlands's most successful football club. The team, founded in 1900, is almost unanimously supported by Amsterdammers. AFC rewards its fans with consistent high-level play, having won both the Dutch Cup and the Dutch Championship in 2002. With 40,000 season ticket holders, the stadium's 12,000 remaining tickets (€30 and up) sell quickly but are usually still available in the weeks before matches. However, games against hated metropolitan rivals like Feyenoord Rotterdam, PSV Eindhoven, and FC Utrecht usually sell out instantly and are often reserved for locals to ensure that diehard fans pack the seats. Be aware that local hooligans occupy the west side of the ArenA (F-Side), where they'll be madly cheering Ajax to victory. A tour of the facility will take you onto the actual field—home to large concerts, an ice skating rink in the winter, and club football matches. The bilingual tour, which also covers the press room and the upper stands, is recommended for those with an interest in European football or stadium design; those without a bloodthirsty passion for kicking around a checkered ball may find it dull. The small museum attached to the stadium gives visitors an impassioned look at the town's pride and joy, delving into the "World of Ajax" through videos, famed uniforms, photographs, and team documents. *(ArenA Boulevard 1. Museum: ArenA Boulevard 3. Metro #50 or 54 or bus #29, 158, 174, 177, or 178 to Strandvliet or Bijlmer/ArenA. 3 zones; 4 strips. Enter on the far side of the stadium, near gate F, across from the Villa Arena mall. Tickets ☎311 1333, 311 1336, or 311 1444; www.amsterdamarena.nl, team website www.ajax.nl. Open Oct.-Mar. M-Sa 10am-5pm, Apr.-Sept. daily 10am-6pm. Guided 1hr. tour of stadium 11am, 12:15, 1:30, 2:45, 4:30pm. Additional tours July-Aug. 12:45, 4, 5pm instead of the 4:30 tour. €9, under 12 and over 65 €8.)*

MUSEUMS

Amsterdam's museums contain enough art and history to arouse even the most indifferent of curiosities. Whether you want to admire Rembrandts, observe cutting-edge photography, pay tribute to Anne Frank's memory, or marvel at sexual oddities, Amsterdam has a museum geared toward every purpose. Above all, however, Amsterdam is an art lover's paradise. The most popular art museums—including the Rijksmuseum and the Van Gogh Museum—fill Museumplein with any and everyone even the slightest bit interested in art. Yet, other neighborhoods also shelter stellar, if somewhat smaller, collections. If you're itching to have your finger on the contemporary pulse of the city's cultural life—or want to take a piece of it home—you should consider spending a morning gallery-hopping (p. 182).

Amsterdam has also witnessed thriving museum counter-culture, best exemplified by a swelling of so-called "alternative art spaces." These extraordinarily compelling spaces, usually housed in formerly squatted buildings, explore a range of artistic expression that includes painting and installation art and goes beyond to performance pieces and innovative mixed media. They are a sometimes elusive part of Amsterdam's artistic life but should not be missed. For more information and listings, see p. 183.

In an entirely different—and frequently non-artistic—vein, the city enjoys a smattering of specific collected artifacts and objects that cater to some truly obscure niche interests; for more information on these curious curators, see **Bizarre Amsterdam,** p. 3.

OUDE ZIJD

Amsterdam is a city of museums, but if you're looking for Rembrandt, Van Gogh, or Rubens, the Oude Zijd will disappoint. The attractions in this neighborhood are less high culture than they are corporeal pleasure, though some sophisticated museums are worth a visit. On the whole, head to the Oude Zijd when looking for a physical distraction from Amsterdam's intellectual scene.

see map p. 340

AMSTERDAMS CENTRUM VOOR FOTOGRAFIE. A brimming forum emphasizing the talents of young photographers, the Amsterdam Center for Photography holds six- to eight-week-long exhibits by up-and-coming artists, following recent (mostly Dutch) art-school graduates through their first post-grad year. The level of talent and breadth of subject matter vary greatly, but there are always some remarkable pieces. The center also organizes frequent photography courses and master classes, but they are all in Dutch; call for more information. (Bethanienstraat 39, between Kloveniersburgwal and Oudezijds Achterburgwal. ☎622 4899. Open July-Aug. Sa 1-5pm; Sept.-June Th-Sa 1-5pm.)

RED LIGHT DISTRICT

Perhaps unsurprisingly, the Red Light District is not home to Amsterdam's most cherished museums. For the most part, the exhibits here focus on predictable topics, considering the location: drugs and sex. Cannabis College, a small resource and information center on the uses and consumption of cannabis, is a worthwhile stop, if only to chat with the smart and enthusiastic staff. A break from the debauchery

see map p. 340

and decadence can be found at Museum Amstelkring, a former clandestine Catholic church that provides a fascinating look into the history of religious persecution in Amsterdam following the Reformation.

■ **MUSEUM AMSTELKRING "ONS' LIEVE HEER OP SOLDER".** After the Protestant Reformation in the 16th century, the Netherlands became an unfriendly place for Catholics. Although Amsterdam maintained a reputation as a relatively tolerant place, many Catholic churches were closed or converted for Protestant use. Catholics could not worship openly, and those who still wanted to congregate were forced to do so in private. The continued persecution led Jan Hartmann, a wealthy Dutch merchant, to convert several canal houses into a secret church (hence, "Our Dear Lord in the Attic"). Completed in 1663 and a museum since 1888, the splendid chapel is housed in the attics of three separate canal houses and includes a fantastic 18th-century Baroque altar with a painting of the Baptism of Christ by famed artist Jacob de Wit. The large antique organ, designed especially for this secret church's unique situation in 1794, is equally impressive. The church makes clever use of its clandestine space, with an ornate pulpit stored under the altar and galleries suspended from the roof by cast-iron rods. On the way up and down, small exhibitions and period rooms re-create life during the Dutch Reformation, embellished by the museum's collection of Dutch painting and antique silver. The church is still active, holding mass six times per year and performing marriages on request; check the website for information on either. *(Oudezijds Voorburgwal 40, at Heintje Hoekssteeg. ☎ 624 6604; www.opsolder.nl. Open M-Sa 10am-5pm, Su and holidays 1-5pm. €7, students €5, ages 5-18 €1, under 5 free.)*

■ **CANNABIS COLLEGE.** If weed piques your interest, your best bet is this staggeringly informative non-academic think tank. For innocuously biased information on the uses of medicinal marijuana, the war on drugs, or the creative applications of industrial hemp (like a wall or a snowboard), it's ounce-for-ounce the equal of the **Hash Museum** (below), just more potent—and free. The staff of volunteers is unbelievably friendly, knowledgeable, and eager to answer any questions. If you think you're enough of an expert and want to spread your reefer know-how, don't be afraid to ask about lending a hand (p. 80). See an artfully designed and adoringly cared-for cannabis garden in the basement for a donation of €2.50, which also entitles you to a demonstration of a vaporizer—bring your own pot, and the staff recommends that you eat something beforehand. *(Oudezijds Achterburgwal 124. ☎ 423 4420; www.cannabiscollege.com. Open daily 11am-7pm. Free.)*

HASH MARIJUANA HEMP MUSEUM. With the free Cannabis College nearby, it's difficult to justify the €5.70 entrance fee to this shrine to ganja. Most of the exhibits here, on topics such as the American war on drugs, pipes of the world, celebrity drug smugglers, or hemp rope making, seem extremely out of date and under-researched, but if you want to ogle a microscopic view of female cannabis flowers or a 1967 issue of *Parade* with the cover story, "Why They Smoke Pot," stop by. The museum's most well-developed attraction is its grow room, which does little more than prove that watching grass grow is indeed as exciting as it sounds. The next-door grow shop, however, is almost worth a visit. *(Oudezijds Achterburgwal 148. ☎ 623 5961; www.sensiseeds.com. Open daily 10am-10pm. €5.70, under 13 free.)*

NIEUWE ZIJD

The collection of museums in the Nieuwe Zijd give even those in Museumplein a run for their money. While the cultural institutions of the south of the city focus largely on art, those in the Nieuwe Zijd also display archaeological findings, historical artifacts, and religious relics. For a taste of all of the culture Amsterdam has to offer, a visit to the Nieuwe Zijd's museums is a must.

NIEUWE KERK. The New Church, the extravagant 15th-century brick-red cathedral at the heart of the Nieuwe Zijd, now serves a triple role as a religious edifice, historical monument, and art museum. The church is most significantly a cultural destination; changing exhibits fill the nooks and crannies of the sacred, cavernous space for several months. Take a moment to stray from the main exhibit and to discover the ornate hexagonal **pulpit**, with its intricate bas-reliefs depicting works of charity and parables from the New Testament. It was carved over 15 years by Albert Jansz Vinckenbrinck. Jacob van Campen, architect of the Koninklijk Paleis, designed the stunning undulating organ case. The paintings on its doors depict scenes from the life of the biblical King David. Be sure to tilt your head upward to catch a glimpse of winged cherubs who appear to be bearing the weight of the vaulted ceiling. **Commemorative windows** are given to the church to honor royal inaugurations and other events; a particularly poignant one is to the right past the gift shop, put in place in 1995 to commemorate 50 years of freedom after WWII. This piece of contemporary art features plain opaque glass and prison bars that evoke the country's struggles during the occupation and celebrate the eventual end of the oppression. Other stained-glass windows include the massive windows above the main entrance (honoring the inauguration of Queen Wilhelmina) and those remembering Queen Beatrix's silver jubilee in 2005. The church, which has been rebuilt several times after several fires, is still used for royal inaugurations and weddings. Queen Wilhelmina was crowned here in 1898, followed by her daughter Juliana in 1948 and granddaughter Beatrix in 1980. In February 2002, Prince Wilhelm Alexander, the heir to the Dutch throne, was married to Argentine belle Maxima in the Nieuwe Kerk's hallowed sanctuary. Check the website before you go; the church closes for two weeks between exhibits. (*Adjacent to Dam Sq., beside Koninklijk Paleis. ☎ 638 6909; www.nieuwekerk.nl. Open daily 10am-5pm. Organ recitals June-Sept. Th 12:30pm, Su 8pm. Call ahead for exact times. €8, ages 6-15 and seniors €6.*)

AMSTERDAMS HISTORISCH MUSEUM. Appropriately for the Amsterdam Historical Museum, the building itself oozes history: the house, constructed in the 17th century, used to be Amsterdam's city orphanage. Even though nothing beats a walk around the city itself, this archival museum offers an eclectic introduction to Amsterdam's historical development by way of ancient archaeological findings, medieval manuscripts, Baroque paintings, and multimedia displays. The collection of artifacts alone provides a useful introduction to the city's importance as a center of trade and culture as well as its rise—and fall—and rise again—from a swampy marshland to a modern city. However, the layout is often needlessly labyrinthine, and the spare wall texts don't provide a coherent narrative. The story is organized into a **Grand Tour** of Amsterdam's history and culture, beginning on the ground floor with "The Young City, 1350-1550," continuing through the Reformation, Industrial Revolution, and finishing in "The Modern City, 1850-2000." The section of the museum that features artistic accounts of gory Golden Age anatomy lessons (Rembrandt's among them) is particularly interesting. The illustrations of Amsterdam's maritime history narrate the curious struggles of the Dutch East India Company. Be sure to catch one of the Historical Museum's **hidden surprises:** in the covered passageway between the museum and the Begijnhof, there is an extensive collection of large 17th-century paintings of Amsterdam's civic guards. During Amsterdam's Golden Age, these pictures were a genre unto themselves, commissioned by the governing boards of municipal bodies seeking painterly immortality. Beyond the passage, the remainder of the museum illustrates Amsterdam's more contemporary history through photography, film, and creative displays. (*Kalverstraat 92 and Nieuwezijds Voorburgwal 357. Tram #4, 9, 14, 16, 24, or 25 to Spui or #1, 2, or 5 to Nieuwezijds Voorburgwal. ☎ 523 1822; www.ahm.nl. Open M-F 10am-5pm, Sa-Su 11am-5pm; closed Queen's Day. €7, ages 6-16 €3.50, seniors €5.25.*)

■STEDELIJK MUSEUM FOR MODERN AND CONTEMPORARY ART. As the Stedelijk's building on Museumplein undergoes extensive renovations, its home until 2009 is a drab 11-story building to the east of Centraal Station overlooking the IJ. The museum has integrated its mission into the space admirably, filling two cavernous floors of the building with exhibits of contemporary art that rotate every three months. These pieces, none of which predate 1968, are sometimes interspersed with masterpieces from the museum's extensive permanent collection of avant-garde and contemporary art. A cafe serves coffee and tea with a beautiful view of the harbor. *(Oosterdokskade 5. ☎573 2745, recorded info 573 2911; www.stedelijk.nl. Open daily 11am-6pm. €9; ages 7-16, over 65, and groups of 15 or more €4.50; under 7 free; families €22.50.)*

ALLARD PIERSON MUSEUM. Experience a classical blast from the past at the University of Amsterdam's archaeological museum, named for a prominent archaeologist and professor at the university in the 19th century. While the well-balanced and handsome collection of artifacts from ancient Egypt, Greece, Mesopotamia, Etruria, and Rome is not exactly world-class, it does have a surprising collection of Roman figurines, Egyptian reliefs, and Greek pottery—as well as some of the city's classiest (albeit 2000-year-old) full-frontal nudes. The museum inhabits the former headquarters (1869-1967) of the Dutch central bank, and the building's classical features, including columns and marble floors, complement the collection well. Although many of the individual captions to the artifacts are only available in Dutch, larger plaques and signs are written in both Dutch and English. The holdings—30,000 excavated objects, 10,000-year-old skulls, and a carefully restored mummy—are worthy attractions for fans of classical antiquity. *(Oude Turfmarkt 127. Located across the Amstel from Rokin, less than 5min. from Dam Sq. ☎525 2556; www.allardpiersonmuseum.nl. Open Tu-F 10am-5pm, Sa-Su 1-5pm. €5; students, ages 4-16, and seniors €2.50; under 4 free.)*

AMSTERDAM SEX MUSEUM. This almost requisite museum will disappoint only those looking for a sophisticated examination of sexuality in all its cultural, economic, legal, regulatory, and generative dimensions. Those looking for a fun, if somewhat unrefined, caricature of sex will be in heaven. Only five minutes on foot from Centraal Station and with an incredibly low admission fee, the Sex Museum won't leave you feeling burned if you find that walls plastered with pictures of bestiality and S&M are not your thing. The first of four floors features some amusing life-size mannequins of pimps, prostitutes, and even one immodest fellow who flashes you from behind his trench coat. With the many moans, whispers, and cackles emitting from these dolls, at times the experience feels more like a horror show than a sexual adventure. The museum features such ancient artifacts as a stone phallus from the Roman age, but the exhibits are hardly informative; the majority is composed of photograph after photograph of sexual acts, some more familiar than others. Watch out for the gallery of fetishes, though: the montage of horses, whips, and nipple clamps is not for the weak of stomach. *(Damrak 18. ☎622 8376; www.sexmuseumamsterdam.nl. Open daily 10am-11:30pm. €3.)*

CANAL RING WEST

Any visit to the Canal Ring West must include the area's magnificent array of museums. The Anne Frank Huis is mere steps away from Westermarkt and the Westerkerk, while the Bijbels Museum and the Theater Instituut Nederlands can be found in their respective magnificent canal houses after a brief stroll.

■ANNE FRANK HUIS. Anne Frank was just 10 years old when WWII began in 1939, but her literary legacy has

see map p. 338

inspired many across the globe. In 1942, the Nazis began deporting all Jews to ghettos and concentration camps, forcing Anne's family and four other Dutch Jews to hide in the *achterhuis*, or annex, of Otto Frank's warehouse on the Prinsengracht. All eight refugees lived in this secret annex for two years, during which time Anne penned her diary, a moving chronicle of her life as a Jew in the Nazi-occupied Netherlands. Translated into over 60 languages, her journal continues to be one of the most widely read books in the world, revealing with its innocent sincerity the destructive consequences of prejudice and hate.

Displays of various household objects, text panels mounted with pages from the diary's first and second copies, and video footage of the rooms as they looked during WWII give some sense of life in that tumultuous time. However, save Anne's original magazine clippings and photos left plastered to the walls, the rooms are unfurnished; the cramped, exposed conditions and lack of privacy described in her writing are left to the visitor's imagination. Footage of interviews with Otto Frank (Anne's father), Miep Gies (an office worker who supplied the family with food and other necessities), and Anne's best childhood friend provide further insights. The original bookcase used to hide the entrance to the secret annex remains, cracked open for visitors to pass through. Especially moving are pencil marks, still visible on the wall, which tracked the height of Anne and her sister Margot Frank while they were in hiding.

After walking through the house, be sure to check out the CD-ROM exhibit, which provides more information about WWII and a virtual tour of the furnished house. Nearby is an interactive display that strives to contextualize the Holocaust in relation to current human rights issues. In the exhibit, visitors watch a film documenting recent civil rights issues.

The endless line stretching around the corner attests to the popularity of the Anne Frank Huis. With extended hours in the summer, there is no reason to wait for an hour in order to get inside—the line is not as long before 10am and after 7pm. *(Prinsengracht 267. Tram #6, 13, 14, or 17 to Westermarkt. ☎556 7100; www.annefrank.nl. Open daily Apr.-Aug. 9am-9pm; Sept.-Mar. 9am-7pm; closed on Yom Kippur. Last entry 30min. before closing. €6.50, ages 10-17 €3, under 10 free.)*

▨BIJBELS MUSEUM. This informative and illustrative museum provides a fascinating examination of ancient biblical culture. Inside two canal houses built by 17th-century architect Philip Vingboons, the museum presents information on both the contents and history of the Bible and the cultural context in which it was written. Opened in 1851 with Leendert Schouten's display of his ancient Israeli Tabernacle, it includes the first Bible ever printed in the Netherlands. Other highlights include a large model of the Temple Mount in Jerusalem, with an exhibit on its significance to Jews, Muslims, and Christians, as well as an authentic Egyptian mummy from 304 BC.

The exhibits benefit from their surroundings; the house is a monument in itself, containing artistic designs that call forth biblical themes and demonstrate the Bible's influence on culture and society. The bottom floor is devoted to the study of canal-house architecture, with emphasis on the ceiling paintings by Jacob de Wit and the elliptical English grand staircase. Make sure to examine the 17th-century kitchen, and don't miss the two **aroma cabinets** that offer samplings of "exalted" fragrances—e.g., lotus and myrrh—and "everyday" scents from biblical times—e.g., fig and pomegranate. The large garden located at the back of the museum is an oasis of calm with its lily pond and arrangement of biblical sculptures. *(Herengracht 366-368. Tram #1, 2, or 5 to Spui. ☎624 2436; www.bijbelsmuseum.nl. Open M-Sa 10am-5pm, Su 11am-5pm. €6, students and children 13-18 €3, under 13 free.)*

HUIS MARSEILLE. This small museum houses a rotating collection of artistic photography. Every three months, a handful of new displays, ranging from 30 to as many as 300 photographs, grace Marseille, a canal house dating from 1665. Only a few prints are selected from each artist, but their works are invariably expressive, informative, and thoughtfully arranged. The museum has a permanent collection of contemporary works by international photographers whose pieces branch out into other forms of visual art. *(Keizersgracht 401. ☎ 531 8989; www.huismarseille.nl. Open Tu-Su 11am-5pm. €5, students €3, under 18 free.)*

MUTABLE MUSEUMS. If you're dead-set on seeing a particular museum and are planning to make an extended trip out of it, make sure to call ahead. Particular artifacts or collections may be away on tour, and museums sometimes close when they are between exhibits.

THEATER INSTITUUT NEDERLAND. Located in five majestic Herengracht canal houses, the Theater Instituut Nederland hosts continually changing exhibits related to all aspects of theater and dance. The main building of the Instituut is **Herengracht 168,** which architect Philip Vingboons transformed in 1638 from a bakery into a resplendent house with the city's first neck-gable (an ornamentation that capped off thin canal houses). The museum also extends into the notable **Bartolotti House,** built in 1617 by Guillelmo Bartolotti. One highlighted permanent exhibit is an intact 17th-century chamber theater. If translations are not next to the exhibits, ask at the reception desk for a printed sheet with the English descriptions. The walls and ceilings of the front reception area are museum pieces in themselves. The landscapes depicted here, painted by artist Isaac de Moucheron, tell the legend of Jefta, the commander of the Israelite army, and the figures, by renowned painter Jacob de Wit, glorify Flora, the Roman goddess of the spring. The building also houses a comprehensive library specializing in Dutch theater. In the back, a well-lit cafe stocks snacks and drinks. *(Herengracht 168-174. Tram #1, 2, or 5 to Dam, then walk up Raadhuisstraat away from the back of the palace. Turn left at Herengracht. ☎ 551 3300; www.tin.nl. Open M-F 11am-5pm, Sa-Su 1-5pm. €4.50, students €2.25, ages 7-16 €2.25, under 7 free.)*

MULTATULI MUSEUM. "I am a coffee broker, and I live at No. 37 Lauriergracht, Amsterdam." So begins *Max Havelaar, or the Coffee Auctions of the Dutch Trading Company*, one of the few 19th-century Dutch novels still popular with contemporary literati. Its author, Eduard Douwes Dekker, has been praised for his visionary political leadership and named the Netherlands's most significant author. He penned *Max Havelaar* after a 20-year stay in Indonesia, during which he realized that the Dutch government's exploitation of the Javanese wasn't as harmless as people seemed to believe. Because the Netherlands profited greatly from colonial spoils, Dekker wavered on whether to publish his controversial beliefs; eventually, he wrote the work in 1860 under the pseudonym *Multatuli*, Latin for "I have endured many things." The novel's critique of colonialism and its sharp witticisms instantly made it a vivid classic, breathing life into the conventional world of mid-19th-century Dutch literature.

Today you can visit the museum dedicated to Dekker's legacy—not on Lauriergracht in the Jordaan, but at the author's birthplace on Korsjespoortsteeg. The museum is used mainly for scholarly research, but the upstairs room displays Dekker's personal book collection, desk, and the sofa on which he died. A fantastically knowledgeable staff of volunteers will eagerly recount Dekker's life. *(Korsjespoortsteeg 20. Tram #1, 2, 5, 13, or 17 to Nieuwezijds Kolk, get off at the Herengracht stop, and walk toward the Shipping Quarter. ☎ 638 1938; www.multatuli-museum.nl/ en. Open Tu and Sa-Su 10am-5pm. Free.)*

NATIONAAL BRILMUSEUM (NATIONAL SPECTACLES MUSEUM). By virtue of its location on one of Amsterdam's quieter side streets, it is easy to overlook the

Nationaal Brilmuseum, perched in the home of a family that has been collecting specs for over four generations. The four-story building, which dates all the way back to 1620, is a tribute to all things ocular. The museum displays everything from models of the eye to a multitude of eyewear in every style. The eye-popping exhibits take you through the history of optical science, craftsmanship, and fashion. While the museum might not catch everyone's eye, the cheap admission fee and its novelty alone certainly make it worth a visit. Inside you'll find famous frames from the past century—such as Schubert's, Buddy Holly's, and Dame Edna's—that have not been worn since their owners bequeathed them to the museum. Visit the shop (p. 217) that occupies the ground floor of the museum if you find yourself squinting at the exhibits. *(Gasthuismolensteeg 7. Take any tram to Dam Sq., walk around to the left of the Palace, turn left, walk ½ block, and turn right onto Paleisstraat, which becomes Gasthuismolensteeg. Cross the Singel; the museum is on the left in the middle of the next block.* ☎ *421 2414; www.brilmuseumamsterdam.nl. Open W-F 11:30am-5:30pm, Sa 11:30am-5pm. €4.50, under 12 €2.50.)*

NETHERLANDS MEDIA ART INSTITUTE, MONTEVIDEO/TIME-BASED ARTS. Founded in 1978, this former canal house functions as an exhibition space, video library, and educational institution devoted to the promotion of time-based media. The **Nederlands Instituut voor Mediakunst,** which also manages De Appel's video holdings, currently has a collection of over 14,000 books and videos available for study in the Mediathèque downstairs. Their collection is one of the largest in the world. The center also curates three or four large exhibitions each year focusing on various aspects of media art. Montevideo organizes lectures, symposia, workshops, and educational programs. Foreigners can serve as interns, helping to manage the extensive video collection; check the website or call for details. *(Keizersgracht 264. Tram #13, 14, or 17 to Westermarkt.* ☎ *623 7101; www.montevideo.nl. Front desk open M-F 9am-5pm; gallery and exhibition space open Tu-Sa 1-6pm; Mediathèque open M-F 1-5pm. Exhibition €2.50, students and seniors €1.50. Mediathèque free.)*

CENTRAL CANAL RING

Visit the thoroughly modern De Appel Museum for a glance at the latest international art or get a taste of life in the Golden lane at the marvelous Van Loon and Willet-Holthuysen canal houses. Take a day or more to experience the neighborhood's amazing offerings; the journey to and from sights around this beautiful area should be nearly as fun as the museums themselves.

see map p. 336

■ **MUSEUM VAN LOON.** The Museum Van Loon provides an exciting look at the history of Amsterdam. Built in 1672 for a Flemish merchant attracted by the international trading boom, it once housed Ferdinand Bol, Rembrandt van Rijn's most famous pupil. The house eventually fell into the hands of the Van Loon family, descendants of Dutch East India Company co-founder Willem van Loon. The Van Loons' portraits, along with the family crest commemorating their connection with the East Indies, adorn the walls of this exquisite residence. Numerous other heirlooms and antique furniture decorate each room. The intricate and opulent Rococo gilt banister along the central staircase has family names subtly worked into its curves. The formal French garden is an oasis as beautiful as the house itself. *(Keizersgracht 672, between Vijzelstraat and Reguliersgracht. Tram #16, 24, or 25 to Keizersgracht.* ☎ *624 5255; www.museumvanloon.nl. Open Sept.-June M and F-Su 11am-5pm; July-Aug. daily 11am-5pm. €5, students €4, under 12 free.)*

■ **FOAM PHOTOGRAPHY MUSEUM.** Housed in a traditional canal house, the Foam Photography Museum fearlessly explores every aspect of modern photography. All genres of the photographed image are welcome here, regardless of message or content. The museum hosts as many as 20 exhibits per year, rendering its galleries as fresh as its spacious, modern wood-and-glass interior. After admiring the engrossing works of international photography giants side by side with those of up-and-coming Dutch students, visit the cafe reading room, which is piled with books and magazines about photography. *(Keizersgracht 609. Tram #16, 24, or 25 to Keizersgracht, between Vijzelstraat and Reguliersgracht. ☎551 6500; www.foam.nl. Open daily 10am-5pm. Cafe open W-Su 10am-5pm. €6, students with ID €5.)*

DE APPEL. Anything goes at De Appel, which showcases and develops contemporary art from around the world. Its multimedia exhibitions and installations are on the cutting edge of the artistic arena. Students from the museum's curatorial school assemble a show once per year, and exhibitions rotate about every month. The first museum to show video art in the Netherlands, De Appel is now a testing ground for the newest, most daring multimedia installations. Check their website for occasional Tuesday programs. *(Nieuwe Spiegelstraat 10. ☎622 5215; www.deappel.nl. Open Tu-Su 11am-6pm. €4. Tu programs 8pm €5)*

MUSEUM WILLET-HOLTHUYSEN. Experience the ways of Amsterdam's Golden Age. Run by the Amsterdam Historisch Museum, this 17th-century canal house has been preserved as a fascinating museum with 18th-century furnishings, so you can see how the wealthy in Amsterdam lived over 300 years ago. In 1895, Sandrina Holthuysen donated the family home she shared with her collector-husband Abraham Willet. Now the marble mansion has been redone in an early 18th-century style, with gilt-edged walls, glittering chandeliers, family portraits, Rococo furnishings, and other signs of conspicuous consumption, including Abraham's collection of fine porcelain, glassware, and silver. Browse through the museum's guidebook to find out the details of daily life here, such as 19th-century water filtration methods. The French Neoclassical garden located behind the house remains as finely manicured as it was in the Dutch Golden Age. *(Herengracht 605, between Amstel and Utrechtsestraat. Tram #4, 9, 14, or 20 to Rembrandtplein or Metro to Waterlooplein. ☎523 1870; www.ahm.nl. Open M-F 10am-5pm, Sa-Su 11am-5pm. €4, ages 6-16 €2, over 65 €3, under 6 free.)*

TORTURE MUSEUM. An impressive and shocking range of medieval instruments of cruel and unusual punishment are on display at the appropriately dark and claustrophobic Torture Museum. Although the array of centuries-old racks, guillotines, and thumbscrews lack much context beyond superficial explanations of their (obvious) uses, their intricate designs shed light on the evolution of sadistic technology throughout history. If the rest of Amsterdam's hedonistic playground—with its mind-boggling collection of brothels, coffee shops, and live sex shows—is simply too cheerful for you, this subdued celebration of torture may be just what the executioner ordered. *(Singel 449. Tram #1, 2, or 5 to Koningsplein; cross the canal and turn right onto Singel. ☎320 6642. Open daily 10am-11pm. €5, children—think twice about this—€3.50.)*

JORDAAN

The Jordaan blends the bizarre with the classic in its fine selection of museums. Electric Ladyland's fluorescent paradise is not to be missed; neither is the smaller but historically relevant Houseboat Museum.

see map p. 338

■ **ELECTRIC LADYLAND: THE FIRST MUSEUM OF FLUORESCENT ART.** Here, owner Nick Padalino has collected a singularly impressive assortment of fluorescent objects from the mines of New Jersey to the heights of the Himalayas. These include gorgeous rocks that glow green in black light, paint kits from the 1950s, and an array of everyday objects that reveal hidden images—Albert Einstein's face hidden on a Dutch credit card, for example. Even better is Padalino's mind-bending fluorescent grotto-like sculpture, which he deems "participatory art." Visitors are encouraged to play with the many switches and buttons that turn various lights on and off; try to find the miniature statues and concealed periscopes all around the sculpture. It took Padalino seven years to make, and he—to whom the adjective "knowledgeable" does not do justice—won't hesitate to spend anywhere from one to three hours explaining the science behind the art. Indeed, a visit to the museum is essentially a private tour with the endearingly eccentric and passionate owner. (If the museum is closed when you arrive, it may be that he is simply downstairs giving a tour—you may have to wait around or come back later.) The other side of the small museum displays the scientific and cultural artifacts in Padalino's collection, and upstairs his fluorescent art—prints, sculptures, cards, etc.—is sold. (2e Leliedwarsstraat 5, below the art gallery, off Prinsengracht between Bloemgracht and Egelantiersgracht. Tram #13, 14, or 17 to Westermarkt; tram #10 to Bloemgracht; or bus #21, 170, or 171 to Westermarkt. ☎420 3776; www.electric-lady-land.com. Check website for how to get there; people often get lost despite written directions. Open Tu-Sa 1-6pm. €5, under 12 free.)

WOONBOOT (HOUSEBOAT) MUSEUM. Houseboats in Amsterdam began as a way to relieve overcrowding and the severe housing shortage that followed WWII. Living on the water is now in vogue, though owning one of the 2500 houseboats that line the canals can be more a labor of love than a practical dwelling, due to the constant maintenance boats require. This houseboat lets you see what the floating life might be like, complete with a tiny bathroom, a play area, and a book-lined living room. A slide show of boats around Amsterdam uses Enya's *Orinoco Flow (Sail Away)* as a soundtrack, and the museum has current listings of houseboats on the market should you feel particularly inspired. Be warned—the boats aren't cheap. (In Prinsengracht canal opposite #296, facing Elandsgracht. ☎427 0750; www.houseboatmuseum.nl. Open Mar.-Oct. Tu-Su 11am-5pm; Nov.-Feb. F-Su 11am-5pm. Closed Jan. 5-30. €3.25, children shorter than 152cm €2.50.)

STEDELIJK MUSEUM BUREAU AMSTERDAM. Tucked away on a quiet Jordaan street, this adjunct of the Stedelijk devotes itself to exhibiting the newest in Amsterdam art; most artists on display here are Dutch or live in the Netherlands. The Bureau's pure white space can be light and breezy or dim and airless, depending on the exhibit. This testing ground for avant-garde artists and material designers hosts six shows per year, which range from traditional art forms like painting and sculpture to performance pieces, installation art, and multimedia. Shows in the Bureau can run anywhere from a weekend to a few months; check website for details. (Rozenstraat 59. ☎422 0471; www.smba.nl. Open Tu-Su 11am-5pm. Free.)

PIANOLA MUSEUM. You wouldn't expect to find a pianola museum, well, anywhere, but least of all tucked into an unassuming corner of bustling Westerstraat. For the uninitiated, the pianola (frequently referred to as a player piano) is an upright piano whose internal mechanism has been partially replaced with machinery that lets it play automatically; different songs are recorded on paper pianola rolls and inserted into the instrument, and air is forced through their holes via an elaborate system of tubing inside the piano. This offbeat curiosity of a museum lets the visitor explore not only the history of the pianola but also the scope of the 1920s, when the popularity of this dodo of musical instruments was at its peak. The collection began as a private obsession but now provides a unique glimpse into this otherwise marginalized niche culture. It also houses a collection of 25,000 vintage player-piano rolls and hosts regular weekend concerts (check website for details). (Westerstraat 106. ☎627 9624; www.pianola.nl. Open Su 2-5pm and by appointment during the week. €5, under 12 €3.)

MUSEUMPLEIN AND VONDELPARK

Just look at the name of the neighborhood: two of the best art collections in the world lie within two blocks of each other here. 'Nuff said.

▨ VAN GOGH MUSEUM

see map p. 342

Paulus Potterstraat 7. Tram #2 or 5 to Paulus Potterstraat. Tram #3, 12, and 16 also stop nearby at the Museumplein. ☎ 570 5252; www.vangoghmuseum.nl. Open M-Th and Sa-Su 10am-6pm, F 10am-10pm. Ticket office and restaurant close 5:30pm; museum shop closes 5:45pm. €10, ages 13-17 €2.50, under 12 free. Ticket price includes admission to the exhibition wing. Audio tours €4. AmEx/MC/V with €25 min. purchase.

For better or for worse, the Van Gogh Museum is one of Amsterdam's biggest cultural tourist attractions and, as such, suffers from some of the longest lines in town. If you think you'll beat the crowd by showing up a few minutes before the museum opens, you're wrong—on weekends, the queue unfurls down the stairs and onto the sidewalk before the cash register even warms up. You'll find the shortest wait if you show up **around 10:30am,** when the initial line has dissipated, or **after 4pm,** when the crowds are heading home. To avoid hassle, you can also reserve your tickets online at www.vangoghmuseum.nl or, for a small service charge, through the Uitburo (www.uitburo.nl). The audio tour available in the lobby is a mixture of historical information and material from Vincent van Gogh's letters and personal writing, but if you can't stomach a dramatic British voice and well-timed classical music, it's best to save your dough. Don't be deterred by logistics: this museum is well worth the wait and the money.

With a new wing completed in 1999 and further renovations to the main building in 2007, the Van Gogh Museum seems to be set on propelling this modern Dutch master to 21st-century stardom. The original 1973 building by *De Stijl* designer **Gerrit Rietveld** has large, white exhibition spaces that reverberate with aloof Modernist cool. Here you'll find the permanent collection, including the meat of the museum, the Van Gogh masterpieces, on the first floor (upstairs from the ticket desk and book shop). The second floor is home to a study area with web consoles and a small library, while the third floor houses a substantial collection of important 19th-century art by Impressionist, post-Impressionist, Realist, and Symbolist painters and sculptors. The partially subterranean **exhibition wing**, designed by Kisho Kurokawa and completed in 1999, is so curvaceous that it's known as "the mussel." This hyper-modern space, encircling an outdoor patio, is the venue for the museum's top-notch traveling exhibitions. The museum is relatively small; count on seeing it all in one morning or afternoon.

FIRST FLOOR. The collection here unfolds in chronological order, beginning with Van Gogh's dark, ponderous, Dutch period. The famous *Potato Eaters* (1885), a depiction of a struggling peasant family at the dinner table, is the crowning achievement of the painter's early work. In 1886, Van Gogh moved to Paris, where he was at last confronted with "modern" (for the time) art. As a result, his paintings became brighter and more experimental. Vincent's love for *japonaiserie* emerged with *The Bridge in the Rain (after Hiroshige)* and *The Courtesan,* in which he incorporated the flatness and stylization of Japanese woodblock prints into his nascent mature style. The last phases of his artistic development coincide with his insanity-induced relocation to Arles, Saint-Remy, and Auvers-sur-Oise; these walls contain some of his most recognizable works. One of the museum's decided gems is the *Bedroom at Arles,* where Van Gogh used thick *impasto* paint and a skewed perspective to bring us inside his private space of rest in the Yellow House, his living quarters in Arles. Despite the then-record US$49 million their sibling fetched at a 1987 auction, his studies of

Sunflowers, made for close friend and rival **Paul Gauguin,** are not the most spectacular works of Vincent's career; masterpieces like *Branches of an Almond Tree in Blossom,* made for his newborn nephew, and *Wheatfield with Crows,* completed just before his suicide in 1890, steal the show.

SECOND FLOOR. This study area attempts some more didactic exhibits on Van Gogh's life and artistry. An excellent collection of smaller works by Van Gogh and his contemporaries—including some unbeatable self-portraits—are hung like specimens behind glass, while a multitude of computers allow you to surf the museum's surprisingly informative and sprawling website. A demonstration of how Van Gogh chose and mixed the colors of his palette provides rare esoteric insight into the minutiae of his craft.

THIRD FLOOR. This collection of European painting and sculpture from 1840-1920 does far more than simply contextualize Van Gogh's painterly development; several of the pieces are masterful in their own right. Don't miss Gauguin's stunning *Self-Portrait with Portrait of Bernard* or the collection of paintings by friend **Emile Bernard,** Symbolist **Odillon Redon,** and Pointillist **Georges Seurat.**

> **TIP** **TGIF.** The Rijksmuseum and the Van Gogh Museum are open until 10pm on Fridays, but the tourist hordes seem to spend that time somewhere else. Take advantage for some personal moments with the world's greatest painters!

 RIJKSMUSEUM AMSTERDAM

Stadhouderskade 42. Tram #2 or 5 to Paulus Potterstraat or tram #6, 7, or 10 to Spiegelgracht. Cross the canal and you can't miss it—it's the huge neo-Gothic castle. The two main entrances off the main building of the Rijksmuseum will be closed for the duration of the museum's renovation; visitors must enter instead through the Philips Wing, around the corner at the intersection of Hobbemastraat and Jan Luijkenstraat. ☎ 674 7000; www.rijksmuseum.nl. Open M-Th and Sa-Su 10am-5pm, F 10am-10pm. Maps available at the ticket counters. €10, under 18 free. Audio tours €4.

Even though the main building of the museum is closed for renovations (due to be completed in 2009), the Rijksmuseum is still a mandatory Amsterdam excursion. During restoration, the smaller Philips Wing will remain open to show masterpieces of 17th-century painting, including works by Rembrandt van Rijn, Johannes Vermeer, Frans Hals, and Jan Steen. Originally opened in 1800, the Rijks—or "state"—museum settled into its current monumental quarters, designed by Pierre Cuypers (also the architect of Centraal Station) in 1885. As the national museum of art and history, it houses an encyclopedic collection of top-notch Dutch art and artifacts from the Middle Ages through the 19th century; a comprehensive exhibit on Dutch history; a collection of Asian art; and an enormous selection of furniture, Delftware, and decorative objects, including two exquisitely detailed dollhouses. Unfortunately, while the museum undergoes renovation, much of this collection will not be on display. However, you may be able to catch a glimpse of some of the museum's holdings on loan elsewhere in the Netherlands, Belgium, and Germany. For information on temporary locations, or if you're wondering about a particular piece, ask at the information desk. Two audio tours are available for visitors: the more historical one is led by the museum's director; the other—dubbed "Jeroen Krabbé's favorites" and led by the famous Dutch actor, painter, and director—is a more personal tour focusing on the artistry of the paintings themselves.

You will find few crucifixion scenes at the Rijksmuseum; traditional Dutch art is distinguished from its traditional European counterparts by its focus on the secular and the everyday. Nearly all 17th-century Golden Age painting in the Netherlands was the product of free-market mercantilism: most of the domestic interiors, civic portraits, landscapes, and vanitas pictures were commissioned by wealthy Dutch merchants for their private homes.

Of this tour-de-force collection, **Rembrandt van Rijn's** gargantuan militia portrait *Night Watch* is a crowning, and deservedly famous, achievement. Equally breathtaking is the museum's collection of paintings by **Johannes Vermeer.** Only 31 paintings by the master of Delft survive; the Rijks possesses four. *The Milkmaid*, from 1668, something of an icon of Dutch genre painting, shows the title woman in front of an open window pouring a pitcher of milk into a bowl. The exquisite light in this painting links it with other painted works of the Dutch Golden Age; *Night Watch* and *The Milkmaid* are the foremost examples of this extraordinary mastery, but the attention to light is evident in paintings throughout the galleries. The museum's other paintings by Vermeer share a similar luminous intensity and voyeuristic intimacy. For more on Vermeer's work, including *The Love Letter*, see **On the Trail of Vermeer,** p. 69.

Hans Bollonger's vanitas painting is a reminder of human ephemerality; this painting of a vase of vibrant tulips was painted two years after the collapse of the tulip market, while the insects on the table serve as a reminder of death. The subversive morality of **Jan Steen's** painting is evident in *The Merry Family*, which depicts a family boisterously singing and drinking—even the young children hold glasses of wine. A hidden message in the rightmost corner of the canvas reads, "as the old song is, so will the young pipe play," a warning to parents that their children will inevitably follow in their footsteps. Be sure not to miss **Pieter de Hooch's** interior scenes (renowned for their "keyhole" details within details), the fine miniature panels of **Gerard Dou, Pieter Saenredam's** paintings of luminous church interiors, or **Frans Hals's** magnificently gestural brushwork.

OTHER MUSEUMS

Although the ⬛**Filmmuseum** is dedicated to the celebration and preservation of film, the "museum" where these films are "exhibited" is a movie theater, and most visitors to the Filmmuseum come to see movies. As the national center for cinema in the Netherlands, the museum's collection of films and books on film claims 35,000 titles stretching back to 1898. In addition to screening several films a day, they have occasional exhibits (€2) and maintain an information center at Vondelstraat 69 (to the right when exiting the Filmmuseum), which houses the Netherlands's largest collection of books and periodicals on film, many in English. Students and aficionados research film in the non-circulating archives or on the computerized databases; anyone can browse the collection, and the friendly staff can help you with any request. The center's staff is constantly at work archiving hundreds of thousands of images, magazines, posters, newspaper clippings, and film soundtracks; much of the work goes on behind the scenes, but anyone with an interest can ask to see some of the older and more valuable works that are kept behind closed doors. Visitors can also screen videos from the museum's collection in the library's booths (€12.50, students €4.50), but you may need to reserve ahead of time. If all you want to do here is sit back and watch a movie, see p. 191. *(Vondelpark 3, in the park between the Roemer Visscherstraat and Vondelstraat entrances. ☎ 589 1400; www.filmmuseum.nl.)*

JODENBUURT AND PLANTAGE

What the Jodenbuurt and Plantage may lack in nightlife, they more than make up for in museums. This neighborhood has one of the highest concentrations of museums in the city, and almost all of them are worth a visit. The Dutch Resistance Museum, close to the Artis Zoo, is a particularly engaging but sometimes overlooked museum. The Rembrandt House, where Rembrandt van Rijn painted many of his most famous masterpieces, and the Jewish Historical Museum, which chronicles the history of Jewish life in Amsterdam, are perennial favorites.

JOODS HISTORISCH MUSEUM (JEWISH HISTORICAL MUSEUM). In the heart of Amsterdam's traditional Jewish neighborhood, the Joods Historisch Museum aims to celebrate Dutch Jewry's rich cultural and historical legacy. The complex links together four different 17th- and 18th-century Ashkenazi synagogues with glass and steel connections, symbolically—and architecturally—bridging past and present. Through exhibits by Jewish artists and galleries of historically significant Judaica, the museum presents the Netherlands's most comprehensive picture of Jewish life—photographs, religious artifacts, texts, artwork, and traditional clothing comprise the permanent collection, accompanied by interactive video monitors that screen film clips and interviews. The excellent children's wing is geared toward educating younger visitors about kosher cooking, Jewish music and art, and the Hebrew alphabet. Some of the more notable artifacts include an ornately embroidered 18th-century Torah mantle and a Holy Ark holding silver Torah shields. The museum makes an effort to examine the present state of Jewish culture in the Netherlands and describes various aspects of Jewish culture, holidays, and foods. Temporary exhibits change every three to four months. *(Jonas Daniel Meijerplein 2-4 at Waterlooplein. Tram #9 to Waterlooplein; museum is near the northwestern corner. ☎ 531 0310; www.jhm.nl. Open M-W and F-Su 11am-5pm, Th 11am-9pm; closed on Yom Kippur. Free audio tour. €7.50, seniors and ISIC holders €4.50, ages 13-17 €3, under 13 free.)*

MUSEUM HET REMBRANDT. Dutch master Rembrandt van Rijn's house at Waterlooplein, which he bought for an astronomical sum in 1639, was sold off by creditors (along with his possessions) in 1658 after Rembrandt failed to pay his mortgage. Fortunately, 350 years later, the building has become the happy home of the artist's impressive collection of 250 etchings. Travel through all four levels of the beautifully restored house—you'll see the studio in which he mentored promising painters; the room where he stored his "art cabinet" full of coral, marble busts, armor and butterflies; and the kitchen in which his mistress is said to have attacked him as they quarreled over alimony. In the upstairs studio, Rembrandt produced some of his most important works. It is rumored that he painted the masterpiece *Night Watch* in the courtyard and rolled the completed project up to fit it out the windows. On display are some of his tools and plates, including an original pot he used to mix paint. Every 45min. on the third floor, artisans reenact the paint-making and printing techniques of his time. The museum contains several impressive paintings by Rembrandt's contemporaries, including works by Pieter Lastman, one of the master's teachers. Enthusiasts should also stop at Rozengracht 184, in the Jordaan, where Rembrandt lived out his life after his eviction. *(Jodenbreestraat 4, at the corner of Oude Schans. Tram #9 or 14 to Waterlooplein, then head northeast across Mr. Visserplein to Jodenbreestraat. ☎ 520 0400; www.rembrandthuis.nl. Open daily 10am-5pm. €8, students with ISIC €5.50, ages 6-15 €1.50, under 6 free.)*

VERZETSMUSEUM (DUTCH RESISTANCE MUSEUM). Germany invaded the Netherlands in May 1940 and, after destroying the port city of Rotterdam with heavy bombing, overran the small nation in only five days. Initially, Dutch authorities cooperated with Germany, and the Nazis treated the Dutch relatively leniently. But, as time went on, the occupation grew harsher—especially for Jews, gays, and gypsies—and resistance increased. The Resistance Museum uses a wide variety of media and presentations to illustrate life under the Nazi occupation and the steps the Dutch took to oppose the German forces. Displays allow visitors to track the occupation and resistance chronologically, ending with an enlightening exhibit on post-war Dutch regeneration. Model streets, buildings, and tape-recorded radio reports recreate the experience, from smug-

TIME: All morning and most of an afternoon—or 700 years, in another sense.

SEASON: Year-round.

This tour will take you on a whirlwind trip around the Centrum and beyond to relive some of its storied past and witness many facets of contemporary life.

1. OOST-INDISCH HUIS. Kloveniersburgwal 48 was once the headquarters of the Dutch East India Company (VOC). The conglomerate established a global trading empire that, at its height, surpassed the wealth of the British East India Company. A vast trade network extended as far as Bengal and Indonesia and dealt mainly in silks, spices, and cotton. Though the facade remains roughly as it did when the VOC prospered, today the building's interior is used as conference rooms, lecture halls, and a library for the University of Amsterdam (p. 144).

2. OUDEZIJDS ACHTERBURGWAL. Experience the liberated 21st-century spectacle of the Red Light District by ambling along this street—the heart of Amsterdam's commercial sex trade. Wall-to-wall window prostitutes pose alluringly for passing patrons, while brothels are the more discreet cousins to the overt sexuality of sex workers behind windows. **Casa Rosso,** at #106-108 and with shops at 46 and 74, features Amsterdam's most famous live sex show (p. 145).

3. OUDE KERK. Like a pocket of salvation in a cesspool of sin, Amsterdam's earliest parish church, constructed in the 14th century, is surrounded by the windows of the Red Light District. The magnificent structure, though, features some beautiful windows of its own—stained-glass that is. The organ, which dates back to 1724, is still played regularly for concerts. The church that once was stripped of its artwork and religious artifacts now houses traveling exhibits (p. 145).

4. PROSTITUTION INFORMATION CENTRE. Find out everything there is to know about the "oldest profession" at this decidedly un-seedy center. Founder and operator Mariska Majoor, a former prostitute, is more than willing to answer any question that you might have (no matter how outlandish) in an attempt to dispel myths about the profession. Take a picture of the replica sex worker booth—something you can't do near the real red lights. The center is unfunded, so be sure to leave a donation (p. 194).

5. MUSEUM AMSTELKRING. Religious resolve is preserved in this Attic Church. During the Alteration, when Protestantism swept through the Netherlands, Catholics were officially banned from practicing their faith; instead, they covertly attended so-called "secret churches" like Amstelkring, a beautiful little chapel that spans the attics of three adjacent buildings. The plain exterior once masqueraded as a shop front but has openly been a museum since 1888 (p. 166).

6A. WAAG. See the ancient Weigh-House, Amsterdam's oldest surviving medieval building, in Nieuwmarkt. The building was initially constructed in 1488 as a gate through the city's fortified walls, and its topmost floor was the setting for Rembrandt's *The Anatomy Lesson of Dr. Tulp.* In 1617, when the city walls were expanded, it became a weigh station, and today the glorious imposing building is home to the ritzy restaurant **In de Waag** (p. 124).

6B. WAAG MARKETS. The Waag presides over an organic food market Saturday from 10am to 3pm and an antiques market Sunday from 9am to 4pm (p. 214).

7. DE BEKEERDE SUSTER. Situated between such great beer-producing countries, the Netherlands is a drinker's paradise, and at this beautiful wood brew house (named the Reformed Sister), the Dutch dedication to heady yet smooth beer is alive and kicking. Four brews are made here at Kloveniersburgwal 6, one of which has an impressive 7% alcohol content. Arrange beforehand to take a tour of the brewing facilities (p. 145).

8. WATERLOOPLEIN. After passing the "Stopera" complex, scramble for bargains at the flea market (M-Sa 9am-5pm). This area was the de facto home of Amsterdam's vibrant Jewish community prior to WWII, when Nazi forces deported over 70,000 Jews (p. 220).

A HISTORY LESSON

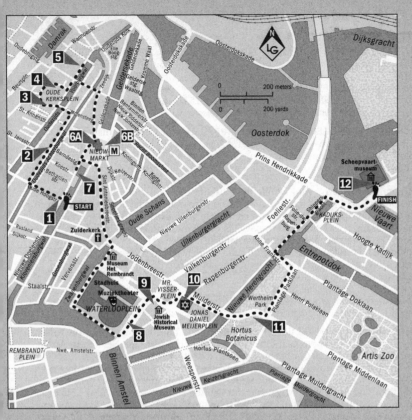

9. JOODS HISTORISCH MUSEUM. Celebrate Jewish culture at the museum dedicated to preserving the religion's cultural legacy with a special focus on the history of Judaism in the Netherlands. The museum links together four different 17th- and 18th-century Ashkenazi synagogues for a comprehensive history of Judaism. Features include an ark (holding a Torah), silver shields, and an excellent children's wing (p. 177).

10. PORTUGUESE SYNAGOGUE. Modeled after Solomon's Temple in Jerusalem, this impressive synagogue miraculously escaped being razed by the Nazis during WWII. It still holds services and features a plain but beautiful *chuppah* (Jewish wedding canopy) crafted from Brazilian jacaranda wood (p. 159).

11. HORTUS BOTANICUS. One of the world's oldest medicinal gardens (established in 1638 to help fight the plague) has over 6000 rare plants, mostly smuggled into the country by members of the Dutch East India Company during the Golden Age. Treasures include a minute Ethiopian coffee plant that spawned many plantations throughout Brazil (p. 158).

12. SCHEEPVAART MUSEUM. The Maritime Museum, though undergoing renovations until 2009, still documents the Netherlands's glorious naval history with the ship *Amsterdam* and the Vereniging Museumhaven Amsterdam, 18 antique boats floating nearby (p. 180).

gling food to issuing counter-propaganda on a printing press. The museum tries to keep the daily lives of average citizens in the forefront of the exhibitions. The Verzetsmuseum is housed in the historic Plancius Building, originally built in 1876 as the social club for a Jewish choir. *(Plantage Kerklaan 61. Tram #6, 9, or 14 to Plantage Kerklaan. ☎620 2535; www.verzetsmuseum.org. Open M and Sa-Su noon-5pm, Tu-F 10am-5pm, public holidays noon-5pm. €5.50, ages 7-15 €3, under 7 free. Tour of neighborhood available by phone or email appointment; €9 per person.)*

SCHEEPVAARTMUSEUM (MARITIME MUSEUM). For lovers of the sea, the vast Scheepvaartmuseum—one of the largest museums of its kind in the world—left no shell unturned in its exploration of the Netherlands's storied seafaring history. Unfortunately for them, the museum will be closed until mid-2009 while it undergoes major renovations. However, plenty of attractions still sit outside the museum on the Oosterdok. While the museum is closed, the full-sized replica of the Dutch East Indian ship *Amsterdam* remains open; it has been moved over to the other side of the NEMO science center. On Wednesdays at 1 and 3pm and Sundays at 11am, 1, and 3pm, actors stage historical reenactments of life on board this ship. The **Vereniging Museumhaven Amsterdam,** a collection of 18 antique boats, lies along the boardwalk between NEMO and the Scheepvaartmuseum. While visitors cannot board these turn-of-the-century vessels, placards explaining the history of each are posted on the docks. Access is free to the wandering passerby. *(Kattenburgerplein 1. From Centraal Station, follow signs past NEMO for about 10min. or bus #22 or 32 to Scheepvaartmuseum. ☎523 2222; www.scheepvaartmuseum.nl. Ship Amsterdam open in summer M 10am-5pm, Tu-Su 10am-5pm. €4, when combined with a NEMO ticket €2, under 3 free.)*

TROPENMUSEUM (MUSEUM OF THE TROPICS). The Tropenmuseum takes guests on an anthropological tour of Oceania, South Asia, the Near East, Africa, Latin America, and the Caribbean. Sponsored by the KIT (Koninklijk Instituut voor de Tropen; Dutch Royal Institute of the Tropics), the museum is situated in a massive, arched-dome building slotted with skylights. Take the elevator up to the second floor and wend your way down through the enormous world tour of ancient artifacts, contemporary objects, and religious pieces. The museum has some extraordinary pieces in its collection, ranging from folk-art portraits of Nelson Mandela to film footage of masked ceremonial dancing in the early 1930s. The first floor is mostly devoted to the dubious history of Dutch colonial expansion in Indonesia, and many of the works on display here were obtained by "explorers" (read: conquerors). On the top floor, the museum attempts more contemporary ethnographic studies, from depictions of life on the streets in Turkey and video footage of the Argentine national soccer team. The museum has a special emphasis on former Dutch colonies, including numerous exhibits describing the Netherlands's relationship with native peoples. *(Linnaeusstraat 2. Tram #9 and bus #22 stop right outside the museum. ☎568 8200; www.tropenmuseum.nl. Open daily 10am-5pm. €7.50, students and seniors €6, ages 6-17 €4, under 6 free. Family ticket (1-2 adults and max. 4 children) €20.)*

The museum is also home to the celebrated **Tropenmuseum Junior.** Open only to children between six and 12 and those accompanying them, the Tropenmuseum Junior tries to provide something for the wee folk to enjoy. Rotating exhibitions combine video footage, music, computer technology, and models to create simulations of real environments, including narrow Indian streets, South American traditional medicine shops, and a Middle Eastern bazaar. *(☎568 8233; www.tropenmuseumjunior.nl. Ages 6-12 €4.50. Special programs in Dutch only; reservations must be made 2 weeks in advance.)*

NEMO (NEW METROPOLIS). If you've tired of static museum exhibits (or if your children are), make your way over to this interactive, educational, and creative exploration center where, miraculously, science is fun! Geared toward children ages six through 16 and their accompanying adults, the massive green building spans four stories and is littered with science exhibits just begging to be poked at, jumped on, and experimented with. The provocative and thoughtfully designed displays at NEMO include permanent fixtures like "Why the World Works," "Machine Park," and "Bamboo House." A massive robotic girl describes the fundamentals of electricity, and the entertaining "Chain Reactions" show is held three times per day on the first floor. Depending on your age, "TEEN Facts" may be able to deliver some pertinent information on sex or body hair, and for the more mature crowd, "Future Fuel" looks closely at where the world is headed in terms of energy consumption. Don't miss the spectacular view of the shipyard and the historic city offered by the museum; on the eastern side of the building, a staircase traverses the structure's slanted roof. *(Oosterdok 2. East of Centraal Station on the Oosterdok.* ☎ *531 3233; www.e-nemo.nl. Open Tu-Su 10am-5pm. €11.50, under 4 free.)*

NATIONAAL VAKBONDSMUSEUM "DE BURCHT" (NATIONAL TRADE UNION MUSEUM "THE FORTRESS").
"The Fortress" is a small museum that both documents the trade-union crusade of Jewish diamond worker Henri Polak and hosts rotating and permanent labor rights exhibits. (But it does not include English translations; a detailed printout of the museum's collection is available at the reception desk.) The building, designed by the famous socialist "community-style" artist Hendrik Petrus Berlage, was the original headquarters for the Algemene Nederlandse Diamantbewerkersbond, the diamond workers' union. Polak wanted the building to be a monument to the workers' struggle, so the design was meant to fit into the populist and socialist underpinnings of trade unionism. Several paintings depicting aspects of Dutch social history are on display as part of the museum's permanent collection. When the eight-hour workday was introduced in 1912, socialist painter Richard Holst created a triptych for the building's board room showing that the day must be divided into three equal parts: work, relaxation, and sleep. On the way out, you'll see the gardens in front of many houses on Henri Polaklaan; at the turn of the century, many of the wealthier Jews in the union moved here and built homes behind what continue to be Amsterdam's only front yards. *(Henri Polaklaan 9. Tram #9 to Artis Zoo.* ☎ *624 1166; www.deburcht.org. Open Tu-F 11am-5pm, Su 1-5pm. €2.30, ages 13-18 and trade unionists €1.15.)*

> **✴ TIP** **RAIN GEAR.** This may not be a shock to you, but you should never bike in a thunderstorm!

GREATER AMSTERDAM

 COBRA MUSEUM. The CoBrA Museum pays tribute to the Netherlands's second great 20th-century art movement (after *De Stijl;* p. 73): the name is an abbreviation of the capital cities of the group's founding members (Copenhagen, Brussels, and Amsterdam). CoBrA was founded after WWII by artists who wanted to rebel against prewar conventions and conservatism, drawing on models of folk art, non-Western art, and abstract Expressionism. The collective included artists like Anton Rooskens, Eugene Brands, Corneille, Constant Nieuwenhuys, and famed Dutchman Karel Appel, all of whom were committed to progressive political activism and the "search for a vital image of reality." After CoBrA disbanded in 1951, the Stedelijk (p. 168) maintained many of their works, but the CoBrA Museum remains the more comprehensive display. The beautiful, modern museum, overlooking a pond and centering on a small "Zen garden," effectively presents a range of the movement's work from Appel's experimentation with sculpture to Corneille's developing interest in color and non-Western worlds. The highlight of the collection is Appel's large *Femmes, Enfants, Animaux* (1951), recently sold to the museum by Metallica drummer Lars Ulrich. The first floor exhibits works from the museum's permanent collection, and the second floor is used for temporary exhibits on everything from advertising to contemporary Chinese art. *(Sandbergplein 1-3, south of Amsterdam in Amstelveen. Tram #5 or bus #170, 171, or 172. The tram stop is a 10min. walk from the museum; after a 15min. ride, the bus will drop you off across the street. ☎ 547 5050, tour reservations 547 5045; www.cobra-museum.nl. Open Tu-Su 11am-5pm. €7, students and seniors €4, ages 6-18 €3. AmEx/MC/V.)*

GALLERIES

The **Jordaan** and **Canal Ring** compete ferociously to be the best destination for top-quality contemporary art. In the former, the area bounded by **Prinsengracht, Lijnbaansgracht, Elandsgracht,** and **Bloemgracht** has myriad galleries that specialize in cutting-edge pieces and installations. In the latter, a stretch of **Lijnbaansgracht** just east of **Vijzelstraat** is home to nine excellent, welcoming galleries. Best of all, the galleries along this convivial canal all hold their openings every few months on the same night: be sure to find out the date and get there early. The best way to plan a gallery-hop of Amsterdam's better spaces is to get your hands on a copy of AKKA's gallery guide and map (www.akka.nl/agenda). The free monthly *Uitkrant* (www.uitkrant.nl), available at the AUB (p. 185) and other locations, also has gallery listings and reviews. Gallery entrance fees range considerably and change often depending on events, installations, and tours.

CANAL RING WEST

De Expeditie, Leliegracht 47 (☎ 620 4758; www.de-expeditie.com). Expect some pop-inspired contemporary art by young Dutch painters. The intriguingly named "hyper-real" style is a De Expeditie favorite. Open W-F 11am-6pm, Sa 2-6pm.

CENTRAL CANAL RING

Van Zoetendaal, Keizersgracht 488 (☎ 624 9802; www.vanzoetendaal.nl). Contemporary Dutch photography overlooking Keizersgracht. Open W-Sa and 1st Su of each month 1-6pm. Closed in July.

Paul Andriesse, Withoedenveem 8 (☎ 623 6237). This well-known gallery has represented Giuseppe Penone, Alex Fischer, and internationally renowned artist Marlene Dumas. Open Tu-F 11am-6pm, Sa 2-6pm, 1st Su of the month 3-5pm.

Galerie Binnen, Keizersgracht 82 (☎ 625 9603). Uber-cool international designers mix up high and low: futuristic Eames-like chairs, molded porcelain tableware, and fluid metal lamps. Open W-Sa noon-6pm. Call ahead for summer hours.

Clement, Prinsengracht 843-845 (☎ 625 1656; www.galerie-clement.nl). The original 1958 print shop that worked with Hockney and Jim Dine has closed, but the exhibition space remains. Contemporary abstract work in a space with beautiful canal views. Open W-Sa 11am-5:30pm.

Galerie Louise Smit, Prinsengracht 615 (☎ 625 9898; www.louisesmit.nl). Beautiful contemporary art-jewelry crosses the line between fashion and gallery art. Open W-F 2-6pm, Sa 1-5pm, or by appointment.

Frozen Fountain, Prinsengracht 629 (☎ 622 9375; www.frozenfountain.nl). Displays colorful, cutting-edge furniture and interior design by young Dutch and international creators. Open M 1-6pm, Tu-F 10am-6pm, Sa 10am-5pm.

Galerie Akinci, Lijnbaansgracht 317 (☎ 638 0480; www.akinci.nl). An international space in the gallery cluster of Lijnbaansgracht, representing world-class artists like Stephan Balkenhol, Axel Hütte, and Ilya Rabinovich. Open Tu-Sa 1-6pm.

Canvas International Art, Fokkerlaan 46 (☎428 6040; www.canvas-art.nl). Art center in the Lijnbaansgracht complex that promotes artists from Latin America, Asia, and Australia. Canvas also sells and leases art to people and organizations. Open Th-Sa 1-6pm or by appointment.

Galerie Lumen Travo, Lijnbaansgracht 314 (☎627 0883; www.lumentravo.nl). Artists from Shirin Neshat to Jimmie Durham. Open W-Sa 1-6pm, 1st Su of the month 2-5pm.

Van Wijngaarden/Hakkens, Lijnbaansgracht 318 (☎626 4970; www.vanwijngaarden-hakkens.nl). Fresh painting, video, photography, and installation work by a small group of Dutch artists. Open W-Sa 1-6pm, 1st Su of the month 2-5pm.

Vous Êtes Ici, Lijnbaansgracht 314 (☎612 7979; www.vousetesici.nl). Young painters from the Netherlands, Germany, and the US exhibit in this friendly space. Open W-Sa 1-6pm, 1st Su of the month 2-5pm, or by appointment.

JORDAAN

Galerie Diana Stigter, Elandsstraat 90 (☎624 2361; www.dianastigter.nl). Sculpture, painting, installation, and photography from artists like Pierre Bismuth, Martha Colburn, and Steve McQueen. 2 of their artists, Saskia Olde Wolbers and Monika Sosnowska, won the Baloise "Artist Statement" prize at the 2003 International Art Fair in Basel. Open W-Sa noon-6pm, 1st Su of the month 2-5pm.

Galerie Fons Welters, Bloemstraat 140 (☎423 3046; www.fonswelters.nl). This skylit gallery's front hall, known as the "Playstation," is a space where young Dutch and European artists are invited to install cutting-edge work. From the street, look for a bulbous green-and-tan facade. Open Tu-Sa 1-6pm, 1st Su of the month 2-5pm.

Annet Gelink Gallery, Laurierstraat 187-189 (☎330 2066; www.annetgelink.nl). Large, airy exhibition space shows contemporary Dutch artists with a few strong international names. The basement of the gallery, nicknamed "The Bakery," serves up work by up-and-coming Dutch student artists. Open Tu-F 10am-6pm, Sa 1-6pm.

Torch, Lauriergracht 94 (☎626 0284; www.torchgallery.com). Heats up with fiery exhibits (including shows like "Icons, Idols, and Fetishes") and super-slick selections of European and American artists (including Loretta Lux, Edward Burtynsky, and Anthony Goicolea). Open Th-Sa 2-6pm.

ALTERNATIVE ART SPACES

Art lovers know Amsterdam for its museums and galleries. However, there are a cluster of institutions (mostly former squats) that host rotating exhibits by contemporary artists. In these "alternative art spaces," artwork is never for sale and entrance is always **free.**

SMART Project Space, Arie Biemondstraat 101-111 (☎427 5951; www.smart-projectspace.net), in the **Oud-West** near Vondelpark. An ambitious arts organization, formed in 1994 and recently relocated. Brand-new cinema, media cafe, and restaurant to be up and running by 2008. Regular exhibitions of Dutch and visiting artists, many of whom work in SMART's studio space. Open Tu-Sa noon-10pm, Su 1-10pm.

W 139, Warmoesstraat 139 (☎622 9434; www.w139.nl), in the **Red Light District.** This former squat is an Amsterdam institution, hosting elaborate, edgy, punky, raucous, awe-inspiring, and politically charged installations that use every inch of this amazing, sprawling space. 6 shows per year. Open W-Su 1-5pm.

ENTERTAINMENT

Amsterdam elates and enthralls visitors with an extraordinary blend of entertainment options. Beautifully rendered arias pour over enraptured audiences, professional jokesters elicit knee-slapping laughter, and cool coffee shops serve as a breezy backdrop for lazy and hazy afternoon delights. This chapter provides a sampling of Amsterdam's various amusements and bemusements in all their forms—from an evening of *film noir* to an afternoon sauna sojourn.

ARTS

Throughout the year, Amsterdam is a whirlwind of artistic activity, providing venues for hundreds of plays, concerts, festivals, and fairs. With so many opportunities, even long-term residents are liable to feel overwhelmed. To thwart such confusion, the **Amsterdams Uit Buro (AUB),** Leidseplein 26, right on the square, is stuffed with free monthly magazines, pamphlets, and tips to help you sift through the seasonal offerings. Although the resources are mostly in Dutch, with a little effort you can figure out the basic information. The most comprehensive publication is the free monthly *Uitkrant,* and, for visitors staying longer, the *Uitgids,* which advertises deals on season tickets and advance purchases. The AUB also sells tickets and makes reservations for just about any cultural event in the city for a commission—around €2 per person per ticket. One of the best deals you'll find in Amsterdam is the half-off tickets at the **Last Minute Ticket Shop,** which is part of the AUB. Visit the office for a list of same-day performances at 50% off; they sell tickets for most venues in the city, but not each one every day. (☎0900 0191; www.amsterdamsuitburo.nl or www.lastminuteticketshop.nl. AUB open M-Sa 10am-7:30pm, Su noon-7:30pm. Last Minute Ticket Shop begins selling tickets daily at noon.) The theater desk at the **VVV,** Stationsplein 10, can also make reservations for cultural events. (☎0900 400 4040, €0.40 per min.; www.amsterdamtourist.nl. Open F-Sa 9am-8pm.) If you're still thirsty for more, the mini-magazine *Boom!,* free at restaurants and cafes around the city, is chock-full of tourist info.

 WEEK SPOTS. *Amsterdam Weekly* is a great English-language paper that's chock-full of interesting articles, entertainment and cultural listings, and an excellent "short list" of worthwhile events (selected by the editors) for the week. You can pick one up for free at many hostels and bookshops.

CLASSICAL MUSIC, OPERA, AND DANCE

Amsterdam is world-renowned for its innovative classical performing arts, especially for its avant-garde, contemporary chamber ensembles. In 1986, the city invested in the construction of the prestigious and controversial **Stadhuis-Het Muziektheater** complex, which now houses both the **National Ballet** and the **Netherlands Opera** in addition to regularly featuring the **Netherlands Philharmonic Orchestra.** At Museumplein, the **Concertgebouw** attracts top-notch performers and is home to one of the world's finest classical orchestras. Tickets for all of these events are available through the AUB (above). **Churches** throughout the city also host regular organ, choral, and chamber music concerts.

Concertgebouw, Concertgebouwplein 2-6 (☎671 8345; www.concertgebouw.nl), across Paulus Potterstraat from the open expanse of the **Museumplein.** Tram #2, 3,

5, 12, or 16 to Museumplein. This gorgeous concert hall, constructed in 1888, is home to one of the world's finest classical ensembles, the **Royal Concertgebouw Orchestra.** Occasional jazz, world, and folk performances are mixed with Mendelssohn and Mozart, and performances from stars like Alfred Brendel and Mitsuko Uchida are common fare. Stop by the hall to get a program of concerts, some of which cost as little as €8.50. There is never a shortage of performances; the theater is one of the world's busiest concert halls, hosting 650 events a year. Su morning concerts with guided tours before the performance are cheaper options, usually running around €12 (tours 9:30am, €3.50). Rush tickets for persons age 26 and under from €7.50. Additional free lunchtime concerts during fall, winter and spring W 12:30pm—no tickets necessary. Ticket office open daily 10am-7pm; until 8:15pm for same-day ticketing. Telephone reservations until 5pm. AmEx/MC/V.

Stadhuis-Het Muziektheater, Waterlooplein (☎625 5455; www.hetmuziektheater.nl) in the **Jodenbuurt.** Tram #9 or 14 or the Metro to Waterlooplein. Also known as the "Stopera" after 1980s protests against its construction, the Muziektheater's gargantuan complex is home to the Dutch National Ballet, the Holland Symfonia, and the Netherlands Opera. Tickets can be bought through either the Muziektheater box office or through the AUB (p. 185). Space is limited, so buy tickets ahead of time. Box office open M-Sa 10am-6pm, Su and holidays 11:30am-2:30pm, or until curtain (usually 8pm) on performance days. Opera tickets start at €20; ballet tickets from €15. For ballet only, €10 student-rush tickets available 30min. before the show. Ballet closed July-Aug. For more information, contact the individual companies: National Ballet (☎551 8225; www.hetnationale-ballet.nl); Holland Symfonia (☎551 8823; www.hollandsymfonia.com); the Netherlands Opera (☎625 5455; www.dno.nl). AmEx/MC/V.

Bimhuis, Piet Heinkade 3 (☎788 2150; www.bimhuis.nl), just east of Centraal Station along the IJ. Amsterdam's premier venue for jazz and improv music for over 20 years, Bimhuis features the famous, the obscure, and the local legend in over 250 concerts per year. Performers from Europe, the Americas, Asia, and Africa unite in the name of unscripted melody. Beyond the bar, the stage is surrounded by benches and a ring of cafe tables. Tickets €12-20, students and seniors €10-18. Open M-Th and Su 7pm-1am, F-Sa 7pm-3am. AmEx/MC/V.

Conservatorium van Amsterdam, Van Baerlestraat 27 (☎527 7550; www.cva.ahk.nl), in the **Museumplein.** Tram #2, 3, 5, 12, or 16 or bus #145, 170, or 197. The Conservatory of Amsterdam's students study here year-round—the jazz, classical, and occasional opera performances are free. In Aug. 2008, the Conservatorium will move to Oosterdok Island, next to Centraal Station and the new main library.

Beurs van Berlage Theater, Damrak 277 (☎671 8345; www.beursvanberlage.nl), in the **Nieuwe Zijd.** This monumental former stock exchange is now an exhibition space and massive function hall (p. 148) with 3 grand concert halls that host the Netherlands Philharmonic Orchestra and the Netherlands Chamber Orchestra. Tickets €15-135; student and senior discounts depending on show. Some tickets are available 45min. before curtain (€7.50) for those under 27. MC/V.

 DUTCH ADO ABOUT NOTHING. Most of the plays and performances in Amsterdam will be in Dutch, but English performances are also sometimes available. If in doubt, call ahead or check online.

Koninklijk Carré Theater, Amstel 115-125 (☎524 9452; www.theatercarre.nl), in the **Plantage.** Tram #4 to Frederiksplein or #6, 7, or 10 to Oosteinde. You can also take the Metro to Weesperplein. Grand, old-fashioned theater with red velvet seats and a columned facade. Opened in 1888 for the family Carré circus and now showing a variety of musicals and musical performances, from Dave Brubeck to Lou Reed to Stomp. Other offerings from touring companies such as smaller pop groups, Chinese acrobatic troupes, and Israeli percussion ensembles. Guided tours of the theater Sa at 11am. €8, under 12 €4. Tickets €15-70, sold at box office or through the AUB (p. 185). Reservations by phone M-F 9am-5pm. Theater box office open daily 4pm-7pm. MC/V.

IJsbreker, Piet Heinkade 1 (☎788 2010 or 788 2000; www.netcetera.nl/ysbreker), just to the right of the entrance to Centraal Station. An avant-garde music center that nourishes Amsterdam's contemporary music scene, playing exclusively 20th-century chamber music. Both local and international talent, as well as experimental programs and a chamber music series. Tickets €6-16, students and seniors about €4 less. MC/V.

Marionette Theater, Nieuwe Jonkerstraat 8 (☎620 8027; www.marionettentheater.nl), on a quiet street north of the **Jodenbuurt.** Performs a full program of Mozart and Offenbach operas entirely with—you guessed it—marionettes. Performances 2-3 times per month. Tickets available by phone, web, or AUB (p. 185). €15, students and seniors €12, under 14 €7.50.

Kit Tropentheater, Linnaeusstraat 2 (☎568 8500; www.tropentheater.nl), in the **Plantage.** Tram #6, 9, or 10. Attached to the Tropenmuseum and part of the same parent organization but under different management. Features a well-curated selection of non-Western performing arts from the Indian Shakespeare Company to Balkan accordion players to Indonesian Gamelan. Occasional documentary film screenings. Tickets €5-20. Box office open M-Sa noon-4pm and 1hr. before performance. MC/V.

LIVE MUSIC

Outside the venues listed below, you can also catch occasional live jazz at **Toomler** (p. 190). World music can sometimes be found at Melkweg, the **Carré Theater,** or the **Tropentheater.** Many nightlife listings also double as live-music venues, including Paradiso, Melkweg, and many not listed here.

🎵 **Alto,** Korte Leidsedwarsstraat 115, on a Leidseplein side street. Hepcats left over from the 50s mingle with young aficionados at this busy nightspot where the vibe is subdued but the jazz is sizzling. Show up early to get a table up front (at the back of the long, skinny space), though you can hear (if not clearly see) the act from the bar. Free nightly jazz (and occasionally blues) M-Th and Su 10pm-2am, F-Sa 10pm-3am. Open M-Th and Su 9pm-3am, F-Sa 9pm-4am. Cash only.

🎵 **The Waterhole,** Korte Leidsedwarsstraat 49 (☎620 8904; www.waterhole.nl), in **Leidseplein.** Take in an all-night jam session by one of Amsterdam's hot local bands or shoot a round of pool with the locals over a

THE LOCAL STORY

ANDRÉ THE GIANT

There are statues of famous Amsterdammers all over the city: Rembrandt van Rijn in Rembrandtplein, Dr. Sarphati in Sarphatipark, and Joost van den Vondel in Vondelpark. These distinguished statues all gaze seriously out over their respective parks and squares, surveying the crush of drunken tourists, joggers, and bicyclists; they're giant, looming figures of history. Then there's André Hazes.

A casual visitor to Albert Cuypmarkt may not notice the small bronze statue among the bustling stalls on the corner of Albert Cuypstraat and 1e Sweelinckstraat. The seated figure gazes dreamily toward the sky with a gold chain around his neck and a microphone raised to his lips. Memorialized here in bronze, André Hazes is one of the best-loved singers and performers the Netherlands has ever known. Hazes was a master of *levenslied*, a simple, sentimental and melodramatic song heavy with cliché. Also called *smartlaps*, they are meant to draw out the deep emotion of everyday life and its love or loss. His funeral, held in a packed ArenA in 2004, was broadcast live on national television to millions of viewers in the Netherlands and Belgium. In September 2005, Hazes's statue was erected in De Pijp, the neighborhood where he grew up. The statue isn't large or imposing, but the icon it represents rests deep in the sentimental heart of the Dutch public.

"frosted pint" of Bavaria lager (€4.20) in this eclectic live-music bar. Don't let the American South motif bumfuzzle you: this bar has a truly Dutch flavor. Music varies by night, with performances ranging from reggae to classic rock. M-W and Su are jam nights, and Th-Sa mostly feature local bands. Music starts nightly around 8:30pm. Open M-Th and Su 4pm-3am, F-Sa 4pm-4am.

■ **Bourbon Street Jazz & Blues Club**, Leidsekruisstraat 6-8 (☎623 3440; www.bourbonstreet.nl), in **Leidseplein**, like everything else, it seems. From Leidsestraat, take the 1st right onto Lange Leidsestraat and turn left onto Leidsekruisstraat. A slightly older tourist crowd dances with abandon to blues, soul, funk, and rock bands. Mostly smaller local bands play this intimate venue, though in the past they have drawn the Stones and Sting. Musicians can join in the Tu and Su blues jam sessions for free (€3 for the rest of us). Call or check the website or the sheet posted in the window to find out what's on. Beer €2.50; pints €5. Cover Th and Su €3, F-Sa €5. Music M-Th and Su 10:30pm-3am, F-Sa 11pm-4am. Open M-Th and Su 10pm-4am, F-Sa 10pm-5am. AmEx/MC/V.

■ **Maloe Melo**, Lijnbaansgracht 163 (☎420 4592; www.maloemelo.com), in the **Jordaan.** Maloe Melo is the best deal in the Jordaan for a night out. The beer is cheap and the bands are too (sometimes even free). Both local and visiting amateur groups play on Tu-W and F-Sa; mostly blues, rock, and alternative country. Stop in and you might catch an act before its big break. Around 4 electric jam sessions per month; music starts at 10pm. Check website for details. Music in the backroom from 10:30pm. Cover F-Sa €5. Open M-Th and Su 9pm-3am, F-Sa 9pm-4am. Cash only.

■ **Paradiso**, Weteringschans 6-8 (☎626 4521; www.paradiso.nl). See listing in **Nightlife** (p. 232).

■ **Melkweg**, Lijnbaansgracht 234A (☎531 8181; www.melkweg.nl). See listing in **Nightlife** (p. 232).

 CULTURE FOR POCKET CHANGE. The **Last Minute Ticket Shop** (p. 185) in Leidseplein offers a whopping 50% discount on tickets purchased on the day of a performance. You can get tickets to amazing jazz shows at the Bimhuis, performances by the National Ballet, or concerts at Melkweg or Paradiso.

Westergasfabriek, Haarlemmerweg 8-10 (www.westergasfabriek.nl), along Haarlemmerweg in **Westerpark**. This group of buildings provides numerous venues for art and culture, from huge open-air concerts in the summer (past artists have included Björk and the Scissor Sisters) to literary festivals to fashion shows. Check the website for information on upcoming events.

Casablanca, Zeedijk 24-26 (☎220 0519; www.cafecasablanca.nl), between Oudezijds Kolk and Vredenburgersteeg, in the **Oude Zijd.** First opened in 1946, Casablanca is one of the oldest jazz clubs in the Netherlands. Popular with locals but also exciting for tourists, with its ornately framed portraits on the ceiling and general vaudevillian atmosphere. At Zeedijk 26, live jazz and funk nightly 9pm, W-Sa karaoke 11pm. Next door at 24, Old World dinner served 4pm-1am (around €17) accompanied by variety shows that dabble in magic, cabaret, drama, and clown acts. Children's magician Su afternoon. Check the website for upcoming performances. €5 cover (Zeedijk 24 only). Open M-Th and Su 8pm-3am, F-Sa 8pm-4am. MC/V.

Cristofori, Prinsengracht 581-583 (☎626 8485; www.cristofori.nl). Tram #1, 2, or 5 to Prinsengracht. Jazz and classical music in an old canal house. Tickets around €17.

De Badcuyp, 1e Sweelinckstraat 10 (☎675 9669; www.badcuyp.nl), on the corner of Albert Cuypstraat in **De Pijp.** This vibrant cobalt-and-yellow restaurant and music venue plays a rotating range of world music—everything from improvisational jazz to flamenco and tango—in a former municipal bathhouse. Tu 8:30pm-midnight experimental free, W 10pm-1am salsa dance €4, F "Tub Club" with live jazz and dance music €8. African dance party last Sa of every month €4. Check website for more events. Open M-F 11am-1am, Sa-Su 11am-3am. MC/V.

Panama, Oostelijke Handelskade 4 (☎311 8686; www.panama.nl), on the outskirts of Amsterdam. Tram #26 to Rietlandpark from Centraal Station. Panama's location—almost as far as its namesake—lures patrons to its opulent playland for the whole night. This restaurant and nightclub usually attracts a mature and stylish crowd in their 30s and 40s. The restaurant, with its high ceilings, contemporary design, and ample terrace space, is a fine spot for a meal (entrees €16-20). Th and Su live music starting at 6 or 7pm. The nightclub, open on the weekends, hosts a variety of theme nights and also attracts an older set. Open M-Th and Su noon-1am, F-Sa noon-4am. AmEx/MC/V.

Club Meander, Voetboogstraat 3B (☎625 8430; www.cafemeander.com). See listing in **Nightlife** (p. 228).

Piano Bar, Leidsekruisstraat 35 (☎624 1920). Sing along with your old friends Elton John and Frank Sinatra at this small club. A jovial piano player leads the enthusiastic patron-chorus in blissful renditions of classic hits. Older crowd translates into slightly more expensive drinks. Heineken €3. M-Th and Su 9pm-3am, Sa-Su 9pm-4am.

THEATER AND COMEDY

If it's live theater or comedy you're after, the AUB is hands down your best resource. Year-round (but especially in the summer), the city is bursting with opportunities to go to the theater, both Dutch and international. There are many different varieties of theater in the city, including **cabarets, musicals, stand-up comedy** (often in English), **spoken dramas,** and **dance.** Ticket prices vary widely.

> **🟊TIP🟊** **CLOSED FOR THE HOLIDAYS.** It is not uncommon for theaters in the Netherlands to close for a period between late July and August, when much of Western Europe goes on holiday. If you're looking to catch a performance during this time, make sure you check ahead.

 Boom Chicago, Leidseplein 12 (☎423 0101; www.boomchicago.nl), right off **Leidseplein.** This bar and restaurant sports an English improv comedy show M-Th and Su 8:15pm (€19.50) and 2 shows per day F-Sa (€23.50). Call ahead for reservations. Enjoy a 2-course meal before the show (appetizers from €5, entrees around €15; last orders taken just before the show starts). Upstairs is a small bar and lounge area decorated with silver bowl chairs and popular with expats and chic locals. Cover M-Th and Sa-Su €8.50; F before 11:30pm €21, after 11:30pm €12. Bring in a copy of *Boom!* (their witty guide to Amsterdam that's distributed free around the city) for a €3 discount on tickets M-Th and Su. Open M-Th and Su 10am-1am, F-Sa 10am-3am.

Stadsschouwburg, Leidseplein 26 (☎624 2311; www.ssba.nl), in **Leidseplein.** The main theater for Dutch-language plays in Amsterdam and the base for the Holland Festival in June. Features some modern dance and opera and hosts the July Dance Festival (www.julidans.com). Theater tickets €10-20. €10 rush tickets 30min. before show for students under 27. Box office open M-Sa noon-6pm. The theater's restaurant, Cafe Cox, is a fashionable spot to grab a drink before or after the performance. AmEx/MC/V.

Bellevue Theater, Leidsekade 90 (☎530 5301; www.theaterbellevue.nl). Tram #1, 2, 5, 6, 7, or 10 to **Leidseplein.** 3 stages for popular theater, musicals, modern dance, and cabaret from a variety of companies. The Bellevue runs experimental theater, mostly in Dutch; check the website for current offerings. While you're waiting for the show to start, sit along the Singelgracht and enjoy a snack from De Smoesshaan, the theater's excellent cafe (☎625 0368; open M-F 11am-1am, Sa-Su 11am-3am). Tickets usually €15-75. Box office open daily 11am-6pm.

De Kleine Komedie, Amstel 56-58 (☎624 0534; www.dekleinekomedie.nl). Tram #4, 5, or 9 to **Rembrandtplein.** Dating from 1786, De Kleine Komedie is Amsterdam's oldest theater and the Netherlands's premiere cabaret spot. Full program of drama and musical theater, most in Dutch. Box office open M-Sa noon-5pm.

Comedy Cafe, Max Euweplein 43-45 (☎638 3971; www.comedycafe.nl). Tram #1, 2, 5, 6, 7, or 10 to **Leidseplein.** A rotating lineup of comics from around the world, but most in Dutch; call or check the web. Performances Th-F 9pm, Sa 9, 11:30pm €15. M-Tu open-mic nights (€3) with a typically unpredictable bag of performances—comics compete for the chance to perform at the W talent show (9pm; €5 cover includes 1 drink). "In Your Face" presents improv in English on Su (9pm; €13). 3-course dinner (€35) includes a ticket to the show; reservation usually necessary. Th and Sa-Su "Spare Ribs" menu includes a big plate of spare ribs (or a vegetarian alternative) and entry (€23). Lunch sandwiches €3-7.50. Variety of dinner entrees (€8.50-15), such as fish stew (€13.50) or vegetarian tortellini (€8.50). Box office open M-F 9am-5pm; otherwise, buy your tickets at the cafe. Cafe open M-Th and Su 9am-1am, F-Sa 9am-3am. MC/V.

Toomler, Breitnerstraat 2 (☎670 7400; www.toomler.nl), next to the Hilton Amsterdam. Tram #16 to Cornelis Schuysstraat; or take tram #5 or 24 to Apollolaan and walk left across the canal for 3 blocks. Bus #15, 145, 170, or 197. Hosts Comedytrain International, a laugh-riot in Dutch, though even English speakers will catch some of the jokes. Features on other nights include live music and more comedy. Occasional performances are in English. Check website for monthly program. €10-15.

Badhuis-Theater de Bochel, Andreas Bonnstraat 28 (☎065 355 3982; www.badhuistheater.nl), in the **Plantage.** Tram #3 to Camperstraat. An irregular schedule of various offbeat productions (experimental theater, children's workshops, dance parties), jazz nights, Brazilian dance classes, and tango lessons in this bathhouse-turned-theater. Also hosts occasional Latin and reggae "swing" parties. Most shows €5-9. Check the website for schedule details and buy your ticket at the door.

Melkweg, Lijnbaansgracht 234A (☎531 8181; www.melkweg.nl), in **Leidseplein.** Along with the cinema, club, and art gallery, Melkweg is a popular venue for touring theater groups. See listing in **Nightlife** (p. 232).

De Balie, Kleine-Gartmanplantsoen 10 (☎553 5100; www.debalie.nl), just off **Leidseplein.** Housed in a former court of justice, De Balie is a center for film, photography, theater, and new media. Interesting contemporary theater is almost a guarantee. See other listing in **Film** (p. 192).

Vondelpark Openluchttheater (☎673 1499; www.openluchttheater.nl), in the center of the park. May-Aug. W-Su afternoons promise free outdoor theater as well as music, dance, and kids' shows.

Marionette Theater, Nieuwe Jonkerstraat 8 (☎620 8027; www.marionettentheater.nl). See listing in **Classical Music, Opera, and Dance** (p. 187).

Casablanca, Zeedijk 24-26 (☎220 0519; www.cafecasablanca.nl). See listing in **Live Music** (p. 226).

FILM

The Dutch love affair with the movies is expansive, encompassing a cinematic range from the tackiest American blockbuster to the most obscure indie art-house flick. The city distinguishes itself with the Filmmuseum, a national cinematic library. Fortunately for tourists and non-locals, films are only rarely dubbed into Dutch, which means that you won't need to have expert lip-reading skills. Bearing this in mind, you must remember that if you're planning to view a non-English film, it will be shown in its original language with Dutch subtitles. Some theaters may offer English subtitles for foreign films, but you should check with the box office first or look for an "EO" or "Engels Ondertitled" sign.

Most movies are released in the Netherlands a few months after their debut in the country in which the movie was produced, although big box office hits will occasionally get to the Dutch screen right away. Check www.movieguide.nl for listings. The best site for Dutch film news is www.filmfocus.nl, which has show-times as well as critical reviews and festival information.

The French company **Pathé** owns three of the bigger cinema houses in the city— Pathé ArenA, Pathé De Munt, and the historic Tuschinski; information for all of these is at www.pathe.nl. Pathé tends to show mainstream films, although there are independent flicks in the lot as well. The standard price for Pathé de Munt is €9; ArenA is €9 but €12 for the IMAX screen; Tuschinski is €9-10, depending on the screen. Pick up the program at any theater for listings to all of Pathé's cinemas or check its website.

Even if you're going to see the lowest of low-brow movies, you should still be aware of cultural differences in Dutch cinema-going. For example, in Amsterdam, people do not eat while watching films, and many theaters do not serve popcorn.

■ **Filmmuseum,** Vondelpark 3 (☎589 1400; www.filmmuseum.nl), between Roemer Viss-cherstraat and Vondelstraat entrances. Walk across Singelgracht from Leidseplein to **Vondelpark** or tram #1 to 1er Constantijn Huygensstraat or #3 or 12 to Overtoom. A grand white mansion overlooking the Vondelpark with at least 4 daily screenings, many of them older classics or organized around a special theme like the works of Fellini, American Westerns, or Hong Kong directors. Every summer, the Filmmuseum shows a retrospective of a film diva, like Sophia Loren or Robert DeNiro (€7.20). F night outdoor screening €3. The complex also houses an extensive information center, with 1900 periodicals and over 30,000 books on film theory, history, and screenplays (p. 176). Pick up a copy of *Zine* magazine for the month's listings or call the main Vondelpark box office. Box office open 9am-10:15pm.

■ **Tuschinski Cinema,** Reguliersbreestraat 26-28 (☎626 2633; www.tuschinski.nl), between **Rembrandtplein** and Muntplein. Step from the gaudy whirlwind of Rembrandt-plein's porno shops and fast-food stands into the Tuschinski Cinema's oasis of Old World elegance. Built in 1921, this ornate movie theater, complete with lush carpeting and ceiling paintings, was one of Europe's first experiments, and successes, with the Art Deco style. Although a group of drunk Nazis once started a fire in the theater's cabaret, the building survived WWII and has remained in operation for over 75 years. Between 1998 and 2002, the building was lovingly restored to its former glory. Includes 3 screens in the main building and 6 more in a modern wing. A ticket to a screening of a Hollywood feature allows you to explore on your own. Theater 1 is the main stage and has private boxes—it tends to show commercial hits while the other screens are devoted to artsy shows. Tuschinski is a Pathé cinema. €9-10, €33 for private balcony for 2, €39 for balcony with champagne.

 HOPE YOU LIKE SUBTITLES. Most movies in the Netherlands are played in their original language with Dutch subtitles scrolled along the bottom. If you don't know Dutch or the film's native language, take heed.

■ **The Movies,** Haarlemmerstraat 159 (☎624 5790; www.themovies.nl), in the **Scheepvaartbuurt.** Bus #18 or 22 or tram #3 to Haarlemmerplein. The Movies, in a restored Art Deco building, is the Netherlands's oldest movie theater and shows a range of engrossing independent films from all genres. Plays recent favorites and dusty classics around midnight F and Sa nights; check the website for screenings and times. A variety of 4-course set menus (€29-36, including the price of a movie ticket M-Th) in the adjacent restaurant and bar, making for an elegant dinner-and-a-movie package. Tickets €8, students and seniors €7. MC/V in restaurant only.

ENTERTAINMENT

■ **Kriterion Theater and Cafe,** Roetersstraat 170 (☎623 1708; www.kriterion.nl), in the **Plantage.** Tram #6, 7, or 10 to Weesperplein. Run entirely by a student collective from the nearby University of Amsterdam, Kriterion is an art-house movie theater with a laid-back bar-cafe where local students come to discuss everything from Bogart to Bond over jazz. Independent and studio films run daily at the theater, and children's movies are also shown regularly throughout the year. Cafe open M-Th 11am-1am, F 11am-3am, Sa noon-3am, Su 1pm-1am. €7, weekends €7.50; students and seniors €5.50/6. Cash only.

■ **SMART Project Space,** Arie Biemondstraat 101-111 (☎427 5951; www.smart-projectspace.net), in the **Oud-West.** Tram #7 or 17 to Ten Katestraat. In addition to featuring a shiny new movie theater, the SMART Project Space doubles as an exhibition space and studio for artists (p. 183) and hosts events in other artistic media. Experimental and independent films in addition to monthly live performances.

De Balie, Kleine-Gartmanplantsoen 10 (Ticket counter ☎553 5100, reception 553 5151; www.debalie.nl), just off **Leidseplein.** Tram #1, 2, 5, 6, 7, or 10 to Leidseplein. An intellectual center in a former courthouse, De Balie offers alternative films (€7, students and seniors €5), theater (€15/12), new media, political debates, and lectures (€8/6). Films are generally independent and non-commercial, on topics such as contemporary life in China. Cafe (see listing in **Food,** p. 130) with monthly rotating art displays and free Wi-Fi with purchase. Ask the box office for info on whether a film is subtitled in English, which is always a plus. Pick up a program in the lobby or check the website for more info. Cash only.

Het Ketelhuis, Pazzanistraat 13 (☎684 0090; www.ketelhuis.nl), in the Westergasfabriek in **Westerpark.** Named for its original location in an old boiler room, the Ketelhuis has undergone renovation and is now a 3-theater movie house, playing Dutch films, documentaries, and a variety of international independent flicks in summer. Also contains a bar and cafe with ample terrace space. €8, children €7. Open W and Sa-Su 1pm until the last movie ends, M-Tu and Th-F 3pm until the last movie ends. Cash only.

Rialto, Ceintuurbaan 338 (☎676 8700; www.rialtofilm.nl), in **De Pijp.** Tram #3, 12, 24 or 25 to Ferdinand Bolstraat/Ceintuurbaan. Wonderful art-house cinema in a newly renovated complex showing a wide variety of international movies on 2 screens. Features an engaging number of retrospectives and series, many in conjunction with the Filmmuseum. M-Th and matinees €7.50, F-Su €8.50. Double features €11. Box office open M-F 7pm-1am, Sa-Su 3pm-1am.

Cinecenter, Lijnbaansgracht 236 (☎623 6615; www.cinecenter.nl), also just off **Leidseplein.** One of the city's larger art-house cinemas, showing a variety of foreign, documentary, and art films. Grab a beer (€2) from the classy bar and enjoy it during the show. Evening screenings €8, students and seniors €6.50; weekday afternoons €7/6; Su 11am, 1:30pm €5.

PROSTITUTION

The "world's oldest profession" has flourished in Amsterdam since the city's inception in the 13th century. Prostitution has always centered on what today is the Red Light District, though it is practiced elsewhere in the city as well. The Red Light District originally grew up in the 13th century around what is now known as Zeedijk, where prostitutes congregated to service sailors who came into port. **Window prostitution,** which grew out of the practice of prostitutes showing off their goods from the front windows of private houses, was officially legalized in 1911. In 2000, the law outlawing brothels was taken off the books, making informal street-walking the only prohibited form of prostitution.

Legal prostitution in Amsterdam comes in three main forms. By far the most visible is window prostitution, where scantily clad women tempt passersby from small chambers fronted by a plate-glass window. These sex workers are self-

KEEP IT MOVIN'. Feel free to look at window prostitutes, but unless you intend to engage in a business transaction, don't stop and stare. You will most likely elicit an angry reaction.

employed and rent the windows themselves, and, accordingly, each sets her own price. This form of commercial sex gave the Red Light District its name, as lamps both outside and inside the windows emit a red glow that bathes the whole area by night. The most popular spot for window prostitution in the Red Light District is between **Zeedijk** and **Warmoesstraat.** There are two more areas: in the **Nieuwe Zijd,** between Spuistraat and Singel, and in **De Pijp** along Ruysdaelkade. Those in the Nieuwe Zijd and De Pijp tend to be more discreet and frequented more by Dutch men than by tourists. Whether shopping or "just looking," be sure to show the women basic respect. Looking is fine and even necessary, but leering and catcalling are absolutely uncalled for. Keep in mind that prostitution is an entirely legal enterprise, and windows are places of business. Most of the prostitutes whom you see belong to a union called "The Red Thread" and are tested for HIV and STIs, although testing is on a voluntary basis. While it's okay to look, **do not take photos** unless you want to explain yourself to the angriest—and largest—man you'll ever see. If you're with a group of tourists, don't crowd in front of a window for a long time; this tends to discourage customers and is thus frustrating to the prostitute.

If you're interested in having sex with a window prostitute, go up to the door and wait for someone inside to open it. Show up clean and sober; prostitutes always reserve the right to refuse their services. Anything goes as long as you clearly and straightforwardly agree on it beforehand. Specifically state what you get for the money you're paying—that means which sex acts, in what positions, and, especially, how much time you have in which to do it. Window prostitutes can set their standards; by no means are they required to do anything you want without consenting to it in advance. Negotiation occurs and money changes hands before any sexual acts take place. Always practice **safe sex;** a prostitute should not and will not touch an uncondomed penis. Be aware that once your time is up, the prostitute will ask you to leave. Don't ask for a refund if you are left unsatisfied; all sales are final. There is no excuse for making trouble; if anyone becomes violent or threatening with a window prostitute, she has access to an emergency button that sets off a loud alarm. Not only does it make an ear-splitting noise, but it also summons the police, who invariably side with prostitutes in disputes. If you feel you have a legitimate complaint or have any kind of question about commercial sex, head to the extremely helpful Prostitution Information Centre (below) and discuss it there.

Increasingly popular are the recently legalized **brothels,** which come in two main flavors. The term usually refers to an establishment centered on a bar; there, women—or men—will make your acquaintance and are available for hour-long sessions. These brothels, also called **sex clubs,** can be pricey. In addition to costly drinks in the bar—solicitors are encouraged by the management to entice patrons into buying bottles of champagne—they charge a cover just to enter the building. A less expensive and more confidential alternative to the sex club is the variation known as the **private house.** In contrast to the bars, in a private house you enter a room and the currently available women walk by for your inspection. Select the one you like (or don't—there's no problem with walking out if none of the prostitutes are to your taste) and rent a room (the cost of which includes the woman's or man's services). Most of these establishments are located in Amsterdam's southern districts. **Escort services** are legal in Amsterdam as well. Offering even more discretion than private houses, these services arrange for a call girl or boy to visit you at your home or hotel room.

The best place to go for information about prostitution in Amsterdam is the **Prostitution Information Centre,** Enge Kerksteeg 3, in the Red Light District behind the Oude Kerk. Founded in 1994 by Mariska Majoor (once a prostitute herself), the center fills a crucial niche in connecting the Red Light District with its eager frequenters. Its friendly, helpful staff can answer any question you might have, no matter how much you blush when you ask it. You can also pick up copies of several informative publications: *The Most Frequently Asked Questions About Amsterdam's Red Light District*, a basic guide to the ins and outs of the window prostitution scene (€2.50); *Best Places to Go in Amsterdam*, five pages of top-shelf establishments (€3.50); and the *Pleasure Guide*, a magazine with ads and articles about commercial sex in the city (€3). The center sells handmade souvenirs and has its own mock-up of a window brothel interior, where you can take pictures—something you can't do at real window-prostitution booths. If you come to poke around, leave a donation; the Prostitution Information Centre is not state-supported and depends on the generosity of visitors to continue its work. An informative way to benefit its worthwhile cause is to take one of its tours of the Red Light District. (☎420 7328; www.pic-amsterdam.com. Open Tu-Sa noon-7pm. 1hr. tours W 7pm and Sa 5pm; €12.50.)

Sex shops and **live sex shows** are related elements of the industry. The former litter the Red Light District, vending pornos (mags and videos), dildos, lubricants, stimulants, lewd souvenirs, and the like. **Porn theaters** abound here as well, where an hour of lurid on-screen sex costs only as much as a movie ticket. Sex shops and porn theaters cluster along **Reguliersbreestraat,** just off Rembrandtplein, as well. Live sex shows are venues where the "performers" on stage will strip and engage in intercourse before your very eyes. There are quite a few live sex show establishments in the Red Light District, but the most famous (and, by some accounts, "classiest") is **Casa Rosso** (p. 145).

RECREATION AND GAMBLING

Sports play a relatively minor role in Dutch culture—with the exception of cheering on local legend Ajax (p. 73 and p. 162), of course. Nonetheless, visitors looking to maintain a healthful lifestyle on the road—or at least catch a good game of pool—can turn to the following venues. For those tired of waiting in long lines or sluggish from all that food, Amsterdam's athletic opportunities are guaranteed to get your blood pumping. Bungee jump into a canal, play a game of squash, lift some weights, or loll back in an indoor pool. Those who prefer betting on athletes (or on their own blackjack skills) can head to the Holland Casino Amsterdam.

■ **De Klimmuur,** De Ruyterkade 160 (☎427 5777; www.deklimmuur.nl), near Centraal Station; it's the enormous, tilted, corrugated block. The unsurpassed indoor wall-climbing facility is sure to entertain (and exhaust) you. €10 per climb, students €8. Equipment rental €15. Open M-F 6-10:30pm, Sa 1-7pm, Su 1-10:30pm. Cash only.

■ **Squash City,** Ketelmakerstraat 6 (☎626 7883; www.squashcity.com). Take bus #18 or 22 to Ketelmakerstraat, dir. Haarlemmerplein. About a 5min. bus ride or 15min. walk west of Centraal Station. Offers squash courts, a gym, and a sauna. Gym or aerobics day cards both €7-10 8:45am-5pm, €11 5pm-closing. Squash day card €7-9.50. Racquet rental €2.50. Squash lessons €24 per session. Tanning bed €8 per session. Student discounts available. Open M-F 8:45am-midnight, Sa-Su 8:45am-9pm.

Holland Casino Amsterdam, Max Euweplein 62 (☎521 1111; www.hollandcasino.nl), in **Leidseplein.** Head through Max Euweplein's columns past a lovely curved fountain and terrace packed with tourists. Though this casino is relatively small, it is the largest and ritziest of the Netherlands's national gaming houses and sits on a lovely spot right along the Singelgracht. The casino generously presents a variety of pocket-emptying diversions: electronic slots, blackjack, roulette, poker, and wily 1-armed bandits. 18+; ID required. Flashy restaurant inside with same hours as casino. Open daily noon-3am. Admission €3.50. Min. wager at some tables €1.30-2, for slots €0.50.

Knijn Bowling, Scheldeplein 3 (☎664 2211; www.knijnbowling.nl), south of **Museumplein and Vondelpark.** Tram #4 to Station RAI. The Dutch aren't famous for bowling, but Knijn makes a noble try. "Twilight Bowling" with luminous balls and pins as well as lighting, smoke, and dance music F 11pm-12:30am, Sa 11:30pm-1am (€11 per person; min. 4 participants). Includes a bar, lounge, and 2 restaurants that serve food at elevated prices. Beer €2. Meals €25-30. Hourly prices for groups of up to 6, including shoe rental: F-Sa 5pm-1am €26.50; M-Th 5pm-1am, Sa noon-5pm, Su and public holidays noon-midnight €24.50; M-F 10am-5pm €18.50. AmEx/MC/V.

Snooker & Poolclub Oud-West, Overtoom 209 (☎618 8019), in **Oud-West.** Tram #1 or 6 to Constantijn Huygensstraat. Full-size snooker in a converted church with 3 pool tables on the balcony, 2 dart lanes, and 8 snooker tables. Considered one of the best snooker halls in the Netherlands; members of its snooker club have repeatedly won the Dutch National Championships. Full bar for added merriment. Beer €2. Monthly membership for use of pool tables €5. Tables €9.50 per hr.; members pay €1.50 less per game. Open M-Th and Su noon-1am, F-Sa noon-2am. Reserve 2 days ahead F-Sa.

Avonturenbaai Sloterparkbad, President Allendelaan 3 (☎506 3506; www.optisport.nl/sloterparkbad). Tram #14 to its end. This beautiful park, which contains both indoor and outdoor pools, is the perfect place to relax or practice your strokes. €4, seniors €3. Open M and Th 2-6pm, Tu and F 2-10pm, W 1-10pm, Sa-Su 10am-6pm.

Garden Gym, Jodenbreestraat 158 (☎626 8772; www.thegarden.nl). With a central location in the **Jodenbuurt,** Garden Gym makes working out truly convenient and inexpensive. Day card (€10) gets you access to equipment and showers; equipment and sauna day card €11. See website for aerobics schedules. Open M, W, F 9am-11pm, Tu and Th noon-10pm, Sa-Su 9am-2pm.

Bungy Jump Holland, Westerdoksdijk 44 (☎419 6005; www.bungy.nl). Supervises jumps from a crane 75m above the IJ canal. You get to choose whether you end up dry or in the drink. 1st jump €55, 2nd €45; duo jump €110. Open Apr. Sa-Su noon-6pm; May-June Th-Su noon-7pm; July-Aug. W-Su noon-8pm; Sept.-Oct. Th-Su noon-6pm.

De Mirandabad, De Mirandalaan 9 (☎546 4444; www.zuideramstel.amsterdam.nl). A water park with a wave pool, beach, and indoor and outdoor pools. €4, seniors €3. Additional charges for some water sports. Open daily 7am-midnight; check website for hours of various facilities.

SAUNAS AND SPAS

Let's Go realizes that travel can be tough. Itineraries have a way of over-scheduling themselves, feet have a tendency to flatten from too many flip-flop-traveled miles, and nerves have been known to fray after a few days cooped up with even one's closest friends. For some folks, saunas and spas offer nonchalant respite from the tourist hordes. Below, we list two varieties of tension-relieving venues: ◢gay saunas, which cater to a gay adult male crowd looking to meet other towel-clad men; and spas, which cater to anyone looking for a bit of mud on the face—but in a smooth, relaxing way.

Thermos Day, Raamstraat 33 (☎623 9158; www.thermos.nl), in the **Jordaan.** Tram #1, 2, 5, 7, or 10 to Leidseplein. From Leidseplein, follow Marnixstraat to Leidsegracht, take a right onto Leidsegracht, and quickly swing left onto Raamdwarsstraat. Raamstraat will be the first right. This is 1-stop shopping for a day of rest, relaxation, and relations with the boys. Open for 40 years, Amsterdam's largest **gay** spa occupies 5 stories of 2 connected buildings and boasts a restaurant, hairdresser, beauty shop, masseur, roof terrace, swimming pool, steam rooms, video cabins, and private upstairs chambers for intimate rendezvous. 2 towels included in admission. Menu in restaurant offers soup, main dish, and dessert for €10. Men only. 18+, but you'll mostly encounter a more mature set. €18, under 24 and over 65 €13.50. Open M-F noon-11pm, Sa noon-10pm, Su 11am-10pm; 1st F of the month also 5-10am.

Thermos Night, Kerkstraat 58-60 (www.thermos.nl), in the **Central Canal Ring.** Tram #1, 2, or 5 to Prinsengracht. Kerkstraat is 1 block north of Prinsengracht. Owned by the same people who run Thermos Day. Feel like letting it all hang out with some ▼**gay** male companions into the wee hours of the night? This is Amsterdam's best bet for a night on the town that won't sap your energy. Smaller size means the Night has fewer amenities than the Day, but nocturnal facilities still include a hot tub, steam room, sauna, small gym, video rooms, and, of course, private cabins. Men only. 18+. €18, over 65 and under 24 €13.50. Open M-Sa 11pm-8am, Su 11pm-10am.

Sauna Deco, Herengracht 115 (☎623 8215; www.saunadeco.nl), in the **Jordaan.** Pamper yourself amid fabulous Art Deco opulence with a massage—deep tissue, hydro-jet, Shiatsu, or reflexology. €30 for 25min., €60 for 55min. Fiery sauna and Turkish bath (both co-ed) hidden among damp tiled columns. Towel rental €2. Open M and W-Sa noon-11pm, Tu 3-11pm, Su 1-7pm. Cash only. Salon next door at Herengracht 117 (☎330 3565) offers facials, manicures, and special "beauty days" from €115. Call ahead to book all salon and massage appointments.

Boomerang, Heintje Hoekssteeg 8 (☎622 6162). On a small side street off Warmoesstraat, just north of the intersection between Warmoesstraat and Lange Niezel. Smaller than Thermos Day or Night, this is a newer ▼**gay** sauna close to the Red Light District and Centraal Station. Caters to a slightly older crowd. 18+. €13. Open daily 9am-11pm.

COFFEE AND SMART SHOPS

> **❗ LET'S GO DOES NOT RECOMMEND DRUG USE IN ANY FORM.** Those who decide to partake should use common sense and remember that any experience with drugs can be dangerous.

As you may know, use of soft drugs, including marijuana and mushrooms, is permissible in the Netherlands. If you choose to indulge in drug tourism, you must follow basic ground rules and take careful safety precautions.

First, be smart about your intake and realize that drug experimentation can cause both short- and long-term damage. **Never buy drugs from street dealers;** they are often strung-out addicts out to mug tourists. **If a friend is tripping, it is important never to leave his or her side.** If there is a medical emergency, call ☎ **112 for an ambulance.** Beware that an ambulance may not arrive as soon as you'd like—authorities are generally fed up with drug tourists who have smoked or eaten too many drugs.

A far cry from your friendly neighborhood Starbucks, Amsterdam's **coffee shops** aren't there for the coffee—in fact, at many, you'll find that the coffeemaker is out of order, and few patrons seem to care. Places calling themselves coffee shops sell hashish, marijuana, and "space" goodies, described in detail below. Look for the green-and-white **BCD** sticker that certifies a shop's credibility. It is a courtesy to tip coffee-shop attendants, even by simply saying, "keep the change." When you move from one coffee shop to another, it is obligatory to **buy a drink** in the next shop even if you already have weed. As long as you're buying drinks, you can stay as long as you want. While it's all right to smoke on the outdoor patio of a coffee shop, **don't go walking down the street smoking a joint** like you're James Dean with a cigarette: it's simply not done. Not only is this an easy way for pickpockets and con artists to pick out a tourist, but locals also consider it offensive.

There is more variety on coffee-shop menus than you might think. **Hashish** comes in three varieties: blonde (Moroccan), black (Indian), and Dutch (Ice-o-Lator; see **On Thin Ice,** p. 203), all of which can cost €4-35 per g. Typically, the cost of the hash is proportional to its quality and strength. Black hash hits harder than blonde, and Ice-o-Lator can send even a seasoned smoker off his or her head. What separates hash from weed is that, while weed is the flower, hash is the extracted resin crystals, which give a different kind of high.

Marijuana is a dried, cured flower also known as 420, Acapulco red, ace, African, airplane, Angola, ashes, assassin of youth, astroturf, atshitshi, Aunt Mary, baby, babysitter, bad seed, bale, bamba, bammy, bar, bash, blanket, blaze, block, blue sage, blunts, bobo, bomber, boo, boom, broccoli, brown, bubble gum, bud, bullyon, burnie, burrito, bush, butter, canamo, canappa, cannabis, catnip, cest, cavite all-star, charge, cheeba, chemo, chillums, chira, Christmas tree, chronic, chunky, churus, citrol, climb, colas, coli, Columbia, cosa, cripple, culican, dagga, dank, dew, ding, dirties, ditch, domestic, Don Juan, donk, doobie, dope, draf, drag weed, duros, DVD, earth, elephant, endo, esra, fallbrook redhair, fatty, feeling, fine stuff, finger, fir, firewood, flower, fraho, freefo, funk, funny stuff, gangster, ganja, garbage, gash, gasper, gates, gauge, geek, giggle smoke, gimme, goblet of jam, golden leaf, GOM (good old marijuana), gong, goodie-goodie, gorge, grass, grasshopper, Greek, greens, greeter, grefa, gremmies, greta, griefs, griffa, gungun, gunney, haircut, happy stick, has, hay, headies, hemp, herb, hocus, homegrown, hooch, hooter, hot stick, hydro, illies, Indian boy, indo, instaga, jay, jive, joints, jolly green, joy stick, ju-ju, jumbos, kabak, kaff, kalakit, kali, Kansas grass, kaya, kee, Kentucky blue, KGB (killer green bud), kick stick, kiff, killer, kilter, kind, king bud, kryptonite, kumba, lamb's bread, laughing grass, leaf, leak, limbo, lid, lima, lime green, llesca, loaf, lobo, locoweed, log, loose shank, love weed, Lucas, lumber, macaroni, machinery, macon, magic ⬛dragon, Manhattan silver, Marley, Mary Jane, Mary Warner, matchbox, meg, messorole, Mexican red, mighty mezz, MJ, mo, modams, mohasky, monte, moocah, mootie, mota, mother, mor a grifa, muggle, nail, northern lights, nuggets, number, OJ, oit, pack, pakaloco, Panama cut, panatella, pasto, pat, Philly blunts, pins, pocket rocket, pod, poke, pot, PR (Panama red), prescription, pretendica, puff, Queen Anne's lace, ragweed, railroad weed, rainy day woman, rangood, rasta weed, red cross, reefer, righteous bush, rip, rockets, root, rope, rough stuff, rugs, salad, salt and pepper, sandwich bag, Santa Maria, sasfras, scissors, scrub, seeds, sen, sezz, shake, siddi, sinse, skunk, snop, spliffs, splim, spruce, stack, stems, stick, sticky icky, stinkweed, straw, stuff, swag, sweet Lucy, taima, tea, tex mex, thirteen, thumb, Tijuana, torch, trauma, tray, trees, triple A, tustin, twist, unotque, vipe, wacky tobacky, weed, whack, wheat, white-haired lady, woo blunts, woodbine, X, yeh, yellow submarine, yen pop, yesca, ying, zambi, or zol. Whatever you call it, it's incredibly strong in the Netherlands, containing 10-25% THC. Any weed with "white" in its name is guaranteed to be strong, such as White Widow, White Butterfly, and White Ice. **Take it easy so you don't pass out.** The Dutch tend to mix tobacco with their pot as well, so joints are harsher on your lungs and throat if you're not a cigarette smoker. Pre-rolled joints are always rolled with tobacco; most coffee shops also offer pure joints at up to twice the cost. Dutch marijuana is the most common and costs €3-15 per g; most coffee shops sell bags in set amounts (€6, €12, etc.). A coffee shop's staff is accustomed to explaining the different kinds of pot on the menu to tourists. It is recommended that you **buy only a gram at a time.** Most places will supply rolling papers and filter tips—Europeans smoke only joints. When pipes or bongs are provided, they are usually for tourists. Another popular way of getting high in Amsterdam is to use a **vaporizer.**

TIME: Most of the day, but you won't notice.

SEASON: Year-round.

Amsterdam's army of coffee shops can be overwhelming to even the most experienced toker. Here is a tour offering a sampling of the city's best coffee shops, munchies, and psychedelic sights. By the end of the tour, you're guaranteed to be stoned and even a bit more cultured—but mostly just stoned.

1. BARNEY'S. Wake and bake, sunshine! Stoners can start the day with Barney's—they have a long trek ahead—and tuck into a hearty breakfast of bacon, eggs, sausages, and toast while smoking their favorite weed. Barney's has received the Cannabis Cup (an award for best weed strain) numerous times (p. 205).

2. ELECTRIC LADYLAND. On the left side of the street, this "First Museum of Fluorescent Art" will befuddle the already-boggled mind. Hippie soulmate/owner Nick Padalino will guide visitors through this collection of fluorescent sculptures, minerals, and everyday objects (p. 172).

3. ABRAXAS. The so-inclined can top off their breakfast with a refreshing hash smoothie. Mellow mood lighting and mosaics make this an enjoyable place to rest. The drink will fortify the venturer for the long, perplexing walk ahead (p. 203).

4. VONDELPARK. Fatigued tokers can take a break and relish the park's soft greenery with other locals who come here to relax—or else marvel at the hilarious street performers (p. 154).

5. VAN GOGH MUSEUM. The stoned will stare at the swirling textures of Van Gogh's masterpieces and chill out in this breezy, bright space. Be warned, though! The sunflowers may look a little strange, and the birds in *Wheatfield with Crows* may seem a bit sinister (p. 174).

6. BOAT TOUR. Tour boats will take customers on a relaxing, immobile, delightfully touristy journey through the Jordaan's winding canals and eventually deposit them at the departure point on Singelgracht outside the Rijksmuseum. With one ticket, you can access tour boats for the entire day without another charge (p. 93).

7. DAMPKRING. Those looking for a high may enjoy this coffee shop, one of the city's classiest. Users choose from 10 pre-rolled joints and relax in a deep blue and golden orange space. Those whose brains have been addled by the day can ask the expert staff for help (p. 202).

8. CANNABIS COLLEGE. Stoners learn everything they've ever wanted to know about the stuff they're smoking—including effects, medicinal uses, and political dimensions—in the company of some hard-core cannabis lovers. Best of all, it's free (p. 166).

9. TASTE OF CULTURE. Munchies starting to kick in? You may be ready for this restaurant's hearty challenge: all you can eat in 1hr. for only €8.50. Greasy Chinese food in all its glory will level diners out for the stumble to the last coffee shop stop (p. 123).

10. GREY AREA. Your last smoke of the day! This tiny shop has a big following. Grey Area has sold great stuff for years—they have received more than 20 awards at the Cannabis Cup since 1996 (p. 206). Those ready to pass out by now can trip on home to their comfy beds; otherwise, this tour leaves its attendees near some of the city's best nightlife. Only minutes away, **Club NL** plays trance music that matches your heightened state (p. 228). Farther out, in the Jordaan, **Café 't Smalle** is ideal for a mellow night of drinks (p. 237).

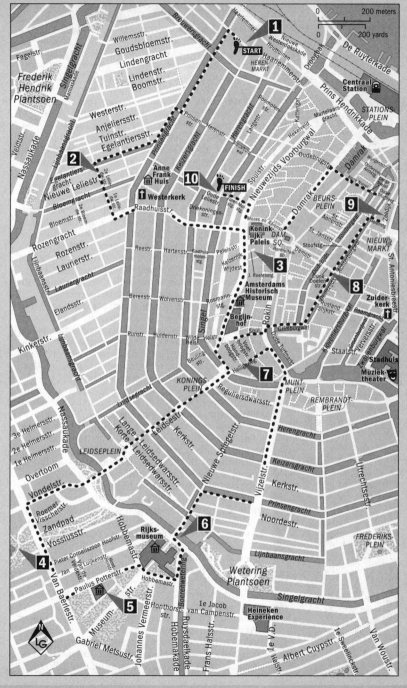

KNOW YOUR BLOW

Don't worry; in the Netherlands, "blow" is just another term for marijuana. There are two main varieties of cannabis sold in Amsterdam's coffee shops. With a little background, you'll be able to make the most of your smoking experience. Here is what you should look for:

Cannabis indica is indigenous to northern climates, such as the mountains of Afghanistan and India. The cool temperatures mean the plants flower earlier and usually reach only about four feet tall, but the flowers are larger and more resinous than southern varieties of cannabis, making this a popular type of plant for the production of hashish. These plants are high in cannabidiol (CBD), which relaxes muscles and creates a more subdued stoned feeling. Popular types of indica found in Amsterdam are Hindu Kush, Shiva, Afghan, and White Widow.

Cannabis sativa is culled from warm equatorial climates like southern Asia, the Caribbean, Latin America, and Africa. Sativa plants have more flowers that grow for a longer period of time, with a higher flower-to-plant ratio. The slower growth creates a sweeter taste and higher quantities of tetrahydrocannabinol (THC), which creates more of a "high" feeling. Amsterdam's sativa selection includes Haze, Kali Mist, and most Thai and African weeds.

These devices heat up cannabis products until the hallucinogenic substances like THC become gaseous, extracting more out of the product than regular burning via cigarettes. Beware that vaporizers are very strong, and those with copper piping may release nasty (and potentially carcinogenic) copper particles.

Space cakes, brownies, and all members of the baked-goods family are made with hash or weed, and the butter used is usually hash- or weed-based. Because the THC only takes effect when it gets into your blood and is digested, the drugs take longer to affect a person and longer to filter out, producing a "body stone" that can take up to two hours or longer to start. **Experts warn against going for a second sweet because you don't feel anything immediately**—start off with half a serving and see how you feel after an hour or two. It's always easier to eat more later than to wait out a higher dose than you can handle. The amount of pot or hash in baked goods cannot be standardized, and it is impossible to know what grade of drugs is in them. This makes ingesting this form of cannabis much more dangerous than smoking, with which you can monitor your intake more closely.

On a slightly edgier level, **smart shops** are scattered throughout Amsterdam and peddle a variety of "herbal enhancers" and hallucinogens like **magic mushrooms ('shrooms).** All 'shrooms have the same psychedelic chemical (psilocybin), but different types of mushrooms offer very different trips. **Mexican** and **Thai** mushrooms are generally used by beginners: they are the least potent and give a laughy, colorful, speedy high with some visual hallucination. **Philosophers' stones** (which have an XTC-like effect) and **Hawaiians** (which give an intensely visual trip similar to LSD) are significantly more intense and should be taken **only by experienced users.** It is currently illegal to "prepare" mushrooms—including drying, baking, or any other kind of handling—because the process concentrates the hallucinogenic chemicals. A mild high is a dose of about 10-15g of fresh 'shrooms; a weak trip has 15-30g; a strong trip has 30-50g. Be sure to ask the salesperson exactly how many grams there are in your purchase.

'Shrooms will start to work around 30-50min. after ingestion, and the effects will last anywhere from three to eight hours, depending on the amount of the dose. The effects you feel will depend on your mood and environment. Your emotions will be heightened such that, as at your high-school prom, you could feel unadulterated bliss, stark fear, or seemingly endless depression. Overall, you will experience a distorted reality: lengths of time will randomly expand or contract; colors, forms, shapes, and experiences will be unpredictably intensified or subdued. Blips will appear on your sensory radar, blinding you to all other realities. Conversely, certain sounds and smells may captivate you such that you become obsessed with their existence. **Do not take more than one dose at a time**—many first-time users take too much because they don't feel anything immediately. A bad trip will occur if you mix hallucinogens or other controlled substances. If you smoke marijuana when 'shrooming, you can have flashbacks up to several days later. Try to avoid eating before taking 'shrooms, since this will likely dull their effect or intensify nausea. Be sure that you take them in a safe surrounding with people you know, preferably outside and during daytime hours—in any strange environment, your neurological worries are bound to affect your high. Avoid balconies, bridges, and rooftops and do not take 'shrooms after a night of little sleep. If you are depressed, pregnant, or on medication, you should not take mushrooms. Don't be ashamed to tell someone should you have a bad trip; you won't be arrested just for using in Amsterdam—it's not a crime here, and locals have seen it all before.

While there are hot spots in Amsterdam that seem to feature as many drug shops as restaurants (i.e., the Nieuwe Zijd and the Red Light District), you'll find that the best offerings aren't necessarily concentrated in any particular location. As a general rule, the farther you travel from the touristed spots, the better value and higher quality the establishments you'll find. When a shop is frequented mainly by Dutch customers, it means they've established a loyal clientele, which in turn means they sell good stuff. There's nothing wrong with walking in and checking a place out before you settle in. When you enter a shop, ask for the menu—establishments are not allowed to advertise their products or leave menus on the tables. Don't be afraid to **take your time** making your selections; it's your money.

 IT'S THE LAW. Although it may seem to the uninitiated that anything goes in Amsterdam, there are in fact very strict regulations regarding drug consumption. For info on the legal ins and outs, call the **Jellinek clinic** (☎570 2378) and see our **Essentials** chapter (p. 25). If your questions pertain only to the drugs themselves, try **Cannabis College** (p. 166). For the latest legislation, check the English-language website http://english.justitie.nl.

OUDE ZIJD

The Centrum's coffee shops are notoriously touristy, and the Red Light District has a monopoly even on those, leaving the Oude Zijd with slim pickings.

see map p. 340

■ **Rusland,** Rusland 16 (☎627 9468). Known as Amsterdam's oldest coffee shop, Rusland is more than just a drug store: choose from over 40 varieties of herbal tea or refreshing yogurt shakes (€2.35). Enjoy your smokes amid walls decorated with sketches of the Kremlin and other Moscow sites. If you enjoy gazing upon the handblown lamps on the walls, head downstairs and admire the selection of handblown pipes while relaxing on the pillowed benches for an afternoon smoke. Pre-rolled joints €2.50-4.50. Especially tasty Afghan bud €7 per g. Space muffins €5. Open M-Th and Su 10am-midnight, F-Sa 10am-1am. Cash only.

RED LIGHT DISTRICT

Despite the proliferation of coffee shops in the area, you're better off looking outside the Red Light District for a quality joint. Because of the heavy tourist traffic, shops don't have to rely on repeat business, so customer satisfaction is a low priority. Shops can sell you lousy weed and get away with it, as

see map p. 340

knowledgeable Dutch smokers will readily affirm. However, some reasonable places do exist if you're craving a hit in the area.

COFFEE SHOPS

■ **Hill Street Blues,** Warmoesstraat 52 (www.hill-street-blues.nl). Don't let the loud rock music wafting into the street drive you away; it's all about leisurely comfort inside at this busy but mellow coffee shop. Add to the liveliness by bringing your own CDs to play at the counter and decorating the graffiti-laden walls with personal messages or postcards. Sit near the back for a great view over Damrak and its canal or downstairs for some more privacy. Space cakes and cookies €3-5. Weed and hash €4.50-11.50 per g. Pre-rolled joints €3. Open M-Th and Su 9am-1am, F-Sa 9am-3am.

The Greenhouse Effect, Warmoesstraat 53 (☎623 7462; www.the-greenhouse-effect.com). Also a hotel and bar, this all-purpose establishment provides almost all of the Red Light District's (non-sexual) thrills, with the crowds you might expect. One of the area's most pleasant and welcoming spots; extremely friendly staff. Smoke on the couches in the back and then head to the bar next door for Happy hour (M-Th and Su 8-10pm). Discounts at coffee shop and bar for hotel patrons. Weed €3.50-14 per g. Hash €3.50-16 per g (including Ice-o-Lator). Pre-rolled joints €3. Pure joints €8. Space chocolate-chip cookies €2. Chocolate cake €4. Vaporizers available. Open daily 9am-1am.

> **TIP** **HARD SELL.** In the Red Light District, it is not uncommon to be approached by drug pushers selling hard drugs such as cocaine and ecstasy. Remember, however, that **all hard drugs are illegal** in Amsterdam.

SMART SHOP

Conscious Dreams Kokopelli, Warmoesstraat 12 (☎421 7000). This smart shop is perhaps the best place in Amsterdam to begin with psychedelic experimentation. Books, gifts, pipes, and lava lamps available with an overwhelming selection of 'shrooms, oxygen drinks, fertility elixirs, vitamins, and herbs. A staff with background in neurobiology and botany is on hand to advise the unknowing consumer. DJs spin tunes F-Sa and sometimes Su 6-10pm. Internet access €1 per 15min. Grow kits €35-65. Herbal XTC €11.50-14. Mushrooms €12.50-17.50 for a colorful variety of effects. €16 for a real "Hawaiian" trip. Discuss all drugs' intensity and safety with the staff first. Open daily 11am-10pm.

NIEUWE ZIJD

The Nieuwe Zijd has one of Amsterdam's highest ratios of coffee shops per sq. km. Listed below are some of Amsterdam's gems.

COFFEE SHOPS

■ **Kadinsky,** Rosmarijnsteeg 9 (☎624 7023; www.kadinsky.nl), a few blocks north of the intersection of Spui and Nieuwezijds Voorburgwal, between the 2 streets. This stylish 3-story joint hidden off an alley near Spui is one of the city's friendliest, hippest, and most comfortable stoneries. A grandiose bouquet of fresh flowers greets you upon entrance, and the window-side bar opens onto the street for indoor and outdoor chillage on sunny days. Joints €3.40-4. Weed €7-11 per g. 20% off 5g purchases. Kadinsky also has 2 small, modish annexes—1 at Langebrugsteeg 7A and the other at Zoutsteeg 14—as well as a cafe at Zoutsteeg 9-11, though nothing beats the original. Open daily 9:30am-1am. see map p. 340

■ **Dampkring,** Handboogstraat 29 (☎638 0705). From Muntplein, take Singel to Heiligeweg and turn right; it's near the corner of Heiligeweg and Handboogstraat. Golden earthy hues and Asian art welcome cannabis fans and backpackers alike to this smoking den. Scenes from the film *Ocean's Twelve* were shot in this shop; 2 video screens show the clips on a continuous loop so that you can't forget. Psychedelic trees hang over the bar, and ambient fluorescent lighting sets the laid-back vibe at this unpretentious spot. Extremely detailed cannabis menu with 10 choices of pre-rolled joints €3.50-8. Same owner as **De Tweede Kamer** (below), with the same excellent value and strong cannabis, like Salad Bowl (€5 per g) or the special NYC Diesel (€8.50 per g). Open M-F 10am-1am.

De Tweede Kamer, Heisteeg 6 (☎422 2236; www.channels.nl/amsterdam/twkamer.html). Head north along Nieuwezijds Voorburgwal from Spui for 1 block, then turn left onto the dinky alleyway that is Heisteeg. You might mistake this *gezellig* smokery's deep burgundy curtains and calligraphic window signs for the facade of a typical Dutch *bruin cafe*. The name refers to a branch of the Dutch parliament, and photographs and blown-up stamps of the House of Orange are an amusing alternative to the psychedelic art typical of so many other shops. The mother store of **Dampkring** (above) with the same fine selection, but attracts fewer tourists and more connoisseurs. A large selection of sativa is available at this small and often very crowded shop. Rifman hash from Morocco is grown without chemicals or additives. Weed €5-10 per g. Open M-Sa 10am-1am, Su 11am-1am.

Route 99, Haringpakkerssteeg 8 (☎320 7562). Big sister to **Route 66,** Warmoesstraat 77. Take a roadtrip through the American West with Elvis, Marilyn, and a White Widow joint. A vibrant mural of highways, cowboys, sand, and outer space decorates the walls of this coffee shop. Extremely popular with tourists for its location right off Damrak and seconds away from Centraal Station. A good place to hang out, with 3 pool tables (€2 per game) in the basement. Internet access €5 per hr. 10 varieties of hash and weed €12 per 1.2-2.5g. Space cakes €4. Open M-Th and Su 9am-midnight, F-Sa 9am-1am.

Abraxas, Jonge Roelensteeg 12-14 (☎625 5763; www.abraxas.tv), between Nieuwezijds Voorburgwal and Kalverstraat, just south of Dam. One of the Nieuwe Zijd's finest coffee shops. Colorful, sprawling mosaics, an undulating tree sculpture growing over the bar, and mood lighting decorate its 2 floors. Serves the full palette of hash and weed products, plus juice and sodas, in a casual, sophisticated, no-pressure atmosphere. Serves shakes (€3) and space cakes (€4), but use caution: Abraxas's spacy baked goods are strong, so ask advice on how to ingest them. Free 15min. of Internet access with any purchase; €1 per hr. thereafter. Wheelchair-accessible. Open daily 10am-1am.

Dutch Flowers, Singel 387 (☎624 7624). From Muntplein, follow the Singel past 2 bridges; Dutch Flowers

ON THE MENU

ON THIN ICE

Ask a coffee shop employer wha the strongest bang for your buck will be and there is invariably one answer: Dutch Ice-o-Lator hash Found in most of Amsterdam's coffee shops, it usually cost around €25 per g. The price may be steep, but it promises the strongest high in town.

Ice-o-Lator hash is created through a synthetic process in which the resin of the marijuana plant is separated from the othe plant parts and re-sifted in ar elaborate system. Ice and wate are added to a filter bag holding the marijuana leaves. A cake mixer is used to dislodge the pollen, which contains the THC. Afte the mixture is chilled, the plant's resin is deposited into a second bag below the filter.

After one or two hours, the bag are removed; the first holds the old marijuana leaves, and the second is left with a small amount of pure resin from the plant. This resin is then packed into small cakes which make their way to Dutch coffee shops. The result is the super potent "Ice-o-Lator," which can be as much as 98% THC.

To put that in perspective, a normal American joint is abou 7% THC (rarely approaching ever 30%). This means that Ice-o-Lato hash is never something to try on your first time out, and even experienced smokers should use extreme caution.

HARM REDUCTION

The Dutch have long regulated and sanctioned practices that are banned in many societies. One personal choice that the government—and Dutch society at large—has indisputably frowned upon is the use of "hard drugs" such as cocaine, speed, and heroin. Yet an unorthodox heroin treatment program recently has emerged in the Netherlands.

The new approach, called "harm reduction," works to keep heroin users safe, healthy, and crime-free. Administrators dole out daily heroin fixes to registered addicts, who are allowed to shoot up in a room stocked with clean needles and sanitary products. This anti-war war on drugs stems from the Dutch belief that drug use is an inevitable social problem in addition to a concern for the individual user and the safety of the community itself.

Mainline is one of the groups at the forefront of the movement. The non-profit organization published *Mainline Lady*, a glossy outreach publication targeted at female drug users. The magazine received government funding and included detailed instructions on how to shoot up, interspersed with sobering personal tales of drug use.

The Netherlands has a very low rate of HIV+ intravenous drug users, as well as a stable and aging number of heroin users, suggesting that the controversial program may hold the key to combatting the problem of drug use.

will be up your right. Ample menu widely considered one of the best in Amsterdam. More than cannabis has gone to their heads, though: as past winners of the coveted "High Life" prize for best hash in Amsterdam's annual Cannabis Cup, the staff can sometimes have a standoffish attitude. But with crooked paintings and shelves on the walls, outside terrace seating along the beautiful Singel canal, and one of Amsterdam's best bakeries around the corner for when you get the munchies (p. 129), Dutch Flowers remains a steadfast purveyor of the high life. Joints €2.80-6.50. Loose weed from €7 per g. Open M-Th and Su 10am-1am, F-Sa 10am-2am.

La Canna, Nieuwendijk 121-125 (☎428 4482; www.lacanna.nl). After following Damrak straight out from Centraal, turn right on Karnemelksteeg and then left on Nieuwendijk. With a bar, coffee shop, smart shop, and restaurant, this jungle-themed party complex is one of Amsterdam's most highly touristed anythings. You're likely to see more La Canna shopping bags on Nieuwendijk than H&M bags. 1st fl. houses a bar with restaurant (snacks €3-5); 2nd fl. has pool tables (€1 per game) and the coffee shop with an irritating minimum of 5g or €20. At the top, there's more pool, another bar, and a tattoo artist—just in case you think getting Jerry Garcia's mug tattooed to your own nether lands seems like a good idea. If the scene starts to run you down, pep up with a house-brewed energy drink (€3). Smart shop on the ground fl. vends magic mushrooms (€14-20) and smart drugs (€10-30). Open M-Th and Su 9am-1am, F-Sa 9am-3am.

Softland, Spuistraat 222 (☎420 9799). From Dam, walk a few blocks south on Spuistraat. Enter the otherworldly Softland intergalactic spaceship, complete with android eye tables, exposed silver piping, and green Martian lighting, for some of their coffee, milk shakes, munchies, space cakes (€6), and, of course, joints (€3-7). This futuristic 2-time Cannabis Cup prize winner is light-years away from the other classy cafes and coffee shops along Spuistraat. Internet access €3 per hr. Open daily 9am-1am.

Coffeeshop Any Day, Korte Kolksteeg 5 (☎420 8698). Take Spuistraat a few blocks north from Dam, and you'll find the store on your right on Korte Kolksteeg. Its 2 floors might be tiny (only 15 seats), but its selection is sizable. Friendly staff is ready to help. Known around town for its pure joints (€4; hand-rolled €7.50-8). The fearless don't miss out on their *verdampers,* or vaporizers, which look like middle-school science projects with a somewhat less virtuous purpose; signs warn that after experiencing their power, "you might not want to smoke anymore." You can buy 1 of your very own for only €250. Hash €2.50-15 per g. Marijuana €5.40-10.80 per g. Coffee and fruit drinks €1.20-1.50. Open daily 10am-1am.

420 Cafe (de Kuil), Oudebrugsteeg 27 (☎623 4848; www.420cafe.com). From Centraal, take Damrak straight out and turn right at Oudebrugsteeg. Though it's only a few blocks from Centraal Station, this coffeehouse provides a mellow escape from the intensity of the city center. A classic rock vibe draws an older crowd that appreciates the Beatles, Hendrix, and house fave Frank Zappa. Hash and pot are sold in increments of 1-5g, ranging from €5-9 per g to €35-60 for 5g. Examine your purchase with the house microscope, through which you can look at the important THC content of the goods. Alternatively, smoke up using one of the bar's 2 state-of-the-art German vaporizers. Joints €4-6. Open M-Th and Su 10am-midnight, F-Sa 10am-1am.

SMART SHOP

Magic Valley, Spuistraat 60 (☎320 3001), just a few blocks north of Dam Sq. Magic Valley offers magic mushrooms, hemp seeds, herbal XTC, energizers, and sex stimulants in a small, colorful shop whose overhanging tree and mushroom sculptures seem to be molded from psychedelic plaster. Potent Hawaiian 'shrooms €18. Mexican (€13) and Thai (€14) 'shrooms less potent but still pack a punch. Ask for help from the well-versed staff. There's a small back section that sells souvenirs from bongs to Amsterdam tourist items. Open M-Th and Su 11am-10pm, F-Sa 10am-10pm. AmEx/MC/V.

SCHEEPVAARTBUURT

The two-block stretch of Haarlemmerstraat just over the Haarlemmersluis and the section of Singel on either side of the bridge are home to the majority of the coffee shops in this area. Though some are just smaller branches of larger chains, a few independent joints attract more discerning pot pilgrims.

Barney's, Haarlemmerstraat 102 (☎625 9761; www.barneys.biz). see map p. 338 Barney's is a hyper-popular tourist spot in the heart of the Shipping Quarter—so popular, in fact, that you might find yourself waiting for a table or sharing one with a backpacker from the hostel down the street. Check out the impressive collection of Cannabis Cup trophies on display behind the counter. Busiest in the mornings, when you can get big breakfasts (omelettes €8, pancakes €6.50). Pot €8-14.50 per g. Hash €7-13 per g. G-13 Haze, winner of the 2006 Cannabis Cup, €13 per g. Pre-rolled joints €4-6. 2 vaporizers free of charge. Open daily 7am-8pm; food served until noon.

CANAL RING WEST

This neighborhood has a few ganja-vending gems that can feel a world apart from the quality—and tourist quantity— of the Centrum.

☒ **Amnesia,** Herengracht 133 (☎638 3003), at the corner of Herengracht and Bergstraat. Slightly larger and significantly more elegant than other coffee shops in the Canal Ring. Boasts a plush red interior and canal-side outdoor seating. Enjoy its wide selection of see map p. 338 drinks, shakes, or snacks. Buy 5 joints (€3-5 each) and get 1 free. For an extra treat, try the Amnesia Haze (€11 per g), a 2004 Cannabis Cup winner. Open daily 9:30am-1am.

☒ **Grey Area,** Oude Leliestraat 2 (☎420 4301; www.greyarea.nl). From Dam Square, follow Raadhuisstraat to Singel; turn right and then left on Oude Leliestraat. Grey Area is the only coffee shop in Amsterdam owned by an American, though his wares are popular with Amsterdammers and Americans alike. The walls are plastered with bumper stickers and pins as well as photos of musicians such as Willie Nelson and Phish who choose to smoke this regular Cannabis Cup award winner's bud when they're in town. Borrow a glass bong to smoke, or hit one of Amsterdam's cheapest pure marijuana joints (€3.50). Juice (€1.50) is also available. Open Tu-Su noon-8pm.

■ **Siberië,** Brouwersgracht 11 (☎623 5909; www.siberie.nl), just past the intersection at Singel. Check out the wacky spiral lamps hanging from the ceiling at this spacious coffee shop. In addition to soft drugs, Siberië features an extensive menu of snacks, including *tostis,* different types of yogurt (€2-2.50), and an assortment of teas. Pre-rolled joints (€4) are especially popular. For something with an extra kick, experienced smokers should try the White Widow Mighty Whitey (€6.50 per g). Live DJ F-Sa 4-9pm. Open M-F 11am-11pm, Sa-Su 11am-midnight.

Extreme Amsterdam, Huidenstraat 13 (☎773 5698; www.coffeeshopXtreme.com), between Herengracht and Keizersgracht. This basement shop boasts a knowledgeable staff and a wide selection. Friendly employees help you navigate the 8 types of grass of various strengths (€4-10 per g). Hash also available. Comfortable couch to relax on while enjoying your joint. Free Internet for up to 30min.—depending on how busy it is. Open M-Th 10am-midnight, F-Sa 10am-1am, Su 11am-midnight.

Tops, Prinsengracht 480 (☎638 4108). A comfortable canal-side coffee shop with a low-key vibe. Cruise the web at one of Tops's 8 Internet terminals available for customers (€1.60 per 20min.) or climb one of the counter's 20 stools to purchase weed. Weed sold in €6, €12, or €24 bags, which get you up to 4.7g of bud. No pre-rolled joints. Open M-Th and Su 11am-1am, F-Sa 11am-3am.

Magic, Herengracht 287 (☎623 0260). This dark, unassuming basement shop is family-owned and operated. Chill at the small counter or relax on one of the cushy benches lining the walls. Choose from 9 types of grass (€6-7 per g) and 9 types of hash (€4-9). Try the house special, 0.4g of White Magic grass mixed with Gold Moroccan (€3)—it comes with a carrying case. Free Internet for customers. Open daily 11am-1am.

Rockland, Raadhuisstraat 8 (☎624 8890; www.rockland.nl). With a neon sign and a large mural of Bob Marley on its facade, this Rastafarian-themed shop is hard to miss. Jamaican marijuana €14 per 2.2g. Nepalese hashish €14 per 2g. In nice weather, enjoy the outdoor seating area. Internet €1 per 15min. Open M-Th and Su 11am-midnight, F-Sa 11am-1am.

 DRUG DICTION. A Dutch slang term for marijuana is "blow," not to be confused with the American-English slang use of the same word to denote cocaine, a hard drug neither tolerated nor legal in the Netherlands.

CENTRAL CANAL RING

The smoking scene here is eclectic and upscale, catering mainly to tourists. Don't hesitate to ask for assistance if you need help deciphering the menu.

COFFEE SHOPS

■ **The Dolphins,** Kerkstraat 39 (☎625 9162). Smoke with the fishes at this underwater-themed coffee shop. Watch huge tropical fishes swim in tanks encrusted into the coral-like walls as you take advantage of the shop's free vaporizers and Wi-Fi. Pre-rolled joints €7. Try the White Dolphin reefer (€10 per g; pure joint €5.50) for an uplifting high. Tea (€5) and space muffins (€7) are popular among visitors. Open M-Th and Su 10am-1am, F-Sa 10am-3am.

■ **Stix,** Utrechtsestraat 21 (www.stix.nl), near Herengracht. Regulars and tourists smoke in style at this small coffee shop with clean wooden tables and park bench-like seating. Large picture windows and high ceilings make for a light, airy feel. The staff at Stix is always happy to let you inspect samples of its high-quality, all-organic smokeables, including hash allegedly favored by Buddhist monks in Nepal. Peruse the illuminated menu for Stix's homemade Gunpowder (pure THC; €12.50 per g), which burns smoothly to produce an uplifting, seriously visual high. Watch out, though—it's not named for nothing. Pre-rolled joints from €3.50. Open daily 11am-1am.

Arabica, Amstelstraat 45. Arabica provides good weed on a budget for locals and tourists alike. Catch the news on the flat-screen TV in back or sink into the loveseats arranged around the large front window to people-watch. Ask the friendly owner for help. Thai joints €2. Arabica €6 per g. Open daily 9am-1am.

The Noon, Zieseniskade 22 (☎422 3669; www.thenoon.net). From Leidseplein, head east on Kleine-Gartmanplantsoen, cross to the south side of Lijnbaansgracht, and continue for about a block. Offers a refuge for a serious crowd looking to escape from the tourist crush of Leidseplein. A Buddha mural, embroidered velvet pillows, and wooden statues of writhing dragons on the bar give the Noon a distinctly Asian flavor. Weed and hash range from standard to extremely powerful; the staff recommends the Blueberry bud (€7 per g; €23 per 5g) and the Honey hash (€10 per g). The Noon Blueberry Ice hash (€27 per g) also comes recommended for an intense smoke. Intense pot-only blueberry joints €7. Open daily 9am-1am.

Coffeeshop Little, Vijzelstraat 47 (☎420 1386). Tram #16, 24, or 25 to Weteringcircuit and backtrack ½ block; it's downstairs on the right. Though certainly not cavernous, plush red couches and a chess table lend a homey appeal to this mellow coffee shop. Hash and weed start at €6-7 per g. Joints €3. Space cakes €3.50. Open M-Th and Su 8am-midnight, F-Sa 8am-1am.

Global Chillage, Kerkstraat 51 (☎777 9977; www.globalchillage.org), between Leidsestraat and Nieuwe Spiegelstraat. Take tram #1, 2, or 5 to Prinsengracht, then walk back along the tram line for 1 block. From there, take a right onto Kerkstraat. Lose yourself in the rhythms of ambient trance music as you partake in Chillage's ample array of puffables. A mural of devious elves, dim lighting, bright purple-and-red booths, and an artificial tree with butterfly-adorned leaves give visitors the sense that they are entering a fantasy world. Joints €4. Space muffins €3.50. Standard array of pot and hash available in €6 and €12 bags, which buys 0.8-1.1g and 1.7-2.2g of goods, respectively. Joints with 0.5g of hash €4. Open daily 10am-midnight.

SMART SHOPS

■ **Conscious Dreams,** Kerkstraat 119 (☎626 6907; www.consciousdreams.nl). Choose from a variety of mushrooms, herbs, vitamins, "dream extracts," and herbal ecstasies at this purveyor of mind- and body-altering substances. Staff is willing to guide your experience; don't hesitate to ask for help before, after, or—if you can form words—during consumption. Mushrooms €12-15. Herbal ecstasy €12 for 2 servings. Affiliated with Conscious Dreams Kokopelli (p. 202). Open daily 11am-10pm. AmEx/MC/V for purchases over €25.

Seeds of Passion, Utrechtsestraat 26 (☎625 1100; www.seedsofpassion.nl). The friendly staff at this upscale store not only sells cannabis seeds from all over the world (€12.50-125 for 10 seeds) but also develops its own seeds that are easier to grow. A huge, impressive specialty selection featuring 100% female seeds (first invented here) makes this the place to go if you're in the market; just keep it in the country, as always. Open M-Sa 11am-6pm. AmEx/MC/V.

LEIDSEPLEIN

With all the hotels, restaurants, bars, and clubs in tiny Leidseplein, you'd think that there would be no room for coffee shops. How wrong you would be: the square lures in even more tourists with its smoking scene. Below are the choicest shops in the area in case you crave a pre-club joint.

see map p. 337

COFFEE SHOPS

🗺 **The Rookies,** Korte Leidsedwarsstraat 145-147 (☎ 639 0978; www.rookies.nl). Part of the restaurant, hotel, and bar combo across the street, this comfortable coffee shop attracts lots of young travelers. Smoke at the counter or while playing a round of pool, at least until new anti-smoking laws force you into a designated room (see **Up in Smoke?,** p. 238). Try their special grass, The Rookies (€15 per 2.4g). Selection of bongs and pipes available for free use. Open daily 10am-1am.

Get Down To It, Korte Leidsedwarsstraat 77. A basement coffee shop where the rock is hard and the soft drugs are strong. Mixed crowd of tourists, locals, and friendly staff. Internet (€1.30 per 30min.) and pool tables available. Hash and weed are sold in €12 and €24 bags; for an intense experience, try the "Dutch Power Hash," 97% pure THC (€12 per 0.8g). White Widow €24 per 3.8g. Open daily 10am-1am.

Crush, Marnixstraat 383 (☎ 420 4435). Crush attracts visitors with a chill, no-frills set-up. Enjoy weed in quiet or play loud pinball. Internet €2.50 per hr. Grass €3-7 per g. Hash €6-8 per g. Open daily 10am-1am.

SMART SHOP

Tatanka, Korte Leidsedwarsstraat 151A (☎ 771 6916). Range of goods includes 'shrooms (Mexican and Thai €12; The Philosopher €15), smart drugs, grow-your-own kits, and hats and T-shirts. A selection of intricate, handmade glass pipes (€18) and glass bongs (€20). Internet €3 per hr. Buy 4 packs of mushrooms, get 1 free. Open daily 10am-10pm.

REMBRANDTPLEIN

Like the other busy squares in Amsterdam, Rembrandtplein has a large collection of coffee shops, and, as in other heavily touristed spots, the quality of these shops varies widely. For the most part, the best spots are removed from the center of the action, away from the statue and out along Reguliersdwarsstraat and on the streets jutting off the Amstel. Most are mainly for smoking and lack many of the accoutrements found, for example, near the Red Light District.

see map p. 336

The Other Side, Reguliersdwarsstraat 6 (☎ 421 1014; www.theotherside.nl). Tram #1, 2, or 5 to Koningsplein. Perhaps Amsterdam's only ■**gay** coffee shop. Colorful, clean, and bright decor and a personable staff make The Other Side feel homey. Very popular with tourists. The music ranges from relaxed to bright and loud pop. Bags of weed are sold in increments of €10, €20, and €35 for everything from 1.5g-13.59g. Pure joints €4.75. Space cakes €5. Open daily 11am-1am.

Free I, Reguliersdwarsstraat 70 (☎ 622 7727). Tram #1, 2, or 5 to Koningsplein. A beach mural atop bamboo walls and calm, laid-back music add nicely to this casual, lazy atmosphere. The shop prides itself on having small quantities of the best-quality smokes. The knowledgeable staff can help with recommendations for any smoker. Afghan hash €7 per g. The ICE hash (€27.50 per g) is especially potent. Joints €3.50. Muffins €5. Open daily 10am-1am.

The Bush Doctor, Thorbeckeplein 28. A 2-time Cannabis Cup winner, this 2-story shop is the place to go for an intense smoke: the shop has one of the largest selections of Ice-o-Lator hash in the city. 6 different varieties of this extra-strong hash (€25) are available. Visit their other location, at Amstel 36, a smaller shop with a more tropical feel. Both shops open daily 9am-1am.

The Saint, Regulierssteeg 1, on an alley off Reguliersbreestraat. Though this small, dark shop isn't the most inviting, its smoothies and shakes ensure a steady stream of both regulars and tourists throughout the day. A ceiling littered with posters and notes and drawings from customers overlook a handful of tables. Bar serves fresh fruit juice and an extensive collection of hash fruit shakes and juices (€7). Hash coffee, tea, and hot chocolate €5. Cannabis sold in 1.4-3g bags (€13). Joints €4-6. Open daily 7am-1am.

JORDAAN

If you want to avoid crowds and loud music, Jordaan coffee shops are the place to toke up. Mirroring the neighborhood's relaxed air, these establishments serve their hash without a side of attitude and are familiar with and friendly to tourists.

see map p. 338

■ **Paradox,** 1e Bloemdwarsstraat 2 (☎623 5639; www.paradoxam-sterdam.demon.nl). This bright, nonchalant coffee shop jives with the neighborhood's relaxed vibe—it has more of a gallery or cafe feel than a typical coffee shop does. Weed from €3.80 per g, hash from €6.50 per g. Bongs for borrowing. Beginning smokers or those looking to unwind can try a "bluff," a light joint (€2). More than just munchies: grab a delicious veggie burger for just €4.50, but be aware: the kitchen closes daily at 3pm. *Tostis* (€1.80) available until 5pm. Freshly squeezed juices and tasty milk shakes €2.30-3.90. Open daily 10am-8pm.

■ **La Tertulia,** Prinsengracht 312 (www.coffeeshopamsterdam.com). La Tertulia's kitsch is of a particularly endearing nature: behind the muraled facade, plants and crystals crowd the 2-story space, the kindly staff sells as much tea as it does marijuana, and friendly patrons get stoned and play board games. The airy terrace looks out over the canal, and the crystals are for sale. Pot brownies €4.50. Pre-rolled joints €3. Bubble gum weed (€5 for 0.6g) is popular. Open Tu-Sa 11am-7pm.

Coffeeshop Sanementereng, 2e Laurierdwarsstraat 44 (☎625 2041). Tucked onto a side street, Sanementereng's leaning storefront is supported by massive tree trunks. Inside, you may want to poke around the 3 floors and 25 years of stuff that the owners of Sanementereng have collected; they've got jewelry, old postcards, Indonesian puppets, cups, barrettes, and an old thermos. Coffee €1.50. Apple pie €2. Pre-rolled joints €3. Popular African Grass €3.50 per g. Haze Highrise €7 per g. Open daily 1pm-1am.

Biba, Hazenstraat 15. Inexpensive weed at this tiny smoke shop, which prides itself on being "the smallest gallery in Amsterdam"—there's room enough for 1 painting in the front of the store! Saddle up to the counter for a quick puff, but don't bring a huge group, since there's only room for 4 or 5 patrons. Free art postcards. Joints €3. White Widow €10 for 1.4g. Open daily 10am-10pm.

Spirit Coffeeshop, Westerstraat 121 (☎625 4650). Named after the American comic-strip character The Spirit (created by Will Eisner), this coffee shop will keep the discriminating stoner busy with pool, tons of arcade games, a jukebox, and foosball (all €0.50). All beverages €1.50-3. Hash from €2.50 per g, weed from €6; varieties from Morocco, Afghanistan, and Jamaica sold in 1g or 5g bags. Pre-rolled joints €2.50-4.55. Open daily 1pm-1am.

The Rokery, Elandsgracht 53 (www.rokerij.net/coffeeshop/elandsgracht/index.html). 4th in a chain of 4 Amsterdam coffee shops, this Rokery's Indian temple theme features relaxing music, high ceilings, and pillowed, mosaic-inlaid, curving benches that facilitate conversations with other smokers. Lots of Buddha statues, too. Large selection of popular herbal teas (€1.80), as well as the chain's Dutch herbs, which can be mixed with weed for a less powerful joint without tobacco. Joints €4.50-5.50. Hash from €6.50 per g, weed from €7.50. Open daily 9am-1am.

African Black Star Coffeeshop, Rozengracht 1A (☎626 9469; www.coffeeshopafrican-blackstar.nl). 2 levels of Bob Marley posters and a red, yellow, and green motif (in reference to the Ghanaian flag). Reggae soundtrack gives it an Afro-Rasta vibe. Bags of African grass for €10 (1.5-3g, depending on the type). Internet access €1 per 20min. Open M-Th and Su 11am-midnight, F-Sa 11am-1am.

ENTERTAINMENT

TIP

SMOKE SCREEN. Amsterdam is set to institute a smoking ban on July 1, 2008, which will also affect coffee shops and their marijuana residue. While this doesn't figure to doom drug tourism, it's a good idea to ask coffee-shop employees where you can smoke after that date has passed. For more information, see **Up in Smoke?,** p. 238.

WESTERPARK AND OUD-WEST

The coffee shops here are fewer and farther between than in the center, but the extended geography also supplies them with a calmer, more local feel. A few quality shops cluster around Jan Pieter Heijestraat, north of Vondelpark.

see map p. 343

■ **Kashmir Lounge,** Jan Pieter Heijestraat 85-87 (☎683 2268). Tram #7 or 17 to Jan Pieter Heijestraat. From the dark Indian-themed interior to the intricate ornamentation on every wall to the large pillow corner, this is the perfect place to sit back and toke up. It's a far way to go if you're staying in the Centrum, but if you want something a little quieter and more laid-back—without sacrificing atmosphere or good prices—make the trip. DJ spins all hours. Hash €3.10-9.10 per g. Marijuana €5.50-18 per g. Pre-rolled joints €2.50. Open M-Sa 10am-1am, Su 11am-1am.

De Supermarkt, Frederik Hendrikstraat 69 (☎486 2497; www.desupermarkt.net). Like its sister coffee shop Siberië (p. 206), De Supermarkt aims more for fresh and artsy than anything else. The work of Amsterdam artists adorns the walls, the cafe has regular DJ events, and the local clientele seems chill and laid-back. Friendly employees walk you through selections of weed and hash (from €4) on display next to the menu. Open M-F 10am-11pm, Sa-Su 10am-midnight.

MUSEUMPLEIN AND VONDELPARK

tWEEDy, Vondelstraat 104 (☎618 0344), just outside the Film-museum entrance to the Vondelpark. Low-key coffee shop with a pool table. Known for its friendly, knowledgeable staff. Great place to grab a joint for a munchies picnic in Vondelpark. NYC Diesel (€11 per g) and Haze (€8.50 per g) are popular varieties of weed, but there are plenty of cheaper options as well. Free Internet. Open daily 11am-11pm.

see map p. 342

DE PIJP

Coffee shops in this area range from middling to unique— *Let's Go* has uncovered the jewels of local smokeries. For the less discriminating smoker, other shops can be found along **Gerard Doustraat.**

see map p. 333

■ **Yo Yo,** 2e Jan van der Heijdenstraat 79 (☎664 7173). Tram #3, 4, or 20 to Van Woustraat/Ceintuurbaan. Yo Yo was founded more than 20 years ago as a feminist coffee shop and has since become one of the most relaxed and welcoming (co-ed) shops in the city. One of the few coffee shops where neighborhood non-smokers can relax, Yo Yo has ample terrace seating and a smoke-free room, perfect for a cup of coffee or a slice of homemade apple pie (€1.75). If you're looking for someplace hip but sublimely laid-back, the ambience here can't be beat. *Tostis,* soup, and (normal) brownies also served. All weed is organic and sold in bags for €5 or €10, with a monthly €3.50 special. Joints €2.50. Open M-Sa noon-7pm.

Katsu, 1e Van Der Helststraat 70. A friendly shop off busy Van Der Helststraat. Specializes in sativa, a marijuana that supposedly provides a more awake, happier high. Northern Night Special hash €5 per 0.6g, pure joints €3. Bud €20 per 2.40-5g. Vaporizers available for use. Open M-Th 11am-11pm, F-Sa 11am-midnight, Su noon-11pm.

Coffeeshop Carmona, 2e Jan van der Heijdenstraat 43. Tram #3, 4, or 20 to Van Woustraat/Ceintuurbaan. This small coffee shop gets its fair share of locals and tourists, but it's nowhere near as crowded or overpriced as shops closer to the center. Comfy couches and a row of 6 computers (Internet €1 per 30min.) might keep you there longer than planned. Hawaiian Haze €8 per g; weed €4-7.50 per g. King hash €9 per g; hash €4-8 per g. Joints €2.50. Drinks €1.50-2.50. ID required. Open daily 10am-1am.

JODENBUURT AND PLANTAGE

With its quieter atmosphere, the Jodenbuurt and Plantage host some great low-key coffee shops. Bluebird, close to the Rembrandt House, is a consistent favorite. If you're in the mood for a bit of a walk, Het Ballonnetje, across from the University of Amsterdam, is a good place to escape from all the tourists.

see map p. 344

■ **Bluebird,** Sint Antoniesbreestraat 71 (☎622 52 32, www.coffeeshopbluebird.nl). 2 stories of azure chill space include a big over-stuffed leather couch for a communal vibe as well as quieter alcoves for a thoughtful smoke. At this companionable spot, the vast menu is presented in 2 thick scrapbooks that include real samples of each variety of hash and marijuana for inspection. Sample the high-quality house blend (1.4g for €12.50) or try the Ice-o-Lator hash (0.4g for €12.50). Space cakes €5 and hash-laced chocolate bonbons €3. A volcano vaporizer and a variety of bongs are available for use. Tasty, fresh juices and smoothies come in a rainbow of fruit flavors (€2-5). Open daily 9:30am-1am.

Green House, Waterlooplein 345 (☎622 5499). Green House took top honors at the 2006 Cannabis Cup; this location, known as "Namaste," is the smallest and quietest of three Green House shops in the city. Relax on the large, winding leather couch, which serves as a good place to meet new people, and take in the trippy murals, which may provide some fodder for conversation. Popular Hawaiian Snow €10 per g. Space cake €7. Collection of seeds €50. Open M-Th and Su 10am-midnight, F-Sa 10am-1am.

Het Ballonnetje, Roetersstraat 12 (☎622 8027). Across the street from the University of Amsterdam. With 35 kinds of tea (€1.40), soup, cookies, and plenty of other home-made goodies, this coffee shop makes an effort to be a comfortable neighborhood shop. Terrariums, houseplants, and a healthy mix of students and locals make the shop a welcome respite from the more commercial coffee shops in the city. The Pac-Man game upstairs can offer a lot of fun post-smoke. Space muffin €5. 9 types of hash and weed. Popular Super Skunk €6 per g. Hash €3-9 per g. Open daily 10am-midnight.

Hortus De Overkant, Nieuwe Herengracht 71 (☎620 6577). It's all business at this no-frills neighborhood shop with an expansive selection. You can order from the long menu and take it to go (nearby Wertheim Park is a popular option), since there's no seating at Hortus, or stand and chat with the locals. Hash runs €3.50-5.20 per g, weed €2-8 per g. Every 6 days, a different kind of weed is 10% off, and there is always a rotating 20% discount on 1 type of hash and 1 type of weed. Open daily 10am-midnight.

Reefer, Sint Antoniesbreestraat 77 (☎623 3615), right on the corner facing the canal. Toke up in front of the massive sculpted tree and the dancing cherubs lining the walls of this bare but sunny shop or try a game of foosball in the small upstairs area. Set prices of €11.50 for hash and weed (sizes and types vary). Space brownies and muffins €5. Open M-Th 11am-11pm, F-Sa 10am-midnight.

SHOPPING

Amsterdam is brimming with specialized boutiques offering all sorts of quirky but well-designed goods. **De Negen Straatjes** (the Nine Streets) are one of the Canal Ring West's biggest claims to fame. These little passageways that cross the three central canals between Raadhuisstraat and Leidsegracht are strewn with fun designs. Together, Reestraat, Hartenstraat, Gasthuismolensteeg, Berenstraat, Wolvenstraat, Oude Spiegelstraat, Runstraat, Huidenstraat, and Wijde Heisteeg form a rectangle containing Amsterdam's trendiest shopping and cafe culture.

Passages in the Jordaan possess similarly charming shops with a vintage vibe. Other roads ripe with goodies include Utrechtsestraat, south of Rembrandtplein; Nieuwe Hoogstraat, in the Oude Zijd; and Haarlemmerstraat, in the Scheepvaartbuurt. Kalverstraat and Nieuwendijk are also two popular pedestrian-packed commercial strips near Dam Sq. The cheapest goods in the city can be found in shops in De Pijp, which brims with bargain finds from all over the world. By contrast, the most prestigious (and expensive) shops are found on **Pieter Corneliszoon Hooftstraat** in Museumplein, which teems with big-name international clothing designers. In comparison to the riot of color that the city's ethnic and vintage shops provide, however, this ritzy area seems rather banal.

Despite the number of quality goods found in specialized boutiques and commercial European chains, Amsterdam's bustling market scene is by far the best option for a pleasant and successful day of bargain hunting. Markets hawking everything from organic produce to random detritus operate daily in the city, including the tulip and bulb market at Bloemenmarkt and the Dappermarkt, which has been claimed by the city's North African and Middle Eastern communities. The true gem of Amsterdam's abundant markets is in De Pijp, at the Albert Cuypmarkt, which merits exploration for its unparalleled abundance of inexpensive treasures.

> **TIP** **DOUBLE DUTCH.** Learn the lingo: in Dutch, *winkel* means shop, and *warenhuis* means department store.

BY TYPE

ANTIQUES
 Nic Nic (216) — CRW

BOOKS
A la Carte (218) — CCR
American Book Center (215) — NZ
Architectura and Natura (217) — CRW
Athenaeum Boekhandel (215) — NZ
The Book Exchange (214) — OZ
English Bookshop (218) — JD
Geografische Boekhandel Pied a Terre (219) — WO
Waterstone's (218) — CCR

CLOTHING AND JEWELRY
Beadies (217) — CRW
Betsy Palmer Shoes (220) — DP
Camilla Matheis (216) — SVB
Episode (220) — JP

De Hoed Van Tijn (214) — OZ
Laundry Industry (215) — NZ
Megazino (219) — JD
Puck (220) — JP
Sjerpentine (220) — DP
Your Cup of T (219) — JD
Zara (217) — CRW

DEPARTMENT STORES
De Bijenkorf (215) — NZ
HEMA (215) — NZ

GIFTS
Brilmuseum (217) — CRW
Cine Qua Non (216) — CRW
Cortina Paper (217) — CRW
De Witte Tanden Winkel (217) — CRW
FA.Kramer/Pontifex (218) — CCR

Hera Kaarsen (219)	WO	Oudemanhuispoort (214)	OZ
De Kinderfeestwinkel (220)	DP	Spui (216)	NZ
La Savonnerie (217)	CRW	Ten Katemarkt (219)	WO
ROB (215)	RLD	Waterlooplein (220)	JP
A Space Oddity (219)	JD	Westermarkt (219)	JD
Witbaard Feestartikelen (220)	DP	**MUSIC**	
HOME GOODS AND FURNITURE		Back Beat Records (219)	JD
De Emaillekeizer (220)	DP	Brutus (218)	CCR
Gallerie Casbah (220)	DP	▧ Concerto (218)	CCR
Kitsch Kitchen (219)	JD	Velvet Music (219)	JD
▧ Maranon Hangmatten (218)	CCR	**SMOKING ACCESSORIES**	
The Purple Onion (216)	SVB	The Old Man (215)	NZ
INTERNATIONAL STORES		**TOYS**	
't Japanse Winkeltje (216)	NZ	De Beestenwinkel (220)	JP
Tibet Winkel (216)	NZ	Juggle Store (215)	OZ
Toko Dun Yong (214)	OZ	**VINTAGE CLOTHING**	
MARKETS		Laura Dols (217)	CRW
▧ Albert Cuypmarkt (219)	DP	Ree-member (217)	CRW
Bloemenmarkt (215)	NZ	Wini (216)	SVB
Dappermarkt (220)	JP	Petticoat (218)	JD
Lindengracht (219)	JD	Time Machine (218)	CCR
▧ Nieuwmarkt (214)	OZ	Zipper (218)	CRW
▧ Noordermarkt (218)	JD		

CRW Canal Ring West **CCR** Central Canal Ring **DP** De Pijp **JP** Jodenbuurt and Plantage **JD** Jordaan **LP** Leidseplein **MV** Museumplein and Vondelpark **NZ** Nieuwe Zijd **OZ** Oude Zijd **RLD** Red Light District **RP** Rembrandtplein **SVB** Scheepvaartbuurt **WO** Westerpark and Oud-West

BY NEIGHBORHOOD

OUDE ZIJD

▧ **Nieuwmarkt** hosts a *boerenmarkt* (organic food market) Sa 10am-3pm, as well as an antiques market May-Sept. Su 9am-4pm.

▧ **De Hoed Van Tijn,** Nieuwe Hoogstraat 15 (☎623 2759). Fedoras, berets, pork pie hats, and every other style of new and old head ornaments are here and range €20-200. Prices are steep, but, when hunting for a stylish chapeau, there's no better place to look. Some handmade in the store. Open M noon-6pm, Tu-F 11am-6pm, Sa 11am-5pm. AmEx/MC/V.

see map p. 340

The Book Exchange, Kloveniersburgwal 58 (☎626 6266), between the Oude Zijd and the Jodenbuurt. Deals in used texts and has a friendly, tasteful, knowledgeable staff. Frightfully good selection of used English-language books, from basic fiction and nonfiction to the more esoteric, all reasonably priced. Also buys used paperbacks; true to its name, the Exchange offers a more favorable deal if you're willing to trade. Open M-Sa 10am-6pm; Su noon-5pm.

Oudemanhuispoort, between Oudezijds Achterburgwal and Kloveniersburgwal. Sells crates of both new and antiquated books, from steamy bodice-rippers to steamed vegetable cookbooks. Books €1-30; most €1. Open M-Sa 11am-6pm.

Toko Dun Yong, Stormsteeg 9 (☎622 1763; www.dunyong.com), on the corner of Geldersekade. 2nd location at Zeedijk 83. A world of Chinese cultural kitsch and cooking goods. Toko's 5 floors burst with foodstuffs, paper fans, decorative lamps, mini ceramic Buddhas, and kitchenware. Open M-Sa 9am-6pm, Su noon-6pm. MC.

Juggle Store, Staalstraat 3 (☎420 1980; www.juggle-store.com). The store for absolutely all of your juggling needs. The expert staff has selected the best products on the market, and all are avid experts on the juggling world. A free split-second juggling lesson is available on request. Open Tu-Sa 12:30pm-5pm.

RED LIGHT DISTRICT

ROB, Warmoesstraat 71 (☎625 4686; www.rob.nl). Disturbingly awe-inspiring selection of rubber toys, leather pants, and fetish-inspiring masks and restraints that make this brazen boutique fun for the whole BDSM family. Men's clothing (jeans, chaps, and vests) also available. Open M-Sa 11am-7pm, Su 1-6pm.

see map p. 340

NIEUWE ZIJD

American Book Center, Spui 12 (☎625 5537; www.abc.nl). A large and well-designed, independently owned English-language book store with a great selection in a well-lit space. 10% discount for students and teachers. Open M-W and F-Sa 10am-8pm, Th 10am-9pm, Su 11am-6:30pm.

see map p. 340

Athenaeum Boekhandel, Spui 14-16 (☎622 6248; www.athenaeum.nl), at the bottom of the Nieuwe Zijd in the Spui. Stocks obscure literary treasures, cultural criticism, and philosophy as well as beautiful coffee-table art books. Most titles in English. Also maintains a newsstand with a very extensive selection of American and British magazines. Open M 11am-6pm, Tu-W and F-Sa 9:30am-6pm, Th 9:30am-9pm, Su noon-5:30pm. AmEx/MC/V.

Bloemenmarkt, on the Singel canal by Muntplein. Dig through rows of flower bulbs and bags of seeds at this floating market. If you want to take the bulbs back home, check customs regulations for your home country; some require a certificate from the seller. Your vendor will know and will be able to help. Open daily 9am-5pm.

Laundry Industry, Spui 1 (☎420 2554; www.laundryindustry.com). The Dutch are proud to call this respected international brand their own. The debonair and crisp, clean-cut suits, semi-casual wear, and lingerie fly off the shelves for middle- to high-range prices. Open daily 11am-6:30pm. AmEx/MC/V.

De Bijenkorf, Dam 1 (☎621 8080). Situated in the heart of Dam Sq., Amsterdam's best-known department store sells books, clothes, and home goods—standard (but classy) department store stock. Open M 11am-7pm, Tu-W 9:30am-7pm, Th-F 9:30am-9pm, Sa 9:30am-7pm, Su noon-6pm.

Magna Plaza, Nieuwezijds Voorburgwal 182 (☎626 9199). A popular shopping mall with high-end fashion boutiques and shops, like Laundry Industry, Mango, the Body Shop, and Toni & Guy. Open M-W and F-Su 11am-7pm, Th 11am-9pm.

The Old Man, Damstraat 16 (☎627 0043). A massive selection near Dam Sq., right in the middle of it all. Glass bongs, wooden pipes, scales, hookahs, and more. Don't miss the Delftware bong shaped like a clog and printed with a windmill, a combination of nearly every Dutch cliche in existence (€40). Upstairs collection of swords and knives for sale. Open daily July-Aug. 10am-9pm; Sept.-June 10am-6pm. AmEx/MC/V.

HEMA, Nieuwendijk 174 (☎638 9963). Compared to De Bijenkorf, HEMA is an affordable department store carrying many of the same items and more household goods. A good bet for just about anything you might need, from a bike seat to a thermos. Open M 10:30am-6:30pm, Tu-W and F-Sa 9:30am-6:30pm, Th 9:30am-9pm, Su noon-6pm.

Tibet Winkel, Spuistraat 185A (☎420 5438; www.tibetwinkel.nl). All proceeds from goods sold in this store (Tibetan music, books, incense, and other cultural items) help to fund the Tibet Support Group. Open M 1-6pm, Tu-Sa 10am-6pm, Su 1-5pm. MC/V.

't Japanse Winkeltje, Nieuwezijds Voorburgwal 177 (☎627 9523; www.japansewinkeltje.nl). Porcelain, kimonos, art, origami, books, and specialty foods from the Eastern island. Open M and Su 1-6pm, Tu-Sa 9:30am-6pm. AmEx/MC/V.

Spui, a market right in the Spui. On Su, local and international artists present their oils, etchings, sculptures, and jewelry here, turning the bustling square into an out-door modern gallery. Open Mar.-Oct. 10am-3pm. On F, the area transforms yet again into a pricey book market that occasionally yields rare editions and 17th-century Dutch romances. Open 10am-6pm.

HELLO, GOODBYE. When entering and leaving a shop, make eye contact with the owner and say hello or goodbye (*dag* will work for both). It's the friendly local custom!

SCHEEPVAARTBUURT

The Purple Onion, Haarlemmerdijk 139 (☎427 3750). Step into this incense-filled shop for a world of eclectic goods imported from India. The owners, a Dutch anthropologist and an Indian scientist, select items made of natural materials, such as wood sculptures and handmade bedspreads. Open Tu-F 11:30am-6pm, Sa 11:30am-5pm. MC/V.

see map p. 338

Wini, Haarlemmerstraat 29 (☎427 9393). Young hipsters shop here for their cool, stylish clothing. Wini also offers a great selection of bags and shoes for both men and women. Open M-W and Sa 10:30am-6pm, Th 10:30am-7pm. V.

Camilla Matheis, Haarlemmerdijk 146 (☎420 4203; www.camillamatheis.nl). A small boutique full of adorable one-of-a-kind clothes and accessories made in Amsterdam and Berlin. Also a small selection of jewelry made by the shop's owner. Open Tu-Sa noon-6pm, Su 10am-6pm. Cash only.

ONE MAN'S GARBAGE FOR POCKET CHANGE. Queen's Day (Apr. 30) is famous for a lot of things, but one of the stranger ones is garage sales. People clean out all their old stuff and sell it on their stoops for pocket change. Head to some of the ritzier neighborhoods, where the "old stuff" people don't want anymore might be a pair of Fendi sunglasses.

CANAL RING WEST

Nic Nic, Gasthuismolensteeg 5 (☎622 8523). Nearly everyone who passes by the exceptionally cluttered window of Nic Nic has to go inside and take a peek—the offerings in this antiques and curiosities shop are simply too unusual to pass up. Everything from Art Deco furniture to 1950s dishware and dolls are on sale for reasonable prices. Take the time to dig through the intimidating piles, and you're sure to surface with an incredible find. Open M-F noon-6pm, Sa 11am-5pm. AmEx/MC/V.

see map p. 338

Cine Qua Non, Staalstraat 14 (☎625 5588). A must-see for film fanatics. Find vintage posters, books, and related ephemera from movies both classic and camp at this small shop devoted to by-products of the film industry. Some DVDs of film classics. Open Tu-Sa 1-6pm. AmEx/MC/V.

Zara, Kalverstraat 67-69 (☎530 4050; www.zara.com). This Spanish establishment may be a chain, but a trip to the spacious store should slake any fashionista's thirst for up-to-the-moment style. Sporty, casual, and dress clothes, accompanied by trendy shoes and chic accessories at pleasantly cheap prices and of adequate quality. Open M and Su noon-6pm, Tu-W and F-Sa 10am-6pm, Th 10am-9pm. AmEx/MC/V.

De Witte Tanden Winkel, Runstraat 5 (☎623 3443). Dentists, you don't have to pinch yourselves; this isn't a dream. A remarkable little shop with toothbrushes sitting in the Ferris wheel in the window. The White Tooth Shop specializes in pampering your pearly whites with novelty brushes and paste from around the world. Open M 1-6pm, Tu-F 10am-6pm; Sa 10am-5pm. AmEx/MC/V.

Laura Dols, Wolvenstraat 6-7 (☎624 9066). 2 shops across the street from each other vend fanciful used men and women's clothing, including tutus and cowboy shirts. A more unusual selection than your average vintage clothing shop. Open July-Aug. daily 10am-6pm, Sept.-June M-W and F-Sa 11am-6pm, Th 11am-9pm, Su 2-6pm. V.

Brilmuseum, Gasthuismolensteeg 7 (☎421 2414; www.brilmuseumamsterdam.nl). 3 generations of spectacle specialists have run this combined eyewear museum (p. 170) and shop. Glasses here aren't secondhand, although many date from the 60s, 50s, or earlier. Retro, art, and antique frames €30-€150. Sunglasses from €9. Ring bell to enter. Open W-F 11:30am-5:30pm, Sa 11:30am-5pm.

Architectura and Natura, Leliegracht 22 (☎623 6186; www.architectura.nl). Can't read Dutch? It doesn't matter, because it's the pictures that make these coffee-table books extraordinary. Heavy and beautiful, the volumes here tend to be expensive. For the truly hopeless, some are in English. Upstairs is a selection of antique Dutch books, also on architecture. Open daily noon-6pm. AmEx/MC/V.

Cortina Paper, Reestraat 22 (☎623 6676). This store is full of elegant stationery, notebooks, and photo albums that make perfect gifts, especially when wrapped in the gorgeous selection of decorative wrapping paper. Pens and ink also available for sale. Open M-F and Su 11am-6pm, Sa 11am-5pm. AmEx/MC/V.

Ree-member, Reestraat 26W (☎622 1329). Well-chosen display of beautiful vintage clothes and 1960s standards like Lacoste polo shirts. Also sells shoes and bags. Good selections of coats, belts, and vests. Open daily 11am-6pm. AmEx/MC/V.

La Savonnerie, Prinsengracht 294 (☎428 1139; www.savonnerie.nl). Exquisite handmade soaps in over 80 colors and scents (€4-5). Cute letter-block soap cubes €1 each. Open M-Sa 10am-6pm. MC/V.

Beadies, Huidenstraat 6 (☎428 5161; www.beadies.com). Provides all the ingredients of a colorful trin-

ON THE MENU

STOP, DROP, AND ROLL

You don't have to be in the Netherlands for a long time to notice its presence: its own shelf at the supermarket, its prominence next to the cashier in the convenience store, its permanent position in the paws of Dutch *kinder*. It is none other than **Drop,** the sweet sensation of the Netherlands.

Drop (rhymes with "pope") is a type of licorice unique to the Netherlands. It bears very little resemblance to its American black and red licorice cousins, which are usually flavored with anise. Drop is infused with a variety of flavors, including honey, menthol, and salt, which renders its taste perhaps unappetizing to the untrained palate.

The candy is made from actual dried licorice roots, which are mixed with water to form syrup and poured into molds, creating "block-Drop." This root of all Drops is then processed through differing techniques to produce six distinct main flavors: plain licorice, honeyed licorice, licorice with a sugar coating, and three types of salty licorice (mild, medium, and double-salted).

The Dutch swear that Drop is not only delicious but also addictive. The dependency starts in childhood, encouraged by the candy's many fun shapes, such as trains and herring. Dutch tots melt the candy in water to make "Dropwater." Drop may not tempt your particular taste buds, but while you're in the Netherlands, it's worth giving the candy a try—at least once.

ket, but plenty of ready-made jewelry is laid out for sale. Bracelets and necklaces from €10 (depending on the cost of beads and clasps). Open M 1-6pm, Tu-W and F-Sa 10:30am-6pm, Th 10:30am-9pm. AmEx/MC/V.

Zipper, Huidenstraat 7 (☎623 7302). 2nd location at Nieuwe Hoogstraat 8 (☎627 0353), in the Jodenbuurt. A good selection of vintage jeans. Also stocks a sizable and well-organized array of youth-oriented, 1970s-esque clothing (Adidas, cut-out T-shirts, big belts) for hipsters to fill the gaps in their wardrobes. Open M noon-6pm, Tu-Sa 11am-6pm, Su 1-5pm. AmEx/MC/V.

CENTRAL CANAL RING

see map p. 336

■ **Concerto,** Utrechtsestraat 52-60 (☎623 5228). Around since 1955 and arguably the best music store in Amsterdam. Sells a broad selection of CDs from 5 adjoining houses: secondhand, dance, pop, jazz/world, and classical. Records downstairs. Good selection of DVDs, too. Listening station where they'll play anything. Across the street, **Get Records,** Utrechtsestraat 105, has the same owners. Open M-W and F-Sa 10am-6pm, Th 10am-9pm, Su noon-6pm. AmEx/MC/V.

■ **Maranon Hangmatten,** Singel 488-490 (☎420 7121; www.maranon.net), right off the flower market. The best place in the city for temporary refuge. Come in for a rest to "test" the colorful, comfortable hammocks hanging from the ceiling. Open M-F 9:30am-5:30pm, Sa 9am-6pm, Su 10am-5:30pm. AmEx/MC/V.

A la Carte, Utrechtsestraat 110-112 (☎625 0679; www.reisboekhandel-alacarte.nl). Tram #7 or 10 to Frederiksplein. A cozy travel bookstore with an impressive collection of maps from around the world, as well as travel books, travel guides, and travel-related gifts. Open M 1-6pm, Tu-F 10am-6pm, Sa 10am-5pm. AmEx/MC/V.

Time Machine, Nieuwe Hoogstraat 26 (☎625 3162). Sister shop of **The End** across the street. Transports you to an age of colorful high-tops and big belts. Good selection of used shoes as well as the usual assortment of track jackets and vintage T-shirts. Open M 1-6pm, Tu-Sa 10:30am-6pm. Cash only.

Brutus, Molsteeg 8 (☎420 6105). A small but focused shop, with lots of well-chosen rock, pop, and alternative CDs, LPs, and music magazines. Open M-W and F-Su 11am-7pm, Th 11am-9pm. Cash only.

FA.Kramer/Pontifex, Reestraat 18-20 (☎626 5274). A combo doll-repair shop and candle store. On one side, broken dolls sit waiting for reanimation; on the other, huge numbers of colorful and curiously scented candles line the walls. Open M-F 10am-6pm, Sa 10am-5pm. Cash only.

Waterstone's, Kalverstraat 152 (☎638 3821), right on the Spui. 4 floors of books and magazines. Open M 10am-6pm, Tu-W 9am-6:30pm, Th 9:30am-9pm, F 9:30am-6:30pm, Sa 10am-6:30pm.v

JORDAAN

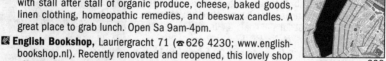

see map p. 338

■ **Noordermarkt** is probably the most upscale of the city's markets, with stall after stall of organic produce, cheese, baked goods, linen clothing, homeopathic remedies, and beeswax candles. A great place to grab lunch. Open Sa 9am-4pm.

■ **English Bookshop,** Lauriergracht 71 (☎626 4230; www.english-bookshop.nl). Recently renovated and reopened, this lovely shop offers coffee and tea to sip while you browse its strong selection of English-language books, from *The Cow Who Fell in the Canal* to a more mature collection of Dutch works translated into English. Open Tu-Su 11am-6pm.

Petticoat, Lindengracht 99 (☎623 3065). Quality secondhand clothing for men and women. Open M-F 11am-6pm, Sa 11am-5pm. Cash only.

Your Cup of T, Westerstraat 77 (www.yourcupoft.com), next to the Albert Heijn. Selection of T-shirts, sweatshirts, and hoodies printed and bedecked with robots, horses, roosters, and phrases like "I wish I was more people, then I could be a rock band." T-shirts from €10. Open M 10am-2pm, W-F 2pm-7pm, Sa noon-6pm. Cash only.

Lindengracht hosts a large market full of the usual wares—biking supplies, food, flowers, and funny clothes—and unusually friendly vendors. Open Sa 9am-4pm.

Westermarkt, on Westerstraat, offers a small selection of various clothes, fabrics, and watches. Open M 9am-1pm.

A Space Oddity, Prinsengracht 204 (☎427 4036; www.spaceoddity.nl). Store owner Jeff Bas has assembled an impressive assortment of sci-fi and comic-book paraphernalia, from old action figures to movie promos. The young at heart will find old and rare toy incarnations of their favorite movies and comic books, from *Star Wars* to *Spider-Man*. Prices start at €10 and skyrocket from there. Open M 1-5:45pm, Tu-F 11am-5:45pm, Sa 10:15am-5pm. MC/V.

Back Beat Records, Egelantiersstraat 19 (☎627 1657). Tightly packed collection of jazz, soul, funk, blues, and R&B. Prices are often steep, but some bargains can be found. New CDs as well as new and used vinyl. Open M-Sa 11am-6pm.

Velvet Music, Rozengracht 40 (☎422 8777; www.velvetmusic.nl). Big selection of new and used CDs, LPs, and DVDs. Occasional in-store performances; call for details. Open M and Su noon-6pm, Tu-W and F-Sa 10am-6pm, Th 10am-9pm. AmEx/MC/V for purchases €40 and up.

Kitsch Kitchen, Rozengracht 183 (☎622 8261; www.kitschkitchen.nl). A walk into the Jordaan will bring you to an explosion of color in the form of offbeat Tupperware, culinary tools, and other home furnishings. Open M-Sa 11am-7pm. AmEx/MC/V.

Megazino, Rozengracht 207-213 (☎330 1031; www.megazino.nl). A designer outlet with name brands (think Valentino, Diesel, and Burberry) for around 30-40% off. Receives new items (sometimes a season or 2 behind) every 2 weeks. Disorderly array of clothes, shoes, and accessories in the 1st fl. shop and the basement outlet. Open M and Su noon-7pm, Tu-W and F-Sa 10am-7pm, Th 10am-9pm. AmEx/MC/V.

WESTERPARK AND OUD-WEST

Hera Kaarsen, Overtoom 402 (☎616 2886). A staggering variety of colorful and curious homemade candles (from €14), shaped into everything from globes to fruits to figurines. Some are even shaped like normal candles. Lamps and glass vases round out Hera Kaarsen's luminous experience. Open Tu-F 11am-6pm, Sa 11am-5pm.

Geografische Boekhandel Pied a Terre, Overtoom 135-137 see map p. 343 (☎612 2314; www.jvw.nl). This excellent map store has all the maps you might need to get around the country by foot, by bike, or in a car, including the superb *Amsterdam Op de Fiets*. They also have lots of books on tourism in the Netherlands, living in Amsterdam, and travel in Europe. Open M 1-6pm, Tu-W and F 10am-6pm, Th 10am-9pm, Sa 10am-5pm. MC/V.

Ten Katemarkt, Ten Katestraat, off Kinkerstraat. This market resembles Albert Cuypmarkt (below) but is far less populated by tourists. Cheap clothes, bike supplies, fruits, veggies, and cheese. Open M-Sa 10am-4pm.

DE PIJP

■ **Albert Cuypmarkt,** the biggest outdoor market in Europe, has almost anything you can think of. Need nail polish, a bra, a fish, or a doghouse? Perhaps some pickles or a rug? Yes, Albert Cuypmarkt has all of those (and more). A great place to pick up

see map p. 333

fresh produce or cheap bags to carry home all those clogs you bought. Also a prime people-watching locale. Open M-Sa 9am-5pm.

Sjerpentine, 1e Van Der Helststraat 33 (☎664 1362). A welcome complement to the largely unwearable clothing selection at the Albert Cuypmarkt, Sjerpentine is bursting at the seams with colorful skirts, shirts, scarves and dresses, all at reasonable prices. Open M noon-6pm, Tu-Sa 10am-6pm. AmEx/MC/V for purchases over €30.

Betsy Palmer Shoes, Van Woustraat 46 (☎470 9795; www.betsypalmer.com) or Rokin 9-15 (☎422 1060) in the Nieuwe Zijd. Heels, sandals, and boots in funky yet elegant styles. Although these chic women's shoes are priced on the high side (€50-100), sales mean they're often 20-50% off. Open M noon-6pm, Tu-F 10am-6pm, Sa 10am-5pm.

De Emaillekeizer, 1e Sweelinckstraat 15 (☎664 1847; www.emaillekeizer.nl), 1½ blocks off Albert Cuypmarkt. Sells bright baskets, colorful woven deck chairs, and other knick-knacks from West Africa and China. Incredibly cheap but cool-looking dishware and teapots. If you're in town for a little while and realize you might need a plate, mug, or pot (no, not that kind), this is the place to go. Open M 1-6pm, Tu-Sa 11am-6pm.

Witbaard Feestartikelen, Ferdinand Bolstraat 22 (☎662 6144). Tram #16, 24, or 25 to Stadhouderskade. A 107-year-old costume shop and party store with 2 floors of everything you might need—should you ever need a gorilla suit or Silly String. Open M 1-6pm, Tu-F 10am-6pm, Sa 10am-5pm. Cash only.

De Kinderfeestwinkel, 1e Van Der Helststraat 15 (☎672 2215). The store to hit when you're planning a child's birthday party. A fantastical shop packed with all sorts of playful, glittery goodies, invitations, toys, party decorations, and children's costumes, all arranged by color. Open M 1-6pm, Tu-Sa 10am-6pm.

Gallerie Casbah, 1e Van Der Helststraat (☎670 3408). Beautifully ornate imports from Morocco. Many pieces, especially tiled fountains and a multitude of ceramic plates, vases, and bowls. Open daily 11am-6pm. MC/V.

STREET MARKETS FOR POCKET CHANGE. Many vendors in the Albert Cuypmarkt hike their prices on Saturdays, when the tourists descend like wealthy and obliging locusts. Save money and visit during the week!

JODENBUURT AND PLANTAGE

Dappermarkt, on Dapperstraat. Tram #3 or 10 to Dapperstraat. If you're hoping to get a glimpse of Amsterdam's Middle Eastern and North African communities, stop by the massive Dappermarkt and sort through piles of some useful, some useless, but all staggeringly cheap stuff. With everything from pharmaceuticals and underwear to fresh produce and cheese, it's worth the trek for the bargain-hunter. Open M-Sa 9am-4pm.

De Beestenwinkel, Staalstraat 11 (☎623 1805). Corner shop specializing in *de beesten:* all manner of children's items, from plush toys to lunchboxes to finger puppets, but with animals on them, of course! Be warned: there's an especially cuddly collection of stuffed animals that you won't be able to resist. Open Tu-Sa 10am-6pm, Su noon-5pm.

Puck, Nieuwe Hoogstraat 1A (☎625 4201). New and used goods in a bright, airy shop. Secondhand clothes are classics and in excellent condition. Best of all, dresses, suits, hats, accessories, linens, kimonos, and children's apparel come without the musty smell of many vintage goods. Open M 1-6pm, Tu-F 11am-6pm, Sa 11am-5pm.

Episode, Waterlooplein 1 (☎320 3000; www.episode.eu). An eclectic selection of inexpensive secondhand clothing awaits your discovery and creative mismatching at this shop located alongside the Waterlooplein flea market. Open M-Sa 10am-6pm. MC/V.

Waterlooplein, an open-air flea market on Waterlooplein. Tapestries, music, and, most of all, used clothing (and lots of it) are all on sale at this large flea market beside the Stadhuis-Het Muziektheater. Open M-F 9am-5pm, Sa 8:30am-5:30pm.

SIZES AND CONVERSIONS

WOMEN'S SHOES

US SIZE	5	6	7	8	9	10	11
UK SIZE	3½	4½	5½	6½	7½	8½	9½
DUTCH SIZE	36	37	38	39	40	41	42

MEN'S SHOES

US SIZE	7	8	9	10	11	12	13
UK SIZE	6½	7½	8½	9½	10½	11½	12½
DUTCH SIZE	41	42	43	44	45	46	47

WOMEN'S CLOTHING

US SIZE	4	6	8	10	12	14	16
UK SIZE	6	8	10	12	14	16	18
DUTCH SIZE	34	36	38	40	42	44	46

MEN'S SUITS/JACKETS

US/UK SIZE	36	37	38	39	40	41	42
DUTCH SIZE	46	47	49	50	51	53	54

MEN'S SHIRTS

US/UK SIZE	14½	15	15½	16	16½	17	17½
DUTCH SIZE	37	38	39	40	41	42	43

SHOPPING

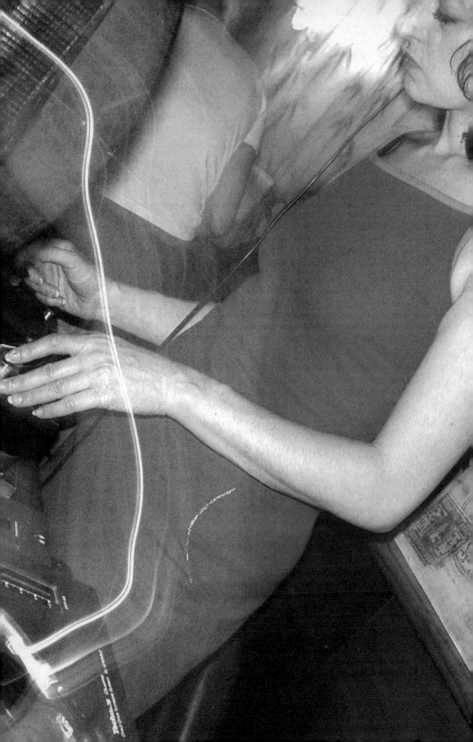

NIGHTLIFE

Amsterdam's reputation as a capital of indulgence is most famously embodied in its coffee shops, but its nightlife provides ample opportunity to do anything or be anyone you want. Clubs cater to gay or straight observers and dancers alike, while bars alternate between classic, old-Amsterdam *bruin cafes* (brown cafes, whose ceilings are weathered and brown from years of tobacco smoke) and their modern counterpart, the fancily named *grandcafe*. Step out into Amsterdam after dark, and you'll acquire first-hand knowledge as to why it's said that the best visit to this city is one that you can't remember.

Though Amsterdam boasts a world-class nightclub scene, it is one that is refreshingly focused on dancing and having a good time rather than posing and outglamming the other clubbers. That said, you'll find a few long lines and discerning bouncers at the most popular establishments, which cluster near **Rembrandtplein** and lie along **Reguliersdwarsstraat.** The clubs closer to the center of town, particularly in the Nieuwe Zijd, are generally bombarded with boisterous tourists. To increase your chances of admission, try one or all of the following: be neatly dressed; be sober in mind and behavior (bouncers revel in throwing out swaying drunks); and be female (unless, of course, you're a man going to a gay bar, in which case you shouldn't have a problem). If you want to return to a club, it's wise to tip the bouncer as you leave to assure his grace on your next visit. Lines are short before midnight, so showing up early can help you get in. Keep in mind, though, that this works well only because people don't show up at clubs until about midnight or 1am. Before then, locals pack into bars to pre-party. While coffee shops may seem attractive for an evening of revelry, they are not popular haunts for local nightlife.

Amsterdam's ☑GLBT nightlife may very well claim the prize as Europe's best, capturing intensity and fun through its many outlets. **Reguliersdwarsstraat** reigns as the undisputed king of the gay party scene, with large clubs that tend to be upbeat, cruise-friendly, and unabashedly flamboyant. For a taste of kinkiness, try the smaller, darker clubs on **Warmoesstraat,** which feature quite a bit of rubber and leather, housing an occasional anything-goes darkroom (so long as it's safe) for the truly intrepid adventurer. There are fewer bars and clubs that cater specifically to lesbians, but those that do exist are popular. They are not always heavily populated, but they have decidedly less attitude than their male counterparts. Many gay clubs host lesbian-themed nights as well, so party-loving ladies can always explore a fair share of options. The distinctive scene does not suggest a separation of sorts, however, as most clubs welcome any sexual orientation, with predominantly straight venues drawing a fair number of gay patrons on any given night.

BY TYPE

BRUIN CAFES		Cafe Menschen (235)	RP
Belgique (228)	NZ	Cafe P96 (239)	JD
Café Brandon (230)	CRW	Cafe Stevens (225)	OZ
Café de Engelbewaarder (225)	OZ	Cafe Thijssen (238)	JD
▨ Café de Jaren (225)	OZ	▨ Café 't Smalle (237)	JD
Café de Tuin (238)	JD	▨ Café Zool (229)	CRW
Cafe Heffer (226)	RLD	De Blauwe Druife (229)	SVB
Cafe Kalkhoven (229)	CRW	▨ Festina Lente (237)	JD

BRUIN CAFES, CONTINUED
Gollem (228) — NZ
Lokaal 't Loosje (225) — OZ
Proust (238) — JD
🏷 Toussaint Cafe (239) — WO
🏷 Wijnand Fockink (226)RLD

COCKTAIL BARS
🏷 Arc Bar (234) — RP
Bamboo Bar (231) — LP
Cafe Lime (225) — OZ
🏷 Chocolate Bar (240) — DP
Ebeling (239) — WO
Finch (238) — JD
Lux (231) — LP
NJOY (231) — LP
Suzy Wong (231) — LP
Vodka Bar The 5th Element (234) — RP
Vuong (231) — LP

DANCE/NIGHTCLUBS
Amsterdamned Café (233) — LP
Arena (241) — JP
Bar Hartje (233) — LP
Brasil Music Bar (233) — LP
Bubbels (232) — LP
🏷 Club NL (228) — NZ
Club Magazijn (227) — RLD
Club Meander (228) — NZ
Club More (239) — JD
🏷 Club Winston (226) — RLD
The Cooldown Café (233) — LP
Dansen Bij Jansen (229) — NZ
De Duivel (237) — RP
🏷 Escape (236) — RP
Jimmy Woo (232) — LP
Korsakoff (239) — JD
La Rumba (233) — LP
The Mansion (240) — MV
🏷 Melkweg (232) — LP
🏷 Odeon (236) — RP
🏷 OT301 (239) — WO
🏷 Paradiso (232) — LP
Party Crew Cafe (236) — RP
Rain (236) — RP

DANCE/NIGHTCLUBS, CONT'D
Royalty (232) — LP
Sugar Factory (232) — LP
Zebra (232) — LP

▼GLBT BARS
Cafe April (235) — RP
Cafe Rouge (236) — RP
Getto (226) — RLD
Habibi Ana Bar (231) — LP
Lellebel (235) — RP
🏷 Montmartre (234) — RP
Saarein II (238) — JD
Soho (235) — RP
Vive La Vie (235) — RP

▼GLBT CLUBS
Cockring (226) — RLD
Exit (237) — RP

GRANDCAFES
🏷 Absinthe (227) — NZ
Bep (227) — NZ
Bloemers (241) — DP
Cafe Berkhout (241) — DP
Cafe de Groene Vlinder (240) — DP
Cafe Krull (240) — DP
🏷 Dulac (229) — SVB
The Getaway (228) — NZ
Kamer 401 (231) — LP
🏷 Kingfisher (240) — DP
🏷 Mankind (230) — CCR
Pirates Bar (231) — LP
Café Soundgarden (238) — JD
🏷 Weber (230) — LP

PUBS
Coco's Outback (235) — RP
Duende (238) — JD
Durty Nelly's Pub (226) — RLD
The Hemp Bar (230) — CCR
O'Donnell's (240) — DP
The Tara (227) — NZ

PUNK
Vrankrijk (227) — NZ

CRW Canal Ring West **CCR** Central Canal Ring **DP** De Pijp **JP** Jodenbuurt and Plantage **JD** Jordaan **LP** Leidseplein **MV** Museumplein and Vondelpark **NZ** Nieuwe Zijd **OZ** Oude Zijd **RLD** Red Light District **RP** Rembrandtplein **SVB** Scheepvaartbuurt **WO** Westerpark and Oud-West

BY NEIGHBORHOOD

OUDE ZIJD

No visit to Amsterdam is complete without a taste of the Oude Zijd at night. This is Amsterdam in all its celebrated, gaudy

see map p. 340

glory: timeless *bruin cafes* fight for space with futuristic bars, huge student dance clubs, and coffee shops thick with marijuana smoke. Garish souvenir stands hawking imitation Dutch clogs compete with sex shops and porno-video supermarkets for tourists' attention. Especially on the weekends, the Oude Zijd does not sleep: when the rest of Amsterdam is getting ready to call it a night, the Oude Zijd begins to stir.

▓ **Café de Jaren,** Nieuwe Doelenstraat 20-22 (☎625 5771). From Muntplein, cross the Amstel and proceed ahead for ½ block. Sweet relief on a hot day; this fabulous 2-floor cafe's air of sophistication doesn't quite mesh with its budget-friendly prices. Gaze at sweeping views of the Amstel through vaulted plate-glass windows or dine in style atop its waterfront deck. Popular with students and staff from the nearby University of Amsterdam. Artfully balances maturity with a youthful hipness. Expansive and airy bottom floor serves the same light menu of soups, salads (€4-6), and sandwiches (€3-6) all day. Full hot meals (vegetarian around €12; meat around €15). Upstairs changes to the dinner menu after 5:30pm (entrees around €14). 2 impressive bars serve mixed drinks and beer (€1.80-3.10). Open M-Th and Su 10am-1am, F-Sa 10am-2am. Kitchen closes M-Th and Su at 10:30pm, F-Sa midnight. MC/V.

Cafe Lime, Zeedijk 104 (☎639 3020), just north of Nieuwmarkt. The ultimate lounge with all the accoutrements of a Space Age bachelor pad—a disco ball casts slivers of light on pleather couches, and a projection of floating globs covers the wall behind the bar. Popular with the pre-club crowd and refreshingly low on attitude. A dramatic change of pace from the raucous sports pubs popular in this area. Soul, house, and jazz tunes make for easy listening. Beer €3. Over 15 mixed drinks (€5-7). Open M-Th and Su 5pm-1am, F-Sa 5pm-3am. AmEx/MC/V.

Café de Engelbewaarder, Kloveniersburgwal 59 (☎625 3772). A hidden jewel just south of the tourist crowds. An enjoyable bar atmosphere any night of the week. No Heineken or Amstel here; the bar serves only Belgian beer (€1.70). Large, welcoming room and exceptionally friendly bartenders round out the experience. Enjoy one of the massive omelettes (€3-4). A new specials menu each week, with entrees around €7. Jan.-June and Sept.-Dec. Su live jazz 4:30-7pm. Open M-Th and Su 11am-1am, F-Sa 11am-3am. Kitchen open noon-3pm and 5:30-10pm. Cash only.

Lokaal 't Loosje, Nieuwmarkt 32-34 (☎627 2635). This quaint bar is beloved by Oude Zijd locals for its mellow come-as-you-are vibe and its well-preserved classic Art Deco wall tiles and mosaic floor. Frequented by a slightly older crowd, Lokaal 't Loosje is a popular spot to sit outside and watch the buzz of Nieuwmarkt ebb and flow around you. Heineken €1.80. Open M-Th and Su 9am-1am, F-Sa 9am-3am. Cash only.

Cafe Stevens, Geldersekade 123 (☎620 6970). A terrific *bruin cafe* right on Nieuwmarkt. A popular place to read a newspaper and to people-watch on a sunny day. In less ideal weather, the long indoor bar makes for easy conversation. Down a *jonge jenever* (€2) or dig into the freshly made apple tarts (€3). Variety of sandwiches around €4. Dinner courses €10-14. Open M-Th and Su 10am-1am, F-Sa 10am-3am. Kitchen closes at 9:30pm.

RED LIGHT DISTRICT

The Red Light District after sunset is the stuff of legend—loud, neon, lustful legend. The most action happens around **Warmoesstraat,** where packs of tourists and locals move from bar to bar to sample competing Happy hours. The street is also home to many of the area's ⬛**GLBT** venues; however, transgendered and cross-dressing visitors should exercise caution in the district. As the night wears on, the crowds tend to head in two directions: students (and those in mixed company) often move south toward Dam Sq. and the big dance clubs, while packs of young men head east to **Oudezijds Voorburgwal,** the heart of the Red Light District.

see map p. 340

NIGHTLIFE

BARS

FOCKINK

■ **Wijnand Fockink,** Pijlsteeg 31 (☎639 2695; www.wynand-fockink.nl), on an alleyway just off Dam Sq. Perhaps the most unique bar you'll visit in Amsterdam. Over 300 years old, and looks it—dusty and creaky floors, dark, antique decor, and no chairs. The hook: unequivocally the best *fockink* (Dutch gin) in the city. Made especially for this tiny bar and available in over 60 flavors, including Walk in the Woods, Hansel in the Cellar, and Forget Me Not. Perhaps even more delicious is the brandy made from fresh fruit. Try a glass of the potent brand (a whopping 20% alcohol) for only €2.10. Bottles of their products are also available for purchase (€17-20). Open daily 3-9pm. Cash only.

Durty Nelly's Pub, Warmoesstraat 115-117 (☎638 0125). From Centraal Station, go south on Damrak, turn right on Brugsteeg, and veer right on Warmoesstraat; Nelly's is 2 blocks down on the left. Below **Durty Nelly's Hostel** (p. 104), this large Irish pub features high-powered A/C, 2 dartboards, 2 pool tables, a foosball table, and a big-screen TV reporting the latest in European sports. A great place to start off the night with friends over a pint of Guinness (€4.60). Good quality pub grub; grab a lighter meal (baked potato loaded with your choice of toppings €6.50) or heartier fare (hamburger with fries €7.50). Pasta of the day €10. Irish stew €7.50. Internet access €5 per hr. Open M-Th and Su 9am-1am (until 4am for hostel guests); F-Sa 9am-3am (until 5am for hostel guests). Kitchen open noon-10pm. Cash only.

Getto, Warmoesstraat 51 (☎421 5151; www.getto.nl). A hip bar and restaurant beloved for its kicky mixed drinks (try Getto Blaster or Thirsty Vampire; €6) and its chic lounge decor. Primarily a ☑**GLBT** establishment, but everyone feels welcome here. Serves appetizers for €3-6 and main dishes like the Delilah veggie burger (€10-15). Tarot card readings Su 8-11pm (about €10). Happy hour daily 5-7pm. Su all-night Cocktail Bash (all mixed drinks €5). Open Tu-Th 4pm-1am, F-Sa 4pm-2am, Su 4pm-midnight. Cafe open daily 6-11pm.

Cafe Heffer, Oudebrugsteeg 7 (☎428 4488; www.heffer.nl), at Beursstraat. Situated in the former house of the city tax collector, the Heffer improves upon the traditional Dutch *bruin cafe* motif. High ceilings, ample light, and a sprawling patio decked with sun umbrellas provide an oasis from the ebb and flow of the pushers and prostitutes in the Red Light District. The beer here is Venloosh (€2.10 per glass). A good place to start drinking before heading for the Red Light District just up the street. Open M-Th and Su 10am-1am, F-Sa 10am-3am. Kitchen closes at 10pm. Cash only.

> **TIP**
> **DEAD-OF-NIGHT DISTRICT.** After the crowds have started to dissipate in the wee hours, the Red Light District becomes increasingly unsavory. Travel in numbers, especially after the clubs let out.

CLUBS

■ **Club Winston,** Warmoesstraat 129 (☎625 3912; www.winston.nl). An eclectic little club with a packed crowd and deceptively large dance floor. The atmosphere can go from laid-back and funky to hot and steamy. Everything from standard DJ/house nights to kimono costume parties and big jazz bands, so there is always something interesting. Cover varies nightly, but usually €3-7. Opening time varies, but usually daily 9pm-3am.

Cockring, Warmoesstraat 96 (☎623 9604; www.clubcockring.com). Just look for the giant cockring on the sign. Lives up to its self-awarded title as "Amsterdam's Premier ☑**Gay** Disco." Straddles the line between a dance venue and a sex club; you can come to dance or to get lucky. DJs play for studly men who readily doff clothing as things heat up. Though packed with a mixed crowd on weekends, weekdays tend to play host to a much smaller, generally older crowd that chats without making much use of the dance floor. Live strip shows Th-Su from 1am. Special "SafeSex" parties 1st and 3rd Su of the month (€7.50, with free condoms; dress code "shoes only" or naked; 3-7pm). Downstairs is a crowded dance floor surrounded by an elevated cruising plank, with mostly techno and dance music; upstairs is a lounge area with a bar and a darkroom. Men only. Cover M-W €2.50, Th-F and Su €3.50, Sa €5. Open M-Th and Su 11pm-4am, F-Sa 11pm-5am.

Club Magazijn, Warmoesstraat 170 (www.clubmagazijn.com). Just off Dam Sq., this large club popular with local students features a huge bar and sweeping dance floor. Pink neon lights and throwback furniture complete the picture. Shake your groove thing to hip hop, Latin, 80s, and more. Check website for special party nights. Cover varies (usually €5-9). Open M-Th 10pm-3am, F-Sa 10pm-4am.

NIEUWE ZIJD

Yes, the Nieuwe Zijd at night should be taken seriously; after all, many tourists come to Amsterdam for its nightlife, and the Nieuwe Zijd is the first neighborhood they step into from the doors of Centraal Station. While its nightlife is by no means tame, the Nieuwe Zijd is a good fallback if the outrageous Oude Zijd and Red Light District are simply on a level you never wanted to reach.

see map p. 340

BARS

Absinthe, Nieuwezijds Voorburgwal 171 (☎320 6780), just south of Dam Sq. The wormwood-laced speciality of this *nachtbar* isn't hard to guess. The whitewashed stone walls and cushioned niches are bathed in light from several disco balls, endowing this popular spot with a subterranean feel—perhaps explaining its attractiveness to visitors of the tourist variety. 17 varieties of absinthe available; it's not cheap (€5-17.50), but just 1 drink is strong enough (55-80% alcohol) to last most of the night. You can consider any absinthe that's more than €8 per shot to be of especially high quality. Open M-Th and Su 10pm-3am, F-Sa 10pm-4am. Cash only.

The Tara, Rokin 85-89 (☎421 2654; www.thetara.com), a few blocks south of Dam. You'll never go thirsty again at this congenial Irish watering hole, the largest bar in Amsterdam. Features a massive, maze-like interior in a number of different styles, from 19th-century hunting lodge to sleek, modern nightspot. Known as more of a wintertime bar, the Tara's cozy fireside armchairs and couches welcome droves of expats throughout the colder months. St. Patrick's Day and soccer season attract equally raucous crowds. 3 bars serve up pints of Guinness. Regular draft beer €2.60-5. DJs or bands (traditional Irish, flamenco, and jazz) usually turn up Sa nights in the fall, winter, and spring months—call ahead or check the website for details. Open M-Th and Su 10am-1am, F-Sa 10am-3am. AmEx/D/MC/V.

Vrankrijk, Spuistraat 216 (☎625 3243; www.vrankrijk.org). 3 blocks north of the Spui; look for the building whose facade is covered by a Lichtenstein-inspired mural. Booming punk music and incredibly cheap drinks (beer €1.20-1.70; mixed drinks €2.50) in a long-standing, well-known squat with few visible tourists. Consider leaving bourgeois accoutrements at home: the mostly amiable crowd consists largely of mohawked, leather-jacketed folks. Sprawl out at tottering tables beneath the graffiti-sprayed walls plastered with political posters. Drink up; all the beer is from small European breweries, and proceeds go to support progressive causes. Ring bell to enter. Free Internet access. M ⚧GLBT night; Tu proceeds go to refugees; Th 8-9:30pm squatter information; Sa disco night. Open M-W 9pm-1am, Th 9:30pm-1am, F 9pm-3am, Sa 10pm-3am, Su "when they feel like it"-1am.

Bep, Nieuwezijds Voorburgwal 260 (☎626 5649). The small, sleek bar is packed with a rotating clientele of hipsters and wannabes jostling for drinks. The slightly older crowd enjoys exotic mixed drinks with metropolitan prices (€6.50-8). Beer €2.20. A full Thai menu is also available for dinner (5:30-10pm). Snacks €4.50-9.50. Entrees €12-16. Open M-Th and Su 5pm-1am, F-Sa 5pm-3am.

ABSINTHE

THE BIG SPLURGE

SUP IN STYLE

In 1999, an investor purchased a cash-strapped underground night-spot and turned it into one of Amsterdam's trendiest. The resulting **Supperclub** has remained one of Amsterdam's most popular escapes, spawning a number of offshoots around the globe.

On a small alley between Kalverstraat and Nieuwezijds Voorburgwal, you'll find Supperclub's unassuming entrance. Inside is a massive, entirely white space. The side walls are furnished with couches, and cushions are everywhere. The design and architecture are sleek and minimalist. On any given night, you're likely to run into fashion designers, artists, models, and musicians—Amsterdam's artistic elite.

While you'll know the price of your five-course dinner (€65), you will have no idea what you will be served. The selection of dishes depends entirely on the whim of the chefs, who are known to try all sorts of irreverent flavor combinations. During and after dinner, you'll be treated to visual art by "VJs," tunes from DJs, and other performances from cabaret artists, dancers, or models.

And don't be surprised by the restroom; the Supperclub doesn't have traditional men's and women's rooms. Rather, its toilets are labeled "Homo" and "Hetero," making bathroom encounters here especially memorable.

Jonge Roelensteeg 21 (☎344 6400; www.supperclub.nl).

Gollem, Raamsteeg 4 (☎676 7117), between Spuistraat and Singel, a few blocks south of Dam Sq. Young, fun, and convivial. Gollem's dripping candles and dark paneling welcome beer aficionados from all walks of life. The bar's beer menu spans 3 walls, with over 200 varieties on tap: most are Belgian, but there are also Czech, Dutch, and German staples (€3.20-12). For something really special, try the Westvleteren (€10-12). Made by monks in Belgium only when they're in the mood, this beer can be purchased only a few crates at a time to keep it from becoming commercialized. Patient bartenders can help you navigate the massive menu. Open M-Th and Su 4pm-1am, F-Sa 2pm-2am.

Belgique, Gravenstraat 2 (☎625 1974), behind the Nieuwe Kerk and between Nieuwendijk and Nieuwezijds Voorburgwal. If you're ready to graduate from keg swill to the real stuff, step up to this bar with over 40 varieties of high-quality (and highly alcoholic) Belgian brew. Popular every night of the week with tourists and locals alike mingling on the benches out front. 8 beers on tap (€2-5), including la Trappe and la Chouffe, fresh from the asceticism of a Trappist monastery and ready to fuel Amsterdam debauchery. The rest come in bottles; after perusing the detailed beer menu, you'll be able to rattle off the names of the monks who packed your brew. Open daily 3pm-1am.

The Getaway, Nieuwezijds Voorburgwal 250 (☎627 1427), 5min. south of Dam. This trendily decorated watering hole is a popular spot for pre-club drinkers. Opened by artists more than 5 years ago, this bar features a creative vibe, with art decorating many of its walls. DJs spin loud music nearly every night in the diminutive 2-story interior. The party usually starts kicking at 11pm. Beer €2.20. Mixed drinks €5. Open M-Th and Su 5pm-1am, F-Sa 5pm-3am.

CLUBS

▨ Club NL, Nieuwezijds Voorburgwal 169 (☎622 7510; www.clubnl.nl), just south of Dam, on the same side of the street. Dress to impress at this upscale club, where the trendy and beautiful flock to sip designer mixed drinks and groove to the happy house tunes of nightly DJs. Fuel your moves with a fresh gourmet mixed drink like the strawberry martini garnished with a twist of black pepper (€8). Attitude may not be everything on the outside, but it is inside—flaunt your stuff to get past the bouncers. Cover F-Su €5. Mandatory €1 coat check. Open M-Th and Su 10pm-3am, F-Sa 10pm-4am. AmEx/MC/V.

Club Meander, Voetboogstraat 3B (☎625 8430; www.cafemeander.com). From Muntplein, take Spuistraat to Heiligeweg; turn right, and then head left on Voetboogstraat. Live bands jam nightly in a number of different genres: top 40, jazz, funk, soul, blues, R&B,

salsa, and DJ-hosted dance sessions (monthly schedule posted on website). Live music 8:30-11pm, DJ from 11pm on. Cover €4-6. Open M-Th and Su 8pm-3am, F-Sa 8pm-4am.

Dansen Bij Jansen, Handboogstraat 11-13 (☎620 1779; www.dansenbijjansen.nl), near Koningsplein. *The* student dance club in Amsterdam, as popular with locals from the nearby University of Amsterdam as with the backpacking set. A great way to meet local university kids. Each night features a different DJ with a distinctive style—a fun, if slightly hokey, blend of R&B, hip hop, disco, and top 40. Dionysian dance frenzy dominates downstairs; a more relaxed bar is upstairs. Scantily clad partygoers abound, but there's not a shred of snooty clubster attitude. You must show a student ID or be accompanied by a student to enter. Beer €1.70-3.30. Mixed drinks from €3.30. Open M-Th and Su 11pm-4am, F-Sa 11pm-5am.

SCHEEPVAARTBUURT

Scheepvaartbuurt isn't the most happening section of town after hours, but it has a few venues that are worth checking out. The islands to the north of Scheepvaartbuurt are home to many of the city's foreign exchange students, who venture south at night in search of a good time. Haarlemmerstraat quiets down in the evening after the restaurants serve their last customers of the day. **Harlem: Drinks and Soulfood** (p. 126) is an exception; it stays open late to make the transition from food to drink.

see map p. 338

▨ **Dulac,** Haarlemmerstraat 118 (☎624 4265). Attracts Amsterdammers and university exchange students with its dimly lit, Art-Deco-gone-wrong interior, pool table, and ample nooks and booths for more private moments. Garden terrace out back for consumables like a pint of beer (€3.50) or tapas (€3-6). Entrees are priced from €7.50-17 and are half-price for student ID holders. Mixed drinks €7. DJ spins F-Sa 10pm-3am. Open M-Th and Su 4pm-1am, F-Sa 4pm-3am. Kitchen open daily until 10:30pm. AmEx/MC/V.

De Blauwe Druife, Haarlemmerstraat 91 (☎626 9897), at Binnen Brouwersstraat. Old-school neighborhood *bruin cafe,* popular with locals since 1733. The whimsical interior alone merits a visit; check out the table, chairs, and piano hanging upside down from the ceiling—the joke is that De Blauwe Druife (The Blue Grape) gets so packed that patrons end up there. The terrace outside is popular on pleasant days. Snacks within budget such as *broodjes* (€2.50-3.50) and *bitterballen* (€4.20). Beer on tap €1.90. Open M-Th and Su noon-1am, F-Sa noon-3am.

CANAL RING WEST

You won't find many ragers in the Canal Ring West. The handful of nightlife establishments here are generally geared toward a more laid-back, local crowd—but this is all the more reason to pay a visit to its low-key scene.

see map p. 338

▨ **Café Zool,** Oude Leliestraat 9 (☎065 131 8542; www.cafezool.nl). This small neighborhood bar has a friendly clientele and a wonderful atmosphere. Ask for Tim or Bas, great sources for information on nightlife and sights around town. Watch out for Bottle, the giant but friendly bar dog. Pints of Palm run €5. Those up for the risk can try a shot of absinthe (€4). Free Internet if you bring a laptop. Open M-Th and Su 4pm-1am, F 4pm-3am, Sa noon-3am. Cash only.

Cafe Kalkhoven, Prinsengracht 283 (☎624 8649). Kalkhoven represents "Old Amsterdam" in all its brown, wooden glory: the old barrels on the wall behind the bar, the chandeliers extending from darkly painted ceilings, and the food selections all have a traditional Dutch flavor. *Tostis* and *appeltas* (apple strudel) both €1.80. Choose a drink from the detailed beer cheat sheet and settle down in the back, where candles light every table. Open daily 11am-1am.

NIGHTLIFE

Café Brandon, Keizersgracht 157. Having re-opened after an 18-year hiatus, Café Brandon is a great place to interact with locals. An older, neighborhood crowd relaxes to Pink Floyd and late-70s English rock. Small bar with a larger backroom and a pool table. Amstel beer on tap (from €1.60). Open M-Th and Su noon-1am, F-Sa noon-3am.

CENTRAL CANAL RING

Most of the nightlife in the Central Canal Ring is concentrated in Leidseplein and Rembrandtplein, though canal-side eating establishments are always great venues for great conversation with locals and a beer with a view.

see map p. 336

 Mankind, Weteringstraat 60 (☎638 4755; www.mankind.nl). Tram #6, 7, or 10 to Speigelgracht or tram #16, 24, or 25 to Weteringcircuit. From Leidseplein, facing the Marriott Hotel, take 1 giant leap down Kleine-Gartmanplantsoen for 2 blocks. This laid-back neighborhood bar brings together tourists and loyal locals to relax and mingle on 1 of its 2 outdoor porches. Standard array of Dutch snacks: *tostis* €2, *bitterballevn* €3.40. Ask for the *dagschotel* (daily special; €8.10) or one of the tasty sandwiches. Mankind Special €4.50. Open daily noon-midnight. Kitchen closes at 8pm. Cash only.

The Hemp Bar, Frederiksplein 15 (☎625 4425; www.hemp-hotel.com). Downstairs from the **Hemp Hotel** (p. 110). A quiet, easygoing spot popular with English-speaking expats and their friends. You can imbibe all manner of booze, but sweet hemp beer is the house speciality (€2; other potables €1.70-2.50). Up to 5 varieties of hemp brew can be available, depending on current hemp laws abroad; however, hemp brew won't get you high because it has no THC. Come here to chat with locals over a beer. Open M-Th and Su 4pm-3am, F-Sa 4pm-4am. V.

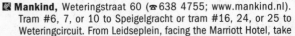

BEER FOR POCKET CHANGE. On weeknights, many clubs and bars offer specials where you can get a small glass of the house draft for €1. It is usually advertised prominently, so keep your eyes peeled or ask your bartender.

LEIDSEPLEIN

For a raucous night out on the Dutch capital, head to Leidseplein. This relatively small district hosts the city's largest concentration of clubs, bars, and concert venues. In a blur of activity, young backpackers rub elbows with local students and yuppie natives, while older crowds shed their inhibitions at blazing jazz joints. Upscale cocktail bars and massive dance halls join traditional Dutch cafes tucked away off the jam-packed streets. Just around the corner, Marnixstraat's string of chic, well-designed bars attract expats and a reasonably large local contingent. In the summer, the sun rises a little before 5am; a Leidseplein-grade night out means you'll still be up for the sunrise.

see map p. 337

BARS

 Weber, Marnixstraat 397 (☎622 9910), between Leidseplein and Leidsegracht. 2 doors down from Lux, its sister bar. All the style and sophistication of Amsterdam's edgiest bars with none of the attitude. Friendly, come-as-you-are bar hosts crowds of both pre-club drinkers and handsome grizzled locals. Though velvet curtains, felt-patterned vintage porn wallpaper, and the occasional Buddha may seem incongruous, somehow it all comes together nicely. Also a popular spot for local musicians and artists; can get very crowded on the weekends. Downstairs grotto provides a spot for chilling and conversations. Beer €2.10. Open M-Th and Su 8pm-3am, F-Sa 8pm-4am. Cash only.

Lux, Marnixstraat 403 (☎422 1412). The borderline tacky mobster motif belies how classy this place actually is. The red plush walls and leopard-print curtains are distinctly ironic when peopled with chatty young people, expats, and a respectable Dutch crowd. There's not much dancing, but the candles, wave lamps, and DJ spinning Th-Su will get you pumped to hit the clubs later on. Beer €2. Mixed drinks €4. Open M-Th and Su 8pm-3am, F-Sa 8pm-4am. Cash only.

Habibi Ana Bar, Lange Leidsedwarsstraat 93 (www.habibiana.nl). This small, unassuming bar has the dramatic distinction of being the only openly ☑gay Arab bar in the world. Arabic for "My Sweetheart," Habibi is a simple bar populated by recent Middle Eastern immigrants. The locals are friendly and welcome visitors into the fun environment. Take in the unique atmosphere over a beer (€2), Arabic tea and coffee (€1.50), or a range of sandwiches and Middle Eastern dishes (around €10). Open M-Th and Su 7pm-1am, F-Sa 7pm-3am. Kitchen closes at 10pm. Cash only.

Suzy Wong, Korte Leidsedwarsstraat 45 (☎626 6769). Same owners as Jimmy Woo across the street and caters to a similarly classy, stylish clientele. Choose from 11 mixed drinks (€7.50-8) as you relax amid red-tinted candles and a mirrored ceiling. Choose from a range of tasty sandwiches (€9). The mood is chill but sharp; dress up a little to blend in. If feeling wild, make friends with the plush, cushioned dance pole. Open Tu-W and Su 6pm-1am, Th 6pm-2am, F-Sa 6pm-3am.

Kamer 401, Marnixstraat 401 (☎320 4580; www.kamer401.nl), between Leidsegracht and Leidseplein. Done up stylishly in chrome and glass with a shiny zinc bar, Kamer boasts a sizable expat contingent and a fashionable professional crowd, competing with next-door Weber and Lux. The small downstairs lounge area provides relief from the crowds near the bar. DJ plays hip hop, soul, and jazz after 10pm on weekends. Dommelsch €2.20. Corona and Hoegaarden €3.50. Mixed drinks €4.50. Open W-Th 6pm-1am, F-Sa 6pm-3am.

Pirates Bar, Korte Leidsedwarsstraat 129. This casual bar is a great place to kick off your nocturnal festivities, especially on €1.30 beer nights (M-F and Su). Check out the gigantic ship chain hanging over the bar. DJ spins the latest top 40, hip hop, and American pop F-Sa. Enjoy the foosball table M-F. Don't forget your eyepatch. Open M-Th and Su 6pm-3am, F-Sa 6pm-4am.

Bamboo Bar, Lange Leidsedwarsstraat 64 (☎624 3993; www.bamboobar.nl). Disco ball and slick hardwood bar share space with tribal masks and tiki torches in a jungle motif that, against all odds, actually works. DJ plays mostly hip hop and salsa. Beer €2. Vast menu of mixed drinks (€4-7.50, most €6.30) includes the down-home Alabama Slamma (€4.50) and Long Island Iced Tea (€7.20). Music courtesy of the next-door Brasil Music Bar (p. 233). Open W-Th and Su 8pm-3am, F-Sa 8pm-4am. Cash only.

NJOY, Korte Leidsedwarsstraat 93 (www.cocktailclubnjoy.nl). Before hitting the clubs, warm up in style at this hip cocktail bar that balances sophistication and verve with a casual ambience. Over 60 mixed drinks on the menu, but the bartenders can prepare up to 200. Sip a Singapore Sling or a Vanilla Sour (€8.50) amid the subtle purple lights. Dance floor and an in-house DJ. Open M-Th and Su 9pm-3am, F-Sa 9pm-4am.

Vuong, Korte Leidsedwarsstraat 51 (☎530 5577; www.vuong.nl). This restaurant and cocktail bar, set behind a black facade facing the square, is yet another place to see, be seen, and most likely feel underdressed. Trendy patrons sip trendy drinks in the undeniably trendy, deep red setting. Venture upstairs for a lounge-like environment. Beer €2.30. Glass of Moët & Chandon €12.50. Open M-Th and Su 11am-1am, F-Sa 11am-3am. Cash only.

 MORE ROOM TO GROOVE. As the weather warms up, most people choose to lounge in the outdoor seating areas of Leidseplein's many cafes and restaurants instead of hitting the dance floor. On these nights, the clubs are often much less crowded, so let the rhythm move you and let loose.

NIGHTLIFE

CLUNS

▨ **Paradiso,** Weteringschans 6-8 (☎ 626 4521; www.paradiso.nl). You can spend a very good Friday in this former church converted to a temple to rock 'n' roll. In the summer, this popular concert hall (and 1960s hippie hangout) hosts a full lineup of big-name rock, punk, New Wave, hip-hop, and reggae acts, from the Wu-Tang Clan to the Stones, who taped their 1995 live album here. After concerts, the space usually becomes a nightclub with multiple dance halls for a variety of music styles; it's cool, accessible, and reliably packed. Concert tickets €5-25; additional mandatory monthly membership fee €2.50. M-Th nightclub cover €6, F-Su €12.50. Open until 2am. Hours vary depending on performances; check the website for showtimes.

▨ **Melkweg,** Lijnbaansgracht 234A (☎ 531 8181; www.melkweg.nl). Tram #1, 2, 5, 6, 7, or 10 to Leidseplein. Turn down the smaller side street to the left of the Stadsschouwburg theater. At this legendary nightspot in an old milk factory (the club's name means "Milky Way"), it's 1-stop shopping for forward-looking live music, food (see **Eat At Jo's,** p. 130), film, and dance parties. There's even a photography gallery (open W-Su 1-9pm; free). Concert tickets €9.50-22 plus €2.50 monthly membership. Prices below include membership. Th popular "Propaganda!" night with "Balkan beatz and Russian Disko" €5; F rotating dance nights around €8; Sa danceable rock, pop, and hip hop midnight-5am €10. Box office open M-F 1-5pm, Sa-Su 4-6pm, show days also 7:30pm to end of show. Check website for details.

Jimmy Woo, Korte Leidsedwarsstraat 18 (☎ 626 3150; www.jimmywoo.com). One of Amsterdam's hottest and most exclusive clubs, Jimmy Woo caters to a bourgeois clientele. Patrons include George Clooney, the Rolling Stones, and the Black Eyed Peas. If you can make it through the phalanx of bouncers—for whom less is more, and black is beautiful—check out the downstairs dancing area, with a ceiling covered with more than 12,000 individual lights, or relax in the lounge at the antique Chinese table. Crack open a bottle of Dom Perignon (€300) or Cristal Champagne (€450) in the lounge: 2 bottles of alcohol get you a table reservation and at least 15min. of fame. For something a little less expensive, bottles of beer run €2.50 and shots come in around €4.50. Cover M-Th and Su €7.50, F-Sa €10. Open M-Th and Su 11pm-3am, F-Sa 11pm-4am.

Sugar Factory, Lijnbaansgracht 238 (www.sugarfactory.nl). Another club aiming for the stylish, well-dressed set, the Sugar Factory aims to provide more than just a place to look good and shake your booty (part of why it calls itself a *nachttheater*). Sweet parties regularly feature a variety of live performances or video; the dance floor and upstairs balcony face a small stage and numerous screens. Check the website for event details. Cover €8-15. Open Th and Su 9pm-4am, F-Sa 9pm-5am.

Zebra, Korte Leidsedwarsstraat 14 (☎ 612 6153; www.the-zebra.nl). A mirrored bar and red-light chandeliers greet you at this fashionable nightclub, a less grandiose version of nearby Jimmy Woo; Zebra isn't as exclusive, but it provides the same kind of sophisticated fun. The upstairs lounge has a larger dance floor, where DJs play lots of house, some top 40, and popular dance music of all stripes. Rent a booth for only 1 bottle of alcohol. Absolut comes with a selection of mixers (€90). Cover Th €7, F-Sa after 1am €10. Open Th and Su 10pm-3am, F-Sa 10pm-4am.

Royalty, Korte Leidsedwarsstraat 28-32 (www.club-royalty.nl). A fun, medium-sized dance and music club fit for kings, queens, and jokers. More locals than most Leidseplein joints. Lots of enthusiasm. Live music F-Sa until 11pm, when it becomes a dance club. A small balcony with a cool view of the dance floor serves as prime perch to view the writhing masses. DJ plays house and top 40. Cover M-Th and Su €3, F-Sa €5; includes 1 drink. Open M-Th and Su 11pm-4am, F-Sa 11pm-6am.

Bubbels, Lange Leidsedwarsstraat 90-92 (☎ 740 4352; www.cafebubbels.nl). A low-profile exterior belies the bubbly crowd inside. Small dance club and bar attracts a fun-loving younger set. DJ spins the standard house, hip-hop, and top 40 selections Th-Su.

Free mixed drinks and shots for women W-Th and Su until 1am. Shots €2.50. Heineken €2.30. A popular drink is the *kootje* (Dutch for "small cow"), a mix of Kahlúa and Sambuca (€3.20). No cover. Open M, W-Th, Su 10pm-4am, F-Sa 10pm-5am.

La Rumba, Korte Leidsedwarsstraat 85-88 (www.larumba.nl). A small club with a Latin flavor. Music is strictly Latin W, F, Su; other nights vary. W salsa party. Open M-Th and Su 10pm-4am, F-Sa 10pm-5am.

Brasil Music Bar, Lange Leidsedwarsstraat 20 (☎626 1500; www.bamboobar.nl). Smaller club boasts a hot menu of Brazilian, salsa, meringue, and R&B beats (many of them by real live performers!). Most nights themed, so call ahead or check the website. W salsa. Often a line for the live Brazilian music F-Sa. Weekend cover €5 for men. Open M-Th and Su 11pm-3am, F-Sa 11pm-4am.

Amsterdamned Café, Korte Leidsedwarsstraat 24A (☎530 5127). A simple club with a long bar and slightly cramped dance floor. Keep an eye on the dance pole or try it out yourself. Nightly DJ plays top 40, house, hip hop, and oldies; don't be surprised if you hear the Macarena. A variety of attractive specials M-Th. Unlimited free mixed drinks for women M and Su. Karaoke Tu after 10:30pm. €1 beer W after 11:30pm. Cover for men €2.50 after midnight (includes a free drink). Happy hour daily 10:30-11:30pm means 2-for-1 drinks. Open M-Th 9pm-3am, F-Sa 9pm-4am, Su 4pm-3am.

The Cooldown Café, Lange Leidsedwarsstraat 116-118 (☎638 3822). Smaller than its sister club on Rembrandtplein, but going for the same *bruin cafe*-turned-nightclub feel. The dark wood paneling and traditional Dutch design give it a distinctive air when compared to the more trend-conscious spots in the area. Small dance floor, but affable atmosphere. Heineken €2.30. Shots €2.80-3.20. DJ plays house and top 40 nightly. Open M-Th and Su 10pm-4am, F-Sa 10pm-5am.

Bar Hartje, Korte Leidsedwarsstraat 64 (☎639 2678). Off the main tourist circuit, but worth a visit if looking for kitschy theme nights from country western to tropical. 2-for-1 drinks before 11pm. W salsa; Th reggaetón and R&B; F theme nights; Sa top 40 and house. Loosen up with a shot of Jägermeister (€2.50). Pint of beer €2.10. Open W-Th 9pm-3am, F-Sa 9pm-4am.

DEAR MR. BARTENDER. Many bartenders and coffee shop employees are well connected to Amsterdam's party scene and trained to work with tourists. Some moonlight as party promoters; many have friends working at nearby clubs. If you're looking for a hot venue for the weekend, start early in the week and ask around. It shouldn't be hard to find your way onto a guest list.

REMBRANDTPLEIN

Rembrandtplein's indisputable draw is its nightlife. Huge dance clubs line the square, with hordes of partygoers strutting their stuff through the wee hours of the morning. The best time to join the peacocking masses is on the weekends, when patrons linger on numerous restaurants' large terraces, leisurely finishing dinner, sipping a beer, or enjoying a smoke. Along with a dizzying concentration of time-tested watering holes, Rembrandtplein boasts some of the best new

see map p. 336

bars in Amsterdam. While other hot spots like De Pijp and the Jordaan have maintained a traditional collection of *bruin cafes*, Rembrandtplein has bars that are increasingly modern, trendy, and fashionable. But the crowds often don't grow thick until after 1am, when the restaurants close and the dance-crazy night owls take over the scene. This is one of the most happening spots in Amsterdam, no question. Refreshingly, everyone is welcome, too: male or female, gay or straight, young or old. The endless selection of clubs of almost

NIGHTLIFE

ON THE MENU

HELLO HERRING, GOODBYE HANGOVER

No trip to the Netherlands is complete without sampling its national delicacy. What could this this country, which has produced such wonders as *bitterballen* and *snert*, possibly do as an encore? The fact is, you haven't truly lived if you haven't tasted that cool, smooth, uniquely Dutch delight: raw herring.

Though this slippery fish may have a substantial gag factor for some, *haring* is low in fat, high in protein, and very functional: locals swear by eating raw herring before and after drinking to prevent a hangover.

Grit your teeth and give *hollandse nieuwe* (as it is known here) a shot: head to one of the dozens of white, blue, and orange herring stands located on many busy streets in Amsterdam. These stands serve salted raw herring chopped up and presented on a piece of cardboard for a paltry €2. The slimy, salty, raw chunks are lowered into one's mouth with the help of an accompanying toothpick. (Onions and pickles on the side are optional.)

Though herring isn't particularly expensive, it is a food the Dutch mostly enjoy on special occasions. After a raging night on Leidseplein, however, look no farther than the *haring* stand to quelch your nausea. You may discover a new favorite snack that soothes your stomach, even if you have to close your eyes and pinch your nose to gulp the fish down.

every variety and size mean there is something for the partier in everyone. The largest (and trendiest) gay bars are located on Reguliersdwarsstraat, west of Vijzelstraat. East of Vijzelstraat the bars are equally hip but more often cater to a straight audience. Throughout Rembrandtplein, however, the atmosphere is accepting and laid-back, making this is a good place to go with mixed company.

BARS

▓ **Arc Bar,** Reguliersdwarsstraat 44 (☎689 7070; www.bararc.com). With a bright red entrance hall, leather lounge chairs, and silver walls, Arc is a hip, cutting-edge choice for a night out with friends. A perfect match for the young, trendy crowd that overtakes the bar weekend nights. Dine on tapas in beige elegance during the afternoon and early evening—popular choices include the oysters (€2) and the mini double hamburger (€4.75). Mixed drinks, including delightfully frilly martinis, caipirinhas, margaritas, mojitos, or Long Island Iced Teas, €7.50-9. On W cocktail night (5pm-1am, all cocktails €5), they serve between 600 and 800 mixed drinks, pretty well drubbing all other bars in the Netherlands. DJs spin every night and dancing begins as early as 6pm on the weekends. Open M-Th and Su 4pm-1am, F-Sa 4pm-3am. AmEx/MC/V.

▓ **Montmartre,** Halvemaansteeg 17 (☎620 7622). Rococo interior inspired by the Garden of Eden with flowers, vines, snakes, apples, and rich draperies make a night at Montmartre one of the wildest parties in Amsterdam for men who love men. Voted best ◤**gay** bar by local gay mag *Gay Krant* 7 years in a row, though it's definitely straight-friendly. Popular with transgendered folks. Don't expect pretense or pressure—just everyone having a good time. Happy hour daily 6-8pm when bartenders serve 2-for-1 beers (beer €2; mixed drinks €4-5.70). The crowd gets younger as the evening wears on and the party rages hardest Th-Su after 11pm, when the boys get down to European or American pop. Be on the lookout for the "surprise" theme parties on a different night each week. Open M-Th and Su 5pm-1am, F-Sa 5pm-3am. Cash only.

Vodka Bar The 5th Element, Reguliersdwarsstraat 41 (☎330 0939; www.the-5th.nl). For a high-class stop, visit this nightspot boasting a classy restaurant and elegant bar where vodka is the specialty. The ultramodern, aluminum bar meshes nicely with the more refined dark wood and contemporary design of the rest of the building. Rub elbows with one of Amsterdam's most fashionable crowds. The appropriately named bar boasts 75 types of vodka (€4-150 per shot). Beer €2. Mixed drinks €5-8. Open W-Th 6pm-2am, F-Sa 6pm-4am. AmEx/MC/V.

Coco's Outback, Thorbeckeplein 8-12 (☎627 2423; www.cocosoutback.com), just east of Rembrandtplein. There's no better place to grab some "lousy food and warm beer" than the Australian Outback at Coco's, complete with plastic crocs, wood ladders, comfy leather couches, and an abundance of handsome Aussie waiters. Part sports bar, part restaurant, part nightclub, Coco's has something for everyone. Wildly popular with tourists on the prowl. During the day, the Outback serves fried favorites and Australian classics like the kangaroo burger (small €12; large €15.20). Kangaroo steak €19. Unlimited chicken and ribs €20. With 15 TVs and 2 projection screens, Coco's is a popular spot for catching a match with friends. After 11pm, the creatures crawl out to play, with DJs spinning Th-Su, pop hits blasting, and British and Australian expats strutting their stuff on the tabletops. Frozen pint €4.50. 20mL shots €2-4.60. Happy hour nightly 5-6pm and 10-11pm (mixed drinks half-price). Open M-Th and Su 11am-1am, F-Sa 11am-3am. Kitchen closes 11pm. AmEx/MC/V.

Cafe April, Reguliersdwarsstraat 37 (☎625 9572; www.cafeapril.eu). Tram #1, 2, or 5 to Koningsplein. Popular ▼**gay** bar that's laid-back by day and increasingly active as the night wears on. It's the brother establishment of popular nightspots **Exit** (p. 237) and **Soho** (p. 235) but not quite as image-conscious. Clusters of tables spill onto the sidewalk out front. The back has a more lounge-like feel, with video screens, darker colors, and a circular rotating bar that is a deservedly huge attraction. Siren lights embedded in the ceiling blast the jingle from *The Price is Right* to signal the start of the popular Happy hour (M-Sa 6-7pm, Su 6-8pm; 2-for-1 drinks), causing a mad rush to the bar. Beer €2. Mixed drinks €6.20. Open July-Aug. M-Th noon-1am, F-Sa noon-3am, Sept.-June M-Th and Su 2pm-1am, F-Sa 2pm-3am. Cash only.

Soho, Reguliersdwarsstraat 36 (☎616 1213; www.pubsoho.eu). Tram #1, 2, or 5 to Koningsplein. Well situated in the thick of Reguliersdwarsstraat, making it ideal for pre-club drinking and lounging. Looks like an old boys' club, but all kinds of characters crowd into this bustling ▼**gay** bar. Leather wallpaper, aged armchairs, and dusty bookshelves line the walls. A number of impressive 2-story mirrors expose all the drama of the night in its fleshy detail. The 1st fl. bar, only open on weekends, has a casual feel, with books lining some of the walls and smaller, more intimate seating arrangements. In the summer, the front doors are flung wide open and the crowd spills into the street. Traditional accoutrements don't quite match the crowd: young and looking to cruise. Happy hour 10-11pm. DJ Th-Sa 10pm-3am, Su live music 9pm. Open M-Th and Su 6pm-3am, F-Sa 6pm-4am. Cash only.

Vive La Vie, Amstelstraat 7 (☎624 0114; www.vivelavie.net), east of Rembrandtplein. Fun, friendly ▼**lesbian** bar with emphasis on good times, good company, and good drinking, all without a shred of attitude. Small, lively, and comfortably packed on weekends. Lined with photos of beautiful female celebrities. Popular with gay men as well. No dance floor, but that doesn't stop the ladies from busting out to jazz, Latin, and feel-good pop anthems. Beer €2.10. Mixed drinks €6. Busiest Th-Sa, when DJs spin after 9pm; Su is more mellow. Open M-Th and Su noon-1am, F-Sa noon-3am. Cash only.

Cafe Menschen, Amstel 202 (☎627 8727), at Amstelstraat. Corner-side bar has great views of the picturesque Blauwbrug and, best of all, pours small but satisfying glasses of Dommelsch beer for a mere €1.20. Locals and tourists take advantage of the cheap booze and relaxed environment, but only true regulars like Eddy, Hans, and Olaf get their names inscribed on plaques on the bar by their favorite stool. Snap a photo and tack it to the wall while you're there; this bar is all about retaining memories. Popular with students from the nearby University of Amsterdam. Pints €3.20. Mixed drinks €4.70-5.20. Open Tu-Th 4pm-1am, F-Sa 4pm-2am. Cash only.

Lellebel, Utrechtsestraat 4 (☎427 5139; www.lellebel.nl), just off the southeast corner of Rembrandtplein. A welcoming local crowd comes to this cozy, campy, vampy ▼**GLBT** bar run by a cadre of outrageous drag queens. Your saucy hostesses Desiree and Susilari tend bar almost every night for their fun-loving crowd of admirers. Attracts a more mature crowd. Women always welcome. Beer €2. Rum and coke €6.50. Theme nights: M "Whatever You Want You Get"—any music request honored; Tu karaoke; W transgender; Th Latin "red-hot salsa"; F open podium contest; Sa popular drag show featuring queens from all over Amsterdam; Su drag queens until midnight and then "Arabian" night. Open M-Th and Su 9pm-3am, F-Sa 8pm-4am.

Cafe Rouge, Amstel 60 (☎420 9881), adjacent to Hotel Monopole. Sa is the busiest night at this ▼gay bar along the Amstel. Generously decorated with portraits of Dutch royalty, black-and-white photos of the owner's family, and autographed photos of celebrities, as well as chandeliers and musical instruments hanging from the ceiling. This bar usually attracts an older crowd than the trendier spots along Reguliersdwarsstraat. Drag nights usually take place on a monthly basis. F-Sa in-house DJ from 8pm. Beer €2. Try the Hengemeng, a favorite Rembrandtplein shot, made with cognac, Tia Maria, and Bailey's (€2.50). Open M-Th 4pm-1am, F-Sa 4pm-3am. Cash only.

 A TIP ABOUT TIPPING. Amsterdam has a very chill clubbing scene; lines are usually short, and covers are rare. Yet if you want to go back to a place, it is customary to tip the bouncer a few euro on your way out.

CLUBS

Escape, Rembrandtplein 11 (☎622 1111; www.escape.nl). Party animals pour into this recently expanded venue for their moment of glory at one of Amsterdam's hottest clubs. 6 bars, a breezy upstairs lounge, and a cafe on the 1st fl. Enormous, sensually charged downstairs dance floor, where impeccably dressed scenesters groove to house, trance, disco, and dance classics. Jump up on one of the platforms scattered around the gigantic dance floor but be prepared to compete with the professional go-go dancers. Lines grow long through 2am; be well dressed and relatively sober to increase your chances of entry. Metal detector, full pat-down, and thorough bag check required before entry. Th "Franchise," a night popular with the stylish student crowd. F continually changes themes to keep the usual crowd entertained. Sa "Framebusters," a hugely popular and fashionable party with Europe's top DJs spinning trance and house. Su "Sundae," a party that channels the energy of Ibiza. Also hosts club nights thrown by private promoters. Beer €2.30. Mixed drinks €7.50. Its new cafe, located just off Rembrandtplein, is the prime spot for people-watching in the square but has the prices to match its ritzy feel. Cover Th-Sa €10-16, students Th €6. Club open Th 11pm-4am, F-Sa 11pm-5am, Su 11pm-4:30am. Cafe open M-Th and Su 10am-1am, F-Sa 10am-3am. Cash only.

Odeon, Singel 460 (☎624 9711). Lose yourself in the mix of techno and club music upstairs or shake it to hip hop downstairs at this upscale club. Dinner before 11pm features delicious cocktails. Dress to impress. Cover M-Th and Su €5, F-Sa €12.50. Open M-W and Su 6pm-1am, Th 11pm-3am, F-Sa 11pm-4am.

Rain, Rembrandtplein 44 (☎626 7078; www.rain-amsterdam.com), directly overlooking Rembrandtplein. One of the latest editions to the city's increasing collection of high-end, exclusive clubs. If you can get past the suit-clad bouncers and door hosts, you'll have a chance to mingle with some of Amsterdam's most bourgeois boogiers. In the early evening, Rain is a fashionable restaurant and lounge, though the menu is a bit limited. The decor is sleek contemporary with lilac accents. Boasts a terrace on which patrons can cast a privileged glance across Rembrandtplein. Mixed drinks start at €8. Weekend themes vary, with quality DJs spinning house, hip hop, and electronic. Often rented for private parties. Dress code: less is more, and even less is even more. Cover F-Sa after 11pm €10. Open M-Th and Su 6pm-2am, F-Sa 6pm-4am. AmEx/MC/V.

Party Crew Cafe, Rembrandtplein 31 (☎623 3740; www.partycrewcafe.nl). 2 large bars (1 only open on weekends) and a peppy atmosphere despite the somewhat bland decor. Packed mostly with tourists from nearby bars as well as some local college students. Smaller than some of the nearby dance clubs, but still a lot of fun. W "Candy Shop"—women get 1 free mixed drink. Open M-Th and Su 10pm-4am, F-Sa 10pm-5am.

Exit, Reguliersdwarsstraat 42 (☎625 8788; www.clubexit.eu). Enter Exit to find one of the most popular ☑**gay** discos in the Netherlands. With a number of stories and styles, Exit attracts a diverse crowd. Mostly male clubbers of different ages end their night here, though female friends often appear. Ground fl. bar plays dance and pop classics for the laid-back boys; more locals hang out here. On the 1st fl. is a DJ-driven, high-energy techno party where a young, handsome crowd sheds its inhibitions. Next floor up plays R&B. Finally, in the back of the top floor, there's a darkroom reserved just for men. Cover F €5, Sa €7. Open M-Th and Su 11pm-4am, F-Sa 11pm-5am. Cash only.

De Duivel, Reguliersdwarsstraat 87 (☎626 6184, www.deduivel.nl). Amsterdam's only club devoted to hip hop, De Duivel ("The Devil") has been visited by Cypress Hill, the Roots, Ghostface, and loads of other musical greats. Small room hosts lively guests who dabble a bit in dancing but mostly just chat over the music. Nightly DJs mix hip hop with an eclectic mix of funk and ska, catering mostly to loyal regulars. A stained-glass devil looks on forbiddingly but can't stop the mellow crowd from enjoying their night. Beer €2. Rum and coke €6.50. Open M-Th and Su 10pm- 3am, F-Sa 10pm-4am.

NIGHTLIFE NEWS. A good resource for the latest on Amsterdam's nightlife and music scene is the free magazine *NL20*, available in most of the city's bars and supermarkets. It boasts a near-complete index of Amsterdam's clubs and bars and has listings of weekly concerts, performances, theme nights, and special shows. The magazine also boasts a "Top Ten" listing for each week. Though in Dutch, the magazine can mostly be deciphered by English-speakers.

JORDAAN

The Jordaan nightlife scene is nothing if not relaxed. Canal boats often moor at bar terraces for a drink, and bar-hoppers sporting everything from T-shirts to designer goods are welcome in this neighborhood's prized blend of the low-brow and the upscale. On warm summer nights in the Jordaan, clubs don't really start swinging until midnight or 1am.

see map p. 338

BARS

▨ **Festina Lente,** Looiersgracht 40 (☎638 1412; www.cafefestinalente.nl). A super-charming bar and cafe that attracts a young, fashionable, and friendly crowd ready to "hurry slowly." Multi-level indoor space filled with books; games of checkers or chess are there for the borrowing. Outdoor canal-side seating shared with a "regular customer" statue. The food here is served as Mediterranean lentini, so that every element of the meal, be it fish, vegetables, or starch, comes separately (€3-5 each). Wine and beer from €2.50. Frequent events like poetry contests (1st Tu of every month) and live concerts—call or check the website for details. Open M 2pm-1am, Tu-Th 10:30am-1am, F 10:30am-3am, Sa 11am-3am, Su noon-1am. Cash only.

▨ **Café 't Smalle,** Egelantiersgracht 12 (☎623 9617), near the corner of Prinsengracht and Egelantiersgracht. A bar rich with its own history, 't Smalle was founded in 1780 as the tasting room of a neighboring distillery of *jenever,* a type of gin. Its fame continues today—a replica of the bar was even made in the "Holland Village" attraction in Nagasaki, Japan. A good place in the afternoon as well as in the evening. Rightfully one of the most popular cafes in the city's west. 't Smalle has tons of canal-side seats in summer and a warm, old-fashioned interior for colder nights. Famous pea soup (€4.35) served in winter. Wieckse Witte €2.45. Open M-Th and Su 10am-1am, F-Sa 10am-2am.

NIGHTLIFE

Café Soundgarden, Marnixstraat 164-166 (☎620 2853; http://home.planet.nl/~nijbo143/soundgarden/ english.htm). Tram #13, 14, or 17 to Marnixstraat or #10 to Rozengracht. One of Amsterdam's true rock 'n' roll joints. Diverse in age and style, but seems to err on the side of grunge. Patrons flock to this classic watering hole to play pool or darts and to listen to a variety of musical genres. Inside are listings of Dutch musical happenings and paintings from local and expat artists; if the dimly lit bar isn't your scene, head to the spacious canal-front terrace. Rotating DJs play everything from classic rock to heavy metal W and Sa night; live acoustic guitar Su 9pm-midnight. Open M-Th and Su 3pm-1am, F-Sa 3pm-3am. Cash only.

Proust, Noordermarkt 4 (☎623 9145). Proust has endured as a place where the beautiful people go to relax. The setting, if not the crowd, is trendier than your average Jordaan *bruin cafe,* and the terrace is packed day and night. Open M-Th and Su 11am-1am, F-Sa 11am-3am. Lunch served until 5pm, dinner 6-10pm. Cash only.

Finch, Noordermarkt 5 (☎626 2461). Chill at this classy lounge bar, whose uber-chic orange-and-white backdrop is a delightful setting for its laid-back crowd. Finch is hopping most nights of the week (especially on market days), keeping the beautiful people in their brew. Beer €2. Organic green-tea *iki* beer €3. Open M 6am-1am, Tu-Th 9:30am-1am, F-Sa 9:30am-3am.

Café de Tuin, 2e Tuindwarsstraat 13 (☎624 4559). Another favorite Jordaan spot. Nestled on a side street away from the hordes. Weekends are especially crowded, though mainly with local faces. Don't ask for Red Bull here; only traditional mixed drinks, wines, and beers (€1.80-2.60) are served in this cool, well-worn *bruin cafe.* Open M-Th and Su 10am-1am, F-Sa 10am-3am.

Duende, Lindengracht 62 (☎420 6692; www.cafe-duende.nl). Free live flamenco music every Sa at 11pm might be what attracts the well-dressed crowd—or perhaps it's the €3-4 tapas. Also a base for flamenco lessons; the bar is often full of women sipping sangria (€3) after a dance workout. No reservations. Open M-Th 4pm-1am, F 4pm-3am, Sa 2pm-3am, Su 2pm-1am.

Cafe Thijssen, Brouwersgracht 107 (☎623 8994; www.cafe-thijssen.nl). After a dinner in one of Lindengracht's many burnished bistros, come here for a tall glass of beer (€1.70-3) on the quiet but beautiful Brouwersgracht. Thijssen is a really unpretentious, classy bar, popular with locals and packed on weekends. Open M-Th and Su 8am-1am, F-Sa 8am-3am. Cash only.

Saarein II, Elandsstraat 119 (☎623 4901), at Hazenstraat. Tram #7, 10, or 17 to Elandsgracht. This relaxed *bruin cafe* has been a ◪**lesbian** establishment for decades. It continues to attract mostly women on weekends, though on weeknights it's filled with all genders and orientations. Full bar (beer €1.75); food during the day. Happy hour F 5-7pm and cash bingo F 7pm. 2nd Su of every month is transgender day. Open Tu-Th and Su noon-1am, F-Sa noon-2am. Cash only.

Cafe P96, Prinsengracht 96 (☎622 1864; www.p96.nl). The locals come out in droves on weekends for this late-night bar on Prinsengracht. The terrace boat, open every evening and weekday, is roomy enough to relax with your favorite brew or your favorite new local friend. Beer €2. Mixed drinks €5. Open M-Th and Su 8pm-3am, F-Sa 8pm-4am. Cash only.

 LEARNED DRINKING. Student travelers: don't forget to ask bartenders if there is a student discount. It's almost always worth a shot.

CLUBS

Club More, Rozengracht 133 (☎528 7459; www.expectmore.nl). Plays host to various organizations and their parties on weekends. Rotating dance nights F; popular salsa nights Sa-Su, when skilled dancers come out to strut their stuff. Cover €8-12. Open F 11pm-4am, Sa-Su 11pm-5am.

Korsakoff, Lijnbaansgracht 161 (☎625 7854). Korsakoff is definitely a goth club, but unless you're dying for some Kanye West and a mojito, don't rule it out for a night out. Industrial, electronic, and hardcore music and strobe lights dominate the dance floor, but upstairs you'll find a slightly more subdued bar (think black lights and Alice in Chains, if you can call Alice in Chains subdued). Bottled beer €2. Open M-Tu and Su 11pm-3am, W-Th 10pm-3am, F-Sa 10pm-4am.

WESTERPARK AND OUD-WEST

Westerpark and Oud-West don't draw many tourists from the sparkly Centrum past sunset, but if you're looking for a laid-back beer with some local faces, there are a number of great places here to throw back a couple of beers. Night spots are fewer in number here, so it's advisable to travel with a destination in mind. If you make the trek, though, you're likely to sip with a Dutch crowd.

see map p. 343

BARS

■ **Toussaint Cafe,** Bosboom Toussaintstraat 26 (☎685 0737). Tram #1 or 6 to 1e Constantijn Huygensstraat or tram #3 or 12 to Overtoom. Walk north from Overtoom 4 blocks on 1e Constantijn Huygensstraat and take a right on Bosboom Toussaintstraat. You won't find a friendlier neighborhood bar in the Oud-West; this cafe bustles with activity during the day and mellows out at night to a calm and candlelit spot for loyal locals to chill. Velvet and dark colors give the space a warm and comfortable feel. The food here is worth mentioning (good sandwiches and veggie options); kitchen closes at 10pm. Open M-Th and Su 10am-midnight, F-Sa 10am-1am. Cash only.

Ebeling, Overtoom 50-52 (☎689 4858), on the block between 1e Constantijn Huygensstraat and Leidseplein. Aims for the young and hip with club-style lighting and slick music. Big on atmosphere, and a nice spot for a mixed drink and a chat; it's got the proximity to Leidseplein without all the crazy crowds. Beer €2. Mixed drinks €5. Open M-Th and Su 11am-1am, F-Sa 11am-3am. Cash only.

CLUB

■ **OT301,** Overtoom 301 (www.squat.net/ot301). One of the larger and more community-oriented legalized squats in Amsterdam. Hosts movie screenings, feminist salons, and live shows. There's also a cinema, gallery space, and cafe, where an organic kitchen serves meals a few times a week. Frequent weekend club nights fill the basement with young, open-minded people ready to dance and have fun. Cover never more than €5. Beer €2. Check the website in advance for events and opening hours.

MUSEUMPLEIN AND VONDELPARK

The Mansion, Hobbemastraat 2 (☎616 6664). Follow Hobbemastraat from the back of the Rijksmuseum toward Leidseplein. The Mansion is like a delicious layer cake—fun to indulge in but not so good for you. A modern Chinese restaurant is stacked on top of three cocktail bars, which in turn are on top of the Dim Sum Club, where DJs spin and the well-coifed crowds dance. Not the place to go for a cheap beer, but if you're willing to dress up, put up with lines, and shell out some cash, you're in for a stylish night. Cover varies. Restaurant open M-Sa 6-11pm; bars open M-Th 6pm-1am, F-Sa 6pm-3am; club open F-Sa 9pm-3am. MC/V.

see map p. 342

DE PIJP

Be sure to return to De Pijp for a night out: its hipster cafes and pubs are swinging on the weekends. Nightlife here is fun with a local flavor, mostly concentrated around Ferdinand Bolstraat and 1e Van Der Helststraat; bars stay open until 3am on weekends. Bars here range from low-key cafes to trendy nightspots, attracting students, young professionals, and expats, along with the occasional tourist. Most De Pijp bars have one thing in common: food! Don't hesitate to peruse the menus at these spots for an inexpensive and tasty bite.

see map p. 333

🏅 **Kingfisher,** Ferdinand Bolstraat 24 (☎671 2395). A local bar with an edge; Kingfisher is low-key and unpretentious but just a little hipper and more stylish than its neighbors. Low-priced, global beer selections include Australian James Boag (€4), Indian Cobra, and, of course, Kingfisher (on tap €2; bottle €3.30). Great food, too. Mixed drinks €6. Frozen fruit smoothies €2. Club sandwiches €4.50. Open M-Th 11am-1am, F-Sa 11am-3am, Su 12pm-1am. Cash only.

🏅 **Chocolate Bar,** 1e Van Der Helststraat 62A (☎675 7672). Tram #16, 24, or 25 to Albert Cuypstraat. In summer, 20-somethings lounge on sofas or padded benches on Chocolate Bar's terrace, heading indoors to enjoy DJs spinning relaxed lounge music on the weekends. 12-15 kinds of mixed drinks run roughly €6.50. Fresh shakes €3. Open M-Th and Su 10am-1am, F-Sa 10am-3am. MC/V.

Cafe Krull, Sarphatipark 2 (☎622 0214). Tram #16, 24, or 25 to Albert Cuypstraat. Boasts ample outdoor seating (across from Sarphatipark), a scrubbed blond wood interior, and enough distance from Van Der Helststraat to feel off the beaten path. An excellent place for a quiet drink or a snack. 10 different draft beers (€1.80), including Guinness (pints €3). *Broodjes* from €3.50. Open M-F 9am-1am, Sa-Su 9am-3am.

Cafe de Groene Vlinder, 130 Albert Cuypstraat (☎470 2500). Tram #16, 24, or 25 to Albert Cuypstraat. The "Green Butterfly" cafe is located on the coveted corner of Albert Cuypstraat and 1e Van Der Helststraat, 2 of De Pijp's most action-packed streets. During the day, its wide picnic-tabled terrace is a great place to take a break from the bustle of the market for a coffee or a salad (€7). Be sure to return at night to hang with De Pijp's chill 20-something crowd. Beer €2. Wine €2.40. Open M-Th and Su 10am-1am, F-Sa 10am-2am. Cash only.

O'Donnell's, Ferdinand Bolstraat 5 (☎676 7786). This Irish pub features a mostly Irish staff and caters to an Anglo-Dutch crowd, showing soccer, cricket, and Gaelic sports on 1 big-screen and 2 small TVs. A bit pricier than other neighborhood bars, but its dark paneling and friendly vibe make up for its €5 pints of Guinness. Other beers €2. The menu features classic food like Irish pie and a traditional roast (€13.50) on Su afternoons after 2pm. Vegetarian options available. Breakfast (omelettes €3.50; full Irish breakfast €8) served M-Sa 11am-5pm, Su 11am-2pm. Lunch €3-5. Shepherd's pie €11. Fish and chips €12. Open M-Th and Su 11am-1am; F-Sa 11am-3am. Kitchen open M-Sa until 10pm, Su until 9pm. AmEx/MC/V.

Cafe Berkhout, Stadhouderskade 77 (☎320 9801), opposite the Heineken Experience (p. 155). This casual joint throws its floor-to-ceiling windows open onto the street in summer, attracting a blend of loyal locals as well as a substantial expat crowd. During the day, tourists make their way over from the Heineken Experience, but the crowd thins out after sundown. Salads €8.50-9.50. Tasty club sandwiches €4-6. Selection of classic, heavy Dutch bar snacks from €4-5. Wash your grub down with a beer (€2-3.60). Open M-Th 11am-1am, F-Sa 11am-3am. MC/V.

Bloemers, Hemonystraat 70 (☎400 4024), on the corner of Ceintuurbaan. Bloemers is a local cafe with a whole host of yuppie and 20-something regulars. Its location on the other side of Sarphatipark gives it a more laid-back feel, but there's no shortage of friendly chatter and free-flowing beer. Pretty colored lights decorate the ocean of outdoor seating. Open M-Th and Su 10am-1am, F-Sa 10am-3am. Cash only.

JODENBUURT AND PLANTAGE

If you're looking for a wild nightlife scene or streets of endless bars, the Jodenbuurt and Plantage are not the place for you. That said, if you value late-night gab sessions more than sweaty interludes in crowded clubs, many of the area's restaurants keep their bars open late. The crown jewel of the neighborhood's nightlife, however, is the wildly popular Arena.

see map p. 344

Arena, 's-Gravesandestraat 51-53 (☎850 2400; www.hotelarena.nl), near Oosterpark. Night bus #76 or 77 or tram #9 to the Tropenmuseum; turn right on Mauritskade and then right on 's-Gravesandestraat. This hotel, bar, restaurant, and nightclub complex is a one-stop shop for fun lovers. The club is bizarrely housed in the chapel of a former Catholic orphanage. The crowd keeps it rockin' through the early hours. A bit touristy, with the pricey Hotel Arena next door, and a bit far away, but more than enough enthusiasm for someone looking for a big night out. Different theme parties F-Su, so do your homework. Cover F-Su €10-25. Occasional public reading or performances, like a recent visit by Miranda July; keep an eye on the calendar. Open F-Sa 11pm-4am.

NIGHTLIFE

DAYTRIPS

With all the fantastical tripping and sights at your fingertips in Amsterdam proper, you may wonder why you would ever want to leave the city. The city appears to be the seat of all things urbane and cultural in the Netherlands, but the popular conception that the remainder of the country offers nothing more than quaint provincialism simply isn't true. The decidedly stereotypical—yet wonderfully so—Zaanse Schans will satisfy hankerings for Dutch clogs and cheese, while a 45min. bus ride out to Aalsmeer will immerse you in more flowers than you ever thought possible. A slightly longer jaunt brings you to Leiden, a bustling university town; to Rotterdam, a modern city with cosmopolitan flavor; or to The Hague and to Delft for the seat of Dutch government and the birthplace of Johannes Vermeer, respectively. A few hours away, the desolate Wadden Islands boast the finest beaches in the Netherlands, and a nature-minded trip to De Hoge Veluwe National Park will reveal the Kröller-Müller museum—the country's best collection outside of Amsterdam (or, arguably, even including the capital).

This guide covers most of the Netherlands, all of which is easily accessible by train, or even bike, from Amsterdam. Biking through the Low Countries is exceptionally easy—they are, after all, largely flat and mostly below sea level. For convenience, you may also take your bike with you on all trains for a €6 fee. Spring, when fields of tulips create a sea of colors along the roads, is an ideal time to see the country in all its stereotypical, but beautiful, glory.

The towns and cities in this chapter are listed by route (so that it's easy to hop from one town to another) and then in order of their approximate distance from Amsterdam. The closer and smaller ones are an easy two-hour excursion, while larger and more distant areas are better seen over a couple of days.

AALSMEER
☎029

Although this small village along Grote Poel Lake seems rather unassuming at first glance, it is actually the epicenter of the world's floral economy: the Aalsmeer flower auction, the village's principal employer, is the largest flower trading floor in the world and plays a critical role in setting flower prices worldwide.

TRANSPORTATION. Aalsmeer can be reached from both Amsterdam and Haarlem by **bus**. From Amsterdam, take bus #172 across from the Victoria Hotel near Centraal Station to the flower auction (Bloemenveiling Aalsmeer) and then on to the town of Aalsmeer. The first bus leaves at 5:12am. (45min.; every 15min.; 6 strips to the flower auction, 2 more to the town.) From Haarlem, take bus #140 to the town of Aalsmeer (45min., every 15-30min., 6 strips) and then transfer to bus #172 to the flower auction. The first bus leaves at 5:25am.

ORIENTATION AND PRACTICAL INFORMATION. Aalsmeer is a very small town; its center can be walked within 15min. The flower auction lies two kilometers away and can be reached without a visit to the town. **Stationsweg,** the main road in what could generously be described as downtown, becomes **Zijdstraat** and continues to the edge of the town. Zijdstraat is the town's main shopping street, boasting a number of shops, cafes, and restaurants. To reach the center of town from the bus stop, continue down Hortensialaan in the direction the bus traveled until Hadleystraat and turn left. Continue down Hadleystraat for two blocks and turn right onto Stommeerweg. Stommeerweg becomes Station-

BIDDING ON BULBS

t may be an understatement to say that flowers are an important national symbol for the Netherlands. Visitors from around the globe come each year to feast their eyes on Dutch tulip fields. What few visitors realize, however, s that these flowers are part of a multi-billion-dollar international ndustry and the Netherlands is one of its most important players.

The Dutch have been flower-crazy for centuries. Tulips, for nstance, arrived in the Netherlands from Constantinople in 1559 and quickly became status symbols for the rich. At first, the bulbs were traded only among ulip aficionados, but soon interest in the precious bulbs spread o speculators, who bought bulbs at low prices and then resold hem at much higher ones. At the peak of the craze in 1637, one bulb went for US$76,000, but within six weeks, the tulip market crashed, sending the entire Dutch economy into shambles.

These days, the Dutch flower market is better organized. The center of this global flower exchange is he **Bloemenveiling Aalsmeer** Aalsmeer flower auction, p. 244). Every day, flower moguls set the world price for flowers in this otherwise sleepy enclave, and it's all done before lunch.

The numbers are staggering. Each morning, 4000 trucks deliver over 19 million flowers and two million plants to the auction's sprawling trading floor, roughly the

sweg. The Aalsmeer **VV,** Drie Kolommenplein 1, is off Stationsweg. This small bureau has a friendly and helpful staff. (☎ 732 5374; www.vvvaalsmeer.nl. Open M-F 9am-12:30pm and 1-5pm).

🎴 **FOOD.** The tiny burg of Aalsmeer manages to keep flower seekers full with a decent set of dining options. Most of the shops and restaurants center on Zijdstraat, which also has a good collection of meat, cheese, and other food shops. For a quick breakfast after visiting the flower auction, there are a few small bakeries at the start of Zijdstraat. In keeping with the hamlet's horticultural claim to fame, **Eetcafe 't Holland Huys ❷,** Zijdstraat 14, sports a gorgeous backyard garden and, inside, bookcases and comfy sofas in a self-described "living room" atmosphere. Try typical Dutch cuisine like *stamppotten*, a traditional meal with mashed potatoes and vegetables. (☎ 734 4602. Lunch sandwiches €2.50-7. Dinner entrees €12-20. Open Tu-Su 10:30am-11pm. Kitchen closes 9pm. Cash only.) **Wapen van Aalsmeer ❸,** Dorpsstraat 15, is a more upscale restaurant offering traditional Dutch meals for around €14-16. Fortunately, lunch is slightly less expensive, with €6-10 sandwiches. (☎ 735 5500. Open daily noon-9:15pm. Lunch served noon-4pm. AmEx/MC/V.) For an inexpensive, no-frills eatery, **O Sole Mio ❶,** Dorpsstraat 28, offers the ultimate in takeout options: pizza and Shawarma. (☎ 733 1440. More than 40 varieties of pizza €5.50-10. Shawarma €4. Lasagna €7.50. Sandwiches €4-6. Open daily 4-10pm. Cash only.)

🟢 **SIGHTS.** Really the only reason to visit Aalsmeer is the **Bloemenveiling Aalsmeer** (Aalsmeer flower auction), Legmeerdijk 313. The Wall Street of the flower industry, this massive warehouse and trading floor hosts thousands of traders every day representing some of the world's largest flower-export companies; it also sets prices for flowers worldwide. Nineteen million flowers and over two million plants are bought and sold daily, with an annual turnover of almost US$2 billion. All of the flowers, often flown overnight from across the globe, go through Aalsmeer's massive trading floor, the size of **150 American football fields** (almost 1 sq. km), making it the largest commercial trading space in the world. The buyers bid on the flowers Dutch-auction style (where the price goes down rather than up) through a complicated system of digital clocking devices. Since the flowers have to make it to their final destination by the end of the day (which includes locales all over the world), almost all the trading is finished by 11am. To see the most action, go between 7 and 9am. The busiest days of the week are Monday and Friday; the quietest day is Thursday. There's always more action around major international holidays such as Christmas and Valentine's Day. The trading floor is visible to tourists via a large catwalk along the ceiling, with audio boxes explaining each step of the process in a variety of languages. This self-guided tour takes approximately an hour to complete, though it lets you flower-gaze at your own pace. It begins with the delivery process, takes you past the auction rooms where the action is, and ends with a description of the shipping process as you watch thousands of flowers are shuffled across the building. (☎739 2185; www.aalsmeer.com. Open M-F 7-11am. €5, ages 6-11 €3, €4 per person for groups over 15. Guides available to hire for €75.)

For those who can still bear the sight of flowers, **Historische Tuin,** Uiterweg 32, is a unique historical garden in a working nursery. It celebrates the Netherlands's botanical history and includes an exhibit on gardening tools and the development of Aalsmeer from a swamp to a town. Exhibits on traditional farm life, 55 varieties of the dahlia flower, an exceptional tree with 13 kinds of pears, and over 150 different types of roses entice nature lovers and insects alike. Look for special flower sales in the spring and be sure to visit the rose greenhouse if you go—the smell alone is worth a linger. (☎732 2562; www.htaalsmeer.org. All captions and information in Dutch. Open Apr.-Oct. Tu-F 10am-4:30pm, Sa-Su 1:30-4:30pm. €3, over 65 €2.50, under 12 €1.50.) Nearby, **Westeinder Rondvaart,** Uiterweg 27, operates an open-air boat that traverses the picturesque lakes west of the city center. Those interested in the history or topography of the region will delight in the tranquil country landscape. The boats pass the islands in the lakes and emphasize the area's history. Though it isn't the most exciting trip, it makes for a pleasant ride. (☎734 1582; www.westeinderrondvaart.nl. Operates May-Oct. Tu-W and F-Sa 1:30, 2:45, 4pm; Su 2:30, 4pm. €6.50, under 12 €3.25, with 15 people or more €5.50.)

ZAANSE SCHANS ☎075

Unleash your inner tourist for a day at delightful Zaanse Schans, a 17th-century town located only 20min. from Amsterdam on the River Zaan. Feel free to fumble clumsily with an oversized map while fiddling with your fanny pack, since Zaanse Schans—with its cheese farm, clog workshop, and working windmills—embraces and encourages a tourist's curiosity. In the 1950s, the residents of the Zaan region were concerned that industrialization was quietly destroying their historic landmarks, so

size of 150 American football fields. Most of the flowers were harvested the night before from farms as close as local tulip fields and as far away as Zambia and Israel.

Thousands of traders, representing some of the world's largest export companies, bid on the plants in four different auction rooms where nine auctions occur simultaneously. The flowers are sold, bundle by bundle, in Dutch auctions, where the price decreases as bidding continues. The action begins at 6am, and in order to allow time for the flowers to reach their final destinations, almost all the trading is completed (and the warehouse is swept and empty) by 11am.

So it is in within these few hours that more than 55,000 transactions take place. It's easy to see, then, how this market is one of the most important centers of the world flower trade, processing one-third of world exports in cut flowers. And though the auction is based in the Netherlands, it's certainly not just for tulips. More than 13,000 types of flowers are traded, with 400 new varieties developed each year. So when you buy your sweetheart a bouquet of roses for Valentine's Day, there's a good chance the flowers went through Aalsmeer.

they transported the wood structures on barges and trucks to this pretty plot of land, making it one-stop shopping for all of the Netherlands's traditional customs. While you walk through the town dodging the numerous group tours, you may feel immersed in a surreal museum village; however, a few inhabitants (about 40 in total, occupying 25 historic houses) do in fact work here, and the town's two windmills sell their products to nearby factories. The town of Zaanse Schans is the perfect destination for that timeless Golden Age feel that you've been searching for throughout the Netherlands.

◲◪ TRANSPORTATION AND PRACTICAL INFORMATION. From Amsterdam Centraal, take the **stoptrein** heading to Alkmaar and get off at Koog Zaandijk (20min., €2.80). From there, follow the signs to Zaanse Schans, a 12min. walk across a bridge. **Biking** to Zaanse Schans takes around 90min.; Bike City (p. 95) plots an easy-to-follow route along well-paved bike paths—you can pick a map up at their shop or on their website. The Museum Zaans ticket desk doubles as the most useful **information center** around Zaanse Schans; you can ask there for a free map or info about the town. The VVV in Amsterdam (p. 93) can provide you with all the information you need for your trip before you leave; otherwise, the closest VVV to Zaanse Schans is the Zaandam office, Ebbehout 31, in the Zaandam train station. (Open M-W 8:30am-4pm, Th 8:30am-7pm, F 8:30am-noon.)

◪◳ ACCOMMODATIONS AND FOOD. Zaanse Schans is really best suited to be a one-day trip, but if you're just begging to stay, try the comfortable, well-run **Hotel Sans Pareil ❹**, Lagedijk 32-34, across the bridge from Zaanse Schans. Their 12 double rooms start at €80 (but can get up to €130 on busy weekends in the summer) and come with TVs, phones, and bath. (☎621 1911; www.sanspareil.nl. AmEx/MC/V.) You'd also be best to bring a picnic lunch, since food doesn't come cheap (and isn't particularly interesting) in the town's few, tourist-oriented restaurants. **De Kraai ❷**, Kraaienpad 1, near the parking lot, is an informal place to grab a bite. (☎615 6403. Coffee €2. Sandwiches from €2.75. *Pannenkoeken* lunch €12.50. Open daily 9am-6pm.)

◪ SIGHTS. The best way to see picturesque Zaanse Schans is just to wander about the town, popping into whichever building that happens to interest you. Most attractions in Zaanse Schans are open daily 10am-5pm in the summer but only on weekends in the winter. The highlights are inarguably the ◪**working windmills,** some of the last remaining ones in the world. You can see the wheels inside grinding raw materials with their breeze-fueled power and then head up to the deck for a dramatic view of the town. Zaanse Schans is home to eight windmills, but only two regularly allow visitors.

The lovely **De Kat windmill,** Kalverringdijk 29, has been grinding plants and chalk into paint pigment for Dutch artists since 1782. Today, you can take a tour of the windmill's inner machinery and climb to the upper balcony for a good view of the River Zaan. Groups can make reservations in advance to see the windmill's 3000kg grinding stones at work. (☎621 0477. Open Apr.-Oct. daily 9am-5pm; Nov.-Mar. Sa-Su 9am-5pm. €2.50, ages 6-12 €1.50, groups of 10 or more €1.50 per person.) Down the road, the **De Zoeker windmill,** Kalverringdijk 31, dating from 1676, is the oldest seed-oil mill in the world, restored to its current condition in 1978; it works by a deafeningly loud beam that will certainly catch your attention. The mill is capable of producing about 100L of oil per day and runs seven days a week, except in bad weather. (☎628 7942. Open Mar.-Oct. daily 9:30am-4:30pm. €2.)

If you're interested in a little context for all the cheese, clogs, and windmills, visit the lovely **Museum Zaans,** Schansend 7. Chronicling the cultural history of the Zaans region through the lenses of wind, water, work, and life, the museum has a

The Netherlands

variety of displays showcasing Dutch life in this rural riverside region in the 17th and 18th centuries. On the top floor, you'll find an expansive view of the area and its windmills. (☎616 2862; www.museumzaans.nl. Open daily 9am-5pm. €5.40, ages 4-12 and over 65 €2.70, under 4 free.) From Schansend, head down Zeilenmakerspad to watch craftsmen mold blocks of wood into attractive but sadly impractical clogs at **Klompenmakerij de Zaanse Schans**, Kraaienest 4. *Klompen* enthusiasts can ake in an informative display that unravels the mystery of the wooden shoe's prominence in Dutch history. Of course, after the short history lesson, there is a humongous gift shop, with strings of endless varieties of clogs in all shapes, sizes, and colors hanging from the walls and ceiling—yours to clunk around in for about €30. (☎617 7121. Open daily 8am-6pm.) Follow your nose (hint: keep going on Zeilenmakerspad toward the water) to the **Cheesefarm Catharina Hoeve**, Zeilenmakerspad 5, a replica of the original cheese farm. Today, the center is more of a large tourist shop, selling endless varieties of Dutch cheese. The shop offers free bite-sized samples of its various homemade products and a small workshop showcasing how the cheese is prepared. Whatever you do, don't say "cheese" when posing for a photo here, but feel free to roll your eyes when someone else inevitably does. (☎621 5820. Open daily 8am-6pm. Free.) On the waterfront road, watch a demonstration on pewter jewelry making at **De Tinkoepel Tinnegieterij**, Kalverringdijk 1. Housed in a Dutch teahouse dating back to 1747, the tiny

BEST OF THE NETHERLANDS (7-9 DAYS)

Leiden (1 day)
One of Europe's most prestigious universities lends Leiden a bipolar personality– a serious intellectual center (with philosophy literally written on the walls) and a hopping party city (p. 260).

Wadden Islands (1-2 days)
As desolate as life gets in the gentrified Dutch countryside, the Wadden Islands present an enviable escape with glorious stretches of sandy white beaches (p. 320).

Haarlem (1 day)
This traditional Dutch town offers churches and other architectural delights to go with the most restaurants per capita in the Netherlands. Hit the beach at nearby Zandvoort or Bloemendaal if you choose, but don't miss the brilliant Frans Hals Museum.

Utrecht (1 day)
Only a 30min. train ride from Amsterdam, this study-by-day and party-by-night university town claims some of the Netherlands's best festivals as well as its own Museum Quarter (p. 298).

Amsterdam ✪

The Hague and Delft (1-2 days)
Brush up on international law at the Hague, the Netherlands's seat of government, home of the royal family, and location of the extraordinary Mauritshuis (p. 269). Delft, the birthplace of painter Johannes Vermeer, is a short tram ride away; it's one of the loveliest and best preserved Dutch towns (p. 279).

Maastricht (1 day)
Maastricht lies at the crossroads of the Netherlands, Belgium, and Germany and has a rich history to match. Its old cobblestoned feel, pub culture, and mysterious caves are worth the long train ride (p. 313).

Rotterdam (1 day)
The biggest port city in Europe, a center for modern architecture, a multicultural city: Rotterdam is as far from the Old World as it gets—at least in the Netherlands (p. 285).

building was moved about five kilometers across the River Zaan to its present location in 1968. The itty-bitty shop has a surprisingly large collection of pewter jewelry and trinkets. The friendly staff prepares the goods right there, explaining each step of the process. (☎616 2263; www.tinkoepel.nl. Open daily Apr.-Oct. 10am-5pm; Nov.-Mar. 11am-4pm. Free.)

Other attractions include the pint-sized **Museum Het Noorderhuis,** Kalverringdijk 17, a restored home that features original costumes from the Zaan region in two reconstructed 19th-century rooms and a display of the wardrobe of an 18th-century lady. (☎617 3237. Open July-Aug. daily 10am-5pm; Mar.-June and Sept.-Oct. Tu-Su 10am-5pm; Nov.-Feb. Sa-Su 10am-5pm. €1, ages 4-11 and seniors €0.50.) Consider cruising around Zaanse Schans with **Rederij de Schans** on a 45min. boat ride through the River Zaan, complete with gorgeous views of overworked windmills. (☎065 329 4467; www.rederijdeschans.nl. Rides Apr.-Sept. daily every hr. 11am-4pm. €6, over 65 €5, under 12 €3.)

HAARLEM ☎023

Haarlem's narrow cobblestone streets, rippling canals, and fields of tulips make for a great escape from Amsterdam's urban frenzy. Most visitors come to the city for its many artistic and historical sights, littered as it is with Renaissance facades, idyllic **hofjes** (almshouses for the elderly), medieval architecture, and the renowned **Frans Hals Museum.** Founded earlier than Amsterdam, Haarlem (pop. 150,000) was once the cultural center of the 16th- and 17th-century Netherlands. But there's more than antiquated charm here—Haarlem beats with a relaxed energy befitting a mid-size urban center. Coffee shops, bars, and the most restaurants per capita of any Dutch city ensure that there's fun to be had after the sun goes down. **Grote Markt** welcomes a bustling marketplace on Monday afternoons, where vendors hawk everything from clothing to flower seeds, usually more cheaply than their big-city counterparts. On the last Saturday in April (sometimes the second to last), make sure to catch the Flower Parade, a joyous affair with floats made entirely of hyacinths, live music, and lots of happy Haarlemmers (see www.bloemencorso.info for more information).

> **⚡TIP** **MARKED MARKT.** Hit Grote Markt on Mondays from 9am to 4pm for inexpensive clothes, jewelry, and other items. To the south, Botermarkt has a general market on Mondays from 9am to 4pm, books for sale Wednesday from 9am to 5pm, and an organic food market Friday from 9am to 4pm.

TRANSPORTATION AND PRACTICAL INFORMATION

Travel to Haarlem from Amsterdam either by **train** from Centraal Station (20min.; €3.60, €6.20 round-trip if returning same day) or by **bus** #80 from Marnixstraat near Leidseplein (20min., 2 per hr., 2 strips). In Haarlem, a **Tickets and Service** center provides schedules for trains and sells tickets and *strippenkaarten.* (Open M-Sa 6:15am-midnight, Su 6:15am-11pm.) There is a bike-rental shop between the train station entrance and the tourist office; it rents bicycles for €6.50 per day or €32.50 per week with a €50 deposit. Look for the **Rijweil Shop** sign. (☎531 7066. Open daily 9am-9pm.)

The **VVV** tourist office, Stationsplein 1, just to your right when you walk out of the train station, sells maps (€2) and finds accommodations for a €5 fee. It also vends discounted passes to the Frans Hals Museum, De Hallen Museum, Teylers Museum, and Het Dolhuys. (☎0900 616 1600, €0.50 per min.; www.vvvzk.nl. Open Oct.-Mar. M-F 9:30am-5pm, Sa 10am-3pm; Apr.-Sept. M-F 9am-5:30pm, Sa

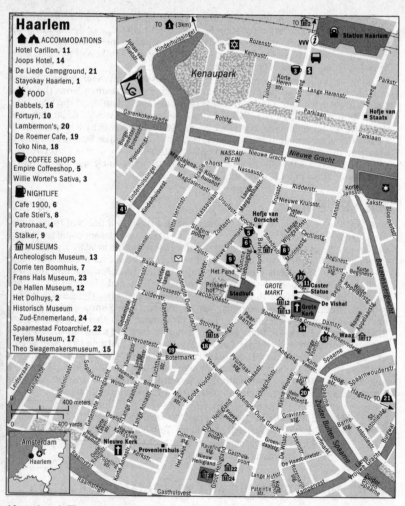

Haarlem

🏠🏠 **ACCOMMODATIONS**
Hotel Carillon, **11**
Joops Hotel, **14**
De Liede Campground, **21**
Stayokay Haarlem, **1**

🍖 **FOOD**
Babbels, **16**
Fortuyn, **10**
Lambermon's, **20**
De Roemer Cafe, **19**
Toko Nina, **18**

☕ **COFFEE SHOPS**
Empire Coffeeshop, **5**
Willie Wortel's Sativa, **3**

🍷 **NIGHTLIFE**
Cafe 1900, **6**
Cafe Stiel's, **8**
Patronaat, **4**
Stalker, **9**

🏛 **MUSEUMS**
Archeologisch Museum, **13**
Corrie ten Boomhuis, **7**
Frans Hals Museum, **23**
De Hallen Museum, **12**
Het Dolhuys, **2**
Historisch Museum
  Zud-Ennemerland, **24**
Spaarnestad Fotoarchief, **22**
Teylers Museum, **17**
Theo Swagemakersmuseum, **15**

10am-4pm.) There is a **post office** branch on Gedempte Oude Gracht, near the intersection with Zijlstraat. (☎0900 767 8526. Open M-F 9am-5pm.)

🏠 ACCOMMODATIONS

Stayokay Haarlem, Jan Gijzenpad 3 (☎537 3793; www.stayokay.com/haarlem). Bus #2 from platform #1 (dir.: Haarlem-Noord; every 10min. until 6pm, every 15min. 6pm-12:30am) to Jan Gijzenpad; the bus stops directly in front of the hostel. The best place to stay in Haarlem is 3km from Haarlem's train station, surrounded by a wooded park and situated on the banks of a placid canal. Rooms are spare but cheery and perfectly clean with bath. The hostel's pub, The Shuffle, is a lively place where the brave can order a 2.5L "boot" of beer (€15). On summer nights, the party spills onto the canal-side patio, where an open fire doubles as a barbecue. Packages for activities at the nearby Noorder sports park available. Bike rental €8 per day (passport or €150 deposit required). Breakfast included. Box lunches €4.15; 3-course dinner served at 6 and 7:30pm €10. Bike rack, bag storage, and laundry room included. Dorms in high season €29; doubles €102. €2.50 HI discount. AmEx/MC/V. ❶

Joops Hotel, Oude Groenmarkt 20 (☎532 2008; www.joopshotel.nl), in the shadow of the giant Grote Kerk, on the entrance side. Centrally located with elegant, fresh-feeling rooms off Egyptian-themed hallways. A few of the hotel rooms are also filled with lavish Nilotic decorations; request one if you want to wake up next to the Sphinx. Spacious rooms and apartments with private bath (some with a tub), DVD player, TV, phone, cream walls, and carpeted floors, all serviced by a Dutch rarity: a spacious elevator. Continental breakfast buffet €12.50. Reception M-Sa 7am-11pm, Su 8am-10pm. Standard doubles €95, larger doubles €115; quads €135; Egyptian hot tub suite €165. Extra bed €30. 1-room studios with bath and kitchenette for 2 people €125; for 3 people €135; for 4 people €145. Apartment with kitchen, bedroom, and bath €145. AmEx/MC/V. ❹

Hotel Carillon, Grote Markt 27 (☎531 0591; www.hotelcarillon.com). Ideally located right in the town square, to the left of the Grote Kerk and 5min. from the train station. Bright, basic rooms make up in cleanliness and neatness what they lack in space. All with TV, shower, and phone. Rooms situated above a classy restaurant and bar with an outdoor patio facing directly onto the square (beer from €1.80; rib-eye steak with fries and salad €11). Breakfast included. Reception and bar open daily in summer 7:30am-1am; in winter 7:30am-midnight. Singles €40, with bath €60; doubles €65/80; triples €102; quads €110. MC/V. ❷

De Liede Campground, Lie Oever 68 (☎535 8666; www.campingdeliede.nl). Take the *stoptrein* that goes between Haarlem and Amsterdam and get off at the Haarlem-Spaarnwoude stop; the campground is just a few min. away. An alternative is bus #2 (dir.: Zuiderpolder); ask the bus driver where to get off. Located on a swimmable canal with a restaurant, pool table, tennis, and campsite shop. Animals allowed. €3.50 per person, €3.50 per tent, €3.50 per car. Cash only. ❶

🍴 FOOD

Haarlem smugly dubs itself the "most delicious city in the Netherlands." The slogan refers to the city's many restaurants, which are definitely satisfying but, unfortunately, rather expensive. For cheaper, casual

LOCAL LEGEND

DIKE DRAMA DEBUNKED

The Netherlands is a land rife with stereotypes: wooden shoes, windmills, and weed, among others. While these images have at least some basis in fact, one of the most ingrained Dutch legends is that of a courageous little boy from Haarlem who saved his town from flooding by stopping up a leak in the town's dike with his chubby finger. This tale, however, is not based in reality; in fact, it isn't even Dutch.

The story of the little boy comes from the popular children's book *Hans Brinker or the Silver Skates*, written by Mary Mapes Dodge in 1865. Dodge was from the US and had never been to the Netherlands; she wrote *Hans Brinker* based on books, magazines, and art about the country. In the story, Hans Brinker's schoolteacher recounts the story of the child who held back the waters of the Atlantic with a small finger and a lot of determination.

It did not matter that it was a fictional story; after it became a hit, the Netherlands was flooded with American tourists in search of its origins. In 1950 (and exasperation), the Dutch Board of Tourism finally placed a statue of the little boy and the dike in the town of Spaarndam. Beneath the statue reads the inscription: "Dedicated to our youth, to honor the boy who symbolizes the perpetual struggle of Holland against the water." In 1954, Dutch author Margreet Bruijn rewrote Dodge's tale in Dutch with the new setting in Spaarndam, thus cementing its place in Dutch lore.

meals, travelers should try the cafes in **Grote Markt** or **Botermarkt,** which have the added advantage of outdoor patios that soak in the stunning city backdrop. Rather expensive restaurants are easy to find, especially on Lange Veerstraat, but even more cheap eateries crowd Gedempte Oude Gracht.

Toko Nina, Koningstraat 48 (☎531 7819; www.tokonina.nl). Opened in 1981, this lovely family-owned Indonesian specialty food shop has cooking ingredients on the shelves and delicious prepared foods behind the deli counter. There are a couple tables for those too hungry to wait. Try the coconut beef, the spicy eggs, or the chicken *satay*, all available as part of various combo meals (white rice with your choice of meat or vegetable dishes; €5.75-8.75). Fried rice and noodles €1 extra. Spring rolls and puff pastries €1 each. Open M 11am-7pm, Tu-F 9:30am-7pm, Sa 9:30am-6pm, Su 1-6pm. Cash only. ❷

Fortuyn, Grote Markt 23 (☎542 1899; www.grandcafefortuyn.nl). One of the smaller *grandcafes* in Grote Markt, so the service is a little more personal and the space less busy. A perfect view of the church rising above to the left, a line of pretty trees to the right, and the square stretching across in front of the relaxed outdoor seating. Sandwiches (salmon €7.05; BLT €4.45) and snacks (olives and cheese €4) served until 5pm, dinner entrees until 10pm (everything from pepper steak to tikka masala; €17.50-22.50). Open M-W and Su 10am-midnight, Th-Sa 10am-1am. Cash only. ❸

Lambermon's, Spaarne 96 (☎542 7804; www.lambermons.nl). From Lange Veerstraat, turn down one of the streets on your left, then turn right; it's 2 blocks down in a 17th-century brick structure adorned with gold lions at the top. 4 chefs whip up a delectable 10-course menu every night; each course (€8.75) is served only once, during its allotted 30min. time slot. 3-5 courses will satisfy, especially when paired with a glass of wine (€4.50), selected to complement each course. Full wine and liquor menus are available as well. The open kitchen functions as a kind of performance-art venue, as guests marvel at the creativity of the numerous chefs. Reservations mandatory on weekends. Open daily 6pm-1am. 1st course at 6:30pm. Kitchen closes at 10:30pm. AmEx/MC/V. ❺

Babbels, Lange Veerstraat 23 (☎542 3578). Walk behind the Grote Kerk and take a right on Lange Veerstraat. Babbels serves a range of meat and fish dishes in an elegant, candlelit setting. The popular restaurant almost feels like an antique toy shop with storybook murals and shelves littered with dolls and trinkets. Prices are slightly lower than those of the upscale restaurants that surround it, and dishes like the *carpaccio* with fresh parmesan (€8.50), chicken skewers in peanut sauce (€13), and spare ribs (€12.50) are satisfying. Main dishes served with salad, french fries, and vegetables (€11.50-17.25). Reasonable appetizers abound (€5-9.75). Open daily 5:30-10pm. AmEx/MC/V. ❸

De Roemer Cafe, Botermarkt 17 (☎532 5267; www.cafederoemer.nl). A typical Dutch cafe on Botermarkt, filled with locals, their kids, and teens preparing to prowl the town by sampling the large selection of specialty beer (€1.80-8.40 per bottle). Music wafts from inside the restaurant to the lively outdoor patio. Appetizer menu includes Thai crab cakes (€5.50). Main dishes €11.40-15.50. Vegetarian daily special €13. Sandwiches €3.10-5.20. *Tostis* (including mozzarella, tomato, and pesto) €2.20-2.60. Open M-Th 10am-1pm, F-Sa 10am-2pm, Su noon-1am. Cash only. ❷

◎ SIGHTS

The action in Haarlem centers on **Grote Markt,** its vibrant main square since the town's founding in 1245. To get to the square from the train station, head south along Kruisweg, which becomes Kruisstraat when it crosses the Nieuwe Gracht. Continue south when Kruisstraat becomes Barteljorisstraat, and you'll soon be bombarded by the square's magnificence. Just north of the Grote Kerk, the five-meter statue of **Laurens Coster** beckons to the public.

FRANS HALS MUSEUM. This breathtaking museum leads you through the art of the Dutch Golden Age with an impressive collection of paintings by masters such as Jacob van Ruisdael, Pieter Saenredam, and one-time (and now permanent) Haarlem resident Frans Hals, many of whom used Haarlem locals as subjects. Housed in a picturesque 17th-century building—used as an almshouse for 200 years and an orphanage for 100 years after that—the museum offers a unique impression of 16th- and 17th-century artwork; the earliest works are 16th-century biblical paintings and some unusual altarpieces, preserved after the beginning of the Reformation, when they were removed from the Grote Kerk. Spread through mostly recreated period rooms, the paintings are displayed as they might have been in the Golden Age: above antique oak tables and between cabinets filled with silver, glass, and porcelain. The sound of beautiful, ticking antique clocks resonates throughout the museum. Along with the dramatic Haarlem landscapes painted by Van Ruisdael and the serene churches depicted by Saenredam, 11 of Haarlem master Frans Hals's works reside here—many of them enormous pieces portraying the city's civic guards. In these works, Hals departed from his contemporaries, as he arranged his militia companies with greater motion and freedom than his colleagues did; most painters of that era preferred to paint portraits with stodgy, rigid poses. In *The Banquet of the Officers of the St. George Militia Company*, look for Hals's self-portrait in the upper-left row of men. His other portraiture work, commissioned by bourgeois merchants, reveals breezy casual brush strokes that were once considered sloppy but are now understood to have been an initial move toward Impressionism. The museum also houses a magnificent, intricate dollhouse and a pristine courtyard garden. *(Groot Heiligland 62. From Grote Markt in front of the church, take a right on Warmoesstraat and go 3½ blocks down. ☎ 511 5775; www.franshalsmuseum.com. Wheelchair-accessible. Open Tu-Sa 11am-5pm, Su noon-5pm. €7, under 19 free, groups €5.25 per person.)*

 TIP **CARPE HAARLEM.** Not sure what those three "V" words sprayed across this tulip country town mean? Haarlem's motto is *vicit vim virtus:* virtue vanquishes violence.

GROTE KERK/ST. BAVO'S. This church's interior glows with light from the enormous stained-glass windows and houses the splendid, mammoth Müller organ and its 5000 pipes, once played by both **Handel** (who came to Haarlem specifically to play it) and **Mozart** (when he was 10 years old). First built in the early 14th century but reconstructed several times, St. Bavo's holds many artifacts, including Haarlem's oldest safe, model ships celebrating the 1219 capture of the city from Spanish hands, a cannonball from the Spanish siege of 1572-73, and a modern statue commemorating Haarlem's resistance during those seven months of besiegement. To the right of the organ is the gated Dog Whipper's Chapel, from which an attendant would emerge to remove troublesome dogs that had entered the church. Make sure to look up to the church's fabulous and delicately painted vaulted wood ceiling. Pieter Saenredam (who painted the church), Jacob van Ruisdael, and Frans Hals are buried here; Hals's tombstone is marked with a lantern. Weary travelers can sip coffee or tea (€1) in the Brewer's Guild memorial section. *(Grote Markt. ☎ 553 2040; www.bavo.nl. Open Nov.-Feb. M-Sa 10am-4pm, Mar.-Oct. Tu-Sa 10am-4pm. €2, children €1.25. Guided tours by appointment €0.50. Organ concerts Tu 8:15pm, June-Sept. also Th 3pm; www.organfestival.nl. €2.50.)*

CORRIE TEN BOOMHUIS. Corrie ten Boom and her family were pillars of strength and generosity in the Dutch Resistance, providing a safe haven for Jews and persecuted Dutch rebels during WWII. This house, despite its location on one of the city's most traveled thoroughfares, served as a secret headquarters for the Resistance. It is estimated that Corrie saved the lives of over 800 people by arranging to have them hidden in houses throughout the city and in the surrounding countryside. She kept the most imperiled refugees in her own house—those who supposedly looked particularly Jewish and others whose poor health meant almost certain death in an extermination camp. When the Ten Boom family's subterfuge was discovered, they were sent to the Ravensbruck concentration camp, and only Corrie managed to survive the slaughter. Following the war, she won global renown for her message of forgiveness and authored the book *The Hiding Place*, the tale of her wartime ordeal, which was later made into a film. The mandatory one-hour tour through the Ten Boom house provides a glance at her moving life, but the most extraordinary sight is undoubtedly the famed hiding spot, an impossibly narrow space located behind a brick wall. Six fugitives hid here from the Gestapo when the Ten Boom family was betrayed, staying in the tiny space for three days without food, water, or facilities before they were rescued by the Dutch police. *(Barteljorisstraat 19. 2min. from Grote Markt. ☎531 0823; www.corrietenboom.com. Open daily Apr.-Oct. 10am-4pm (last tour 3:30pm); Nov.-Mar. 11am-3pm (last tour 2:30pm). Tours every 30min., alternating between Dutch and English; call or check the clock outside for times. Free, but donations accepted.)*

TEYLERS MUSEUM. Named after Pieter Teyler van der Hulst, a textile manufacturer who left his fortune for the promotion of arts and sciences, this museum, opened in 1784, is the oldest in the Netherlands. It feels like an oversized cabinet of curiosities, complete with a Gregorian reflecting telescope, a mammoth skull, a beautiful celestial globe, a giant elephant bird egg, a 40kg chunk of smoky quartz from the Alps, a Plesiosaurus fossil, and much more—all crammed together into the bottom floor of the massive building. One wing houses rotating exhibitions, more thoughtfully curated and on related topics like optical illusions. There are old coins, obsolete scientific instruments, and a room of 19th-century paintings alongside the jaws of a Mosasaurus and the "Diluvian man" (a salamander fossil once mistaken for an undiscovered species of human, *Homo diluvii testis*). Make sure to ask for the free English audio tour on your way in. The Classical facade is a formidable sight along the canal-side houses, and the museum also houses a small cafe that faces out to a serene landscape of open green. *(Spaarne 16. From Grote Markt, walk behind the church to Damstraat and then take a left at the river. ☎531 9010; www.teylersmuseum.nl. Wheelchair-accessible. Open Tu-Sa 10am-5pm, Su noon-5pm. €7, ages 6-17 €2, groups of 20 €5 per person.)*

HET DOLHUYS. This new national museum of psychiatry opened in 2005 on the initiative of several psychiatric hospitals, which transferred their historical artifacts to this exhibition space to "bridge the gap between the mental health care sector and the general public." The hugely inventive exhibits use video, audio, slide shows, computer terminals, and innumerable artifacts to represent mental illness through the ages. Here, you can marvel at treatments from cupping and herbal treatments (meant to cure a bodily imbalance) to Freudian psychoanalysis (meant to heal the mind). The downside to this museum is that all audio recordings, wall texts, and videos are in Dutch. It's still worth a look, though, especially for anyone interested in the subject, and a well-written and comprehensive English guidebook helps you pick this museum's brain. *(Schotersingel 2. Cross through to the back of the train station, cross the street, and follow Kennemerbrug, which is on your right, until you reach Schotersingel. Take a left and follow past the park to the museum. ☎541 0670. €7.50, ages 13-18 and seniors €5. Open Tu-F 10am-5pm, Sa-Su noon-5pm.)*

DE HALLEN MUSEUM (VLEESHAL AND VERWEYHAL). Now owned by the Frans Hals Museum, Haarlem's collection of modern art is housed in the 17th-century

Dutch Renaissance *vleeshal*, an indoor meat market built in the early 1600s for sanitation purposes. The building is a magnificent sight in Grote Markt, with a reminder of its old purpose suitably displayed in the ox and sheep heads adorning the exterior. The museum hosts changing exhibitions of modern and contemporary art, giving special attention to contemporary photography and displaying a large collection of works by 20th-century artist **Kees Verwey;** the adjoining hall is named after this Haarlem painter, who died in 1995. A roof terrace provides a sweeping view over Haarlem but is not always open for visitors. *(Grote Markt 16, just to the right of the Grote Kerk. ☎ 511 5775; www.dehallen.com. Open Tu-Sa 11am-5pm, Su noon-5pm. €5, under 18 free.)*

HISTORISCH MUSEUM ZUD-ENNEMERLAND. This cozy museum explores Haarlem's fascinating past. Most of the museum's wall cards are in Dutch, but the highlight of the museum, an engaging 10min. film in English narrated by "Laurens Coster" (who died in 1484) explains noteworthy aspects of city history. Rotating exhibits on noteworthy aspects of Haarlem's history feature black-and-white photos and antiquated objects. *(Groot Heiligland 47. Opposite the Frans Hals Museum. ☎ 542 2427. Open Tu-Sa noon-5pm, Su 1-5pm. €1, under 18 free.)*

OTHER SIGHTS. The city has 19 **hofjes,** or almshouses, which have provided the elderly with free housing for over five centuries. Many of the *hofjes*—all of which are still in operation—surround beautiful garden courtyards that visitors can sometimes stroll through (but keep in mind that these are people's homes). Check out the **Hofje van Oorschot,** where Kruisstraat becomes Barteljorisstraat, whose gorgeous courtyard of lavender and roses contains a statue of Eve before original sin. *(Kruisstraat 44. Open M-F 10am-5pm.)* Another timeworn *hofje* worth noting is the **Proveniershuis,** on Grote Houtstraat, home to the small cafe **Juffrouw Zonder Zorgen,** which serves well-priced sandwiches, salads, and soups in a beautiful setting. *(Grote Houtstraat 142. juffrouwzonderzorgen@tiscali.nl. Open M-Sa 10am-6pm.)* **Hofje van Staats,** near the train station, is one of the larger and grander *hofjes* in Haarlem. *(Jansweg 39. Take a right out of the station and then a left on Jansweg. Open M-Sa 10am-5pm.)* At the west end of Grote Markt looms the glorious medieval **Stadhuis,** once the hunting lodge of the Count of Holland. It was built in the 14th through 17th centuries, the varying architectural styles reflected in its bricolage of spires and statues. In a small space right by the Grote Kerk is **De Vishal,** a gallery space displaying contemporary multimedia art. Its name, "The Fish Hall," derives from its original use in 1603 to contain the stench of freshly caught fish brought in from Zandvoort to be sold at market. Exhibits of paintings, photography, sculpture, and fashion change frequently but do not diminish in their experimentation; most artists are local members of an artists' association, but international and Dutch artists from farther afield occasionally visit. *(Grote Markt 20. ☎ 532 6856; www.devishal.nl. Open Tu-Sa 11am-5pm, Su 1-5pm. Free.)* Underneath the De Hallen Museum to the right of the Grote Kerk is the **Archeologisch Museum,** displaying centuries of archaeological artifacts through exhibits that change every six months. *(Grote Markt 18K. ☎ 542 0888 or 531 3135. Open W-Su 1-5pm. Free.)* The **Theo Swagemakersmuseum,** between Koningstraat and Gedempte Oude Gracht, houses 200 of the 20th-century portrait painter Theo Swagemakers's works, including still lifes and landscape watercolors. The ground floor is a gallery with exhibits that rotate every three months; the third floor is a tiny toy museum. *(Stoofsteeg 6. ☎ 532 7761; www.swagemakersmuseum.nl. Open W-Su 1-5pm. €3.50, ages 5-15 and seniors €2.)* Upstairs from the Historisch Museum is the **Spaarnestad Fotoarchief,** and next door is its free gallery with changing exhibits of contemporary documentary photographs and selections from a permanent collection of four million photos. *(Groot Heiligland 37. ☎ 518 5152; www.spaarnefoto.nl. Photo archive open M-F 9:30am-5pm by appointment only. Gallery open Tu-Su 1-5pm. Free.)* To the left of the Teylers Museum is the 1598 **Waag** (weigh-house), which was formerly used for weighing goods during trade on the Spaarne River. Across the Spaarne sits the stately **Amsterdamse Poort,** built around 1400, the last segment of the city's fortifications still standing from when a defensive wall encircled the whole town. To reach the Poort, cross the bridge to the left of the Teylers Museum, take your second left on Spaarnwouderstraat and follow until you reach the Poort. The **Nieuwe Kerk,** situated amidst rows of residential houses on Korte Annastraat, is an impressive rectangular structure designed in the 1640s by Jacob van Campen. It peaks with a quirky tower conceived a generation earlier in 1613 by Lieven de Key in the Dutch Renaissance style. *(No entrance allowed.)*

COFFEE SHOPS

Haarlem's coffee shops lack the creative ambience of Amsterdam's style-conscious versions, but they aren't hard to find and offer good deals.

Empire Coffeeshop, Krocht 8 (☎531 4453), just off Barteljorisstraat. The long, thin space in the front opens up into a games area in the back, with a pool table (€1), foosball (€0.50), and speedy but expensive Internet access (€1.30 per 15min.) in a comfortable cafe environment. Usually full of locals. Weed and hash €6-12 for 0.8-3g. Pre-rolled joints €3. Open daily 10am-midnight.

Willie Wortel's Sativa, Kruisweg 46 (☎531 7770), conveniently located across from the train station. This tourist-friendly shop comes fully equipped with comfortable booth seating and efficient staff. Popular sativa Amnesia Haze €13 per g. Ridiculously cheap pure joints €2.40-3.50. Bongs available for use (€0.60 or free with drink purchase). Free Internet access. Open M 10:30am-midnight, Tu-Sa 9:30am-midnight, Su 11am-11pm.

NIGHTLIFE

Haarlem's nightlife doesn't rock as hard as Amsterdam's, but the bars and clubs are more accessible and less crowded. On summer weekends, you may want to consider taking a bus to nearby Bloemendaal aan Zee instead for dinner, drinks, and music on the beach (p. 258).

Cafe Stiel's, Smedestraat 21 (☎531 6940; www.stiels.nl), just northwest of the city center. Stylish, candlelit drinking den and music venue that grows hugely active as the night progresses. Extremely popular with locals who appreciate dancing to the quality music that explodes from a powerful stereo system. M-Th and Su live bands play soul, R&B, covers, and acid jazz, while F-Sa 20-somethings boogie to DJs spinning dance classics. Crowded after 11pm with very few seats. Beer €2. Mixed drinks €5. Open M-Th and Su 6pm-2am, F-Sa 6pm-4am. Cash only.

Patronaat, Zijlsingel 2 (☎517 5858; www.patronaat.nl). Follow Zijlstraat away from Grote Markt until you hit the Zijlsingel canal; cross it, and Patronaat will be 2 buildings down on your left. An excellent live music venue in Haarlem, playing local and international acts. 2 concert halls accommodate a range of nightly performers and events, from DJ sets to after-parties to crooning singer-songwriters. Check the website for programming before you go; Patronaat is not open every evening. Tickets for concerts run from free shows in the cafe to €30 in the main hall. Cover for parties and events €5-12.50. Cafe open W-Th and Su 8pm-1am, F 5pm-3am, Sa 8pm-3am.

Stalker, Kromme Elleboogsteeg 20 (☎531 4652; www.clubstalker.nl), just off Zijlstraat. Located in a former warehouse, Stalker is one of the few bona fide clubs in Haarlem; locals keep the party bumpin' until dawn. Huge dance floor downstairs; upstairs lounge provides comfortable seating, a separate DJ, and a bar. House, techno, garage, and French disco play for the dancing crowd. Out-of-towners should show up early to ensure admittance. Cover Th €6; F €7; Sa €8-9; Su €3. Open Th-F and Su midnight-5am, Sa 11pm-5am. Cash only.

Cafe 1900, Barteljorisstraat 10 (☎531 8283), just northwest of Grote Markt. Dark, bustling cafe that serves a light lunch throughout the day (salads and sandwiches €3-7) and then morphs into a chill bar by night. Room for dancing, but patrons prefer to sink back into plush booths to socialize over drinks. Open M-Th 9am-12:30am, F-Sa 9am-3am, Su 11am-1am.

ZANDVOORT AAN ZEE ☎023

Just seven miles from Haarlem, the seaside town of Zandvoort draws gaggles of sun-starved Germans and Dutch to its expansive stretch of sandy beaches during summer. The ocean water is generally too cold for prolonged swimming, though bodies of all shapes and sizes can be found in the surf on nice days, particularly when it goes above 20°C in August.

TRANSPORTATION AND PRACTICAL INFORMATION. Take a **train** from Amsterdam's Centraal Station (30min.; 3 per hr.; €4.70, round-trip €8.40) or from Haarlem (10min., round-trip €3.20). Rent **bikes** at the train station at Stationsplein (☎571 2600) or at Vondelaan 16 (☎572 0000). To find the shore from the train station, walk straight out from the station and keep walking until you trip over a fresh fish stand onto the sand. The **VVV** tourist office, Schoolplein 1, is just east of the town square off Louisdavidstraat and about eight minutes from the beach and the train station. From the station, take a left on Stationsstraat, a left onto Zeestraat, and a right onto Schoolstraat; follow that until you hit Schoolplein. The VVV is a great place to start your visit unless you're just planning to plop down in the sand and never move again. The friendly staff can provide a guide to the beaches and accommodations, a map of hiking and biking trails in nearby Kennemerland National Park, and lots of information on the city. Their website lists accommodations options, so you can book online. (☎571 7947; www.vvvzk.nl. Open Oct.-Mar. M-F 9am-12:30pm and 1:30-4:30pm, Sa 10am-2pm; Apr.-Sept. M-F 9am-12:30pm and 1:30-4:30pm, Sa 10am-4pm.)

ACCOMMODATIONS AND FOOD. There are quite a few hotels in Zandvoort, many of them located on Hogeweg or Haltestraat, including **Hotel Arosa ❸,** Hogeweg 48, which features very clean, comfortable digs and a friendly proprietor. (☎571 3187; hotel_arosa@hotmail.com. Breakfast and city tax included. Small doubles €60, large doubles €72; triples €90. AmEx/MC/V.) Otherwise, you can book inexpensive B&B rooms through the VVV for a €3 fee. In Zandvoort, B&Bs are generally in private residences; bookings can be made up to three weeks in advance. Zandvoort's **restaurants** can bankrupt you in true beach-resort style, but some budget deals line the streets radiating from **Raadhuisplein.** On sunny days, the best choice might be one of the many **food trucks** that park along the beach strip, vending seafood (fried or raw) fresh from the Atlantic (meals €3.50-7). One particularly reliable choice is **Boudewijns Visservice ❶,** which usually parks at Badhuisplein right near the path down to the beach and serves delicious fried fish and seafood. (☎061 220 4648. Open daily 11am-8pm.) Kerkstraat and Haltestraat in particular are packed with eateries, most of which feature tranquil outdoor patios during the day that transform into lively bars at night. **De Pannenkoeken Farm ❶,** Kerkstraat 10A, serves over 100 species of hot and fluffy pancakes topped with warm, friendly service. (☎571 9498. *Pannenkoeken* €6-9; in summer, all *pannenkoeken* €5. Open daily noon-10pm. Cash only.)

◙♫ SIGHTS AND ENTERTAINMENT. You can stake out a spot on the sand for free, but most locals catch their rays through the comfort of **beach clubs,** wood pavilions that run along the shore with enclosed restaurants, outdoor patios, and rows of *chaises longues* for sunbathing. These clubs open early each morning, close at midnight, and are only in service during the summer. Each offers a distinct personality and food, with themes ranging from Australian to tapas; admission is free as long as you're buying drinks or food. The unclothed head to one of several nudist beach clubs on the **Naaktstrand,** about 20min. south of the main beach (to the left when facing the water). Just north of town lies the **Kraansvlak Dune Reserve,** a quiet hideaway for a walk or bike ride and part of Zuid Kennemerland National Park. (☎0900 796 4736; www.pwn.nl. Open M-Sa 9am-6pm, Su 10am-6pm.) For a wilder time, try out the **Holland Casino Zandvoort,** Badhuisplein 7, featuring the likes of roulette, blackjack, and slot machines. Wednesday is Ladies' Day, with free entry and a free drink for women. (☎574 6574; www.hollandcasino.nl/zandvoort/nl. Open daily 12:30pm-3am.) There is also a free **circus,** Gasthuisplein 5, with games, miniature rides, and a movie theater. The bottom floor is dubbed Familyland and is stuffed with every imaginable arcade game. (☎571 8686; www.circus-zandvoort.nl. Movie tickets €7.50, under 12 €6.) To the right when walking toward the beach is **Yanks,** Dorpsplein 2, off Kerkstraat, a rowdy, two-story, cowboy-themed coffee shop decorated with an excess of Native American headdresses and tipis. (☎571 9455; www.yanks.nl. Weed and hash from €3 per g. Open daily in summer 9am-3am; in winter 10am-3am. MC/V.) **Grand Cafe 25,** Kerkstraat 25, features a classy bar and comfy, multicolored linen chairs ideal for lounging with a colorful mixed drink for only €5. (☎571 3510. Open daily 11am-3am. Cash only.)

BLOEMENDAAL AAN ZEE ☎023

In recent years, Bloemendaal aan Zee has transformed from a quiet stretch of beach into the site of the Netherlands's largest and most popular beach party. While Zandvoort aan Zee is backed immediately by the bustling town of Zandvoort, Bloemendaal proper is kilometers away from the beach and hardly worth visiting. Bloemendaal aan Zee, *aan* the other hand, is a purely hedonistic collection of fashionable and fabulous beach clubs and draws Amsterdam's most stylish fun-seeking revelers. Local club **Woodstock 69** is the granddaddy of them all, clocking in at almost 15 years old. There is a distinct hippie feel here; there are hammocks, tiki torches, a small stage for events, and lots of color and loose clothing. The club is divided between an area with couches and beds for lounging outside and a large bar area inside. They host parties several times a week, each with a different theme, DJ, and crowd; check the website for information. Look for a palm tree marking the club, to the right of the entrance when you're facing the water. (☎573 8084. Open daily 10am-midnight.) Since its founding in 1994, Woodstock has found itself surrounded by more beach clubs of the same ilk; the newer clubs cater more to the sophisticates from the big city but have similarly laid-back decor, atmosphere, and beach parties. **Bloomingdale** reclines in chic elegance with black and tan sofas and plush pillows thrown into a background of pulsing music. With its cool grace, Bloomingdale tends to be the favorite of most locals. (☎573 7580; www.bloomingdaleaanzee.com. Open daily 10am-midnight.) In general, the day crowd is more relaxed than those who come for Bloemendaal's nightlife. By law, the clubs must close at midnight, but the parties don't sacrifice any fun to the early closing time. For a slight change of pace, you can ride along lovely bike trails through the dunes farther from the coast in **Zuid Kennemerland National Park.** Bloemendaal boasts the Kopje van Bloemendaal (nicknamed the "Bride of Haarlem"), the highest sand dune in the Netherlands. Stay on marked trails because the park doubles as a nature sanctuary. The VVV in Zandvoort can sell you a good map of hiking and biking trails, and the park's Visitors Center is another good source of maps and information—if a bit out of the way. To get there, follow the marked bike trails from Haarlem toward Bloemendaal, and you'll pass the Visitors Center on your right. Otherwise, you can take a train to Overveen and follow signs from the station. (☎541 1123. Open Tu-Su 10am-5pm.)

If you can't get enough of the beach, spend a few nights camping at **Bloemendaal ❶**, Zeeweg 72. (☎573 2178; www.campingbloemendaal.nl. Reception open daily 9am-9pm. €20 with tent and car.) **Lakens ❶**, Zeeweg 60, is a larger option. (☎0900 384 6226; www.kennemerduincampings.nl. Open daily 9am-4am. €26.15 includes car, tent, and tax.) There are no hotels in Bloemendaal aan Zee, but Zandvoort is only a 10min. bike ride down the beach. The many beach clubs serve satisfying-enough meals, but if you're looking for something cheaper and more informal, try **Café Restaurant 't Eindpunt ❶**, Zeeweg 82, near the entrance to the clubs. Here you can grab sandwiches for around €3, *pannenkoeken* for €5.75, and soups for €4.50. (☎573 2170; www.eindpunt.nl. Open daily 8am-9pm.)

Bloemendaal is best reached from one of the larger cities around it. To get to the madness from Zandvoort, take a 30min. walk or 10min. bike ride to the north of the beach (to your right when facing the water) or board bus #81 from Haarlem or Zandvoort. There is also a scenic bike or walking route through the dunes from Haarlem; follow the signs or ask for a map from the VVV in Haarlem.

LISSE ☎0252

A sleepy village just outside Amsterdam, Lisse's main (and indeed sole) attraction is horticulture—specifically, that renowned Dutch flower, the tulip (which is, ironically, not native to the Netherlands). For this florid reason, Lisse is a seasonal town; the best time to visit (even though the town is filled with tourists) is between late March and mid-May, when the tulip fields are in full bloom. Lisse stays quiet the rest of the year, a small settlement surrounded in all directions by endless fallow fields.

🖃 🎵 TRANSPORTATION AND PRACTICAL INFORMATION. Several **bus** lines service Lisse, but the easiest way to get there is to take the **train** either to Leiden or to Haarlem. From there, take bus #50 or 51 toward Lisse (20min., 5 strips or €3.50); bus #54, the Keukenhof Express, can also be accessed from either the Leiden or Lisse stations. The town's **VVV**, Grachtweg 53, gives information on the town's sights. It's a short list, so a stop here won't take you very long. (☎41 42 62; www.lisse.nl. Open M noon-5pm, Tu-F 9am-5pm, Sa 9am-4pm.)

🖸 FOOD. Most of Lisse's restaurants are located along **Kanaalstraat,** the main street that also has a good collection of shops, and around the **Vierkant,** at the center of town. If you're looking for an alluring atmosphere, try the gorgeous garden at **Restaurant De Vier Seizoenen ❸**, Heereweg 224, which provides the perfect setting for a delicious meal for (unlike Lisse) all "four seasons." (☎41 80 23. Entrees €7-21. Open daily noon-2pm and 5:30-9:30pm. AmEx/MC/V.)

🖾 🎵 SIGHTS AND NIGHTLIFE. Lisse is the capital of tulip country, so when the tulips are in bloom, this village is a must-see. If you're around the Netherlands in late April, be sure to go see the **Flower Parade,** a 25 mi. procession from Noordwijk to Haarlem that goes right through Lisse and includes more than 20 tulip-covered floats. (☎42 82 37; www.bloemencorso-bollenstreek.nl.) The unquestionable highlight of the comfortable town of Lisse is the breathtaking **Keukenhof Gardens,** Stationsweg 166A, which in late spring become a kaleidoscope of color as millions of bulbs explode into life. Designed in 1949 by the creators of Vondelpark, the gardens were a priority of the town's mayor, who wanted a permanent space for

RITING ON THE WALLS

Since the founding of its university n 1575, Leiden has been a vibrant intellectual center for inventors, artists, and authors. Throughout its rich history, the city has served as the home of several notable authors, including Maarten Biesheuvel, J.C. Bloem, Maarten 't Hart, Piet Paaltjens, and Jan Wolkers. To commemorate this literary and academic legacy, a private foundation began painting poems on the walls of Leiden's buildings in 1992. Until he project was completed in 2005, several new poems were inscribed onto the facades of Leiden's buildings each year.

Exactly 101 poems now adorn the backs and sides of Leiden's buildings, meant to blend in rather than to stand out. The poems come from a variety of cultures and are written in several languages, often with a translation (in English and Dutch) printed on a plaque below. The collection includes works from such masters as Matsuo Basho, e.e. cummings, and John Keats. Moreover, the inscriptions themselves are works of art: each poem is hand-painted, with an emphasis on blending the painted text with the tone and message of the poem. An attempt to find all of Leiden's wall poems can be a fun and interesting way to learn more about the city, its quieter corners, and this fascinating cultural project.

annual open-air flower exhibitions. Now the world's largest flower garden, Keukenhof boasts impeccable grounds with fountains, a windmill, and bronze sculptures. Feel free to steal (ideas) from all seven "inspirational gardens," themed sectors meant to give you an epiphany for your own front yard. From Keukenhof, you can also take in views of the area's surrounding tulip fields, whose long strips of color are the pride of the Dutch. April 11-13, 2008, marks the annual Summerbulb Weekend. Opening times and dates change every year, depending on the flower crop. (☎46 55 55; www.keukenhof.nl. Open daily late Mar.-late May 8am-7:40pm; tickets on sale until 6pm. Open also in mid-Oct. for the sale of bulbs; check website for more information. €13.50, ages 4-11 €6, over 65 €12.50.) The **Zwarte Tulp Museum,** Grachtweg 2A, details the historical cultivation and scientific evolution of "bulbiculture," or tulip raising, through photos, drawings, artifacts, and tools. The small "Black Tulip Museum" is best seen as a complement to the lovely tulip fields of Lisse; there is little here to draw the average tourist independent of flowering season. (☎41 79 00; www.museumdezwartetulp.nl. Open Tu-Su 1-5pm. €3, ages 6-12 and over 65 €2. Guided tours €12.50.) Older than any standing structure in Amsterdam, the **Dever House,** Heereweg 349A, with its tower and dungeon, was built in 1375 by Reinier Dever, a knight and vassal of Count Van Beieren. The ancient building, after undergoing a massive restoration and reopening in 1978, now holds a small collection of medieval artifacts. (☎41 14 30. Open Tu-Su 2-5pm. Free.)

For a local bar, try **De Kroeg,** Heereweg 196, whose name translates, straightforwardly enough, into "the bar." Decorated with dessert wall murals and marked with its distinctive chalkboard sign, De Kroeg lets you bop to a DJ the last Saturday of each month for a €3.50 cover. (☎41 23 11. Open Tu-Th and Su 4pm-1am, F-Sa 4pm-2am. Cash only.)

LEIDEN   ☎070

Home to one of the oldest and most prestigious universities in Europe, Leiden (pop. 120,000) brims with bookstores, flowing canals, windmills, gated gardens, antique churches, hidden walkways, and some truly outstanding museums. Approximately 40km southwest of Amsterdam, near the North Sea on the Rhine River, Leiden has historically been the Netherlands's primary textile producer and today stands as one of Europe's intellectual centers. Many of the city's buildings are painted with famous excerpts from the writings of William Shakespeare, Paul Verlaine, and Matsuo Basho, and Rembrandt's birthplace and the site of Europe's first tulips are both within the city limits. As quaint and serene as Amsterdam is cosmopolitan and fast-paced, Leiden offers visitors a picturesque gateway to flower country alongside a rewarding glance at Dutch history.

▐ TRANSPORTATION

Trains haul into Leiden's slick, translucent Centraal Station from Amsterdam (35min.; 8 per hr.; €7.60, round-trip €14) and The Hague (20min.; 4 per hr.; €3.10, round-trip €5.10). Be careful as you're exiting the station: there are two exits, one down near platforms one and two leading toward the city center and the other heading for the Museum Naturalis and the University of Leiden Medical Center.

✦ ? ORIENTATION AND PRACTICAL INFORMATION

The city center lies southeast of Leiden Centraal, and the most interesting sights are enclosed roughly within the **Maresingel** canal in the north, the **Witte Singel** in the west and south, and the **Herengracht** in the east. This core can be enjoyably explored on foot and has no shortage of picturesque canals, spectacular sights, informative museums, and specialized restaurants. A crowded marketplace overtakes the banks of the Rhine, along Nieuwe Rijn and Botermarkt, every Wednesday and Saturday from 9am to 4:30pm, offering everything from antique goods to flowers to secondhand clothing.

> **✦TIP** **WALKING LEIDEN.** Leiden is a small city with an easily walkable center. A good way to get acquainted with the city is to follow one of several walking tours Leiden's tourist office has prepared. At the VVV (below), ask for a map and description of the various routes; the more popular walks include the haunts of a young Rembrandt, Leiden's 35 almshouses, and important Pilgrim sites.

To get to the **VVV,** Stationsweg 2D, walk for five minutes on Stationsweg from the train station's south exit toward the city center. The office sells maps and brochures (€2-5) and can help find hotel rooms (€2.25 fee for 1 person, €1.75 for each additional person). Be sure to ask about Leiden's walking tours, which cover various aspects of Leiden's past. (☎516 1211; www.hollandrijnland.nl. Open M 11am-5:30pm, Tu-F 9:30am-5:30pm, Sa 10am-4:30pm; Apr.-Aug. also Su 11am-3pm.)

▐ ACCOMMODATIONS

Leiden is an academic and intellectual center, and many of the hotels in the area cater to professional travelers visiting the area for conferences, exhibitions, or research at the city's several academic institutions, museums, and hospitals. As a result, many hotels are slightly more upscale and expensive. But Leiden is also a student-centered city, and some deals also exist for the younger budget traveler.

 Hotel Pension Witte Singel, Witte Singel 80 (☎512 4592; www.pension-ws.demon.nl). Head south on the street that changes from Turfmarkt to Prinsessekade to Rapenburg to (finally) Kaiserstraat until it hits Witte Singel; the Hotel Pension Witte Singel is across the water on your right. The owners of this 7-room guesthouse are friendly and the home they share with their guests is elegant and clean. A series of large, well-appointed, and immaculate rooms have an excellent view overlooking Leiden's gorgeous gardens and canals. Breakfast included; some rooms have bathrooms and others a sink. Free Wi-Fi. Competitive prices make it a popular spot; in summer, book at least a week in advance. Singles €43.50-49.50; doubles €63.50-85. MC/V with 2% surcharge. ❷

Hotel de Doelen, Rapenburg 2 (☎512 0527; www.dedoelen.com). From the south exit of Centraal, take Steenstraat until you can turn left onto Morsstraat and then head right onto Prinsessekade. This former mansion on Rapenburg is more centrally located and classier than the Hotel Pension Witte Singel but has higher prices to match. Stately reception with wall carvings. Rooms sparkle with luxury and comfort; all with bathroom, phone, and TV. Satisfying breakfast (€7.50) served in bright, elegant surroundings. Free Wi-Fi. Singles €75-95; doubles €95-125. Extra bed €15. AmEx/MC/V. ❸

Hotel Nieuw Minerva, Boommarkt 23 (☎512 6358; www.nieuwminerva.nl). From the south exit of the train station, take Steenstraat until you can turn left onto Morsstraat. Then go right onto Prinsessekade and left again onto Boommarkt. This hotel, a collection of 6 interconnected 16th-century townhouses right on the De Rijn canal, has some of the finest rooms in Leiden's city center. The homey reception is inviting and the staff attentive. Stay in either a standard room or one of the luxury rooms, which have themes like "The Rembrandt Room," "The Hunter's Room," and "The Classical Room." All rooms with bathroom, phone, and TV. Breakfast included. Free Wi-Fi. Standard singles €80, luxury singles €96, luxury singles with bath €108; doubles €110/125/135; triples €140; quads €170. AmEx/MC/V. ❹

▐ FOOD

For a small city, Leiden is chock-full of diverse dining options. Several cafes and larger restaurants cluster around the fork in the Rhine, near City Hall, along Nieuwe Rijn, and the streets around the Hooglandse Kerk. For a quick bite on the go, stop by the **Super de Boer** supermarket, Stationsweg 40, located opposite the train station. (Open M-F 7am-9pm, Sa 9am-8pm, Su noon-7pm.)

Annie's Verjaardag, Hoogstraat 1A (☎512 5737). Right at the confluence of the Oude Rijn and the Nieuwe Rijn canals, this restaurant and cafe is a favorite with locals and students. An underground space with vaulted ceilings and one of the best-located canal-side terraces in the city mean the view here is tough to beat. During the day, choose from a selection of salads and sandwiches (€2.75-8.50). In the evening, pick one of the reasonably priced fish, meat, or vegetarian options (€12.50-15.75) or just stop by for a drink and enjoy the surroundings. Open M-Th and Su noon-1am, F noon-2am, Sa 11am-2am. MC/V. ❷

De Waterlijn, Prinsessekade 5 (☎512 1279). From the station, take Steenstraat south to Morsstraat, turn left, and head right onto Prinsessekade. This bright glass cafe with incredible views of the town floats serenely atop a canal. Serves light fare including *tostis* (€2.50-3). The apple tart is a real Dutch treat (€3). If weather permits, head out to the wicker-chaired patio for an unobstructed view of the waterfront, which is especially gorgeous at sunset. Open daily 10am-8pm. Cash only. ❶

Olive Garden, Vrouwenkerkplein 1 (☎512 2529; www.olivegarden.nl). Though Leiden's Olive Garden does serve classic Italian fare, this is far from your neighborhood restaurant chain. Quality food in an intimate atmosphere pops out of an open kitchen. 10 types of bruschetta (€6-6.75), salads (€8-9), and pasta (€9-12) are all fresh, tasty, and reasonably priced. Finish off your dinner with a cappuccino (€1.75). Open Tu-Su 5-10pm. AmEx/MC/V. ❷

Camino Real, Doelensteeg 8 (☎514 9069; www.caminoreal.nl), north of the Hortus Botanicus. Vibrant red and sky blue and adorned with mosaic tiles. Pretty back garden offers a nice respite in which to relax in summer. Lunch dishes such as *pain fez* (Turkish bread stuffed with mincemeat) fall well within budget range at €5-5.25 and are served noon-3pm from a sleek bar. Dinner appetizers make for a light but delicious meal. *Sashimi* salad €10. Sushi platter €10. Choose 6 tapas from a selection of 10 for €14.50. Most main courses €16.50-17.50. Many people just drop in for a drink (beer from €2; mixed drinks €6). Open M-Sa noon-12:30am, Su 3pm-12:30am. AmEx/MC/V. ❷

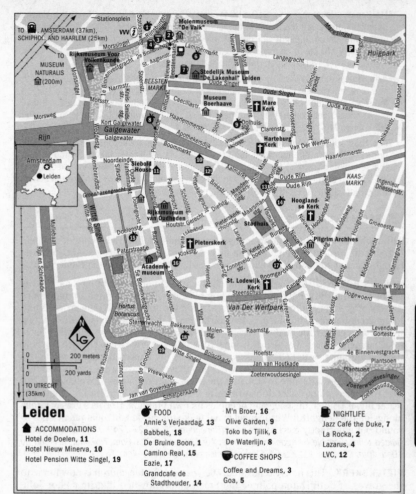

Leiden

♠ ACCOMMODATIONS
Hotel de Doelen, **11**
Hotel Nieuw Minerva, **10**
Hotel Pension Witte Singel, **19**

🍓 FOOD
Annie's Verjaardag, **13**
Babbels, **18**
De Bruine Boon, **1**
Camino Real, **15**
Eazie, **17**
Grandcafe de
  Stadthouder, **14**

M'n Broer, **16**
Olive Garden, **9**
Toko Ibo Tjilik, **6**
De Waterlijn, **8**

☕ COFFEE SHOPS
Coffee and Dreams, **3**
Goa, **5**

🍷 NIGHTLIFE
Jazz Café the Duke, **7**
La Rocka, **2**
Lazarus, **4**
LVC, **12**

Grandcafe de Stadthouder, Nieuwe Rijn 13 (☎514 9275; www.stadthouder.nl). A delightful restaurant highlighted by its floating patio on the canal out front. On ugly weather days, the colorful indoor lounge beckons, enhanced by spherical chandeliers, wood ceiling beams, and subtle candlelight. For lunch (11am-5pm), feast on sandwiches, *tostis*, omelettes, soup, or pancakes, almost all under €6. A number of dinner entrees fits the budget range at €8; other main courses around €15, including a number of Indian-inspired dishes. Open daily 11am-12:30am. Kitchen closes at 10pm. MC/V. ❷

Babbels, Boisotkade 1 (☎514 0002), along the Witte Singel. Steps away from some of the University of Leiden's major buildings. Attracts a variety of students and university affiliates. Lovely patio seating at the edge of the Witte Singel. Lunch sandwiches €2.50-4.80. Specialty sandwiches €6-10. For dinner, try the escargot appetizer (€6.20) and the *satay* beef with peanut sauce (€13.50). Children's menu €6.50-7.50. 4 draft beers (€1.75-3.60). Open daily 11:30am-midnight. Lunch served 11:30am-1pm. Dinner served 7-10pm. Cash only. ❷

M'n Broer, Kloksteeg 7 (☎512 5024), just off Rapenburg, across from the Hortus Botanicus and down the street from Pieterskerk. French-inspired, this dark dinner spot with romantic candlelight will delight with its tantalizing flavors. Grab a vegetarian entree for €10. Menu changes seasonally, but consistent favorites include the prime filet of steak (€18.50). Open daily 5pm-midnight. MC/V. ❸

Eazie, Breestraat 157 (☎513 8867). A hip hangout that feeds students Asian rice, salads, and some sushi. Slurp Asian noodles or enjoy a Crazy Coconut smoothie (€3) in the sleek green-and-black decor. Choose from the Eazie Menu, noodles or rice in a variety of sauces with vegetables and meat (€6-7.25), or try sushi (€3.30-9) or a salad (€5). Open M-Sa 12:30-10pm, Su 3-9:30pm. ❶

Toko Iboe Tjilik, Lammermarkt 9 (☎513 4372). This small Indonesian takeout spot prides itself on authenticity; its food tastes like it's fresh from Jakarta. Choose from the selection of *rames,* full meals with rice or noodles, vegetables, and meat (from €6.25). No seating; bring your food to the benches along the De Valk windmill across the street. Open Tu-F 1-8pm, Sa-Su 2-8pm. Cash only. ❷

⊙ SIGHTS

Although the town is home to many extraordinary collections, Leiden's appeal extends beyond its museums: the city is awash with lovely canals, covered bridges, stately mansions, 35 almshouses, and parks carpeted with greenery.

HORTUS BOTANICUS. The most impressive of Leiden's natural havens, Hortus doubles as the University of Leiden's botanic gardens, which offer an impressive display of greenery with over 400 years of plant life cultivated on the grounds and in the greenhouses. The oldest botanical garden in the Netherlands, it was opened in 1587 as a center for medical research and botanical instruction, allowing Carolus Clusius to plant Western Europe's first tulips in his research with Turkish medicinal plants. A not-to-be-missed highlight is the **Clusius Garden,** a wonderful reconstruction of his verdant 1594 workshop that showcases tube plants and rare 200-year-old trees. Be sure to stop into the tropical greenhouses as well, which feature first-class plant collections primarily from Asia. The Victoria lily, a gigantic water lily, is truly a must-see and occupies its own building. Hortus's grassy knolls alongside the delightful Witte Singel canal make the garden an ideal picnic spot to round out a perfectly easy afternoon. *(Rapenburg 73. ☎527 7249; www.hortusleiden.nl. Guided tours available by appointment. Open Apr.-Oct. daily 10am-6pm; Nov.-Mar. M-F and Su 10am-4pm. €5, ages 4-12 €2.50. Clusius Garden open M-F 10am-4pm. Free.)*

PIETERSKERK. This newly renovated, 500-year-old Gothic church is now home to the graves of both Dutch painter Jan Steen and renowned Pilgrim pastor John Robinson. Founded in 1121 by the Count of Holland, it is dedicated to St. Peter, whose keys to heaven's gate appear in Leiden's ubiquitous coat of arms. The church also possesses an important link to the US as the site where the Pilgrims conducted their services after fleeing to the Netherlands from England and before moving to the New World. Be sure to take note of the two plaques commemorating the Pilgrims who are buried there, including Robinson. *(Kloksteeg 16. ☎512 4319; www.pieterskerk.com. Tours in Dutch Su 2pm. Open daily 1:30-4pm. Free.)*

OTHER SIGHTS. From Pieterskerk, backtrack toward Hortus and turn left on Rapenburg, following the curve of the canal for a few blocks. The welcoming, lush **Van Der Werfpark** will be on your right as you walk. This soft, green space, with a small cafe at its northwestern edge, was the site of a gunpowder storage facility that exploded in 1807 and destroyed the surrounding city blocks. Miraculously, **St. Lodewijk Kerk,** located across the canal from the eastern side of the park, survived almost entirely unscathed. From the church, make your way up Gangetje as it becomes Hartesteeg and turn left on Nieuwe Rijn. After a few blocks, you will notice the tall spires of the **Hooglandse Kerk,** founded in 1314 as a small wood chapel; construction of the massive stone Gothic church began in 1366. Its roof was once used during droughts to catch rain to save as drinking water. Several small shops, cafes, and pool halls surround the church. *(Middelweg 2. ☎514 9636; www.hooglandsekerk.com. Open Tu-Sa 11am-8pm. Music Sa 1:30-2:15pm.)* Continue north from the church along Nieuwstraat and you'll come to the **Burcht.** Built on an artificial hill and situated right in the middle of the city center, this castle dates to the 11th century and is thought to have been constructed for the protection of the settlement for the Count of Holland. The Burcht is located within a small park and is freely accessible. From the Burcht, continue back along Nieuwstraat and turn right onto Burgsteeg. Follow this street and cross the canal. In front of you will be the **Stadhuis,** the city hall. Continue around to the front for the best view. This building, which dates to the 14th century and acquired its monumental facade in the 16th century, has served as the office of the burgomasters (town magistrates) since its founding. Much of the building was destroyed in 1929 by fire but was thereafter restored.

🏛 MUSEUMS

A center of learning for over four centuries, Leiden is a haven for museum-goers, with many must-see collections. Make sure you have a Museumjaarkaart to get into many of them for free (see **More Museums for Less,** p. 7).

▨RIJKSMUSEUM VOOR VOLKENKUNDE (NATIONAL MUSEUM OF ETHNOLOGY). Full of ethnic treasures brought back by Dutch explorers and academics since 1837, this anthropological museum displays Incan sculptures, Chinese paintings, African bronzes, and Indonesian artifacts. Totems and togs, swords and statues, and masks and mukluks overflow in this regal, grandiose complex. In all, the collection holds more than 200,000 artifacts depicting the dress, customs, and artwork of myriad indigenous cultures—a must for those interested in anthropology and social history. Though some of the exhibits are a bit cursory, others, including those detailing Indonesia and civilization in the Pacific islands, are true treasures. Recent renovations lend technological sophistication to the exhibits; interactive touchscreens offer explanations in English and in Dutch, and guides give illuminating presentations on the international collection. Impromptu performances and modern interpretations of ethnology on display in the museum gardens provide additional intrigue. *(Steenstraat 1, just over the canal from the VVV. ☎516 8800; www.volkenkunde.nl. Open Tu-Su 10am-5pm. €7.50, ages 4-12 and over 65 €4.)*

▨MUSEUM NATURALIS. This prize museum brings natural history to life through modern and visually exciting displays that explore the history of the earth and its various inhabitants. With stunning exhibits of animals, plants, minerals, rocks, and fossils—all brilliantly explained on English and Dutch panels—this is an absolute must-see for nature lovers. Even those who don't normally enjoy museums will appreciate the awe-inspiring wealth of colors and shapes, improved by the scientific and anthropological tales designed to appeal to audiences of all ages. Youngsters, though, will especially enjoy the museum, with its many hands-on displays and activities. New exhibits crop up every year. Free guided tours, children's exhibits, and a domed theater make this museum an exhilarating experience for the whole family. *(Darwinweg. From the northern exit of Leiden Centraal, near platform 9, follow the signs that lead to the museum between Leiden University Medical Center and the large parking complex to its right. ☎568 7600; www.naturalis.nl. Open July-Aug. daily 10am-6pm; Sept.-June Tu-F 10am-5pm, Sa-Su 10am-6pm. €9, ages 4-17 €5, under 3 free.)*

■ **RIJKSMUSEUM VAN OUDHEDEN (NATIONAL MUSEUM OF ANTIQUITIES).** This branch of the Rijksmuseum focuses on the cultures of Ancient Egypt, Greece, and Rome as well as the ancient beginnings of the Netherlands. The fascinating collection, which includes more than 6000 items on display, showcases everything from mummies and sarcophagi from North Africa and Europe to outstanding Dutch artifacts from the Roman Empire. Be sure to examine the **Egyptian Temple of Taffeh,** a gift to the Dutch removed from the reservoir basin of the Aswan Dam when it overflowed. It is one of the only complete Egyptian temples outside of Egypt. Free English-language guide available for Dutch-impaired visitors. *(Rapenburg 28. ☎516 3163; www.rmo.nl. Open Tu-F 10am-5pm, Sa-Su noon-5pm. €8.50, ages 4-17 €5.50, over 65 €7.50.)*

■ **STEDELIJK MUSEUM "DE LAKENHAL" LEIDEN (MUNICIPAL MUSEUM OF LEIDEN).** This museum, smaller than the local national museums, is housed in **De Lakenhal,** the former cloth hall that was vital to Leiden's economic development as one of the centers of cloth production in Europe. It provides a glimpse into the history and development of the city through a carefully chosen collection that includes masterpieces by Rembrandt van Rijn, Lucas van Leyden, and Jan Steen, as well as decorative arts. In these finely styled surroundings, the museum makes Leiden's development interesting and informative. The hallmark of the museum is its second floor, which includes restored rooms that were part of the original Lakenhal, where the quality of Leiden cloth was checked. Be sure to visit the **Syndics' Room,** where those in charge of dyeing cloth would meet. Its walls are covered in gilt leather. On the top floor, you'll find displays explaining the importance of various sites around the town; it even contains parts of a Catholic chapel that were installed here in 1929. *(Oude Singel 28-32. ☎516 5360. Open Tu-F 10am-5pm, Sa-Su noon-5pm. €4, under 18 free.)* In addition, the museum also oversees the **Scheltema Complex** only one block away. Housed in a former factory, this collection includes contemporary art in evocative surroundings. *(Marktsteeg 1. Open Tu-Su noon-5pm. Free.)*

MOLENMUSEUM "DE VALK". Scale steep staircases to inspect the innards of a functioning windmill from 1743 at this unique museum, which sells the whole-wheat flour ground in its mill (€1 per kg). The living quarters on the mill's ground floor have been preserved from their last habitation, with paintings and photographs displayed to depict the life of a 19th-century miller. The next set of floors detail the importance of the grain and flour trade and the process by which millers produced the flour. Video presentations and wall panels explain the craftsmanship, history, and technology of a windmill. A climb to the top grants visitors a sweeping view of Leiden's green expanses. *(2e Binnenvestgracht 1. ☎516 5353; http://home.wanadoo.nl/molenmuseum. Open Tu-Sa 10am-5pm, Su 1-5pm. €2.50.)*

MUSEUM BOERHAAVE. Science buffs tired of art and anthropology museums will appreciate this museum, named for 16th-century physician Herman Boerhaave. The Dutch National Museum of Science and Medicine, it has a well-organized and impressive collection spanning more than four centuries of Dutch scientific learning, from human and animal skeletons to antique microscopes, fitness equipment, medical instruments, telescopes, and even an early fire engine. *(Lange Sint Agnietenstraat 10. ☎566 2640; www.museumboerhaave.nl. Open Tu-Sa 10am-5pm, Su noon-5pm. €6, ages 6-18 and over 65 €3.)*

SIEBOLD HOUSE. Within a restored canal house, this small museum hosts a collection of Japanese porcelain, ceramics, clothing, and other material objects collected by Philipp Franz von Siebold, a physician posted in Japan by the Dutch government who came to amass an incredible collection of artifacts. Housed over three floors, the objects are beautifully showcased in vivid displays that shed light on both Japanese art and history as well as on Von Siebold's own work. Temporary exhibits portray and examine various aspects of modern Japanese art and design. *(Rapenburg 19. ☎512 5539; www.sieboldhuis.org. Open Tu-Su 10am-5pm. €7.50, ages 4-12 and over 65 €4.)*

■ COFFEE SHOPS

Leiden isn't the wildest or most touristy town, so good coffee shops can be scarce. Below are a few places for a smoke for those who simply can't go without.

Goa, Korte Mare 8 (☎522 6476). Take Steenstraat south and turn left at Beestenmarkt, following Oude Singel a few blocks to Korte Mare. Neighborhood coffee shop with an Indian motif. The owner prides himself on keeping his shop open at the same times 365 days a year. Enjoy the pool table while you take in the polychromatic wall murals. *Primera* (Moroccan hash) €9 per g. Haze weed €7.50 per g. Pre-rolled joints €3.25-3.75. 10% discount for purchases above €15; 20% above €25. Open daily 4-10pm.

Coffee and Dreams, Beestenmarkt 32. More of a counter than a coffee shop. Take advantage of the €24 deal: get €30 worth of pot for €24 or get 6 joints for the price of 5. Open daily 4-10pm. Cash only.

■ NIGHTLIFE

The city is undoubtedly a university town, but most students hit up the bars and discos only after they've had their share of private fraternity events. If you're looking to bar- or club-hop, head to the upper stretch of **Nieuwe Beestenmarkt,** just south of the formidable windmill, which is packed with bustling bars, clubs, and coffee shops. A collection of larger cafe-restaurants serves alcohol on large terraces along **Nieuwe Rijn,** and some pool halls and smaller bars dot **Hooglandse Kerkgracht.** At the beginning of **Breestraat,** near Prinsessekade and Rapenburg, are a number of restaurants and cafes that are popular with teenagers.

LIVIN' LARGE IN LEIDEN. For up-to-date information on Leiden's entertainment scene, grab a copy of the free magazine *L.O.S.*, which provides features on bars, restaurants, theme nights, and nightlife news. Look for *L.O.S.* in snack shops, grocery stores, and restaurants.

LVC, Breestraat 66 (☎514 6449; www.lvc.nl). Party with a student-heavy crowd at this popular dance spot and nightclub with prices to match a student's budget. Run almost entirely by volunteers; if you help out too, you can get in for free. The large space, which includes a graffiti-covered lounge, hosts everything from concerts and comedy acts to dancing. Themes and music vary from 60s Beach Party or Salsa Lounge to Caribbean Night or New Alternative; check website for details. Beer €1.80. Mixed drinks €4.50. Cover €5-9. Open Th-Sa; times vary with theme, ranging from 10-11pm for opening and 2-5am for closing. Cash only.

La Rocka, Beestenmarkt 32, next door to **Coffee and Dreams** coffee shop. A laid-back bar across from the De Valk windmill. Chill out in their bright, glass-enclosed terrace or play a game of pool (€2). Heineken €2. For something a little kinkier, try the €3 Blow Job (vodka and Tia Maria with whipped cream). Rum and Coke €6. Open M-Th and Su 3pm-1am, F-Sa 3pm-2am. Cash only.

Lazarus, Nieuwe Beestenmarkt 32 (☎512 2849). This bar is a haven for rock and metal fans who tire of the lounge or dance music played elsewhere. Recently renovated upstairs bar open Sa after 11pm. Th live music with a metal band. Beer €2.10. Open M-Th and Su 3pm-1am, F-Sa 3pm-2am. Cash only.

Jazz Café the Duke, Oude Singel 2 (☎512 1972; www.jazzcafetheduke.nl). The interior of this small but popular cafe sets the melodic mood, with old jazz-album covers,

Miles Davis posters, and a ceiling covered with antique instruments. The menu is limited but offers a variety of snacks (€3-5) and sandwiches (€8.50-10.50). Nightly live music starting around 10pm, although it's not always blues. M jam session. Open M-Th 3pm-5am, F-Su 1pm-5am. Cash only.

NOORDWIJK AAN ZEE   ☎ 071

Beautiful beaches can be found about an hour from Amsterdam and The Hague in the town of Noordwijk aan Zee (pop. 25,000). While this stunning hamlet on the coast of the Netherlands has always been a favorite resort for Dutch vacationers, tourists from outside of the Netherlands and Europe are beginning to discover its wonders—visit before the town is overrun by traveling hordes. Less crowded and commercial than Scheveningen (p. 277) is, Noordwijk aan Zee hosts outdoor activities galore; visitors can go horseback riding through dunes and woods, surf brisk coastal waters, or toss Frisbees over 13km of sparkling white sand.

▐▌ TRANSPORTATION AND PRACTICAL INFORMATION. To get to Noordwijk from Amsterdam, first take a **train** to Leiden Centraal (35min.; 8 per hr.; €7.60, round-trip €14). Outside the station in Leiden is a terminal where you can catch **bus** 40 or 42 to Noordwijk (30min., 5 strips or €2.20). A better (but lesser known) bet is the Flying Pig summertime shuttle bus (€3) that leaves from their downtown hostel in Amsterdam (p. 106) daily at 10:30am, 1:30, 7, 10pm and from the Vondelpark hostel (p. 116) 15min. later. The bus will drop you off at the Flying Pig Beach Hostel in downtown Noordwijk aan Zee (p. 268). The return bus leaves from the hostel for Amsterdam at 9:30am, 12:30, 6, 9pm. (☎362 2533. Reservations required, taken up to 2 days in advance.) Noordwijk aan Zee is easily walkable; however, renting a bike is an engaging way to take in the nearby dune trails or to leave the sand-bound crowds behind. Bike, scooter, and roller-skate **rentals** are available at **J. Mooijekind,** Schoolstraat 68, starting at €6 per day. (☎361 2826. Open daily 8:30am-6pm.)

To visit the town's **VVV,** get off the bus at the Pickeplein stop and head in the direction of the massive Hotel Huis ter Duin. The VVV will be on your right. Here you can pick up a free map to the town. (☎0900 222 2333, €0.60 per min.; www.vvvnoordwijk.nl. Open Apr.-May M-F 10am-6pm, Sa 9am-4pm, Su 10am-2pm; June-Aug. M-F 10am-6pm, Sa 9am-5pm, Su 10am-2pm; Sept.-Oct. M-F 10am-5:30pm, Sa 9am-4pm; Nov.-Mar. M-F 10am-5:30pm, Sa 10am-2pm.) The beach is just a four-minute walk from the bus stop—**Koningin Wilhelmina Boulevard** is the street that runs parallel to the beach along the center of town, while its adjacent neighbor is conveniently named **Parallel Boulevard.** Wilhelmina turns inward and becomes **De Grent** at the police station on the beach while **Koningin Astrid Boulevard** continues south along down the coast.

▐▌ ACCOMMODATIONS AND FOOD. If you've boarded the Flying Pig—shuttle, that is—to Noordwijk, chances are you know of at least one place to spend the night: the ☒**Flying Pig Beach Hostel ❶,** Parallel Blvd. 208. Located in the center of town and two minutes from the beach, the Beach Hostel is a rare find among budget accommodations, offering excellent service and clean, brightly decorated lodgings. It's a favorite among backpackers who want to meet other young travelers in a fun, laid-back ambience. Staff members prepare home-cooked meals for guests every Saturday night (€6). Ask for help with any activities you have planned. For those getting to Noordwijk on their own, take bus #40 or 42 to Vuurtorenplein, or Lighthouse Sq.; face south with the lighthouse to your right. The Pig is 100m up on your left. (☎362 2533; www.flyingpig.nl. Full kitchen facilities. Breakfast included. Free safety deposit lockers. Free Internet access. Key deposit €15. Reception 9am-2am at bar. Open Mar.-Oct. Dorms €19-27.50; queen-size bed in dorm €28.50-31.50; doubles €55.50-64. MC/V.)

Hoofdstraat, a two-minute walk from the Flying Pig, is lined with small shops and restaurants. There are a number of cafes lining De Grent, before the VVV, as well as snack spots along the beach. In addition, the cafes and bars on Koningin Wilhelmina Blvd. offer terraces that overlook the North Sea. The best of these is **Chicoleo ❸**, Koningin Wilhelmina Blvd. 7B. This colorful Mexican restaurant and Argentinean steakhouse is a local favorite; wicker furniture is spread outside, and bright lights jazz up the interior. Stop in on the weekend and catch some live music (Sa-Su 7-11pm) to add some spice to your salsa. The lunch specials are unbeatable—with any and all options you could desire, from quesadillas to wraps to taco salads—for only €5.50-5.75. (☎361 2121; www.chicoleo.nl. Dinner burritos, tacos, and chimichangas €12-13.50. Vegetarian dishes €14.50-15.75. Steak €17.50-19.50. Open M-Th 1pm-midnight, F-Su 1pm-1am. Kitchen closes at 11pm. AmEx/MC/V.) **Restaurant de Filosoof ❷**, De Grent 4, next to the VVV, attracts its fair share of both tourists and locals with slightly expensive but satiating food in a cheerful, upscale setting. Sit on the large outdoor terrace and watch the kids play minigolf across the street. The menu changes often, but tasty fare like Thai beef (€16.75) is always guaranteed—and topped with fresh desserts. (☎364 9003; www.defilosoof.nl. Lunch sandwiches €4.50-8. Salads €11.75-12. Open daily 11am-2am. Kitchen closes at 10:30pm. AmEx/MC/V.) No meal, however, could be complete without the superb ice cream of **Vivaldi's ❶**, Koningin Wilhelmina Blvd. 17. Stuff your toppling cone with one of 50 homemade flavors, including hazelnut and pear. (☎361 6704. 1 scoop €1; 5 scoops €3.25. Open daily in summer noon-10:30 or 11pm. Cash only.) For nighttime nourishment, **Harbour Lights ❷**, Koningin Wilhelmina Blvd. 9, is an intimate bar and grill where you can swig a beer while playing a harrowing game of darts. This seaside pub attracts locals and tourists of all ages, most of whom rely on it to serve up a mean pint of Guinness (€4.40). Other beers (14 varieties on tap and 19 in bottles) will cost you slightly less. (☎361 7705; www.harbourlights.nl. Vegetarian entrees €10. Spare ribs €12.50. Other entrees €10-15. Open daily 4pm-1am.)

⬛ SIGHTS. Visitors come to Noordwijk for the beach, but they refuse to merely laze under the beating sun. The waves are perfect for surfing—boards, wetsuits, and all other equipment are always available for rent. For some less strenuous fun, take bus #90 toward The Hague and get off at Willem van den Bergh to reach the **Space Expo**, Keplerlaan 3, a permanent exhibit at the Visitors Center of the ESTEC, the largest branch of the European Space Agency. (☎364 6489; www.space-expo.nl. Open Tu-Su 10am-5pm. €9, ages 4-12 €6.) Across from the VVV is **Mini Golf Huis ter Duin,** De Grent 3, whose competitive game the Dutch tactfully call "midget golf." (☎361 8859. Open in summer daily 10am-midnight; in winter Th 10am-midnight. €3.50, children €2.50.)

THE HAGUE (DEN HAAG) ☎070

Words cannot do justice to The Hague. Whereas Amsterdam is the cultural and commercial center of the Netherlands, The Hague (pop. 480,000) is without a doubt the political nucleus. Since the city—whose official name is 's-Graven-hage, or "Count's Domain"—was not granted municipal rights until 1806, it was perfectly situated to become the neutral seat of political power in the Netherlands. In 1248, Willem II moved his royal residence to The Hague, and when Prince Maurits transferred his court to the *stadhouder*'s residence on the Binnenhof (p. 274) in 1585, the city became the permanent home of the royal House of Orange. These days, all of the Netherlands's important governmental institutions find their homes in The Hague: Queen Beatrix's royal residence off Noordeinde, the Dutch government in the Binnenhof, and the headquarters of the Netherlands's important government ministries all reside in the city's old center.

The Hague is best known, however, as the world's epicenter for international law. The Vredespaleis (Peace Palace), a gift from American steel mogul Andrew Carnegie, houses the Permanent Court of Arbitration and the International Court of Justice, the United Nations's official judicial arm. The Hague is also home to the International Criminal Court and the EU's international police force, Europol.

With all its international lawyers, elected officials, embassies, and imposing government buildings, The Hague might seem a bit stiff in the collar. And while some of the city's monuments will appeal primarily to those with a particular interest in politics and international affairs, The Hague has much more to offer. World-class art museums (the stunning Mauritshuis in particular), a lively (if a bit confusing) city center, high-class shopping, and more parks per square kilometer than almost any other Dutch city combine to make the Netherlands's political hub anything but boring. If you need a break from sightseeing, The Hague's carefree neighbor on the North Sea, Scheveningen (p. 277), is a short tram or bike ride away.

 ## TRANSPORTATION AND PRACTICAL INFORMATION

Trains roll in from Amsterdam Centraal (50min.; 1-6 per hr.; €9.60, round-trip €17.70) and Rotterdam Centraal (30min.; 1-6 per hr.; €4.20, round-trip €7.30) to both of The Hague's major stations, Den Haag Centraal and Holland Spoor. Centraal Station is right on the eastern edge of The Hague's downtown; Holland Spoor is a 10min. walk south of the city center but is conveniently near the Stayokay hostel. Trams #1, 9, 12, and 15 connect the two stations. Good **bikes** are available at both; at Centraal, look for a blue-and-yellow sign and go down into the bike garage under the station. **Rijwielshop Den Haag,** Koningin Julianaplein 10, rents single-speed bikes for €6.50 per day, but a €50 deposit is required. Three-speed bikes are €8 per day with a €100 deposit. (☎385 3235. Open daily 5:30am-2am.) Another good option for bikes (without the hefty deposit) is **Du Nord Rijwielen,** in nearby Scheveningen (p. 277).

> **HAGUE HEADACHES.** When traveling to The Hague by train, most passengers should get off at Den Haag Centraal, which is much closer to the city center and main attractions than Holland Spoor, which is most convenient only for guests at the Stayokay. From Amsterdam, the stop for Holland Spoor comes first, so just stay on to reach Centraal.

The Hague's central **VVV** tourist office, Hofweg 1, is across the street from the Binnenhof; it's not terrifically well labeled, but look for it next to the Novotel. Staffers book rooms for an €8 fee and sell highly detailed maps of the city center (€2); they have lots of city guides, bicycle maps, and guidebooks for sale in their shop, and the desk can arrange canal, carriage, and city tours (€10-27.50). For comprehensive listings of The Hague's cultural events, pick up a free copy of the monthly publication *The Hague Magazine,* which also has extensive restaurant and shop listings for the city. (☎361 8888; www.denhaag.com. Open M-F 10am-6pm, Sa 10am-5pm, Su noon-5pm.) Also helpful is the **Haags Uitburo,** in the same office as the VVV, which offers information about cultural events in the area and publishes a free and very thorough monthly magazine of culture listings. It also sells last-minute tickets on the day of performances for 50% off. (☎0900 828 2999; www.haagsuitburo.nl. Open same hours as the VVV.) An option for **Internet** is **O₂,** Grote Marktstraat 51. (€3 for 1hr., €5 for 2hr. Open M-W and F-Sa 10am-

The Hague

ACCOMMODATIONS
Hotel 't Centrum, 2
Stayokay City Hostel
Den Haag, 16

FOOD
Cafe de Bok, 5
De Oude Mol, 4
Giuliano's, 9
Harvest, 15
HNM Café, 3
Juliana's Café and
Restaurant, 7
Los Argentinos, 11
La Place Menagerie, 12

COFFEE SHOPS
The Game, 10

NIGHTLIFE
Boterwaag, 14
Danzig, 8
De Paap, 6
De Paas, 17
O'Casey's Bar, 1
Paard van Troje, 13

Amsterdam
The Hague

6:30pm, Th 10am-9pm, Su noon-6pm.) The **post office**, Kerkplein 6, is next to Grote Kerk. (Open M 11am-5pm, Tu-Sa 9am-5pm.)

ACCOMMODATIONS

The Hague is a serious city, with many accommodations geared toward business travelers: diplomats, politicians, and lawyers. A few good deals exist, especially the Stayokay City Hostel, which hangs back outside the city center. *Let's Go* does not recommend staying in one of the overpriced hotels lining **Stationsweg**.

Stayokay City Hostel Den Haag, Scheepmakerstraat 27 (☎315 7888; www.stay-okay.com/denhaag). Turn right from Holland Spoor, follow the tram tracks, turn right at the big intersection, and Scheepmakerstraat is 3min. ahead and on your right. From Centraal Station, tram #1 (dir.: Delft), 9 (dir.: Vrederust), or 12 (dir.: Duindorp) to Rijswijksplein (2 strips); cross to the left in front of the tram, cross the big intersection, and Scheepmakerstraat is straight ahead. One of the best Stayokay hostels in the Netherlands, the City Hostel Den Haag has spacious, sparkling rooms with private baths, a remarkably helpful staff, and lots of space in which to lounge around. Downstairs in-house restaurant, **Brasserie Backpackers** (p. 272). Also an in-house bar and an airy library area. Breakfast buffet included 7:30-9:30am. Locker rental €2 for 24hr. Internet €5 per hr. Reception 7:30am-10:30pm. Bar open daily 4pm-midnight. Special night keycard (and deposit) required to stay out later than 1am. 4- to 8-person dorms €25.25; singles €55.25; doubles €61-66; triples €94; quads €113. €2.50 HI discount. €2.50 surcharge on the weekends. MC/V. ❶

Hotel 't Centrum, Veenkade 5-6 (☎346 3657), right by Paleis Tuin. Tram #3. A classy hotel with a spacious lobby and dining area. A little bit off the main drag, but still an easy walk to the city center. Rooms are lovely and have everything you might need—except a phone. Apartments are also available and come with kitchenettes. Breakfast €10. Singles €35, with bath €60; doubles with bath €70; 1-person apartments €70; 2-person apartments €85; 3-person apartments €100. AmEx/MC/V. ❶

▣ FOOD

The best restaurants in The Hague cluster in the neighborhood of Grote Kerk; try **Lange Poten** and **Korte Poten,** two streets that run behind the Binnenhof, for takeout joints where you can grab a quick falafel, Shawarma, or *döner* kebab. North of Grote Kerk, along **Oude Molstraat,** additional small restaurants, cafes, and pubs cluster. Follow Schoolstraat one block south of Grote Kerk for a collection of good bars and casual eating at **Grote Markt. Wagenstraat,** to the south, is home to an abundance of relatively inexpensive Chinese restaurants. For more upscale dining, head over to the canals to the north of the city center, along **Hooikade** and **Hooigracht.** For outdoor terrace eating (should there ever be a sunny day), **Buitenhof Square** has some large (and pricey) restaurants.

▨ **HNM Café,** Molenstraat 21A (☎365 6553). A creative and happy take on the *bruin cafe*, HNM has floor-to-ceiling windows, brightly colored chairs and walls, and a big bowl of Thai noodle soup (€7) on the menu. Lots of locals, and lots of sidewalk seating for nice weather. Sandwiches (BLT €4) and salads (€8) round out the menu. Open M-W noon-midnight, Th-Sa noon-1am, Su noon-6pm. Cash only. ❶

Harvest, Sint Jacobstraat 1 (☎392 0960), on the corner with Wagenstraat. Calls itself a dim sum restaurant, and although you'll indeed reap the benefits of delicious dim sum all day long, there are all manner of soups, rice and noodle dishes, and even a banana split on the menu. The service here is to the point, the clientele a mix of Chinese, Dutch, and English speakers, and most importantly, the food great. Dim sum €2.50-4; other dishes around €8. Open daily noon-midnight. Kitchen closes at 10pm. Cash only. ❶

Tapaskeuken Sally, Oude Molstraat 61 (☎345 1623). Tram #3 to Grote Halstraat. Walk through the pavilion to your right, where you'll hit Oude Molstraat; follow it for 2 blocks, and the restaurant will be on the right. Upstairs from **De Oude Mol** bar (p. 277), this excellent restaurant is one of The Hague's best-kept dining secrets. Here you'll find delicious tapas (€2.50-7) accompanied on M nights by live rock, Cajun, and world music. Open W-Sa 5:30-10:30pm. Cash only. ❷

Los Argentinos, Kettingstraat 14 (☎346 8523; www.los-argentinos.nl). There's nothing subtle about Los Argentinos, but locals agree with its claim that it boasts "the best steak in town." Prices are surprisingly reasonable here, and the staff is very friendly to out-of-towners. Not the best place for a vegetarian—or anyone with a particularly critical eye for interior design—but a great place for a generously portioned meal. Steaks €8-18; other main dishes (including grilled salmon) around €13. Open daily 3pm-midnight. AmEx/MC/V. ❸

Brasserie Backpackers, Scheepmakerstraat 27. Restaurant for the young crowd at the **Stayokay** (p. 271). Excellent and healthy dinner meals—like a veggie burger or niçoise salad—for only €6.60. Open daily 4pm-1am. Kitchen closes at 9pm. ❶

Cafe de Bok, Papestraat 36 (☎364 2162). Charming, British-style cafe with a comforting menu of familiar favorites. Dishes like vegetarian quiche (€9) and French onion soup (€6.50) are good non-meat options, while sausage with eggs and chips (€9.50) is a bit heartier. Join friendly locals for a glass at the bar; British, Dutch, Irish, and Scottish beers around €2.25. Big Irish or veggie breakfast Su €12.50. Open Tu-F 12:30-2:30pm and 5:30-10pm, Sa 1-10pm, Su noon-5pm. MC/V. ❷

La Place Menagerie, Spui 3 (☎0900 235 8363), just inside the V&D mall; enter from Spuistraat, just off the Spui on your left. Looking for a quick, cheap bite? Go to this sprawling food complex, with sandwiches (€2.60-4), pizzas (€3 per slice), a big salad bar (€1.30 per 100g), cakes and pies (€2.20 per slice), and freshly squeezed juices (€2), as well as bread, fruit, candy, and nuts. Locals duck in here for a nibble after shopping on Spuistraat and Vlamingstraat. Certainly one of the most wallet-friendly places to find good, fresh food in the Centrum. Ample seating available. Open M 11am-6pm, Tu-W and F-Sa 9:30am-8pm, Th 9:30am-9pm, Su noon-6pm. Cash only. ❶

Juliana's Café and Restaurant, Plaats 11 (☎365 0235; www.julianas.nl). Don't come to Juliana's just for the food, but also for the beautiful, peaceful seating out in the square. It's the perfect place for a drink or a snack, to see and be seen, and to pass an afternoon. Lunch sandwiches from €3, salads from €8. French onion soup €4.50. Cheese fondue with fruits and veggies €12.50. Open daily 9:30am-midnight. Kitchen closes at 11pm. AmEx/D/MC/V. ❷

Giuliano's, Schoolstraat 13A (☎345 5215), just south of Grote Kerk. Authentic Italian food in an intimate, candlelit dining room. Enjoy the slightly eccentric collection of antique swords, cooking utensils, and musical instruments decorating the wall and ceiling. Prices won't hurt, with almost every pasta dish €10-12. 7 different kinds of spaghetti €10. Open M-Th 5-11pm, F-Su noon-3pm and 5-11pm. AmEx/MC/V. ❷

📷 SIGHTS

Although it might seem more staid than its happening neighbor to the north (or, for that matter, its other neighbors to the west, east, or south), The Hague is home to some truly worthwhile sights. If you're here for more than a day, take the list below and run with it. Even if your stay is more limited, be sure to make a stop at some of this city's gems. Everyone from government buffs to modern art fanatics should find themselves satisfied in the Count's Domain.

📷 PEACE PALACE (VREDESPALEIS). The opulent home of the International Court of Justice and the Permanent Court of Arbitration was founded under the original initiative of Russian Tsar Nicholas II, financed by Andrew Carnegie, and opened in 1913 with three fewer towers than originally planned. Even making do with the towers it has, the palace is an extraordinarily grand and impressive building. It has served as the site of international arbitrations, peace-treaty negotiations, and high-profile conflict resolutions. The 45min. tour focuses more on the building's remarkable objects (donated by member states) and artwork than on the workings of the courts. You'll see a gorgeous Finnish fountain in the courtyard, a pair of massive Ming vases (gifts from China) in—where else?—the Japanese Room, and a Russian marble statue so heavy that the floor beneath it had to be reinforced. The building is surrounded by impeccably kept grounds and gardens that are closed to the public, but if you are interested in further acquaintance with the court's work, you can apply to study at the summer **Hague Academy of International Law** (p. 86). Although the Permanent Court of Arbitration is closed to the public, hearings of the International Court of Justice are free to attend; call far in advance for details on hearing times and dates. *(Carnegieplein 2. Tram #17 (dir.: Statenkwartier) for 3min. or tram #8 (dir.: Scheveningen) to Vredespaleis stop. ☎302 4242, guided tours 302 4137; www.vredespaleis.nl. Tours M-F 10, 11am, 2, 3pm. Book 1 week in advance. No tours when the court is in session. €5, under 13 €3. Cash only.)*

■**MAURITSHUIS.** With only two modest stories, this is one of the most beautiful small museums anywhere. Originally constructed in 1644 and rebuilt by Jacob van Campen in 1822 in the Dutch Neoclassical style, the Mauritshuis has a near-perfect collection of Dutch Golden Age art. Not counting the precious selection of paintings by Peter Paul Rubens, Jacob van Ruisdael, Jan Steen, Hans Holbein, and Judith Leyster, the museum has in its possession several excellent Rembrandts, including one of his last self-portraits (from 1669, the year of his death) and his famous *The Anatomy Lesson of Dr. Tulp*. The showstopping pieces are, without hesitation, two absolutely gorgeous paintings by Johannes Vermeer: *Girl with a Pearl Earring* and *View of Delft*, the latter of which is one of the lushest and most stunning depictions of light in landscape ever painted (see **On the Trail of Vermeer**, p. 69). You will not be disappointed. *(Korte Vijverberg 8, just outside the northern entrance of the Binnenhof. Tram #1, 3, 7, 8, 9, 10, 12, or 16; bus #4 or 22 from Centraal Station. ☎302 3435; www.mauritshuis.nl. Open Tu-Sa 10am-5pm, Su 11am-5pm. Free audio tour. €9.50, under 18 free. Entrance to the Picture Gallery of Prince Willem V, "the Netherlands's first museum" due to re-open by 2008; free with ticket to Mauritshuis.)*

BINNENHOF AND RIDDERZAAL. Beside the Hofvijver reflecting pool lies the "home of Dutch democracy," the Binnenhof parliament building; *binnenhof* means "inner courtyard." Built in the 13th century as a hunting lodge for Count Floris IV, it has a long history as home to many of the Netherlands's most prominent historical figures. Show up at Binnenhof 8A (tucked behind Ridderzaal, in the center of the courtyard) for a guided tour, which covers both the historic Ridderzaal (Hall of Knights) and the **Second Chamber of the States-General,** the Netherlands's main legislative body. The latter, in a new wing designed in 1992, is in modern shades of blue and green and is somewhat less impressive than the Ridderzaal. Because Dutch democracy needs its quiet, tours don't run when Parliament is in session, but if you show up early you can sit in on the proceedings. The tour is in Dutch, though an English translation is provided on paper. If you're not interested in learning about the Dutch political system, skip the tour and just wander around the courtyard, one of The Hague's most photogenic sights. While in the courtyard, catch a glimpse of the regal Ridderzaal, where Queen Beatrix opens Parliament from her throne each year on the third Tuesday in September, traveling to the Binnenhof in a gilded carriage. *(Binnenhof 8A. The most central point in the city, accessible by trams #1, 2, 3, 6, 7, 8, 9, and 17. ☎364 6144; www.eerstekamer.nl or www.tweedekamer.nl. Open M-Sa 10am-4pm. Last tour leaves 3:45pm. Parliament is often in session Tu-Th, and you can enter the Second Chamber only if you show up with a passport or driver's license. Entrance to courtyard free. Tours €5, seniors and children €4.30. Cash only.)*

GEMEENTEMUSEUM. The best reason to visit Gemeentemuseum is for the museum's collection (the world's largest) of paintings by Piet Mondrian, 280 in all. The Gemeentemuseum has a remarkably complete assortment of the *De Stijl* painter's work, whose development you can trace in his move from symbolic figuration to completely abstract "neo-Plasticity." The museum recently acquired the highlight of his resume and his last work, the eye-popping *Victory Boogie Woogie*, finished with paint and colored tape. The exhibition that shows the Mondrians is always changing, with paintings going on tour or coming out of storage—call ahead if you're looking forward to something in particular. In any case, it would be a shame not to glance at the other highlights of the collection, which include a room of brush strokes by Francis Bacon, Wassily Kandinsky, Karel Appel, Pablo Picasso, and László Moholy-Nagy as well as a small selection of works by American minimalists like Sol LeWitt and Donald Judd. Much of the museum is devoted to regional art (especially in the New Hague School), which is sometimes interesting but often alike. The **Wonder Kamers** in the basement display a mishmash of 20th-century work by Odilon Redon, Picasso, and lesser-known artists mixed in with shoes, cell phone cases, and all manner of wondrous material objects. An extensive collection of ancient applied arts from China, Indonesia, Japan, and Rome and a small collection of 17th-century Delft blue pottery round out the museum's holdings. Everything in the museum except the period rooms and the Wonder Kamers is continually changing; you might see an exhibit on avant-garde furniture one month and on German painting since 1900 the next. *(Stadhouderslaan 41. From Holland Spoor, tram #10; from Centraal Station, bus #4. Both stop in front of the museum complex. ☎ 338 1111; www.gemeentemuseum.nl. Open Tu-Su 11am-5pm. €8.50, seniors €6.50, Museumjaarkaart holders free.)*

GEM/FOTOMUSEUM. If you've made it all the way to the Gemeentemuseum, it would be a mistake not to stop in at this cutting-edge, if somewhat bizarre, modern art museum next door. The Gem Museum of Contemporary Art (KHEM) holds provocative rotating exhibitions on contemporary sculpture, video, photography, and painting by artists like Yoshimoto Nara, Gavin Turk, and other people you've probably never heard of. Still, you'll be glad you got a chance to see them here first. Gem also awards the annual Prix de Rome to the most innovative young European artists exploring issues in sculpture and public space. The Fotomuseum is one of the best places to go for creative photography by artists from Edward Curtis to Tracey Moffat. *(Stadhouderslaan 43, to the left of Gemeentemuseum in the far wing of the same building. Gem ☎ 338 1133; www.gem-online.nl. Fotomuseum ☎ 338 1144; www.fotomuse-umdenhaag.nl. Open Tu-Su noon-8pm. €5, students and seniors €3, under 18 and Museumjaar-kaart holders free. For film screenings, events, and parties, check the website or call in advance.)*

MADURODAM. All the big sites in the Netherlands—except smaller! If this idea excites you, head immediately to Madurodam, a short tram or bike ride from the Hague and on the way to Scheveningen. Although you might find it a bit hokey, you'll be surprised by just how much time you can spend wandering among the detailed miniature recreations (scale 1:25) of almost all of the Netherlands: working trains, boats, drawbridges, windmills, ferries, and even water-skiers are in constant motion throughout Madurodam's insanely miniaturized expanse. You'll lord over picturesque models of Utrecht's Domtoren, Dam Square in Amsterdam, and the local Binnenhof—most enjoyable if you've already been to the real thing. But for the sake of judiciousness, the park's designers have included a host of decidedly non-scenic monuments, including a concrete mixing plant, an insurance company, and a power station in Nijmegen. Bring your camera; this miniature world provides several fun photo opportunities. *(George Maduroplein 1. Tram #1 or 9 (dir.: Scheveningen) to Madurodam or bus #10 or 20 to Dr. A. Jacobsweg. ☎ 416 2400; www.madurodam.nl. Open daily Mar.-June 9am-8pm; July-Aug. 9am-10pm; Sept.-Feb. 9am-6pm. Ticket office open until 1hr. before closing. €12, over 65 €11, ages 3-11 €8.75, under 3 free. Includes free guide booklet.)*

ESCHER IN HET PALEIS. Rather like M.C. Escher's work itself, this small museum provides a non-traditional and quirky take on viewing art; it's worthwhile if you've ever admired Escher's work or even if you have an hour to spend and feel up to some tessellations. Nearly all of Escher's prints are held here in the Lange Voorhout Palace, a building that has been owned by the Dutch royal family for almost a century. It still largely resembles a residence and features several special chandeliers designed by Hans van Bentem in 2003. The prints range from woodcuts of Italian landscapes, produced after Escher's lengthy stays on Corsica and in Abruzzo, to the more famous *Hand With Reflecting Sphere* (1935) and *Convex and Concave* (1955). There are posters, advertisements, and book covers designed by Escher here, some colored chalk drawings, and many mezzotints (the first method of intaglio printing that allowed for a tonal range). Upstairs, you may take your picture in an optical illusion (€5) or experience Escher's work in a nine-minute virtual reality experience—the technology is somewhat dated, but that's part of what makes it fun. *(Lange Voorhout 74. Tram #16 or 17 to Korte Voorhout or bus #4, 5, or 22 to Kneuterdijk. ☎427 7730; www.escher-inhetpaleis.nl. Open Tu-Su 11am-5pm. €7.50, ages 7-15 €5, under 7 free.)*

OTHER SIGHTS. It's too bad that the 15th-century church **Grote Kerk** isn't open more regularly. Nevertheless, it's still one of The Hague's most impressive sights from the outside, even if it now has to tower over the myriad department stores that lie at its feet. *(Kerkplein. ☎302 8630. Open only during public events; check at entrance or call for information.)* Across the street from Mauritshuis, the **Haags Historisch Museum** is a lengthy exploration of the Netherlands's history (from the 1560 Dutch rebellion against Spain, led by William III of Orange, to the WWII occupation by Germany), using paintings, weapons, furniture, and other artifacts as guides. Look for the teeny tiny kitchen utensils in the *poppenhuis* (dollhouse) and the massive tortoise-shell portrait of ruler Frederik Hendrik, posing after his 1629 capture of 's-Hertogenbosch. *(Korte Vijverberg 7. ☎364 6940; www.haagshistorischmuseum.nl. Open Tu-F 10am-5pm, Sa-Su 11am-5pm. €3.60, seniors €3.20, under 18 free.)*

♫ ENTERTAINMENT

Perhaps unsurprisingly for a city organized around and animated by international law, The Hague hosts far fewer coffee shops per capita than most free-lighting Dutch cities. Nonetheless, some quality joints dot the cityscape, including **The Game,** Nieuwstraat 4. This coffee shop prides itself on its diverse clientele of expats, lots of locals, and some tourists. (☎345 0574. White Widow €8 per g. Pre-rolled joints €3. Open M-Th 11am-1am, F-Sa 11am-1:30am, Su 2pm-1am. Cash only.) More conventional entertainment can be found at:

Parkpop (☎523 9064; www.parkpop.nl). Hosts what the Dutch hail as the largest free public pop concert in Europe. Held on 3 big stages in Zuiderpark during late June every year. Past acts include the Dandy Warhols, Suzanne Vega, and the Bloodhound Gang.

Theater aan het Spui, Spui 187 (ticket office ☎880 0333, main office 880 0300; www.theateraanhetspui.nl). Tram #16 or 17 to Spui. Experimental theater, opera, jazz and blues, world-class classical ensembles, indie music, and modern dance all find a home at the Spui, with its funky stage design and overall hip approach to entertainment. There are regular concerts featuring the latest cutting-edge sound. Some plays in Dutch. Check website for latest offerings. Pick up a free schedule of events at the box office or the VVV. Closed late June-Aug. Ticket office open Tu-Sa 11am-6pm.

Filmhuis Den Haag, Spui 191 (☎345 9900; www.filmhuisdenhaag.nl). The Hague's only art-house cinema, playing a wide range of new releases and older classics. Occasional retrospectives and special events; check the website or pick up a monthly program at the theater. €7.50, matinees €6.50. Box office open daily 4-10pm.

◈ NIGHTLIFE

The Hague's laid-back sophistication translates into fewer clubs and more bar-cafes for diplomats to drown their geopolitical troubles; the best place to find them is around the **Grote Kerk** area, with a few old-style international *bruin cafes* along **Oude Molstraat** and a whole group of more boisterous and excellent bars with outdoor terraces on **Grote Markt,** just south of the church.

▧ **De Paas,** Dunne Bierkade 16A (☎360 0019; www.depaas.nl). De Paas is about as cozy and pleasant as a bar can be, and on warm nights the good times roll out to a plant-covered platform floating on the canal. There are 11 unusually good beers on tap here,

170 or so more available in bottles, and about as many friendly faces around the bar; it's a young, hip crowd, but not a see-and-be-seen atmosphere. Beers start at €1.70. Open M-Th and Su 3pm-1am; F-Sa 3pm-1:30am. Cash only.

Paard van Troje, Prinsegracht 12 (☎360 1838; www.paard.nl). This huge building (nicknamed "the Barn") is home to the "Trojan Horse," a popular club and frequent rock, pop, and reggae concert venue. People come here to dance, but, just like the siege of Troy, don't expect it to get started before midnight. Student night Th; more of a mixed crowd F-Sa nights. Check website for upcoming concerts. Mixed drinks €5. Th no cover with student ID; F-Sa cover around €7. Box office open daily noon-5pm. Club open Th-F 11pm-4am, Sa 11pm-5am. Cash only.

Boterwaag, Grote Markt 28 (☎362 3862; www.boterwaag.nl). Grote Markt is the place to be on weekend nights, but if you want a little more breathing room than most of the bars here provide, head across the *plein* to Boterwaag. The high, vaulted ceilings give the illusion of monumental space, and the vibe is chill. Beer €2. Open M-Th and Su 10am-1am, F-Sa 10am-3am. Cash only.

De Paap, Papestraat 32 (☎365 2002; www.depaap.nl). The hottest rock cafe in town; stylish 20-somethings come for the jazz, punk, funk, and occasional hip-hop acts—there's a pretty varied mix, so check the website before you go. Best of all, there's usually no cover. On nights with no band, there are still bumpin' beats and lots of beer. Live music W-Sa, and sometimes Tu, 10pm-1am. Beer €2. Bar open in summer Tu-Th 7pm-3am, F 4pm-5am, Sa 7pm-5am; in winter, also open Su 7pm-1am. Cash only.

De Oude Mol, Oude Molstraat 61 (☎345 1623), downstairs from **Tapaskeuken Sally** (p. 272). Tram #3 to Grote Halstraat. Follow directions to Sally. Opened in 1868, one of the oldest bars in The Hague. Decorated with colorful Mexican oil-cloth paintings, a Rococo beer pump, and lavender ceilings. Open M-W and Su 5pm-1am, Th 5pm-1:30am, F-Sa 5pm-2am. Cash only.

Danzig, Lange Houtstraat 9 (☎364 8464; www.danzig.nl). Danzig is a hipper-than-thou dance club with a fancy-pants clientele and an intimidating doorman. Don't let him scare you, though—go on in, even if your pants aren't that fancy. TV screens, colored lights, and lots of room to lounge or get your groove on. Beer €2. Mixed drinks from €7. Open Th 9pm-3am, F-Sa 9pm-5am. Cash only.

O'Casey's Bar, Noordeinde 140 (☎363 0698; www.ocaseys.net). Owned by a former European football (soccer) player, O'Casey's is an Irish bar with what could conservatively be described as an emphasis on sports. In nice weather, bring your beverages out back to the garden, regally situated just behind the back wall of the Dutch queen's palace. Enjoy the darts or the big-screen TVs playing the latest football and rugby matches. Irish drinking songs on the stereo. Th quiz nights 8:30pm. Best pint of Guinness in The Hague €4. Pub food such as ham and cheese rolls €4.50. Irish favorites such as baked potatoes (€6.50) or battered cod (€10). Open M-Th noon-1am, F-Sa noon-2am. Kitchen closes M-Th at 9:30pm, F-Su at 8pm. MC/V.

SCHEVENINGEN ☎070

For non-Dutch speakers, pronouncing the name of this beach town due north of The Hague is usually an exercise in futility. (Pick your poison—*Let's Go* has heard SHKHE-ven-ikh-er, SHAY-fen-ing-ger, and SKHAY-vuh-ning-gen. Attempt at your own risk.) Luckily, Scheveningen is easier done than said: a popular summer vacation spot for the Dutch, this carefree, libertine oasis is a hop, skip, and a jump from The Hague's cultivated seriousness. Running right along the coast of the North Sea, Scheveningen's main drag, **Strandweg,** is a long boardwalk packed end to end with hopping bars, nightclubs, restaurants, and souvenir stands. On most sunny summer days, the beaches are packed with all manner of little kids,

DAYTRIPS

tourists, locals, beach bums, and sunbathers, while the nightlife, focused around these themed beach bar-cafe-dance clubs, runs almost year-round.

⊡⛻ TRANSPORTATION AND PRACTICAL INFORMATION. To reach Scheveningen from Amsterdam, you'll have to at least pass through The Hague, from which **trams** #1 and 9 trace the path to the sea; just look for the hordes of bathing-suit-clad commuters on hot days. For sprightlier beach bums, well-marked paths provide a great hike or 30min. **bike** ride from The Hague (rent from Holland Spoor or Centraal Station, €6.50 per day), which you can then extend into a shoreline cycle trek. For bicycle rental in Scheveningen, your best bet is **Du Nord Rijwielen,** Keizerstraat 27-29, just off Strandweg, to the west of Gevers Deynootweg. (☎/fax 355 4060. Rentals from €7 per day, €35 per week. Open Apr.-Oct. daily 10am-6pm; Nov.-Mar. Tu-Sa 10am-6pm.) The Scheveningen branch of the **VVV,** Gevers Deynootweg 1134, has info on rooms and can help book them for an €8 fee. Outside the office is a 24hr. **Internet** terminal that will set you back €0.10 per min. (☎0900 340 3505, €0.40 per min. Open Apr.-June and Sept. M-F 10am-6pm, Sa 10am-5pm, Su 10am-3pm; July-Aug. M-Th 10am-6pm, F 9am-7:30pm, Sa 10am-5pm, Su 10am-3pm; Oct.-Mar. M-F 10am-6pm, Sa 10am-5pm.)

⛻⛉ ACCOMMODATIONS AND FOOD. Accommodations in a beach resort like Scheveningen don't come cheap. The large hotels along the beachfront cater to family vacationers and to more heavy spenders. Just off the main stretch, however, lie some noteworthy exceptions. Several more affordable hotels are located along **Gevers Deynootweg,** past the main boardwalk area, going back toward The Hague. In nice weather, it's a good idea to book in advance. **⛨Hotel Mimosa ❷,** Renbaanstraat 18-24, is one such hotel only a five-minute walk from the beach. To get there, follow Rotterdamsestraat from Gevers Deynootweg and take a right onto Renbaanstraat. Its comfortable rooms come with TV and phone, access to a lovely breakfast room and back patio, and a nice, quiet location; everything is well run here. (☎354 8137; www.hotelmimosa.nl. Smaller singles with sink €52.50, larger singles with bath €85; doubles €75/115; triples €165.) If you don't feel like biking that far, stay right above the Du Nord Rijwielen bike shop at the **Empire Hotel ❶,** Keizerstraat 27A-29. Rooms here are a good deal—completely basic, completely clean, and just steps from the beach. (☎350 5752; www.hotelempire.nl. Shared bath and shower. Breakfast included. Singles €35; doubles €65; triples €85. Cash only.) Closer to the VVV, you'll find the **Hotel de Stern ❷,** Gevers Deynootweg 68, with its good selection of smaller and larger rooms at competitive prices. It's nothing fancy, but with friendly, personal service two minutes from the beach, it's got it where it counts. (☎350 4800; www.hoteldestern.nl. Breakfast included. Parking €8 per day. Singles €45-70; doubles €60-90; triples €120; quads €140. Cash only.) For those craving a big beachside hotel, **Hotel Nordzee ❸,** Seinpostduin 24, has very standard rooms with TV, phone, and bath. Downstairs, the bar is open from 3pm to 3am, and a restaurant fires up the ovens during the week. Next door is a comfortable old wood house with larger rooms, operated by the same staff and owner. (☎352 3500. High-season singles €75; doubles €95; triples €120. Low-season singles €65; doubles €85. AmEx/MC/V.)

For picnicking supplies, the most basic stop is **Albert Heijn** supermarket, Keizerstraat 342. (Open M-Sa 8am-10pm, Su 10am-6pm.) Next door, **Arjan van Leeuwen,** Keizerstraat 338, is a charming cheese shop to complement your buys. (☎358 4845. Open M-Sa 8am-6pm, Su 8am-5pm.) Dining in Scheveningen is best done at any of the fresh-fish vendors that roll up to Strandweg and sell *broodjes* (around €4) and meals of cod, calamari, perch, and pike (€3-5). If you can't land a vendor, **Simonis ❶,** Strandweg 77-79, near the Scheveningen Pier, operates a snack shack just on the other side of the boulevard where you can get good fried fish and chips and snacks for around €4.50. (☎306 1619. Open daily 9am-9pm.) Most restaurants along Strandweg tend to double as bars and triple as dance clubs, and each one has a particularly garish theme, from the South Seas to giant gorillas to crazy pianos. (If you're looking for nightlife that can be taken seriously, go back to The Hague.) Dinner at these places isn't cheap, with main dishes running €10-20. If you want to get off the beachfront, nearby Keizerstraat, decorated with flags from around the world, also has some places to shop and to eat, including bakeries, falafel and kebab shops. **Brada's ❶,** Keizerstraat 158, is a source for Surinamese selections. (☎322 6623. Open M 1-9pm, Tu-Sa 11am-9pm, Su 4-9pm.) If you want something slightly fancier, the Indonesian sit-down restaurant **Lombok,** Stevinstraat 174, has delicious food in a comfortable, quieter, and less beachy environment. (☎355 9349. Open M-Tu and Th-Su 4pm-11pm. AmEx/MC/V.)

☑ SIGHTS. Strandweg stretches along the beach, scattered with outdoor terraces and a few carnivalesque attractions, including a small merry-go-round. The beach itself is dotted with beach clubs that serve food and have space where you can recline with a beer and catch some rays. These pre-fabricated huts change yearly, but the best ones tend to cluster at the less crowded northern end of the Strand. From the tram stop Circustheater, follow Badhuisweg to Gevers Deynootweg, then continue to the left until Harteveltstraat. A sculpture museum "on the sea" that advertises itself as "a silent sensation," **Beelden-aan-Zee,** Harteveltstraat 1, houses no big names, and the pieces, culled from the slightly oddball collection of a family of Dutch industrialists, are mostly figurative work from the mid- to late 20th century. But it's not just the art that you should come here to see: the museum, built under the foundations of a 19th-century pavilion and carved literally out of the sand, is a work of art itself. Large skylit galleries curve seamlessly around airy outdoor patios and push up against the sand of hilly beachside dunes. The panoramic views over the ocean offered by this unique space manage to obscure the roiling mess of street vendors and beach-hoppers on Strandweg below, giving the impression of stillness and quiet. (☎358 5857; www.beeldenaan-zee.nl. Open Tu-Su 11am-5pm. €7, students and ages 5-18 €3.50.) Though the **Scheveningen Pier** dates back some 100 years, its recent renovations have erased the ravages of time. The walkway extends several hundred meters out above the ocean. Upstairs, you can walk in the open air, looking out over the sea and faraway windsurfers in one direction and the beach and its colorful clubs in the other. On the bottom level of the pier is a covered walkway filled with kitschy souvenir shops, a restaurant, and even a casino. An entry fee is required here. Bungee jumping over the North Sea is an option for the less faint of heart. (☎306 5500; www.pier.nl. Pier €1. Open daily 10am-10pm. Bungee €50. Open in summer noon-11pm.) If you're looking for some family-friendly entertainment while in Scheveningen, try to visit **Sea Life,** Strandweg 13, on the way to the pier from Beelden-aan-Zee. This aquarium boasts an impressive collection of eels, sharks, sea turtles, and rays. Many of the fishes are native to the North Sea, but there is also an exhibit on the rainforest with piranhas, tropical fishes, and sea horses. (☎354 2100; www.sealife.nl. Open daily 10am-6pm. €11.50, ages 3-11 €7.50, over 65 €10.)

DAYTRIPS

DELFT ☎015

The lilied canals and stone footbridges that still line the streets of picturesque Delft (pop. 100,000) make up one of the loveliest retreats from the urban buzz of The Hague or Amsterdam. Delft is famously the birthplace and hometown of the 17th-century Dutch painter **Johannes Vermeer,** whose sumptuous *View of Delft,* now in the Mauritshuis in The Hague (p. 269), is a rare tribute to the town's luminous medieval charm. However, Vermeer was not the only Golden

Age artist drawn to Delft's placid canals, quiet canal houses, and colorful markets: painters like Jan Steen, Carel Fabritius, Pieter de Hooch, and Willem van Aelst all spent time here. Over the centuries, the city also held court as a royal retreat and is the birthplace of the famous blue-and-white ceramic pottery known as Delftware. A thriving commercial metropolis in the 1400s, Delft has also seen its fair share of tragedy: two-thirds of Delft was decimated by fire and plague in 1537, and in 1583 the city witnessed the assassination of national hero William I, Prince of Orange, as he sought refuge during the Eighty Years' War (p. 58). Today, the city is a center for science and technology in the Netherlands: Delft is home to one of the finest engineering schools in the country. Six hundred national monuments, enlightening museums, nightlife that caters to nearly 13,000 students, and three working Delftware factories make the city a popular destination for tourists. Thursdays and Saturdays, when townspeople flood to the bustling marketplaces, are the best days to visit. Thursday's market on Markt runs from 9am to 5pm, and there is also a flower and plant market held at the same time on Hippolytusbuurt. On Saturday, the general market sits on Brabantse Turfmarkt. (Open 9am-5pm.) In the first weeks of August, Delft hosts the **Delft Chamber Music Festival.** (☎ 020 640 4555; www.delftmusicfestival.nl. Single tickets €26, reductions for multiple-event tickets.)

 VERMEER IN DELFT. To find out more information about Vermeer's life in Delft, visit www.johannesvermeer.info.

☰❓ TRANSPORTATION AND PRACTICAL INFORMATION

The easiest way into Delft is the 15min. ride on **tram** #1 from The Hague (2 strips) to Delft station; alternatively, you can catch the **train** from either of the two train stations in The Hague (8min., €2), which is a faster option. Trains also arrive from Amsterdam (1hr., €9). The best way to see Delft is on foot, but **Rondvaart Delft,** Koornmarkt 113, runs water bike tours through the canals. (☎ 212 6385; www.rondvaartdelft.nl. Tours depart Apr.-Oct. daily on the hr. 11am-5pm. €5.75, ages 3-12 €3, under 3 free.)

The **Tourist Information Point,** Hippolytusbuurt 4, just by the Stadhuis, has free **Internet** terminals for tourists (essential for your sanity, since there are no Internet cafes in Delft), as well as free maps and information on sights and events. They also offer walking tours and can book a hotel free of charge. To get there from the train station, head left along the canal, turn right onto Sint Agathaplein, walk straight, cross two bridges, and turn right on Hippolytusbuurt. (☎ 215 4015; www.delft.nl. Open M and Su 10am-4pm, Tu-F 9am-6pm, Sa 9am-5pm.)

▟ ACCOMMODATIONS

There aren't any rock-bottom budget accommodations in Delft; if you're on a shoestring, you can always stay in The Hague and take the train.

Herberg de Emauspoort, Vrouwenregt 9-11 (☎ 219 0219; www.emauspoort.nl). It's a bit pricey, but with a location just across from the Nieuwe Kerk, you'll be sleeping next to royalty (William of Orange). This friendly, old Dutch-style hotel is located above a pastry shop and rests on an idyllic canal. Best of all, if you plan ahead, you can stay in 1 of 2 exceptionally clean caravans (€75-85). Also remarkable is the new Vermeer room, with an ensuite loft all decked out in the style of Vermeer's era. Atmospheric and lovely, it's a unique experience that stops just short of being gimmicky. All rooms with bath, TV, and phone. Breakfast included, with baked goods from the pastry shop. Singles €88; doubles €99; triples €137.50; Vermeer room €150. Extra bed €35. ❹

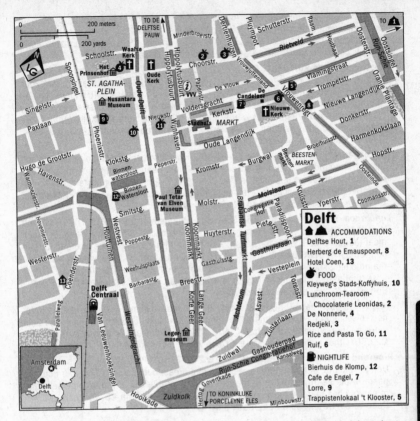

Delft

🏠🏠 ACCOMMODATIONS
Delftse Hout, **1**
Herberg de Emauspoort, **8**
Hotel Coen, **13**

🍴 FOOD
Kleyweg's Stads-Koffyhuis, **10**
Lunchroom-Tearoom-
    Chocolaterie Leonidas, **2**
De Nonnerie, **4**
Redjeki, **3**
Rice and Pasta To Go, **11**
Ruif, **6**

🍺 NIGHTLIFE
Bierhuis de Klomp, **12**
Cafe de Engel, **7**
Lorre, **9**
Trappistenlokaal 't Klooster, **5**

Hotel Coen, Coenderstraat 47 (☎214 5914; www.hotelcoen.nl), right behind the train station. Let the rumble of passing trains lull you to sleep at this family-run hotel. All the comforts, including bathroom, TV, phone, and even a free sauna 6-8pm. The rooms are large but lack decoration. Don't worry if you can't get enough Delftware—the baths are tiled with it. Breakfast €12. Singles from €70; doubles from €105; quads €130. AmEx/MC/V. ❸

Delftse Hout, Korftlaan 5 (☎213 0040; www.delftsehout.nl). Campgrounds about 15min. west of the center of town. Bus #64 stops right in front. Cabins are more expensive (€39), but campsites are €21.50-25.50 for 2 people. ❶

🍴 FOOD

While a good meal can turn up almost anywhere in Delft, restaurants line **Volderstraat** and **Oude Delft** in particular.

Ruif, Kerkstraat 22-24 (☎214 2206; www.ruif.nl). With a tiny boat terrace and verdant canal-side seating, Ruif may just have the loveliest spot to enjoy a light meal or a glass of beer in Delft. Students and young professionals meet for drinks or a full meal in the youthful ambience. Rustic-chic, candlelit dining room with exposed brick walls and ranch equipment hanging from the ceiling is ideal when the weather gets colder. If you don't speak Dutch, ask your server to translate some of the humorous titles given to each of the dishes on the menu. Appetizers €4-8. Main courses €12.70-16, such as pork tenderloin with *satay* sauce (€13). Vegetarian specialty of cheese, pears, tomatoes, almonds, and spinach €14.20. Daily entree special €8. Open M 3pm-1am, Tu-Th and Su 11:30am-1am, F-Sa 11:30am-2am. Kitchen closes at 10pm. ❸

Kleyweg's Stads-Koffyhuis, Oude Delft 133-135 (☎212 4625; www.stads-koffy-huis.nl). A perfect place for lunch. Coffeehouse with a boat terrace and a gorgeous backyard garden known for its interesting coffees (with ginger €2.40). Menu lists an enormous selection of pancakes (€7.75-10.50) with a vast array of sweet and savory toppings that could make any crepe jealous. Check out the fancifully ornamented bathrooms, where fragments of Delftware cups and bowls emerge from the walls. Open M-F 9am-8pm, Sa 9am-6pm. Cash only. ❷

De Nonnerie, Sint Agathaplein (☎212 1860), across the canal from the Oude Kerk and through the gate. Located just off one of the most beautiful courtyards in Delft, this downstairs lunchroom has brick-vaulted ceilings and a meandering upstairs garden terrace. Get thee to De Nonnerie, even just for a drink on a warm day. Sandwiches start at €4. Open Tu-F 10am-5pm, Sa-Su 11am-5pm. ❶

Lunchroom-Tearoom-Chocolaterie Leonidas, Choorstraat 24 (☎215 7821), just off Hippolytusbuurt. Many names and just as many services. Sit down for a quiet Dutch meal (sandwiches €4.50; basil soup €5) by the fig trees and ferns of the inner garden terrace or treat yourself to high tea (€17.50). Chocoholics will want to indulge at the adjoining shop where you can buy bonbons by the boxful (starting at €1.75 per box), though it's cheaper to buy by the bag. Open M-Th and Sa 9am-6pm, F 9am-9pm, Su 11am-5pm. AmEx/MC/V. ❶

Redjeki, Choorstraat 50-56 (☎212 5022; www.redjeki.com). A small, upscale Indonesian restaurant. Good deals are available, especially if you're traveling with 2 or more people. Vegetarian *rijsttafel* for 2 €12.50. Special "Redjeki" *rijsttafel* for 2 €22.50. Other main courses €5-15. Open Tu-Su 5-10pm. AmEx/MC/V. ❸

Rice and Pasta To Go, Nieuwstraat 5 (☎212 7940). Pretty much sums itself up. Don't expect to sit down; there are no seating areas, but you can bring your rice and pasta to the nearby Markt or to the canals. Unbeatable value, with a large selection of sandwiches under €2. Variety of pasta dishes €3. Lasagna €6. Thai curry €3.40. Open Tu-Sa 1-9pm, Su 4-9pm. Cash only. ❶

👁 SIGHTS

The famous blue-on-white designs of 🔲**Delftware** pottery came into being from local artisans in the 16th century to compete with the newly imported Chinese counterpart. Delftware has been sought after ever since. In the 18th century, there were over 35 factories in Delft alone; today only three remain: **De Candelaer, Koninklijke Porceleyne Fles,** and **De Delftse Pauw,** all open for visitors.

🔲**HET PRINSENHOF.** Visit the building that William of Orange, father of the Netherlands, used as his headquarters during the Dutch resistance to Spain in the 16th century (p. 58). In 1584, an assassin hired by Spanish King Philip II killed William of Orange on this spot. The bullet holes are still visible, preserved behind protective glass. The gorgeous old building now houses a museum chronicling the life of William, with exhibits on other important figures in early Dutch history such as the Duke of Alva and Philip II. Its dramatic telling of the story of William and Philip's early friendship degenerating over the liberty of the Netherlands and ending in William's death is one of the most exciting soap operas you'll ever see. The museum also holds a collection of paintings, Delftware, and other artifacts from the Dutch Golden Age. After you visit the building, stroll through the meticulously kept garden next door, with a life-size statue of William of Orange. *(Sint Agathaplein*

*1, in the Centrum off Oude Delft, north of Centraal Station.
☎ 260 2358; www.prinsenhof-delft.nl. Open Tu-Sa 10am-5pm,
Su 1-5pm. €5, ages 12-16 €4, under 12 free.)*

■ OUDE KERK. The Oude Kerk, built around 1200, is smaller than the Nieuwe Kerk but much lovelier, with its simple but bright interior. Be sure to admire the 27 stained-glass windows, designed by famous artist Joep Nicolas. Most of the windows have a religious theme, but there is also one commemorating the Netherlands's 1945 liberation and even a special window honoring William of Orange (which is stained more colors than just orange). The three antique organs are also worth an examination. The church is also the gravesite for celebrated naval hero **Piet Hein,** scientist **Anton van Leeuwenhoek** (the inventor of the microscope), and famed Dutch painter **Johannes Vermeer.** The church's tower is approximately 75m high and leans a staggering—and slightly unnerving—1.96m out of line. *(Heilige Geestkerkhof 25, across the canal from Sint Agathaplein. ☎ 212 3015; www.oudekerk-delft.nl. Open Apr.-Oct. M-Sa 9am-6pm; Nov.-Mar. M-F 11am-4pm, Sa 10am-5pm. Entrance to both Nieuwe Kerk and Oude Kerk €3, ages 3-12 €1.50, seniors €2.)*

NIEUWE KERK. Built in 1381, Delft's Nieuwe Kerk, recognizable from Vermeer's sumptuous painting *View of Delft* (on view at the Mauritshuis in The Hague; p. 269) has a unique but quite stark brick interior different from many cathedrals of the day. It's also home to the remains of the members of the House of Orange, the Netherlands's royal family. The mausoleum of Dutch liberator and Delft's adopted hero, William of Orange, at the end of the nave, is a sight in itself; the elaborate black-and-white marble work was magnificently restored in 2001. It includes a sculpture of the ruler's dog, which, upon William's murder, supposedly starved itself to death in an astonishing show of loyalty. A collection of impressive stained-glass works, several of which honor different members of the Dutch royal family, completes the exhibit of adoration. The 36-bell carillon frequently plays elaborate melodies. The church still hosts regular Sunday services that are open to the public. *(On the central Markt. ☎ 212 3025; www.nieuwekerk-delft.nl. Church open Apr.-Oct. M-Sa 9am-6pm; Nov.-Mar. M-F 11am-4pm, Sa 10am-5pm. Carillon usually chimes Tu, Th, Sa at noon. Entrance to both Nieuwe Kerk and Oude Kerk €3, ages 3-12 €1.50, seniors €2. Tower closes 1hr. earlier and can be climbed for an additional €2.50, ages 3-12 €1. AmEx/MC/V.)*

DE CANDELAER. The smallest and most centrally located Delftware factory makes the stuff from scratch. Visitors can listen to a free explanation of the process. The factory workers perform their work in an

THE LOCAL STORY

KNOW YOUR DELFTWAR

Not only in Delft, but indeed throughout the Netherlands, souve nir shops hawk the blue-and-white pottery known as "Delftware." Man unsuspecting tourists, however, car be tricked into thinking they are buying something they aren't. Usu ally, the pottery purchased in sou venir shops is not authentic Delf pottery but rather mass-produced imitations. Here's how to check the porcelain's authenticity.

Since the name Delft is reserved for only factories approved by the Chamber of Commerce, imitation manufacturers use names like "Delfts," "Delft Blue," or "Delft Ware." Phrases like "hand-deco rated" and "hand-painted" are equally suspect; they may onl mean that a few brush strokes were added to printed-on designs Authentic Delftware should have a **model number,** the **initials** of the painter etched into the bottom, and the factory's signature **logo.** In Delf itself, only three factories are licensed to make genuine Delftware so be able to identify the logos of **D Candelaer, Koninklijke Porceleyne Fles,** and **De Delftse Pauw.** Prices usually run around €25-30 for smal plates and tiles, €30 for smal objects, €50-75 for larger plates and €100-175 for medium-size vases. If you're interested in antique Delftware, be sure to have you potential purchase checked out by a neutral third party or get a written statement of authenticity from the antiques dealer.

open room adjoining the shop and, if they have time, are generally happy to show off whatever part of the process they are engaged in. Each piece comes with a certificate of authenticity. *(Kerkstraat 13, just off Markt, to the left of Nieuwe Kerk.* ☎ *213 1848; www.candelaer.nl. Open daily 9am-6pm. Will ship to the US. AmEx/MC/V.)*

KONINKLIJKE PORCELEYNE FLES. "Royal Delft," founded in 1653, is the last remaining 17th-century Delftware factory, and it's the official designer of Delftware for the Dutch royal family. The center offers guided tours, painting workshops, demonstrations, and an extensive museum, with a large collection of Delftware antiques and an impressive re-creation of Rembrandt's famed *Night Watch* painted entirely on tile in the Delftware style. You can also fulfill a lifelong dream and paint your own tile. *(Rotterdamseweg 196. Tram #1 away from The Hague or bus #63, 121, or 129 to the TU Aula stop.* ☎ *251 2030; www.royaldelft.com. Open Apr.-Oct. daily 9am-5pm. Nov.-Mar. M-Sa 9am-5pm. €4, under 12 free. Paint-your-own Delftware €32.50, children under 12 €17.50.)*

DE DELFTSE PAUW. If your thirst for Delftware still isn't quenched, head north to the outskirts of town to see how the "Delft Peacock" factory does it. You'll be rewarded for the somewhat long trip with free Delftware demonstrations. *(Delftweg 133.* ☎ *212 4920; www.delftsepauw.com. Tram #1 to Vrijenbanselaan. Open Apr.-Oct. daily 9am-4:30pm; Nov.-Mar. M-F 9am-4:30pm, Sa-Su 11am-1pm.)*

NUSANTARA MUSEUM. Nusantara is post-colonialism at its best (if it can be positive at all), housing a small but gorgeous collection of objects from the former Dutch colonies, with special emphasis on Indonesia. The building, which is the former home of several Portuguese princesses, creates a backdrop for the era of Dutch colonial power against which the exhibit is artfully shown. Masks, musical instruments, and votive objects from Papua New Guinea, Sumatra, Bali, and Borneo complement a full gamelan orchestra that is played every Saturday. The exhibit begins with a display of VOC (Dutch East Indies Company) artifacts and moves on to displays of indigenous arts. A small gallery by the ticket desk sells objects to interested collectors. All information is in Dutch, but the friendly staff can answer your questions. *(Sint Agathaplein 4-5.* ☎ *260 2358; www.nusantara-delft.nl. Open Tu-Sa 10am-5pm, Su 1-5pm. Gamelan concerts every Sa 11am-1:30pm. €3.50, ages 12-16 and seniors €3, under 12 and Museumjaarkaart holders free. Combination ticket to the Nusantara Museum and Het Prinsenhof €6, ages 12-16 and seniors €5. AmEx/MC/V.)*

OTHER SIGHTS. Opposite the Oude Kerk and across the canal is Sint Agathaplein; through the gate of this square is the **Waalse Kerk** (Walloon Church), in use as a French church since 1584. *(Oude Delft 179-181.)* The **Stadhuis**, across Markt from the Nieuwe Kerk, is a gorgeous early 17th-century facade designed by famous architect Hendrick de Keyser. A must-see for military buffs, the strangely cheerful **Legermuseum** (Military Museum) features an extensive display on the history of the Dutch military and the House of Orange, explaining the story of Dutch armed combat from the 17th century onward. Original costumes, weapons, armor, and paintings are on display, ranging from exhibits on Roman legions to restored WWII-era tanks, as well as explanations of Dutch military operations in Indonesia and modern UN peacekeeping missions. Much of the museum is in Dutch, but a translation sheet is available at the reception desk for the major exhibits. *(Korte Geer 1.* ☎ *215 0500; www.legermuseum.nl. Open M-F 10am-5pm, Sa-Su noon-5pm. €5, over 65 €3, under 12 and Museumjaarkaart holders free.)* The **Paul Tetar van Elven Museum** was the home of 19th-century academy painter and collector Paul Tetar van Elven. Magnificent period rooms, curiosities, paintings, drawings, and furniture are on display for visitors. *(Koornmarkt 67.* ☎ *212 4206. Open Apr. 21-Oct. 28 Tu-Su 1-5pm. €2.50, ages 12-18 €1, under 12 free.)*

NIGHTLIFE

Trappistenlokaal 't Klooster, Vlamingstraat 2 (☎212 1013). Named after an order of 18th-century Belgian monks who set up a brewery in their monastery to raise money, Klooster is a place for the serious beer drinker. Choose from over 100 varieties of beer (from €1.70) and enjoy this tiny bar's warm Old World feel. Play one of the numerous board games or simply talk to the many students who pack this bar nightly. If you're curious about anything in the realm of beer, talk to the vastly knowledgeable and enthusiastic bartender. Open M-Th 4pm-1am, F-Sa 4pm-2am, Su 5pm-1am. Cash only.

Cafe de Engel, Markt 66A (☎213 5708), at the foot of the entrance to the Nieuwe Kerk on Markt. Enjoy a beer (€1.80) on the small terrace in the late afternoon or head inside when the large projection TV beams the latest football or tennis match. The staff knows its liquor, with 35 beers and 25 varieties of whiskey available. If you have 1 cocktail while in Delft, make it the "flat liner," a house special with tequila, Sambuca, and a lining of Tabasco sauce—a drink for the truly adventurous (€3). Snacks €2-7. *Tostis* €2-3.40. Homemade soups €3.40. Open M-Sa 10:30am-2am, Su 11am-1am. Cash only.

Lorre, Phoenixstraat 30 (☎215 0027). Tired of running into middle-aged tourists? Your best remedy may be Lorre, a dance club operated by and for students at the Delft Technological University. The beer is cheap (€3) and the hours are late, but the true draw is the chance to rub shoulders with real-life Dutch university students. Generally a small cover charge, but the bigger hurdle may be the required student ID. If you are a university student somewhere in the world, flash that ID—it will probably work. If not, however, you'll need to be escorted by someone with one. A fun fact: Lorre is the word in Dutch for the sound that parrots make. Open Th 11pm-5am, Sa 11pm-4am, though hours are flexible and will often run later.

Bierhuis de Klomp, Binnenwatersloot 5 (☎212 3810; www.bierhuisdeklomp.nl), just off Oude Delft. Time stands still at this charming little pub. First opened in 1652, de Klomp is one of the oldest bars in the Netherlands, replete with an accordion hanging from the ceiling, peanut shells crunching underfoot, old velvet seats, Delftware on the walls, and a statue of the Virgin Mary. A charming local hangout after more than 360 years in service. Beer from €1.75. Open M-Th and Su 4pm-1am, F-Sa 4pm-2am. Cash only.

ROTTERDAM ☎010

Marked by a razor-sharp skyline, countless steamships, and darting high-speed trains, Rotterdam (pop. 590,000) is a city reborn out of tragedy. Bombed flat by the Nazis in May 1940, Rotterdam focused its primary efforts in the following years on asserting itself as a modern—and modernizing—European center and a model for reconstruction. Its urban design—eclectic, eccentric, and often terrifically dated—is a veritable architectural manifesto for post-war urban renewal. An arsenal of experimental architects converted the bombed-out debris into an urban center unlike any other in the Netherlands. Even if you look hard, you'll find few quaint locales in this thoroughly modern city of steel, concrete, and glass. But it's precisely Rotterdam's high-spirited creativity that draws visitors to the city today: structures like the new Netherlands Architectural Institute, the Erasmus Bridge, or the Schouwburgplein are some of Europe's most impressive modern architectural achievements.

Yet there is more to Rotterdam than its urban design. Festivals, art galleries, and extremely dynamic nightlife make Rotterdam a lively center of cultural activity and the hippest, most up-and-coming city in the Netherlands. It's also the country's most exciting multicultural capital, with the largest traditional immigrant population in the Netherlands. But Rotterdam isn't a completely clean slate: a walk along

DAYTRIPS

the old harbor, a trip up the Euromast, and a visit to the Maritiem Museum are all great ways to learn about Rotterdam's history as the busiest port in Europe. Make no mistake, though; despite Rotterdam's ultra-modern appearance, it is no urban jungle: beautiful and serene parks grace many areas of the city, meaning there is always the chance to relax in nature before hitting up the next trendy bar or club.

⬛ 🔼 TRANSPORTATION AND PRACTICAL INFORMATION

Trains run into Rotterdam Centraal daily from Amsterdam (1¼hr.; 1-5 per hr.; €12.70, round-trip €22.80) and The Hague (30min.; 1-4 per hr.; €4.20, round-trip €7.30). Rotterdam has a network of buses, trams, and two Metro lines (**Calandlijn** and **Erasmuslijn**) that intersect in the center of the city at Beurs station. Metro tickets are equivalent to two strips on the *strippenkaart* and are valid for two hours.

The neighborhood to the west of **'s-Gravendijkwal** should be avoided at night, as should **Chinatown** (the area to the north of West Kruiskade and west of Batavierenstraat). The area around Centraal Station (the strip to the north of Weena and east of Batavierenstraat) is also a no-no after hours. The **VVV**, Coolsingel 5, opposite the Stadhuis, books rooms for a small fee. Free maps of public transportation, as well as maps of the city, are also for sale (€1 for a sightseeing map, but the €1.50 map is more user-friendly). The VVV also has tourist guidebooks (€2) and copies of *R'Uit*, with its listings of cultural events and information about tram, bike, and boat tours. (☎0900 271 0120, €0.35 per min.; from abroad 414 0000; www.vvvrotterdam.nl. Open M-Th 9:30am-6pm, F 9:30am-9pm, Sa 9:30am-5pm.) For more information on Rotterdam, you can also stop by the student-oriented 🔳**Use-it Rotterdam**, Conradstraat 2. It also publishes the extremely useful budget guide to Rotterdam, *Simply the Best*, which is stuffed with excellent—and candidly honest—advice on cheap accommodations, vintage shopping, architecture, restaurants, and upcoming events. You can pick up a copy of their publication at the VVV or most hostels and hotels. (☎240 9158; www.use-it.nl.) Also useful is the free *Rotterdam In Your Pocket!* guide, generally found wherever *Simply the Best* is.

🔼 ACCOMMODATIONS

Rotterdam is a working city, with more hotels catering to business travelers than to leisurely tourists. These hotels, however, can offer good value and spacious rooms for all walks of life, and the Stayokay presents a solid budget option.

Hotel Bazar, Witte de Withstraat 16 (☎206 5151). Turn onto Schilderstraat from Schiedamsedijk and follow the street until it turns into Witte de Withstraat. If you're tired of Europe, you can escape to the Middle East, Africa, or South America in one of Bazar's 27 hip, extremely well-decorated rooms, each with its own design. Try to book any of the newly designed rooms on the African floor. Elevator access. All rooms with bath and TV. Breakfast included. Check-in M-Sa 8am-11pm, Su 9am-11pm, or until the restaurant closes. Book 2 weeks in advance for weekend reservations. Singles €60-100; doubles €75-120. Extra bed €30. AmEx/MC/V. ❸

Stayokay Rotterdam, Rochussenstraat 107-109 (☎436 5763; www.stayokay.com/ rotterdam). M: Dijkzigt. Friendly, knowledgeable staff and clean, comfortable rooms help create a pleasant and relaxed atmosphere. A great place to meet other young travelers. In April 2008, this location will shut its doors but will reopen in a series of the famed cube houses, at Overblaak 85-87, taking its comfort and convenience into the trendiest of Rotterdam's architectural attractions. Kitchen, upstairs TV lounge, downstairs bar with pool table, bike rental (€7.50 per day), and laundry (€4.50). Internet access €5 per hr. Reception 24hr. Meals in the cafeteria 5:30-8:30pm

Rotterdam

▲ **ACCOMMODATIONS**
Home Hotel, **11**
Hotel Bazar, **12**
Stayokay Rotterdam, **21**

🍴 **FOOD**
Bagel Bakery, **10**
Bazar, **13**
Ciao Pirandello, **17**
De Pannenkoekenboot
Rotterdam, **22**
Wester Paviljoen, **18**
Zin, **1**

☕ **COFFEE SHOPS**
Desire, **19**
Lachende Paus, **16**
Witte de With, **15**

🎭 **NIGHTLIFE**
De Apres Skihut, **3**
Dizzy, **20**
Off_Corso, **2**
De Regenboog, **7**
Rotown, **9**
Stalles, **8**
Stockholm, **5**
Strano, **6**
Villakakel Bont, **4**
De Witte Aap, **14**

DAYTRIPS

(€3.50-7.50, €10 for 3 courses). Dorms €22.50; singles €39.75-44.25; doubles €55.50-64.50. €2.50 HI discount. AmEx/MC/V. ❶

Home Hotel, Witte de Withstraat 38 (☎414 2150; www.homehotel.nl). Follow directions to Hotel Bazar; Home Hotel is just past it. Located right on Rotterdam's coolest street, Home boasts exceptionally large rooms with couches, kitchenettes, private bathrooms, TV, and phone. Very helpful front office offers lots of sightseeing advice. Internet access €10 per day. Reception M-Sa 8:30am-10pm, Su 9:30am-10pm. Singles €80; doubles €100; triples €130; quads €145. Prices do not include 5.5% city tax. Special rates for longer stays. AmEx/MC/V. ❹

🍴 FOOD

For inexpensive gastronomic delights, head to **Witte de Withstraat,** where you can easily grab a meal for under €5—generally Chinese takeout or Shawarma. Try **Lijbaan** and **Oudehaven** for pubs and bars. Find your essentials and groceries at **Spar,** Witte de Withstraat 36, next to the Home Hotel. (Open M-F 8:30am-7pm, Sa 8:30am-5pm.) Closer to the center of town, you'll find a large **Albert Heijn** supermarket near Beurs. (Open M-F 8am-8pm, Sa 8am-6pm, Su noon-6pm.)

🍽 **Bazar,** Witte de Withstraat 16 (☎206 5151; www.hotelbazar.nl), on the 1st fl. of the hotel by the same name. In the middle of Rotterdam's hippest street, Bazar attracts nightly crowds with glittering colored lights, bright blue tables, and satisfying Middle Eastern fusion cuisine. Don't expect the world's most attentive service, but the pleasant bustle and huge portions of tasty food make up for not feeling coddled by the waitstaff. Several vegetarian options, such as the *gh'ti kuku* (artichoke filled with feta cheese, falafel, tomato, green and yellow kuku, onions, and olives). The candlelit basement is a little more intimate, but come prepared for a lively, festive atmosphere to the tune of North African techno. Sandwiches €4. Special of the day dinner entree €8. Breakfast and lunch are served all day. Reservations recommended for dinner. Open M-Th 8am-1am, F 8am-2am, Sa 10am-2am, Su 10am-midnight. AmEx/MC/V. ❷

🍽 **Bagel Bakery,** Schilderstraat 57A-59A (☎412 1560). A fashionable New York cafe that far outstrips its somewhat pedestrian name. A popular stop for nearby architecture students with artfully topped bagels in a well-lit and hip environment. During the day it's a lunch stop; in the evening it becomes more formal, with a wide range of dinner entrees. Try the *mezze* (rotating Israeli-style tapas, with a variety of small Middle Eastern dishes with Dutch flair; small €7.50, large €13), or the *chullent* (traditional Jewish meat stew; €14.50). Whatever you do, don't leave without trying their delicious freshly baked *liefdesbrood* (true love bread), fragrant with onions, orange peel, and cumin and served with their unique homemade hummus. Open Tu-Th 9am-9pm, F-Sa 9am-10pm, Su 10am-9pm. Cash only. ❷

Wester Paviljoen, Nieuwe Binnenweg 136 (☎436 2645; www.westerpaviljoen.nl), on the corner of Mathenesserlaan. Housed in one of the few buildings in Rotterdam to survive WWII. The expansive, bustling terrace of this large old-style cafe feels like a little bit of Paris in the middle of Rotterdam. Omelettes €4.70-5.30. Sandwiches €3.10-6. Pasta dishes €8-9.40. Breakfast until 3pm; lunch and dinner noon-10:30pm. Open M-Th 8am-1am, F-Sa 8am-2am, Su 9am-1am. Kitchen closes M-Th and Su at 11pm, F-Sa at midnight. Cash only. ❶

Ciao Pirandello, Nieuwe Binnenweg 147 (☎436 4263; www.ciaopirandello.nl). Say "hello" to delicious, hearty portions of Italian food in a pleasant atmosphere. A whole meal can come in at under €10. Home-baked lasagna €8. Over 20 varieties of pizza €7-12. Extensive selection of pasta dishes €6.50-9. Delivery to nearby hotels. Open M-W 3-11pm, Th-Sa 3pm-midnight. Cash only. ❷

De Pannenkoekenboot Rotterdam, Parkhaven (☎436 7295; www.pannenkoekenboot.nl), right across from the Euromast. Tram #8 to Euromast. Definitely touristy, but nevertheless a lot of fun. Rotterdam's "Pancakeboat" doesn't fall flat with its series of daily buffet-tours where you can eat as many pancakes as you want while the vessel cruises the harbor for 1-3hr. Call ahead for reservations. Buffet W and F 4:30, 6pm; Sa-Su 1:30, 4:30, 6pm (€13.50, children €8.50). Harbor sightseeing Pancake Cruise Sa 8-11pm (€21, children €16). Discount with proof of entrance to the Euromast (p. 290). Cash only. ❸

Zin, Lijbaan 40 (☎281 0910; www.zinrotterdam.nl), just off Weena. A short walk from Centraal Station or M: Stadhuis. If you're not afraid to show just how cool you are (and pay for it), then come mingle with Rotterdam's scene makers over delicious tapas (€4-9). The bar is famous for its mixed drinks, offering courses to the staffs of Rotterdam's other bars. 20-30 different mixed drinks €5-7. Global menu, with culinary curiosities from Japan to Italy. Main courses from €12. *Broodjes* from €4. Reservations through website. Open M-Th and Su noon-midnight, F-Sa noon-2am; June-Aug. opens at 11am. Kitchen closes at 10:30pm, though hours are flexible. AmEx/MC/V. ❸

◎ SIGHTS

Rotterdam's historic center was completely destroyed in WWII, meaning Amsterdam's neighbor to the south is not exactly the place for historic buildings or traditional European designs. The city's extensive rebuilding, however, created some fantastic new buildings, and Rotterdam has become one of the leading architectural centers in Europe. As such, the main attractions in Rotterdam center on building, art, and design. Many of the museums that chronicle Rotterdam's extraordinary revitalization also serve as sights of interest.

▧ MUSEUM BOIJMANS VAN BEUNINGEN. Without a doubt Rotterdam's finest art museum, Boijmans van Beuningen is even in the upper echelon of Dutch collections, but its massive size and maze-like set-up mean only the extremely ambitious should attempt to see it all in one day. On the ground floor, you'll find post-war work by artists like Andy Warhol, Claes Oldenburg, Joseph Beuys, and Bruce Nauman. The second floor is home to a large selection of Surrealist paintings, including work by Salvador Dalí, Max Ernst, and René Magritte (check out his famous *Le Modèle Rouge*), as well as Expressionist pieces by Wassily Kandinsky, Oskar Kokoschka, and Edvard Munch, plus several Claude Monets. This floor also has an impressive collection of Dutch and Flemish art, with two rooms with paintings and drawings by Peter Paul Rubens, Dirk Bouts's 15th-century *Head of Christ*, Pieter Bruegel's *The Tower of Babel*, and various works by the likes of Hans Memling, Anthony van Dyck, Jan Steen, Frans Hals, and Rembrandt van Rijn. *(Museumpark 18-20. M: Eendrachtsplein or tram #4 or 5 to Eendrachtsplein. Across the street from the Architectuurinstituut. ☎441 9400; www.boijmans.nl. Open Tu-Sa 10am-5pm, Su 11am-5pm. €9, seniors €3.50, under 18 and Museumjaarkaart holders free. Library open M-F 10am-4pm; free with entrance ticket.)*

▧ NEDERLANDS ARCHITECTUURINSTITUUT. Architect Jo Coenen's 1992 design for the new Netherlands Architecture Institute (NAI) beat out that of superstar Rem Koolhaas—and the building is now one of the most extraordinary in all of Rotterdam. The multi-leveled glass and steel construction—which traverses a manmade pool and looks out onto Museumpark—is home to several exhibition spaces, a world-class archive, a reading room with 39,500 books, and the new **Architecture Biennale,** which brings architects and designers together every two years for exhibitions and research. *(www.biennalerotterdam.nl.)* The rotating exhibits—always innovative, if perhaps a bit much for casual architecture admirers—explore issues in contemporary architecture but place a greater emphasis on urban design and landscape planning. A small permanent display explores "200 years of Dutch architecture" through models, photographs, and a short video. The exhibit also includes extensive information on Amsterdam's architecture and urban development. Entrance to the museum grants access to the ■Sonnenveld House, a former private mansion restored to the way it would have looked in 1933. *(Museumpark 25. On the northern end of Museumpark. Tram #4 or 5 to Eendrachtsplein. M: Eendrachtsplein or bus #32 to Rochussenstraat. ☎ 440 1200; www.nai.nl. Open Tu-Sa 10am-5pm, Su 11am-5pm. Library and reading room open Tu-Sa 10am-5pm. €8, students and seniors €5, ages 4-12 €1, under 15 and Museumjaarkaart holders free. Sonnenveld House free with ticket.)*

EUROMAST. The tallest structure in the Netherlands, this popular site is the best way to take in a breathtaking panoramic view of Rotterdam's jagged skyline. Originally built in 1959, it was extended to 185m in 1970 in order to hold onto its distinction as the highest structure in Rotterdam. From the 112m viewing deck, you can take the **Euroscoop** (sounds like "scope"), a revolving capsule that ascends to the 185m mark, where you can see all the way to Delft, The Hague, and even—they claim—the North Pole. More adventurous travelers can try abseiling or rope sliding from the top (both €42.50; book at www.abseilen.nl), two ways to descend from the tower without waiting for the elevator. An expensive restaurant (entrees around €15) resides at the 100m mark, but if you really want to linger near the spectacular view, you can spend a night in one of the two luxury hotel suites at the viewing deck, a privilege that grants you exclusive after-hours access to the observation area. *(Parkhaven 20. Tram #8 to Euromast. ☎ 436 4811; www.euromast.nl. Open daily Apr.-Sept. 9:30am-11pm; Oct.-Mar. 10am-11pm. Euroscoop open Jan.-Feb. Sa-Su 10am-5pm; Mar. and Oct.-Dec. daily 10am-11pm; Apr.-Sept. daily 9:30am-11pm. €8, ages 4-11 €5.20.)*

KUBUSWONIG (CUBE HOUSES). For a dramatic example of Rotterdam's eccentric urban design, check out architect Piet Blom's unusual housing complex on the old harbor. Built in 1982 and nicknamed **Het Blaakse Bos** (the Blaak Woods, after its street address), the tilted, yellow, cube-shaped houses are mounted on one corner on tall concrete columns and are designed to resemble a forest. Though they've been inhabited as private homes for over 20 years, a **Show Cube (Kijk-Kubus),** fitted with custom-made furniture, is open to the public. For a more intimate view of the cube houses, stay in the Stayokay Rotterdam hostel (p. 286), which in April 2008 will move into some of the six-sided lodgings. *(Overblaak 70. M: Blaak or tram #1 to Blaak. Exit, turn left, and look up. ☎ 414 2285; www.cubehouse.nl. Open Mar.-Dec. daily 11am-5pm; Jan.-Feb. Sa-Su 11am-5pm. €2, ages 4-12 and seniors €1.50.)*

KUNSTHAL ROTTERDAM. Designed by famous Dutch architect Rem Koolhaas and built in 1993, the large, modern Kunsthal building is one of Rotterdam's premier venues for contemporary art, with a wide range of exhibits. The museum also has traveling exhibitions on early modern and 19th-century painting and sculpture. Don't miss the eclectic design of the museum itself, such as the seemingly floating banisters or the apparently hair-covered walls of the cafe. *(Westzeedijk 341. On the southern end of Museumpark; enter on either Westzeedijk or from the park. ☎ 440 0300, info 440 0301; www.kunsthal.nl. Open Tu-Sa 10am-5pm, Su 11am-5pm. €8.50, over 65 €8, ages 16-18 €2, under 16 free.)*

TENT AND WITTE DE WITH. This address houses two avant-garde art spaces under one roof. Tent and Witte de With both show work by up-and-coming and international contemporary sculptors, painters, videographers, and multimedia artists. On the ground floor, the Tent space specializes mostly in works by younger Dutch artists. Upstairs, Witte de With's more international exhibits include frequent lectures and debates on a wide variety of art-related subjects. The helpful staff (mostly artists) can give advice about viewing art in Rotterdam. *(Witte de Withstraat 50. Tent: ☎ 413 5498; www.tentplaza.nl. Witte de With: ☎ 411 0144; www.wdw.nl. Both open Tu-Su 11am-6pm. €4, students and seniors €2. Museumjaarkaart holders free.)*

MUSEUMPARK. Of the many parks in the Netherlands, few are as enjoyable as Museumpark. Conceived by Rem Koolhaas's Office for Metropolitan Architecture in Rotterdam, Museumpark seamlessly integrates art and urban landscape architecture. The park features a number of sculptures, mosaics, and monuments—designed by some of the world's foremost artists and architects—interwoven among serene fountains and hedgerows. Nearby **De Heuvel Park,** just across the street toward the Euromast, is also worth a visit. *(Tram #5 or 8 until the park. Free.)*

ST. LAURENSKERK. Though it was bombed and almost completely destroyed on May 14, 1940, the Grote, or St. Laurenskerk, has since been restored to its medieval splendor. While there are no eye-dazzling stained-glass windows or stunning sculptures to be seen here, the church's three organs make it worth the visit. The great red-and-gold organ at the back of the church is the largest mechanical organ in Europe. In the summer, the church holds organ concerts. There is also a permanent exhibit that looks back on the bombing of Rotterdam with video footage and photographs. *(Grote Kerkplein 15. M: Blaak. ☎ 413 1494; www.laurenskerkrotterdam.nl. Open Tu-Sa 10am-4pm, Su 1-4pm. Services Su 9, 10:30am, 5pm. Guided tours available in the summer at 11am, noon, 1, 2pm. Services free. Tours €2.)*

MARITIEM MUSEUM. With close to 30,000 ships docking here every year, Rotterdam is by far the largest port in Europe and, after Singapore and Shanghai, the third largest port in the world. Learn how Rotterdam's labyrinthine port works through interactive multimedia displays, exhibits that show what it's like to be inside a ship, and hundreds of model ships constructed with amazing detail. For a computer-based look at the history, check out the **Wereldhaven** (World Port) room, where you can use computer consoles to navigate through 500 years of Rotterdam harbor's history in images, interviews, and amazing 1880 film footage of the docklands at work. On the top floor, **Professor Plunge,** a children's playground, is a popular stop for those ages 10 and under. A stop aboard the *De Buffel*, a restored 19th-century turret ship, is included with admission. When you're done, swing by the **Verscheurde Stad** (Torn City) monument behind the museum, designed by sculptor Ossip Zadkine. The figure with a hole in his heart writhing in agony was erected in 1951 to remember the WWII bombings 11 years earlier. The **Havenmuseum,** with a collection of old Rotterdam port boats, is also right next door. *(Leuvehaven 1, a 5min. walk from Coolsingel. M: Beurs or tram #1, 8, 20 or 23. ☎ 413 2680; www.maritiemmuseum.nl. Wheelchair-accessible. Open July-Aug. M-Sa 10am-5pm, Su 11am-5pm; Sept.-June Tu-Sa 10am-5pm, Su 11am-5pm. €5, ages 4-15 €3, under 4 free. AmEx/MC/V.)*

OTHER SIGHTS. No trip to Rotterdam would be complete without admiring the futuristic ingenuity and flair of the city's architecture and urban design. In addition to viewing the NAI, Kunsthal, and the cube houses, stop by the centrally located **Schouwburgplein** for one of the more impressive sights in Rotterdam. Designed by architect Adriaan Geuze in 1997 and built using wood, rubber, epoxy, steel, concrete, and stone, the huge open space includes the angular and lurching **Pathé cinema building** as well as four moveable, fire-engine-red lanterns that crane over the open square with a steel floor. *(M: Centraal or tram #3, 4, 5, or 8.)* Ben van Berkel's **Erasmusbrug,** which swoops dramatically across the harbor from the city center to Rotterdam Zuid, has been nicknamed *de Zwaan* (the swan) by residents for its graceful, stark white support structure. *(M: Leuhaven or tram #20 or 23.)* A less eccentric architectural monument is the **Nationale Nederlanden Building,** whose 151m of reflective glass make it by far the tallest building in the Netherlands. *(Weena 30, next to Centraal Station.)* For more information about Rotterdam's unique architecture—as well as news of future city developments—stop by the **City Information Center,** which has extensive information about several of Rotterdam's best buildings as well

DAYTRIPS

as a small-scale model of the entire city with an exhibit about Rotterdam's built history. *(Coolsingel 197. ☎ 489 7777; www.cic.rotterdam.nl. Open M 1-5:30pm, Tu-F 9am-5:30pm, Sa 11am-5:30pm.)* Explore Rotterdam's history and contrast the times before and after 1940 at the **Museum Het Schielandshuis** (Historical Museum), one of the only buildings in Rotterdam's center to survive the German onslaught. Exhibits focus on all aspects of Rotterdam, from shopping and eating to architecture. Exhibits, however, are only in Dutch. Check out their well-landscaped garden courtyard. *(Korte Hoogstraat 31. To get there from Churchill-plein, turn right on Westblaak, and Korte Hoogstraat is on the left. ☎ 217 6767; www.hmr.rotter-dam.nl. Open Tu-Su 11am-5pm. €3, ages 4-16 and over 65 €1.50, under 4 and Museumjaarkaart holders free.)* Photography enthusiasts should visit the **Nederlands Foto Museum,** which features rotating photography exhibits and hosts additional exhibits across the street. *(Wilhelminakade 32. ☎ 203 0405; www.nederlandsfoto-museum.nl. Open Tu-F 10-5pm, Sa-Su 11am-5pm. €6.)* And, if you haven't gotten enough harbor history at the Maritiem Museum, you can head a few meters south on Schiedamsedijk to the free **Havenmuseum** (Harbor Museum), where you can walk through a small shipyard exhibition. *(Leuvehaven 50-72. ☎ 404 8072; www.havenmuseum.nl. Open M-F 10am-5pm, Sa-Su 11am-5pm.)* The giant whale skeleton in the front lobby may be the most impressive aspect of the **Natuurhistorisch Museum,** which has a collection of birds, butterflies, and small animals. The museum is relatively small but can be a welcome distraction from all the Golden Age paintings that seem to overload many Dutch museums. *(Westzeedijk 345. In the southwestern corner of Museumpark, near the Euromast. Tram #5 or 8 to Museump-ark. ☎ 436 4222; www.nmr.nl. Open Tu-Sa 10am-5pm, Su 11am-5pm. €4, ages 5-15 and over 65 €2, under 4 and Museumjaarkaart holders free.)*

♫ ENTERTAINMENT

A trip to Rotterdam that doesn't take in some of the city's fantastic performance art would be a big mistake. For up-to-date information on concerts and theater in Rotterdam, pick up a free copy of the monthly magazine **R'Uit** at the VVV or most performance venues. The **Rotterdamse Schouwburg,** Schouwburgplein 25, serves as Rotterdam's main theater venue, with over 200 performances of opera, musical theater, modern dance, classical ballet, theater, and family performances. The theater is located in the extravagantly modern Schouwburgplein, which is an architectural sight all on its own. (☎411 8110; www.rotterdamse-schouwburg.nl.) **De Doelen,** Doelen Schouwburgplein 50, is the biggest concert hall in the Netherlands. The venue is home to classical, jazz, and new and world music concerts as well as to the **Rotterdam Philharmonic Orchestra.** (☎217 1717; www.dedoelen.nl. Philharmonic ☎217 1707; www.rpho.nl.)

Coffee shops in Rotterdam are in general more basic than those in Amsterdam: expect to find few pillow-lined lounges. Nevertheless, for the highest density, check out the **Oude** and **Nieuwe Binnenweg,** especially between 's-Gravendijkwal and Hobokenstraat.

Lachende Paus, Nieuwe Binnenweg 139A (☎436 2932). A smart shop with everything you might need to get your feet off the ground. The "Laughing Pope" (as its name translates) has a very Zen (and un-Catholic) atmosphere, with little Buddhist and Hindu statues everywhere. Open daily 10am-midnight.

Desire, Nieuwe Binnenweg 148 (☎204 3134). The earliest opening hours of any coffee shop around. Head here if you desire an early-morning smoke. Simple decor with foosball and a pool table. All joints hand-rolled (€3). 10 types of hash and weed €7-12. Open M-Th and Su 7am-1am, F-Sa 7am-2am. Cash only.

Witte de With, Witte de Withstraat 92. A simple basement shop with foosball and pool tables and a chill atmosphere. Joints €2.50. Bongs available. Pipes for sale. Open daily 9am-1am. Cash only.

NIGHTLIFE

Rotterdam's nightlife pulses with energy. Dancing, live music, and a large GLBT presence help this large port rival Amsterdam as the Dutch party capital. Bars and clubs line **Mauritsweg, Oude** and **Nieuwe Binnenweg,** and **Witte de Withstraat. Oude-haven,** east of the city center, also has lively, student-friendly nightlife.

> **TIP**   **MAPPING GAY ROTTERDAM.** For a comprehensive listing of all of Rotterdam's GLBT nightclubs, bars, and saunas, pick up a copy of *The Gaymap,* a detailed map of gay Rotterdam with many GLBT establishments well marked. Inquire about a copy at any of the city's GLBT establishments. The most up-to-date map can also be found at www.gaymap.info.

Dizzy, 's-Gravendijkwal 127 (☎477 3014; www.dizzy.nl). M: Dijkzigt or tram #4 to 's-Gravendijkwal. Rotterdam's premier jazz cafe for 25 years, Dizzy hosts frequent jam sessions and has hosted internationally known performers such as Chet Baker. The backdoor patio garden, lined with bamboo and ivy, is modern and unconventional but functional and appealing. Sept.-June M jam session 10pm-1am. Tu jazz concert 10pm. Beer €1.80. Whiskey €5.20. Restaurant serves salads (€4-9) and entrees (€8-15) daily until 11pm. Restaurant reservations recommended on weekends. Open M-Th noon-1am, F-Sa noon-2am, Su noon-midnight. AmEx/MC/V.

Off_Corso, Kruiskade 22 (☎280 7359; www.offcorso.nl). This abandoned movie theater got a new lease on life in 2001 when 4 young local residents gave birth to what has become Rotterdam's hottest nighttime phenomenon. Art exhibitions share the bill with regular dance parties. Specific theme nights and covers change often. Hours depend on the event; check the website to see what's on the agenda.

De Witte Aap, Witte de Withstraat 78 (☎414 9565; www.dewitteaap.nl). Of all the small, trendy bars that line Witte de Withstraat, The White Ape (whose logo is a primate with headphones) is one of the coolest. The nightspot's namesake is incorporated into the design and decor tastefully and cleverly, and wall-sized windows look out onto the street. But the real draw is one of Rotterdam's most diverse and interesting crowds, which spills onto the street on weekends. A popular spot after other clubs have closed. Beer €2. Open M-Th and Su 4pm-4am, F-Sa 4pm-5am. Cash only.

Rotown, Nieuwe Binnenweg 19B (☎436 2669; www.rotown.nl). A diverse clientele of hip 20-somethings crowds the terrace but heads to the back of the building when there's live reggae, rock, hip hop, and alternative playing. During the day, the stage leads into an sunlit dining room. Sandwiches €3-4. Dinner entrees around €10, but with 10 live shows a month, the primary attraction is the music. Th indie rock; F-Sa DJ. Cover F-Sa €3.50. Bar open M-W and Su 11am-2am, Th-Sa 11am-3am. AmEx/MC/V.

De Regenboog, Van Oldenbarneveltstraat 148A. A funky and patriotic ▼**gay** bar known for its mixed clientele and karaoke nights. The place to go for an upbeat, energetic night out on the town with a fun atmosphere and friendly staff, decked out with intense disco lights. Beer from €2. Open W-Th and Su 4pm-1am, F-Sa 4pm-2am. Cash only.

Stockholm, Spaansekade 12 (☎414 7295; www.stockholmbar.nl). A new and very appealing bar that adds a bit of sophistication to the many other bars on Spaansekade. The modern and effective Scandinavian design and drinks with an interesting twist (Swedish Spring Punch made with currant vodka; €7.50) will make you think you've left the Netherlands for a neighbor to the north. Cocktails €7.50. Wine €3.50 per glass. Open M-Th and Su 5pm-1am, F-Sa 4pm-2am.

Strano, Van Oldenbarneveltplaats 154 (☎412 5811; www.strano.nl), on the corner with Mauritsweg. Small **gay** bar and dance club set against a permeating trendy red glow. An older following shows up late when most of Rotterdam is closed. Friendly staff can tell you about Rotterdam's GLBT scene. Happy hour daily 11pm-midnight (2-for-1 drinks). Beer €2.30. Mixed drinks €6.20. Open M-Th 4pm-2am, F-Su 4pm-4am.

Villakakel Bont, Spaansepoort 73 (☎413 2050). A popular student bar that also serves food. The terrace is a popular place to have some drinks before moving on to one of the late-night dance clubs. Big sandwiches €5-6. Salmon filet €10.50. Salads €8.50-9. Beer €2. Open M-Th and Su noon-2am, F-Sa 2:30pm-4am. Be warned, however: their hours are flexible and can vary depending on weather and other factors. Kitchen closes at 10pm. AmEx/MC/V.

Stalles, Nieuwe Binnenweg 11A (☎436 1655; www.cafestalles.nl). A good place to grab a meal or a drink before checking out the concert at nearby Rotown. Cheap dinners around €7-10. M-Tu pizzas €4-6. Beer €2. Large collection of over 30 specialty whiskeys €5-7. Open M-Th and Su noon-1am, F-Sa noon-2am. Kitchen closes at 10pm. Cash only.

De Apres Skihut, Stadhuisplein 29 (☎213 3846; www.deapresskihut.nl). Fake ice hanging from the ceilings and a ski-lodge theme give this big restaurant, bar, and dance club a bit of a hokey feel, but the packed crowds don't seem to mind. This is the place to find a party any night of the week: unlike the more laid-back bars that dominate the Rotterdam nightlife scene, this is the domain of loud Dutch pop music (complete with a crowd singing along with every word) and a constantly blaring air horn. The bartenders, both male and female, seem to spend much of the night dancing on the bar. Cover for men F-Sa €5. Open M-Th and Su 11am-4am, F-Sa 11am-5am.

GOUDA ☎018

Gouda (pop. 75,000) is anything but cheesy. It is the quintessential Dutch town, complete with canals, narrow and winding brick-paved alleys, a windmill, and odd pronunciation (HOW-da). In the 14th century, much of the town's infrastructure and fortifications were already developed, and, up until the 15th century, it rivaled Amsterdam in size and prestige. Known for knife making, *stroopwafels* (see **One Wafel, Extra Stroop,** p. 135), stained glass, and, of course, its famous cheese, Gouda was also the birthplace and home of **Erasmus.** The medieval humanist scholar was educated and took his vows here in town. With its large, heart-shaped central square and lovely architecture, Gouda remains an idyllic place to get away from the more fast-paced Dutch cities, but if your visit coincides with its Thursday market, you will find that Gouda has an energy all its own.

◪◪ TRANSPORTATION AND PRACTICAL INFORMATION. Trains roll into town from Amsterdam (1hr.; €9.20, round-trip €17.20) and Rotterdam (20min.; €4.10, round-trip €7.30). From the station, follow signs to the left toward the **VVV,** Markt 27: cross the bridge over the canal and walk straight into **Kleiweg,** a principal shopping and commercial street. Kleiweg turns into **Hoogstraat** and leads to **Markt** and the tourist office. (☎0900 46 83 28 88; www.vvvgouda.nl. Open M-F 9am-5pm, Sa 10am-5pm; in summer also Su noon-3pm.)

◖ FOOD. Great options for food surround the inner square of Gouda, with culinary genres ranging from traditional Dutch to Mexican to Asian fusion. For an elegant but unpretentious meal or glass of wine, try **Ratatouille ❶,** Markt 16. Along with its appealing outer terrace on Markt, the restaurant boasts an attractive interior of exposed brick and lovely artwork on the walls. (☎252 9522. Soups €4.

Broodjes €4-10.50. House wine €3.20 per glass. AmEx/MC/V.) For a bit more history, head toward **De Zalm ❷**, Markt 34. Located in what it claims is the oldest inn in the Netherlands, De Zalm continues that tradition of hospitality with excellent salads and entrees in a surprisingly untouristed venue (considering its prime location on Markt). Try their special *Goudse kaassoep* (Gouda cheese soup) for €4.50. (☎268 6976. Salads and warm lunches €5.50-13.50. Dinner €14.50-21.50. Open daily 9am-1am. AmEx/MC/V.) Those more interested in delectable Dutch sweets can try **De Vlaam ❶**, Markt 69, tucked in among the many a bar and *pannenkoekenhuis.* This bakery is famous for its take on *stroopwafels*, the delicious local specialty which will cost you a mere €1.40 for a package of five.) While these syrupy waffles are delicious all over the Netherlands, De Vlaam uses a special old recipe rendering their version slightly crisper than those of their chewy competitors. For a more traditional pastry, try a special *apfel kanjer* (€1.30), a delicious and delicate apple turnover drenched in powdered sugar. (☎251 3359. Open M-W and F 8:30am-6pm, Th 8:30am-9pm, Sa 8am-5pm.)

◙ SIGHTS. In the summer, visitors can witness old-time trading procedures (like the hand-clapping agreements made between salesmen while bartering) during the **cheese market** held in central Markt (Th 10am-12:30pm). The market features a number of tourist treats, among them cheese-making demonstrations and free samples presented by Gouda's cheese maidens. A good starting point for dairy tourists is the **Kaaswaag Gouda,** Markt 35-36, in the central Markt area. Merchants and farmers have been weighing and selling cheese for centuries at this 17th-century weigh-house. Staffers provide information about Gouda's dairy mainstay. The Kaaswaag features a small but delightful permanent exhibition on Gouda and the history of its cheese trade, as well as a fun feature where you can weigh yourself in cheese. Don't miss the video on the third floor detailing the traditional production of cheese with the accompaniment of a dramatic soundtrack. On the second floor beckon the long and beautifully curved stems of ceramic pipes made and hand-painted by artisans. (☎252 9996. Open Apr. 9 -Oct. 29 Tu-W 1-5pm, Th 10am-5pm, F-Su 1-5pm. €3.50, under 12 €3.) If you haven't had enough of those large yellow wheels, every Thursday at 2pm you can join the **Cheese Walk** through town. (Meets at the VVV. €3.50.) While you're along central Markt, you won't want to miss the spectacular late Gothic **Stadhuis,** right in the center of the square, with its red-and-white clapboard shutters. It is sporadically open to the public—although, since it still functions as the city hall, don't expect exhibits or English explanations for anything in the building. Don't fret if it's closed, though; the building is perhaps most impressive when viewed from the outdoor terrace of one of the many cafes that ring the square. Its mechanical clock has puppets that are set into motion at two and 32 minutes past the hour. (Entrance €0.75.) Tucked within a small square just behind the Stadhuis and Markt sits the gargantuan late Gothic **St. Janskerk,** Achter de Kerk 16. This impressive church has managed to maintain its collection of 16th-century stained-glass windows, despite attacks by both the elements and Reformation iconoclasts. At nearly 130m, it is also the longest church in the Netherlands. (☎251 2684; www.st-janskerkgouda.nl. Open M-Sa Mar.-Oct. 9am-5pm; Nov.-Feb. 10am-4pm. €2.75, students and seniors €2.50, ages 12-18 €2, ages 5-12 €1.) Gouda's pride and joy, the city museum, **Museum Het Catharina Gasthuis,** Achter de Kerk 14, houses a collection that explores the history of Gouda, using everything from Flemish art and early surgical instruments to period furniture, dolls, and weaponry. Be sure to admire the museum's unique collection of 16th-century altarpieces, some of the few that survived the Netherlands's Protestant Reformation. To give it resonance, the Gasthuis is located in a former chapel. There's also an adjoining torture chamber that is less uplifting. After inspecting the artwork, enjoy a cup of coffee in their beautiful little garden, a peaceful alcove just beside Sint

DAYTRIPS

Janskerk. (☎233 1000; www.museumgouda.nl. Open W-F 10am-5pm, Sa-Su noon-5pm. €4, under 18 and Museumjaarkaart holders free.)

UTRECHT ☎030

Smack-dab in the center of the Netherlands lies Utrecht (pop. 290,000), a town first settled in AD 50 and now a mecca for history buffs and student partiers alike. The swarms of fraternity boys that fill the city's outdoor cafes are a visible testament to Utrecht's status as the Netherlands's largest university town, with a student population pushing 60,000. Utrecht is also a cultural hub: visitors come here for lively festivals, museums, nightlife, and winding, tree-lined canals. Historically the Christian capital of the Low Countries, Utrecht brims with relics from its religious past. **Domtoren,** the country's tallest church tower, dominates the provincial landscape, while **Museum Catharijneconvent** displays the region's religious artifacts. Even the canals are visitor-friendly: lying below street level, their concrete banks are ideal strolling territory. The **Museumkwartier** boasts no fewer than seven museums in one area, rendering it a perfect choice for an afternoon walk.

 THE REAL DEAL. The center of Utrecht can be very commercial, but if you go down Oudegracht past Hamburgerstraat, you'll find many small boutiques, quirky shops, and cozy cafes. —*Ravi Ramchandani*

▐ TRANSPORTATION

Take the **train** from Amsterdam (30min.; 3-6 per hr.; €6.40, round-trip €11.70). When you arrive, you'll be in a building connected to the Netherlands's largest shopping mall, the **Hoog Catharijne.** It's easiest to follow the signs through the mall toward **Vredenburg** (the marketplace and music hall) near the center of the city. Turn left out of the mall and walk along the market until **Lange Viestraat,** then turn right and walk one block to the center over **Oudegracht,** Utrecht's main canal. The city is small enough to be crossed on foot (about 20-40min. across the city center), but if you're itching to put foot to pedal, rent a bike at **Bicycle Shop Tusveld,** Van Sijpesteijnkade 40. (☎293 2679. Bikes €7.50 per day.) **Schuttevaer,** Bemuurde Weerd Oostzijde 17, offers **canal tours** that leave from the corner of Oudegracht and Lange Viestraat every 30min. from 11am to 5pm. (☎272 0111; www.schuttevaer.com. Open daily 11am-6pm. €7.50, under 12 €5.75.) For a **taxi,** call ☎230 0400 or pick one up near Centraal Station.

◄▌ ▐ ORIENTATION AND PRACTICAL INFORMATION

The pulsing center of Utrecht is known as the **Museumkwartier,** a five-minute walk from Utrecht Centraal's Vredenburg exit. Generally speaking, the Museumkwartier is the area bordered on the east and west by Oudegracht and **Nieuwegracht.** On Oudegracht, you'll find countless churches, museums, fashionable shops, restaurants, art galleries, theaters, and coffee shops. To check up on any museum listing, go to www.utrecht-city.com. The main west-east thoroughfare is the many-named **Vredenburg/Lange Viestraat/Potterstraat** stretch. The center of the city is very commercial, but a stroll farther in any direction will yield more provincial regions. **Beware: the area around Centraal Station should be avoided at night;** in all emergencies, dial ☎112.

To find the **VVV,** Domplein 9, from Lange Viestraat, turn right on Oudegracht and follow it down on the easternmost side until Servetstraat; turn left. The VVV is in a building called the **RonDom,** a Visitors Center for cultural history, across from the

Domkerk. Pick up a free map of the city and a complete listing of museums and sights; the desk can even suggest and book a hotel based on your budget. (☎0900 128 8732, €0.50 per min.; www.utrechtyourway.nl. Open Apr.-Sept. M-Sa 10am-5pm, Su noon-5pm; Oct.-Mar. M-F and Su noon-5pm, Sa 10am-5pm.) The best way to get **Internet** access is to use free computers at hostels, but cheap rates (€3 per hr.) can be found at the **Centrale Bibliotheek** (Central Library), Oude-gracht 167, north of Domtoren. (☎286 1800; www.utrecht.nl/bibliotheek. Open M 1-9pm, Tu-W and F 11am-6pm, Th 11am-9pm, Sa 10am-5pm.)

ACCOMMODATIONS

Budget accommodations in Utrecht are everything hostels should be; they provide inexpensive room and board along with a friendly community of travelers.

> **TIP** **TOO TIRED TO STAND?** For an extended, cost-free stay in Utrecht, head to the squatters' meeting held every Wednesday from 8 to 9pm at the ACU Politiek Cultureel Centrum (p. 301) to learn about finding your very own squat.

▨ **Strowis Hostel,** Boothstraat 8 (☎238 0280; www.strowis.nl). From Centraal, head east on Vredenburg until it becomes Lange Jansstraat, turn left onto the tree-lined square at Janskerkhof, and turn left again at Boothstraat; the hostel is on your left. Laid-back staff, convenient location right around the corner from the ACU Politiek Cultureel Centrum (p. 301), and unbeatable prices. This former squat feels more like a homey country villa, complete with high ceilings, comfy antique furnishings, and French doors leading to an outdoor terrace overlooking a garden and a tiny pond. Dorms are neatly packed with bunk beds; women-only dorms available. Rooms and bathrooms are kept very clean. A kitchen well equipped with pots and pans is also available. Breakfast €5. Sheets and blanket €1.25. Free Internet access. Free lockers. 2-week max. stay. Curfew M-F 2am, Sa-Su 3am. 14-bed dorms €14.50; 8-bed dorms €15.50; 6-bed dorms €16.50; 4-bed dorms €17.50; doubles €57.50; triples €69. ❶

B&B Utrecht City Centre, Lucasbolwerk 4 (☎065 043 4884; www.hostelutrecht.nl), next to the park. Head down Vredenburg, crossing the city center until it turns into Nobelstraat, and turn left on Lucasbolwerk. There's nothing on the outside indicating that you're in front of a hostel—you have to ring the bell to be let into this spacious, 3-story lodging that feels like a utopian commune. B&B Utrecht operates under a unique set of ideals. For a flat fee (€16.50), you get a dorm bed, 24hr. food (the fridge is stocked continually with eggs, bread, meat, and pasta), a music corner full of instruments, and a home video system (with hundreds of videocassettes and a few DVDs). The rooms are strictly no-frills, and the showers are in need of updating. Sheets €2.50. Free Wi-Fi. Cheap bike rental (€5 per day). Stay for free in exchange for a few hours of work around the building each day. Reserve by phone or online. Dorms €16.50; singles €55; doubles €65; triples €90; quads €120. MC/V. ❶

⚫ FOOD

Utrecht's affluence is nowhere more apparent than in its lack of extensive budget dining options. For cheap eats, try the pizzerias, pubs, and sandwich shops on **Nobelstraat** (Lange Viestraat's stage name east of the Museumkwartier) or **Voorstraat,** closer to the center. Otherwise, you may want to splurge at one of the canal-side restaurants lining **Oudegracht,** near **Domplein.**

▨ **Het Nachtrestaurant,** Oudegracht 158 (☎230 3036), right on the east bank of the canal, just north of the Stadhuis. Enter through the underground passage in the middle of Ganzenmarkt. Co-owned by the popular **De Winkel van Sinkel** *grandcafe* (p. 302), this "night restaurant" has a decadent, pillow-lined cellar dining room, while the flashier clientele crowds the canal-side terrace until late. Tapas €3-6. Open M-Sa 6-11pm or later, depending on the weather. Becomes a nightclub Sa 11pm. AmEx/MC/V. ❷

Toque Toque, Oudegracht 138 (☎231 8787), just off Vinkenburgstraat. Red walls, aluminum details, and bright modern art lend a bohemian chicness to this eatery that manages to be refined yet unpretentious. Ask to be seated on the canal-side terrace. Peruse the 9-page wine list while nibbling a delicious range of salads and fresh pastas (€11-14). The lunch menu consists largely of sandwiches and soup (€4.50-7.50). Meat entrees from €15.20. Open M-W and Su 10am-midnight, Th-Sa 10am-1am. Kitchen open daily 10am-10pm. AmEx/MC/V. ❸

Venezia, Voorstraat 8 (☎231 2903; www.venezia.nl). Utrecht's favorite ice-cream parlor. Winner of many awards, Venezia has a charm that will appeal to adults and kids alike. Sundaes from €3, single scoop €1.10. Heaping 3-scoop cones €2.70. Try the ice-cream lasagna, ice-cream pizza, or the countless number of special sundaes, including the "Coupe Royale" and the "Gondola." There is also a Venezia ice-cream stand along the canal at Oudegracht 105. Parlor open daily noon-10pm. Stand open M-W and F-Su noon-6:30pm, Th noon-7:30pm. Cash only. ❶

🅖 SIGHTS

The Museumkwartier contains the core of Utrecht's extended family of museums. For more general information, check out www.utrecht-city.com.

DOMKERK AND DOMTOREN. Utrecht's Domtoren is impossible to ignore: the city's most beloved landmark is also the highest church tower in the Netherlands. The 112m tower presides over the province with magnificent spires and 26,000kg of bronze bells. The carillon on the top third of the tower consists of 50 bells that play a short melody every 15min., a longer tune at half-past, and a full song each hour. Begun in 1321 and finished 150 years later in the French Gothic style, the brick-red Domkerk (Dom Church) was attached to the tower until an errant tornado blew away the nave in 1674. Climb the tower's 465 steps to take in panoramic views of Amersfoort and Amsterdam—on clear days, Rotterdam and The Hague are also visible. During the hour-long tour, you'll learn about the history of the church and get a glimpse of the church's bells. The number of visitors to the tower must be regulated carefully, so if you want to climb the tower during the heavily trafficked summer months, it is essential to check in advance. For a peaceful rest, be sure to visit the Cathedral Courtyard on Servetstraat, next to the Domtoren. (*Achter de Dom 1. From Lange Viestraat, turn right on Oudegracht, following it down on the easternmost side until Servetstraat; turn left. ☎231 0403. Open Oct.-Apr. M-F 11am-4pm, Sa 11am-3:30pm, Su 2-4pm; May-Sept. M-F 10am-5pm, Sa 10am-3:30pm, Su 2-4pm. Free concert every Sa 3:30pm. Domtoren accessible only through 1hr. tours in English and Dutch; other languages depending on demand. Tours daily Oct.-Mar. M-F noon, 2, 4pm, Sa every hr. 10am-5pm, Su every hr. noon-5pm. Apr.-Sept. M-Sa every hr. 10am-5pm, Su every hr. noon-5pm. Domkerk free. Domtoren €7.50, ages 4-12 €4.50.)*

CENTRAAL MUSEUM. Visitors enter this former medieval cloister's labyrinth of pavilions to experience a range of Dutch art spanning everything from Roman and medieval archaeological finds to old masterpieces to modern art. The old masters section includes works by the Utrecht **Caravaggists**, including Hendrick ter Brugghen, Dirck van Baburen, and Gerrit van Honthorst, but the museum's most noteworthy collection is the range of modern art, featuring work by **Magic Realists** Pyke Koch and Carel Willink, as well as some by the **Surrealist** Johannes Moesman. The museum oversees the world's largest collection of work by *De Stijl* designer Gerrit Rietveld, but many of these objects have been transferred to the avant-garde **Rietveld Schroderhuis,** a UNESCO World Heritage Site. Designed

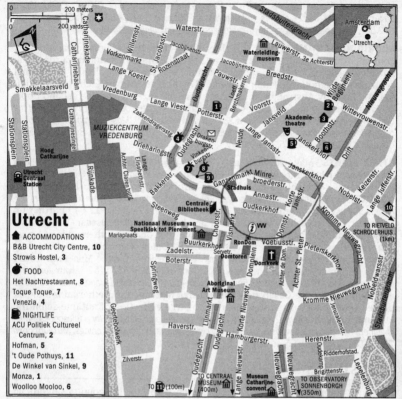

Utrecht

🏠 ACCOMMODATIONS
B&B Utrecht City Centre, **10**
Strowis Hostel, **3**

🍎 FOOD
Het Nachtrestaurant, **8**
Toque Toque, **7**
Venezia, **4**

🍷 NIGHTLIFE
ACU Politiek Cultureel
 Centrum, **2**
Hofman, **5**
't Oude Pothuys, **11**
De Winkel van Sinkel, **9**
Monza, **1**
Woolloo Mooloo, **6**

by Rietveld and constructed in 1924, the house is located east of the city. It is accessible only by guided tour through the Centraal Museum, so call ahead for reservations. (*Nicolaaskerkhof 10. From Domplein, head south on Korte Nieuwstraat, which becomes Lange Nieuwstraat. Turn right onto Agnietenstraat; it becomes Nicolaaskerkhof.* ☎ *236 2362 or 236 2310 for Rietveld Schroderhuis; www.centraalmuseum.nl. Open Tu-Th and Sa-Su noon-5pm, F noon-9pm. Audio tour free. €8, students €3, under 12 free.*)

 WALTZ OF THE FLOWERS. The best time to walk along the main canal in Utrecht is on Saturday from 8am to 5pm, when a canal-side flower market makes the experience that much more beautiful.

MUSEUM CATHARIJNECONVENT. In honor of Utrecht's religious history, the Museum Catharijneconvent, a converted 16th-century monastery, has assembled a survey of Dutch Christianity through works of visual art. The museum's permanent collection focuses on the history of Christian art and influences in Dutch society and includes illuminated manuscripts, jeweled book bindings, and paintings from the Dutch Golden Age by artists like Rembrandt van Rijn and Frans Hals. Items from the permanent collection juxtapose with modern renditions of similar Christian themes. The museum also hosts impressive temporary exhibits on its upper floor that include full English captioning and free English and Dutch audio tours. *(Lange Nieuwstraat 38. ☎ 231 3835; www.catharijneconvent.nl. Open Tu-F 10am-5pm, Sa-Su 11am-5pm. €8.50, seniors and students €7.50, ages 6-17 €4.50, under 5 free; families €22.50. Some special exhibits may require extra admission. AmEx/MC/V.)*

ABORIGINAL ART MUSEUM. This three-story collection of acrylic paintings by contemporary Australian Aboriginal artists is the first of its kind in Europe. The museum hosts two to three rotating exhibits every year that display Aboriginal art from throughout Australia as well as Western art influenced by the Aboriginal. Art films by Australian Aboriginal artists are screened on the second floor. The museum also has a gallery with paintings for sale. *(Oudegracht 176. South of the Dom on the east side of Oudegracht. ☎ 238 0100; www.aamu.nl. Most information is in Dutch, but ask for the walk-through English-language pamphlet. Open Tu-F 10am-5pm, Sa-Su 11am-5pm. €8, under 12 and seniors €5. AmEx/MC/V.)*

OTHER SIGHTS. Make sure to leave time for the **Nationaal Museum van Speelklok tot Pierement** (the National Museum of Musical Clocks and Street Organs) and its collection of noisemakers from the 17th through 20th centuries. *(Buurkerkhof 10. ☎ 231 2789; www.museumspeelklok.nl. Open Tu-Sa 10am-5pm, Su noon-5pm. Guided tours during which you can see the instruments in motion every hr. €7, ages 4-12 €4.)* Farther up Oudegracht, those thirsty for more will find the **Waterleidingmuseum** (Waterworks Museum), situated in a 39m water tower from 1895 on the northern side of Lange Viestraat. Here you can dive into four floors of Dutch water history delivered by former employees of the water company. Use a restroom in the Museumkwartier before the 5min. walk to the waterworks. *(Lauwerhof 29. ☎ 232 1152; www.waterleiding-museum.nl. Open Tu-F and Su 1:30-5pm, Sa 11am-4pm. €2, ages 6-11 and seniors €1.)* For astronomy buffs, the **Observatory Sonnenborgh Museum,** the Netherlands's oldest domed observatory, has telescopes and a large collection of antique scientific instruments. *(Zonnenburg 2. ☎ 230 2818; www.sonnenborgh.nl. Space for a telescope viewing is limited; call or visit the website to make a viewing reservation for the evenings. Museum open Tu-F and Su 11am-5pm. €5, seniors €3.50, ages 4-17 €3.)*

※ FESTIVALS

As the geographical center of the Netherlands, Utrecht is the country's unofficial festival capital. Free events abound throughout the year; check the *UitLoper* magazine—which can be found in pubs and cafes across the city or at www.uitloper.nl—or get a free copy of *Experienz Magazine* at the tourist office. On Sundays during the summer, Utrecht organizes a series of cultural events, such as concerts, museum events, and other performances throughout the city.

TWEETAKT. Every year in the middle of March, Utrecht hosts the national youth theater festival. The festival aims to bring established performers and new talent together for some of the most exciting and most innovative youth theater in the Low Countries. *(☎ 799 0080; www.tweetakt.net.)*

NIGHT FEVER. On the second weekend in June, the entire city heats up for Night Fever, a celebration of all things dance and disco. At different cafes, clubs, and other public locations, residents and visitors alike come together to get down with a number of traditional and cutting-edge musicians. *(www.night-fever-utrecht.nl.)*

MIDZOMERGRACHT. Roughly the third week of June is the Midsummer Canal Party, Utrecht's famously zesty ☑**GLBT** cultural festival, with free movies, concerts, and events. *(☎ 062 869 5041; www.midzomergracht.nl.)*

FESTIVAL OUDE MUZIEK. In late August, the city hosts the Old Music Festival, with Baroque and Classical ensembles playing period instruments. *(☎ 232 9000; www.oudemuziek.nl.)*

NETHERLANDS FILM FESTIVAL. During September and October, Utrecht is home to the Dutch version of the Academy Awards. It comes complete with red carpets, Dutch film stars, and the "Gouden Kalf" award, the highest Dutch honor given out in categories like best actor and best director. (☎230 3800; www.filmfestival.nl.)

HOLLAND ANIMATION FILM FESTIVAL. Every other November (in even-numbered years), the Holland Animation Film Festival screens everything from anime to feature films. Expositions and lectures round out this festival, which aims to honor Dutch animation as a unique art form. (☎233 1733; http://haff.awn.com.)

SMARTLAPPEN. During the second week of November, Utrecht's cafes and pubs open their doors to a less high-brow tradition: the Smartlappen festival celebrates folk singing and beer drinking. (www.smartlappenfestival.nl.)

🎵 NIGHTLIFE

For those not satisfied with stargazing at the observatory, the Netherlands's largest college town has no shortage of nightlife. Pick up a copy of *UitLoper* at bars or restaurants to scout the bar and arts scenes—both stay lively seven days a week. As with most student bars and clubs in the Netherlands, big nights are Wednesday through Friday; on Saturday many students leave town to visit family outside of Utrecht or to indulge in Amsterdam's libidinally charged landscape.

> **TIP** **WOOHOO WOOLLOO.** After partying it up at Woolloo Mooloo (p. 302), check www.woofoto.nl to see if any pics of you shaking your moneymaker made it online. Also, make friends with Sir Fred, the bouncer, who's worked at the club since it opened in the early 1970s—he's got the scoop on the Dutch royal family members who have partied away many a late night and early morning there.

 't Oude Pothuys, Oudegracht 279 (☎231 8970). Head down winding stone steps to this candlelit music cafe, whose name refers to its history as a storehouse for pots and pans as early as 1621. Uninhibited patrons have been known to jump off the bar's canal-side terrace into the Oudegracht after a long night of festivities. Live music nightly 11pm. Come early for a dinner fondue (€12.25 per person, €10 on M); wash your cheese down with a beer for €2. Open M-W and Su 3pm-2am, Th-Sa 3pm-3am. AmEx/MC.

ACU Politiek Cultureel Centrum, Voorstraat 71 (☎231 4590; www.acu.nl). Head east on Lange Viestraat from Oudegracht and turn left onto Voorstraat. Dreadlocked volunteers work the bar and the door at this former squat-turned-political/cultural center with a friendly anti-capitalist vibe. Hosts live music W and F (mostly hardcore, punk, and some folk; cover €5-6), a political discussion group (M 8pm-2am), and a movie night (Su; €1.70). Vegan dinners (€6.50-7.50) Tu-Th and Su 6-9pm. Beer €1.70. Open M and Su 8pm-2am, Tu-W 6pm-2am, Th 6pm-3am, F-Sa 9pm-4am. Cash only.

Hofman, Janskerkhof 17A (☎230 2470; www.hofman-cafe.nl), in a tree-lined square just next to the Akademietheater. Utrecht's theater school, Hofman, is packed with students and 20-somethings throughout the week. Take advantage of student-friendly events like a free Argentine Tango night (Tu 9pm), a cocktail night with a new cocktail every week (Th 9pm), dance parties (F-Sa 11pm-3:30am), and live music (M and Su 5pm). Beer €2. Open M-Th and Su 11am-2am, F-Sa 11am-3:30am. Cash only.

Monza, Potterstraat 16-20 (☎065 539 3184; www.clubmonza.nl). This former theater is now one of the Netherlands's most popular dance clubs. 3 nights per week, Monza brings DJs into a space filled with 2 bars, 3 video screens, and professional dancers. Th "Zoo" students get in free. Last Su of the month features "Super Sunday," a DJ battle. Beer €2. Cover €5-15 depending on DJ. Open Th-Sa midnight-5am. Cash only.

Woolloo Mooloo, Janskerkhof 14 (☎236 0860; www.woolloomooloo.nl). Run by a local fraternity, this is where Utrecht's student population migrates after everything else closes; show up after 1am on weekdays for the most fun, since many students go home on the weekends. Student ID required for entry into the dance hall. DJs spin dance music nightly. Beer tokens from vending machines outside the dance floor €1.10. Cover €3. Open daily 11pm until as late (early) as 7am. Cash only.

De Winkel van Sinkel, Oudegracht 158 (☎230 3030; www.dewinkelvansinkel.nl). The city's most popular *grandcafe* in an old canal-side warehouse turns into a nightclub on weekends. The huge, mandarin-colored complex with martini glasses lining the walls and a hyper-kitsch newsprint menu attracts tourists during the day and an older crowd at night. Entertainment includes live music, Tu knitting club 7:30-11pm, and W "Orakel Cafe" (free tarot readings). Extensive wine selection; glasses from €2.60. Beer from €2.30. *Grandcafe* open M-W 11am-midnight, Th-F 11am-1am, Sa 11am-10:30am, Su noon-midnight. Dancing Sa 11pm-5am. AmEx/MC/V.

ARNHEM   ☎026

Arnhem's nightlife may not compare to Utrecht's, but this sleepy city (pop. 150,000) on the Lower Rhine is a must-see for those interested in WWII history. Arnhem was the site of the ill-fated **Operation Market Garden,** in which Allied troops famously went "a bridge too far" and were subsequently crushed by the Germans. The capital of the province of **Gelderland** is encircled by parks and is home to lots of middling stores and some good restaurants.

TRANSPORTATION AND PRACTICAL INFORMATION. Trains pull in daily from Amsterdam's Centraal Station (1¼hr.; every 15min.; €14, round-trip €24.60). The city center of Arnhem lies to the south of the main street, **Jansbuitensingel,** which runs east-west from the exit of the train station. It is bounded on the east by **Velperbuitensingel** and on the west by **Willemsplein,** which runs down from just in front of the train station. Much of the area within this region is for pedestrians only. On the southeast corner is Eusebiuskerk, the 15th-century church destroyed in the 1944 Battle of Arnhem and restored thereafter.

EARN YOUR STRIPS. When traveling around Arnhem—to De Hoge Veluwe, your hostel, Apeldoorn, etc.—remember to buy a *strippenkaart* in 15- or 45-strip denominations. It's always cheaper than buying a ticket on the bus.

As of August 2007, Arnhem's **VVV** had closed but figured to be resurrected in a new location in 2008. Meanwhile, the **Tourist Information Kiosk,** Velperbuitensingel 25, lies on the outskirts of the city center. To get there, exit the train station, cross the street and turn left. On Jansstraat, turn right and continue until Vijzelstraat. Turn left and follow Vijzelstraat past the many shops and department stores as it takes on the alibis of Ketelstraat and then Roggestraat. At the next major intersection, cross the street to find the information kiosk on the side of the Musis Sacrum, a concert hall. (☎0900 112 2344, €0.45 per min.; www.arnhemavontuur.nl.)

ACCOMMODATIONS AND FOOD. Your best bet for accommodations in Arnhem is the **Stayokay Arnhem ❶,** Diepenbrocklaan 27. Take bus #3 from the station on platform M toward Alteveer or Burger's Zoo (10min., €1 one-way) to the Rijnstate Hospital stop. From the bus stop, turn right as you face the hospital (Ziekenhuis Rijnstate) and cross the street at the intersection. From here, you can follow the signs up Wagnerlaan, turn left on Waterbergseweg, and veer left again on Diepenbrocklaan. The other option is the much faster shortcut: turn left on Cattepoelseweg. Then, about 150m ahead, turn right up the brick steps and turn right at the top. The Stayokay will be straight ahead. This hostel's exceptionally clean rooms appeal to a slightly older crowd. The bar (pints €2.50) and reading room close at midnight. (☎442 0114; www.stayokay.com/arnhem. Breakfast included. Laundry €3.50; dryer €2. Linens included. Free safe box at reception. Reception 8am-11pm. No curfew, but buses stop running at midnight, so be prepared to take a cab if you plan to stay out late. 6-person dorms €22.20-31.60; 4-person dorms €24.40-35; doubles €63-90. €2.50 HI discount. AmEx/MC/V.)

There are a number of restaurants and cafes on Jansplein, a small square dominated by the octagonal Koepelkerk. From the train station, cross the street, turn left, and continue until Jansstraat. At Jansstraat turn right, continue for one block, and turn left on Jansplaats. Continue forward until you reach the square. On the southeast corner of Jansplein, **Zilli & Zilli ❸**, Marienburgstraat 1, is one of the most popular spots in Arnhem. The cafe-bar on the ground floor is elegant yet inviting, with stark white walls, a deep red ceiling, and plenty of lounge seating. (☎442 0288; www.zillizilli.nl. Sandwiches €4.50-8.50; salads €7-12. Pasta entrees €7.50-13.50. Meat entrees €15.50-22. Lunch served 11:30am-4:30pm. Dinner served after 5pm. Open M-Th and Su 11:30am-1am, F-Sa 11:30am-2am. AmEx/MC/V.) Several cheap, greasy sandwich stops and Shawarma stands can be found along the bustling Korenmarkt directly southeast of the train station. **Pizzeria Pinoccio ❷**, Korenmarkt 25B, serves up inexpensive pies in a faux-ivy-trimmed, candlelit setting in the heart of the city with plenty of statues of the famous wood puppet. Sit outside on the square to watch revelers heading to adjacent bars. (☎443 2208. Personal pizzas €5.60-11. Pasta and meat entrees also available. Open M-W 5-9:30pm, Th-F 5-10pm, Sa 4-10pm, Su 4-9:30pm. AmEx/MC/V.) **Proef Lokaal de Waag ❸**, Markt 38, at Walburgstraat, is just south of Eusebiuskerk on the southeast end of the city. Lunch means soups and sandwiches at this two-floor restaurant in a restored, all-wood mansion from 1761, though dinner is served too. (☎370 5960; www.proeflokaaldewaag.nl. Veggie lasagna €13.50. Well-portioned rack of lamb €19. Open M-Sa 10am-11pm.) For traditional ethnic food, start at the train station and turn left on the main street and right at Nieuweplein. A left on Rijnstraat and then another quick left put Varkensstraat on your right. **Pasam ❷**, Varkensstraat 33, is a basic Middle Eastern snack bar with ample seating. The friendly staff keeps this joint open super late. (☎446 0758. Sandwiches €2-6.50. Falafel €3.20. Shawarma €5.50. Kebabs and main dishes €7-12. Open daily noon-5am.)

 FRESHER IS BETTER. For fresh food, check out Arnhem's bustling market on Saturday from 9am to 5pm, in Markt across from Proef Lokaal de Waag.

◙ **SIGHTS.** In September 1944, the Nazis bombed the town in what has become known as the Battle of Arnhem. Like many Dutch cities, Arnhem had to be completely rebuilt after the war. After its 15th-century tower crashed to the ground during the blitz, the grand church **Eusebiuskerk,** Kerkplein 1, was restored in the neo-Gothic style and is now the town's most conspicuous sight. Today its Eusebiustoren, the 93m tower whose 53-bell carillon is the heaviest in the Netherlands, lords over a frighteningly empty square. During restoration, a glass elevator was installed to take visitors up to the beautiful views. (☎443 5068. Open Tu-Sa 10am-5pm, Su noon-5pm. Elevator €2.50, under 14 €2.) The hideous gray building behind the church is Arnhem's city hall, **Stadhuis,** which was built in 1964. Against Walburgstraat and between the church and Stadhuis, you'll find **Duivelshuis** (Devil's House), Koningstraat 1. This mansion, with distorted faces and animal-like human statues carved into its sides, was built in 1545. Untouched by the bombings, it was owned by a successful Dutch warmonger who sculpted the images to protest the town hall's prohibition of gold-coated front steps. Later owners reconciled themselves with town authorities, and the house has been linked to City Hall through a passage since 1830. Continue down Walburgstraat past the Duivelshuis and the Stadhuis. Go toward the right and continue around St. Walburg's church. At the intersection, cross the street and turn right. Keep going right along the path. Approximately 40m beyond the bus stop, you will reach the **John Frostbrug.** Rebuilt since it was destroyed during World War II, the famous "bridge too far" has been renamed for John Frost, commander of the Allied forces who attempted to secure it in September 1944. Frost's small force was the only group of Allied soldiers to reach the bridge on September 17, while most other troops landed much farther away and were unable to assist. His battalion held the bridge for an amazing four days before surrendering to Nazi forces on September 21. Though there is no major memorial at the sight, you can visit a small plaque dedicated to Frost and his men at the start of the bridge.

■ **NIGHTLIFE.** Arnhem may seem like a sleepy town during the day, but Korenmarkt's back-to-back bars and clubs get wild and crazy before they shut down at 2am. **5th Avenue,** Korenmarkt 26, packs its three floors with New Yorker wannabes sipping designer mixed drinks (€7.50) and groovin' to 70s, 80s, and 90s tunes (spun Th-Sa) on the top-floor dance floor. If you're under 21, look elsewhere; there is a bouncer-enforced age limit at this upscale joint. (☎442 8107; www.5avenue.nl. M-Th and Su 2pm-1am, F-Sa 2pm-2am.) Students need look no further than two doors down, however, where **Aspen Valley,** Korenmarkt 25, serves €1 beers to those with a student ID on Thursdays (€2 for those without). On weekends, this faux ski lodge is populated by a slightly older crowd. Thursday through Saturday nights resound with dance music, and DJs spin every night after 10pm. (☎443 0413; www.aspenvalley.nl. Open W-Su 8pm-2am. Cash only.) For a laid-back atmosphere and good food, cross the street to **Le Grand Cafe,** Korenmarkt 16. Moose heads, fake Greek statuary, and contemporary furnishings co-exist harmoniously in this low-key but somewhat hip bar with a spacious terrace. (☎442 6281. Sandwiches, soups, and salads €6.75-12.75. Beer €2. Open M-W 10am-1am, Th-Sa 10am-2am, Su 11am-1am. Cash only.)

APELDOORN   ☎055

While not a magnificent town in itself, Apeldoorn (pop. 160,000), some 25km north of Arnhem, is another gateway to **De Hoge Veluwe National Park.** Apeldoorn is home to the stunning ◪**Museum Paleis Het Loo,** a 17th-century palace that was the summer home of many King Williams of Orange. The three royal bedchambers, the stateliest rooms in the palace, are worth lingering over. The sizable grounds are a monument to geometrical excess: the pristine gardens—full of Neoclassical sculptures, fountains, and colonnades—have been pedantically and symmetrically trimmed for almost 350 years. Be sure to visit the stables, which house carriages and cars still in use by the royal family, and check out the peacocks, roosters, and hens that traipse around outside. From the train station, walk 40min. or take bus #102 or 104 (20min., 2 strips) to get to the museum; the bus stops outside the entrance. (☎577 2400; www.paleishetloo.nl. Open Tu-Su 10am-5pm. Guided tours in English by appointment only. Tours €1.20 per person for up to 20-person groups; reserve at least 2 weeks in advance. €9, ages 6-17 €3. MC/V.) Also nearby is ◪**Apenheul** (Apes' Refuge), an interactive zoo in Berg and Bos nature reserve, with 30 different species of apes. Take bus #2 or 3 (10min., 2 strips). Gorillas, orangutans, and bonobos live on islands throughout the park,

while smaller apes dwell in the area around the many walking paths, often interacting with guests. You're likelier to get pickpocketed here than in Amsterdam
Centraal—and, as such, the park provides special **ape-proof money belts.** (☎357
5757; www.apenheul.com. Open daily Apr.-June and Sept.-Oct. 9:30am-5pm; July-
Aug. 9:30am-6pm; €16, seniors and ages 3-9 €12.)

Trains run into Apeldoorn station from both Amsterdam (1hr.; every 30min.;
€13, round-trip €23.10) and Arnhem (1hr.; every 30min.; €7.40, round-trip
€13.70), though the latter involves a train change at Deventer. The easiest and
cheapest trip from Arnhem is by bus #91 or 231 (45min., 8 strips). The **VVV** tourist
office, Deventerstraat 18, is a short walk from the train station; walk down Stationsstraat for about 10min., then turn left onto Deventerstraat and continue until the
end of the block. The VVV here is an fine source for advice as well as for bike
maps. (☎526 0200; www.vvvapeldorn.nl. Open M-F 9am-6pm, Sa 9am-5pm.)

DE HOGE VELUWE NATIONAL PARK ☎0318

De Hoge Veluwe (pop. hundreds of plant and animal species) is a far cry from
the urban buzz of Amsterdam: at 13,565 acres, the nature reserve is the largest in
the Netherlands. Exploration through the park reveals wooded areas, moors,
grassy plains, and—extraordinarily—sand dunes. While the flat landscape may
not offer the most dramatic hiking, it is the ideal natural habitat for bicycles.
Over 36km of extensively mapped bike paths cross the reserve, and 1700 white
bikes, available free of charge at five convenient spots in the park, make travers-
ing the grounds a real treat. The handful of lakes and shady glens also make the
park ideal for picnicking. Venture to the southern end to watch the wildlife; early
morning and late afternoon are the best times to catch a glimpse of the deer,
wild boars, and numerous birds that inhabit the park.

🖪🔁 TRANSPORTATION AND PRACTICAL INFORMATION. Apeldoorn and
preferably Arnhem (both 15km from the park) are both good bases for exploring
De Hoge Veluwe. From the **Arnhem** train station, take bus #105 (Harderwijk, Platform S) to Otterloo and transfer to bus #106, a shuttle bus, into the park. (M-F 10
per day 8:03am-4:02pm, Sa 9 per day 8:03am-4:02pm, Su 7 per day 10:03am-
4:02pm; €4.80 or 6 strips). From **Apeldoorn,** hop on bus #108 at the train station to
the main Hoenderloo entrance (25 min.; every hr. 9:51am-10:51pm; €4.20 or 6
strips). To go deeper into the park, transfer to shuttle bus #106 at the entrance.
Begin by picking up a map (€2.50) at any of the park entrances or at the De Hoge
Veluwe Visitors Center, known as the **Bezoekerscentrum.** (☎59 16 27; www.hogev-
eluwe.nl. Open daily Apr.-Oct. 9:30am-6pm, Nov.-Mar. 9:30am-5pm.) Note that
bike paths, car roads, and hiking trails are separated throughout the park. Be
sure to read the map legend carefully.

🏠🍴 ACCOMMODATIONS AND FOOD. Camping is available at a campground
near the Hoenderloo entrance. (☎055 378 2232. Open Apr.-Oct. €4 per person,
ages 6-12 €1.75. Electricity €2.)

The most economical and enjoyable way to refuel during a day in the park is
with a picnic lunch. There are, however, two restaurants within the park. **De Koperen Kop ❷,** a self-service, cafeteria-style restaurant at the center of the park and
next to the Visitors Center, offers specials (€11-14) for every season, in addition to
cheaper crepes and salads (€3.75-4.75) and larger entrees. (Open same hours as
the Visitors Center. AmEx/MC/V.) A kiosk next to De Koperen Kop sells ice cream,
snacks, and cold drinks in the warmer months. The more upscale **Rijzenburg ❺,**
much farther away from the center (toward the southernmost end of the park),
has a three-course menu from €25. (☎443 6733; www.rijzenburg.nl. Open daily

Apr.-Oct. 10am-10pm, Nov.-Mar. 10am-9pm.) **Monsieur Jacques ❶,** located inside the Kröller-Müller Museum, is a less expensive option. It sells sandwiches and drinks at only slightly inflated prices, and the outdoor terrace makes it worth a stop. (☎59 16 57; www.monsieurjacques.nl. Open same hours as the museum.)

🖪 **SIGHTS.** The park's extensive biking trails are its main attraction. There are two major bike paths. Path #1 (10km) goes to the major sights in the park: the Bezoekerscentrum, the Kröller-Müller Museum, and the St. Hubert Hunting Lodge in the north of the park. The more extensive route is #2 (2-3hr. round-trip, 26km). Begin at the Kröller-Müller Museum and follow the route down past the sand dunes; be sure to pull over and check out the animal tracks, wind-blown streaks of sand, and desert-like flora. For a shorter route, turn left at the major intersections to make a smaller circle. Make your first left and continue straight ahead, veering again to your left: you will pass by the **Deelense Veld's** beautiful lakes on your right. Take the first and second left turns to get back to the Museum or the Otterloo entrance. For the full route, continue all the way down to Schaarsbergen. (Grounds open daily Apr. 8am-8pm; May and Aug. 8am-9pm; June-July 8am-10pm; Sept. 9am-8pm; Oct. 9am-7pm; Nov.-Mar. 9am-6pm. €7, ages 6-12 €3; 50% discount May-Sept. after 5pm. Cars €6. V.)

It's both a blessing and a curse that the world-class 🖪**Kröller-Müller Museum** is tucked deep within the park's beautiful expanses. The museum's collection, which began with the private holdings of heiress Helene Kröller-Müller, boasts an astounding 87 paintings and 180 drawings by **Vincent van Gogh,** including *Four Sunflowers Going to Seed* and *Pink Peach Trees.* The true scene-stealer, though, is his famous *Terrace of a Cafe at Night.* Yet the sprawling, modern complex is also home to work by other early Modernist masters like Piet Mondrian, Juan Gris, Alberto Giacometti, Georges Seurat, Fernand Leger, and Georges Braque. The museum also situates itself firmly in its natural surroundings. Whole galleries look out onto adjacent woodlands, and the gorgeous sculpture garden—with moving large-scale works by Richard Serra, Mario Merz, Carl Andre, and Tony Smith—is an astonishing amalgam of natural and manmade materials. Be sure not to miss **Jean Dubuffet's** *Jardin d'email*—a walk-through environment in white and black; look for the towering, cartoonish tree or pick up a free map to the garden. The museum and its grounds—both worthy of all hyperbole—should not be missed. (☎59 12 41; www.kmm.nl. Open Tu-Su 10am-5pm; sculpture garden closes 4:30pm. €7, ages 6-12 €3.50, under 6 free.)

A few kilometers north, the central tower of the **St. Hubert Hunting Lodge** rises up out of the landscape like a large, brick-red ostrich. Designed by **Hendrik Petrus Berlage,** the castle is open daily for free guided tours. There is also a suggested walk (follow the signs) circling the lodge that rambles past a meditation garden, peat bog, water mill, and sheep meadow. Spots for the lodge tours are limited and fill up especially fast in summer. Reserve early on the day of the tour at the Visitors Center. (Lodge grounds open same hours as park. Tours Tu-Su noon-3:30pm.) Also check out the visually inventive **Museonder,** an underground museum that's an earth scientist's dream come true. Located in the Visitors Center, this kid-friendly museum teaches visitors about the park's flora and ecosystems beneath the ground, focusing on animal and plant life living in the earth as well as the gradual development of geological formations. (Open same hours as Bezoekerscentrum. Free with park ticket.)

GRONINGEN   ☎050

Groningen (pop. 185,000), easily the most happening city in the northern Netherlands, pulses with rejuvenated spirit. While the city is far older than Amsterdam—earliest mentions of the city's primitive name *Cruoninga* date from 1040—the attitude here is strictly forward-looking. Heavily bombed in WWII, Groningen rebuilt itself completely. Yet unlike some other Dutch cities, Groningen managed to retain its Old World feel alongside its bland 1950s architecture. Some beautiful and venerable sights remain, including Martini-kerk, Stadhuis, and Prinsenhoftuin, but the priority is now cutting-edge archi-tecture and design, as evidenced by the adventurous **Groninger Museum** and **Rem Koolhaas's** milk-glass public urinal (among many other things). The city gates—nine markers that spell out the city's ancient name—were conceived by architect **Daniel Libeskind** in 1990 to celebrate Groningen's 950th anniversary. More than half of the city's inhabitants are under 35, due in no small part to the Rijksuniversiteit Groningen (University of Groningen) and the Hanzehoge-school (Institute for Higher Professional Education). As a result, Groningen is known throughout the Netherlands as a party city.

TRANSPORTATION

The **train** from Amsterdam is one of the longer trips you'll take in the Nether-lands, and you must transfer in Amersfoort (2½hr., with an additional 30min. between trains; about 2 per hr.; €27, round-trip €38.60). If you need to hit the road within Groningen, a bus system reaches all parts of the city (bring your *strippenkaart*). Call for **taxis** (☎549 4940).

ORIENTATION AND PRACTICAL INFORMATION

Groningen's old center is easily walkable and no bigger than a sq. km. Bordered by public transit in the south and canals in the east, north, and west, the center is a 10min. walk from the train station. To get there, go out to the main street, turn right, and cross the second bridge on your left. After crossing, follow Her-estraat until its end at Groningen's historic **Grote Markt.** Though Groningen, like virtually every other Dutch city, boasts a network of canals, here they are referred to as *diep* rather than *gracht*.

The **VVV** tourist office, Grote Markt 25, is in the southeast corner of the Grote Markt next to the Martinitoren. The friendly and enthusiastic staff books accom-modations for a fee of roughly €5 and gives guided walking tours throughout the year; reserve in advance. (☎900 202 3050, €0.45 per min.; www.vvvgroningen.nl. Open M-W 9am-6pm, Sa 10am-5pm; July-Aug. also Su 11am-3pm. Walking tours are available at varying times throughout the year. Call in advance for more specifics.) Get your email fix at the **@ease Internet Cafe,** Herestraat 94. (☎589 3563. €2.50 per hr. Open M and Sa-Su noon-10pm, Tu-F 10am-10pm.)

ACCOMMODATIONS

▨ **Simplon Jongerenhotel,** Boterdiep 73-2 (☎313 5221; www.simplon-jongerenhotel.nl). Bus #1 (dir.: Korrewegwijk) from the train station to Boterdiep. Look for the sign above a driveway entrance. Pulls in fun, young residents with its clean lodgings, rock-bottom prices, homey feel, and friendly staff. Breakfast (8:30-11am; €4.50) and linens (€2.50) included with private rooms. Free lockers with €10 deposit. Laundry €4. Reception 24hr. Lockout noon-3pm. Bike rentals €6. 5 dorms (4 co-ed, 1 women-only). Large dorm €13; small dorm €17.50; singles €32.50-39; doubles €49.50-55; triples €69.50; quads €100; quints €120; 6-person room €132. Cash only. ❶

Martini Hotel, Gedempte Zuiderdiep 8 (☎312 9919; www.martinihotel.nl). From the station, cross the canal at the Groninger Museum and follow that street a few blocks to

Gedempte Zuiderdiep. Turn right; Martini is on your right. About halfway between the train station and Grote Markt, this large hotel from 1871 was recently renovated with a classy new lobby. Some rooms are a little cramped, but all have private bath and TVs. Buffet breakfast (€9) served in the spacious bar and lounge adjoining the reception area. Internet access €3.50 per 15min. Bar open 4:30pm-midnight. Singles €77.50; doubles €77.50-87.50; triples €87.50; quads €100. AmEx/MC/V. ❹

Hotel Friesland, Kleine Pelsterstraat 4 (☎312 1307). 5-10min. walk from the train station; cross the canal at the Groninger Museum (on your right as you exit the station) and walk up Ubbo Emmiusstraat. Turn right on Gedempte Zuiderdiep, left on Pelsterstraat, and right onto Kleine Pelsterstraat. Not nearly as barbaric as the name might imply. Most rooms with TV. Shared bathrooms are clean, if dated. All rooms with sink. Breakfast included. Singles €40; doubles €65; triples €92; quads €114. AmEx/MC/V. ❷

🍴 FOOD

🍴 **Ben'z,** Peperstraat 17 (☎313 7917; www.restaurantbenz.nl). This lovingly managed restaurant provides a unique dining experience. The Mediterranean cuisine is a potpourri of dishes from North Africa, Europe, and the Middle East. Dinner is served on low tables in a lantern-lit Bedouin tent while guests lounge upon Turkish cushions. Appetizers €2.60-4. Entrees €10-17. 5-course menu €32.35. Special rates for groups, as well as the option of ordering a belly dancer; special student menu offered during the week (fries, salad, soup, bread, and a main dish; €7.60-9.10). Open daily 4:30pm-midnight. Kitchen closes 9pm. Cash only. ❸

De Kleine Moghul, Nieuwe Boteringstraat 62 (☎318 8905). Entirely organic, well-prepared Indian cuisine that's very popular with the locals. In a setting that can only be described as hippie or Indian chic with bright neon colors and pastel walls. It's a bit of a walk from the center, but convenient to the Noorderplantsoen. Appetizers €3-3.75. Entrees €9-12. Takeout available. Open daily 5-10pm. MC/V. ❷

Satehuis, Herestraat 111 (☎311 2865). Savor Indonesian flavors in this medium-size eatery in an upscale bamboo-bedecked atmosphere with provincial prices. 6 sticks of beef or chicken *satay* with rice, sides, and access to the stocked salad bar from €11.25. 4 sticks of *satay* from €7.50. Special movie deal (€17.75) buys a meal, drink, and ticket to the cinema across the street. Takeout available. Open M 5-10:30pm, Tu-Th 4-10:30pm, F-Sa noon-11pm, Su noon-10pm. AmEx/MC/V. ❷

👁 SIGHTS

GRONINGER MUSEUM. The Groninger Museum, in a multi-colored, multi-faceted, multi-shaped building, presents modern art, traditional paintings, and ancient artifacts. Brought to you by Italian architects and famed French designer Philippe Starck, the museum's steel-trimmed pavilions and cafe create a futuristic laboratory vibe for its exhibits. It's a museum defined by risk, both architecturally and artistically; there are some Golden Age paintings detailing the early history of Groningen, but the point here is revolutionary design and contemporary art. No distinction is made among fashion, painting, photography, sculpture, and design. Expect to see any and all artistic disciplines displayed deliberately alongside one another. *(Museumeiland 1. In the middle of the canal in front and to the right of the train station. Walk across the blue pedestrian bridge. ☎366 6555; www.groninger-museum.nl. Open Sept.-June Tu-Su 10am-5pm; July-Aug. M 1-5pm, Tu-Su 10am-5pm. €8, seniors €7, children €4.)*

NOORDELIJK SCHEEPVAART EN NIEMEYER TABAKSMUSEUM (SHIPPING AND TOBACCO MUSEUM). With two fascinating museums in one, the **Noordelijk** is a fun, cheap, hour-long diversion consisting of an incredible collection of artifacts.

Groningen

▲ ACCOMMODATIONS
Hotel Friesland, **13**
Martini Hotel, **12**
Simplon Jongerenhotel, **2**

🍎 FOOD
Ben'z, **5**
De Kleine Moghul, **1**
Satehuis, **15**

☕ COFFEE SHOPS
Dee's Cafe, **8**
The Glory, **11**
De Vliegende Hollander, **14**

🍸 NIGHTLIFE
Cafe de Vlaamsche Reus, **4**
Cafe de Zolder, **9**
Jazzcafe de Spieghel, **3**
Sally O'Brian's, **7**
Vera, **10**

The Scheepvaart, full of every type of nautical equipment or instrument imaginable, focuses on the history of Dutch trade from the Middle Ages. Whole ship's cabins are recreated for your maritime pleasure. The smaller **Tabaksmuseum** celebrates the important commercial and political history of the tobacco trade and displays fabulous ivory and crystal pipes. Unfortunately, most of the information is in Dutch (a short English guide is available to the Tobacco Museum), though much of the content can be understood visually, and it is a treat just to wander through the meandering building itself, constructed in 1450. *(Brugstraat 24-26. Head up Ubbo Emmiusstraat and keep going, as it becomes Folkingestraat, until Vismarkt. Turn left on the 2nd street leaving Vismarkt from the west; after 2 blocks, that street becomes Brugstraat. ☎312 2202. Open Tu-Sa 10am-5pm, Su 1-5pm. €3, ages 7-14 and over 65 €1.60, under 7 free.)*

MARTINIKERK. While its middle, Romanesque section dates from the 13th century, the Gothic rest of this originally Catholic church was added in the 15th century. When Protestants took over the church in the late 16th century, they whitewashed the original frescoes, some of which have been recovered with modern-day restorations. The church's organ, dating from 1480 with additions through the 18th century, is one of the largest Baroque organs in Northern Europe. Above, the 97m **Martinitoren** offers the best views of Groningen. Miraculously, it survived WWII untouched, unlike its neighbors on the northern and

UNDER THE HOSPICES OF GRONINGEN

Though Groningen is known for its all-night bars, contemporary architecture, and fashionable shopping, some 30 almshouses lie within the bustle. These buildings where "undesirables" once lived are standing connections to Groningen's medieval past.

1 Heiligen Geest Gasthuis, built by the order of the Holy Spirit in the 13th century. The identifying mark of this group is the double St. Andrew's Cross visible throughout the building. This hospice was once both an inn and an almshouse.

2 St. Anthony Gasthuis, home to plague victims and the mentally ill from 1517. The hospice itself was originally outside the city walls.

3 St. Geertruids Gasthuis, used for the poor, the sick, the elderly, and pilgrims. It includes a courtyard, a church, and several other buildings as part of its extensive complex.

eastern sides of Grote Markt, which suffered total destruction. Climb the winding spiral staircase to midway up the tower, where you can pull cords and push buttons to simulate bell ringing. Let your feet leave the ground, and the rope will pull you upward. You can also see the real bells, under which people were occasionally tied as torture, up close and personal. Finally, at the top, enjoy a stunning view of the city. (*Southeast corner of Grote Markt. Church open June-Aug. Tu-Sa noon-5pm, Sept.-Nov. Sa noon-5pm. €1. Tower open daily Apr.-Oct. 11am-5pm; Nov.-Mar. noon-4pm. €3, under 12 €2. Buy tickets at the VVV, across the street, or on the tower's 1st fl. when VVV is not open.*)

STRIPMUSEUM (COMIC MUSEUM). This comic extravaganza begins with a 10min. film in a rotating theater with five screens (narrated by Dutch comic-book characters) to the right of the entrance. From there, displays of original and in-progress comics line undulating walls, and brightly colored nooks and crannies bring cartoons and full-size models of comic-book characters to life. Most of the exhibits care mostly about Dutch artists and their creations, but some feature old faves like Donald Duck. Afterward, hit the studio to draw your own comics—or just color inside the lines of one. Pick up a map of the museum, drawn completely in comic-book style. (*Westerhaven 71. ☎317 8470; www.stripmuseumgroningen.nl. Open Tu-Su 10am-5pm. €7, ages 3-11 €5.75, under 3 free.*)

OTHER SIGHTS. While in the area of Martinikerk, look to the western side of the square and you'll see the **Stadhuis**, Groningen City Hall, erected in 1810. The Stadhuis prevails over the **Grote Markt,** which becomes a real marketplace every Tuesday and Saturday. Behind the Stadhuis, catch a glimpse of the **Goudkantoor (Gold Office).** This building once functioned as the city's tax-collection office and is beautifully restored in glittering detail as a restaurant. Continue along behind it to the 1865 **Korenbeurs (Corn Exchange),** which now appropriately holds an Albert Heijn supermarket. For a rare display of open-air urination, continue along the road. In a few blocks, it becomes Brugstraat; right before the first canal, turn left onto Kleine der A. There, take in the opaque glass **urinoir,** decorated with bejeweled blue dancers and designed by Rem Koolhaas so men can go about their business in style. With that out of your system, backtrack along the same canal past Brugstraat and take it easy at **Noorderplantsoen,** a rolling, fountained park in the northwestern corner of the city (follow the canal north of Brugstraat and turn left across the last canal before it bends away to the right). The park hosts the annual **Noorderzon Festival** (Northern Sun) for theater in late August.

North of Brugstraat, follow Turftorenstraat, turn left on De Laan, and head right on Uurwerkersgang. Down the road sits the Harmonie Complex, which houses academic buildings. They tip you off that you're approaching **Academieplein,** the complex that houses **Rijksuniversiteit Groningen,** the 35,000-student university that fuels the city's boisterous nightlife. As you walk up the street, on your left is **Academiegebouw,** the administrative center, and on your right lies the university's main library. After Academieplein, turn left onto Oude Boteringestraat for some unique dwellings: the house with 13 temples (#23), the former District Court (#36-38), and the one-time residence of the Queen's Commissioner (#44) all lie along the street. Follow the canal to the right until just after Kattenhage, where you can escape the city's post-war urbanity in the **Prinsenhoftuin (Princes' Court Gardens),** originally designed in 1625 with a rose garden and covered paths. When in bloom, the fragrant roses make it impossible not to linger, especially when the **Theeschenkerij Tea Hut** inside the garden tempts you to order a cup of tea (€0.80) and lounge in the sun or under one of the canopied underpasses. *(Tea hut open M-F 10am-6pm, Sa-Su noon-6pm.)* On your way out, ponder the advice of the Latin inscription on the sundial above the entrance: *Tempus praeteritum nihil. Futurum incertum. Praesens instabile. Cave ne perdas hoc tuum* ("The past is nothing, the future uncertain, the present unstable; ensure that you do not lose this time, which is yours alone").

◪ COFFEE SHOPS

Groningen's streets possess a total of 14 coffee shops, almost all of which offer better prices than those in Amsterdam.

Dee's Cafe, Papengang 3 (www.cafedees.nl). Tucked unassumingly in a small alley between the city's party streets. Neon-blue light scheme, rock music, and foosball and pool tables (both €0.50) make it a perfect spot for night owls. The owner of the shop has been in the coffee-shop business for over 25 years and ensures that her weed and hash are grown and cut without chemicals or other additives. Especially popular with the younger crowd. Weed sold in €5 and €12 denominations. Internet access €1 per 30min. Space cakes €2.70. Some outdoor seating. Open M-W 11am-midnight, Th 11am-1am, F-Sa noon-3am.

The Glory, Steentilstraat 3 (☎312 5742). A mishmash of fake flowers, hanging lanterns, international flags, and smoking aliens adorn The Glory's walls and ceilings, giving the shop an out-of-this-world feel. Clients chill in movie-theater-style seats around small tables or around the projection screen at the rear of the shop while reggae blasts nonstop. Space cakes or joints €2.50. Bud and hash in €5 and €15 increments. Open M-W noon-1am, Th-F noon-2am, Sa 11am-3am.

De Vliegende Hollander, Gedempte Zuiderdiep 63 (☎314 4807; www.de-vliegende-hollander.nl). You knew it was only a matter of time before you stumbled upon a place named "The Flying Dutchman." Select your goodies, which come in €5 and €15 packets, from a touch computer screen at this linoleum-styled, impersonal coffee shop. The shop's specialty hash, Te Tafelberg (available Dec.-Jan.; €10 per g), received 2nd place at the 2004 Cannabis Cup. 6-pack of joints €12.50. Open daily 10am-10pm.

◪ NIGHTLIFE

Groningen parties beyond its size; there are 160 pubs and discotheques crammed into this medium-size city. The best bets for a night on the town lie just off the southeast corner of Grote Markt on **Poelestraat** and **Peperstraat.** The bars and restaurants on these two streets are literally packed shoulder-to-shoulder and offer good prices and a buzzing atmosphere to the mainly student crowd. The students boast that the bars close only when the people stop drinking—usually around 4am on weekends. For outdoor nightlife, try the bars overlooking the Grote Markt.

Vera, Oosterstraat 44 (☎313 4681; www.vera-groningen.nl). Billing itself as the "club for the international pop underground," this center for live music and cinema of all stripes is a not-to-be-missed local party nearly every night. Pick up a copy of *Verakrant,* the newsletter in the box outside, for a schedule of events. Some gigs start at 1am. Events from €4-11. Open daily 10pm-3am, sometimes later.

Jazzcafe de Spieghel, Peperstraat 11 (☎312 6300). Intimate, candlelit cafe with 2 bars and 1 large stage for live jazz, funk, or blues nightly at 11pm or later. M 10:30pm open jazz session is a tradition, and big names in jazz (well, big for the Netherlands) have been known to stop by and play impromptu sets. Pick up a free copy of *UitLoper* from the VVV to find out what's on. Wine €2.20 per glass. Open daily 8pm-4am.

Cafe de Zolder, Papengang 3A (☎318 8607). No sign marks the entrance to this rowdy 2-story bar, which is through an arched doorway and up a flight of graffiti-covered stairs to the right as you face Dee's Cafe. Head over to Cafe de Zolder for a chat with wild company of all ages. Beer €2.10. Shots €2-2.80. Tu 12:30am reggae jam session. Live music most weekends. Open M-W 5pm-3am, Th-Sa 5pm-4am, Su 5pm-2am.

Cafe de Vlaamsche Reus, Poelestraat 15 (☎314 8313). A pleasant nightspot that's never too packed or too empty. A young crowd keeps things lively, with students on both sides of the long bar. Beer €2. Open daily from 9:30pm until people start leaving; Th-Sa as late as 5 or 6am.

Sally O'Brian's, Oosterstraat 33 (☎311 8039). This dark, smoky, and spacious pub is proud to be one of the only Irish pubs in Groningen. Attracts an international, mainly Anglophone crowd and is especially popular with Irish and English students, as well as with area expats. Beer €2. Irish pints €4. Th 10pm live acoustic music. Open M-W 6pm-2am, Th 2pm-3am, F 2pm-4am, Sa 1pm-4am, Su 2pm-1am.

HOOGHALEN
☎0593

Hooghalen is not a tourist town; in fact, with a population hovering around 1000, it's barely a town at all. However, this hamlet hides one of the Netherlands's most important sites, nestled appropriately deep in the Dutch forest. Originally built in 1939 as a refugee camp for fleeing Germans, **Kamp Westerbork,** Oosthalen 8, quickly transformed into the most dreaded locale in the country. Used as a detainment camp for Jews from 1942 until liberation, Kamp Westerbork held more than 100,000 Dutch Jews before sending them east to the concentration camps. The transport camp was the last stop on Dutch land for virtually all of the country's Jews, including the Frank family in 1944. The **Herinneringscentrum (Memorial Center)** runs a museum that documents life inside the camp through clothing, letters, documents, maps, photos, and movies. Displays at the end of the exhibit reveal the contents of some of the suitcases brought to Westerbork by Jewish families. Though most of the information is in Dutch, there are a few panels in English. About three kilometers from the Herinneringscentrum is the actual camp, accessible by Westerbork shuttle (every 20min. M-F 11am-5pm, Sa-Sa 1:10-5pm; round-trip €1.75). Not much remains here but open fields and the remnants of former barracks, but there are several memorials, including a set of railway tracks rising off the ground, splintered and twisted, at the back of the camp. The memorials were designed by Westerbork inmate and Theresienstadt survivor Ralph Prins. At the former roll-call site, 102,000 rocks sit in stony silence—one for each detainee who perished in the concentration camps. On the drive, look for five stone coffins on your right, representing the five concentration camps to which Jews were sent from here. On one side of the coffin is the number sent, and on the other is the number exterminated. The exhibits and displays are in Dutch, but a 700m walk to the far end of the camp, where a watch tower and barbed wire are still intact, will give you some idea of life inside Westerbork. After WWII, the site was used as a refugee camp for 12,500 Moluccans. A small population inhabiting the eastern tip of Indonesia, Moluccans joined the drive for Indonesian independence but found the Dutch government unsympathetic to their nationalist cause. They remained an independent community within the Netherlands by living in Westerbork with the hope that they would return home en masse. The Moluccans ultimately integrated into the Dutch population. (☎59 26 00; www.kampwesterbork.nl. Open Feb.-June and Sept.-Dec. M-F 10am-5pm, Sa-Su 1-5pm; July-Aug. M-F 10am-5pm, Sa-Su 11am-5pm. Tours July-Aug. daily noon, 2pm. €4.50, ages 8-18 €2.)

To pay your respects, take a train from Groningen to Beilin (25min.; 2 per hr.; €7, round-trip €13), then a €5 taxi straight to Westerbork's Herinnerings-centrum. The taxi can be summoned from a kiosk at the train station and usually arrives within 10min. Call ahead for the ride back.

MAASTRICHT   ☎043

Maastricht's (pop. 120,000) name, derived from the Latin *Mosae Trajectum* ("crossing of the Maas"), marks it as an important crossroads of the Low Countries. The city was originally settled by the Romans en route to Cologne as a convenient spot to ford the River Maas. In a little pocket of land surrounded by Belgium and Germany, Maastricht's strategic location has made it a hotbed of military conquest. After its defensive walls went up in 1229, the town was besieged 22 times and captured by the Spanish in 1579 and by the French in 1673. In 1814, it joined the Kingdom of the Netherlands and then resisted siege by the Belgians. After being occupied by the Germans during WWII, Maastricht was one of the first towns to be liberated. This past of international convergence gives Maastricht resonance as the site of the 1991 treaty that established the European Union.

As one of the oldest and richest cities in the Netherlands, Maastricht has a pleasingly sedate, Old World feel; neither the rise of many modern buildings on the east side of the city nor an active student population manage to take away the city's medieval charm. Old brick fortifications, cobblestone streets, well-preserved churches, and an astounding, vast subterranean defense system (the Caves of Mt. St. Pieter) make Maastricht an appealing place to live and to visit.

▐ TRANSPORTATION   € 40

Trains to Maastricht (2½hr.; every 30min.; €26.50, round-trip €38.10) leave from Centraal Station in Amsterdam. If you plan on making long trips across town, you can rent a bike at **Aon de Stasie**, on the Stationsplein, to your left just outside the train station. (☎321 1100. €7.50 per day; €50 or 100 deposit and ID required.) For longer trips, Maastricht has a **bus** system; information is available at a booth outside the train station, or you can buy a map at the VVV. **Taxi** ranks are located at Vrijthof, Markt, and the train station; sometimes it is cheaper to pick one up at these stops rather than hailing it on the street.

▮▮ ORIENTATION AND PRACTICAL INFORMATION

Maastricht is bisected by the River Maas, and the old town (with most of the sights) lies on the western side of the water, across the river from the train station. The heart of the town is **Vrijthof**, a large square dominated by two churches, although **Markt** and **Onze Lieve Vrouweplein** are also important public squares. The best way to see Maastricht is to discover its medieval alleyways on foot, and it's

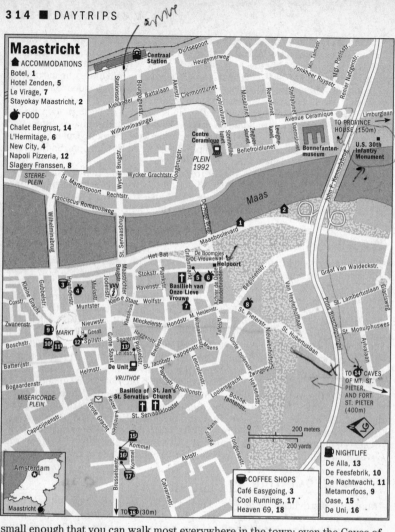

Maastricht

🏠 ACCOMMODATIONS
Botel, **1**
Hotel Zenden, **5**
Le Virage, **7**
Stayokay Maastricht, **2**

🍴 FOOD
Chalet Bergrust, **14**
L'Hermitage, **6**
New City, **4**
Napoli Pizzeria, **12**
Slagery Franssen, **8**

☕ COFFEE SHOPS
Café Easygoing, **3**
Cool Runnings, **17**
Heaven 69, **18**

🍷 NIGHTLIFE
De Alla, **13**
De Feesfebrik, **10**
De Nachtwacht, **9**
Metamorfoos, **9**
Oase, **15**
De Uni, **16**

small enough that you can walk most everywhere in the town; even the Caves of Mt. St. Pieter, which lie on the outskirts, are just a 30min. walk.

To get to the **VV**, Kleine Staat 1, go straight on Stationsstraat, cross the bridge, and walk for another block. When you hit a wall, take a right; the tourist office is one block down on your right. Be sure to pick up a map (€1.25) of the city center or the hefty €2.20 tourist booklet. (☎325 2121; www.vvvmaastricht.nl. Open May-Oct. M-Sa 9am-6pm, Su 11am-3pm; Nov.-Apr. M-Th 9am-6pm, Sa 9am-5pm.) **Centre Ceramique**, Ave. Ceramique 50, in Plein 1992 just off De Hoge Brug, contains an exhibition space and public library that offers free **Internet** access and Wi-Fi on its second floor. (☎350 5600; www.centreceramique.nl. Open Tu and Th 10:30am-8:30pm, W and F 10:30am-5pm, Su 1-5pm.) **De Unit,** Leliestraat 19, also offers Internet access in the old town. Walk off Vrijthof onto Paleisstraat and take a left onto Leliestraat, a narrow alley. (€3 per hr. Open M-F noon-7pm, Sa

FALSTAFF - Bar - lo beers etc
(large variety of bottled beers)

noon-6pm.) For information on free and special events, check the free monthly magazines *Uit in Maastricht* or *Week In, Week Uit* (both in Dutch). Both are available at the VVV or in hotels and pubs.

 # 6 Sint Amorspelein

♦ ACCOMMODATIONS

For a small fee (€3.50 per room in person, €6.50 over the phone), the VVV can book rooms in private B&Bs (doubles from €32); many are near the center but rent only one or two rooms total. In general, budget accommodations in Maastricht can be difficult to find.

Stayokay Maastricht, Maasboulevard 101 (☎750 1790; www.stayokay.com/maastricht). From the train station, walk straight down Stationsstraat and cross the bridge. Walk down several blocks with the river to your left. This brand-new hostel is your best bet for budget digs in Maastricht. Right on the River Maas, it boasts a waterside terrace, clean rooms, a small bar, and a restaurant. All rooms with bath. Breakfast and linens included. Towels €1.25. Internet access €5 per hr. Bike rental €11.50 per day. 6-person dorms €21-30; 4-person dorms €23-33; 2-person dorms €28-40. Prices change with the season; check website for exact pricing. €2.50 HI discount. AmEx/MC/V. ❶

Botel, Maasboulevard 95 (☎321 9023), just before the Stayokay on Maasboulevard. Enjoy a night and morning over the River Maas. This hotel on a moored boat may not offer the most polished service, but these tiny cabins adjoining a cozy deck room lounge are solid budget digs in this town. Try to get one of the rooms above deck—they're the same price but much cheerier. Breakfast €4. Reception 24hr., but show up early since night hours are especially unreliable after the gate closes at midnight. Singles €27, with bath €31; doubles €42/46; quads €92; 6-person room €138. Cash only. ❶

Le Virage, Cortenstraat 2-2B (☎321 6608; www.levirage.nl), facing the *basiliek* on the right-hand corner of Onze Lieve Vrouweplein. A little pricey, but the upscale atmosphere matches the elevated costs. 4 spacious, spotless suites for 2 with bedroom, living room, fridge, and bathroom. The owners live minutes away, so reception hours are spotty: W-Th and Su 5-10:30pm, F-Sa noon-10:30pm, or by request. Doubles M-Th and Su €79, F-Sa €99. AmEx/MC/V. ❹

Hotel Zenden, Sint Bernardusstraat 5 (☎321 2211; www.zenden.nl). This small hotel with a brick interior doubles as a fitness center for locals, with classes, equipment, and even a pool (membership is separate). A terrific value for those able to book 1 of the 5 double rooms, many of which have leather couches. All rooms with bath. Breakfast included. M-Th and Su €79 for 1, €89 for 2; F-Sa €109 for 2. Cash only. ❹

♦ FOOD

Maastricht is known for its *eetcafes*, pubs that serve traditional food but still don't forget the beer. The best areas to find these establishments are around the **Onze Lieve Vrouweplein, Sint Amorsplein,** and **Vrijthof,** but prices in Maastricht are fairly high across the board. For an economical but hardly glamorous solution, stop by the various snack and sandwich stands that surround Vrijthof or **Markt.** Streets north and south of Markt also contain a number of fast-food and kebab restaurants. Delifrance outlets and other snack or Shawarma shops also offer cheap options. Several student-oriented restaurants with slightly lower prices line Brusselsestraat toward the western edge of the city. Maastricht is also known for its collection of more luxurious (and expensive) French-influenced restaurants.

New City, Hoenderstraat 11 (☎326 1031). The best deal in town. Snarf a tasty Indonesian and Chinese buffet with hot, fresh dishes prepared in the kitchen right next to the seating area. All-you-can-eat buffet €7. Open daily noon-10pm. Cash only. ❶

L'Hermitage, Sint Bernadusstraat 20 (☎325 1777; www.texmexfood.nl), off the south-east corner of Onze Lieve Vrouweplein. Friendly Tex-Mex cafe that's a hit with students and locals. Tacos €11. Enchiladas €14.50. Shrimp €16. Quesadillas €7.50. In keeping with the name, French dishes round out the cuisine. Open daily 5pm-midnight. ❸

Napoli Pizzeria, Markt 73 (☎325 5594). This small Italian restaurant, right in the heart of Markt, is a student favorite. The extensive menu includes salads (€5-9), soup (€5), pasta (€8.70-12.50) and their very popular personal pizzas (€6-13). Come early; there can be a wait for a table. Open daily 11am-11pm. Cash only. ❷

Chalet Bergrust, Luikerweg 71 (☎325 5421), next to the VVV ticket booth for the Caves of Mt. St. Pieter to the south of the city (p. 316). A good post-spelunking stopover on perhaps the only hilltop in the Netherlands. Beautiful view over the town. Lunch options (sandwiches, pancakes, omelettes) about €4. Larger entrees around €12. Open Apr.-Oct. daily 11am-10pm (kitchen closes at 8pm); Nov.-Mar. M, W, F-Su 11am-8pm. ❷

Slagery Franssen, Sint Pieterstraat 42 (☎321 2900). This small takeout deli lays out an appetizing display case full of economical options. Choose from an array of hot and cold sandwiches (€1.75-4), chicken stew (€3), traditional Dutch meat-filled rolls (€3), and large portions of homemade soups (€2.75-3.25). Family-owned for 4 generations; all food is prepared on the premises, including bread baked daily. No tables. Open Tu-F 8am-6pm, Sa 8am-4pm. Cash only. ❶

◉ SIGHTS

Maastricht's vast network of underground caves and its beautiful churches are the main vestiges of its 1000-year history. If you're in the mood for more contemporary sights, visit the **Province House** to see where the European Union was formed.

◪ **CAVES OF MT. ST. PIETER.** The manmade caves of Mt. St. Pieter began life as a Roman limestone quarry; over centuries, the Dutch expanded it into the **world's second largest underground complex** with more than 20,000 passages totaling 200km. Capable of sheltering up to 40,000 people at a time, this enormous underground labyrinth was used repeatedly as a defensive hideaway during the many sieges of Maastricht, earning the town the nickname "the Iron City." The French commandeered the caves for their own use in the 18th century, as did the Nazis in the 20th. During WWII, the Germans hid several important Dutch paintings, including Rembrandt's *Night Watch*, in Mt. St. Pieter's tunnels. Similar passages were used to shelter Dutch civilians from Nazi invasion; wells, a chapel, and a bakery have all been constructed within for those in hiding.

Nearly 2000 years of history are written on the walls. Graffiti, carvings, and charcoal drawings from as early as Roman times cover the miles and miles of limestone. Visitors can even walk around the bedrooms, feeding troughs, and ovens dug out of the porous stone by local farmers during extended sieges. While the Zonneberg tour focuses more on WWII history, the Grotten Noord concentrates on the local farmers' defense efforts. The caves average a temperature of 9°C—wear a coat or sweater. *(Go to the VVV in the city center for exact information; tour times and hours vary from season to season. There are 2 entrances to the vast system of caves; the most convenient starting point is Grotten Noord, Luikerweg 71, accessible by foot or by bus #4 from Markt or the train station. Plan to arrive 15min. before tour departs to buy your ticket from the VVV window by the restaurant. ☎325 2121; www.pietersberg.nl. €4.25, under 12 €3.25; combination with entrance to Fort St. Pieter €5.50/3.50. 1hr. English tours, Apr.-June and Sept.-Oct. Sa-Su 2pm, depending on demand. The Zonneberg Caves, Slavante 1, are more difficult to reach; ask at the VVV for walking directions or take the boat from the dock at the corner of Maasboulevard and Graanmarkt. English tours June-Aug. daily 1:55pm—plan to arrive at the docks at 1pm. Prices same as Grotten Noord; combination boat trip and visit €10.45, children €7.15. V.)*

PROVINCE HOUSE. The official seat of government for the Dutch province of Limburg, this sleek, modern building was constructed in 1986; Limburg's Provincial Council meets here monthly. The building has an impressive collection of modern artwork mostly by local artists, including sculptures, tapestries, and paintings. Most famously, in December 1991, European leaders reached an agreement regarding a common European political and monetary union in the Banqueting Hall. On February 7, 1992, the leaders of 12 European nations met to sign the **Maastricht Treaty** at the small table in the center of the Council Chamber. The historic treaty established the modern European Union, leading to a common European currency, the euro, and countless internal squabbles. There is a small plaque on the table commemorating the mammoth event. *(Limburglaan 10. Cross the River Maas and walk past the Bonnefantenmuseum under the John F. Kennedybrug along the Maaspuntweg. The Province House will be directly ahead on your right on a small island in the river just off the shoreline. It can be reached by crossing the bridge at the far end of the island.* ☎ *389 9999; www.limburg.nl. Open M-F 8am-5pm. If you come early enough, you may be able to get a private guided tour. Otherwise, ask for a self-guided tour booklet at the security desk.)*

BASILICA OF ST. SERVATIUS. This beautiful church, a central Maastricht landmark, fuses architectural and ecclesiastical history. It is the only church in the Netherlands to be built over the grave of a saint, St. Servatius (died AD 384), the first bishop of the Netherlands. The original church was built over his tomb (c. AD 570); the remains have since been excavated. Of the building that stands today, the inner Romanesque part was built in the 11th century, while the outer Gothic structure was constructed in the 14th and 15th centuries. In a chamber opposite the entrance, there is a tiled labyrinth on the floor; see if you can get from "one of the four corners of the earth" (Rome, Constantinople, Cologne, or Aachen) to the "celestial city" of Jerusalem. (Hint: you must go by St. Servatius.) The church surrounds a lovely lavender-lined inner courtyard featuring a huge (7000kg) bell from 1515, affectionately known as the **Grameer** (grandmother). On your way into the church, you will pass its treasury, which contains a bare-bones golden reliquary—literally. The holy innards within include part of St. Servatius's skeletal remains (and other possessions of his) as well as a silver arm containing a bone of the apostle Thomas. Restoration work in the 1980s revealed important archaeological discoveries like burial sites and the walls of earlier churches, parts of which can be seen in the treasury

LOCAL LEGEND

THE FOURTH MUSKETEER

On a stroll through the Aldenhofpark back to central Maastricht from the Caves of Mt. St. Peter, you might be surprised to see a statue of one of the heroes of Alexandre Dumas's 19th-century novel *The Three Musketeers*, d'Artagnan. The inscription underneath the statue reads *"un pour tous, tous pour un"*—"one for all, all for one"—and d'Artagnan stands ready to strike with his sword. Don't be too frightened—d'Artagnan was fictional, after all, but he was inspired by a real man who possessed a very intimate link to Maastricht.

Dumas's d'Artagnan, the unofficial fourth musketeer, was based on the real Count d'Artagnan, a captain-lieutenant of Louis XIV's Musketeers, an important company of military officers. Dumas borrowed liberally from the count's life in writing his d'Artagnan trilogy: *The Three Musketeers, Twenty Years After,* and *The Vicomte of Bragelonne.*

The real d'Artagnan, like the fictional version, died during the French siege of Maastricht in 1673, which the statue commemorates. A musket bullet to the throat did d'Artagnan in, but the French ultimately succeeded, and Maastricht surrendered after 13 days. However, the victory was short-lived. Within five years, the French were forced to relinquish Maastricht, and the city once again became a part of the Dutch domain.

galleries. *(The huge church on Vrijthof. The entrance is to the right on Keizer Karelplein. www.sintservaas.nl. Open Jan.-June and Sept.-Dec. 10am-5pm; July-Aug. 10am-6pm. €3.50, over 65 €2.10, ages 6-12 €1, under 6 free.)*

BONNEFANTENMUSEUM. Lying across the River Maas from the city center, next to the John F. Kennedybrug, this 1995 building by Aldo Rossi looks like a cross between a soft-boiled egg and a rocket ship. With a sizable selection of Southern Dutch and Flemish art on long-term loan from the Rijksmuseum in Amsterdam, the Bonnefanten's collection offers a good range of medieval votive woodcarvings, 17th-century Baroque paintings, and 20th-century Minimalist, Conceptual, and post-Conceptual art. Its holdings of mainstream American and European contemporary art are impressive: a good Richard Serra installation fills one of the courtyards; Sol LeWitt, Robert Ryman, Joseph Beuys, and Marcel Broodthaers are also well represented. The museum makes a concerted effort to collect pieces by up-and-coming Dutch artists, giving it a slightly regional feel as well. Nevertheless, there is a good mix between older and more modern art forms, and the museum is worth a visit for any art lover visiting Maastricht. *(Ave. Ceramique 250. Walk down the river on the side of the train station for 10min.; it's the huge building that looks like a missile silo. ☎329 0190; www.bonnefanten.nl. Open Tu-Su 11am-5pm. €7.50, students and ages 13-18 €3.50, under 13 free. AmEx/MC/V.)*

BASILIEK VAN ONZE LIEVE VROUWE (BASILICA OF OUR DEAR LADY). The most striking thing about this church is the number of visitors who regularly come to offer their prayers. You'll feel like you've traveled to the Middle Ages in this ancient basilica honoring the Virgin Mary, with a dark, dank feel punctuated by beautiful stained glass. Parts of this cruciform church date to the 11th century. Mary is here affectionately termed **Star of the Sea** because she is said to have saved the lives of sailors at sea during a storm around 1700. See the hundreds of votive candles now placed around her statue in devotion to her miracle-working power. There is a small information center in the church's old crypt. The square outside the church is perhaps the most beautiful in Maastricht. *(Follow signs to Onze Lieve Vrouweplein. ☎325 1851. Open Easter-Oct. M-Sa 11am-5pm, Su 1-5pm. Mass in English Su 5pm in crypt. Church free. Treasury €3, over 65 €2, children €1.)*

OTHER SIGHTS. St. Jan's Church, a Gothic structure to the left of the St. Servatius Basilica, has been a Flemish-speaking Protestant church since 1632. The church's red tower, at 236 ft., provides a magnificent view of the entire city. *(Open Mar.-Sept. M-Sa 11am-4pm. Church free. Tower €1.50, under 12 €0.50.)* On the outskirts of the old center lies the **Helpoort,** the only city gate from 1229 still standing. Stroll along the city's old cannons on the Onze Lieve Vrouwe rampart and climb a treacherous, ancient spiral staircase to learn about the history of the fortified city from the knowledgeable staff. *(Sint Bernardusstraat 24B. Open daily mid-Apr. to Oct. 1:30-4:30pm. Free.)* While walking along the Maas between the Bonnefantenmuseum and the Province House, take a look at the small monument to the **US 30th Infantry Division.** The monument marks the spot where "Old Hickory" (as the division is known) crossed the River Maas to liberate the city of Maastricht on September 14, 1944. More military sights are at the pentagonal **Fort St. Pieter,** across from the Grotten Noord, which provided protection for the city starting in 1702. *(Luikerweg 80. Check with VVV for exact tour availability. The timing and frequency of tours changes throughout the year. €4.25, children €3.25.)* Markt takes on an extra vowel when it hosts a **market** on Wednesday and Friday mornings from 8am-1pm and a Friday fish market on Boschstraat. On Thursdays, there is a market on Stationsstraat near the train depot; on Saturdays from 10am-4pm, it's a flea market. You can also take **boat trips** with the Rederij Stiphout starting at €6.20 for a basic tour on the River Maas. *(☎351 5300; www.stiphout.nl.)*

☕ COFFEE SHOPS

A steady stream of visitors from nearby Belgium, Germany, and France endow Maastricht with a relatively high number of coffee shops. Although there are several to choose from, Maastricht's joints usually lack the pomp and circumstance of Amsterdam's coffee shops, so expect a more laid-back, low-key atmosphere. If you're looking to buy mushrooms or plant seeds (no, not for gardening), several smart shops line **Oude Tweebergenpoort.**

☑ **Heaven 69,** Brusselsestraat 146 (☎325 3493; www.heaven69.nl), toward the east end of town. This coffee shop doubles as a serious restaurant. "The Breakfast" (€8) includes fruit, corn flakes, a croissant, orange juice, and coffee. Smaller continental breakfast €6. Lunch is mostly sandwiches (cheeseburger and french fries €5.70). Dinner boasts a selection of big pasta dishes (€5.70-9) along with more expensive fare such as lamb chops (€15). 3 types of marijuana and 4 types of hash (€7-10 per g). Pre-rolled joints €4-5. Open daily 9am-midnight. Kitchen closes 10pm.

☑ **Cool Runnings,** Brusselsestraat 35. A fun place with an extensive food menu, Cool Runnings has something for everyone. The upstairs is cheerier, with posters of Bob Marley, a Jamaican color scheme, and a foosball table, while the basement is darker, with loud music and graffiti covering literally every surface. Jasmina pre-rolled joints €4. Happy Brother weed, the house specialty, is some of the strongest pot in Maastricht—puff with caution (€13 per g). Pizza and hot dogs €2. Milk shakes €2.75. Open M-Th 10am-midnight, F-Sa 10am-2am, Su 2pm-midnight. Cash only.

Cafe Easygoing, Hoenderstraat 8 (☎321 1845). Though smaller than some of the other coffee shops in Maastricht, Cafe Easygoing, with a joint-smoking turtle as its mascot, prides itself on the quality of its product. Their most potent, Jack Haze, sells for €2 per g. Sandwiches, soup, and coffee are available (€1.30-2.50). Open daily 10am-11pm.

🎵 NIGHTLIFE

Maastricht is a college town, and, in the great spirit of college towns the world over, there is always something to do at night here. For the best value, try the student-run bars. Run by groups of fraternity brothers and filled with hordes of local students, the bars offer visitors a chance to see Maastricht up close and personal. The only downside to the volunteer staff is that the bars usually close in July and August when students are home for the summer. At many of the student-run bars, a €10 card buys you 10 beers. In addition, there are a number of bars on Platielstraat, right off Vrijthof, that attract locals and students alike.

☑ **De Uni,** Brusselsestraat 31 (www.deuni.nl). Opened in 1997 by 2 fraternities at the University of Maastricht, this bar has evolved into an unbeatable spot for imbibing with locals. Beer €1. Shots €1-1.50. Mixed drinks €2. €5 or €10 cards buy 5 or 10 beers. Open W-Th 9:30pm-2am, F-Sa 9:30pm-3am. Closed mid-July to mid-Aug. Cash only.

☑ **Oase,** Brusselsestraat 25. Next door to De Uni, this bar is also run by a fraternity from the University of Maastricht. With a raucous crowd, Oase pulses with beer-fueled energy. Beer €1. Same €5 and €10 card deal. Shots €1. Open July-Aug. W, F, Su 9pm-2am; otherwise Tu-Th and Su 9pm-2am, F 9pm-3am. Cash only.

De Feesfebrik, Markt 25 (☎321 5612; www.feesfebrik.nl). With a name that translates to "party factory," this cafe-bar is one Maastricht's most popular nightspots. The crowd, mostly students, rolls in after midnight and keeps the party going until the sun comes up. "Piek fest" (2-3am) offers 2 beers for €1. Live DJs spin an eclectic mix of music nightly. Open M-Sa 10am-6am. Cash only.

De Nachtwacht, Markt 22 (☎321 9837). 2 doors down from Feesfebrik, this bar and cafe attracts a large crowd of its own. With a more traditional feel and decor, it's popular with older locals and students alike. Open M-Tu 9am-midnight, W and F-Sa 9am-5am, Th 9am-2am. Cash only.

Metamorfoos, Kleine Gracht 40-42 (☎321 2714; www.metamorfoos.nl). During the school year, students stay out late to drink at this cafe-brasserie. It's particularly popular with Maastricht's large exchange-student population and hosts a number of student events throughout the year. Main dishes €9-12.50, vegetarian €8.50. Drinks here are pricier than at the student-run bars. Beer €1.80, shots €2-2.50. Open Tu and Th-Sa 4pm-5am, W and Su 4-11pm. Cash only.

De Alla, Leliestraat 9 (☎325 4724; www.alla.nl). This late-night club is a classic student hangout. After 2am, the dance floor fills with 20-somethings rolling in from the nearby bars. DJ plays mostly house and top 40. Open M-F and Su midnight-6am, Sa 11am-6am. Cash only.

WADDEN ISLANDS (WADDENEILANDEN)

Tucked away off the northwestern coast of the Netherlands and inauspiciously named (*wadden* means "mud flat"), the Wadden Islands are an unassuming vacation destination. The Dutch wouldn't have it any other way; they're happy to keep these idyllic islands to themselves. Even when Netherlanders flock here during the summer, the islands feel sleepy and isolated. Deserted bike paths wind through stretches of grazing land and lead to some of Europe's most pristine nature reserves. The islands offer excellent beaches where the sun-warmed shallows of the Waddenzee make for temperate swimming. Though transit can tax the wallet of the budget traveler, abundant campsites, good hostels, and legion picnic sites render a trip to these resplendent islands affordable.

The islands arc around the northwest of the Netherlands. **Texel,** closest to Amsterdam, is the largest and most populated. **Vlieland** is a sleepy stretch of endless beaches. **Terschelling,** the middle of the five, bustles with nightlife and nature preserves. The fourth and fifth islands, remote **Ameland** and remoter **Schiermonnikoog,** fill out the archipelago. Most people travel from the mainland town of Den Helder to Texel and from Harlingen to the others; island hopping is possible but sometimes difficult with the ferry schedules, so plan in advance.

WHEEL AND DEAL. Consider spending a few extra euro to rent a bike with more than one gear, especially if you're visiting multiple islands, to help take you up and down the paths through the dunes with ease. If you're staying more than a few days, negotiate a better rate than the daily price.

TEXEL   ☎0222

Because of its proximity to Amsterdam and the painless 20min. ferry ride, Texel is the most touristed of the Wadden Islands. While its four siblings are certainly quieter by degrees, Texel is no less charming for its relative popularity. Though other Wadden Islanders may scoff at Texel's traffic lights and road systems, it is truly accessible in a single day and offers all the amenities of the mainland in a remote-feeling setting. The diversity of landscape here is dazzling, and its dunes, woods, heaths, salt marshes, and mud flats are all entirely bikeable. There are two major villages among the various clusters of thatched-roof houses lining the

Wadden Islands

0   10 kilometers

0   10 miles

Schiermonnikoog

Ameland   Nes   Schiermonnikoog

Terschelling

Terschelling-West

Lauwersoog

Holwerd   N361

N356   N361

Oost-Vlieland

Waddenzee

N361   N356   N355

Vlieland

A31

Leeuwarden

Texel   De Cocksdorp

Harlingen

E22 A7

De Koog

N31   N32

Den Burg

Afsluitdijk

Sneek

E22 A7

Amsterdam

Den Helder

N250   E22 A7   IJsselmeer

Heerenveen

N32

landscape of Texel: while the quiet Den Burg is located in the center of the island, the more party-loving De Koog lines Texel's northern shore.

TRANSPORTATION AND PRACTICAL INFORMATION. To reach Texel, take the **train** from Amsterdam to Den Helder (1½hr., €11) and then grab **bus #33** right next to the train station (2 strips or €1); it will drop you off at the docks, from which a **Teso ferry** will take you to Het Horntje, the southernmost town on Texel (20min.; every hr. 6:30am-9:30pm; round-trip €3, under 12 €1.50, additional €2.50 for bikes). You can find Teso's main office, Pontweg 1, in the Texel town of Den Hoorn. (☎36 96 00; www.teso.nl.) **Buses** depart from the ferry dock to various locales throughout the island; purchase a **Texel Ticket,** which allows unlimited one-day travel on the island-wide bus system (runs mid-June to mid-Sept., €4.50). Be warned: the buses arrive at a given stop only about once an hour, even in high season, and buses to more remote locations (like De Cocksdorp) stop running at 6pm. Pick up a schedule on any bus or at the tourist office. The best way to travel, however, is to rent a **bike** from **Rijwielverhuur Veerhaven,** Pontweg 2, in Het Horntje, opposite the ferry dock. (☎31 95 88. From €5 per day. Open Apr.-Sept. daily 8:30am-6pm; Oct.-Dec. and Mar. M-F 9am-5pm, Sa-Su 9:30am-5pm; Jan.-Feb. M-F 9am-5pm, Sa 9:30am-5pm.)

The island of Texel is not merely one town. From Het Horntje, Pontweg, the main road, winds north first to Den Burg and then to beachside De Koog. De Cocksdorp is a remote village on the northern tip of the island, and Oudeschild is a vintage hamlet on the east coast. Den Hoorn, in the southern interior, and Oosterend, north of Oudeschild, are two other town names you might hear. The **VVV,** Emmalaan 66, is located just outside Den Burg about 300m south of the main bus stop; it's a short walk to the left down Emmalaan from the Stayokay hostel. (☎31 47 41; www.texel.net. Open M-F 9am-5:30pm, Sa 9am-5pm.) **Internet** is available at **Internet Cafe Texel,** Badweg 3, in De Koog, just off Dorpsstraat near Le Berry, for €1.50 per 30min. (☎31 75 11. Open daily 10am-10pm.)

ACCOMMODATIONS AND FOOD. The massive **Stayokay Texel ❶,** Haffelderweg 29, one of the newest Stayokays in the Netherlands, is the island's cheapest and most reliable accommodations option. Take bus #28 from Het

Horntje and disembark at the nearby Elmert bus stop. In addition to immaculately kept dorms and private rooms, the hostel boasts a small playground, a football pitch, a large restaurant and bar, and a lounge area filled with giant beanbags. Guests also have the option to rent a bike (€5 per day), but the hostel is a convenient 10min. walk from the center of Den Burg. (☎31 54 41. Breakfast and linens included. Wholesome buffet dinner €10; arrange in advance at reception. Internet access €1 per 30min. Reception 8am-8pm. Bar open 5pm-midnight. 4- to 6-bed dorms €30; 2-bed dorms from €35.) Another possibility is to have the tourist office direct you to a B&B, pension, or bungalow, all of which dot the island; the VVV has an extensive directory of such options and their contact info, but you must make your own reservation. There are over 30 homes willing to let out rooms to visitors on Texel, often for prices (€20-60) comparable to the Stayokay's. **Campgrounds** are an inexpensive and adventurous way to commune with the island's nature. Ask the tourist office about reservations.

The **Albert Heijn** supermarket, Waalderstraat 48, in Den Burg, is the best place for self-caterers to grab food and sundries. (Open M-Th 8am-8pm, F 8am-9pm, Sa 8am-6pm, Su 9am-noon.) In De Koog, you can also head to **Super de Boer** supermarket on Nikadel, just through the pedestrian walkway from Dorpsplein. (Open M-Th and Sa 8am-6pm, F 8am-8pm.) To sit down in Den Burg, walk anywhere in the center to find a bite; fresh seafood is served in most restaurants. The pub **De 12 Balcken Tavern ❶**, Weverstraat 20, in Den Burg, has a cozy *bruin cafe* feel and serves heavenly marinated or grilled spare ribs with salad and a heaping bowl of french fries (€12.50-13.50; feeds 2 people). You can also sample a shot of *'t Juttertje*, the island's popular licorice-flavored schnapps that is fermented from herbs and wheat (€2.20). For lunch (10am-5pm), try a homemade hamburger (€5) or a salad (€4-5.25). Weekends are busy, so reserve ahead. (☎31 26 81. Open M-Sa 10am-3am.) **Pizzeria Venezia ❶**, Kogerstraat 7, in Den Burg, offers traditional pizzas (€5.50-10.75) and salads (€4.50-6.75) in a homey, candlelit setting. Six varieties of soup make great starters (€3-4), and lots of vegetarian options are available. (☎31 25 70. Open daily Apr.-Oct. noon-11pm; Nov.-May 4-11pm. MC.) In De Koog, venture down Dorpsstraat, the town's main drag, for all manner of beach bars, cafes, Shawarma huts, *pannenkoekenhuizen*, and ice cream stands. De Koog caters more to tourists and less to locals, and food can be pricey to match.

◨ SIGHTS. Texel's greatest treasures lie outdoors. Its **bike paths** curve along the shoreline, through its pristine nature reserves, and past some of the best beaches in the Netherlands. The isle's stretch of sand runs largely uninterrupted up the western coast and is divided into strands, called *paals*, which run in ascending numerical order from south to north. The most popular strands lie near De Koog; **paal 20** is especially well loved. Just west of town, you'll find numerous and varied beach clubs and lots of folks sunning and splashing. Uncrowded kilometers of beach can be found to the north and south of *paal* 20, including some local favorites. All beaches are open to the public, and the water becomes friendly to swimmers when it warms in July and August. At the northern and southern tips of the islands, nude beaches tempt the uninhibited; you can bare it all near *paal* 9 (0.5km south of Den Hoorn) or *paal* 28 (1km south of De Cocksdorp). All along the northwest shore is the **Nationaal Park Duinen van Texel** (Dunes of Texel National Park), with its magnificent wind-sculpted sand dunes. (www.npduinenvantexel.nl.)

No need to worry if the sun fails to shine, though, since Texel boasts five fine museums. Take bus #28 to the **Ecomare Museum and Aquarium**, Ruijslaan 92, two kilometers south of De Koog, just off the Ruijslaan bike path or down Californieweg from Pontweg. Its exhibits and small aquarium aim to spread the word about Texel's ecology. A seal refuge at the center houses around 30 seals per year, which are rehabilitated before being released back into the Waddenzee;

they are fed (to the delight of huge crowds) at 11am and 3pm. There are three trails in the dunes behind the museum, and an audio tour (€2) can be rented from the reception desk for information on the habitat. The staff can also arrange tours of the surrounding nature reserves with outside organizations. Each reserve focuses on specific ecological niches, such as native birds and tide pool life. For information on tours, call or check the board at the museum. The Visitors Center for Dunes of Texel National Park is in the same building as Ecomare, and there is a free exhibit near the reception desk. (☎31 77 41; www.ecomare.nl. Open daily 9am-5pm. €8, ages 4-13 €5, under 4 free.) The **Schipbreuk- en Juttersmuseum Flora,** Pontweg 141, on the main road between Den Burg and De Koog just south of the turn-off for Ecomare, is a wonderful showcase of almost 70 years of beachcombing. Jan Uitgeest, the owner and busy beachcomber, has filled four barns with huge chunks of sea glass, a crate full of notes and photographs from Britain and beached on Texel, some of the more than 70 TVs that washed ashore in 2005, and a few of the 250,000 shoes that ended up on Terschelling in 2006. There is a video (in Dutch) explaining the life of a beachcomber and yet another barn full of photographs and descriptions of shipwrecks around the island. (☎32 12 30. €4, under 16 €2.50. Open M-Sa 10am-5pm. Cash only.) On the other side of the island is the quaint burg of Oudeschild, where a windmill marks the site of the **Maritiem en Jutters Museum** (Maritime and Beachcombers Museum), Barentzstraat 21. Visitors can climb into the windmill or stroll across a constructed canal to peer into life-size replicas of smiths' and fishermen's houses from turn-of-the-century Oudeschild. Indoor displays include hundreds of letters found in bottles washed up on the Texel shores. Messages range from requests for pen pals to last-ditch SOS attempts, both of which seem likely to have been unsuccessful. (☎31 49 56; www.texelsmaritiem.nl. Open Sept.-June Tu-Sa 10am-5pm; July-Aug. M-Sa 10am-5pm. €5, under 14 €3.50.)

◼ NIGHTLIFE. After the sun sets on the beaches of Texel, the young and sunburned masses migrate to shore-side De Koog for its sprightly nightlife. **Le Berry,** Dorpsstraat 3, has the air of a pub and caters to a slightly older crowd. There is dancing most nights, though, especially on weekends in the summer. Big-screen TVs broadcast sports during the day. (☎31 71 14; www.leberry.nl. DJ W-Su nights. Open noon-4am. Dancing from 11pm.) To the right of Le Berry is **De Blauwe Piste,** a nightclub offering two rooms: an apres-ski-esque dance floor (complete with snow

THE LOCAL STORY

GO TAKE A WADLOPEN

The Dutch have waged a wa against the advances of the sea for centuries. In the Wadder Islands, this age-old struggle is carried out on a personal leve through the traditional activity o *wadlopen.* It may not make oceans recede, but it provides a definite sense of conquest.

Wadlopen is an extreme spor of a different color, calling on childhood skills to wade through the whims of the great puddle known as the Wadden Sea. In the summer, registered guides take groups of tourists and exper enced *wadlopers* on treks through the mud surrounding the thre northernmost islands in the Wac den Island archipelago. Guides are armed with long poles, com passes, and walkie-talkies as the shepherd their flocks on poten tially deadly treks fraught with sinkholes and unpredictable weather. Mud mercilessly seeps into shoes and clothing up to one's waist, and crossing colc channels of strong currents is a somewhat harrowing reminder o the sea's force.

Tours usually range three to five hours, and the longest anc most arduous walk is along Sch ermonnikoog, which is abou 20km long. Walks of all intensi ties, however, provide dazzling encounters with the flora anc fauna of the Wadden Sea.

Book tours at local VVs or contac the Netherlands Board of Tourisn (p. 16) for more information.

machine) and a beach bar. The chalkboard outside advertises its regular DJ and live music offerings. (☎20 06 00. Dance floor open daily 10pm-4am. Beach bar open daily 5pm-4am.) **Cafe Sam-Sam,** Dorpsstraat 146, always knows how to have a good time. The more relaxed crowd of tourists and some locals enjoy eight beers on tap (4 in low season) while grooving to 70s, 80s, and 90s beats. (☎31 75 90. Beer €1.80. Mixed drinks €4.50. Kitchen open noon-9:30pm. Open daily 10am-3:30am.) Den Burg possesses something of a scene, too, though young people tend to stay in De Koog. In Den Burg, nightclubs and bars cluster just off the town square along Kantoorstraat. **De Pilaar,** Kantoorstraat 5, draws a hip crowd with occasional live music, running the gamut from country and blues to rock and soul. Pilaar's main draw is its wide selection of Belgian and locally brewed beer, all for €1.60. (☎31 40 75. Open daily 8pm-3am. Doors close at 2am.)

VLIELAND   ☎0562

Vlieland is a true escape. The farthest island from the mainland, it is second in the constellation and is characterized by a serene, untouched feel. In the center, 700 acres of forest shade mostly unpaved bike paths, while the long and skinny shape of the island is conducive to beaches along the northern coast; the distance across the width of the island is a mere kilometer. Oost-Vlieland, the closest thing to a village on the island, is a single tree-lined street that is, miraculously, chock-full of facilities for travelers while still retaining its isolated charm. Any traveler to Vlieland will soon realize, however, that its seclusion is not a coincidence. Getting to and from Vlieland can be a nightmare, and, as such, parts of our coverage for Vlieland (and its neighbor Terschelling) have not been updated since 2005.

█▰ TRANSPORTATION AND PRACTICAL INFORMATION. Traveling to Vlieland is often an unpredictable and maddening experience. From Amsterdam, you must first get to Harlingen via **train** (3hr., €28.30) or to Texel (above). Vlieland can be reached from the mainland via the ferry from Harlingen either by the standard **Oost-Vlieland ferry** (1¾hr.; 3 per day; €13, ages 4-11 €7) or by the **fast ferry.** (☎44 20 02; www.doeksen.nl.) You can also take the **Vriendschap** ferry from De Cocksdorp on Texel (25min.; May-June and Sept. Tu-Th and Su 2 per day, July-Aug. 3 per day; €13, ages 4-11 €7.50, under 4 €1.50), which takes you to the eastern side of the island. From the dock, a huge yellow truck will pick you up and take you over the beach to the main part of the island, where you can rent a bike or take a bus to Oost-Vlieland, Vlieland's main town. The ride is included in your ferry ticket. (☎0222 31 64 51; www.waddenveer.nl.) Unlike on Texel, no tourist cars are allowed on the island. A **bus** leaves from the ferry dock once per hour, hitting most major stops on Vlieland, and exorbitantly expensive **taxis** run throughout the island (☎45 12 22). Rent a bike at **Fietsverhuur Jan Van Vlieland,** Dorpsstraat 8, with storage across the ferry dock. (☎45 15 09. From €4 per day. Open daily 8:30am-7pm.) An alternative is **Zeelen Rijwiel Verhuur,** Dorpsstraat 2. (☎45 10 90. From €4 per day. Open July-Aug. daily 9am-9pm; Sept.-June M-F 9am-6pm, Su 9am-5pm.)

The **VV** tourist office, Havenweg 10, is located opposite the ferry dock at the edge of the village of Oost-Vlieland. (☎45 11 11; www.vlieland.net. Open M-F 9am-12:30pm and 1:30-5pm.) There is an **ATM** next to the **post office,** Dorpsstraat 120 (open M-F 9:30am-noon and 1:30-5:30pm, Sa 9:30-noon). **Internet** access (€1.60 per 30min.) is available at **Informatiecentrum de Noordwester** (below).

▮◩ ACCOMMODATIONS AND FOOD. Lodging in Vlieland usually falls into one of two categories: village or beach. Staying in one of the many hotels and pensions in Oost-Vlieland means ready access to modern conveniences, while the hotels on the dunes practically have private beaches as their backyard. **Hotel de Bosrand ❸**, Duinkersoord 113, is a beautiful and well-kept hotel that's one of the best deals on the dunes. Take bus #110 from the ferry to Bosrand, dropping your baggage on the free transport wagon first. (☎45 12 48; www.hoteldebosrand.nl. All rooms with bath. Breakfast and access to tanning studio and sauna included. Singles €71; doubles €94; fully equipped apartments for 2-5 people €430-590 per week. Cash only.) In the village, **Pension de Veerman ❶**, Dorpsstraat 173, is clean, comfortable, and homey. (☎45 13 78; www.pensiondeveerman.nl. Breakfast included. All rooms with shared bath. Singles €34; doubles €54; apartments €300-600 per week. Cash only.) Reserve ahead for **campgrounds** on Vlieland. **Stortemelk ❶**, Kampweg 1, lies about a kilometer north of the village and is Vlieland's largest campground. The site is right next to the beach and even has its own small supermarket. (☎45 12 25; www.stortemelk.nl. €5.60, under 10 €2.75; tent fee €4.05-7.30.) **Lange Paal ❶**, three kilometers west of Oost-Vlieland amid grasslands and sand dunes, is an equally viable, if smaller, option. (☎45 16 39; www.langepaal.com. €5, ages 3-12 €3.40.)

Fill up on provisions at the **SPAR** supermarket, Dorpsstraat 38. (☎45 13 47. Open M-F 8:30am-12:30pm and 1:30-6pm, Sa 8:30am-12:30pm and 1:30-5pm.) Nearly identical restaurants, each serving fish, mussels, and spare ribs at Amsterdam-style prices, line Dorpsstraat, Oost-Vlieland's lone street. Pick up sandwiches and milk shakes (€1.20-3) at **'t Smulpunt ❶**, Dorpsstraat 70. (☎45 33 62. Open daily noon-10pm.)

◪ ▮ **SIGHTS AND NIGHTLIFE.** The entire northern coast of the island offers unspoiled **beaches** that, at their most crowded, boast about 25 people. Book nature excursions of all kinds at **Informatiecentrum de Noordwester,** Dorpsstraat 81. (☎45 17 00; www.denoordwester.nl. 2hr. excursions usually €5. Call ahead for English-language tour. Open May and Oct. M-F 1:30-5pm, Sa 2-5pm, Su 1-4pm; June and Sept. M-F 10am-noon and 12:30-5pm, Sa 2-5pm, Su 1-4pm; July-Aug. M-F 10am-5pm, Sa 2-5pm, Su 3-6pm; Nov. Tu-Th 1:30-5pm, Sa 2-5pm, Su 1-4pm; Dec. Tu and Th 1:30-5pm, Sa 2-5pm, Su 1-4pm.) The best view of the island, if you're willing to trek up the stairs, is at the **Bezichtiging Vuurtoren** (lighthouse), just west of the village. (Open Jan.-Mar. and Nov.-Dec. daily 10:30am-noon; Apr. M-W 10:30am-noon and 2-4pm, Th-Su 10:30am-noon; May-June and Sept.-Oct. M-F 10:30am-noon and 2-4pm, Sa-Su 10:30am-noon. €1.75.)

Nobody comes to Vlieland for the parties, but if you desperately need to hit the town, a few *bruin cafes* can be found in Oost-Vlieland. **Oude Stoep,** Dorpsstraat 81, even promises dancing. (☎45 14 95. Open daily in high season 10pm-2am.)

TERSCHELLING ☎0562

With 80% of the island covered by protected nature reserves, Terschelling offers secluded beaches that stretch around the western tip and across the northern coast of this long, narrow island. Civilization on this island is traced back to at least the 13th century, but today human habitation takes a back seat to an extraordinary variety of plant and bird species. The second largest of the Wadden Islands, Terschelling can compete with Texel's range of activities, though parts of this large island retain Vlieland's seclusion. As with Vlieland, parts of our Terschelling coverage have not been updated since 2005.

▮ ▮ **TRANSPORTATION AND PRACTICAL INFORMATION.** Take a **train** from Amsterdam directly to Harlingen (3hr., €28.30); it drops you at the **ferry** landing, where regular-speed (2hr.; 4-6 per day; €13, ages 4-11 €6) and fast ferries depart for Terschelling. (☎44 20 02; www.doeksen.nl.) There is a **bus** at every ferry arrival, leaving once per hour and reaching most major spots; bring your strippenkaart. To explore the island's striking scenery, rent a bike from **Haantjes Fietsver-huur,** Willem Barentszkade 23. (☎44 29 29. From €4.50 per day, €20 per week.) The **VVV** tourist office, Willem Barentszkade 19A, is opposite the ferry landing. (☎44 30 00; www.vvvterschelling.nl. Open M-F 9:30am-5:30pm, Sa 10am-3pm.)

⌐◻ ACCOMMODATIONS AND FOOD. The **Terschelling Stayokay Hostel ❶,** Burgemeester van Heusdenweg 39, is located on the waterfront, just out of town. With your back to the harbor, take a right, walk along the pier, and continue for just over a kilometer on the bike path to Midsland. The hostel is on the right, where the paved road curves away from the ocean. The bar (open in summer daily 4:30pm-midnight) and many guest rooms feature sweeping ocean views, and the kitchen serves up a great *dagschotel* for €9.05 (served 6-6:45pm), which you can enjoy on the spacious terrace overlooking the sea. Renovations have made most of the dorms into smaller, 2-, 4-, and 6-person rooms. (☎44 23 38; www.stay-okay.com/terschelling. Breakfast included 8-10am. Linens included; towels €1.50. Laundry €3.50. Internet access €0.13 per min. Reception 9am-10:30pm. High-season 6-person dorms €30; 4-person dorms €32.20; 2-person dorms €40. Low-season 6-person dorms €21; 4-person dorms €22.60; 2-person €28. €2.50 HI discount.) Campgrounds abound on Terschelling, especially along the Midslander Hoofdweg on the southwestern coast. Try **Camping de Kooi ❶,** Hee 9, for its prime location and great amenities. (☎44 27 43; www.campingdekooi.nl.) However, there are 12 campsites on the island, and all are fairly equal in quality.

Campers can pick up groceries and other supplies at the **SPAR** supermarket, Boomstraat 13. (Open M-F 8am-8pm, Sa 8am-6pm.) Terschelling's best food experience, however, is at ◼**The Heartbreak Hotel ❶,** Oosterend, a shrine to all things Elvis. There's free live rock 'n' roll, starring the Elvis-impersonating owner, every night from the end of July through August. Break out your blue suede shoes for the huge Elvis Memorial Day party on August 16. Diner-style food abounds; the "Burning Love Burger" is only €4.50, and the frothy cranberry milk shake (€3.50) is made from the island's own berries. Post-meal, relax or take a dip at the bustling beach in front of the restaurant. (☎44 86 34; www.heartbreak-hotel.nl. Open daily 10am-1am. Cash only.) **Zeezicht ❸,** Willem Barentszkade 20, next to the VVV, across from the ferry landing, offers a pleasant, relaxed atmosphere in which to enjoy French-oriented cuisine with a sweeping view of the ocean. The main courses are pricey (€12-16.50) but come in enormous portions with sides of potatoes and salad, guaranteed to satisfy the heartiest appetite. Fresh mussels served with salad and bread are an affordable seasonal favorite at €14.50. (☎44 22 68. Open daily 10am-midnight. Kitchen closes at 9:30pm. AmEx/MC/V.) Follow your nose to the sandwiches and freshly squeezed juice at **De Dis ❶,** Boomstraat 17. Gourmet sandwiches are €2.30-6; the Caprino *broodje*—brown bread stuffed with goat cheese, honey, and walnuts—is a sweet treat on the beach (€5.80). Pre-made salads start at €1.40 per 100g. (☎44 34 43. Open M-Sa 9am-9pm, Su 11am-9pm.)

◙◼ SIGHTS AND NIGHTLIFE. Hills are rare in the Netherlands, but rolling expanses define Terschelling and make for great mountain biking; the VVV can help book organized bike tours. Less strenuous biking is also possible thanks to the island's numerous bike rental shops (above) and paved and pebbled bike paths. **Beaches** stretch across the northern coast, where, as on the other Wadden Islands, you can go long stretches without encountering another soul. Don't miss the view from the western tip of the island; to get there from the ferry landing, turn left out of the landing dock and walk until you can walk no farther. There you'll behold an unparalleled view of lilting sailboats floating placidly on infinite blue waves. **Oerol,** a huge experimental theater festival, packs the island with revelers every year during the third week of June; book accommodations in advance. (☎ 44 84 48; www.oerol.nl.) Although it will take you a bit away from the town, a trip to the ▨**Wrakkenmuseum**, Formerum Zuid 13, is worth it if only for the eight-kilometer bike ride past some of the island's most picturesque fields. To get there, follow the bike path to Formerum; once in Formerum, take a left at the small statue of Rembrandt van Rijn; the museum is five minutes ahead. The Shipwreck Museum displays finds from shipwrecks around Terschelling; a boat and a pirate castle built of driftwood behind the museum make this a great destination for kids. Signs are in Dutch. Try a slice of tangy cranberry tart at the museum's cafe for only €2.25. (☎ 44 93 05; http://wrakkenmuseum.nl. Open in summer 10am-11pm, in winter 10am-8pm. €2.) Closer to the main drag, the **Zee-aquarium and Natuurmuseum**, Burgemeester Reedekerstraat 11, is a cut above the average taxidermy shop. Though the signs are all in Dutch, most exhibits speak quite well for themselves. (☎ 44 23 90. Open Apr.-Nov. M-F 7am-5pm, Sa-Su 2-5pm; Nov.-Feb. Sa-Su 2-5pm. €4, ages 4-11 €3.)

Dutch teenagers flood Terschelling during the summer, accounting for the island's surprisingly active nightlife. A night bus runs around 10pm-2am in the high season, transporting drunken revelers home. **Cafe de Zeevaart**, Torenstraat 22, possesses a seaside grog-house feel. A plate of *bitterballen* is €4.50; during the day, meatballs are especially popular and a steal at €2.30 for a bowl. (☎ 44 26 77. Open daily 10am-2am. Cash only.) Velvet curtains separate the pub area from the youth-packed dance floor at **Braskoer**, Torenstraat 32. (☎ 46 21 97. Beer €2. Cover €5 after 9pm. Open daily 10am-2am. Dancing from 11pm.)

DAYTRIPS

APPENDIX

CLIMATE

Amsterdam's weather is mild and temperate but unpredictable. Like in much of Northern Europe, the mostly snowless winters are chilly and wet, and the summers are warmish and wet. Because the country is so flat, blustery winds can enter from all directions, sweeping away morning clouds or bringing in late-afternoon showers, all without warning.

Month	Avg. High Temperature		Avg. Low Temperature		Avg. Rainfall		Avg. Number of Wet Days
January	4°C	39°F	-1°C	30°F	79mm	3.1 in.	13
February	6°C	43°F	-1°C	30°F	43mm	1.7 in.	12
March	9°C	48°F	1°C	34°F	89mm	3.5 in.	13
April	13°C	55°F	3°C	37°F	38mm	1.5 in.	13
May	17°C	63°F	7°C	45°F	51mm	2.0 in.	12
June	20°C	68°F	10°C	50°F	61mm	2.4 in.	12
July	22°C	72°F	12°C	54°F	74mm	2.9 in.	10
August	22°C	72°F	12°C	54°F	61mm	2.4 in.	11
September	19°C	66°F	9°C	48°F	81mm	3.2 in.	13
October	14°C	57°F	7°C	45°F	104mm	4.1 in.	14
November	9°C	48°F	3°C	37°F	76mm	3.0 in.	15
December	6°C	43°F	1°C	34°F	71mm	2.8 in.	11

MEASUREMENTS

The Netherlands uses the metric system. The basic unit of length is the **meter (m)**, which is divided into 100 **centimeters (cm)** or 1000 **millimeters (mm)**. One thousand meters make up one **kilometer (km)**. Fluids are measured in **liters (L)**, each divided into 1000 **milliliters (ml)**. A liter of pure water weighs one **kilogram (kg)**, the unit of mass that is divided into 1000 **grams (g)**. One **metric ton** is 1000kg.

1 inch (in.) = 25.4mm	1 millimeter (mm) = 0.039 in.
1 foot (ft.) = 0.305m	1 meter (m) = 3.28 ft.
1 yard (yd.) = 0.914m	1 meter (m) = 1.09 yd.
1 mile (mi.) = 1.609km	1 kilometer (km) = 0.62 mi.
1 ounce (oz.) = 28.35g	1 gram (g) = 0.035 oz.
1 pound (lb.) = 0.454kg	1 kilogram (kg) = 2.205 lb.
1 fluid ounce (fl. oz.) = 29.57ml	1 milliliter (mL) = 0.034 fl. oz.
1 gallon (gal.) = 3.785L	1 liter (L) = 0.264 gal.

LANGUAGE

Dutch is the official language of the Netherlands, but in Amsterdam most natives speak English—and speak it well. Thanks to mandatory English education in schools and to English-language media exports, most locals have impeccable grammar, vast vocabularies, and a soft Continental accent that makes conversing relatively easy. Knowing a few key Dutch words and phrases can't hurt, particularly in smaller towns where English is not spoken as widely. Dutch spellings frequently resemble German, but pronunciation is very different. To initiate an English conversation, politely ask, *"Spreekt u Engels?"* (SPRAYKT oo ANG-les?). Even if your conversational counterpart speaks little English, he or she will usually try to communicate, an effort you can acknowledge by thanking them: *"Dank u wel"* (DAHNK oo vell).

PRONUNCIATION GUIDE

Most Dutch consonants, with a few notable exceptions, share their sounds with their English versions, sometimes rendering Dutch into a phonetic version of English with a foreign accent. Vowels are a different story. The combinations "e," "ee," "i," and "ij" are occasionally pronounced "er" as in "mother." Here are the other counterintuitive pronunciations:

PHONETIC UNIT	PRONUNCIATION	PHONETIC UNIT	PRONUNCIATION
au, ou, or ui	ow, as in "now"	g or ch	kh, as in "loch"
oo	oa, as in "boat"	ie	ee, as in "see"
v	between f and v	j	y, as in "yes"
w	between v and w	ee, ij or ei	ay, as in "layer"
aa	a longer a than in "cat"	oe	oo, as in "shoo"
eu	u, as in "hurt"	uu	a longer oo than in "too"

DUTCH PHRASEBOOK

ENGLISH	DUTCH	PRONUNCIATION
Hello!/Hi!	Dag!/Hallo!	Dakh!/Hallo!
My name is...	Mijn naam is...	Mayn nahm iss...
Do you speak English?	Spreekt u Engels?	Spraykt oo ANG-les?
I don't speak Dutch.	Ik spreek geen Nederlands.	Ik sprayk khayn NAY-der-lans.
I don't understand.	Ik begrijp het niet.	Ik ber-KHRAYP het neet.
Good morning!	Goedemorgen!	KHOO-der-mor-khern!
Good afternoon!	Goedemiddag!	KHOO-der-mid-akh!
Good evening!	Goedenavond!	KHOO-der-na-fondt!
Goodbye!	Tot ziens!	Tot zeens!
Yes.	Ja.	Yah.
No.	Nee.	Nay.
Maybe.	Misschien.	Miss-kheen.
Please/You're welcome.	Alstublieft.	Als-too-BLEEFT.
Thank you.	Dank u wel.	Dahnk oo vell.
Excuse me? (Getting attention)	Pardon?	Par-DON?
Excuse me! (To apologize)	Neemt u mij niet!	Naymt oo may neet!
Sorry!	Sorry!	SOR-ee!
Wooden shoes	Klompen	KLOM-pern
EMERGENCY		
Go away!	Ga weg!	Kha vekh!
Help!	Help!	Help!
Stop!	Stop!	Stop!

ENGLISH	DUTCH	PRONUNCIATION
Call the police!	Bel de politie!	Bel der poh-LEET-see!
Get a doctor!	Haal een dokter!	Haal ayn DOK-ter!
I'm sick.	Ik ben ziek.	Ik ben zeek.
I'm lost.	Ik ben verdwaald.	Ik ben ferd-VAHLDT.
QUESTIONS		
Who?	Wie?	Vee?
What?	Wat?	Vat?
When?	Wanneer?	Van-AYR?
Why?	Waarom?	VAR-ohm?
Where is...?	Waar is...?	Vahr iss...?
How do I get to...?	Hoe kom ik in...?	Hoo kom ik in...?
...the museum	...het museum	...het muh-say-um
...the church	...de kerk	...de kerk
...the bank	...de bank	...de bahnk
...the hotel	...het hotel	...het ho-TEL
...the shop	...de winkel	...de VIN-kerl
...the market	...de markt	...de markt
...the consulate	...het consulaat	...het kon-sul-AAT
...the train station	...het station	...het staht-see-OHN
...the bus stop	...de bushalte	...de BUS-hahlter
...the tourist office	...de VVV	...de fay fay fay
...the toilet	...het toilet	...het tva-LET
What time is it?	Hoe laat is het?	Hoo laht iss het?
When does...open?	Waneer gaat...open?	Van-AYR khaht...OH-pern?
Do you have...?	Heeft u...?	Hayft oo...?
How much does this cost?	Wat kost het?	Vat kost het?
ACCOMMODATIONS		
I have a reservation.	Ik heb een reservering.	Ik hep ayn res-er-VAY-ring.
Single room	Eenpersoonskamer	AYN-per-sohn-kah-mer
Double room	Tweepersoonskamer	TVAY-per-sohn-kah-mer
How much per night?	Hoeveel kost het per nacht?	Hoo-FAYL kost het per nakht?
Yesterday	Gisteren	KHIS-ter-ern
Today	Vandaag	Fan-DAKH
Tomorrow	Morgen	MOR-khern
FOOD		
Restaurant	Restaurant	Rest-oh-RAHNT
We have a reservation.	We hebben gereserveerd.	Vay HEP-bern kher-ay-ser-VAYRT.
Waiter/waitress	Meneer/mevrouw	Mer-NAYR/me-FROW
I'd like...	Ik wil graag...	Ik vil krakh...
May I have the check, please?	Mag ik de rekening?	Makh ik der RAY-kern-inkh?

MAP APPENDIX

Central Canal Ring and Rembrandtplein **336**
De Pijp **333**
Jodenbuurt and Plantage **344**
Leidseplein **337**
Museumplein and Vondelpark **342**
Nieuwe Zijd, Oude Zijd, and The Red Light District **340**
Scheepvaartbuurt, Canal Ring West, and Jordaan **338**
Transportation Overview **334**
Westerpark and Oud-West **343**

OTHER MAPS

Amsterdam Neighborhoods **VIII**
Best of the Netherlands **248**
Delft **281**
Groningen **309**
Haarlem **250**
The Hague **271**
Leiden **263**
Maastricht **314**
The Netherlands **247**
Rotterdam **287**
Utrecht **299**
Wadden Islands **321**

APPENDIX

MAP LEGEND

⊞ Hospital	✈ Airport	♨ Theater	⌂ Museum
℞ Pharmacy	🚌 Bus Station	♠ Hotel/Hostel	📖 Library
✚ Police	🚆 Train Station	⛺ Camping	Park
✉ Post Office	M Metro Station	♣ Restaurant	Water
ⓘ Tourist Office	Ⓢ Light Rail Station	☕ Coffeeshop	
$ Bank/ATM	Ⓣ Tram Stop	▮ Nightlife	Building
⚑ Embassy/Consulate	☐ Internet Cafe	★ Entertainment	
▪ Site or Point of Interest	✝ Church	⚓ Ferry Route/Landing	The Let's Go compass always points NORTH.
☎ Telephone Office	✡ Synagogue	Pedestrian Zone	
	⛩ Buddhist Temple	Stairs	

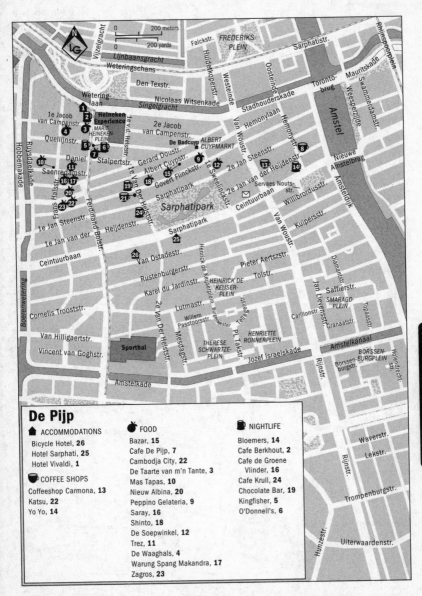

0 200 meters
0 200 yards

N
LG

Vlizelgracht
Lijnbaansgracht
Weteringschans
Weteringlaan
Den Texstr.
Nicolaas Witsenkade
Singelgracht
Falckstr.
FREDERIKS-
PLEIN
Sarphatistr.
Huidekoperstr.
Westeinde
Oosteinde
Stadhouderskade
Van Woustr.
Hemonylaan
Hemonystr.
Toronto-
brug
Weesperzijde
Mauritskade
Swammerdamstr.
Rhinspoorplein
Amstel
Nieuwe
Amstelbrug
Amsteldijk

1e Jacob
van Campenstr.
Quellijnstr.
Daniel
Stalpertstr.
Saenredamstr.
Frans Halsstr.
1e Jan Steenstr.
1e Jan van der
Ceintuurbaan
Cornelis Troostr.
Van Hilligaertstr.
Vincent van Goghstr.
Amstelkade

2e Jacob
van Campenstr.
Gerard Doustr.
Albert Cuypstr.
Govert Flinckstr.
Sarphatipark
Heijdenstr.
Sarphatipark
Van Ostadestr.
Rustenburgerstr.
Karel du Jardinstr.
Lutmastr.
Willem
Passtoorsstr.
Mesdagstr.
Sporthal

MARIE
HEINEKEN
PLEIN
De Badcuyp
ALBERT
CUYPMARKT
2e Jan Steenstr.
2e Jan v.d. Heijdenstr.
Servaes Noutsstr.
Ceintuurbaan
Willibrordusstr.
Kuipersstr.
Van Woustr.
Pieter Aertszstr.
Tolstr.
Henrick de Keijserplein
HEINRICK DE
KEIJSER-
PLEIN
Burgemeester
Tellegenstr.
Jozef Israelskade
Rijnstr.
Jan Lievensstr.
Saffierstr.
SMARAGD-
PLEIN
Granaatstr.
Carillonstr.
Diamantstr.
Topaasstr.
Amstelkanaal
BORSSEN-
BURGPLEIN
Borssen-
burgstr.
Hoiendrecht-
str.

2e van Der Helststr.
Ferdinand Bolstr.
2e Van Der Helststr.
1e v.d. Helststr.

Heinekenen
Experience

Hobbemakade
Ruysdaelkade
Boerenwetering

THERESE
SCHWARTZE-
PLEIN
HENRIETTE
RONNERPLEIN
Pl. Takstr.

Waverstr.
Lekstr.
Rijnstr.
Trompenburgstr.
Humzestr.
Uiterwaardenstr.

APPENDIX

De Pijp

🏠 ACCOMMODATIONS
Bicycle Hotel, 26
Hotel Sarphati, 25
Hotel Vivaldi, 1

☕ COFFEE SHOPS
Coffeeshop Carmona, 13
Katsu, 22
Yo Yo, 14

🍎 FOOD
Bazar, 15
Cafe De Pijp, 7
Cambodja City, 22
De Taarte van m'n Tante, 3
Mas Tapas, 10
Nieuw Albina, 20
Peppino Gelateria, 9
Saray, 16
Shinto, 18
De Soepwinkel, 12
Trez, 11
De Waaghals, 4
Warung Spang Makandra, 17
Zagros, 23

🍸 NIGHTLIFE
Bloemers, 14
Cafe Berkhout, 2
Cafe de Groene
Vlinder, 16
Cafe Krull, 24
Chocolate Bar, 19
Kingfisher, 5
O'Donnell's, 6

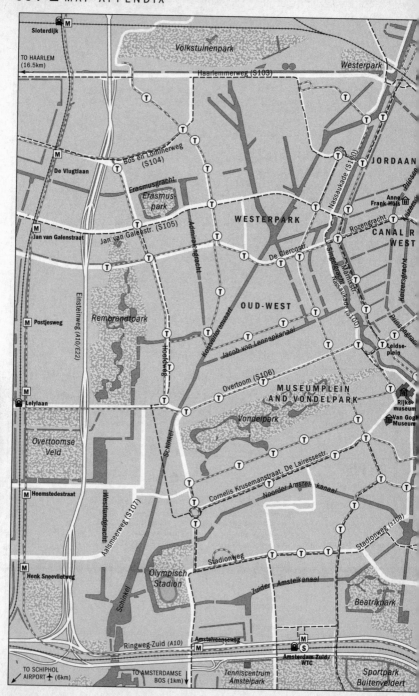

Transportation Overview

- ┄┄┄ Railway lines
- ▦▦▦ Metro lines
- ▨▨▨ Tram lines
- ╌╌╌ Bus lines
- 🚆 Railway stations
- Ⓢ Light rail stations
- Ⓜ Metro stations
- Ⓣ Tram stops

Het IJ

0   500 yards
0   500 meters

't Houttuinen

Het IJ

De Ruyterkade

IJ-Tunnel

SCHEEPVAART-BUURT

Centraal

Piet Heinkade

IJhaven

Singel

Herengracht

Damrak

Nieuwe Kerk

Oude Kerk

Oosterdok

Prins Hendrikkade

NEMO

Koninklijk Paleis

Nieuwmarkt

NIEUWMARKT

Oude Schans

CENTRUM

Rokin

JODENBUURT

Nieuwe Vaart

PLANTAGE

Het Muziektheater

Stadhuis

WATERLOO-PLEIN

Plantage Middenlaan

Artis Zoo

Zeeburgerdijk

Rembrandt-plein

Amstel

Weesperstr.

CENTRAL CANAL RING

WEESPERPLEIN

...kade (S100)

Oosterpark

Muiderpoort

Linnaeus-str.

Stadhouderskade (S100)

Heineken Experience

Ferdinand Bolstr.

Sarphatipark

DE PIJP

Amstel

Amsteldijk (S110)

WIBAUT-STRAAT

Watergraaf-smeer

Middenweg (S113)

Amstelkanaal

Van Wou...

Vrijheidslaan

AMSTEL

Hugo de Vrieslaan

Nieuwe Ooster Begraafplaats

Scheldestr.

Roosevelthaan

Amstel

Goolsewag (S112)

TO AMSTERDAM ARENA (2.5km)

President Kennedy-laan

Spaklerweg

Sportpark Drie Burg

Europaplvd.

Martin Luther King Park

Spaklerweg

Ringweg-Zuid

RAI

Zorgvlied

TO UTRECHT (40km)

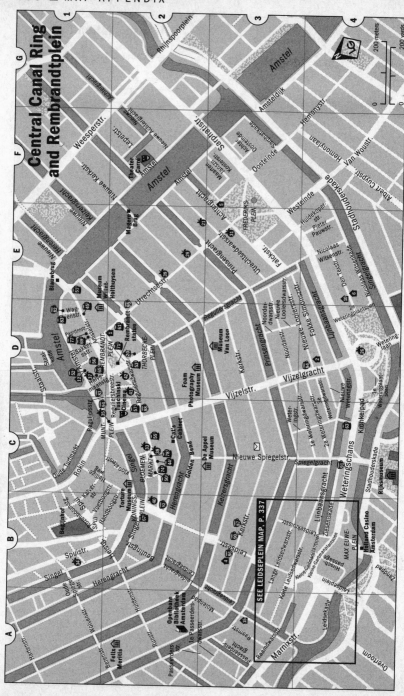

Central Canal Ring
and Rembrandtplein

SEE LEIDSEPLEIN MAP. P. 337

200 meters
200 yards

Central Canal Ring, Leidseplein, and Rembrandtplein

🏠 ACCOMMODATIONS

City Hotel,	1	D2
Euphemia Budget Hotel,	2	D4
Freeland,	3	H6
The Golden Bear,	4	B3
Hemp Hotel,	5	F3
Hotel Asterisk,	6	E4
Hotel La Boheme,	7	I6
Hotel de la Haye,	8	H5
Hotel Impala,	9	H6
Hotel Kap,	10	E4
Hotel Kooyk,	11	H6
Hotel Monopole,	12	D1
Hotel de Paris,	13	H5
Hotel Titus,	14	H6
International Budget Hostel,	15	A3
King Hotel,	16	H6
Leidseplein Hotel,	17	J5
Marnix Hotel,	18	H5
Quentin Hotel,	19	H6
Thorbecke Hotel,	20	D2

🍎 FOOD

Axum,	21	E2
Belgica,	22	K6
Bojo,	23	K5
Bombay Inn,	24	I5
Café Americain,	25	I6
Carousel Pancake House,	26	D4
Chicanos,	27	K5
Coffee and Jazz,	28	E2
De Balie,	29	J6
Eat at Jo's,	30	I6
Golden Temple,	31	E3
J.J. Ooyevaar,	32	K5
La Margarita,	33	C2
Lanskroon,	34	B1
NOA,	35	H5
The Pantry,	36	K5
Ristorante Pizzeria Firenze,	37	D1
Rose's Cantina,	38	C2
Tashi Deleg,	39	E2
Thai Restaurant Phuket,	40	B2
Tomo Sushi,	41	D2
Van Dobben,	42	D2

🍺 NIGHTLIFE

Amsterdamned Café,	43	J5
Arc Bar,	44	C2
The Back Door,	45	D1
Bamboo Bar,	46	I5
Bar Hartje,	47	K5
Brasil Music Bar,	48	I5
Bubbels,	49	J5
Cafe April,	50	C2
Café Menschen,	51	E1
Cafe Rouge,	52	D1
Coco's Outback,	53	D2
The Cooldown Café,	54	K5
De Duivel,	55	C2
Escape,	56	D1
Exit,	57	C2
Habibi Ana Bar,	58	I5
Jimmy Woo,	59	I5
Kamer 401,	60	I6
Lellebel,	61	D2
Lux,	62	I6
Mankind,	63	C4
Melkweg,	64	I5
Montmartre,	65	D1
NJOY,	66	J5
Odeon,	67	B2
Paradiso,	68	K6
Party Crew Cafe,	69	D1
Pirates Bar,	70	K5
Rain,	71	D2
Royalty,	72	J5
La Rumba,	73	J5
Soho,	74	C2
Sugar Factory,	75	I5
Suzy Wong,	76	I5
Vive La Vie,	77	D1
Vodka Bar The 5th Element,	78	C2
Vuong,	79	I5
Weber,	80	I5
Zebra,	81	I5

☕ COFFEE SHOPS

Arabica,	82	D1
The Bush Doctor,	83	D1
Coffeeshop Little,	84	D4
Crush,	85	H5
Dolphins,	86	B3
Conscious Dreams,	87	B3
Free I,	88	C2
Get Down To It,	89	J5
Global Chillage,	90	B3
The Noon,	91	C4
The Other Side,	92	B2
The Rookies,	93	J5
The Saint,	94	C1
Stix,	95	D2
Tatanka,	96	J5

⭐ ENTERTAINMENT

Alto,	97	K6
Bourbon Street Jazz & Blues Club,	98	K5
Cinecenter,	99	I5
Piano Bar,	100	K6
The Waterhole,	101	I5

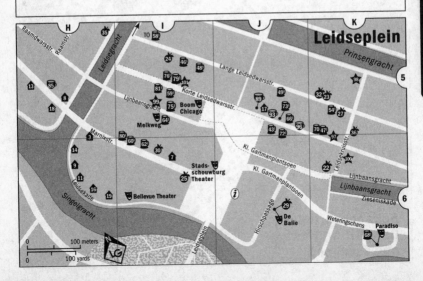

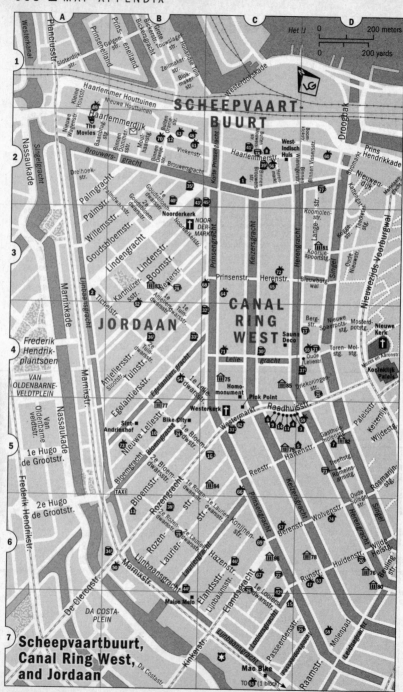

SCHEEPVAART-
BUURT

JORDAAN

CANAL
RING
WEST

Het IJ

0   200 meters
0   200 yards

**Scheepvaartbuurt,
Canal Ring West,
and Jordaan**

Scheepvaartbuurt, Canal Ring West, and Jordaan

♠ ACCOMMODATIONS
Frédéric Rent a Bike,	1	C2
Hotel Acacia,	2	A3
Hotel Di Ann,	3	D5
Hotel Aspen,	4	C5
Hotel Belga,	5	D5
Hotel Clemens,	6	C5
Hotel Hegra,	7	D5
Hotel My Home,	8	C2
Hotel Pax,	9	C5
Hotel Van Onna,	10	B5
Nadia Hotel,	11	C5
Ramenas Hotel,	12	B2
The Shelter Jordan,	13	B6
Westertoren Hotel,	14	C5
Wiechmann Hotel,	15	C7

☕ COFFEE SHOPS
African Black Star Coffeeshop,	16	C5
Amnesia,	17	D4
Barney's,	18	C2
Coffeeshop Sanementereng,	19	B6
Extreme Amsterdam,	20	D6
Grey Area,	21	D4
La Tertulia,	22	C6
Magic,	23	D5
Paradox,	24	B5
Rockland,	25	D4
The Rokery,	26	C6
Siberië,	27	D2
Spirit Coffeeshop,	28	B3
Tops,	29	D7

■ NIGHTLIFE
Café Brandon,	30	C4
Cafe Kalkhoven,	31	C5
Cafe P96,	32	C4
Café 't Smalle,	33	B4
Café Soundgarden,	34	B6
Cafe Thijssen,	35	B2
Café de Tuin,	36	B4
Café Zool,	37	D4
Club More,	38	B6
De Blauwe Druife,	39	C2
Duende,	40	B2
Dulac,	41	C2
Festina Lente,	42	C6
Finch,	43	B2
Korsakoff,	44	B6
Proust,	45	C2
Saarein II,	46	C6

🍎 FOOD
Bakkerij Paul Année,	47	D6
Balraj,	48	B2
Bakkerij Mediterrane,	49	A1
Ben Cohen Shawarma,	50	B6
Cafe de Koe,	51	C7
Cinema Paradiso,	52	B4
De Kaaskamer,	53	D6
De Reiger,	54	B4
Foodism,	55	D4
Harlem: Drinks and Soulfood,	56	C2
Hein,	57	C6
Het Molenpad,	58	D7
Il Panorama,	59	D5
Jay's Juice,	60	D2
Jordino,	61	B2
Koh-i-noor,	62	C5
Padi,	63	B2
The Pancake Bakery,	64	C3
Prego,	65	C3
Rainarai,	66	C5
Rakang,	67	C6
Restaurant de Bolhoed,	68	C3
Roem,	69	C6
Small World Cafe,	70	B2
Spanjer en Van Twist,	71	C4
Top Thai,	72	C3
De Vliegende Schotel,	73	B5
Wolvenstraat 23,	74	D6

🏛 MUSEUMS
Anne Frank Huis,	75	C4
Bijbels Museum,	76	D6
Electric Ladyland,	77	B5
Felix Meritis,	78	D6
Huis Marseille,	79	C5
Institute for War Documentation,	80	D6
Multatuli Museum,	81	D3
Nationaal Brilmuseum,	82	D5
Pianola Museum,	83	B3
Stedelijk Museum Bureau Amsterdam,	84	C5
Theater Instituut Nederland,	85	C4
Woonboot Museum,	86	C6

Nieuwe Zijd, Oude Zijd, and Red Light District

Nieuwe Westerdokstr.
Nieuwe Haarlemmer Houttuinen
Buiten Brouwers-str.
Boom-kloksstr.
Haarlemmerstr.
Binnen Brouwers-str.
Binnen Wieringerstr.
Binnen Visserstr.
Brouwers-gracht
Roomolenstr.
Langestr.
Stromarkt
Kattengat
Korsjespoortstg.
Herenstr.
Blauwburgwal
Singel
Bergstr.
Herengracht
Oude Lelistr.
Torenstg.
Mol-stg.
Nieuwe Spaarpot-stg.
Mesderd-nietstg.
Zwartehandstg.
Gravenstr.
Driekoningenstr.
Raadhuisstr.
Spuistr.
Paleisstr.
Gasthuis-molenstg.
Keizerrijk
Wijdesteeg
Jonge Roelensteg.
Treeftstg.
Gemeinsarm-stg.
Huidenstr.
Heisstg.
Wilde Heisstg.
Beulingstr.
Herengracht

Prins Hendrikkade
Droogbak
Open
STATIONS-PLEIN
Centraal Station
Oosterdokskade
Haven Front
Prins Hendrikkade
Oosterdoksstr.
Oudezijds Kolk

Nieuwendijk
Martelaarsgracht
Nieuwezijds Voorburgwal
Nieuwendijk
Oude Braak
St. Jacobsstr.
Kolksteeg
Oudebrugsteeg
Mandenmakersteeg
Dirk van Hasseltssteeg
Onze L. Vrouwesteeg
Nieuwe Nieuwstr.
St. Nicolaasstr.
Spuistraat
Nieuwe Nieuwstr.
Beurs-passage
Beurs-straat
Papenbrugsteeg

NIEUWE ZIJD

Nieuwe Armst.
Haringpakkers-stg.
Amsterdam Sex Museum
Damrak
Warmoesstraat
Oudezijds Armst.
Oudezijds Voorburgwal
Sint Nicolaaskerk
Wingaardseatie
Oudezijds Armst.
Vreden-Spoelstg.
Zeedijk
Geldersekade
Henkel
Hoeksstg.
Oude Niezel
Stormstg.
Monnikenstr.
Oude Hoogstr.
Oude Doelenstr.
Hash Marijuana Hemp Museum

Beurs van Berlage
Paternosterstg.
Wijde Kerkstg.
BEURS-PLEIN
Oude Kerk
Museum Amstelkring
Oude Kerksplein
Trompettersteeg
St. Annenstr.

RED LIGHT DISTRICT

Nieuwe Kerk
Mozes en Aaronstr.
Magna Plaza Shopping Center
Koninklijk Paleis
DAM SQ.
Nationaal Monument
Damstr.
Pijlstg.
Warmoesstraat
Damrakstg.
Vatkensstr.
Hermietenstr.
Nadorststr.
Pieter Jacobszstr.
Papenbroekssteeg
Spaarpotssteeg
Rokin
St. Pietersstr.
St. Pieterspoortstg.
St. Pietershalstg.
Gaperstr.
Wijde-lombardstg.
Enge-lombardstg.
Spinhuissstg.
Rusland
Slijkstr.
Sint Agnietenkapel
St. Luciensteeg
Kalfsvel-Barberenstg.
Kulperssstg.
Grimburgwal
Grimburgwal
Turfdraagsterpad
Vendelstr.
Staalstr.
Binnen-gasthuisstr.
Binnen Amstel

OUDE ZIJD
Nieuwe Hoogstr.
Koestr.
Bethaniënstr.
Trippenhuis
Oost-Indisch Huis
Raamgracht
Groenburgwal
Verversstr.
Zwanenburgwal
Zwanenburgwal
St. Antoniesbreestr.

Casa Rosso
Barndesstr.
Cannabis College
NIEUWMARKT
Fo Guang Shan He Hua Temple
St. Antoniesbreestr.

Kreupel-stg.
Molensteeg
Bloedstr.
St. Jansstr.
Oudezijds Achterburgwal
Oudezijds Voorburgwal
Kloveniersburgwal

Amsterdams Historisch Museum
Enge Kapelstg.
Wijde Kapelstg.
Kalfsvelstg.
N.Z.
Begijnensteeg
Waterstg.
Rozenboomstg.
Taksstg.
Begijn-hof
SPUI
Kalverstr.
Handboogstr.
Voetboogstr.
Heiligeweg
Torture Museum
KONINGS-PLEIN
Bloemenmarkt
Nieuwezijds Kapelsteeg
Olieslagerssteeg
Duifjessteeg
Enge Kapelstg.
Allard Pierson Museum
Oude Turfmarkt
Rokin
Amstel
MUNT-PLEIN
REMBRANDT-PLEIN
Binnen Amstel

Oude Spiegelstr.
Oude Spiegelstr.
Rosmarijnsteeg
Raamstg.
Singel

0   200 meters
0   200 yards

Nieuwe Zijd, Oude Zijd, and Red Light District

♠ ACCOMMODATIONS

Aivergo Youth Hostel,	1	B2
ANCO Hotel,	2	D3
Bob's Youth Hostel,	3	B3
Budget Hotel Tamara,	4	B4
Durty Nelly's Hostel,	5	C4
Flying Pig Downtown,	6	C2
Frisco Inn,	7	C3
The Greenhouse Effect Hotel,	8	D3
Hotel Brian,	9	B3
Hotel Brouwer,	10	B3
Hotel Continental,	11	C3
Hotel Cosmos,	12	B3
Hotel The Crown,	13	D3
Hotel Groenendael,	14	B2
Hotel Hoksbergen,	15	A6
Hotel Internationaal,	16	D3
Hotel Nova,	17	B5
Hotel Old Quarter,	18	C3
Hotel Rokin,	19	B5
Hotel Royal Taste,	20	D4
Hotel Vijaya,	21	D3
Meeting Point Youth Hostel,	22	D2
Old Nickel,	23	D2
De Oranje Tulp,	24	D6
Stayokay Amsterdam	25	B3
Stadsdoelen,	26	C4
Tourist Inn,	27	C3
The Winston Hotel,	28	C3
De Witte Tulp Hostel,		

♣ FOOD

Aneka Rasa,	29	D3
Frood,	30	B3
La Fruteria,	31	B4
Green Planet,	32	A4
Cafe Latei,	33	D4
In de Waag,	34	D4
Nam Kee,	35	D3
New Season,	36	C3
Pannenkoekenhuis Upstairs,	37	C6
La Place,	38	C7
Poco Loco,	39	D4
Ristorante Caprese,	40	A6
Sie Joe,	41	B4
Taste of Culture,	42	D3
Theehuis Himalaya,	43	C3

♫ NIGHTLIFE

Absinthe,	44	B5
Belgique,	45	B4
Bep,	46	B5
Café de Engelbewaarder,	47	D5
Café de Jaren,	48	C7
Cafe Heffer,	49	C3
Cafe Lime,	50	D4
Cafe Stevens,	51	D4
Casablanca,	52	D3
Club Magazijn,	53	C4
Club Meander,	54	B7
Club NL,	55	B5
Club Winston,	56	C4
Cockring,	57	C3
Dansen Bij Jansen,	58	B7
Durty Nelly's Pub,	59	C4
The Getaway,	60	B5
Getto,	61	D3
Gollem,	62	A6
Lokaal 't Loosje,	63	D4
The Tara,	64	C6
Vrankrijk,	65	A5
Wijnand Fockink,	66	C4

☕ COFFEE SHOPS

420 Cafe (de Kuil),	67	C3
Abraxas,	68	B5
La Canna,	69	C3
Coffeeshop Any Day,	70	B3
Conscious Dreams Kokopelli,	71	D2
Dampkring,	72	B7
Dutch Flowers,	73	A7
The Greenhouse Effect,	74	D3
Hill Street Blues,	75	C3
Kadinsky,	76	B6
Magic Valley,	77	B3
Route 99,	78	C2
Rusland,	79	C5
Softland,	80	A5
De Tweede Kamer,	81	A6

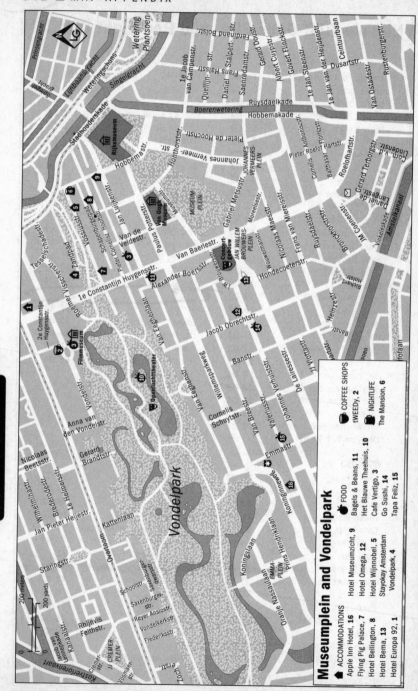

Museumplein and Vondelpark

♦ ACCOMMODATIONS
Apple Inn Hotel, **16**
Flying Pig Palace, **7**
Hotel Bellington, **8**
Hotel Bema, **13**
Hotel Europa 92, **1**
Hotel Museumzicht, **9**
Hotel Omega, **12**
Hotel Wijnnobel, **5**
Stayokay Amsterdam
Vondelpark, **4**

♣ FOOD
Bagels & Beans, **11**
Het Blauwe Theehuis, **10**
Cafe Vertigo, **3**
Go Sushi, **14**
Tapa Feliz, **15**

☕ COFFEE SHOPS
tWEEDy, **2**

☂ NIGHTLIFE
The Mansion, **6**

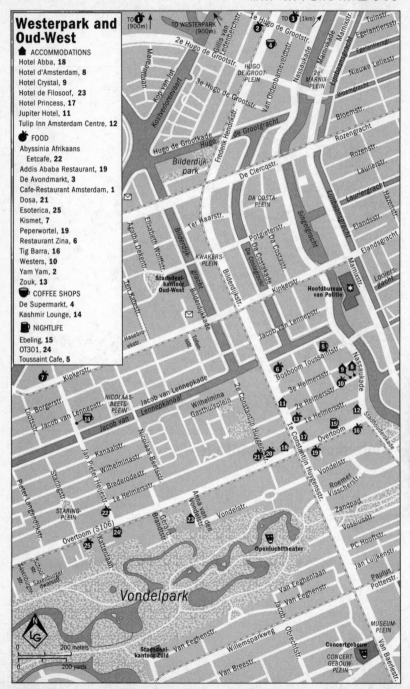

Westerpark and Oud-West

ACCOMMODATIONS
Hotel Abba, **18**
Hotel d'Amsterdam, **8**
Hotel Crystal, **9**
Hotel de Filosoof, **23**
Hotel Princess, **17**
Jupiter Hotel, **11**
Tulip Inn Amsterdam Centre, **12**

FOOD
Abyssinia Afrikaans
Eetcafe, **22**
Addis Ababa Restaurant, **19**
De Avondmarkt, **3**
Cafe-Restaurant Amsterdam, **1**
Dosa, **21**
Esoterica, **25**
Kismet, **7**
Peperwortel, **19**
Restaurant Zina, **6**
Tig Barra, **16**
Westers, **10**
Yam Yam, **2**
Zouk, **13**

COFFEE SHOPS
De Supermarkt, **4**
Kashmir Lounge, **14**

NIGHTLIFE
Ebeling, **15**
OT301, **24**
Toussaint Cafe, **5**

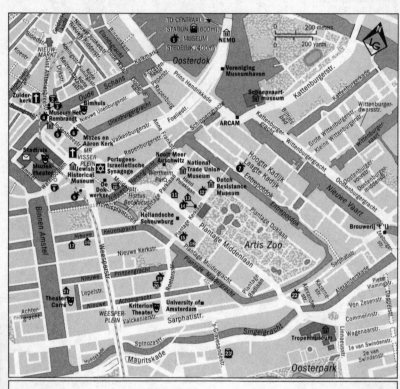

Jodenbuurt and Plantage

🛏 ACCOMMODATIONS
The Bridge Hotel, **21**
Hotel Adolesce, **16**
Hotel Barbacan, **18**
Hotel Plantage, **13**
Hotel Rembrandt, **11**
Luckytravellers Fantasia Hotel, **17**

🍎 FOOD
Abe Veneto, **15**
Aguada, **19**
Bloem, **7**
Café Koosje, **14**
De Groene Olifant, **22**
Eetkunst Asmara, **9**
Nam Tin, **6**
Plancius, **12**
Sea Palace, **1**
Soup En Zo, **5**
TisFris, **4**

☕ COFFEE SHOPS
Bluebird, **2**
Green House, **8**
Het Ballonnetje, **20**
Hortus De Overkant, **10**
Reefer, **3**

🍺 NIGHTLIFE
Arena, **23**

INDEX

A

Aalsmeer. See **Daytrips.**
Abe Veneto 140
Aboriginal Art Museum 300
abortion 30
Absinthe 227
Academy of Fine Arts 86
Accommodations 99–119
  by neighborhood 103
  by price 102
ACU Politiek Cultureel
  Centrum 301
AIDS 30
airport. See Schiphol.
Ajax 73
Albert Heijn 121, 278, 322
alcohol 25
Allard Pierson Museum 168
Alteration 58
alternative art spaces
  SMART Project Space 183
  W 139 183
Alto 187
Ameland 320
American Express 20, 47, 94
Amnesia 205
Amnesty International 79
Amstel Diamonds 153
Amsterdam Canal Garden
  Foundation 152
Amsterdam Op de Fiets. See
  publications.
Amsterdam School (art) 66
Amsterdam Sex Museum 168
Amsterdam Weekly. See
  publications.
Amsterdams Centrum voor
  Fotografie 165
Amsterdams Historisch
  Museum 167
Amsterdamse Bos 161
Amsterdamse Poort 256
*Anatomy Lesson of Dr. Tulp,
The* 72, 143, 274
ANCO Hotel and Bar 104
Anne Frank Huis 168
Annet Gelink Gallery. See
  galleries.

ANWB 43
apartments 101
Apeldoorn. See **Daytrips.**
Apenheul 304
apotheek. See pharmacies.
Appel, Karel 73
Appendix 329–331
  climate 329
  language 329
  measurements 329
Arc Bar 234
ARCAM (Architectuurcentrum
  Amsterdam) 161
Archeologisch Museum 255
architecture 65
Architecture Biennale 289
Arnhem. See **Daytrips.**
art. See visual art.
Artis Zoo 159
ATMs. See money.
au pair work 89
AUB 185
Avonturenbaai Sloterparkbad
  195

B

Badhuis-Theater de Bochel
  190
Bagel Bakery 288
Balkenende, Jan Peter 63
banks 94
Barney's 205
Bartolotti House 170
baseball 74
Basilica of St. Servatius 317
Basiliek van Onze Lieve
  Vrouwe (Basilica of Our Dear
  Lady) 318
Batavi 55
Bazar 137, 288
beaches
  Bloemendaal aan Zee 258
  Noordwijk aan Zee 268
  nude 258, 322
  Scheveningen 279
  Terschelling 326
  Texel 322
  Vlieland 325

  Zandvoort aan Zee 258
bed & breakfasts 100
Beelden-aan-Zee 279
Begijnhof 146
Begijnhofkapel 146
Bellevue Theater 189
Ben'z 308
Berlage, Hendrik Petrus 66,
  306
Beurs van Berlage 148, 186
Beyond Tourism 77–90
  studying 83
  volunteering 78
  working 87
Bezichtiging Vuurtoren
  (lighthouse) 325
Bezoekerscentrum 305
Bicycle Hotel 118
Bijbels Museum 169
Bike City 95
bikes 38
  rental 95
  tours. See tours.
Bimhuis 186
Binnenhof 274
bitterballen 74, 128, 230
Bizarre Amsterdam 3
Blauwbrug 152
Bloemendaal aan Zee. See
  Daytrips.
Bloemenveiling Aalsmeer
  244
Bluebird 211
boats 35
Bombay Inn 130
Bonnefantenmuseum 318
Boom Chicago 189
Boom! See publications.
Boomerang 196
Bos en Lommer 6
Bosmuseum 162
Bourbon Street Jazz & Blues
  Club 188
broodjes 74, 130, 133, 240
brothels 193
Brouwerij 't IJ 160
BTW. See value added tax.
budget 22

Bungy Jump Holland 195
Burcht 265
Burgundian Dynasty 57
buses. See public
  transportation.

C

Café 't Smalle 237
Café de Jaren 225
Cafe De Pijp 137
Cafe Latei 123
Cafe Vertigo 136
Café Zool 229
Cafe-Restaurant Amsterdam
  134
calling cards 45
Canal Ring West 4
  accommodations 109
  coffee shops 205
  food 127
  museums 168
  nightlife 229
  shopping 216
  sights 149
Cannabis College 80, 166
Canvas International Art. See
  galleries.
car insurance. See driving.
Casa Rosso 145, 194
Casablanca 188, 190
Cat's Cabinet 152
Caves of Mt. St. Pieter 316
cellular phones. See phones.
Celts 55
Centers for Disease Control
  (CDC) 28
Centraal Museum 298
Centraal Station 39
Central Canal Ring 4
  accommodations 110
  coffee shops 206
  food 129
  museums 171
  nightlife 230
  shopping 218
  sights 152
Centrum 2
Charlemagne 56
charter flights. See flights.
Cheese Walk 295
Cheesefarm Catharina Hoeve
  247
chess 152
Chocolate Bar 240

Christian Democratic Appeal
  (CDA) 63, 79
Cinecenter 192
City Hotel 113
classical music 185
Clement. See galleries.
climate. See **Appendix.**
Club Meander 189
Club NL 228
Club Winston 226
CoBrA 73, 181
CoBrA Museum 181
COC 50, 80
Cockring 226
coffee shops 196–211
comedy 189
Comedy Cafe 190
con artists 27
Concertgebouw 185
Concerto 218
Conscious Dreams 207
Conservatorium van
  Amsterdam 186
consulates. See embassies.
Cool Runnings 319
Corrie ten Boomhuis 253
Coster Diamonds 155
costs. See budget.
courier flights. See flights.
credit cards. See money.
cricket 74
crisis lines 96
Cristofori 188
Cube Houses 290
cuisine 74
currency exchange. See
  money.
customs 18
Cuypers, Pierre 65
cycling 74

D

Dam Square 147
Dampkring 202
dance 66, 185
Daytrips 243–327
  Aalsmeer 243
  Apeldoorn 304
  Arnhem 302
  Bloemendaal aan Zee 258
  De Hoge Veluwe National Park
    305

Delft 279
Gouda 294
Groningen 306
Haarlem 249
The Hague 269
Hooghalen 312
Leiden 260
Lisse 259
Maastricht 313
Noordwijk aan Zee 268
Rotterdam 285
Scheveningen 277
Terschelling 325
Texel 320
Utrecht 296
Vlieland 324
Zaanse Schans 245
Zandvoort aan Zee 257
De Appel 172
De Baarsjes 6
De Badcuyp 188
De Balie 190, 192
De Candelaer 283
De Delftse Pauw 284
De Doelen 292
De Expeditie. See galleries.
De Hallen Museum 254
De Heuvel Park 291
De Hoed Van Tijn 214
De Hoge Veluwe National
  Park. See **Daytrips.**
de Keyser, Hendrick 65
De Kleine Komedie 190
de Klerk, Michel 66
De Klimmuur 194
De Mirandabad 195
De Paas 276
De Pijp 7
  accommodations 118
  coffee shops 210
  food 137
  nightlife 240
  shopping 219
  sights 155
De Stijl 73
De Tinkoepel Tinnegieterij
  247
De Tweede Kamer 203
De Uni 319
De Vishal 255
De Vlaam 295
De Vliegende Schotel 133
debit cards. See money.
dehydration 28
Dekker, Eduard Douwes. See

Multatuli.
Delft Chamber Music Festival 280
Delft. See **Daytrips.**
Delftware 282
Democrats 66 79
Den Haag. See The Hague.
Dever House 260
diarrhea 29
dietary concerns 51
Dirk van den Broek 121
disabled travelers 50
Discover 1–8
  biking tours 8
  facts and figures 1
  neighborhoods 2
  walking tours 8
  when to go 1
diseases
  food- and water-borne 29
  insect-borne 28
Dizzy 293
Dockworker, The 159
doctors 30
  See also health.
Dolphins, The 206
Domkerk 298
Domtoren 298
driving 41–43
  buying a car 43
  insurance 41
  leasing a car 42
  permits 41
  renting a car 41
  safety 26
drugs
  law 25
  See also coffee shops.
Duivelshuis 303
Dulac 229
Durty Nelly's
  Hostel 104
  Pub 226
Dutch
  phrasebook 330
  pronunciation 330
Dutch East India Company (VOC) 59
duty-free 18

E

Eat at Jo's 130
Ecomare Museum and Aquarium 322
ecotourism 48
eetcafe 74
Eighty Years' War 58
Electric Ladyland 172
Elfstedentocht 74
email. See Internet.
embassies
  abroad 15
  in the Netherlands 16
emergency 96
encephalitis 29
Engelsekerk 146
English Bookshop 218
Entertainment 185–211
entrance requirements 15
environmental conservation 81
Erasmus 57
Erasmusbrug 291
Escape 236
Escher in Het Paleis 275
Escher, M.C. 73, 275
escort services 193
Essentials 15–53
  getting around the Netherlands 37
  getting to the Netherlands 31
  keeping in touch 44
  other resources 52
  planning your trip 15
  safety and health 24
  specific concerns 47
Eurail Pass. See railpasses.
Euromast 290
European Union (EU)
  euro 20
  freedom of movement 17, 18
  history 62
Eusebiuskerk 303
exchange rates. See money.

F

Federal Express 47
Felix Meritis 149
female travelers. See women travelers.
Festina Lente 237
festivals 75
  film 67
film 66, 190
Filmhuis Den Haag 276
Filmmuseum 176, 191
financial matters. See money.
flights 31–35
  charter 35
  commercial 33
  courier 34
  fares 31
  standby 34
Flower Parade 259
Flying Pig
  Beach Hostel 268
  Downtown 106
  Palace 116
Fo Guang Shan He Hua Temple 144
Foam Photography Museum 171
Food 121–141
  by neighborhood 123
  by type 121
Foodism 127
football 73
Fort St. Pieter 318
Fortuyn 252
Fortuyn, Pim 63
Frank, Anne 61, 68, 168
Franks 56
Frans Hals Museum 253
Frédéric Rent a Bike 95, 108
Freeland 111
frikandel 74
Frisians 55
frostbite 28
Frozen Fountain. See galleries.

G

gabber 68
galleries
  Annet Gelink Gallery 183
  Canvas International Art 183
  Clement 182
  De Expeditie 182
  Frozen Fountain 182
  Galerie Akinci 182
  Galerie Binnen 182
  Galerie Diana Stigter 183
  Galerie Fons Welters 183
  Galerie Louise Smit 182
  Galerie Lumen Travo 183
  Paul Andriesse 182
  Torch 183
  Van Wijngaarden/Hakkens 183
  Van Zoetendaal 182
  Vous Êtes Ici 183
gambling 194

Garden Gym 195
gasoline 43
Gassan Diamonds 158
gay marriage 64
Gay Pride Festival 64
gay travelers. See GLBT.
Gem/Fotomuseum 275
Gemeentemuseum 274
General Delivery. See Poste
  Restante.
Girl with a Pearl Earring 72,
  274
GLBT
  accommodations 99
  coffee shop 208
  life in Amsterdam 64
  nightlife 224
  resources 49
  saunas 195
  travelers 49
Golden Age. See history.
Golden Bear, The 110
Golden Bend 65, 152
Gorris, Marleen 67
Gothic 65
Gouda. See **Daytrips.**
Goudse kaassoep 295
grachtengordel 4
Greater Amsterdam
  museums 181
  sights 161
Greenhouse Effect
  coffee shop 202
  Hotel 104
Greenpeace 81
Grey Area 205
Groningen. See **Daytrips.**
Groninger Museum 308
Grote Kerk/St. Bavo's 253
guesthouses 100
GVB 39

H

Haags Historisch Museum
  276
Haags Uitburo 270
Haarlem. See **Daytrips.**
The Hague. See **Daytrips.**
Hague Magazine, The. See
  publications.
Hakkens. See Van
  Wijngaarden/Hakkens.
Hals, Frans 72, 253

Harlem Drinks and Soulfood
  126
Hash Marijuana Hemp
  Museum 166
hashish 197
Havenmuseum (Harbor
  Museum) 292
health. See **Essentials.**
Heartbreak Hotel, The 326
heat exhaustion 28
heat stroke 28
Heaven 69 319
Hein 127
Heineken Experience 155
Helpoort 318
Hemp Bar 230
Hemp Hotel 110
Herengracht 2
Herinneringscentrum 312
Hermans, Willem 68
Het Dolhuys 254
Het Houten Huys (The
  Wooden House) 146
Het Ketelhuis 192
Het Lievertje (The Little
  Urchin) 148
Het Nachtrestaurant 297
Het Prinsenhof 282
Hill Street Blues 202
Historical Museum. See
  Amsterdams Historisch
  Museum.
Historisch Museum Zud-
  Ennemerland 255
Historische Tuin 245
history 55–62
  Golden Age 58
hitchhiking 43
HIV. See AIDS.
HNM Café 272
Hofje van Oorschot 255
Hofje van Staats 255
Hofman 301
holidays 75
Holland 56
Holland Casino
  Amsterdam 194
  Zandvoort 258
Hollander, Xaviera 68
Hollandsche Schouwburg
  159
Holocaust 61

Holy Roman Empire 56
home exchange 101
Homomonument 153
Hooft, Pieter Corneliszoon 67
Hooghalen. See **Daytrips.**
Hooglandse Kerk 265
Hortus Botanicus 158
Hortus Botanicus (Leiden)
  264
hospitality clubs 101
hostels 99
  Hostelling International (HI) 99
Hotel Abba 114
Hotel Asterisk 110
Hotel Bema 116
Hotel Brouwer 106
Hotel Clemens 109
Hotel de Filosoof 114
Hotel Impala 111
Hotel Mimosa 278
Hotel The Crown 104
Hotelrunners 104
hotels 100
Huis aan de Drie Grachten
  144
Huis Marseille 169
hutspot 74, 131
hypothermia 28

I

ice skating 74
identification 18
IJsbreker 187
immunizations 27
injera 129, 140
Institute for War
  Documentation 149
International Court of Justice
  (ICJ) 62
International Driving Permit.
  See driving.
Internet 44
  access 97
  resources 52
internships 87
Ivens, Joris 67

J

jenever 225
Jimmy Woo 232
Jodenbuurt and Plantage 7

accommodations 118
coffee shops 211
food 140
museums 176
nightlife 241
shopping 220
sights 158
John Frostbrug 304
Joods Historisch Museum 177
Jordaan 5
accommodations 113
coffee shops 209
food 132
museums 172
nightlife 237
shopping 218
sights 153

K

Kaaswaag Gouda 295
Kadinsky 202
Kamp Westerbork 312
Kashmir Lounge 210
Keizer Culinair 86
Keizersgracht 2
Keukenhof Gardens 259
King Hotel 111
Kingfisher 240
Kit Tropentheater 187
Kleine Trippenhuis 144
Klompenmakerij de Zaanse Schans 247
Knijn Bowling 195
Koninklijk Carré Theater 186
Koninklijk Paleis (Royal Palace) 147
Koninklijke Porceleyne Fles 284
Koolhaas, Rem 310
korfball 74
kosher 52
Kramer, Piet 66
Kriterion Theater and Cafe 192
Kröller-Müller Museum 306
Kubuswonig. See Cube Houses.
Kunsthal Rotterdam 290

L

L.O.S. See publications.
La Tertulia 209

Labor Party 79
language schools 85
language. See **Appendix.**
Lanskroon 129
laptop computers 44
Last Minute Ticket Shop 185
laundry 96
Legermuseum (Military Museum) 284
Leiden University 85
Leiden. See **Daytrips.**
Leidseplein 5
accommodations 111
coffee shops 207
food 130
nightlife 230
sights 152
library 96
Life and Times 55–75
life 62
times 55
Lisse. See **Daytrips.**
literature 67
live music 187
Lodewijk Kerk 264
Luckytravellers Fantasia Hotel 118
Lyme disease 29

M

Maastricht Treaty 62, 317
Maastricht. See **Daytrips.**
Madame Tussaud's Wax Museum 147
Madurodam 275
Magere Brug 152
Magna Plaza Shopping Center 146
mail 47
Maloe Melo 188
Mankind 230
Maranon Hangmatten 218
marijuana 197
Marionette Theater 187, 190
Maritiem en Jutters Museum (Maritime and Beachcombers Museum) 323
Maritiem Museum 291
markets
Albert Cuypmarkt 219
Bloemenmarkt 215
Dappermarkt 220

Lindengracht 219
Nieuwmarkt 214
Noordermarkt 218
Oudemanhuispoort 214
Spui 216
Ten Katemarkt 219
Waterlooplein 220
Westermarkt 219
Martinikerk 309
Martinitoren 309
MasterCard 20
Mauritshuis 274
Max Euweplein 152
Max Havelaar 67, 170
measurements. See **Appendix.**
medical outreach 80
medical services 97
MedicAlert 30
Melkweg 188, 190, 232
Metro. See public transportation.
Midzomergracht 300
The Milkmaid 72, 176
minority travelers 51
Model Mugging 26
Molenmuseum 266
Mondrian, Piet 73, 274
money
ATMs 20
credit cards 20
currency exchange 19
debit cards 21
traveler's checks 19
Montmartre 234
mosquitoes 28
Movies, The 191
Mozes en Aaronkerk (Moses and Aaron Church) 161
Mr. Visserplein 158
Mulisch, Harry 68
Multatuli 67, 170
Multatuli Museum 170
Municipal Information Center for Physical Planning and Housing 160
Museonder 306
Museum Amstelkring 166
Museum Boerhaave 266
Museum Boijmans van Beuningen 289
Museum Catharijneconvent 299
Museum Het Catharina

Gasthuis 295
Museum Het Noorderhuis 249
Museum Het Rembrandt 177
Museum Het Schielandshuis 292
Museum Naturalis 265, 266
Museum Paleis Het Loo 304
Museum Van Loon 171
Museum Willet-Holthuysen 172
Museum Zaans 246
Museumpark 291
Museumplein and Vondelpark 6
  accommodations 116
  coffee shops 210
  food 136
  museums 174
  nightlife 240
  sights 154
Museums 165–183
mushrooms 200
music 68
Muziektheater. See Stadhuis-Het Muziektheater.

N

Nadia Hotel 109
Nationaal Brilmuseum (National Spectacles Museum) 170
Nationaal Monument 147
Nationaal Museum van Speelklok tot Pierement 300
Nationaal Park Duinen van Texel 322
Nationaal Vakbondsmuseum 181
National Ballet 185
Natuurhistorisch Museum 292
Nazis. See World War II.
Neder Pop 68
Nederlands Architectuurinstituut 289
Nederlands Foto Museum 292
Nederlands Instituut voor Mediakunst 171
Nederlandse Spoorwegen

(NS) 40
neighborhood overviews 2
NEMO (New Metropolis) 180
Neoclassicism 65
Netherlands Board of Tourism 16
Netherlands Media Art Institute, Montevideo/Time-Based Arts 171
Netherlands Opera 185
Netherlands Philharmonic Orchestra 185
New City 315
Nic Nic 216
Nieuwe Kerk 167
Nieuwe Kerk (Delft) 283
Nieuwe Zijd 3
  accommodations 105
  coffee shops 202
  food 124
  museums 166
  nightlife 227
  shopping 215
  sights 146
Nieuwmarkt 143
night buses. See public transportation.
Night Fever 300
Night Watch 71, 176
Nightlife 223–241
  by neighborhood 224
  by type 223
Nine Streets. See Canal Ring West.
NL20. See publications.
NOA 129
Nooit Meer Auschwitz (Auschwitz Never Again) 160
Noordelijk Scheepvaart en Niemeyer Tabaksmuseum (Shipping and Tobacco Museum) 308
Noorderplantsoen 310
Noorderzon Festival 310
Noordwijk aan Zee. See **Daytrips.**
NS. See Nederlandse Spoorwegen.
Nusantara Museum 284

O

Oase 319

Observatory Sonnenborgh Museum 300
Odeon 236
Oerol 326
oliebollen 74
Oost-Indisch Huis (East Indies House) 144
opera 185
Oranje 73
OT301 239
Oude Kerk 145
Oude Kerk (Delft) 283
Oude Zijd 2
  accommodations 103
  coffee shops 201
  food 123
  museums 165
  nightlife 224
  shopping 214
  sights 143
Oudemanhuispoort 144
Oud-West. See Westerpark and Oud-West.

P

Padalino, Nick 172
painting. See visual art.
Panama 189
pannenkoeken 74, 124, 130
Pannenkoekenhuis Upstairs 124
Paradiso 188, 232
Paradox 209
paramaribop 68
Parkpop 276
passports 16
Pathé 191
Patriot Movement 60
Paul Andriesse. See galleries.
Paul Tetar van Elven Museum 284
Peace Palace (Vredespaleis) 273
pensions 100
Peperwortel 134
pharmacies 96
phone cards. See calling cards.
phones 45
  cellular phones 46
  pay phones 46

Piano Bar 189
Pianola Museum 173
pickpockets 27
Pieterskerk 264
Pink Point 153
Plantage. See Jodenbuurt and Plantage.
poffertjes 74
police 96
political activism 78
politics 63
Portugees-Israelietische Synagoge 159
post offices 97
Poste Restante 47
Post-Impressionism 72
Practical Information 93–97
 emergency and communications 96
 local services 95
 tourist and financial services 93
prime minister. See Balkenende, Jan Peter.
Prinsengracht 2
Prinsenhoftuin (Princes' Court Gardens) 311
Prostitution Information Centre 194
Proveniershuis 255
Province House 317
Provo movement 62
public transportation 39
publications
 Amsterdam Op de Fiets 160
 Amsterdam Weekly 185
 Boom! 185, 189
 Hague Magazine, The 270
 L.O.S. 267
 NL20 237
 Rotterdam In Your Pocket! 286
 Simply the Best 286
 Uitgids 185
 Uitkrant 182, 185

Q

Queen Beatrix 62
Queen Wilhelmina 61
Quentin Hotel 111

R

rabies 30
railpasses
 Benelux Tourrail Pass 40
 Eurail Pass 36
 Holland Railpass 40
 InterRail Pass 37
 national 40
Rainarai 133
recreation 194
Red Cross
 American 28
 Dutch 80
Red Light District 2
 accommodations 103
 coffee shops 201
 food 123
 museums 165
 nightlife 225
 shopping 215
 sights 144
religion 64
Rembrandt van Rijn 71, 176, 177
Rembrandtpark 6
Rembrandtplein 5
 accommodations 113
 coffee shops 208
 food 131
 nightlife 233
 sights 153
Resistance 61, 177
Reve, Gerard 68
Rialto 192
Ridderzaal 274
Rijksmuseum Amsterdam 175
Rijksmuseum van Oudheden (National Museum of Antiquities) 266
Rijksmuseum voor Volkenkunde (National Museum of Ethnology) 265
Rijksuniversiteit Groningen 311
rijsttafel 124, 126
Ristorante Caprese 125
Ristorante Pizzeria Firenze 131
Rococo 65
Romanesque 65
Romans 55
Rookies, The 208
Rotterdam In Your Pocket! See publications.

Rotterdam. See **Daytrips**
Rotterdamse Schouwburg 292
roundworms 29
Royal Concertgebouw Orchestra 186
Ruif 281
Rusland 201

S

safety. See **Essentials.**
Sauna Deco 196
Saxons 56
Scheepvaartbuurt 4
 accommodations 108
 coffee shops 205
 food 125
 nightlife 229
 shopping 216
 sights 148
Scheepvaartmuseum 180
Scheveningen Pier 279
Scheveningen. See **Daytrips.**
Schiermonnikoog 320
Schipbreuk- en Juttersmuseum Flora 323
Schiphol 31
Sea Life 279
self-defense 27
Sex Museum. See Amsterdam Sex Museum.
sexually transmitted diseases. See STIs.
sexually transmitted infections. See STIs.
Shipping Quarter. See Scheepvaartbuurt.
Shopping 213–221
 by neighborhood 214
 by type 213
shrooms. See mushrooms.
Siberie 206
Siebold House 266
Sights 143–163
Simplon Jongerenhotel 307
Simply the Best. See publications.
Singel 2
Singelgracht 2
Sint Agnietenkapel 144
Sint Nicolaaskerk 143
Sint-Andrieshof 153

sizes and conversions 221
skating. See ice skating.
SMART Project Space 192
  See also alternative art
  spaces.
smart shops. See coffee
  shops.
Smartlappen 301
snert 74
Snooker & Poolclub Oud-
  West 195
soccer. See football.
social activism 79
solo travelers 48
Sonnenveld House 290
Spaarnestad Fotoarchief
  255
Space Expo 269
spas 195
sports 73
Spui 147
Squash City 194
squats 62, 239, 301
St. Bavo's. See Grote Kerk/
  St. Bavo's.
St. Hubert Hunting Lodge
  306
St. Janskerk 295
St. Laurenskerk 291
Stadhuis-Het Muziektheater
  160, 186
Stadsschouwburg 189
standby flights. See flights.
States-General 57, 63, 274
Stayokay
  Amsterdam Stadsdoelen 103
  Amsterdam Vondelpark 116
  Arnhem 302
  City Hostel Den Haag 271
  Haarlem 250
  Maastricht 315
  Rotterdam 286
  Terschelling 326
  Texel 321
STDs. See STIs.
Stedelijk Museum Bureau
  Amsterdam 173
Stedelijk Museum for
  Modern and Contemporary
  Art 168
Stedelijk Museum Leiden
  266
Steen, Jan 176
STIs 30

Stix 206
Stopera. See Stadhuis-Het
  Muziektheater.
Stripmuseum (Comic
  Museum) 310
strippenkaart 39
stroopwafels 74, 129, 295
Strowis Hostel 297
study abroad
  alternative 86
study abroad. See **Beyond
  Tourism.**
subway. See public
  transportation.
sunburn 28
sustainable travel 47

T

Taste of Culture 123
taxes 22
telephones. See phones.
Tent 290
terrorism 25
Terschelling. See **Daytrips.**
Texel. See **Daytrips.**
Teylers Museum 254
theater 66, 189
Theater aan het Spui 276
Theater Instituut Nederland
  170
theehuis 74
Theo Swagemakersmuseum
  255
Thermos Day 195
Thermos Night 196
Thomas Cook 20, 37
ticks 28
time zones 46
tipping 22
Toko Nina 252
Toomler 190
Torch. See galleries.
Torture Museum 172
tostis 74, 128, 131, 230
tourist offices 16
  See also VVV.
Tours
  A History Lesson 178
tours
  bike 94
  boat 93
  bus 94

Toussaint Cafe 239
trains
  in the Netherlands 40
  international 35
  See also railpasses.
trams. See public
  transportation.
transportation 31–44
  See also bikes, boats, driving,
  public transportation, trains,
  walking.
Trappistenlokaal 't Klooster
  285
travel advisories 26
travel agencies 32
traveler's checks. See
  money.
Travelex 20, 94
Trippenhuis 144
Tropenmuseum 180
Tuschinski Cinema 191

U

Uitgids. See publications.
Uitkrant. See publications.
uitzendbureaus 90
universities 84
University of Amsterdam 85
urinoir 310
US State Department 21
Use-it Rotterdam 286
Utrecht University 85
Utrecht. See **Daytrips.**

V

vaccinations. See
  immunizations.
value added tax (VAT, BTW)
  22
van den Vondel, Joost 67
van der Keuken, Johan 67
van der Mey, Johan 66
Van Der Werfpark 264
van Diem, Mike 67
Van Dobben 131
van Eyck, Johannes 68
Van Gogh Museum 174
van Gogh, Theo 64, 67
van Gogh, Vincent 72, 174,
  306
Van Wijngaarden/Hakkens.
  See galleries.

Van Zoetendaal. See galleries.
vaporizers 197
VAT. See value added tax.
vegetarianism 51
Vereniging Museumhaven Amsterdam 180
Vermeer, Johannes 72, 176, 274, 279, 283
Verzetsmuseum 177
Vikings 56
Visa 20
visas 17
  student 83
  work 87
visual art 68–73
  Golden Age 71
Vlieland. See **Daytrips.**
VOC. See Dutch East India Company.
volunteering. See **Beyond Tourism.**
Vondelpark 154
Vondelpark Openluchttheater 190
Vous Êtes Ici. See galleries.
Vredespaleis. See Peace Palace.
VVV
  Aalsmeer 244
  Amsterdam 93
  Apeldoorn 305
  Arnhem 302
  Gouda 294
  Groningen 307
  Haarlem 249
  The Hague 270
  Leiden 261
  Lisse 259
  Maastricht 314
  Noordwijk aan Zee 268

  Rotterdam 286
  Scheveningen 278
  Terschelling 326
  Texel 321
  Utrecht 296
  Vlieland 324
  Zandvoort aan Zee 257

W

W 139. See alternative art spaces.
Waag 143
Waalse Kerk 284
Wadden Islands 320–327
  See also **Daytrips.**
Waterhole, The 187
Waterleidingmuseum 300
Waterlooplein 158
Weber 230
Wertheim Park 160
West India Company (WIC) 59
Westergasfabriek 154, 188
Westerkerk 149
Westerkerkstoren 149
Western Union 21
Westerpark 154
Westerpark and Oud-West 6
  accommodations 114
  coffee shops 210
  food 134
  nightlife 239
  shopping 219
  sights 154
West-Indisch Huis (West Indies House) 149
WIC. See West India Company.
Wi-Fi 44

Wijnand Fockink 226
William I, Prince of Orange 58, 282
William III of Orange 59
windmills 246
window prostitution 192
Witte de With 290
women travelers 49
women's health 30
Woonboot Museum 173
work permits 17
  See also visas.
working abroad. See **Beyond Tourism.**
World Cup 73
World War I 60
World War II 61
Wrakkenmuseum 327

Y

Yo Yo 210

Z

Zaanse Schans. See **Daytrips.**
Zandvoort aan Zee. See **Daytrips.**
Zeeaquarium and Natuurmuseum 327
Zilli & Zilli 303
zones (public transportation) 39
Zuid Kennemerland National Park 258
Zuiderkerk 160
Zwarte Tulp Museum 260

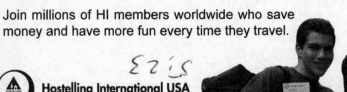

"A wonderful surprise. . . . *In a Father's Place* is a beautiful book, making emotions as vivid and rich in perspective as a loved landscape."
—**John Casey, *New York Times Book Review***

"Astonishingly balanced storytelling. . . . Tilghman writes with precision, grace and honesty. . . . In the end, he seems like a wonderfully versatile musician who can not only sing ballads and the occasional up-tempo number, but can also play some serious, wild, blues guitar."
—**Steve Kettman, *San Francisco Chronicle***

"Plainly one of the strongest fictional debuts in some time. . . . The characters are full-blooded, full-emotioned, and so firmly rooted in family and their own pasts as to seem almost a part of the land themselves."
—**Gary Krist, *Philadelphia Inquirer***

"The debut of the year. . . . Tilghman's stories are modest and muscular, utterly lacking in pretension. . . . They have a simple, classic feel, as if written from deep in the American grain."
—**Matthew Gilbert, *Boston Globe***

"Tilghman's first collection unfolds at a serene pace, the calm born of devoted interest in small details, which open onto larger spaces. . . . Landscape matters in these stories. . . . History haunts them. . . . Tilghman catches his characters at moments of transition . . . and leaves them with a new perspective not just on themselves, but on the world—an unusual push beyond psychological drama to social observation and then to moral reflection."
—**Ann Hulbert, *The New Republic***

"Audacious. . . . For good or ill, nature shapes these characters' lives and invests them with a believable grandeur. As a result, they possess an almost Dickensian sense of drama and possibility."
—***Newsweek***

"Tilghman has accomplished what only a true storyteller can do: make the impossible inevitable. . . . Tilghman's ladders, rising like Yeats', out of the human heart . . . give a glorious view."
—**Richard Eder, *Los Angeles Times***

"Christopher Tilghman's first book announces one of the year's most significant debuts . . . filled with surprises, along with a profound sense of place, character and incident."
—***Time***